P9-AOT-032

THE ∞INFINITY WAR

INFINITY WAR. Contains material originally published in magazine form as INFINITY WAR #1-6, MARVEL COMICS PRESENTS #108-111 and WARLOCK AND THE INFINITY WATCH #7-10. Eighth printing 2018. ISBN 978-0-7851-2105-3. Published by MARVEL WORLDWIDE, INC., a subsidiary of MARVEL ENTERTAINMENT, LLC. OFFICE OF PUBLICATION: 135 West 50th Street, New York, NY 10020. Copyright © 2006 MARVEL No similarity between any of the names, characters, persons, and/or institutions in this magazine with those of any living or dead person or institution is intended, and any such similarity which may exist is purely coincidental. **Printed in the U.S.A.** DAN BUCKLEY, President, Marvel Entertainment; JOHN NEE, Publisher; JOE QUESADA, Chief Creative Officer; TOM BREVOORT, SVP of Publishing; DAVID BOGART, SVP of Business Affairs & Operations, Publishing & Partnership; DAVID GABRIEL, SVP of Sales & Marketing, Publishing; JEFF YOUNGQUIST, VP of Production & Special Projects; DAN CARR, Executive Director of Publishing Technology; ALEX MORALES, Director of Publishing Operations; DAN EDINGTON, Managing Editor; SUSAN CRESPI, Production Manager; STAN LEE, Chairman Emeritus. For information regarding advertising in Marvel Comics or on Marvel.com, please contact Vit DeBellis, Custom Solutions & Integrated Advertising Manager, at vdebellis@marvel.com. For Marvel subscription inquiries, please call 888-511-5480. **Manufactured between 5/23/2018 and 6/12/2018 by QUAD GRAPHICS SARATOGA, SARATOGA SPRINGS, NY, USA.**

10 9 8

THE ∞INF
W

Writer: **Jim Starlin**

Pencilers: **Ron Lim, Tom Raney, Angel Medina,**
Larry Alexander & Shawn McManus

Inkers: **Al Milgrom, Terry Austin, Keith Williams,**
Bob Almond, Tim Tuohy & Shawn McManus

Colorists: **Max Scheele, Ian Laughlin, Evelyn Stein,**
John Kalisz, Kevin Tinsley & Sarra Mossoff

Letterers: **Jack Morelli, Ken Lopez, Janice Chiang,**
Michael Higgins, Steve Dutro & Dave Sharpe

Editors: **Craig Anderson & Terry Kavanagh**

Cover Art: **Ron Lim**

INITY
AR

Collection Editor: **Mark D. Beazley**
Assistant Editor: **Caitlin O'Connell**
Associate Managing Editor: **Kateri Woody**
Associate Manager, Digital Assets: **Joe Hochstein**
Senior Editor, Special Projects: **Jennifer Grünwald**
VP Production & Special Projects: **Jeff Youngquist**
SVP Print, Sales & Marketing: **David Gabriel**
Production: **ColorTek & Joe Frontirre**
Book Designer: **Jhonson Eteng**
Editor in Chief: **C.B. Cebulski**
Chief Creative Officer: **Joe Quesada**
President: **Dan Buckley**
Executive Producer: **Alan Fine**

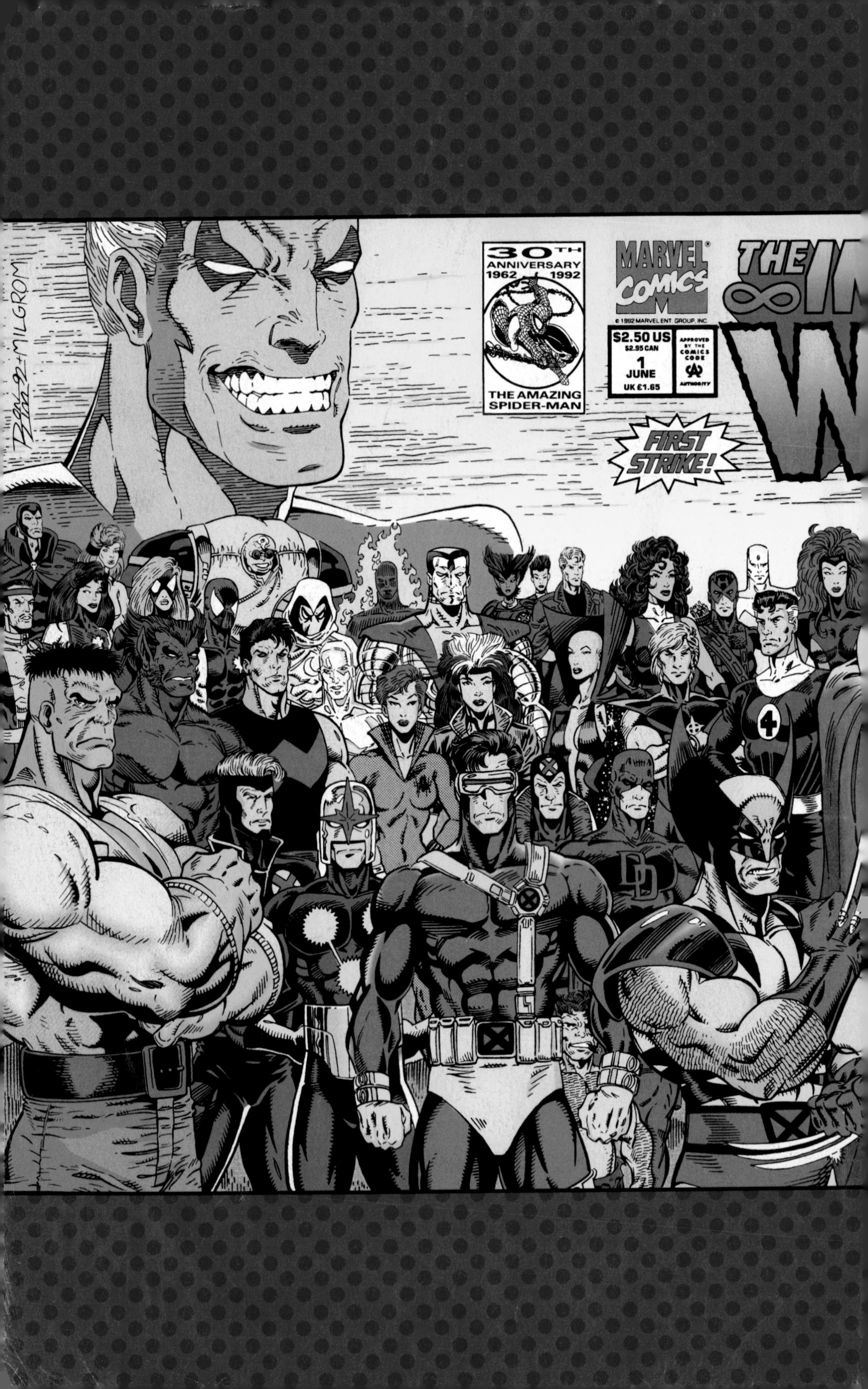
30TH
ANNIVERSARY
1962 1992
THE AMAZING
SPIDER-MAN
MARVEL COMICS
© 1992 MARVEL ENT. GROUP, INC.
$2.50 US
$2.95 CAN
1
JUNE
UK £1.65
APPROVED BY THE COMICS CODE AUTHORITY
FIRST STRIKE!

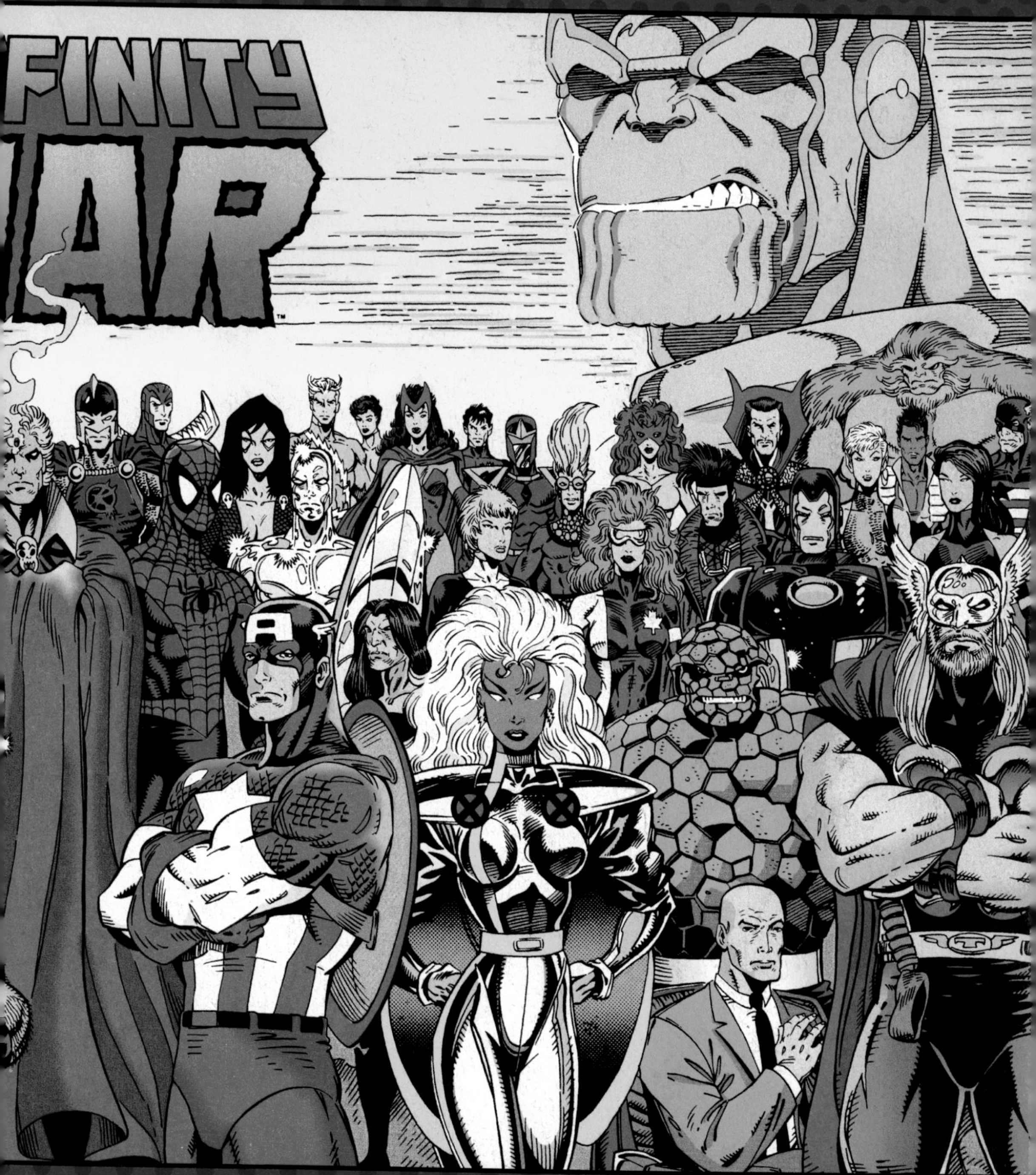
FINITY
AR

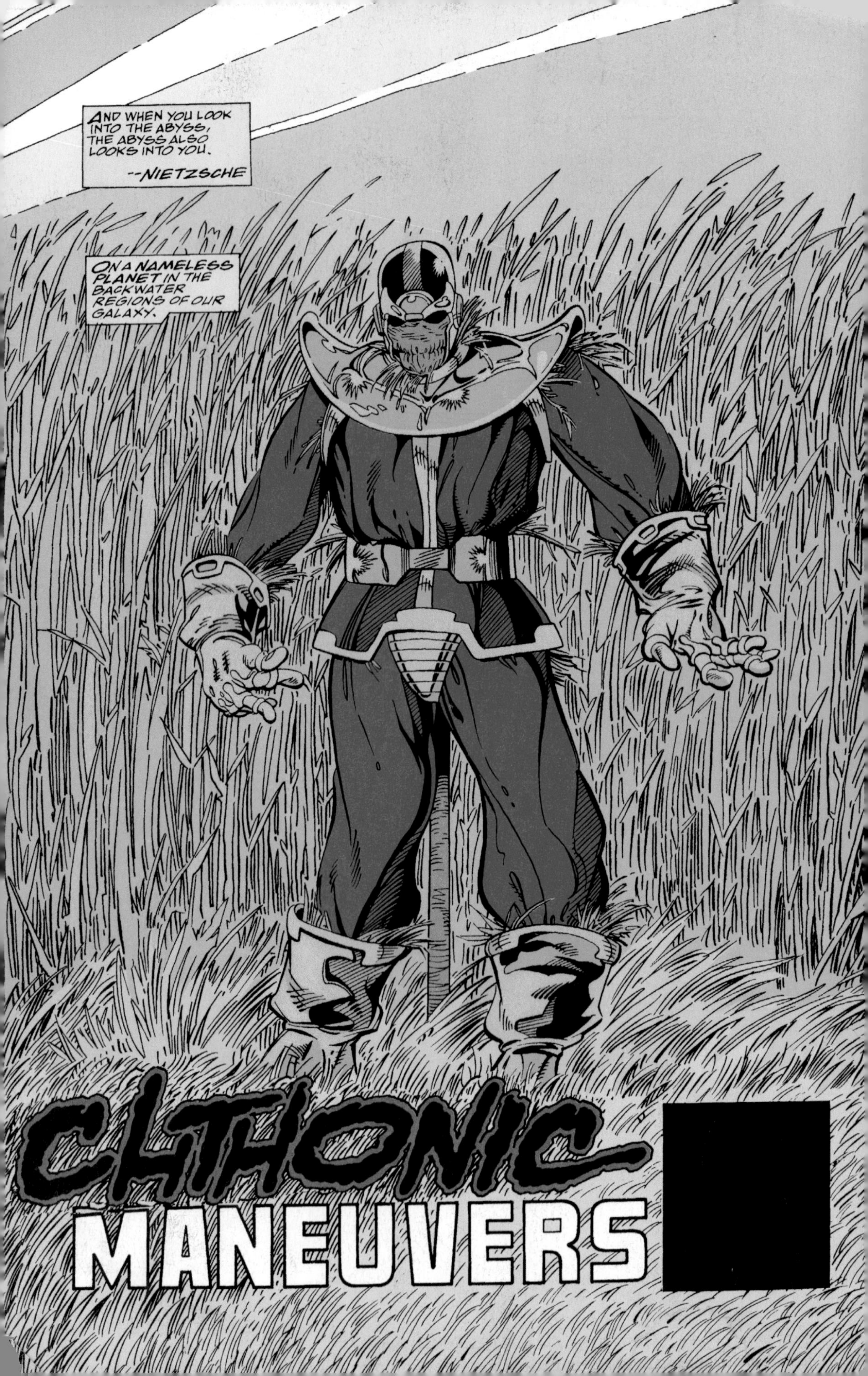
AND WHEN YOU LOOK INTO THE ABYSS, THE ABYSS ALSO LOOKS INTO YOU.
--NIETZSCHE
ON A NAMELESS PLANET IN THE BACKWATER REGIONS OF OUR GALAXY.
CHTHONIC MANEUVERS

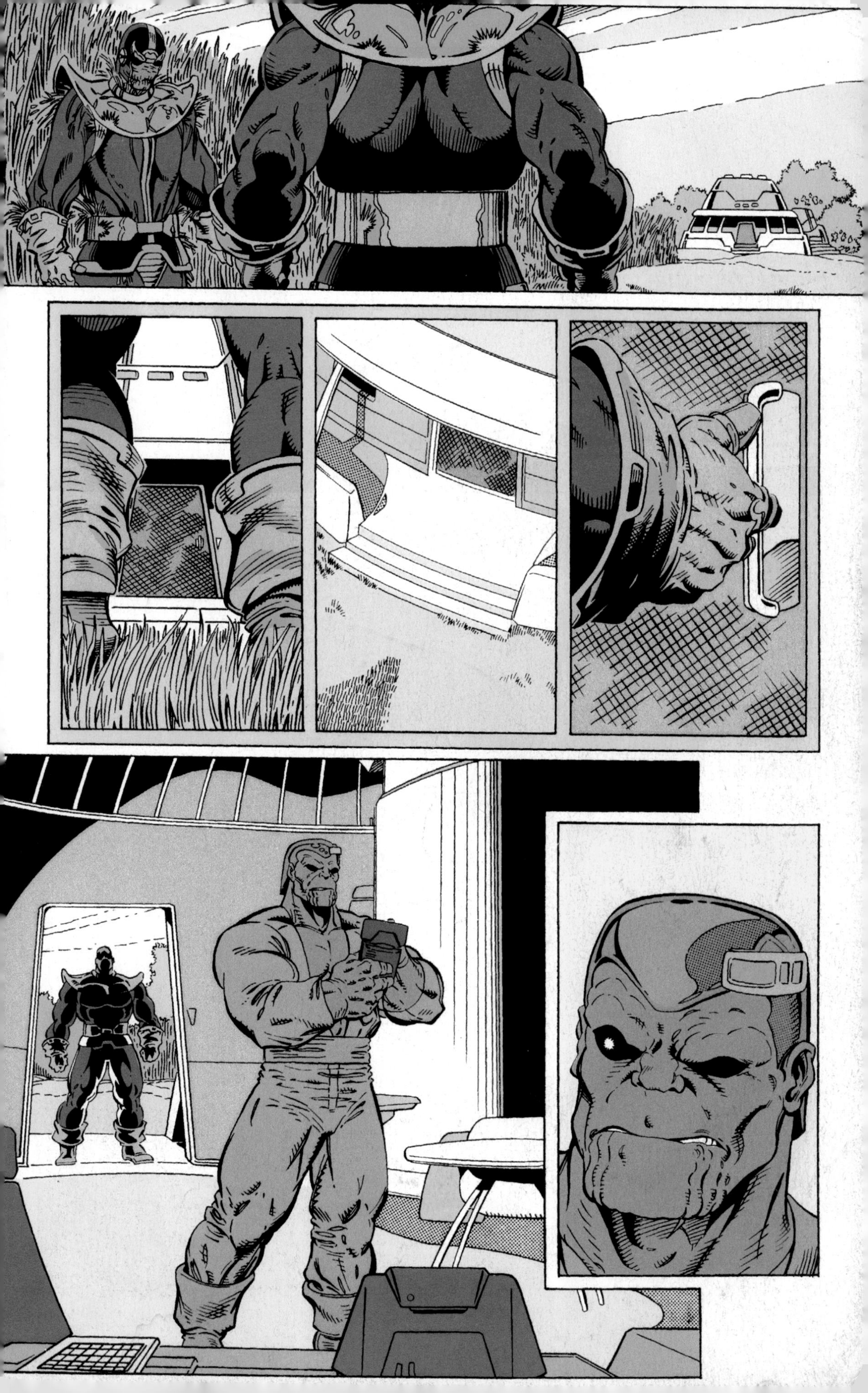

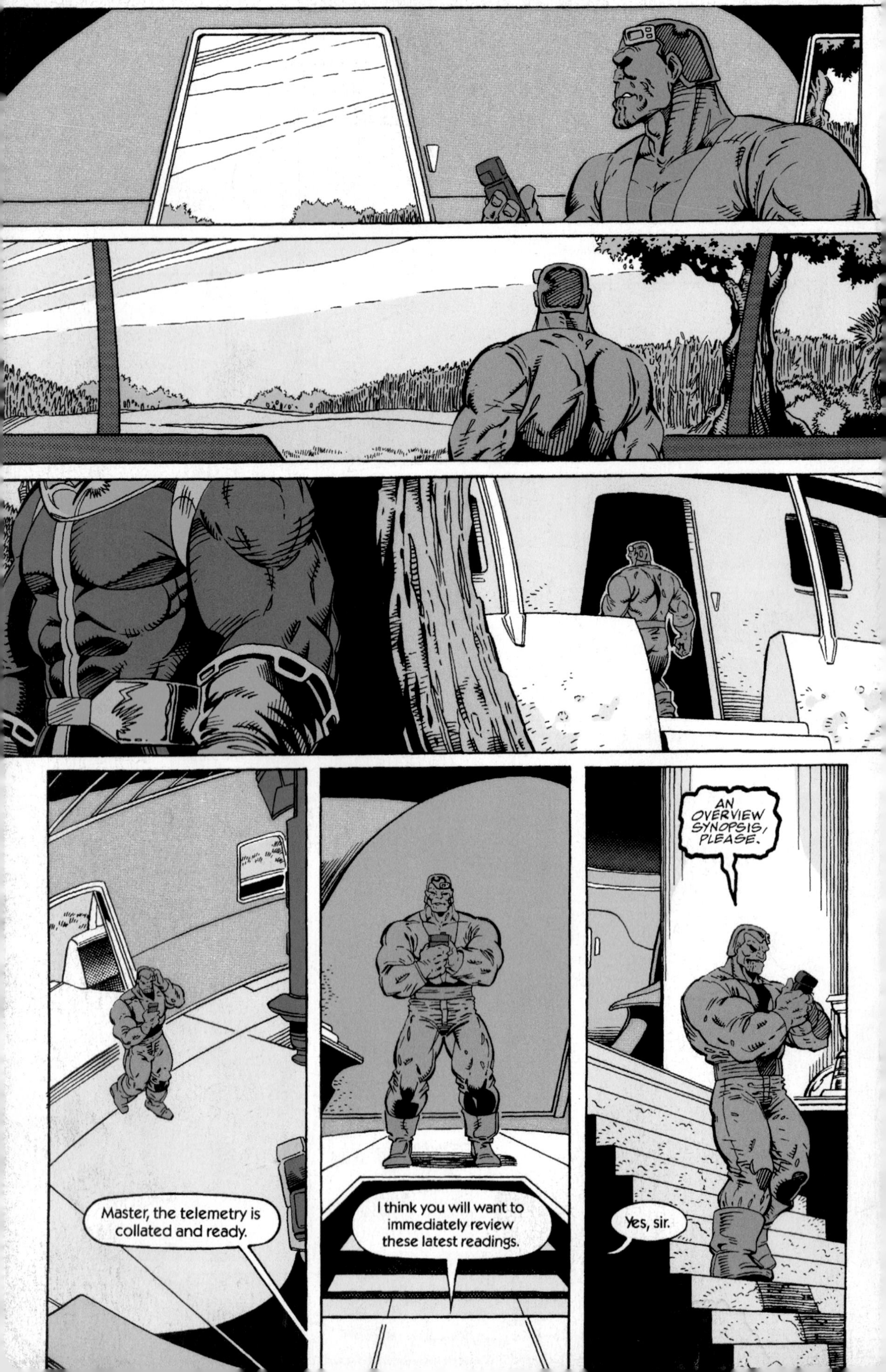
Master, the telemetry is collated and ready.
I think you will want to immediately review these latest readings.
AN OVERVIEW SYNOPSIS, PLEASE.
Yes, sir.

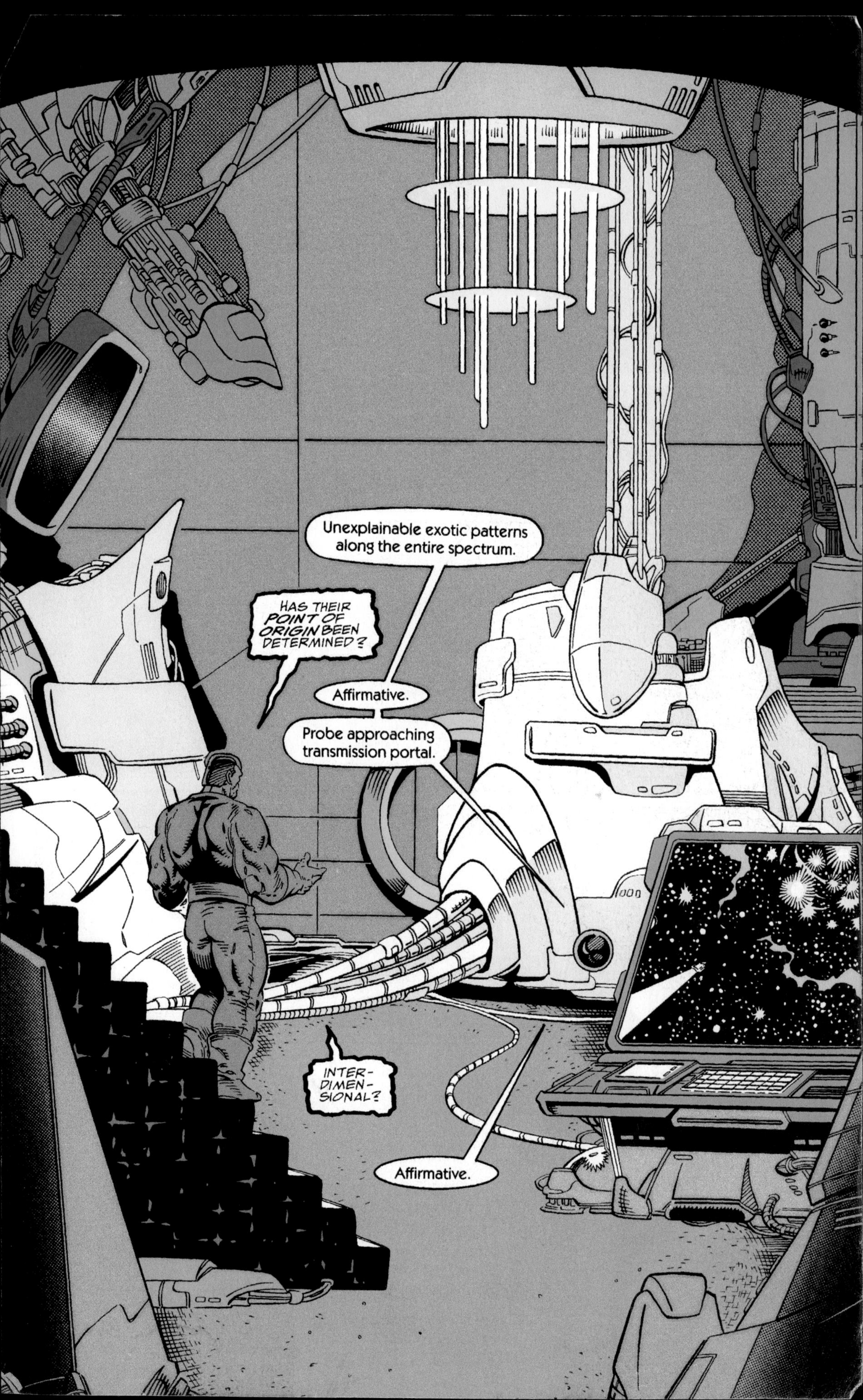

Unexplainable exotic patterns along the entire spectrum.
HAS THEIR POINT OF ORIGIN BEEN DETERMINED?
Affirmative.
Probe approaching transmission portal.
INTER-DIMEN-SIONAL?
Affirmative.

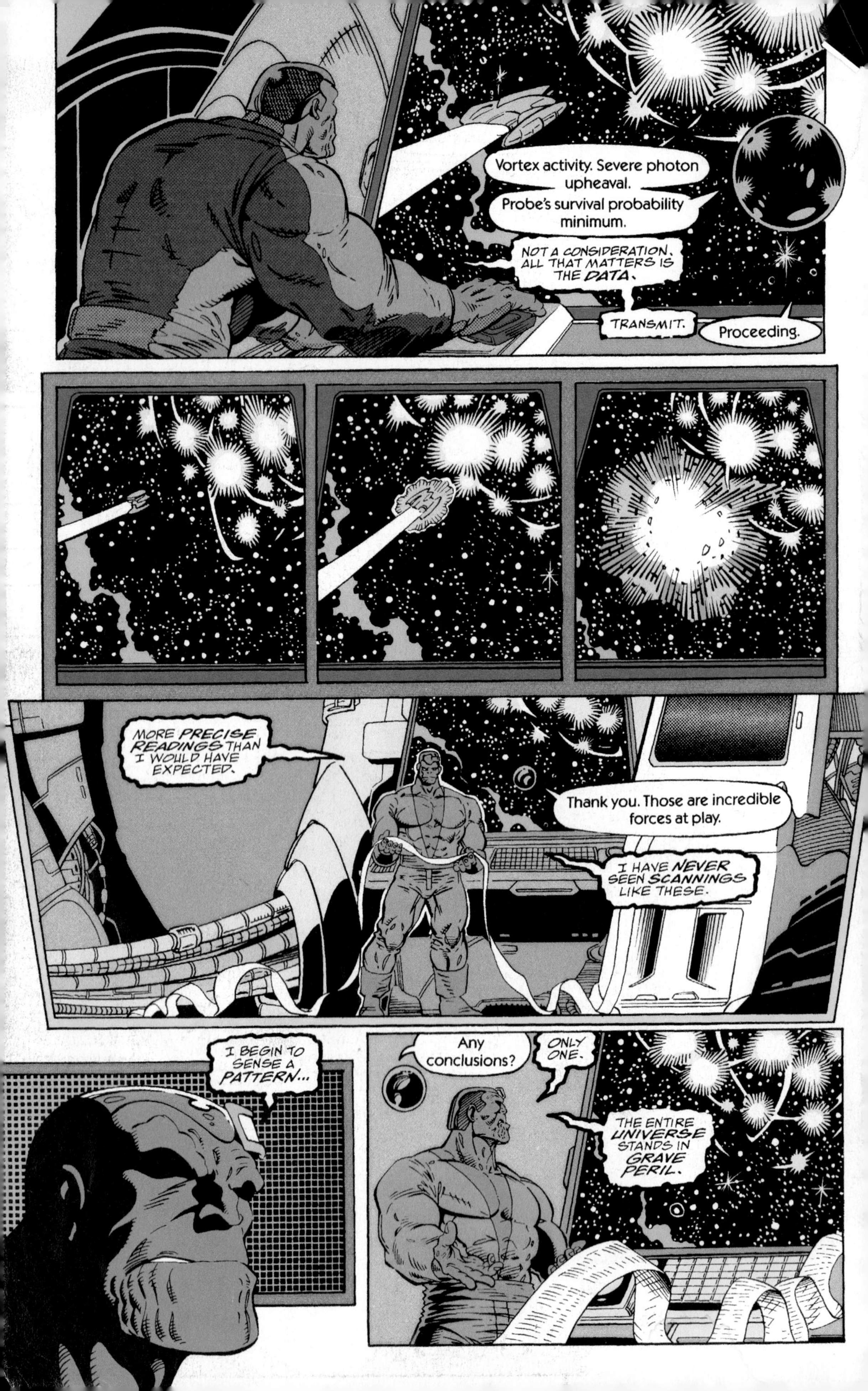
Vortex activity. Severe photon upheaval.
Probe's survival probability minimum.
NOT A CONSIDERATION. ALL THAT MATTERS IS THE DATA.
TRANSMIT.
Proceeding.
MORE PRECISE READINGS THAN I WOULD HAVE EXPECTED.
Thank you. Those are incredible forces at play.
I HAVE NEVER SEEN SCANNINGS LIKE THESE.
I BEGIN TO SENSE A PATTERN...
Any conclusions?
ONLY ONE.
THE ENTIRE UNIVERSE STANDS IN GRAVE PERIL.

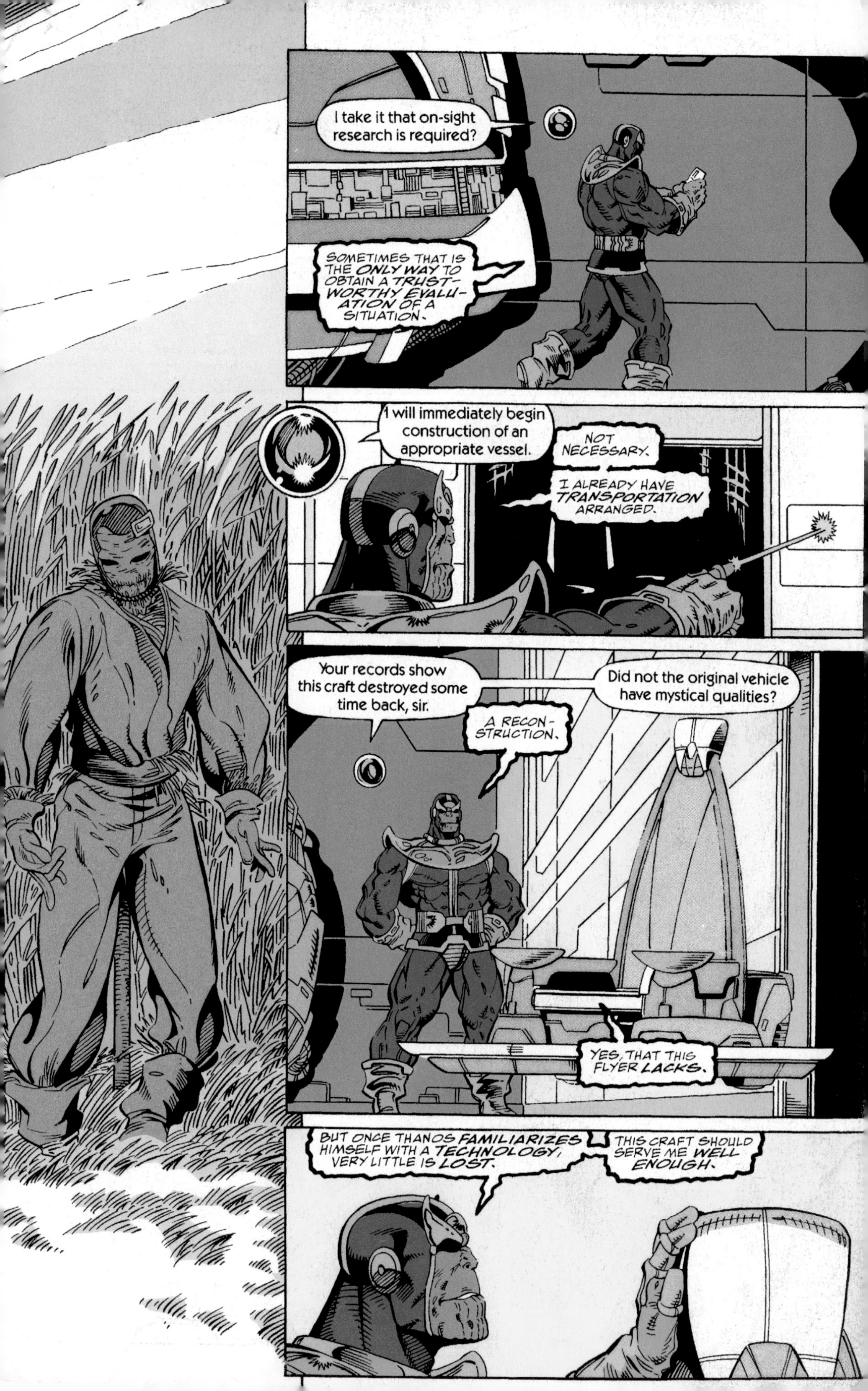
I take it that on-sight research is required?
SOMETIMES THAT IS THE ONLY WAY TO OBTAIN A TRUST-WORTHY EVALU-ATION OF A SITUATION.
I will immediately begin construction of an appropriate vessel.
NOT NECESSARY.
I ALREADY HAVE TRANSPORTATION ARRANGED.
Your records show this craft destroyed some time back, sir.
A RECON-STRUCTION.
Did not the original vehicle have mystical qualities?
YES, THAT THIS FLYER LACKS.
BUT ONCE THANOS FAMILIARIZES HIMSELF WITH A TECHNOLOGY, VERY LITTLE IS LOST.
THIS CRAFT SHOULD SERVE ME WELL ENOUGH.

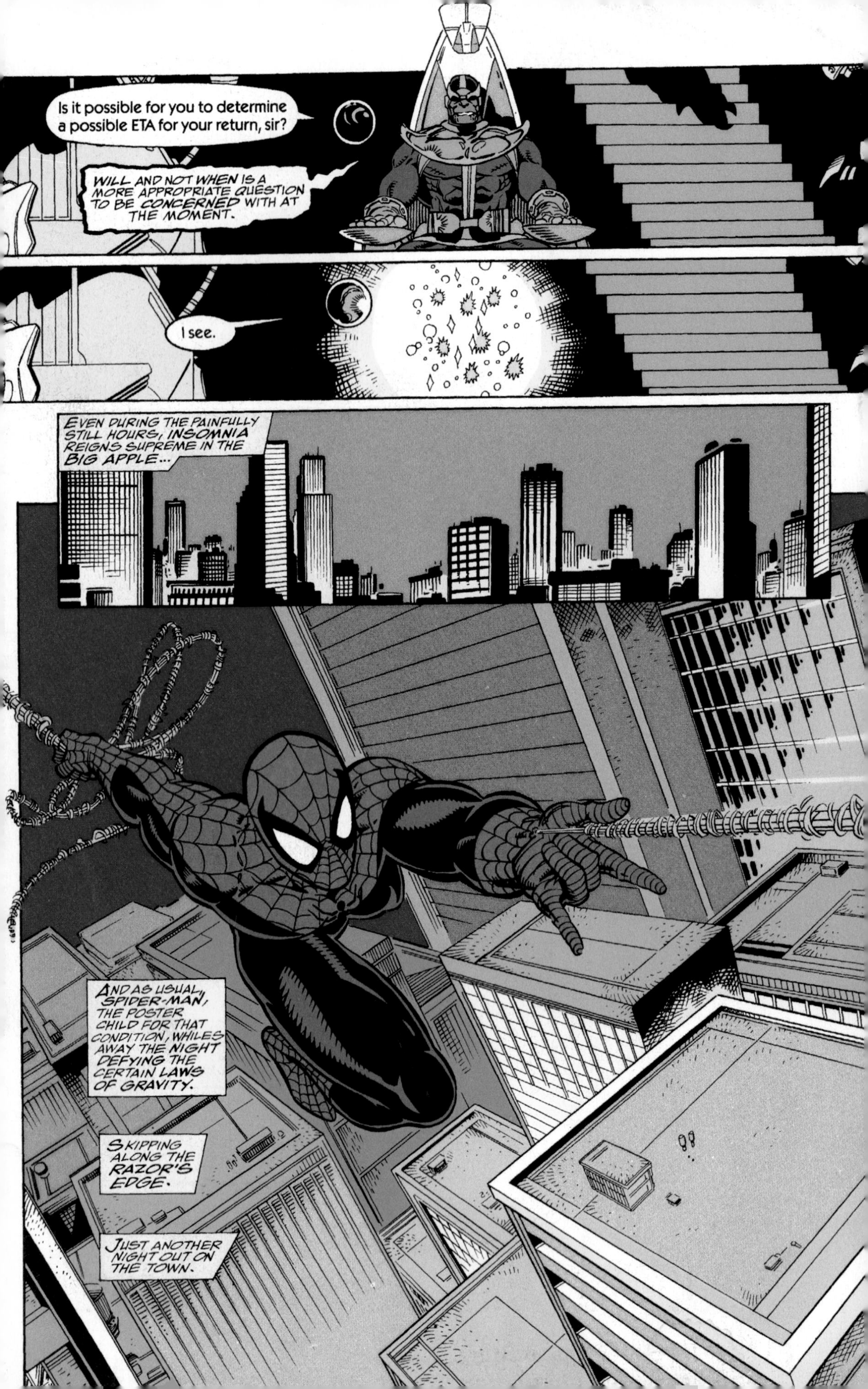
Is it possible for you to determine a possible ETA for your return, sir?
WILL AND NOT WHEN IS A MORE APPROPRIATE QUESTION TO BE CONCERNED WITH AT THE MOMENT.
I see.
EVEN DURING THE PAINFULLY STILL HOURS, INSOMNIA REIGNS SUPREME IN THE BIG APPLE...
AND AS USUAL, SPIDER-MAN, THE POSTER CHILD FOR THAT CONDITION, WHILES AWAY THE NIGHT DEFYING THE CERTAIN LAWS OF GRAVITY.
SKIPPING ALONG THE RAZOR'S EDGE.
JUST ANOTHER NIGHT OUT ON THE TOWN.

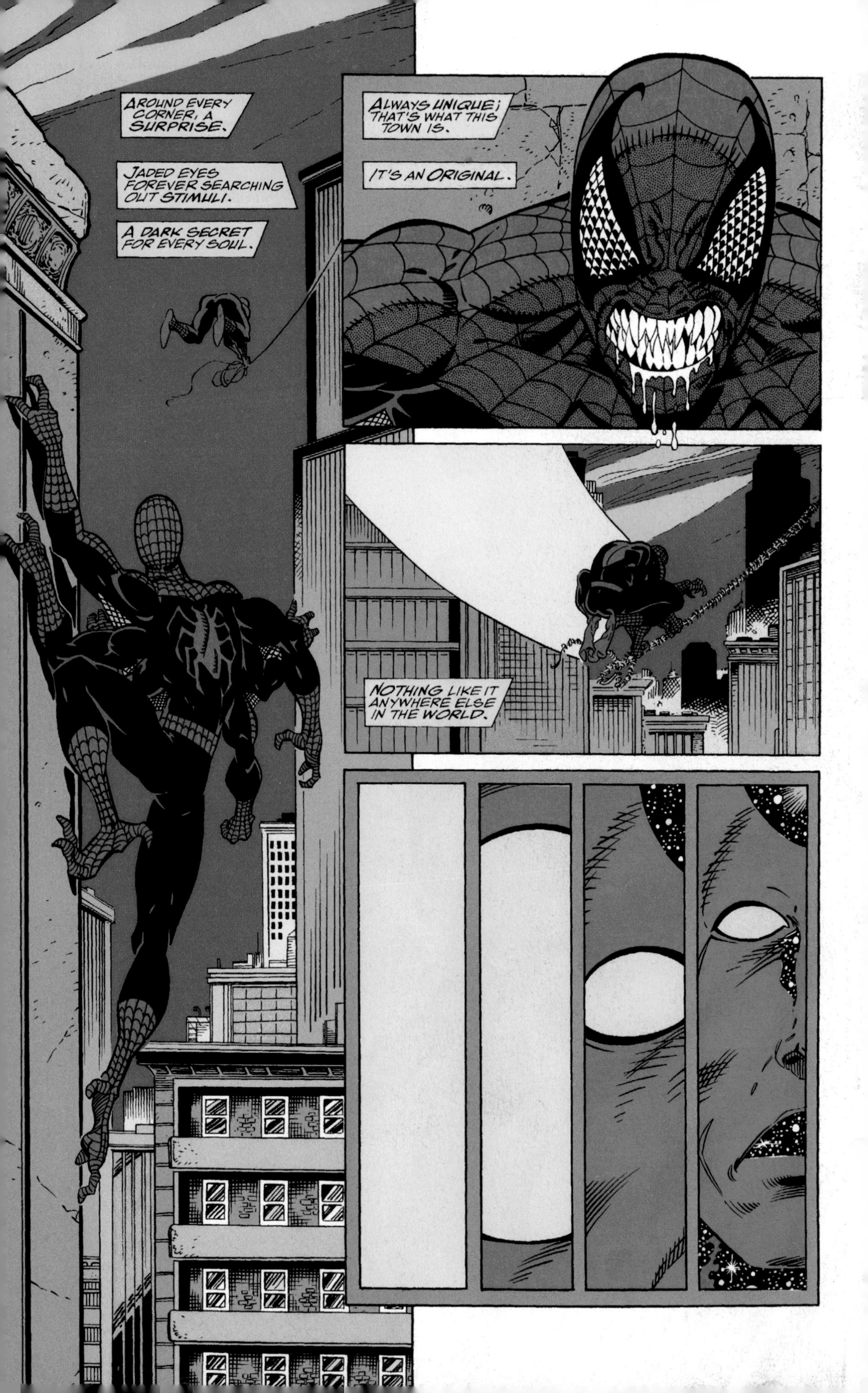
AROUND EVERY CORNER, A SURPRISE.
JADED EYES FOREVER SEARCHING OUT STIMULI.
A DARK SECRET FOR EVERY SOUL.
ALWAYS UNIQUE; THAT'S WHAT THIS TOWN IS.
IT'S AN ORIGINAL.
NOTHING LIKE IT ANYWHERE ELSE IN THE WORLD.

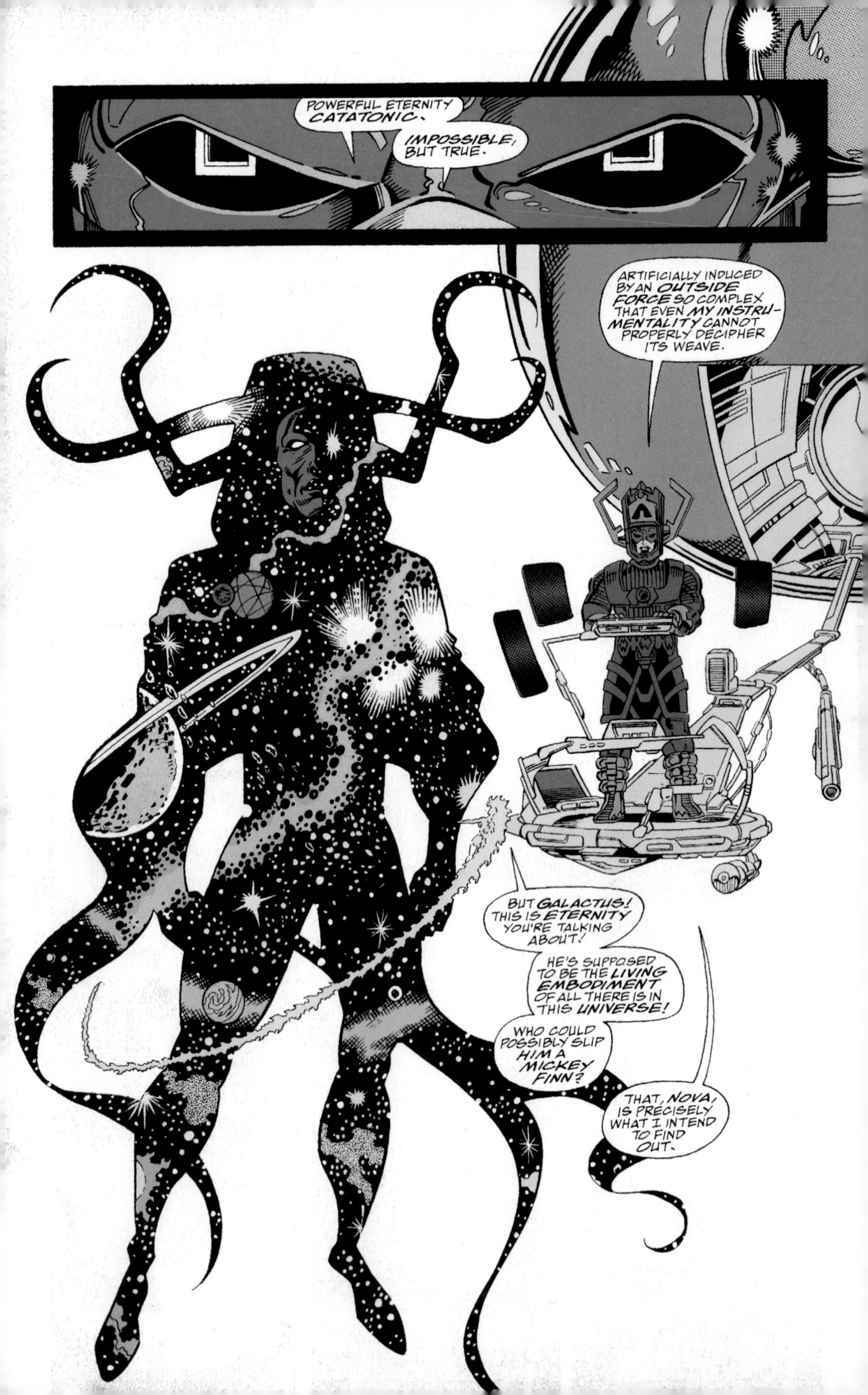
POWERFUL ETERNITY CATATONIC.
IMPOSSIBLE, BUT TRUE.
ARTIFICIALLY INDUCED BY AN OUTSIDE FORCE SO COMPLEX THAT EVEN MY INSTRUMENTALITY CANNOT PROPERLY DECIPHER ITS WEAVE.
BUT GALACTUS! THIS IS ETERNITY YOU'RE TALKING ABOUT!
HE'S SUPPOSED TO BE THE LIVING EMBODIMENT OF ALL THERE IS IN THIS UNIVERSE!
WHO COULD POSSIBLY SLIP HIM A MICKEY FINN?
THAT, NOVA, IS PRECISELY WHAT I INTEND TO FIND OUT.

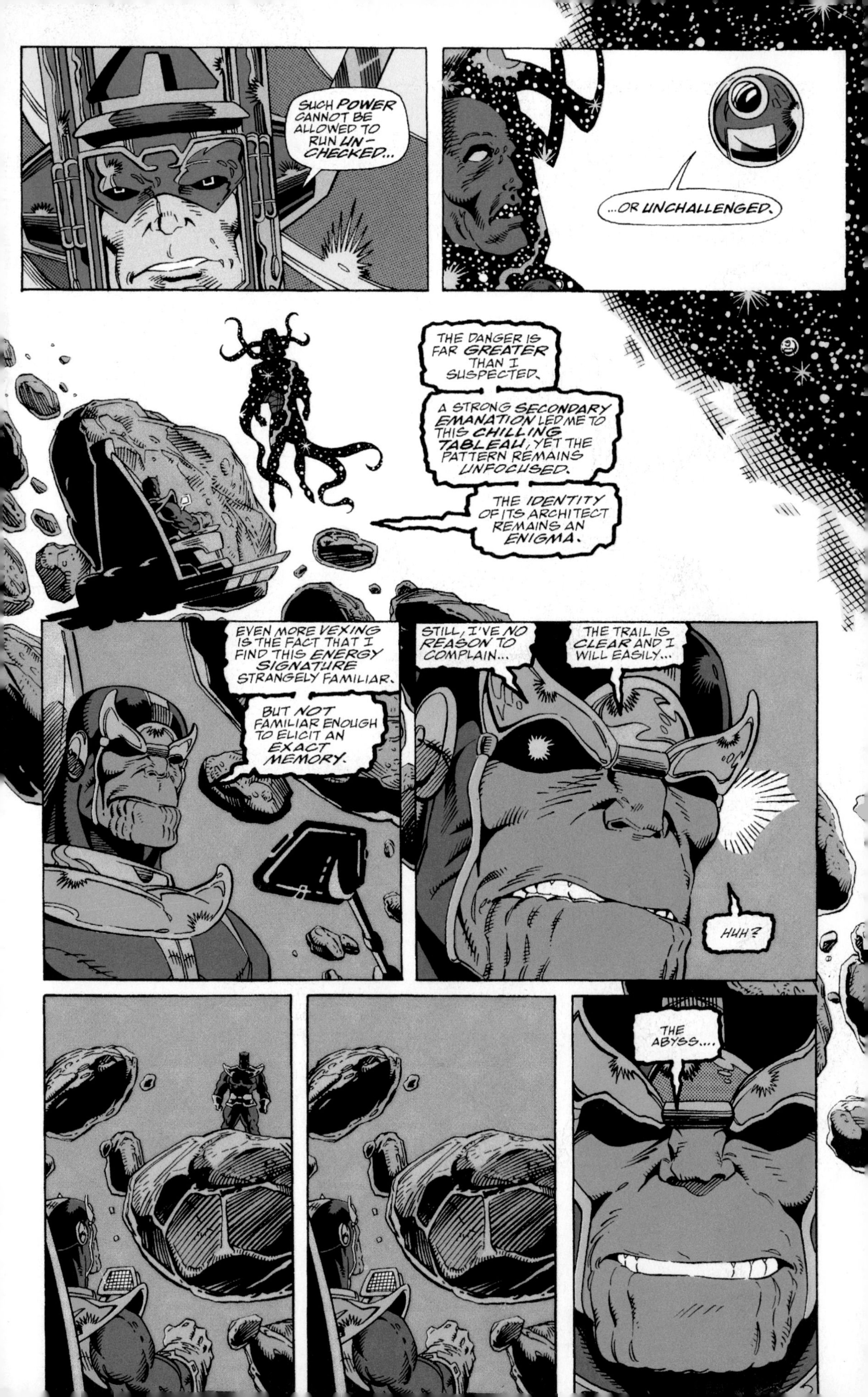
SUCH POWER CANNOT BE ALLOWED TO RUN UN-CHECKED...
...OR UNCHALLENGED.
THE DANGER IS FAR GREATER THAN I SUSPECTED.
A STRONG SECONDARY EMANATION LED ME TO THIS CHILLING TABLEAU, YET THE PATTERN REMAINS UNFOCUSED.
THE IDENTITY OF ITS ARCHITECT REMAINS AN ENIGMA.
EVEN MORE VEXING IS THE FACT THAT I FIND THIS ENERGY SIGNATURE STRANGELY FAMILIAR.
BUT NOT FAMILIAR ENOUGH TO ELICIT AN EXACT MEMORY.
STILL, I'VE NO REASON TO COMPLAIN...
THE TRAIL IS CLEAR AND I WILL EASILY...
HUH?
THE ABYSS....

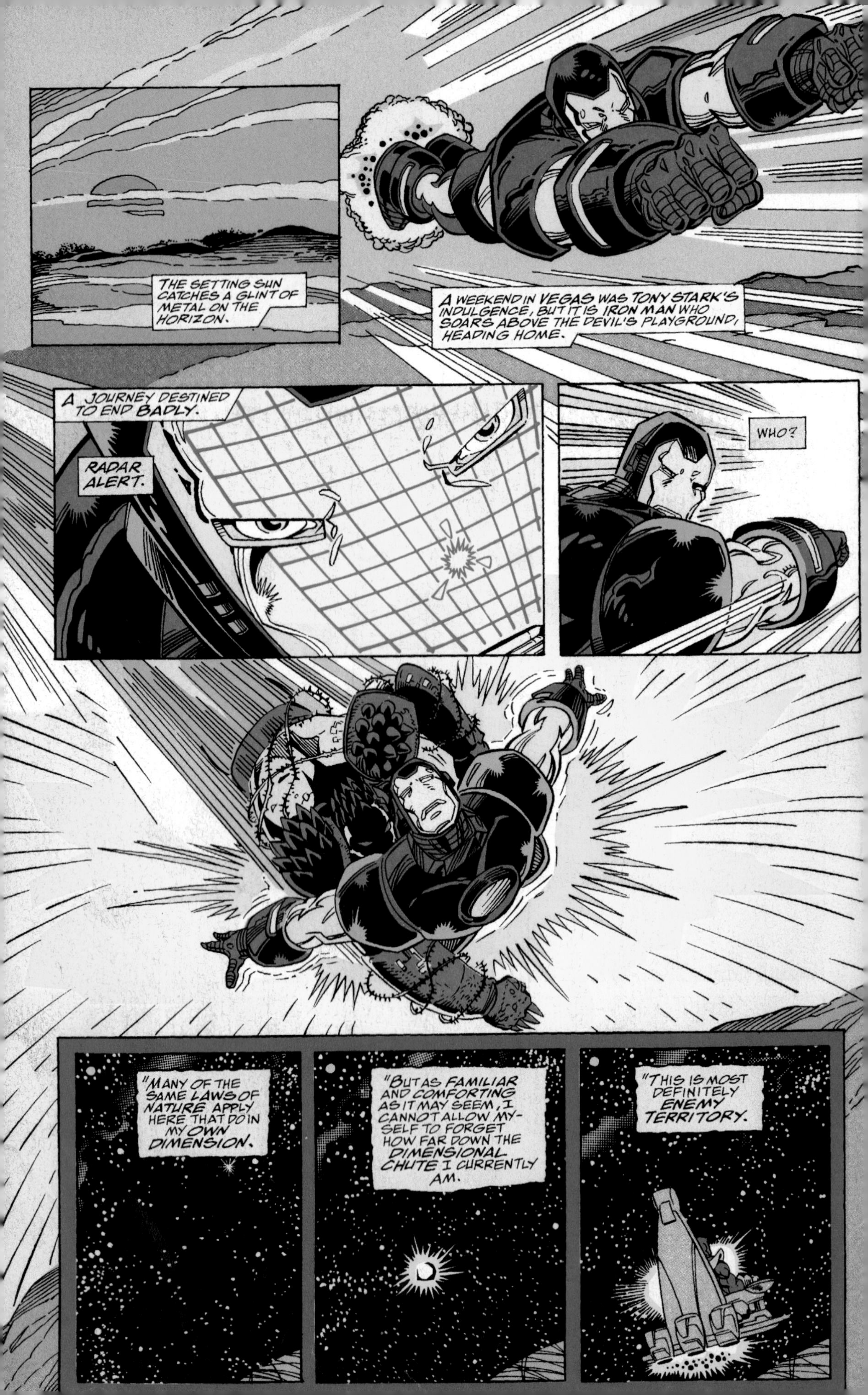
THE SETTING SUN CATCHES A GLINT OF METAL ON THE HORIZON.
A WEEKEND IN VEGAS WAS TONY STARK'S INDULGENCE, BUT IT IS IRON MAN WHO SOARS ABOVE THE DEVIL'S PLAYGROUND, HEADING HOME.
A JOURNEY DESTINED TO END BADLY.
RADAR ALERT.
WHO?
"MANY OF THE SAME LAWS OF NATURE APPLY HERE THAT DO IN MY OWN DIMENSION.
"BUT AS FAMILIAR AND COMFORTING AS IT MAY SEEM, I CANNOT ALLOW MY-SELF TO FORGET HOW FAR DOWN THE DIMENSIONAL CHUTE I CURRENTLY AM.
"THIS IS MOST DEFINITELY ENEMY TERRITORY.

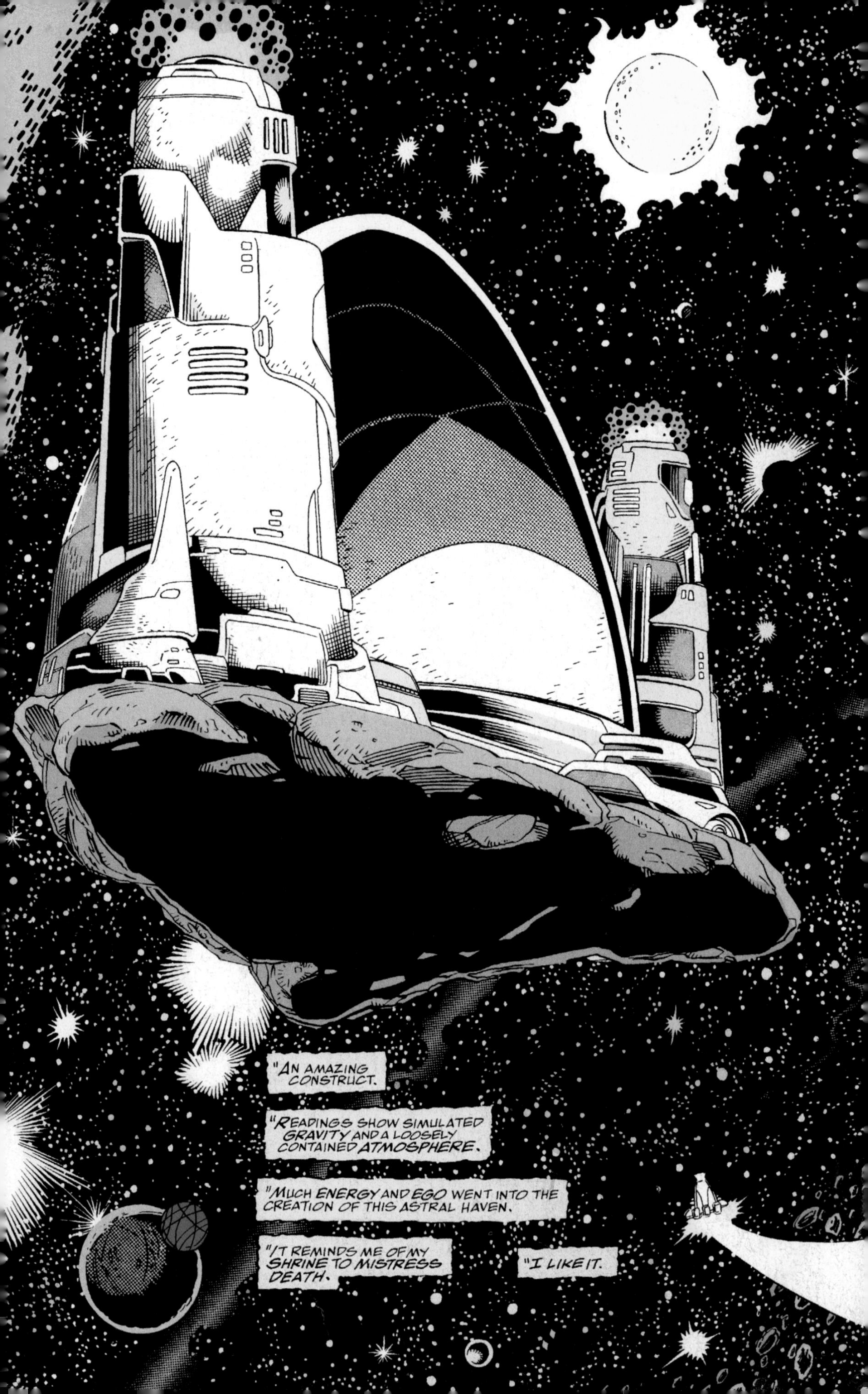
"AN AMAZING CONSTRUCT.
"READINGS SHOW SIMULATED GRAVITY AND A LOOSELY CONTAINED ATMOSPHERE.
"MUCH ENERGY AND EGO WENT INTO THE CREATION OF THIS ASTRAL HAVEN.
"IT REMINDS ME OF MY SHRINE TO MISTRESS DEATH.
"I LIKE IT.

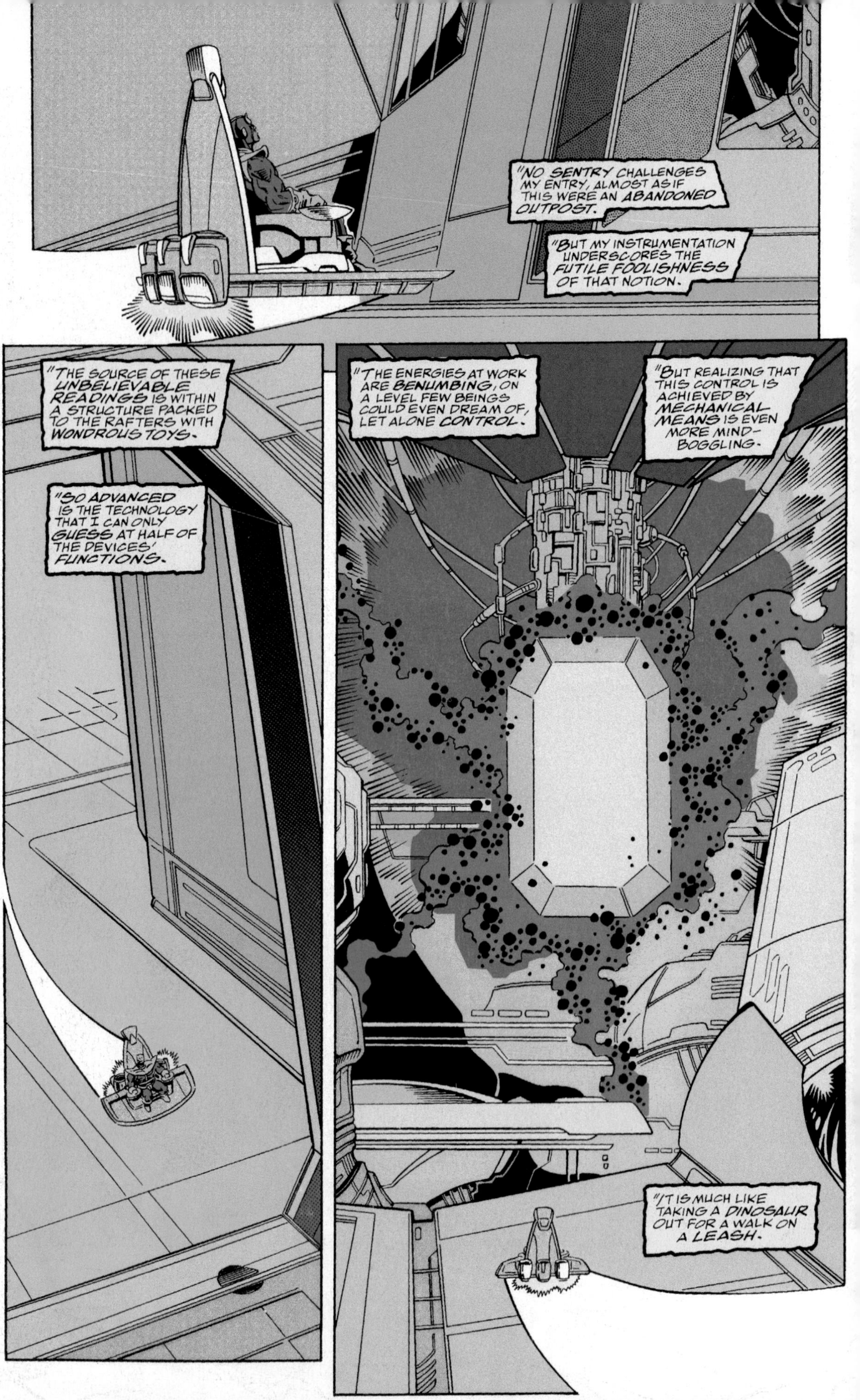
"NO SENTRY CHALLENGES MY ENTRY, ALMOST AS IF THIS WERE AN ABANDONED OUTPOST.
"BUT MY INSTRUMENTATION UNDERSCORES THE FUTILE FOOLISHNESS OF THAT NOTION.
"THE SOURCE OF THESE UNBELIEVABLE READINGS IS WITHIN A STRUCTURE PACKED TO THE RAFTERS WITH WONDROUS TOYS.
"SO ADVANCED IS THE TECHNOLOGY THAT I CAN ONLY GUESS AT HALF OF THE DEVICES' FUNCTIONS.
"THE ENERGIES AT WORK ARE BENUMBING, ON A LEVEL FEW BEINGS COULD EVEN DREAM OF, LET ALONE CONTROL.
"BUT REALIZING THAT THIS CONTROL IS ACHIEVED BY MECHANICAL MEANS IS EVEN MORE MIND-BOGGLING.
"IT IS MUCH LIKE TAKING A DINOSAUR OUT FOR A WALK ON A LEASH.

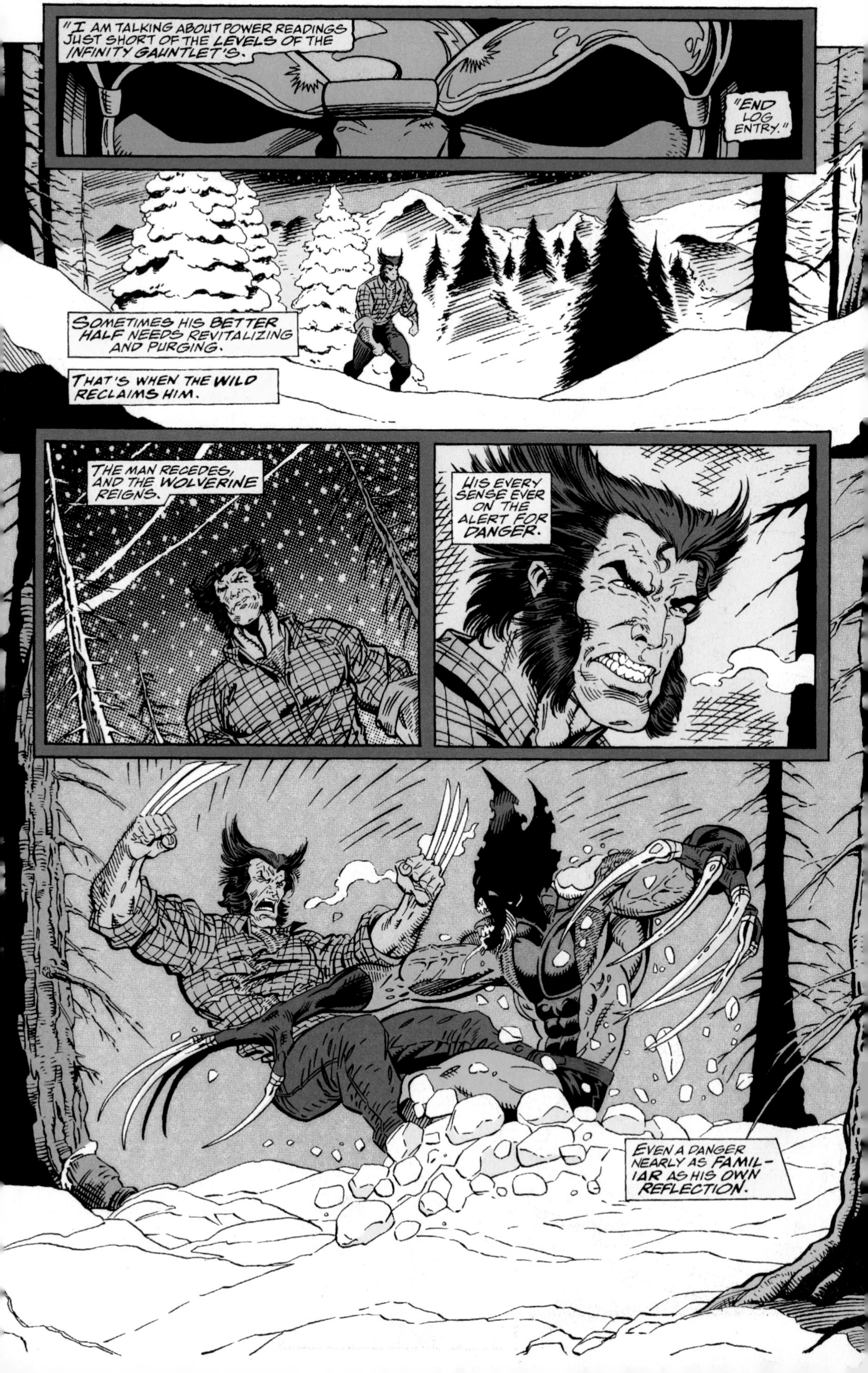
"I AM TALKING ABOUT POWER READINGS JUST SHORT OF THE LEVELS OF THE INFINITY GAUNTLET'S.
"END LOG ENTRY."
SOMETIMES HIS BETTER HALF NEEDS REVITALIZING AND PURGING.
THAT'S WHEN THE WILD RECLAIMS HIM.
THE MAN RECEDES, AND THE WOLVERINE REIGNS.
HIS EVERY SENSE EVER ON THE ALERT FOR DANGER.
EVEN A DANGER NEARLY AS FAMIL-IAR AS HIS OWN REFLECTION.

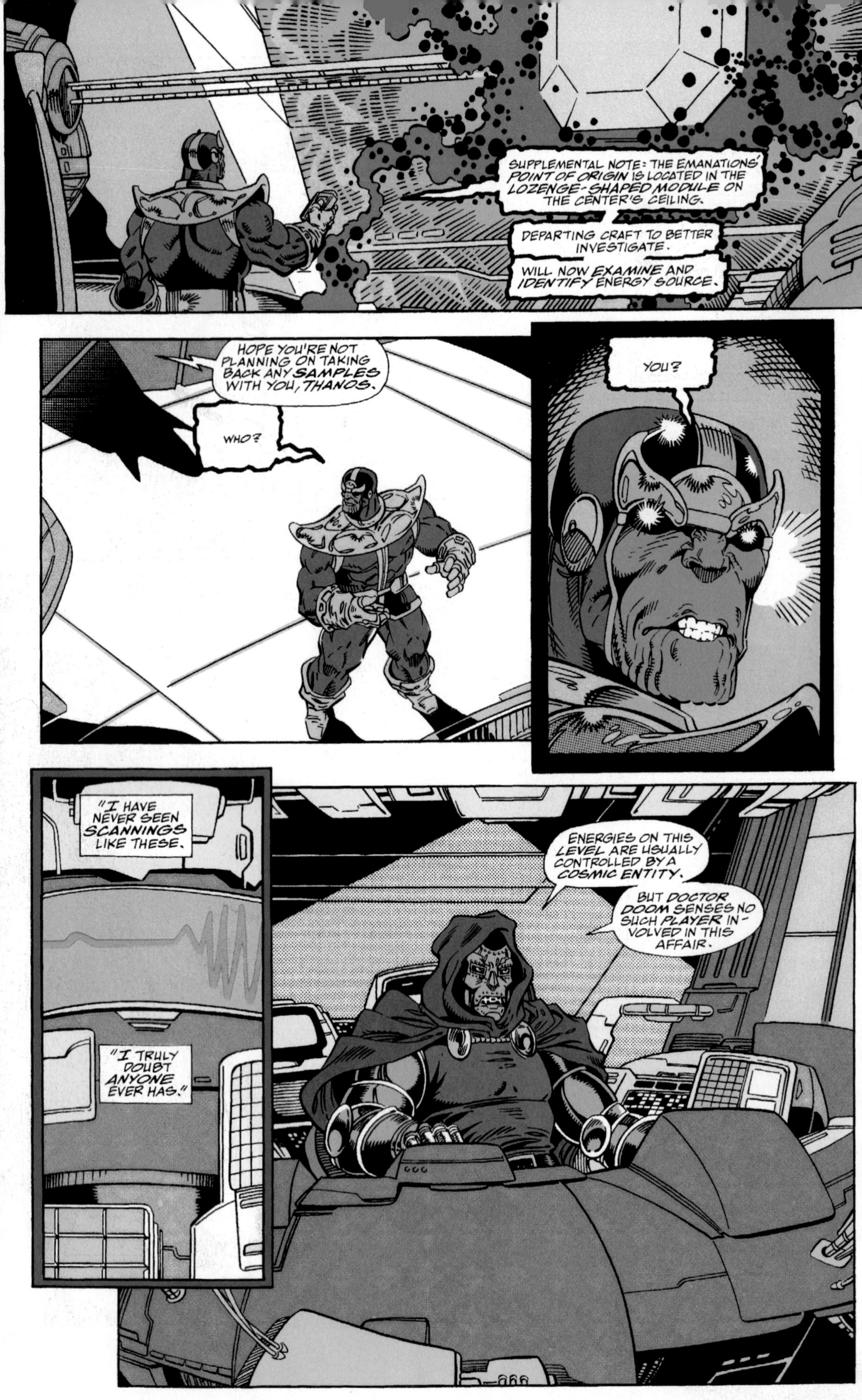
SUPPLEMENTAL NOTE: THE EMANATIONS' POINT OF ORIGIN IS LOCATED IN THE LOZENGE-SHAPED MODULE ON THE CENTER'S CEILING.
DEPARTING CRAFT TO BETTER INVESTIGATE.
WILL NOW EXAMINE AND IDENTIFY ENERGY SOURCE.
HOPE YOU'RE NOT PLANNING ON TAKING BACK ANY SAMPLES WITH YOU, THANOS.
WHO?
YOU?
"I HAVE NEVER SEEN SCANNINGS LIKE THESE.
"I TRULY DOUBT ANYONE EVER HAS."
ENERGIES ON THIS LEVEL ARE USUALLY CONTROLLED BY A COSMIC ENTITY.
BUT DOCTOR DOOM SENSES NO SUCH PLAYER IN-VOLVED IN THIS AFFAIR.

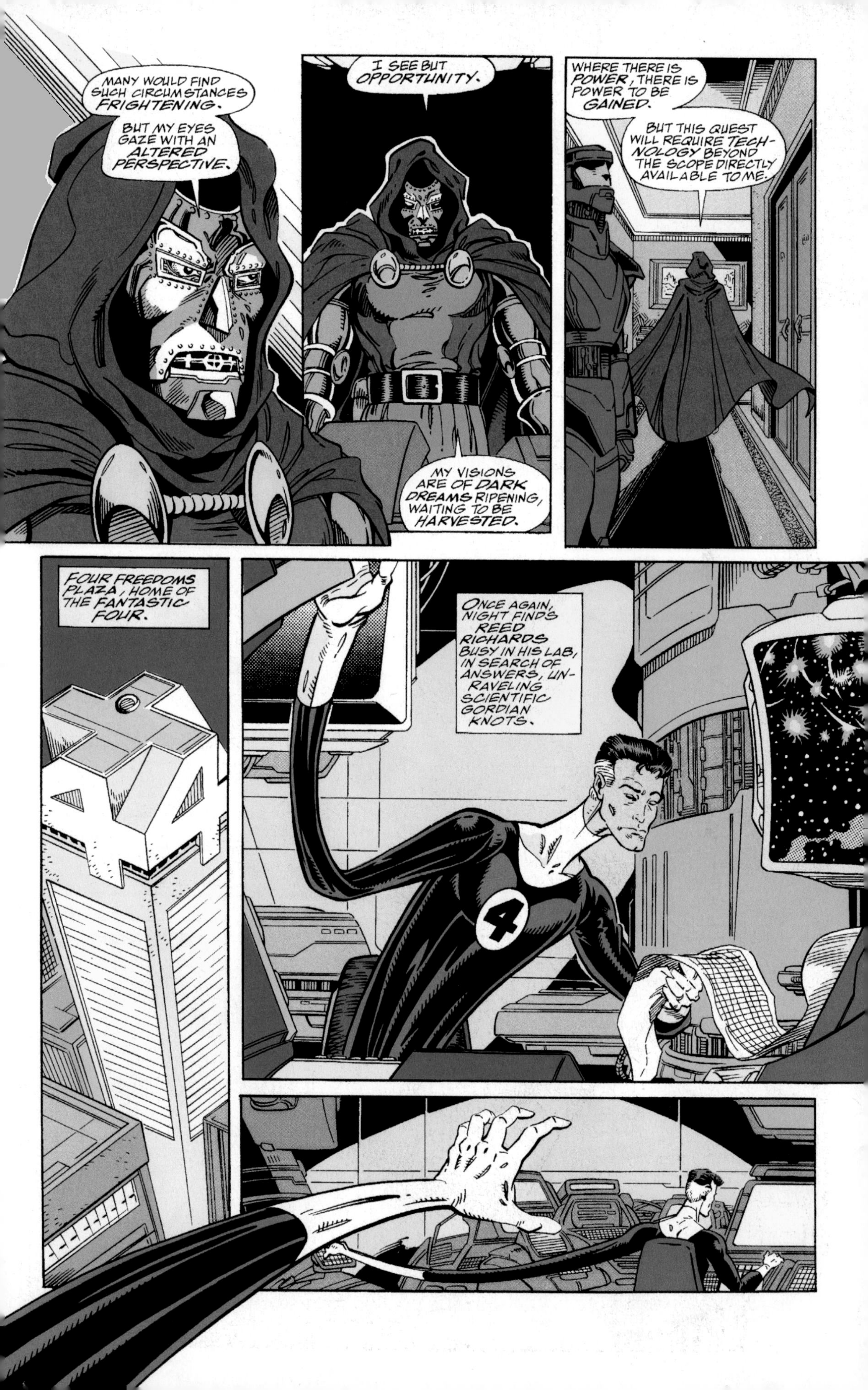
MANY WOULD FIND SUCH CIRCUMSTANCES FRIGHTENING.
BUT MY EYES GAZE WITH AN ALTERED PERSPECTIVE.
I SEE BUT OPPORTUNITY.
MY VISIONS ARE OF DARK DREAMS RIPENING, WAITING TO BE HARVESTED.
WHERE THERE IS POWER, THERE IS POWER TO BE GAINED.
BUT THIS QUEST WILL REQUIRE TECH-NOLOGY BEYOND THE SCOPE DIRECTLY AVAILABLE TO ME.
FOUR FREEDOMS PLAZA, HOME OF THE FANTASTIC FOUR.
ONCE AGAIN, NIGHT FINDS REED RICHARDS BUSY IN HIS LAB, IN SEARCH OF ANSWERS, UN-RAVELING SCIENTIFIC GORDIAN KNOTS.

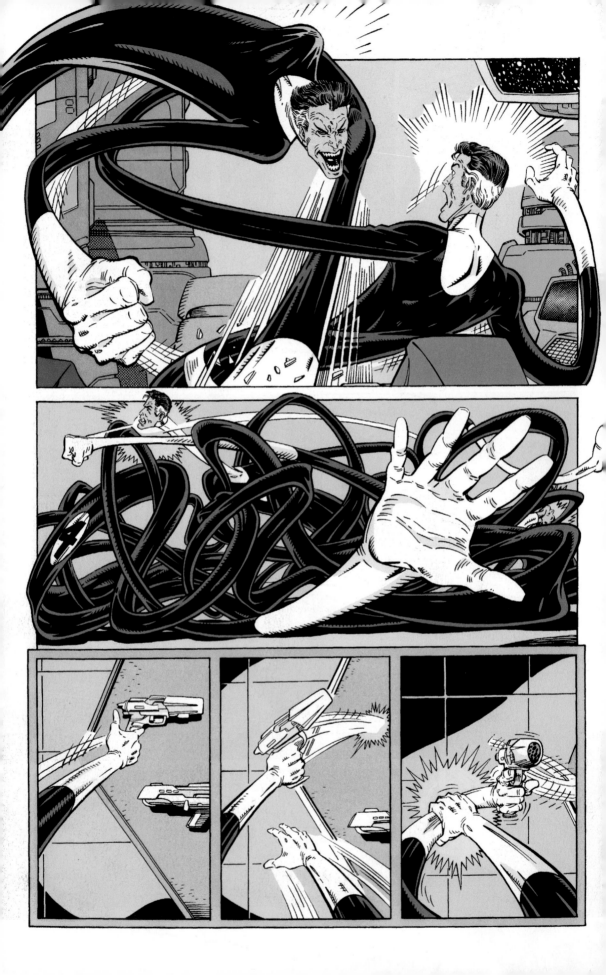

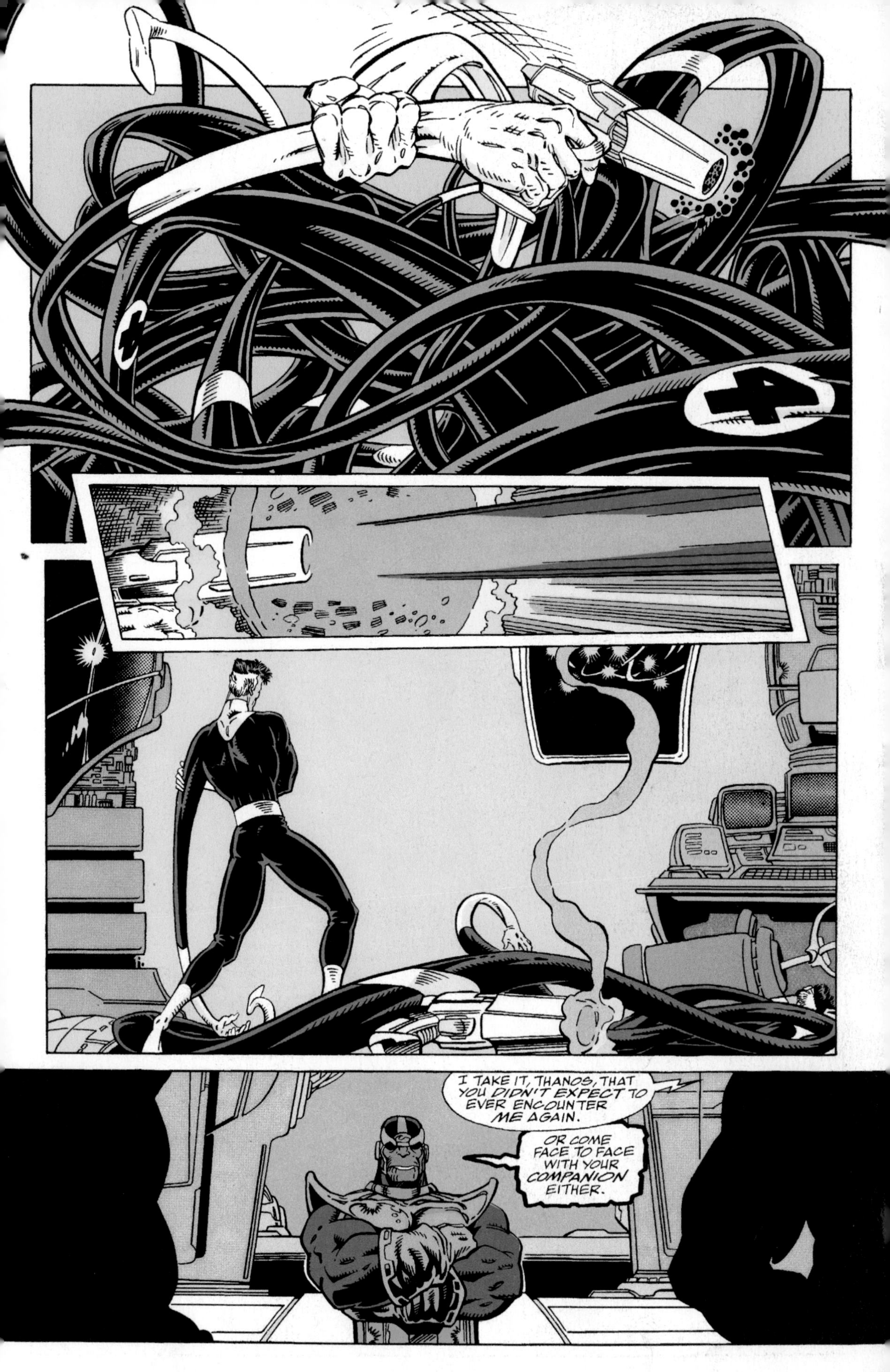
I TAKE IT, THANOS, THAT YOU DIDN'T EXPECT TO EVER ENCOUNTER ME AGAIN.
OR COME FACE TO FACE WITH YOUR COMPANION EITHER.

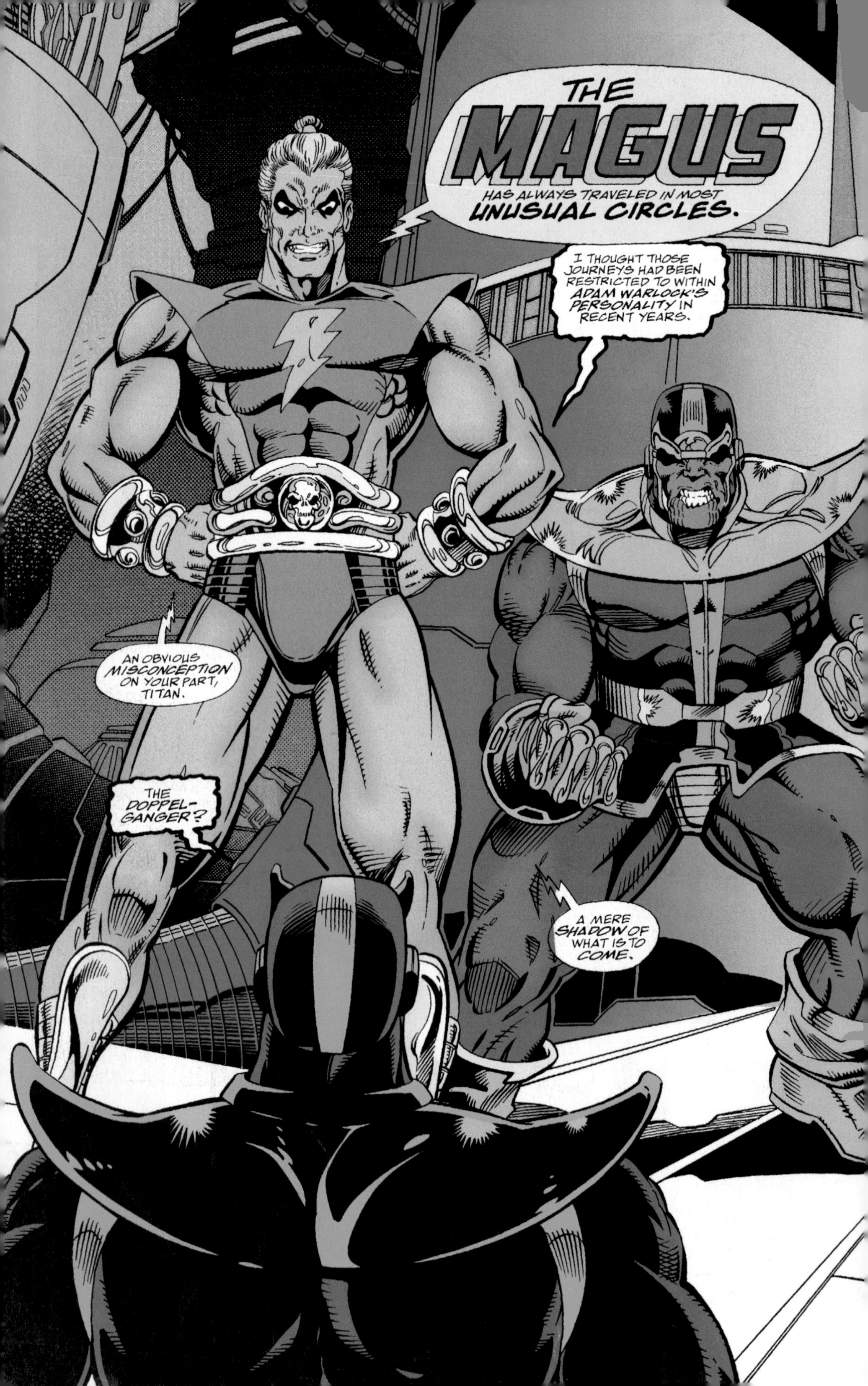
THE MAGUS HAS ALWAYS TRAVELED IN MOST UNUSUAL CIRCLES.
I THOUGHT THOSE JOURNEYS HAD BEEN RESTRICTED TO WITHIN ADAM WARLOCK'S PERSONALITY IN RECENT YEARS.
AN OBVIOUS MISCONCEPTION ON YOUR PART, TITAN.
THE DOPPEL-GANGER?
A MERE SHADOW OF WHAT IS TO COME.

I WAS WITH WARLOCK WHEN YOUR *TIME LINE* WAS DESTROYED.

THERE ARE MANY *PATHS* LEADING TO *GRANDEUR*.

THAT SENTIMENT HAS A *FALSE* RING TO IT.

DOUBT?

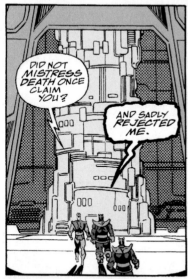

DID NOT *MISTRESS DEATH* ONCE CLAIM YOU?

AND SADLY *REJECTED* ME.

PERHAPS *DIVINE GUIDANCE* ALSO HAD A HAND IN YOUR *RESURRECTION.*

NOW YOU ARE AN *INSTRUMENT* OF THE *ALMIGHTY?*

MOCK IF YOU WILL...

... BUT YOU WILL EVENTUALLY COME TO SEE THAT *MY FLAME* IS DESTINED TO *BLAZE* THROUGHOUT THE HEAVENS.

SOME MISTAKES ARE JUST *TOO TEMPTING* NOT TO *REPEAT.*

ME, A MISTAKE?

THEN PERHAPS *ANOTHER SHADOW?*

YOU TRY MY *PATIENCE*, TITAN.

BE WARNED, FANNING THE *EMBERS* OF MY WRATH COULD PROVE A *TERRIBLE ERROR.*

REMEMBER, SOME MISTAKES ARE *FATAL*,

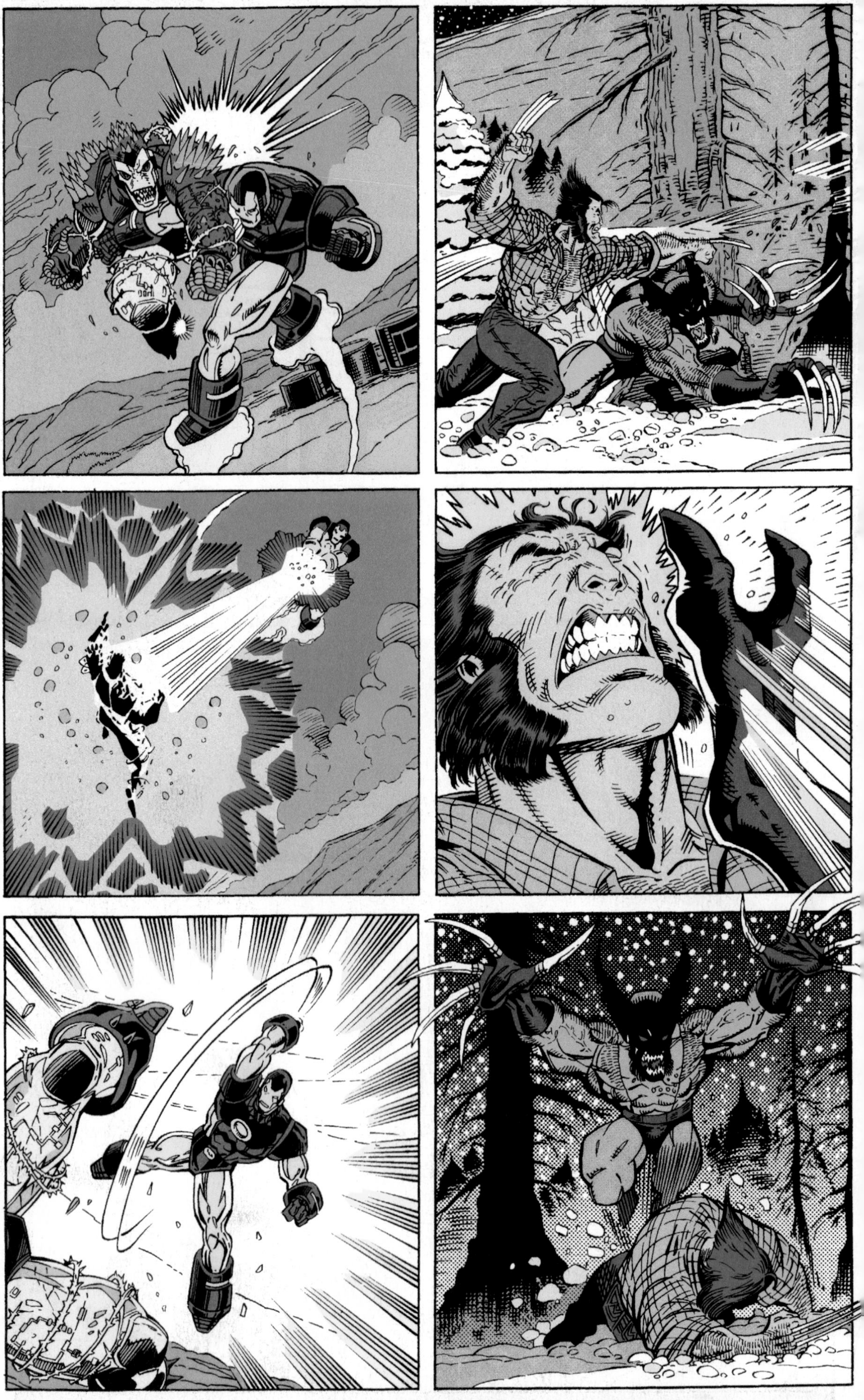

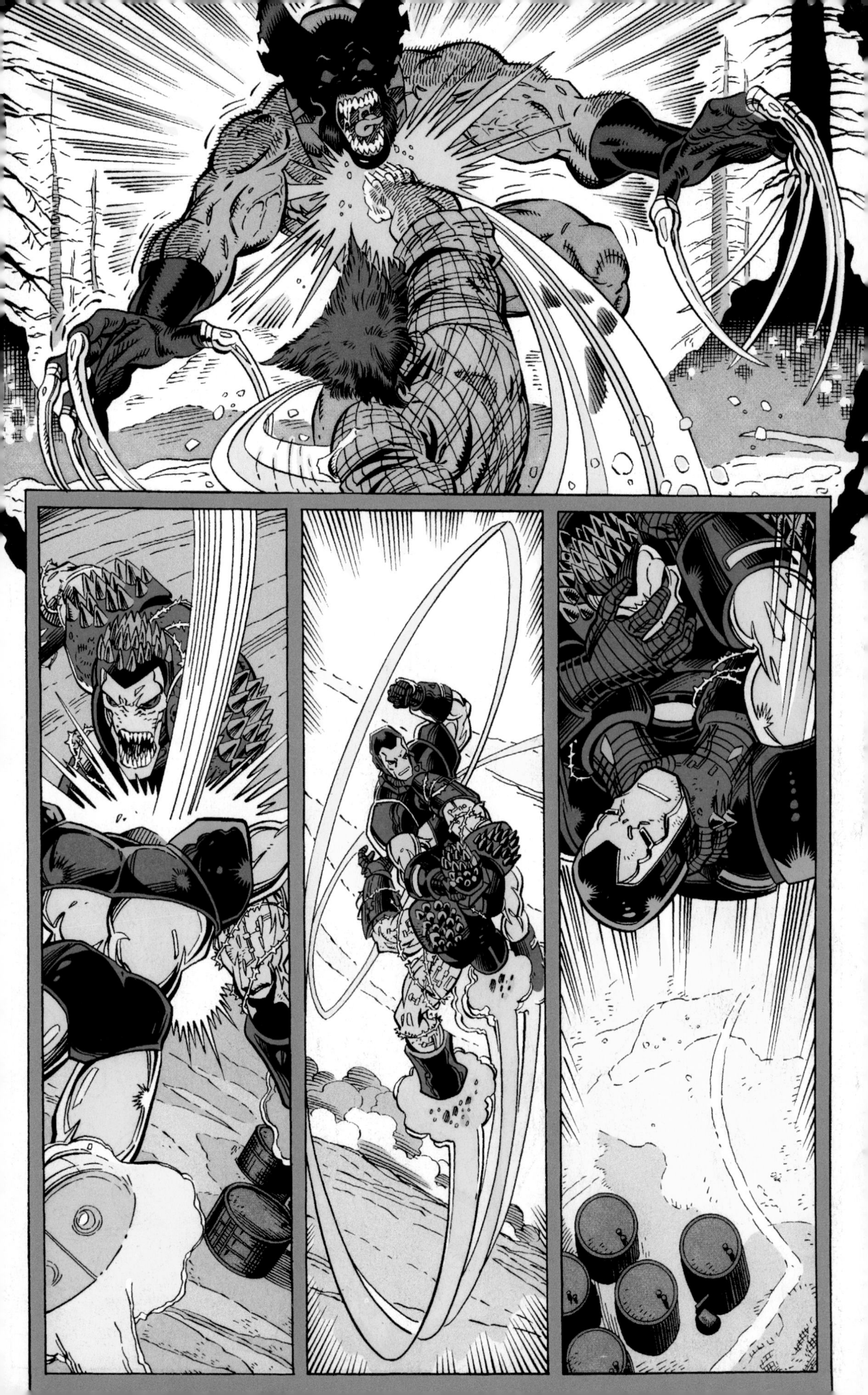

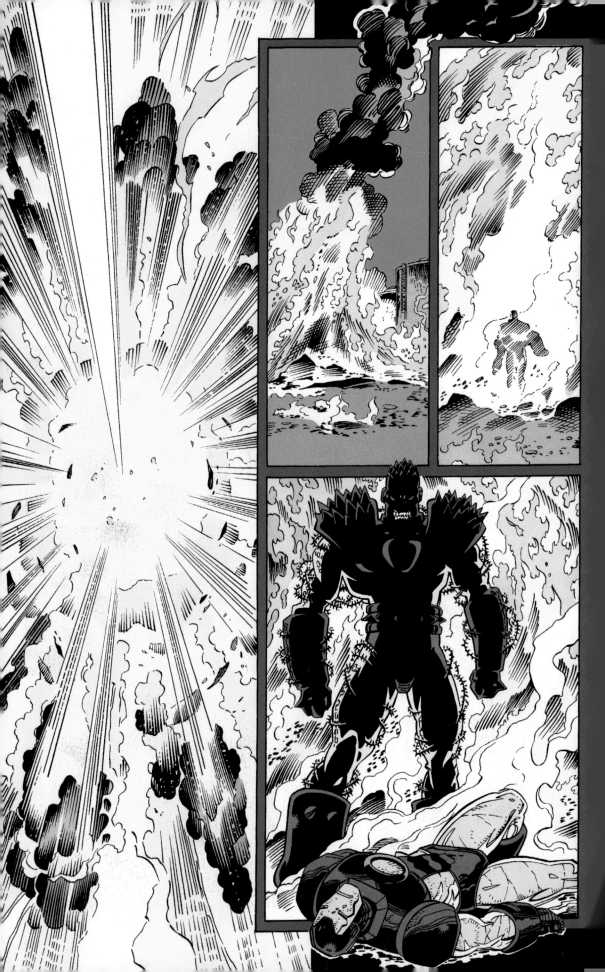

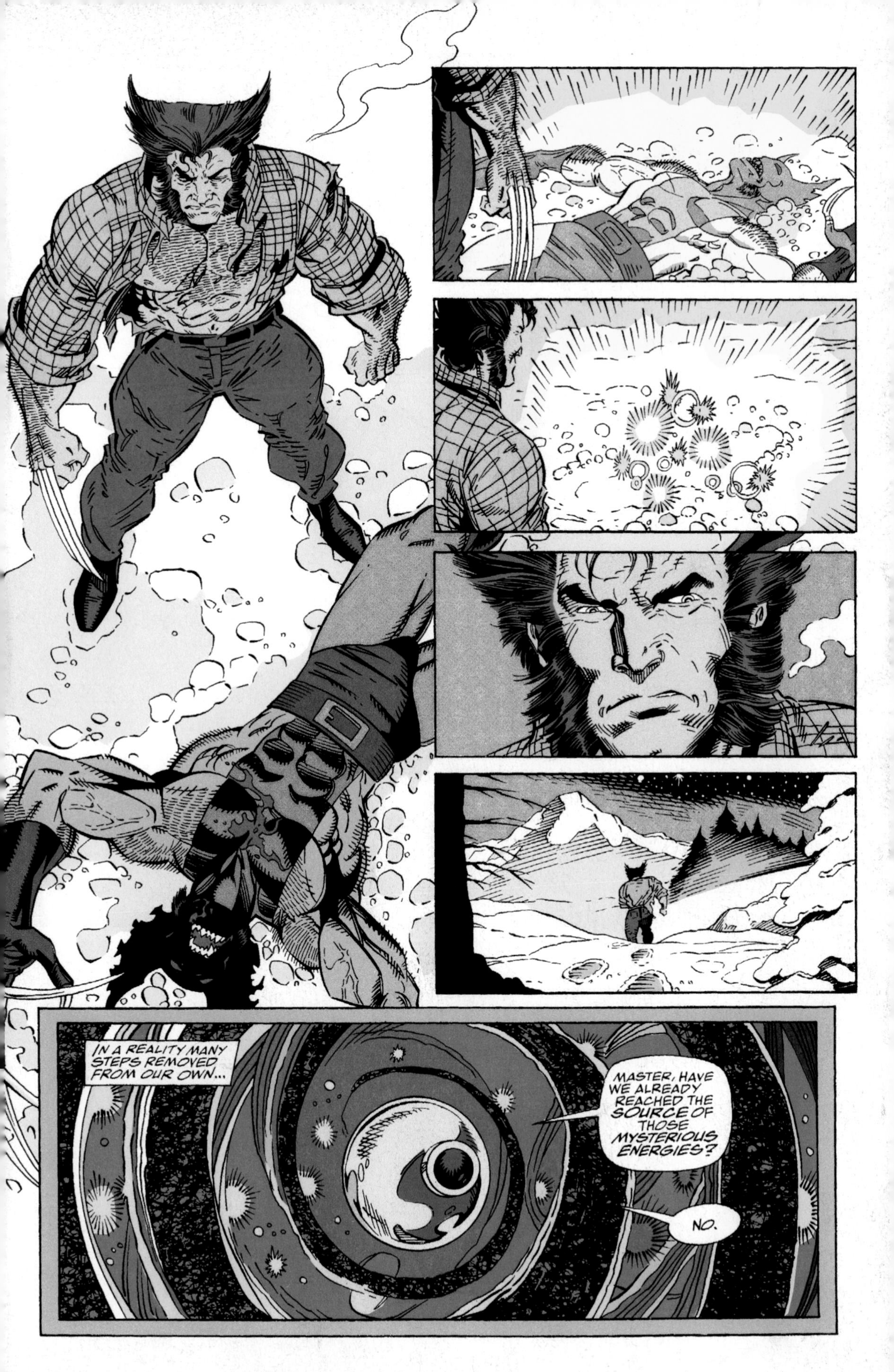
IN A REALITY MANY STEPS REMOVED FROM OUR OWN...
MASTER, HAVE WE ALREADY REACHED THE SOURCE OF THOSE MYSTERIOUS ENERGIES?
NO.

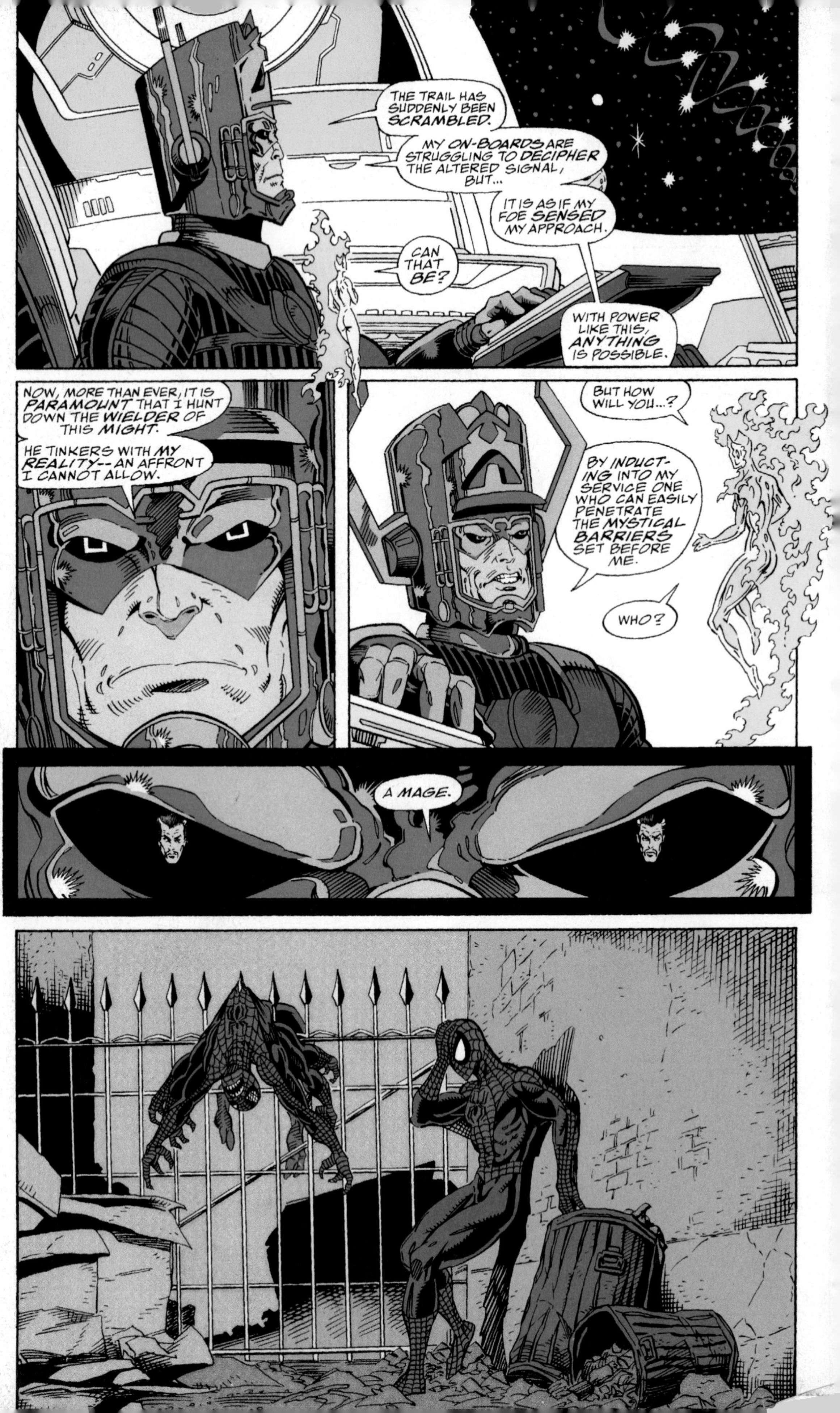

THE TRAIL HAS SUDDENLY BEEN SCRAMBLED.
MY ON-BOARDS ARE STRUGGLING TO DECIPHER THE ALTERED SIGNAL, BUT...
IT IS AS IF MY FOE SENSED MY APPROACH.
CAN THAT BE?
WITH POWER LIKE THIS, ANYTHING IS POSSIBLE.
NOW, MORE THAN EVER, IT IS PARAMOUNT THAT I HUNT DOWN THE WIELDER OF THIS MIGHT.
HE TINKERS WITH MY REALITY-- AN AFFRONT I CANNOT ALLOW.
BUT HOW WILL YOU...?
BY INDUCTING INTO MY SERVICE ONE WHO CAN EASILY PENETRATE THE MYSTICAL BARRIERS SET BEFORE ME.
WHO?
A MAGE.

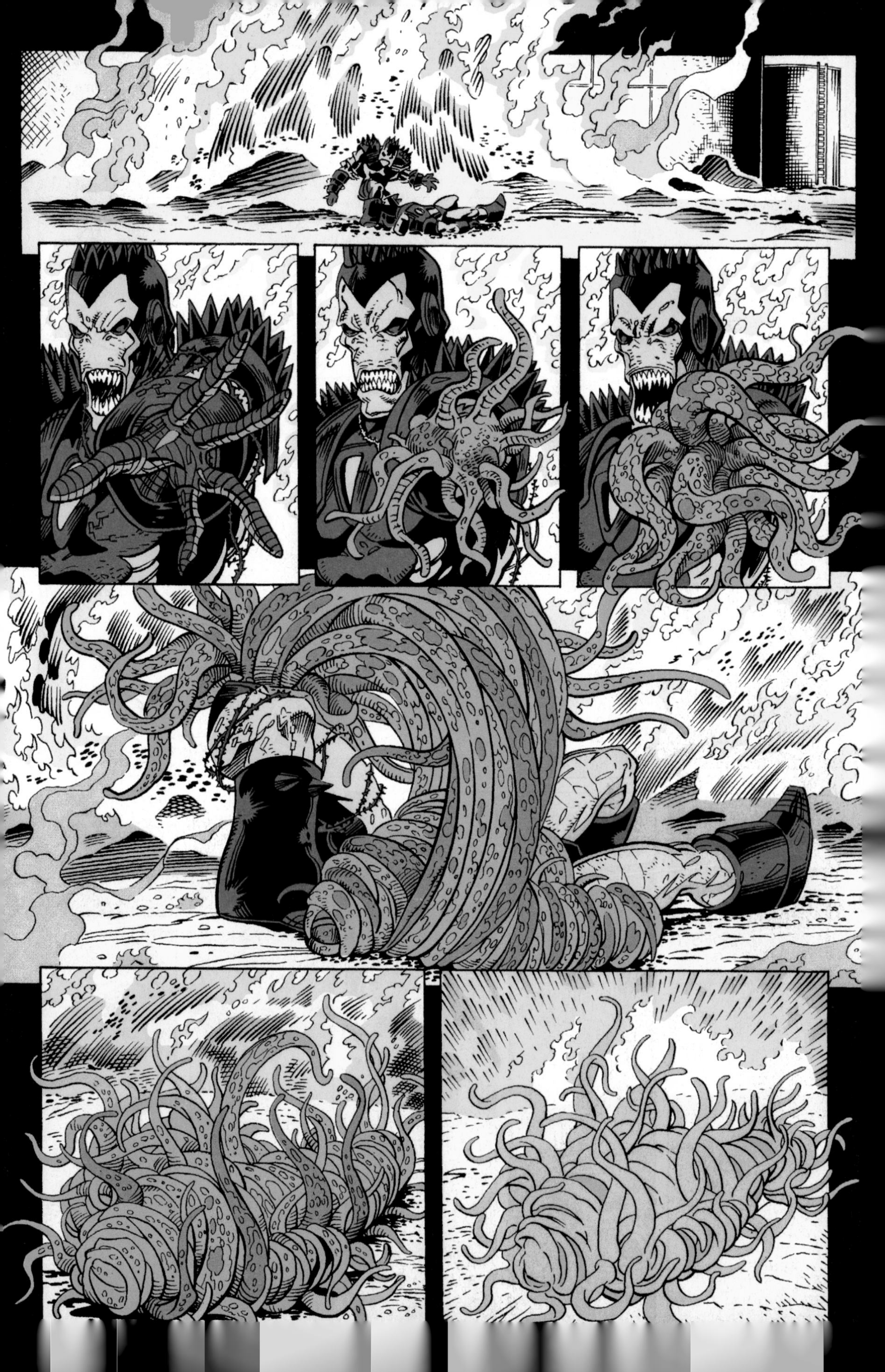

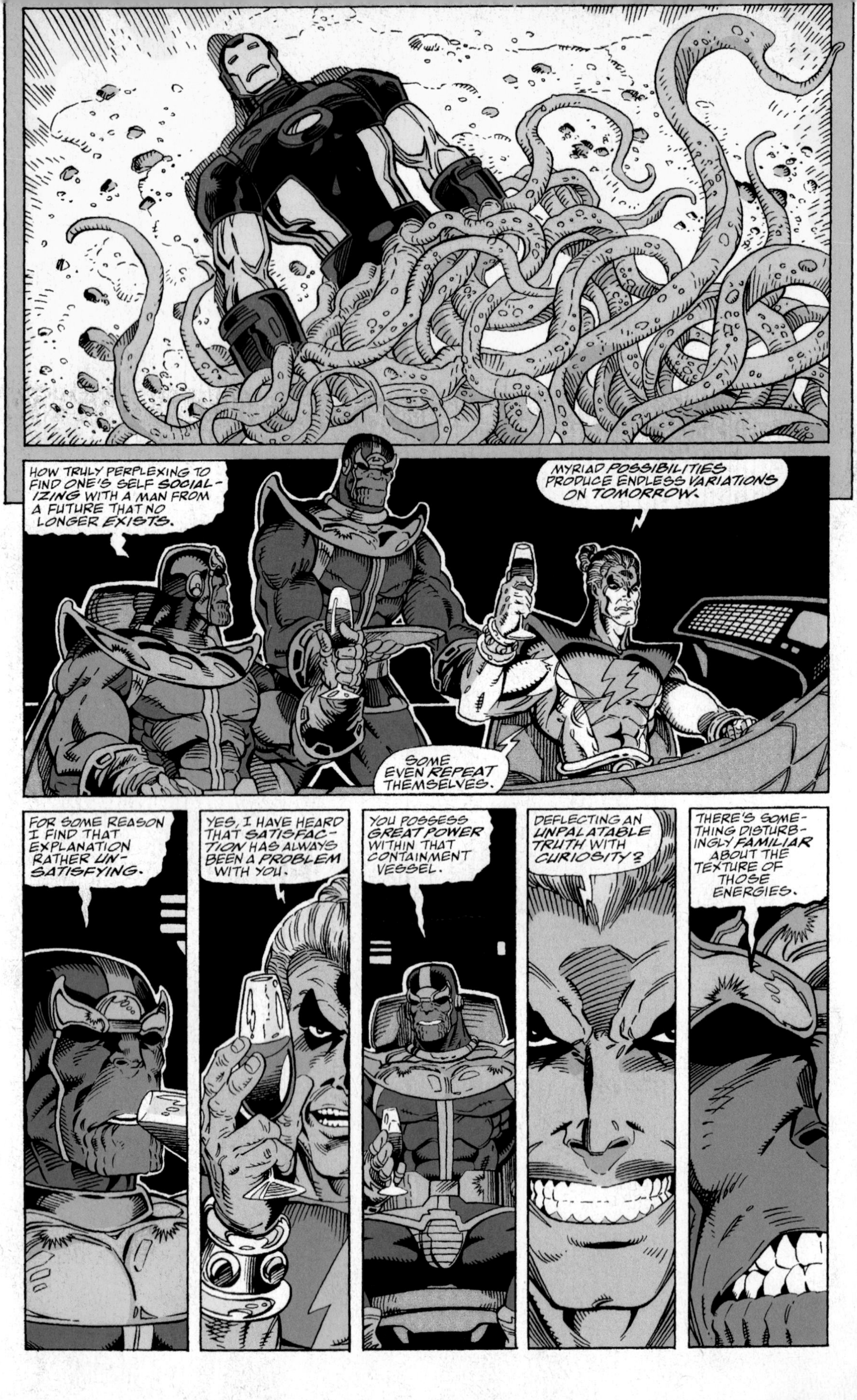
HOW TRULY PERPLEXING TO FIND ONE'S SELF SOCIALIZING WITH A MAN FROM A FUTURE THAT NO LONGER EXISTS.
MYRIAD POSSIBILITIES PRODUCE ENDLESS VARIATIONS ON TOMORROW.
SOME EVEN REPEAT THEMSELVES.
FOR SOME REASON I FIND THAT EXPLANATION RATHER UNSATISFYING.
YES, I HAVE HEARD THAT SATISFACTION HAS ALWAYS BEEN A PROBLEM WITH YOU.
YOU POSSESS GREAT POWER WITHIN THAT CONTAINMENT VESSEL.
DEFLECTING AN UNPALATABLE TRUTH WITH CURIOSITY?
THERE'S SOMETHING DISTURBINGLY FAMILIAR ABOUT THE TEXTURE OF THOSE ENERGIES.

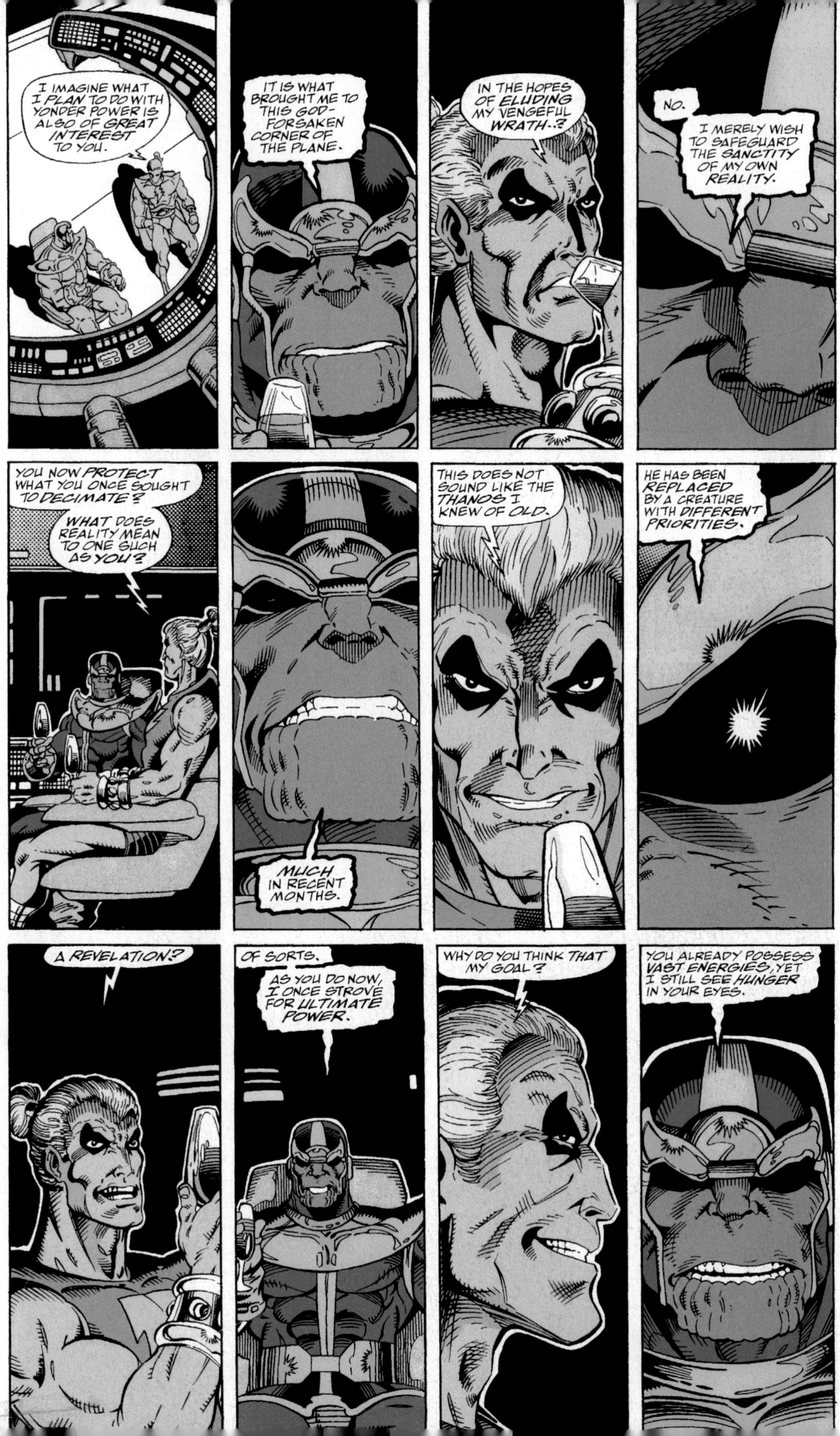
I IMAGINE WHAT I PLAN TO DO WITH YONDER POWER IS ALSO OF GREAT INTEREST TO YOU.
IT IS WHAT BROUGHT ME TO THIS GOD-FORSAKEN CORNER OF THE PLANE.
IN THE HOPES OF ELUDING MY VENGEFUL WRATH..?
NO.
I MERELY WISH TO SAFEGUARD THE SANCTITY OF MY OWN REALITY.
YOU NOW PROTECT WHAT YOU ONCE SOUGHT TO DECIMATE?
WHAT DOES REALITY MEAN TO ONE SUCH AS YOU?
MUCH IN RECENT MONTHS.
THIS DOES NOT SOUND LIKE THE THANOS I KNEW OF OLD.
HE HAS BEEN REPLACED BY A CREATURE WITH DIFFERENT PRIORITIES.
A REVELATION?
OF SORTS.
AS YOU DO NOW, I ONCE STROVE FOR ULTIMATE POWER.
WHY DO YOU THINK THAT MY GOAL?
YOU ALREADY POSSESS VAST ENERGIES, YET I STILL SEE HUNGER IN YOUR EYES.

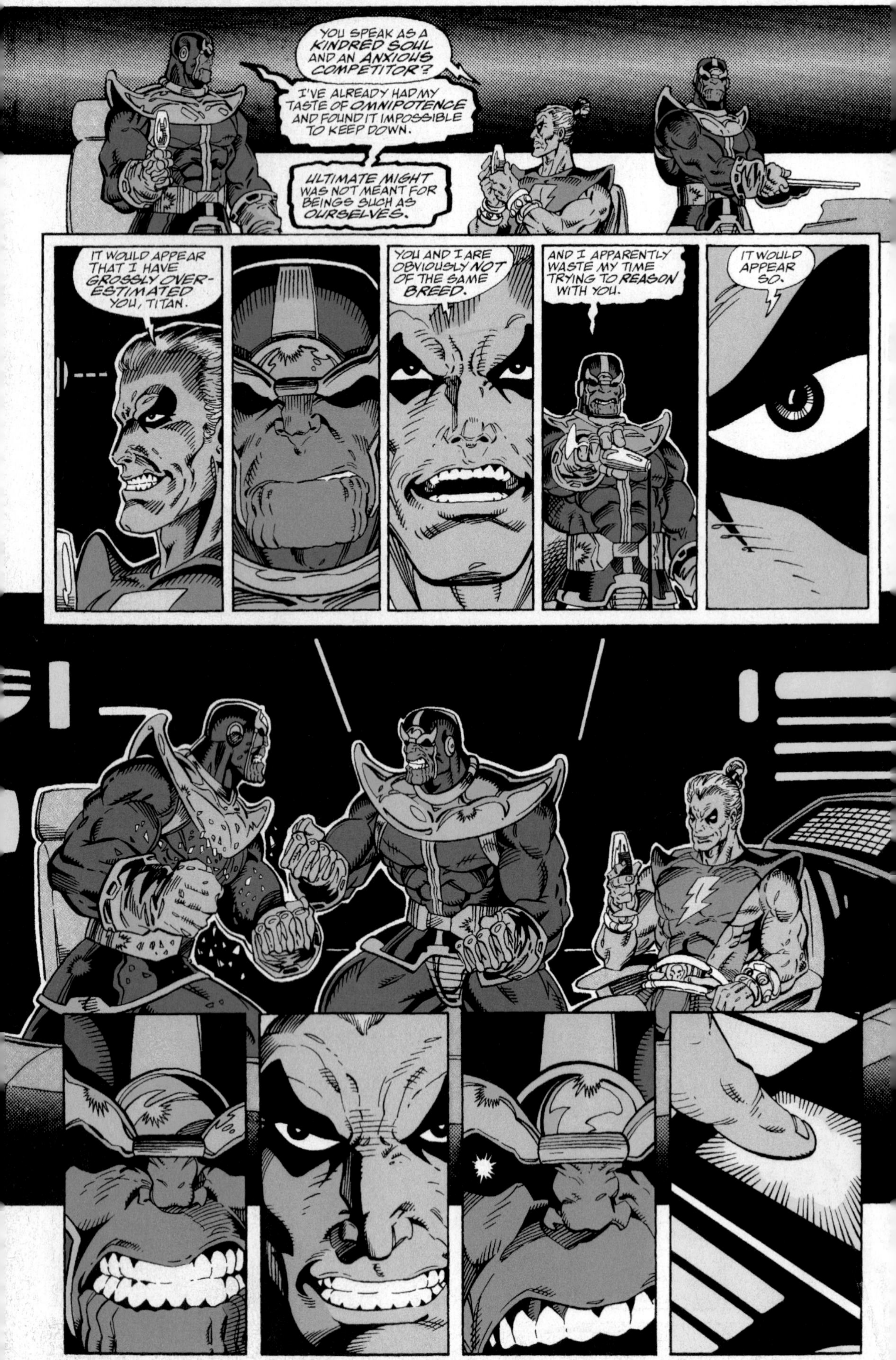
YOU SPEAK AS A KINDRED SOUL AND AN ANXIOUS COMPETITOR?
I'VE ALREADY HAD MY TASTE OF OMNIPOTENCE AND FOUND IT IMPOSSIBLE TO KEEP DOWN.
ULTIMATE MIGHT WAS NOT MEANT FOR BEINGS SUCH AS OURSELVES.
IT WOULD APPEAR THAT I HAVE GROSSLY OVER-ESTIMATED YOU, TITAN.
YOU AND I ARE OBVIOUSLY NOT OF THE SAME BREED.
AND I APPARENTLY WASTE MY TIME TRYING TO REASON WITH YOU.
IT WOULD APPEAR SO.

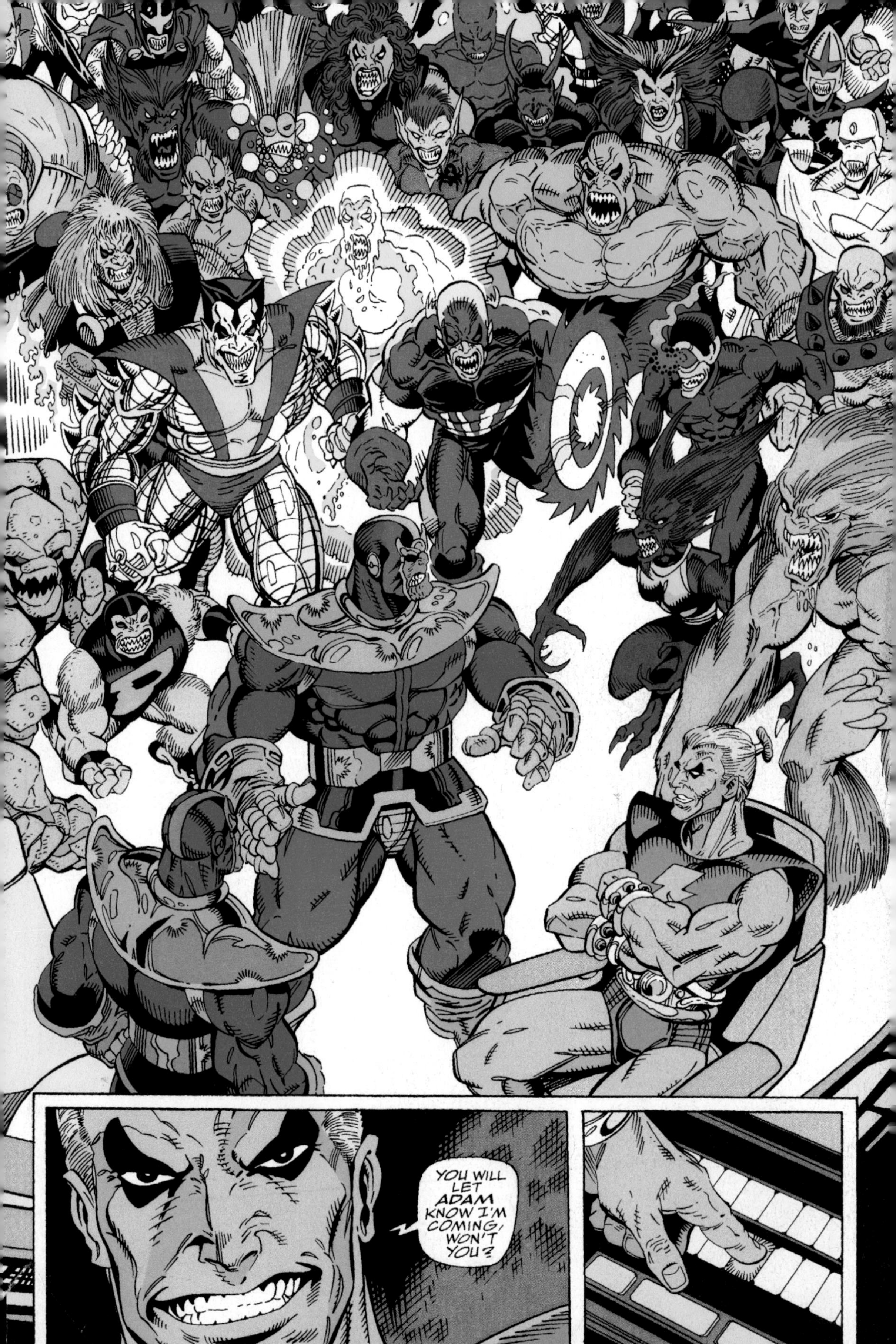
YOU WILL LET ADAM KNOW I'M COMING, WON'T YOU?

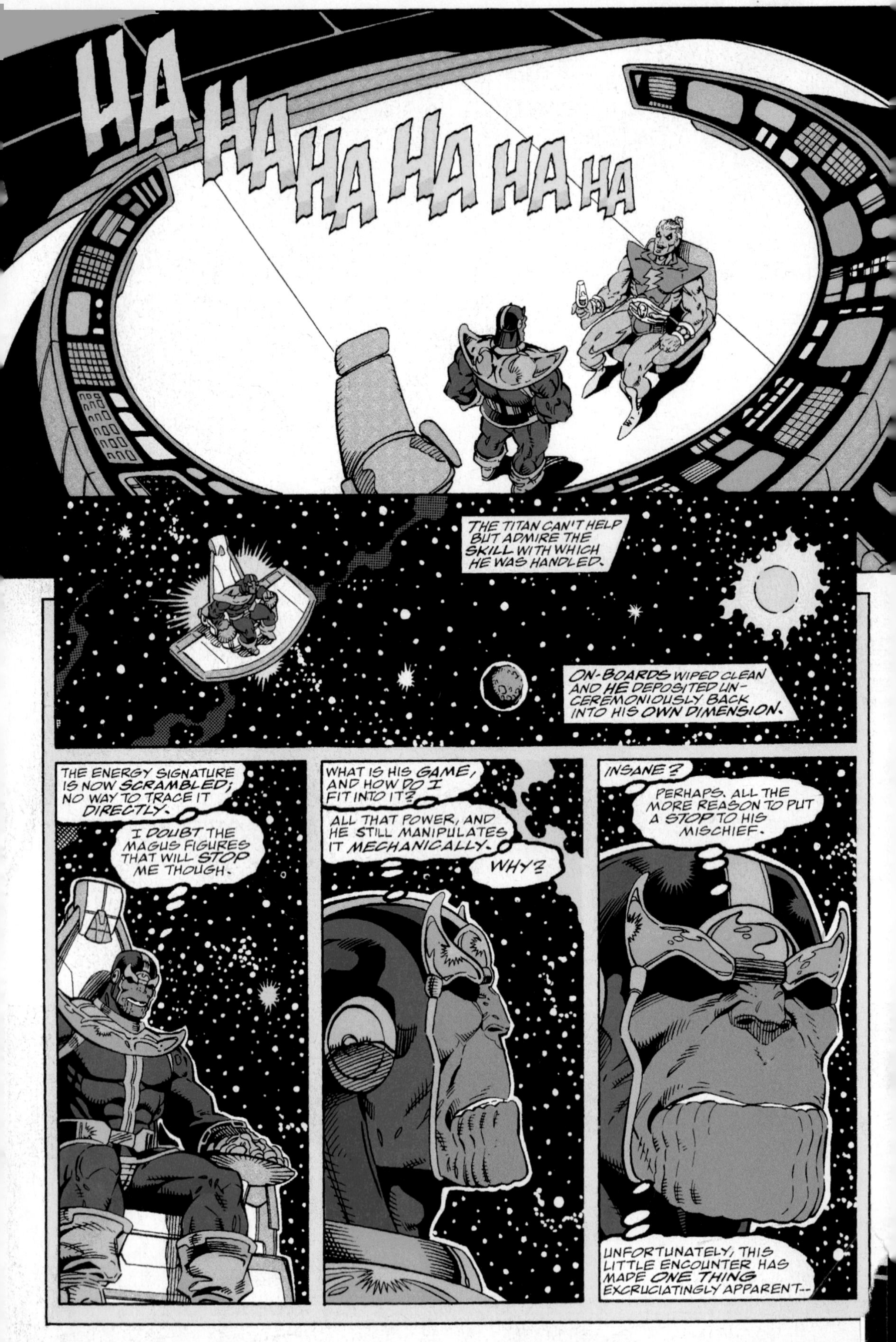
HA HA HA HA HA HA HA HA
THE TITAN CAN'T HELP BUT ADMIRE THE SKILL WITH WHICH HE WAS HANDLED.
ON-BOARDS WIPED CLEAN AND HE DEPOSITED UN-CEREMONIOUSLY BACK INTO HIS OWN DIMENSION.
THE ENERGY SIGNATURE IS NOW SCRAMBLED; NO WAY TO TRACE IT DIRECTLY.
I DOUBT THE MAGUS FIGURES THAT WILL STOP ME THOUGH.
WHAT IS HIS GAME, AND HOW DO I FIT INTO IT?
ALL THAT POWER, AND HE STILL MANIPULATES IT MECHANICALLY.
WHY?
INSANE?
PERHAPS. ALL THE MORE REASON TO PUT A STOP TO HIS MISCHIEF.
UNFORTUNATELY, THIS LITTLE ENCOUNTER HAS MADE ONE THING EXCRUCIATINGLY APPARENT--

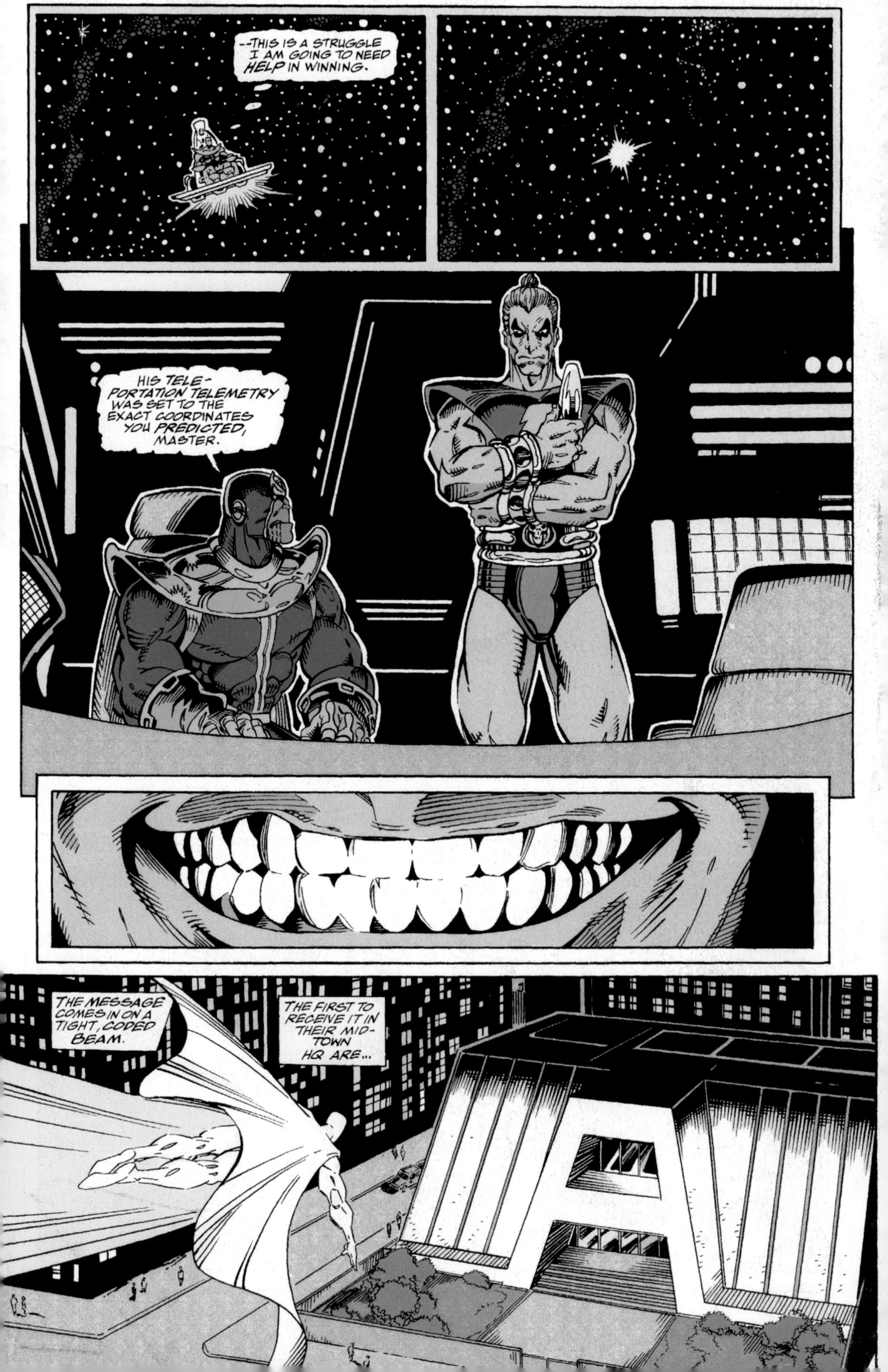
--THIS IS A STRUGGLE I AM GOING TO NEED HELP IN WINNING.
HIS TELE-PORTATION TELEMETRY WAS SET TO THE EXACT COORDINATES YOU PREDICTED, MASTER.
THE MESSAGE COMES IN ON A TIGHT, CODED BEAM.
THE FIRST TO RECEIVE IT IN THEIR MID-TOWN HQ ARE...

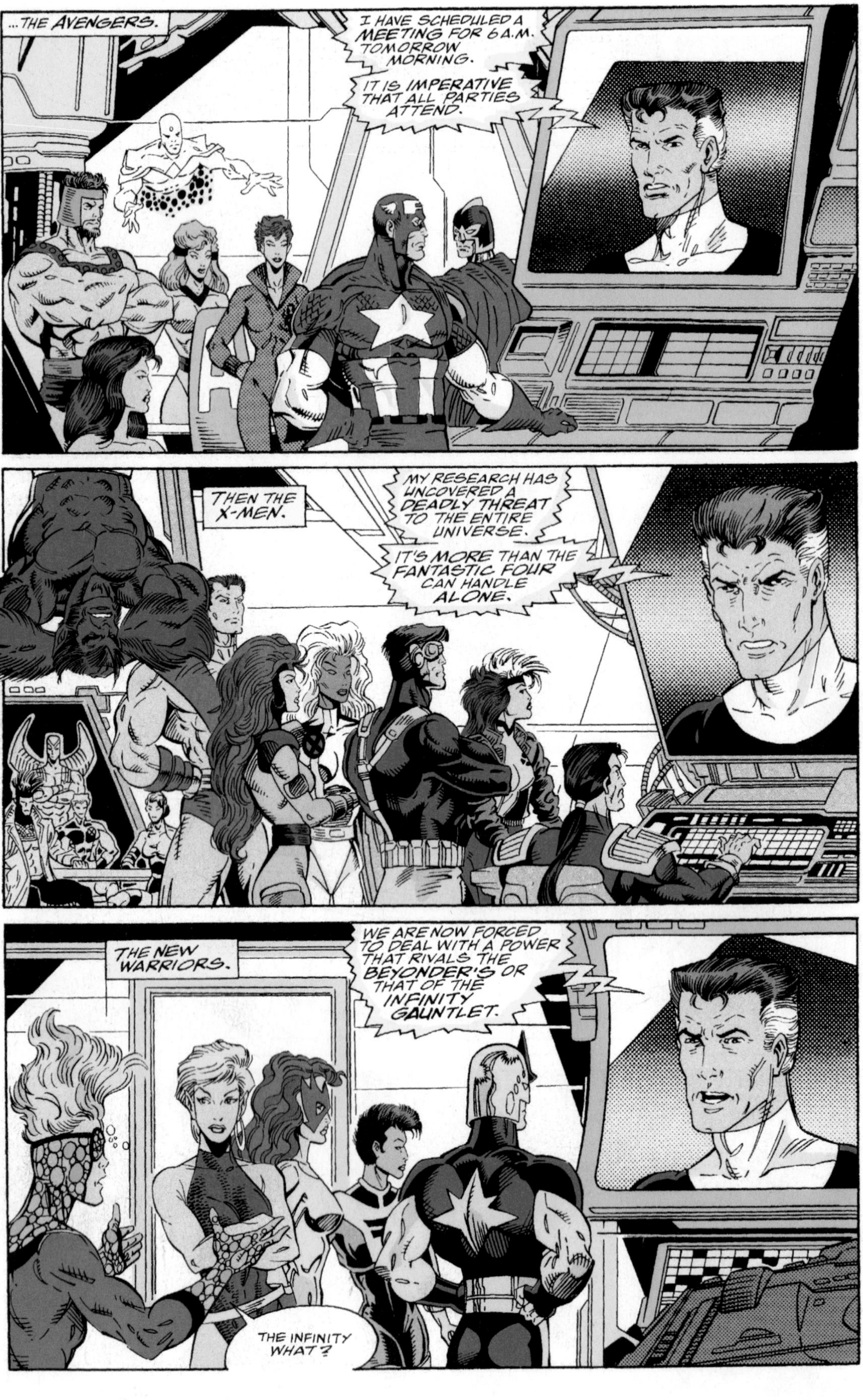
...THE AVENGERS.
I HAVE SCHEDULED A MEETING FOR 6 A.M. TOMORROW MORNING.
IT IS IMPERATIVE THAT ALL PARTIES ATTEND.
THEN THE X-MEN.
MY RESEARCH HAS UNCOVERED A DEADLY THREAT TO THE ENTIRE UNIVERSE.
IT'S MORE THAN THE FANTASTIC FOUR CAN HANDLE ALONE.
THE NEW WARRIORS.
WE ARE NOW FORCED TO DEAL WITH A POWER THAT RIVALS THE BEYONDER'S OR THAT OF THE INFINITY GAUNTLET.
THE INFINITY WHAT?

THE WEST COAST AVENGERS.

IT'S GOING TO TAKE A CONCERTED EFFORT ON ALL OUR PARTS TO INSURE THIS UNIVERSE'S SURVIVAL OVER THE NEXT FEW DAYS.

X-FACTOR.

CAN WE GET ANY PARTICULARS NOW...?

NOT OVER THE WIRE.

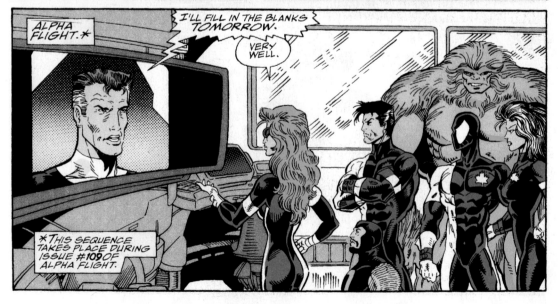

ALPHA FLIGHT.*

I'LL FILL IN THE BLANKS TOMORROW.

VERY WELL.

*THIS SEQUENCE TAKES PLACE DURING ISSUE #109 OF ALPHA FLIGHT.

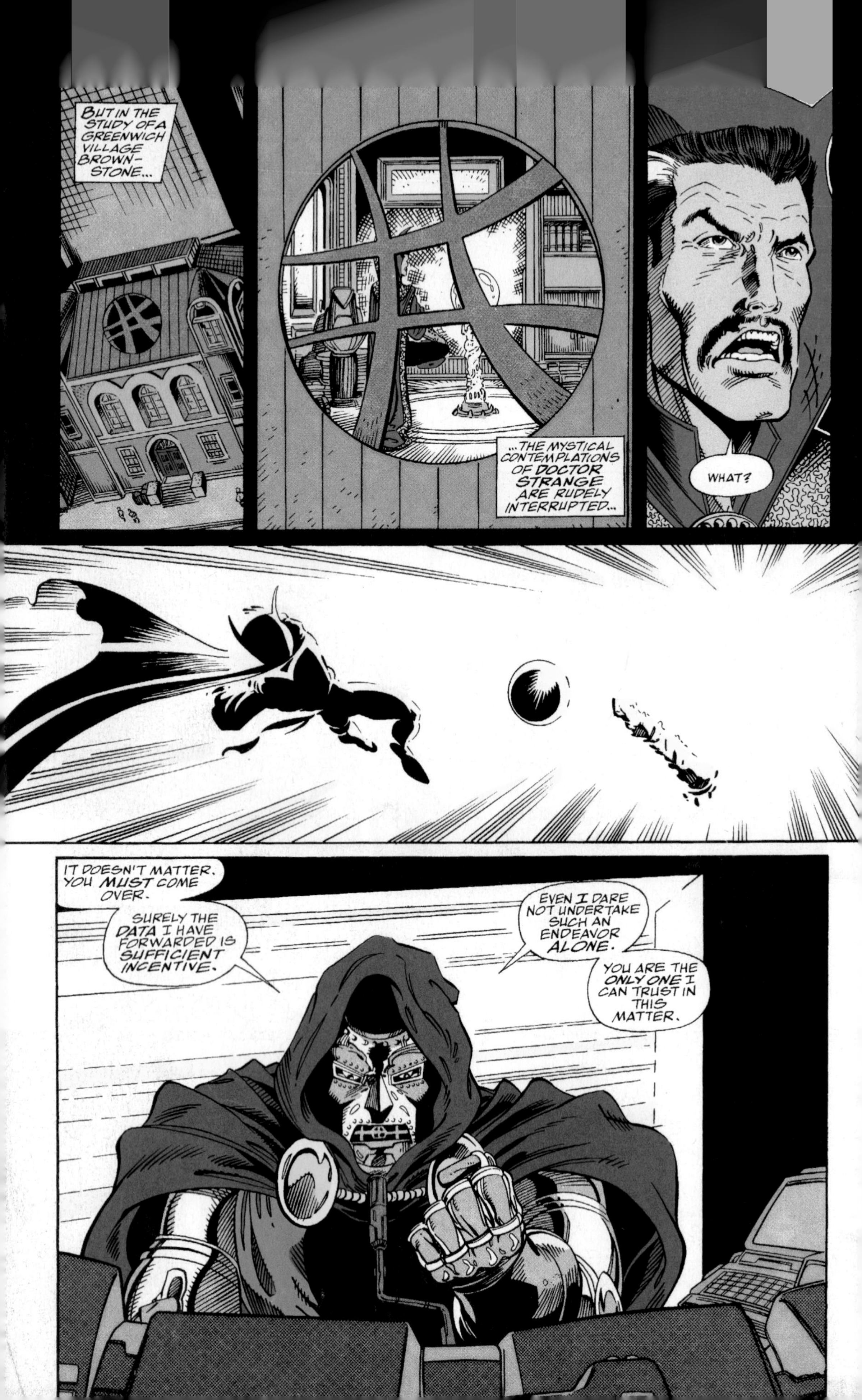
BUT IN THE STUDY OF A GREENWICH VILLAGE BROWN-STONE...
...THE MYSTICAL CONTEMPLATIONS OF DOCTOR STRANGE ARE RUDELY INTERRUPTED...
WHAT?
IT DOESN'T MATTER. YOU MUST COME OVER.
SURELY THE DATA I HAVE FORWARDED IS SUFFICIENT INCENTIVE.
EVEN I DARE NOT UNDERTAKE SUCH AN ENDEAVOR ALONE.
YOU ARE THE ONLY ONE I CAN TRUST IN THIS MATTER.

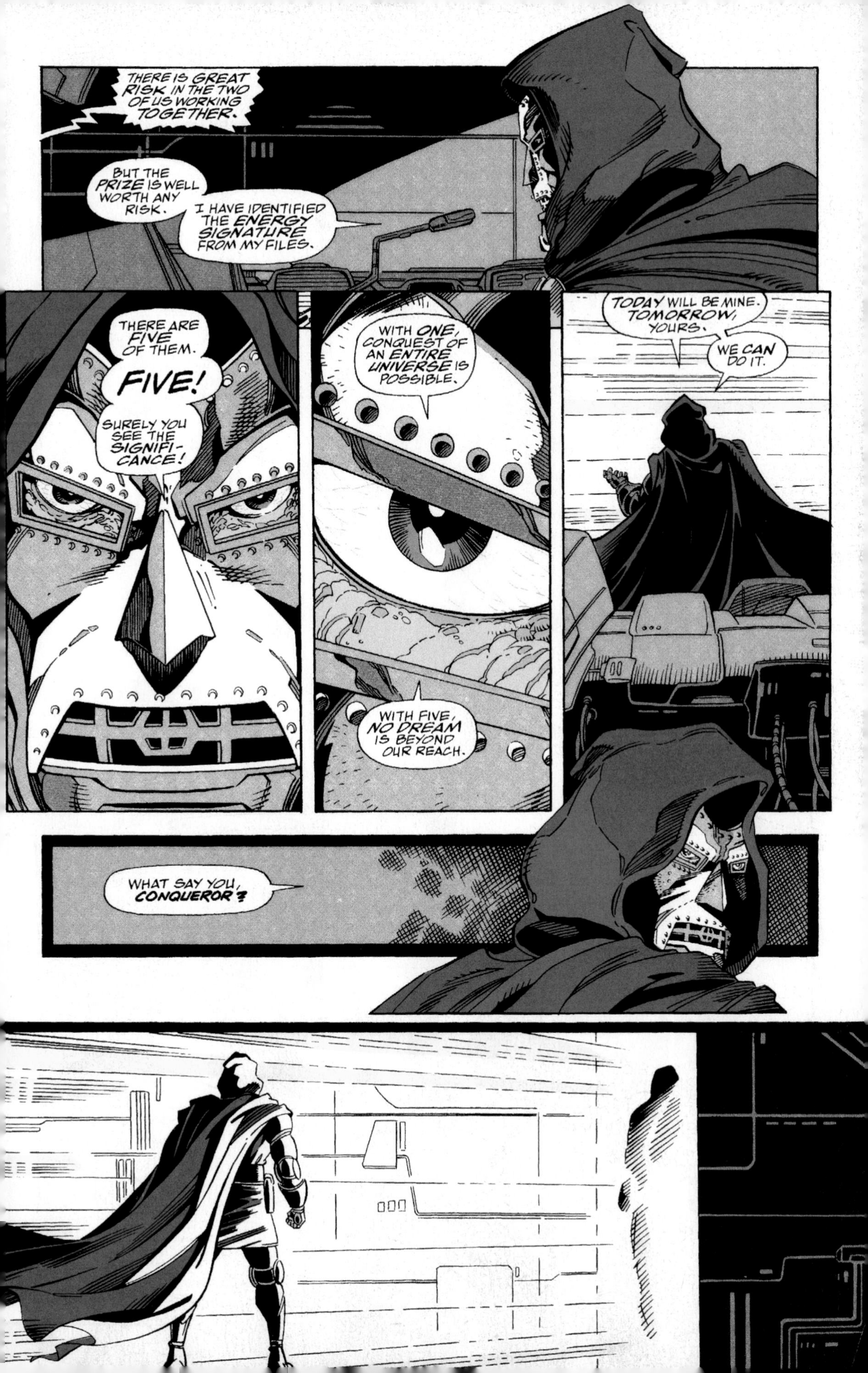
THERE IS GREAT RISK IN THE TWO OF US WORKING TOGETHER.
BUT THE PRIZE IS WELL WORTH ANY RISK.
I HAVE IDENTIFIED THE ENERGY SIGNATURE FROM MY FILES.
THERE ARE FIVE OF THEM.
FIVE!
SURELY YOU SEE THE SIGNIFI-CANCE!
WITH ONE, CONQUEST OF AN ENTIRE UNIVERSE IS POSSIBLE.
WITH FIVE, NO DREAM IS BEYOND OUR REACH.
TODAY WILL BE MINE. TOMORROW, YOURS.
WE CAN DO IT.
WHAT SAY YOU, CONQUEROR?

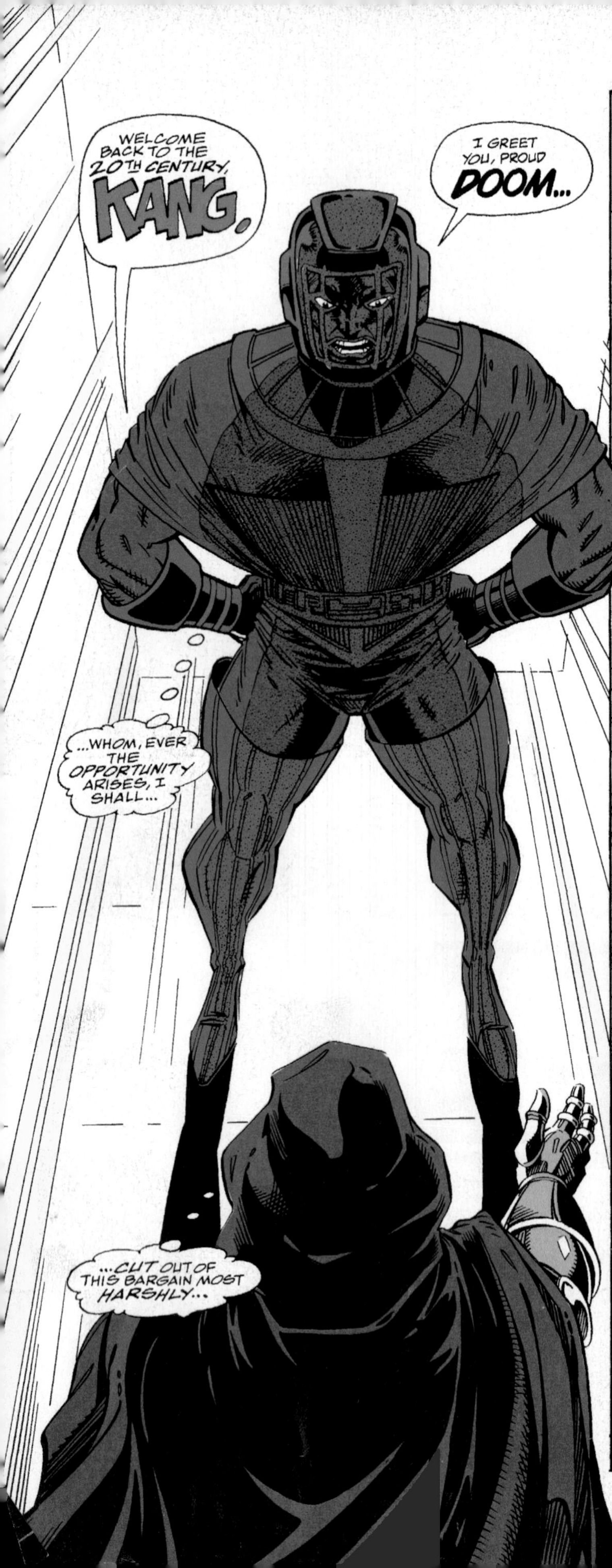
WELCOME BACK TO THE 20TH CENTURY, KANG.
I GREET YOU, PROUD DOOM...
...WHOM, EVER THE OPPORTUNITY ARISES, I SHALL...
...CUT OUT OF THIS BARGAIN MOST HARSHLY...
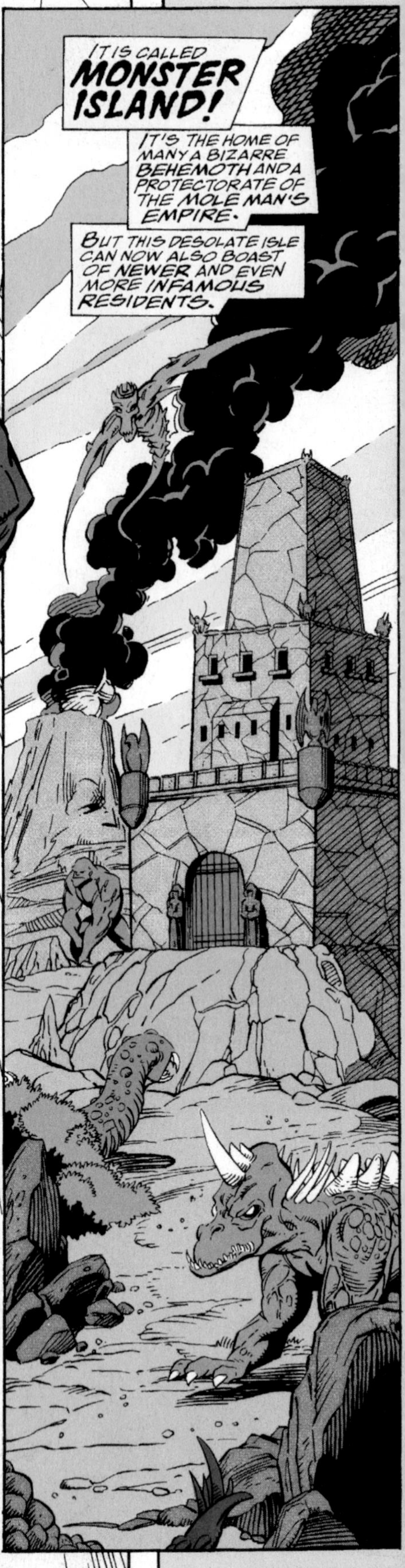
IT IS CALLED MONSTER ISLAND!
IT'S THE HOME OF MANY A BIZARRE BEHEMOTH AND A PROTECTORATE OF THE MOLE MAN'S EMPIRE.
BUT THIS DESOLATE ISLE CAN NOW ALSO BOAST OF NEWER AND EVEN MORE INFAMOUS RESIDENTS.

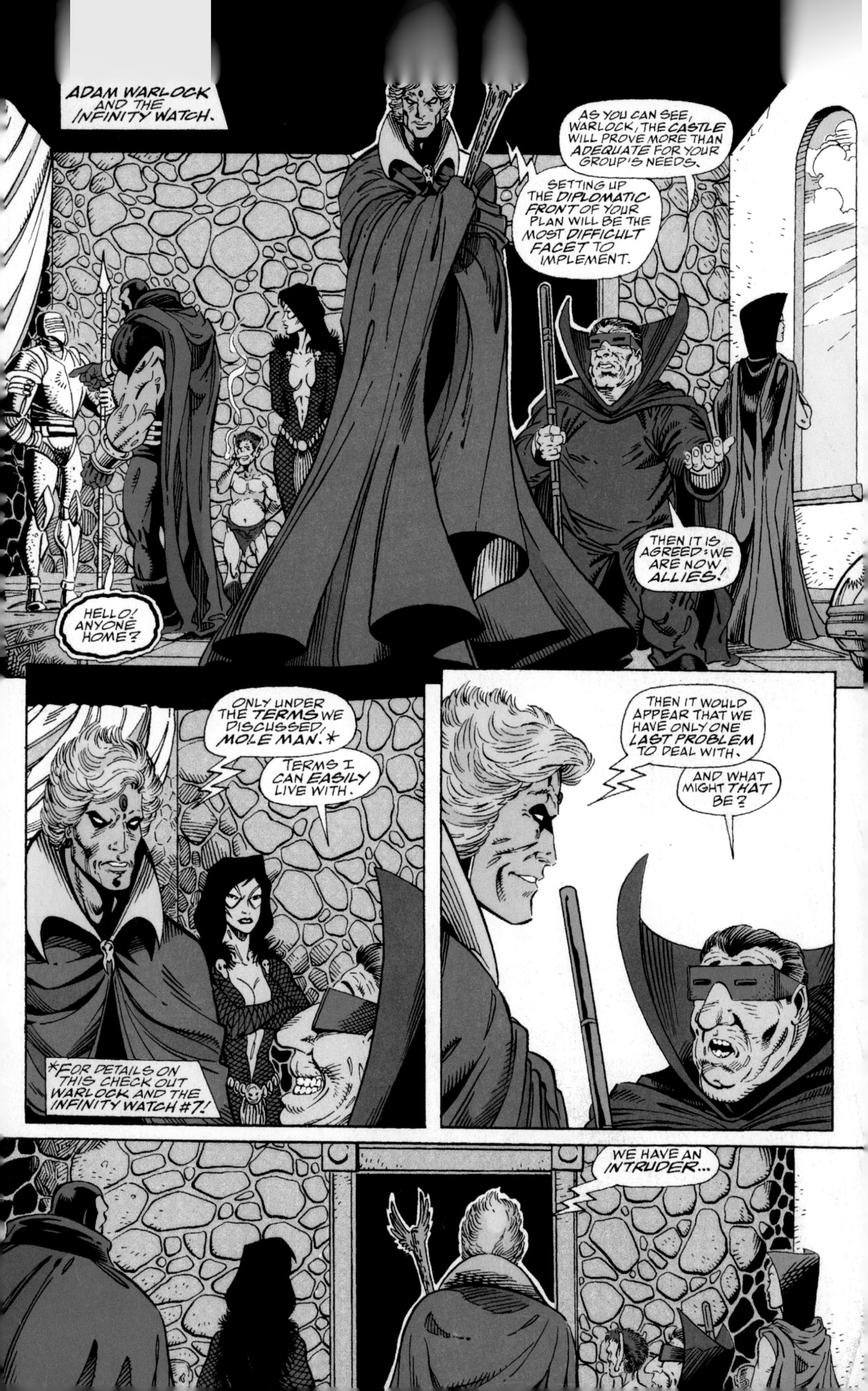
ADAM WARLOCK AND THE INFINITY WATCH.
AS YOU CAN SEE, WARLOCK, THE CASTLE WILL PROVE MORE THAN ADEQUATE FOR YOUR GROUP'S NEEDS.
SETTING UP THE DIPLOMATIC FRONT OF YOUR PLAN WILL BE THE MOST DIFFICULT FACET TO IMPLEMENT.
THEN IT IS AGREED: WE ARE NOW ALLIES!
HELLO! ANYONE HOME?
ONLY UNDER THE TERMS WE DISCUSSED, MOLE MAN.*
TERMS I CAN EASILY LIVE WITH.
*FOR DETAILS ON THIS CHECK OUT WARLOCK AND THE INFINITY WATCH #7!
THEN IT WOULD APPEAR THAT WE HAVE ONLY ONE LAST PROBLEM TO DEAL WITH.
AND WHAT MIGHT THAT BE?
WE HAVE AN INTRUDER...

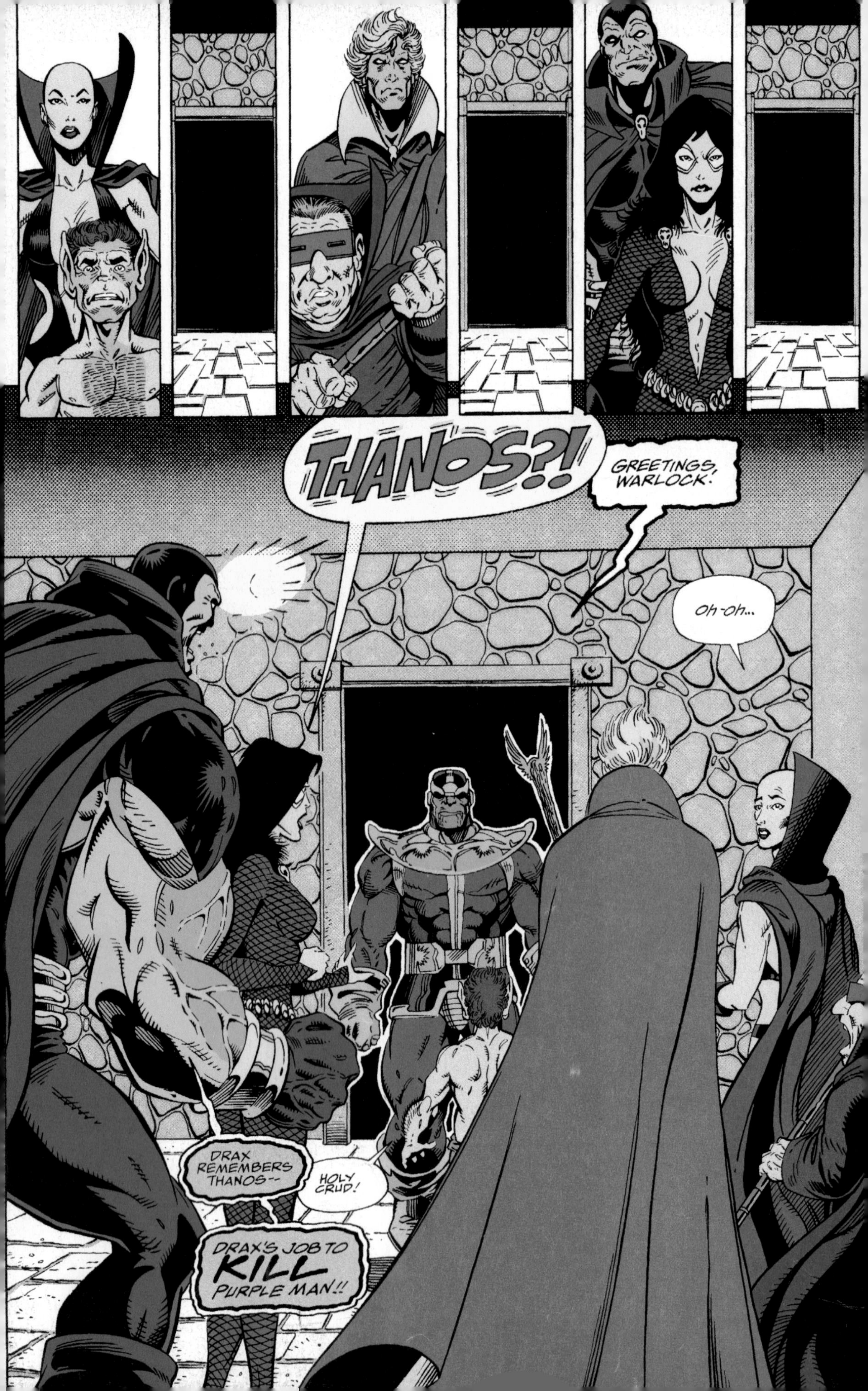
THANOS?!
GREETINGS, WARLOCK.
Oh-oh...
DRAX REMEMBERS THANOS--
HOLY CRUD!
DRAX'S JOB TO KILL PURPLE MAN!!

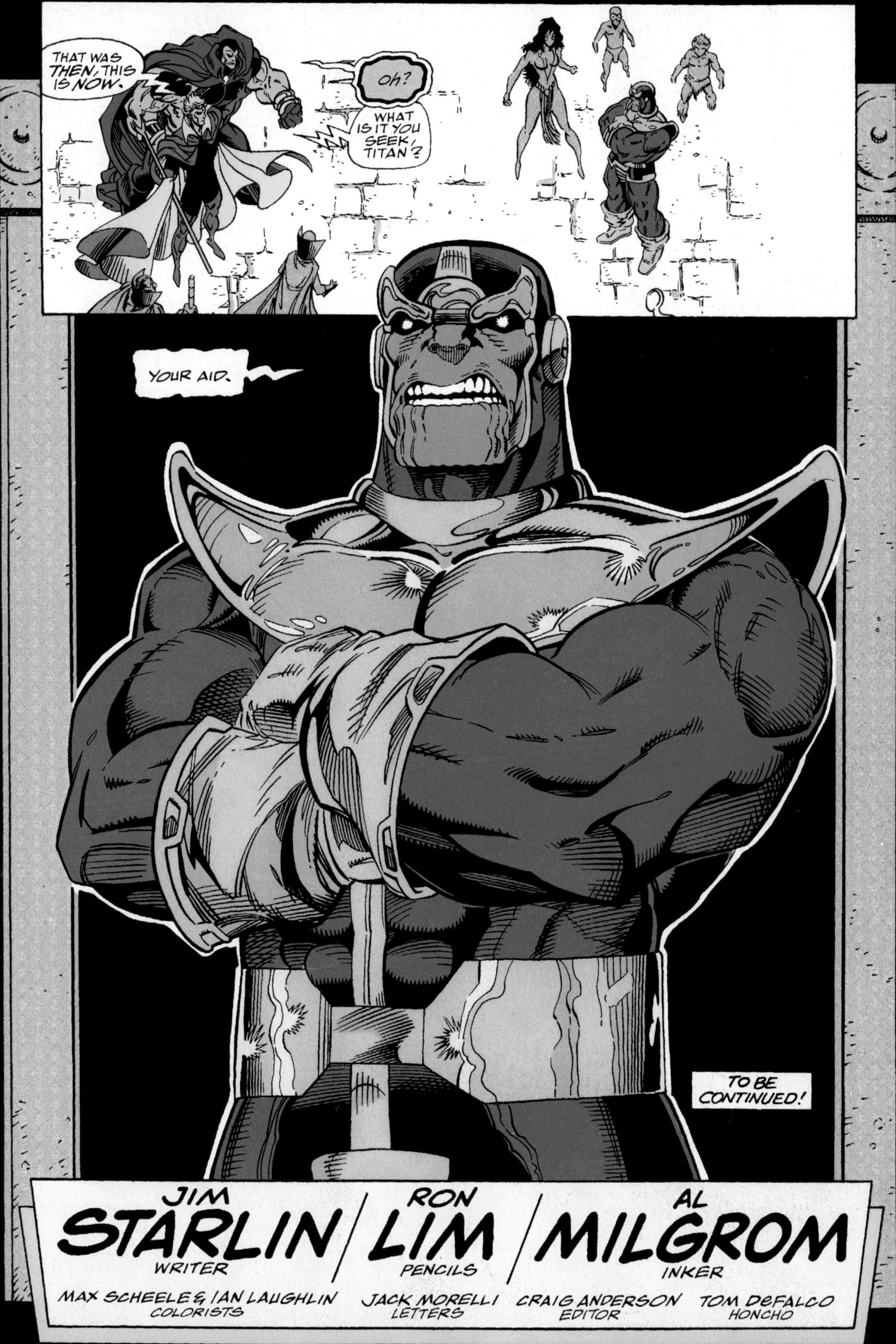
THAT WAS THEN, THIS IS NOW.
Oh?
WHAT IS IT YOU SEEK, TITAN?
YOUR AID.
TO BE CONTINUED!
JIM STARLIN WRITER
RON LIM PENCILS
AL MILGROM INKER
MAX SCHEELE & IAN LAUGHLIN COLORISTS
JACK MORELLI LETTERS
CRAIG ANDERSON EDITOR
TOM DeFALCO HONCHO

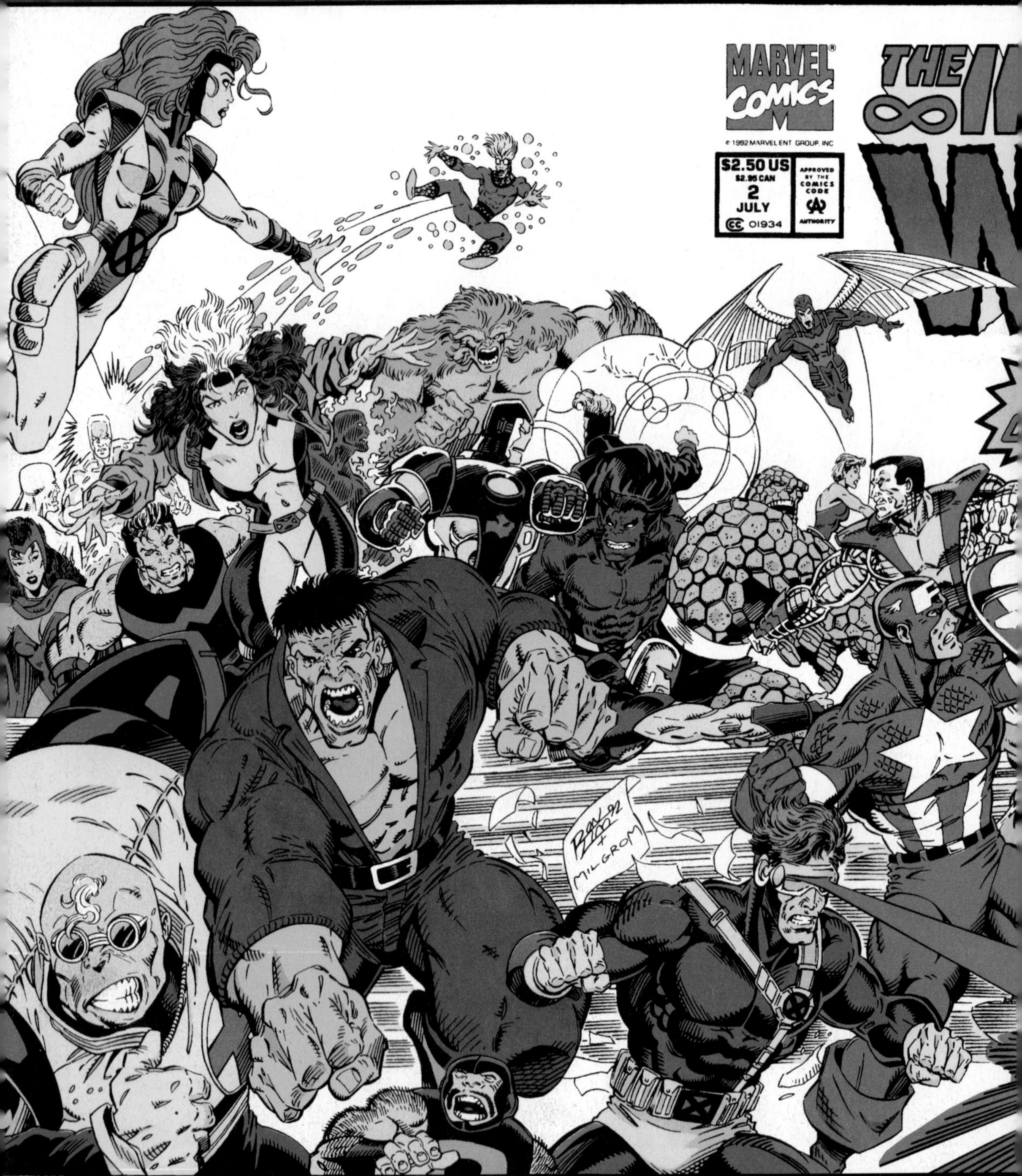
MARVEL COMICS
© 1992 MARVEL ENT. GROUP, INC.
$2.50 US
$2.95 CAN
2
JULY
01934
APPROVED BY THE COMICS CODE AUTHORITY
THE
MILGROM

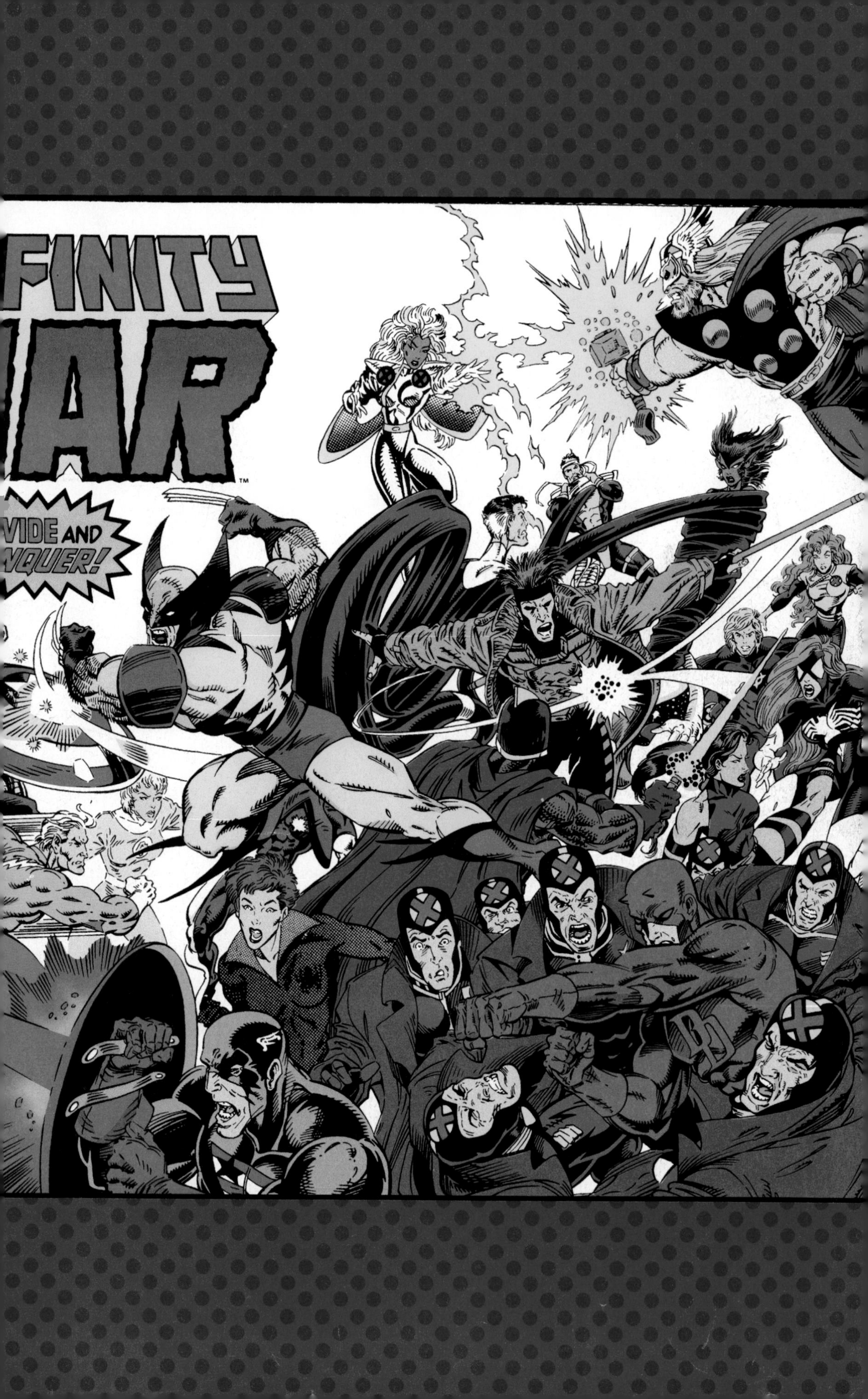
FINITY
AR™
VIDE AND
NQUER!

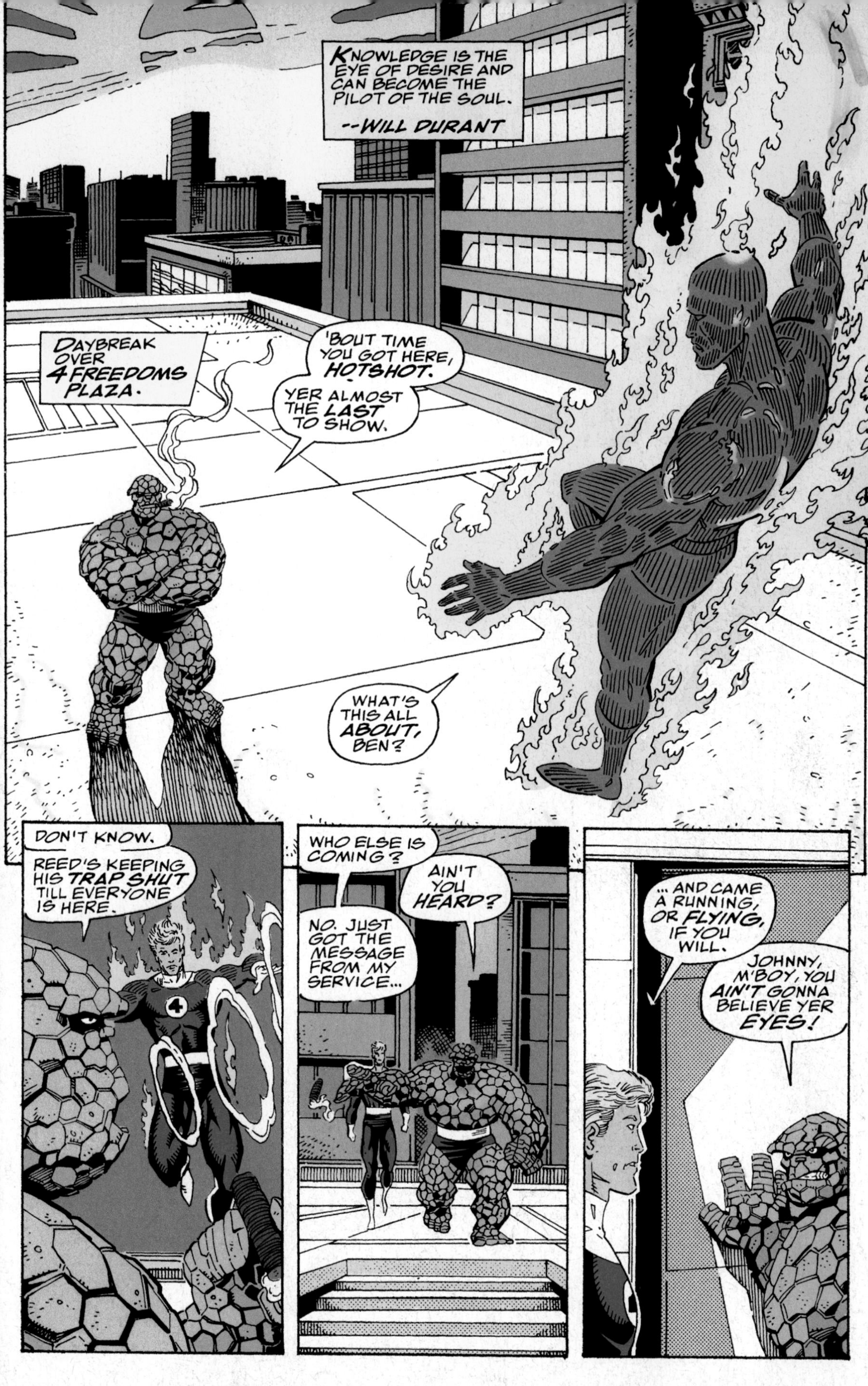
KNOWLEDGE IS THE EYE OF DESIRE AND CAN BECOME THE PILOT OF THE SOUL.
--WILL DURANT
DAYBREAK OVER 4 FREEDOMS PLAZA.
'BOUT TIME YOU GOT HERE, HOTSHOT.
YER ALMOST THE LAST TO SHOW.
WHAT'S THIS ALL ABOUT, BEN?
DON'T KNOW.
REED'S KEEPING HIS TRAP SHUT TILL EVERYONE IS HERE.
WHO ELSE IS COMING?
AIN'T YOU HEARD?
NO. JUST GOT THE MESSAGE FROM MY SERVICE...
...AND CAME A RUNNING, OR FLYING, IF YOU WILL.
JOHNNY, M'BOY, YOU AIN'T GONNA BELIEVE YER EYES!

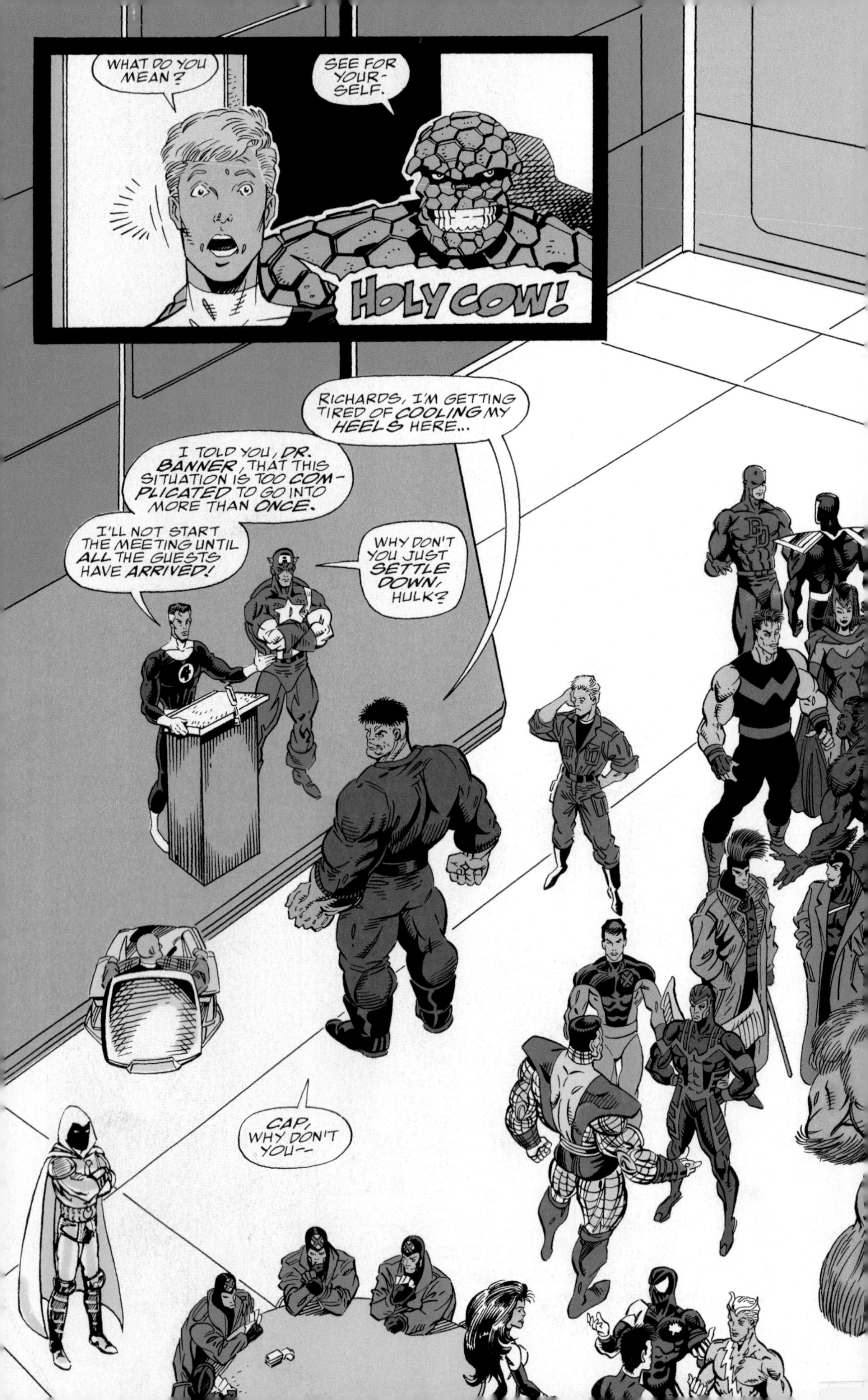

WHAT DO YOU MEAN?
SEE FOR YOUR-SELF.
HOLY COW!
RICHARDS, I'M GETTING TIRED OF COOLING MY HEELS HERE...
I TOLD YOU, DR. BANNER, THAT THIS SITUATION IS TOO COM-PLICATED TO GO INTO MORE THAN ONCE.
I'LL NOT START THE MEETING UNTIL ALL THE GUESTS HAVE ARRIVED!
WHY DON'T YOU JUST SETTLE DOWN, HULK?
CAP, WHY DON'T YOU--

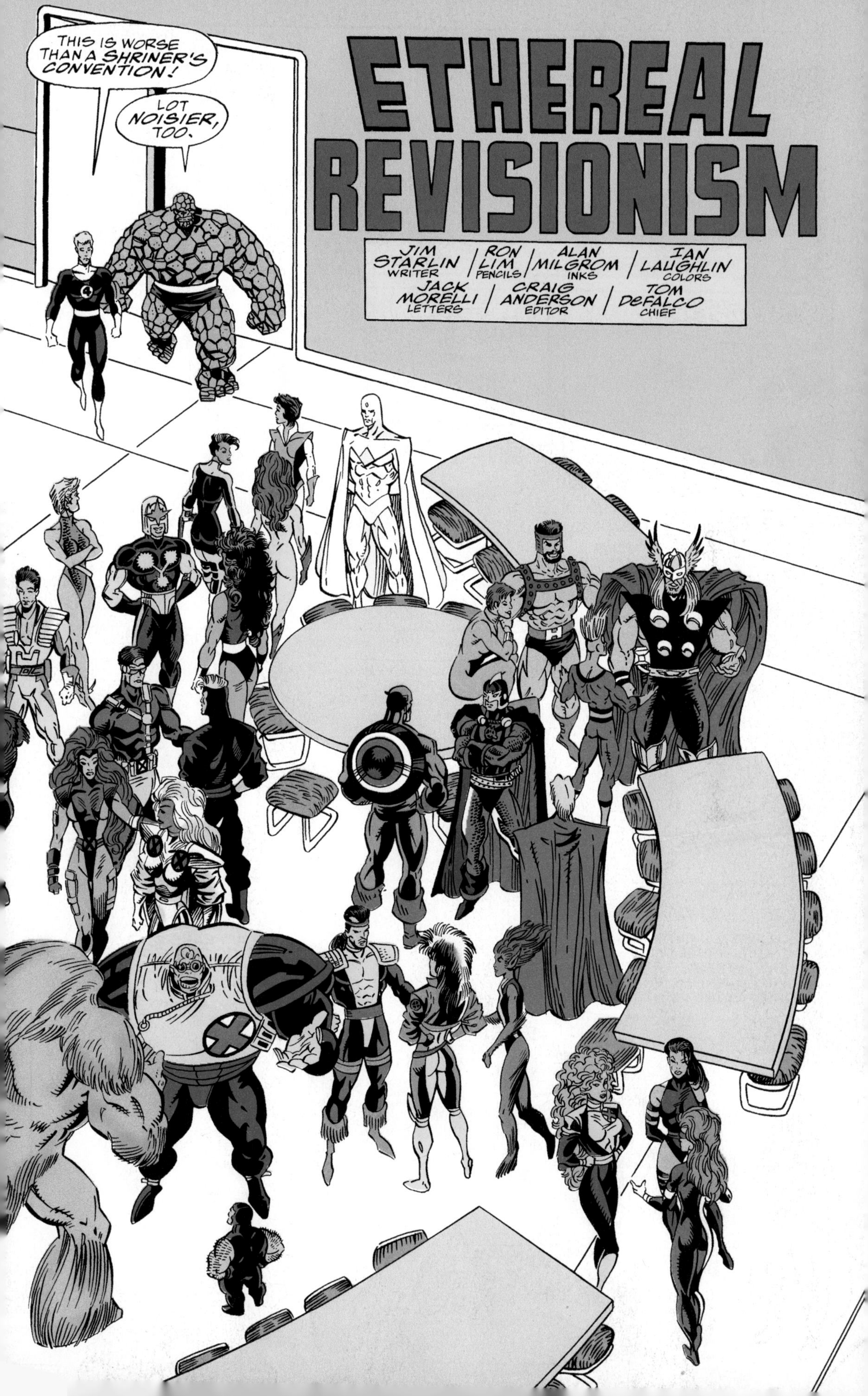
THIS IS WORSE THAN A SHRINER'S CONVENTION!
LOT NOISIER, TOO.
ETHEREAL REVISIONISM
JIM STARLIN WRITER
RON LIM PENCILS
ALAN MILGROM INKS
IAN LAUGHLIN COLORS
JACK MORELLI LETTERS
CRAIG ANDERSON EDITOR
TOM DeFALCO CHIEF

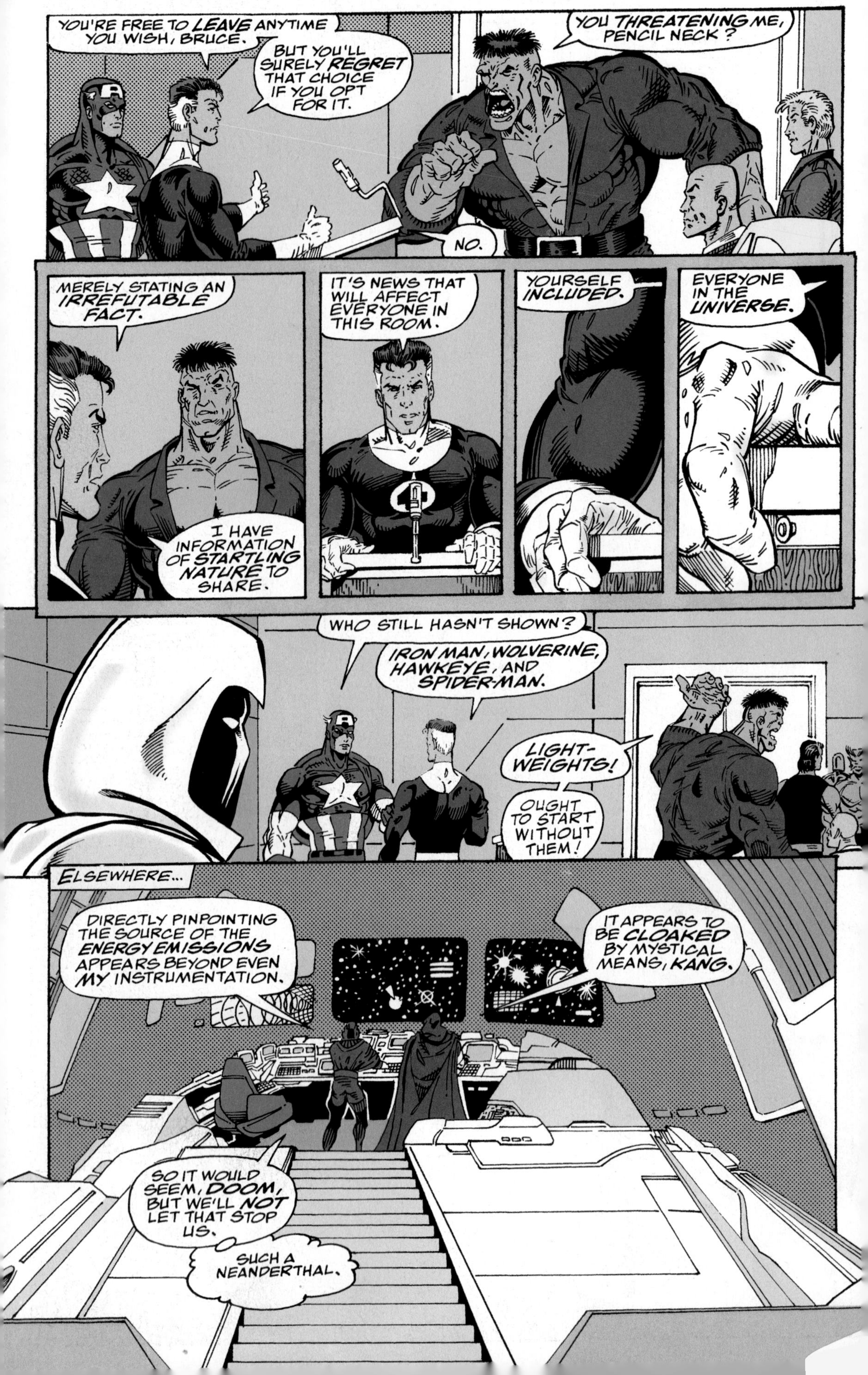

YOU'RE FREE TO LEAVE ANYTIME YOU WISH, BRUCE.
BUT YOU'LL SURELY REGRET THAT CHOICE IF YOU OPT FOR IT.
YOU THREATENING ME, PENCIL NECK?
NO.
MERELY STATING AN IRREFUTABLE FACT.
I HAVE INFORMATION OF STARTLING NATURE TO SHARE.
IT'S NEWS THAT WILL AFFECT EVERYONE IN THIS ROOM.
YOURSELF INCLUDED.
EVERYONE IN THE UNIVERSE.
WHO STILL HASN'T SHOWN?
IRON MAN, WOLVERINE, HAWKEYE, AND SPIDER-MAN.
LIGHT-WEIGHTS!
OUGHT TO START WITHOUT THEM!
ELSEWHERE...
DIRECTLY PINPOINTING THE SOURCE OF THE ENERGY EMISSIONS APPEARS BEYOND EVEN MY INSTRUMENTATION.
IT APPEARS TO BE CLOAKED BY MYSTICAL MEANS, KANG.
SO IT WOULD SEEM, DOOM, BUT WE'LL NOT LET THAT STOP US.
SUCH A NEANDERTHAL.

PERHAPS IF WE APPROACH THE PROBLEM FROM THE *OPPOSITE DIRECTION.*

THE ENERGIES ARE BEING FUNNELED TO *MYRIAD* SITES THROUGHOUT THE HEAVENS.

MYRIAD?

THE POMPOUS *FOOL.*

YES. OBSERVE THIS *CHART* OF THE GALAXY. NOW IF I...

...SUPERIMPOSE THE LOCATION OF EVERY *RECEPTION POINT*...

THEY ARE *IDENTICAL!*

AND EACH STAR'S PLANET ALSO HAS A *SECONDARY RECEIVER.*

OF COURSE YOU *REALIZE* WHAT THIS *MEANS.*

THAT *EVERY MOMENT* COUNTS.

IF WE WISH TO WREST *POWER* FROM OUR *SECRET ADVERSARY*...

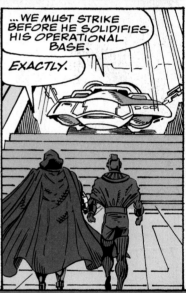

...WE MUST STRIKE BEFORE HE SOLIDIFIES HIS OPERATIONAL BASE.

EXACTLY.

MONSTER ISLAND, HOME OF ADAM WARLOCK AND THE INFINITY WATCH.

AND I TELL YOU THAT I SPOKE *FACE TO FACE* WITH HIM!

WARLOCK, I SAW HIS OPERATION AND FELT HIS *MIGHT!*

THE **MAGUS** LIVES!

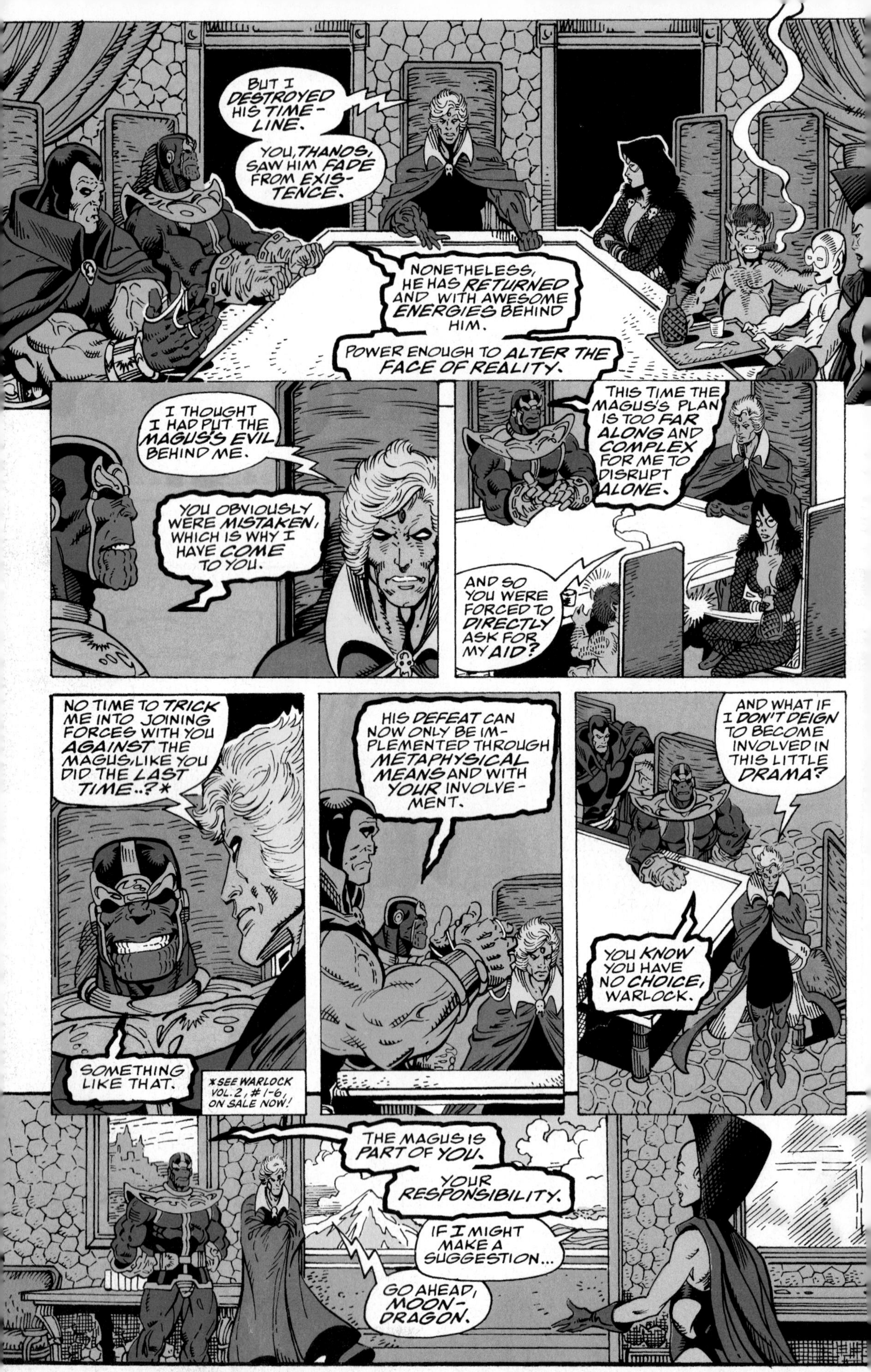
BUT I DESTROYED HIS TIME-LINE.
YOU, THANOS, SAW HIM FADE FROM EXISTENCE.
NONETHELESS, HE HAS RETURNED AND WITH AWESOME ENERGIES BEHIND HIM.
POWER ENOUGH TO ALTER THE FACE OF REALITY.
I THOUGHT I HAD PUT THE MAGUS'S EVIL BEHIND ME.
YOU OBVIOUSLY WERE MISTAKEN, WHICH IS WHY I HAVE COME TO YOU.
THIS TIME THE MAGUS'S PLAN IS TOO FAR ALONG AND COMPLEX FOR ME TO DISRUPT ALONE.
AND SO YOU WERE FORCED TO DIRECTLY ASK FOR MY AID?
NO TIME TO TRICK ME INTO JOINING FORCES WITH YOU AGAINST THE MAGUS, LIKE YOU DID THE LAST TIME..?*
SOMETHING LIKE THAT.
*SEE WARLOCK VOL. 2, #1-6, ON SALE NOW!
HIS DEFEAT CAN NOW ONLY BE IMPLEMENTED THROUGH METAPHYSICAL MEANS AND WITH YOUR INVOLVEMENT.
AND WHAT IF I DON'T DEIGN TO BECOME INVOLVED IN THIS LITTLE DRAMA?
YOU KNOW YOU HAVE NO CHOICE, WARLOCK.
THE MAGUS IS PART OF YOU.
YOUR RESPONSIBILITY.
IF I MIGHT MAKE A SUGGESTION...
GO AHEAD, MOON-DRAGON.

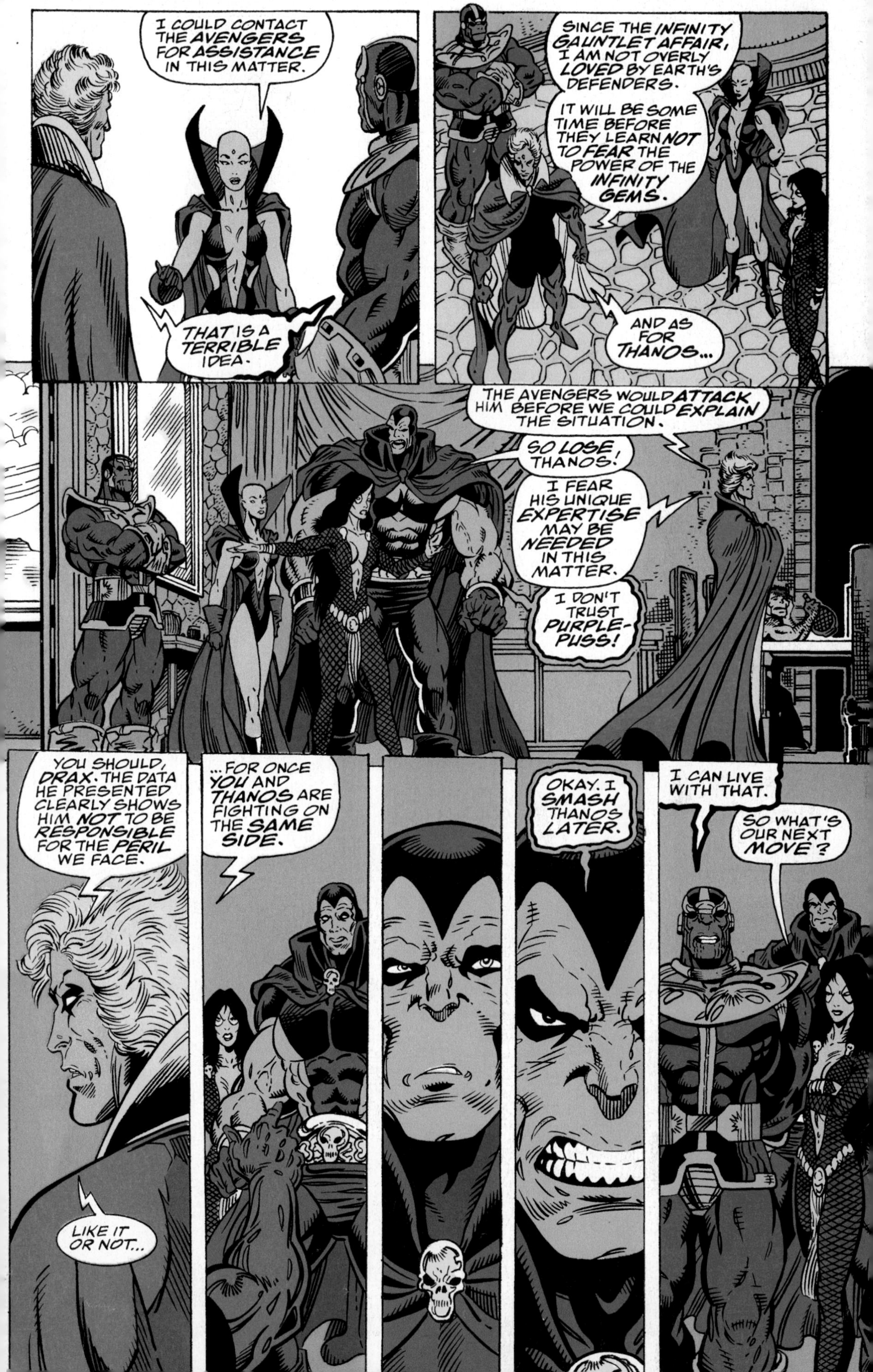
I COULD CONTACT THE AVENGERS FOR ASSISTANCE IN THIS MATTER.
THAT IS A TERRIBLE IDEA.
SINCE THE INFINITY GAUNTLET AFFAIR, I AM NOT OVERLY LOVED BY EARTH'S DEFENDERS.
IT WILL BE SOME TIME BEFORE THEY LEARN NOT TO FEAR THE POWER OF THE INFINITY GEMS.
AND AS FOR THANOS...
THE AVENGERS WOULD ATTACK HIM BEFORE WE COULD EXPLAIN THE SITUATION.
SO LOSE THANOS!
I FEAR HIS UNIQUE EXPERTISE MAY BE NEEDED IN THIS MATTER.
I DON'T TRUST PURPLE-PUSS!
YOU SHOULD, DRAX. THE DATA HE PRESENTED CLEARLY SHOWS HIM NOT TO BE RESPONSIBLE FOR THE PERIL WE FACE.
LIKE IT OR NOT...
...FOR ONCE YOU AND THANOS ARE FIGHTING ON THE SAME SIDE.
OKAY. I SMASH THANOS LATER.
I CAN LIVE WITH THAT.
SO WHAT'S OUR NEXT MOVE?

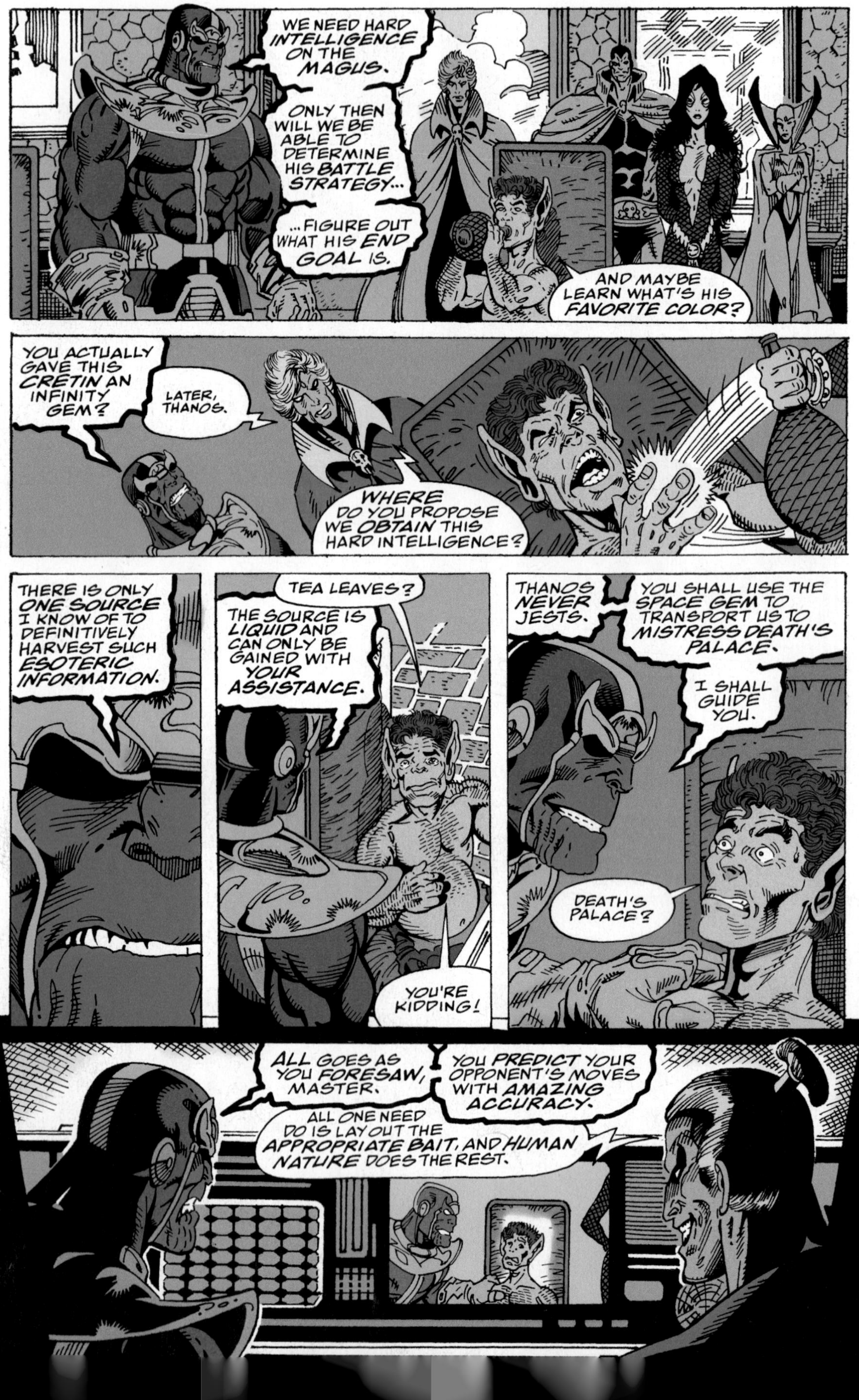

WE NEED HARD INTELLIGENCE ON THE MAGUS.
ONLY THEN WILL WE BE ABLE TO DETERMINE HIS BATTLE STRATEGY...
...FIGURE OUT WHAT HIS END GOAL IS.
AND MAYBE LEARN WHAT'S HIS FAVORITE COLOR?
YOU ACTUALLY GAVE THIS CRETIN AN INFINITY GEM?
LATER, THANOS.
WHERE DO YOU PROPOSE WE OBTAIN THIS HARD INTELLIGENCE?
THERE IS ONLY ONE SOURCE I KNOW OF TO DEFINITIVELY HARVEST SUCH ESOTERIC INFORMATION.
TEA LEAVES?
THE SOURCE IS LIQUID AND CAN ONLY BE GAINED WITH YOUR ASSISTANCE.
YOU'RE KIDDING!
THANOS NEVER JESTS.
YOU SHALL USE THE SPACE GEM TO TRANSPORT US TO MISTRESS DEATH'S PALACE.
I SHALL GUIDE YOU.
DEATH'S PALACE?
ALL GOES AS YOU FORESAW, MASTER.
YOU PREDICT YOUR OPPONENT'S MOVES WITH AMAZING ACCURACY.
ALL ONE NEED DO IS LAY OUT THE APPROPRIATE BAIT, AND HUMAN NATURE DOES THE REST.

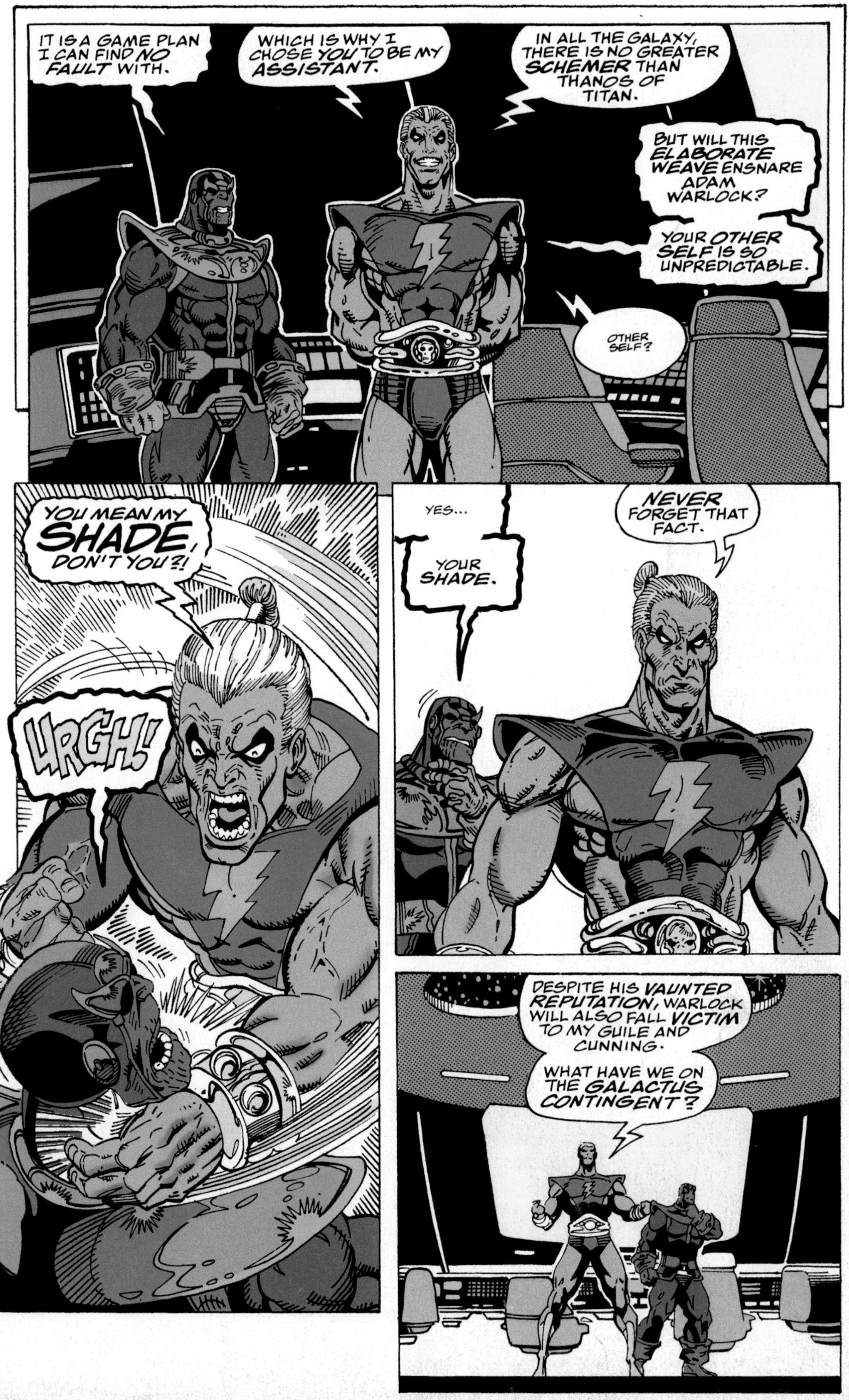
IT IS A GAME PLAN I CAN FIND NO FAULT WITH.
WHICH IS WHY I CHOSE YOU TO BE MY ASSISTANT.
IN ALL THE GALAXY, THERE IS NO GREATER SCHEMER THAN THANOS OF TITAN.
BUT WILL THIS ELABORATE WEAVE ENSNARE ADAM WARLOCK?
YOUR OTHER SELF IS SO UNPREDICTABLE.
OTHER SELF?
YOU MEAN MY SHADE, DON'T YOU?!
URGH!
YES...
YOUR SHADE.
NEVER FORGET THAT FACT.
DESPITE HIS VAUNTED REPUTATION, WARLOCK WILL ALSO FALL VICTIM TO MY GUILE AND CUNNING.
WHAT HAVE WE ON THE GALACTUS CONTINGENT?

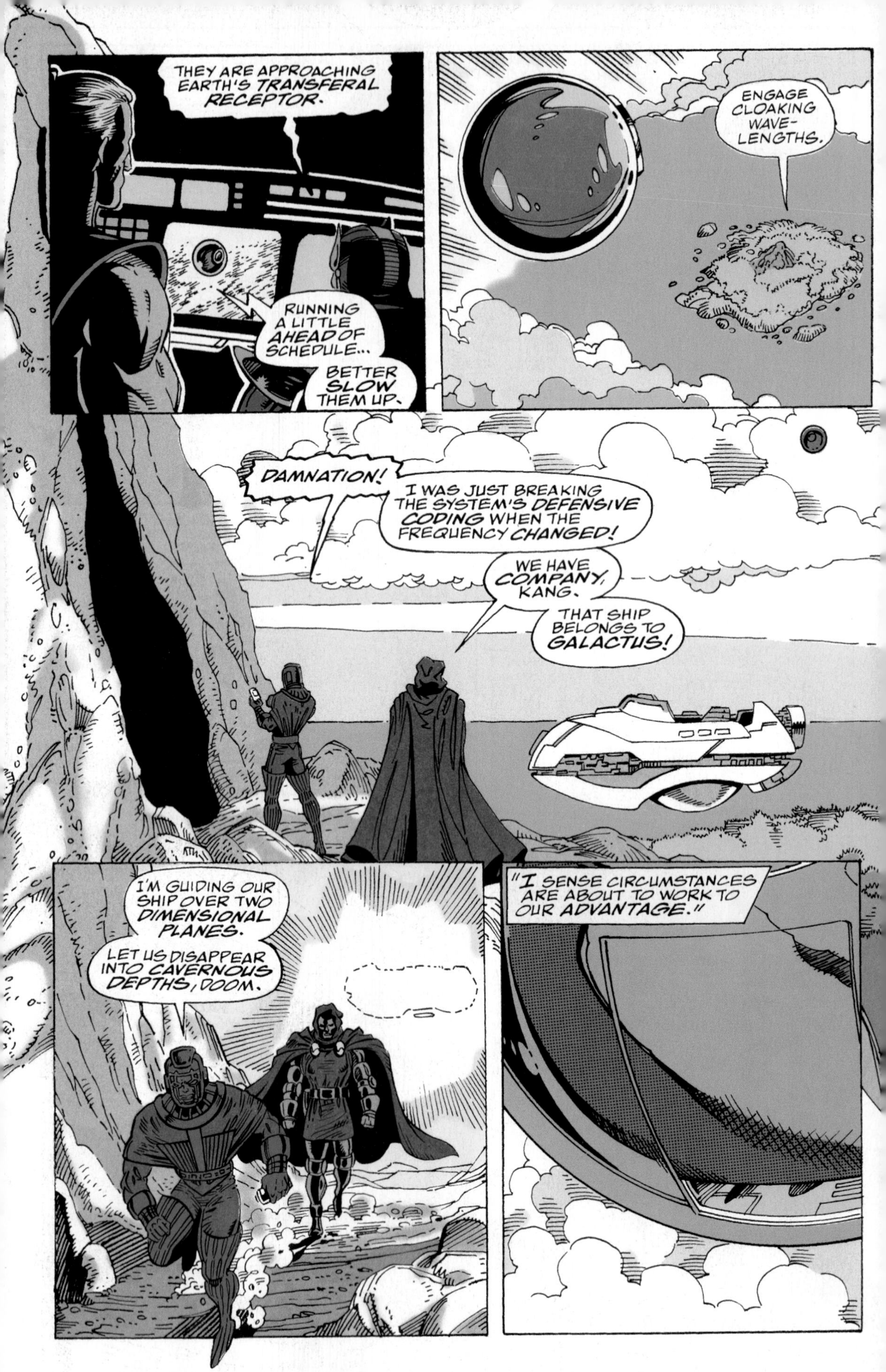
THEY ARE APPROACHING EARTH'S TRANSFERAL RECEPTOR.
RUNNING A LITTLE AHEAD OF SCHEDULE...
BETTER SLOW THEM UP.
ENGAGE CLOAKING WAVE-LENGTHS.
DAMNATION!
I WAS JUST BREAKING THE SYSTEM'S DEFENSIVE CODING WHEN THE FREQUENCY CHANGED!
WE HAVE COMPANY, KANG.
THAT SHIP BELONGS TO GALACTUS!
I'M GUIDING OUR SHIP OVER TWO DIMENSIONAL PLANES.
LET US DISAPPEAR INTO CAVERNOUS DEPTHS, DOOM.
"I SENSE CIRCUMSTANCES ARE ABOUT TO WORK TO OUR ADVANTAGE."

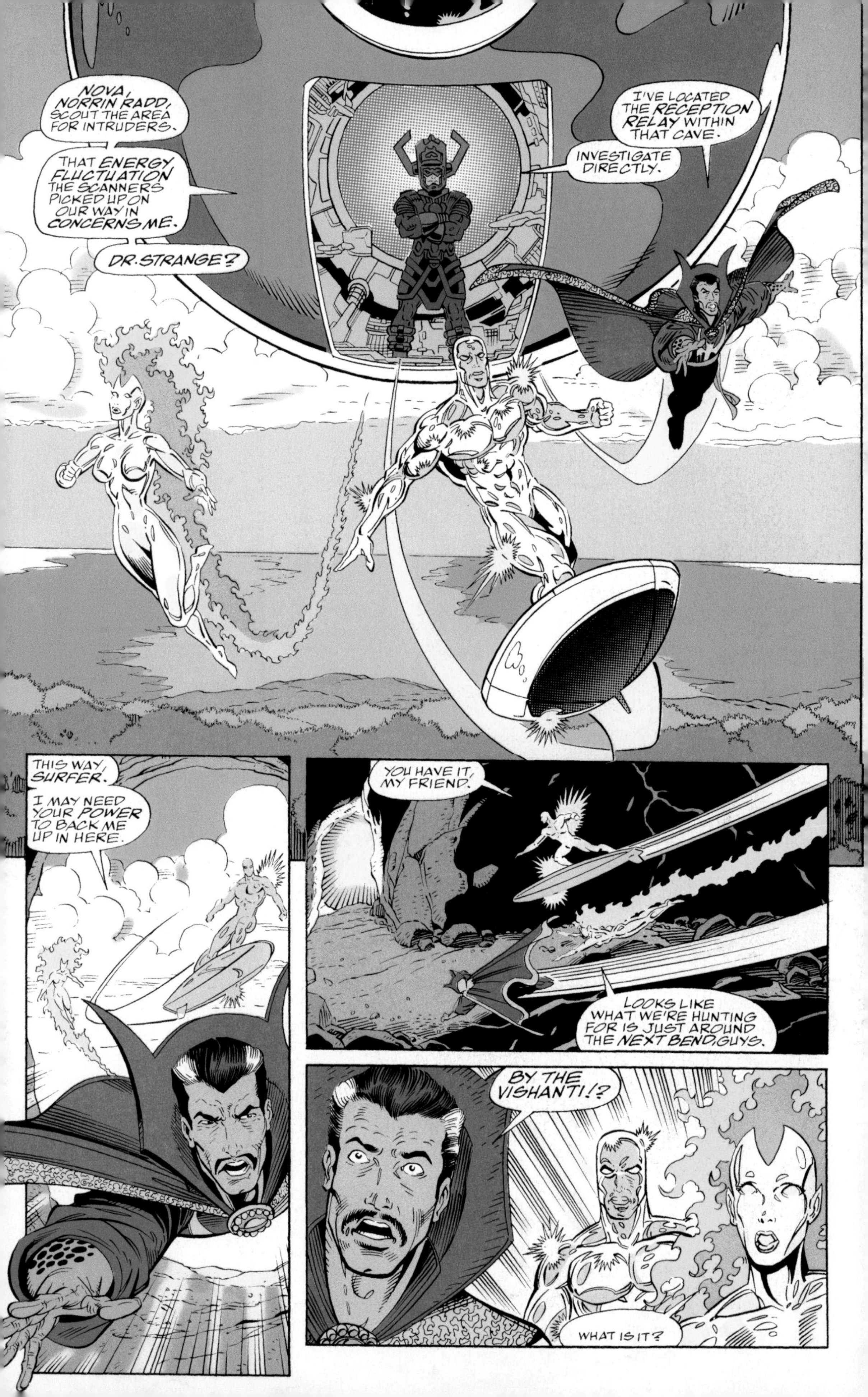
NOVA, NORRIN RADD, SCOUT THE AREA FOR INTRUDERS.
THAT ENERGY FLUCTUATION THE SCANNERS PICKED UP ON OUR WAY IN CONCERNS ME.
DR. STRANGE?
I'VE LOCATED THE RECEPTION RELAY WITHIN THAT CAVE.
INVESTIGATE DIRECTLY.
THIS WAY, SURFER.
I MAY NEED YOUR POWER TO BACK ME UP IN HERE.
YOU HAVE IT, MY FRIEND.
LOOKS LIKE WHAT WE'RE HUNTING FOR IS JUST AROUND THE NEXT BEND, GUYS.
BY THE VISHANTI!?
WHAT IS IT?

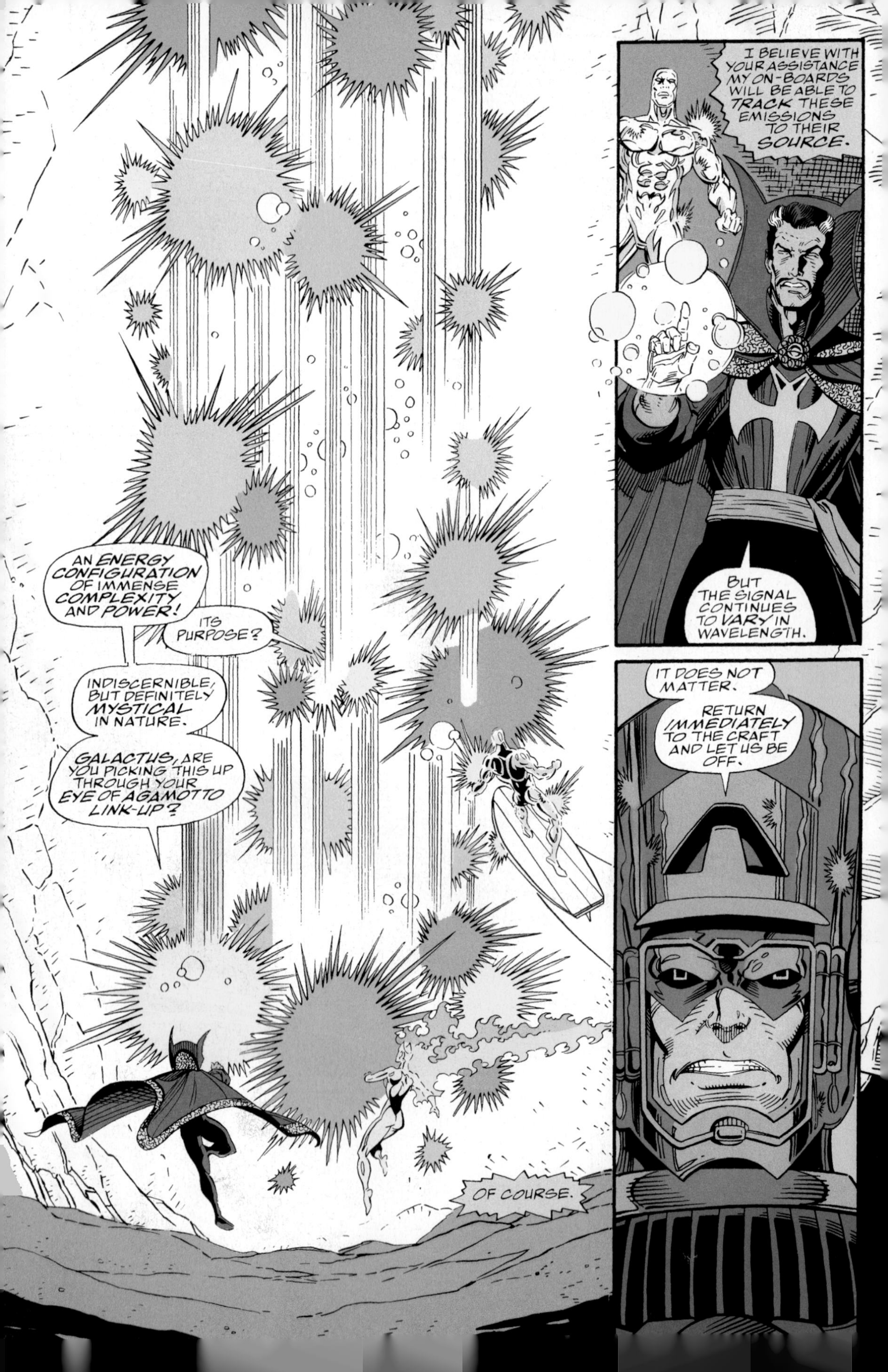

AN ENERGY CONFIGURATION OF IMMENSE COMPLEXITY AND POWER!
ITS PURPOSE?
INDISCERNIBLE, BUT DEFINITELY MYSTICAL IN NATURE.
GALACTUS, ARE YOU PICKING THIS UP THROUGH YOUR EYE OF AGAMOTTO LINK-UP?
OF COURSE.
I BELIEVE WITH YOUR ASSISTANCE MY ON-BOARDS WILL BE ABLE TO TRACK THESE EMISSIONS TO THEIR SOURCE.
BUT THE SIGNAL CONTINUES TO VARY IN WAVELENGTH.
IT DOES NOT MATTER.
RETURN IMMEDIATELY TO THE CRAFT AND LET US BE OFF.

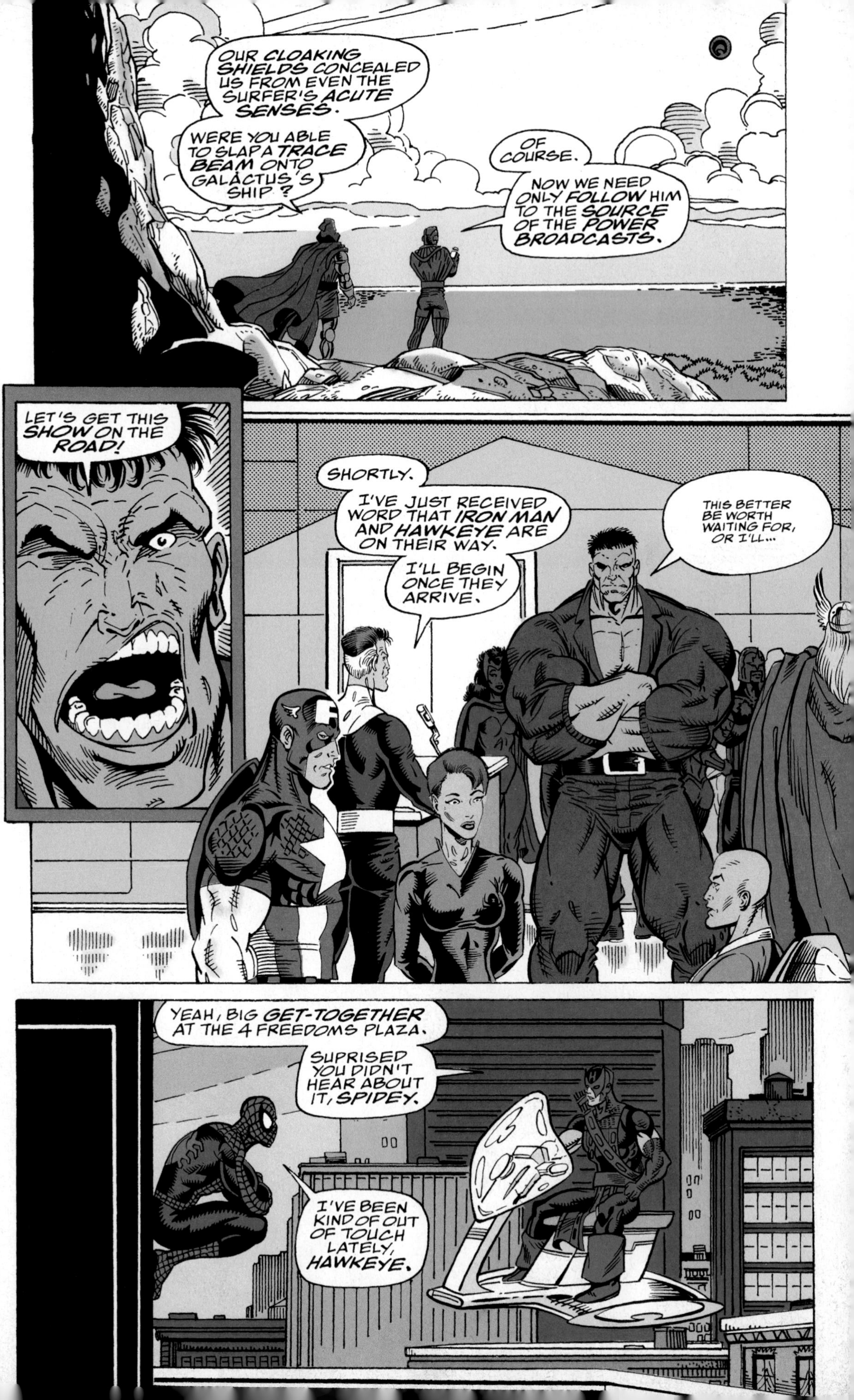
OUR CLOAKING SHIELDS CONCEALED US FROM EVEN THE SURFER'S ACUTE SENSES.
WERE YOU ABLE TO SLAP A TRACE BEAM ONTO GALACTUS'S SHIP?
OF COURSE.
NOW WE NEED ONLY FOLLOW HIM TO THE SOURCE OF THE POWER BROADCASTS.
LET'S GET THIS SHOW ON THE ROAD!
SHORTLY.
I'VE JUST RECEIVED WORD THAT IRON MAN AND HAWKEYE ARE ON THEIR WAY.
I'LL BEGIN ONCE THEY ARRIVE.
THIS BETTER BE WORTH WAITING FOR, OR I'LL...
YEAH, BIG GET-TOGETHER AT THE 4 FREEDOMS PLAZA.
SUPRISED YOU DIDN'T HEAR ABOUT IT, SPIDEY.
I'VE BEEN KIND OF OUT OF TOUCH LATELY, HAWKEYE.

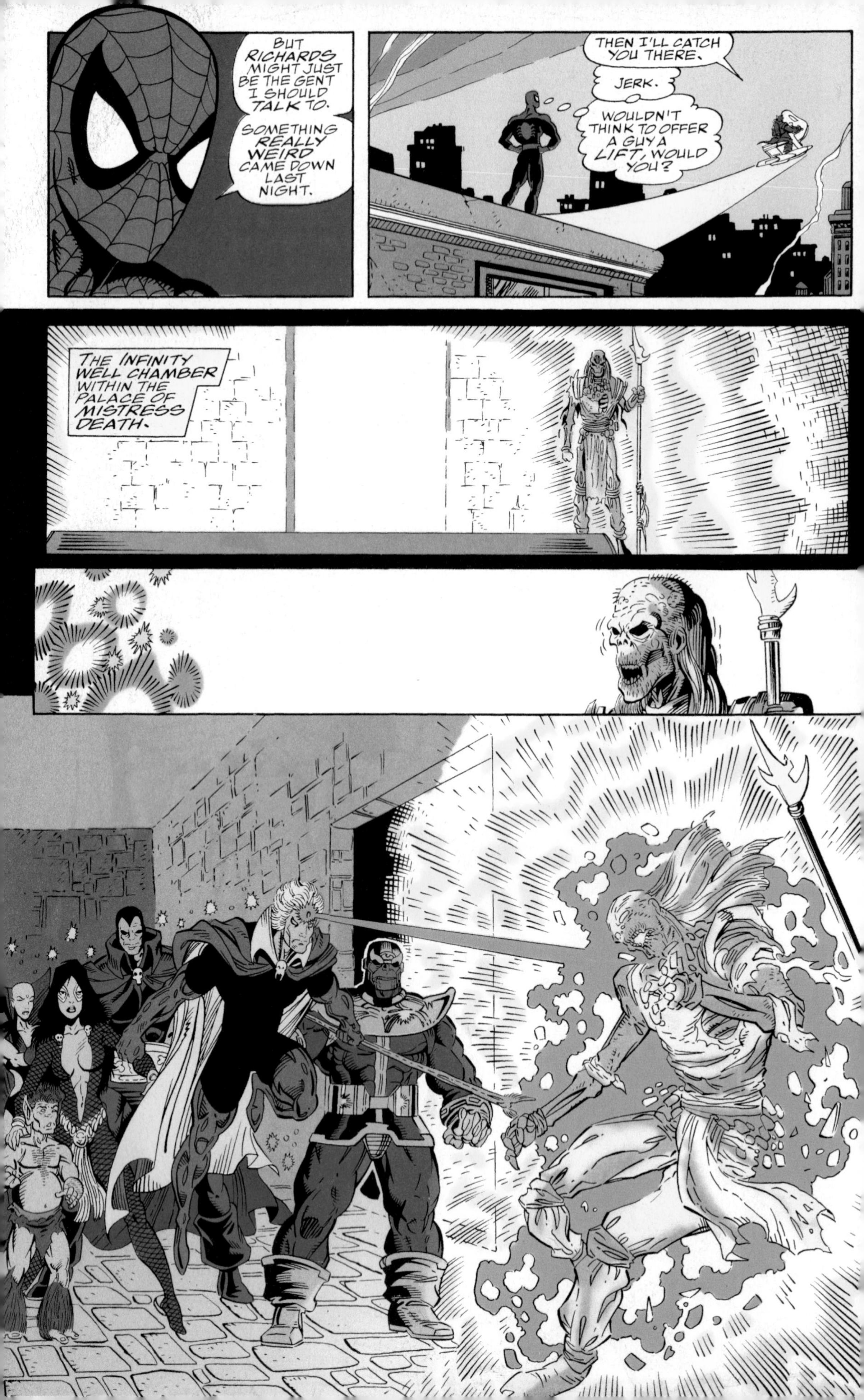
BUT RICHARDS MIGHT JUST BE THE GENT I SHOULD TALK TO.
SOMETHING REALLY WEIRD CAME DOWN LAST NIGHT.
THEN I'LL CATCH YOU THERE.
JERK.
WOULDN'T THINK TO OFFER A GUY A LIFT, WOULD YOU?
THE INFINITY WELL CHAMBER WITHIN THE PALACE OF MISTRESS DEATH.

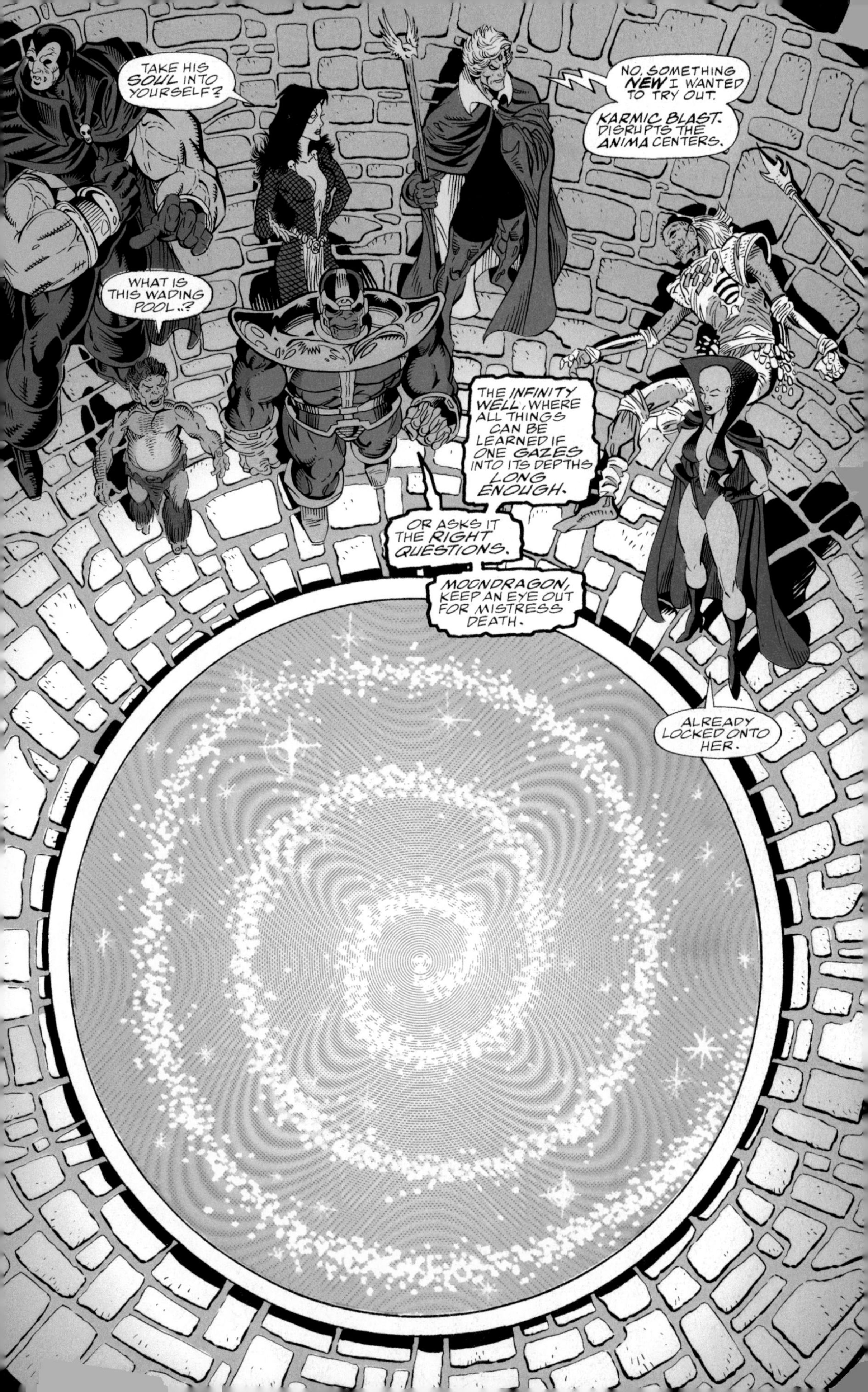
TAKE HIS SOUL INTO YOURSELF?
NO, SOMETHING NEW I WANTED TO TRY OUT.
KARMIC BLAST. DISRUPTS THE ANIMA CENTERS.
WHAT IS THIS WADING POOL..?
THE INFINITY WELL, WHERE ALL THINGS CAN BE LEARNED IF ONE GAZES INTO ITS DEPTHS LONG ENOUGH.
OR ASKS IT THE RIGHT QUESTIONS.
MOONDRAGON, KEEP AN EYE OUT FOR MISTRESS DEATH.
ALREADY LOCKED ONTO HER.

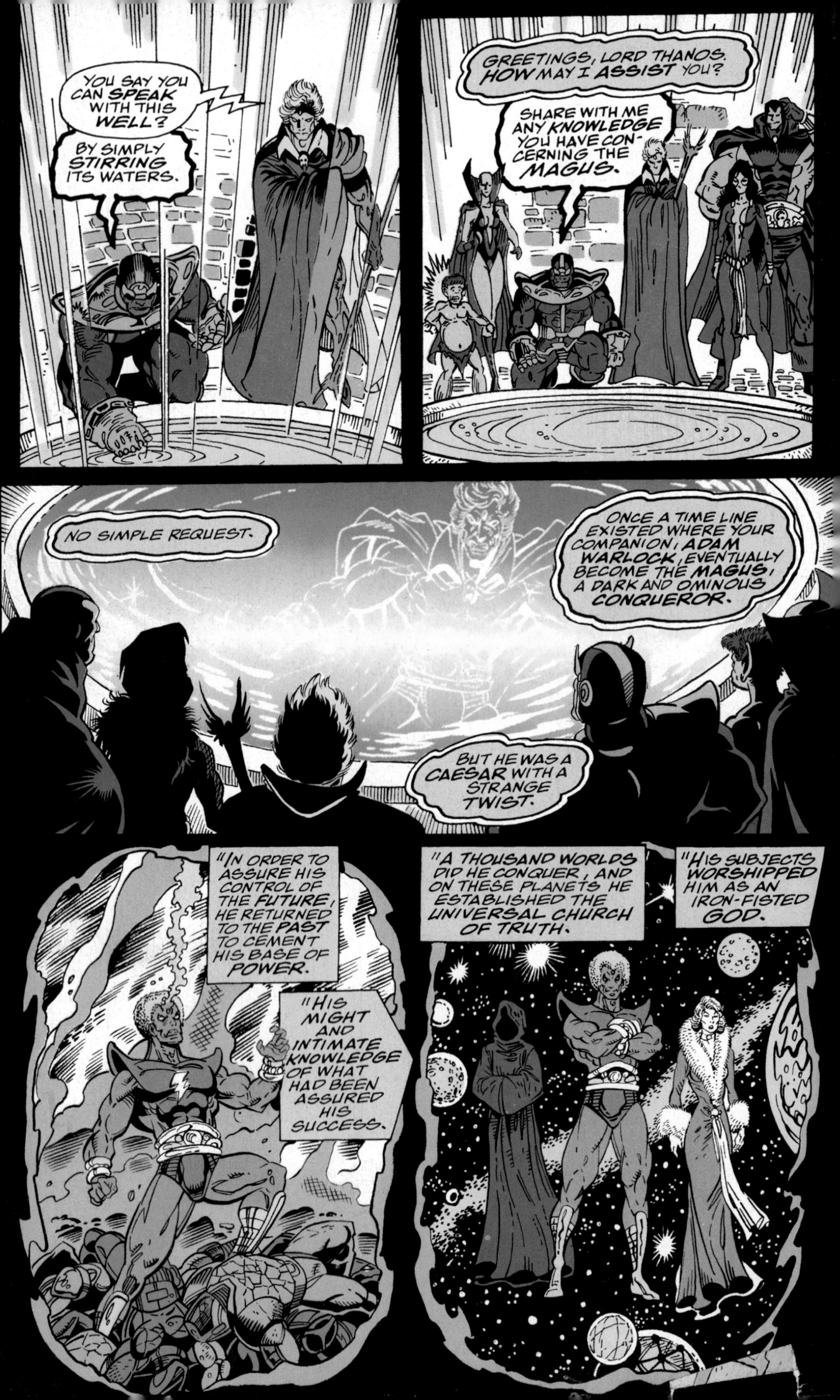

YOU SAY YOU CAN SPEAK WITH THIS WELL?
BY SIMPLY STIRRING ITS WATERS.
GREETINGS, LORD THANOS. HOW MAY I ASSIST YOU?
SHARE WITH ME ANY KNOWLEDGE YOU HAVE CONCERNING THE MAGUS.
NO SIMPLE REQUEST.
ONCE A TIME LINE EXISTED WHERE YOUR COMPANION, ADAM WARLOCK, EVENTUALLY BECOME THE MAGUS, A DARK AND OMINOUS CONQUEROR.
BUT HE WAS A CAESAR WITH A STRANGE TWIST.
"IN ORDER TO ASSURE HIS CONTROL OF THE FUTURE, HE RETURNED TO THE PAST TO CEMENT HIS BASE OF POWER.
"HIS MIGHT AND INTIMATE KNOWLEDGE OF WHAT HAD BEEN ASSURED HIS SUCCESS.
"A THOUSAND WORLDS DID HE CONQUER, AND ON THESE PLANETS HE ESTABLISHED THE UNIVERSAL CHURCH OF TRUTH.
"HIS SUBJECTS WORSHIPPED HIM AS AN IRON-FISTED GOD.

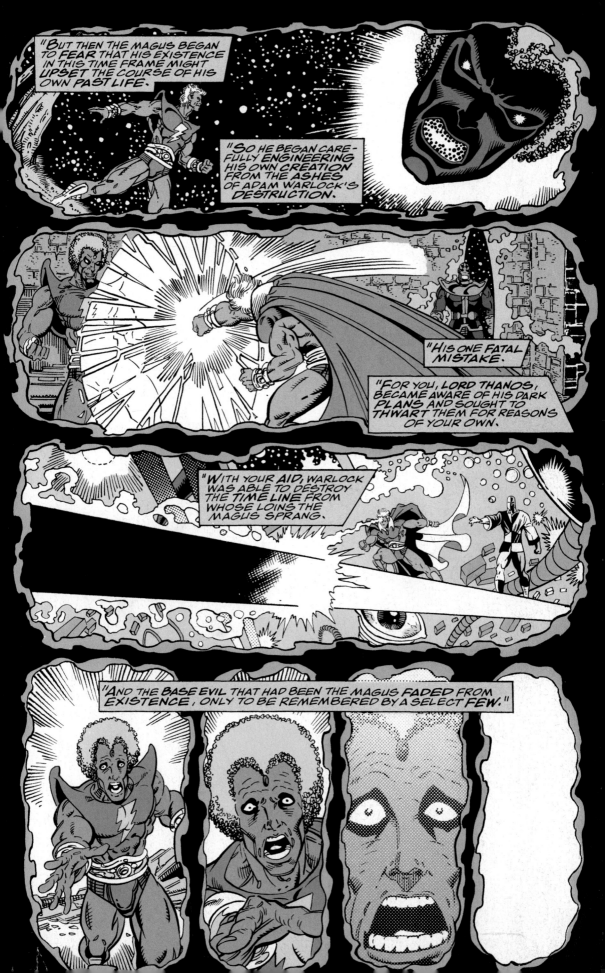

"BUT THEN THE MAGUS BEGAN TO FEAR THAT HIS EXISTENCE IN THIS TIME FRAME MIGHT UPSET THE COURSE OF HIS OWN PAST LIFE.

"SO HE BEGAN CAREFULLY ENGINEERING HIS OWN CREATION FROM THE ASHES OF ADAM WARLOCK'S DESTRUCTION.

"HIS ONE FATAL MISTAKE.

"FOR YOU, LORD THANOS, BECAME AWARE OF HIS DARK PLANS AND SOUGHT TO THWART THEM FOR REASONS OF YOUR OWN.

"WITH YOUR AID, WARLOCK WAS ABLE TO DESTROY THE TIME LINE FROM WHOSE LOINS THE MAGUS SPRANG.

"AND THE BASE EVIL THAT HAD BEEN THE MAGUS FADED FROM EXISTENCE, ONLY TO BE REMEMBERED BY A SELECT FEW."

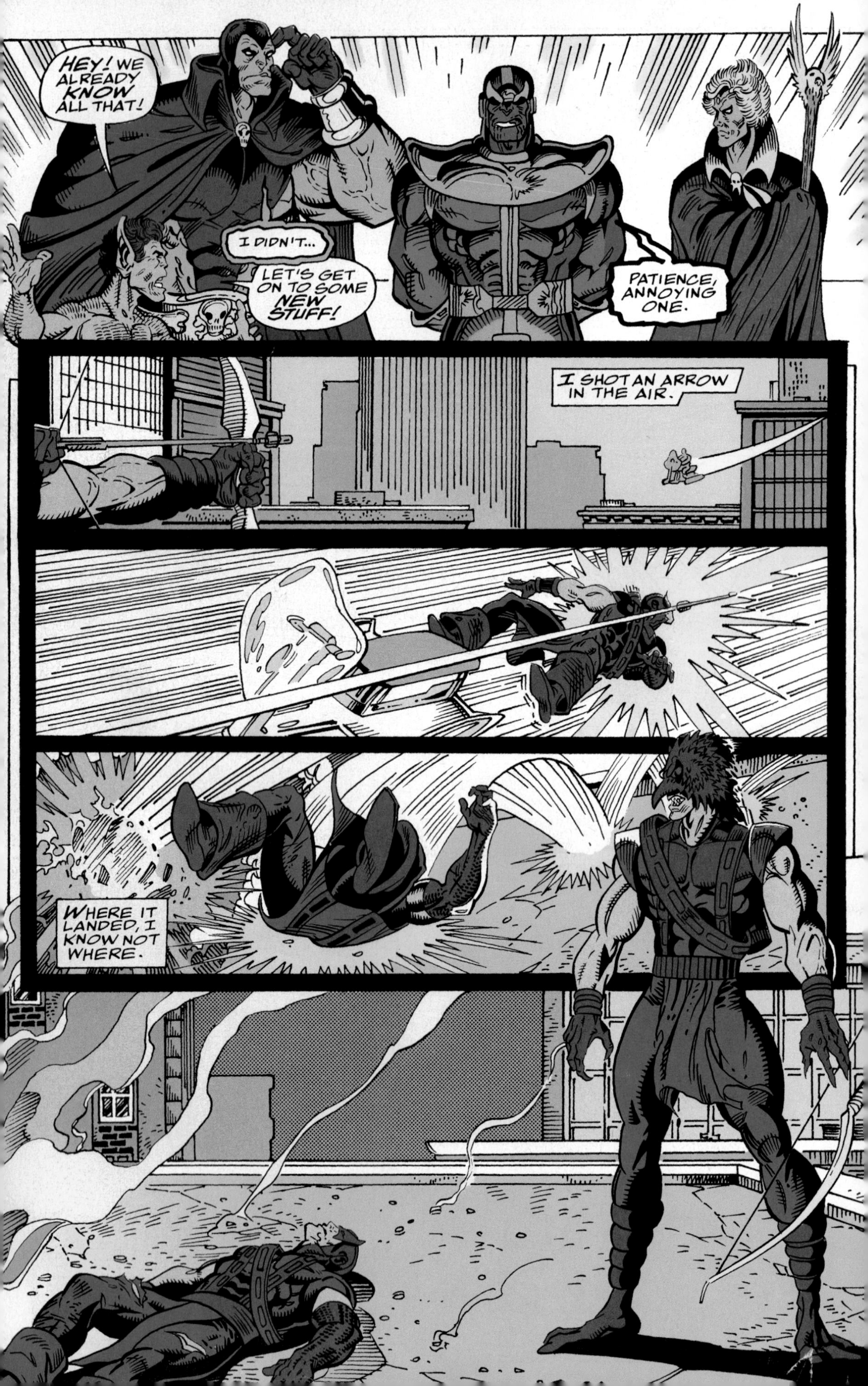
HEY! WE ALREADY KNOW ALL THAT!
I DIDN'T...
LET'S GET ON TO SOME NEW STUFF!
PATIENCE, ANNOYING ONE.
I SHOT AN ARROW IN THE AIR.
WHERE IT LANDED, I KNOW NOT WHERE.

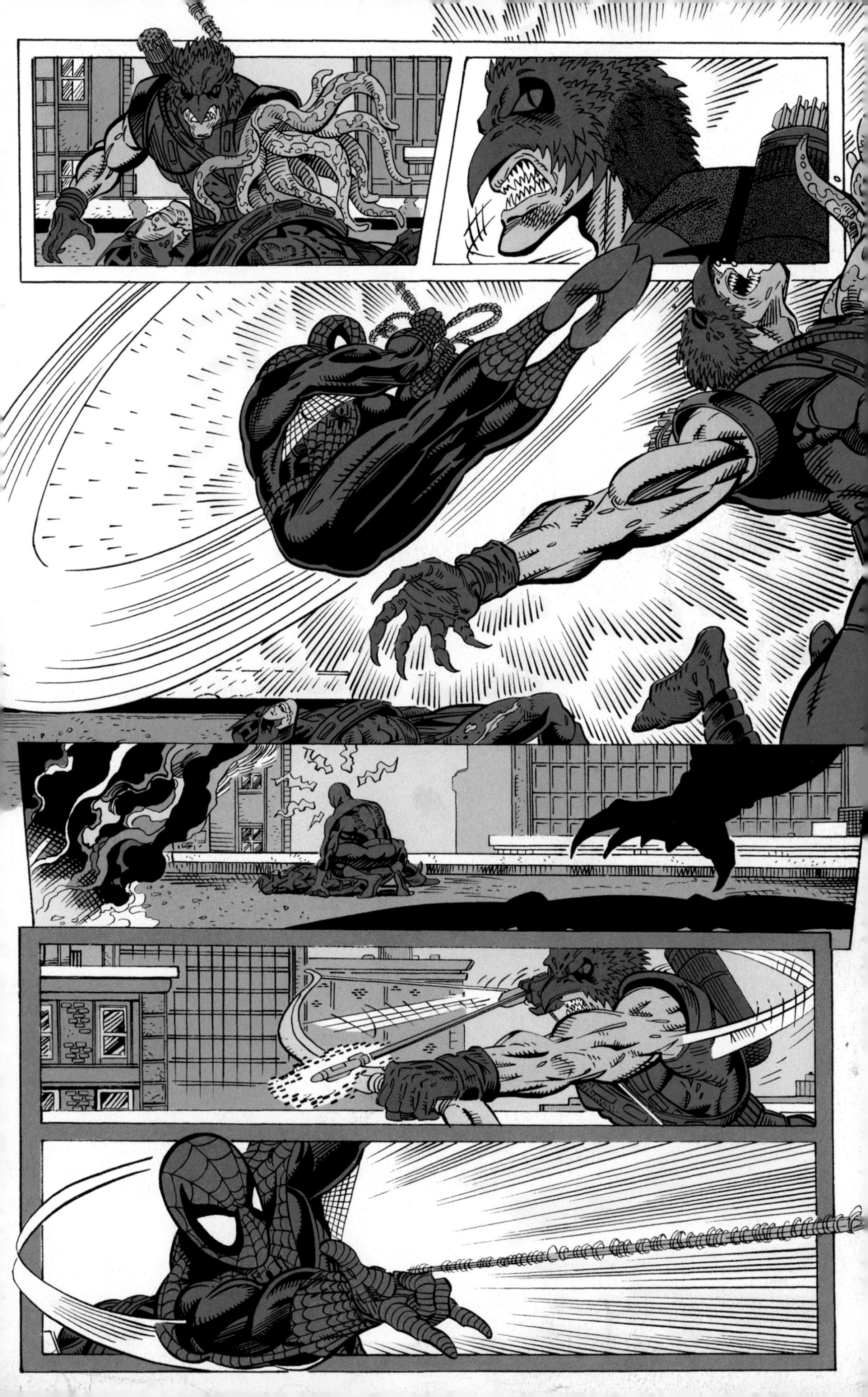

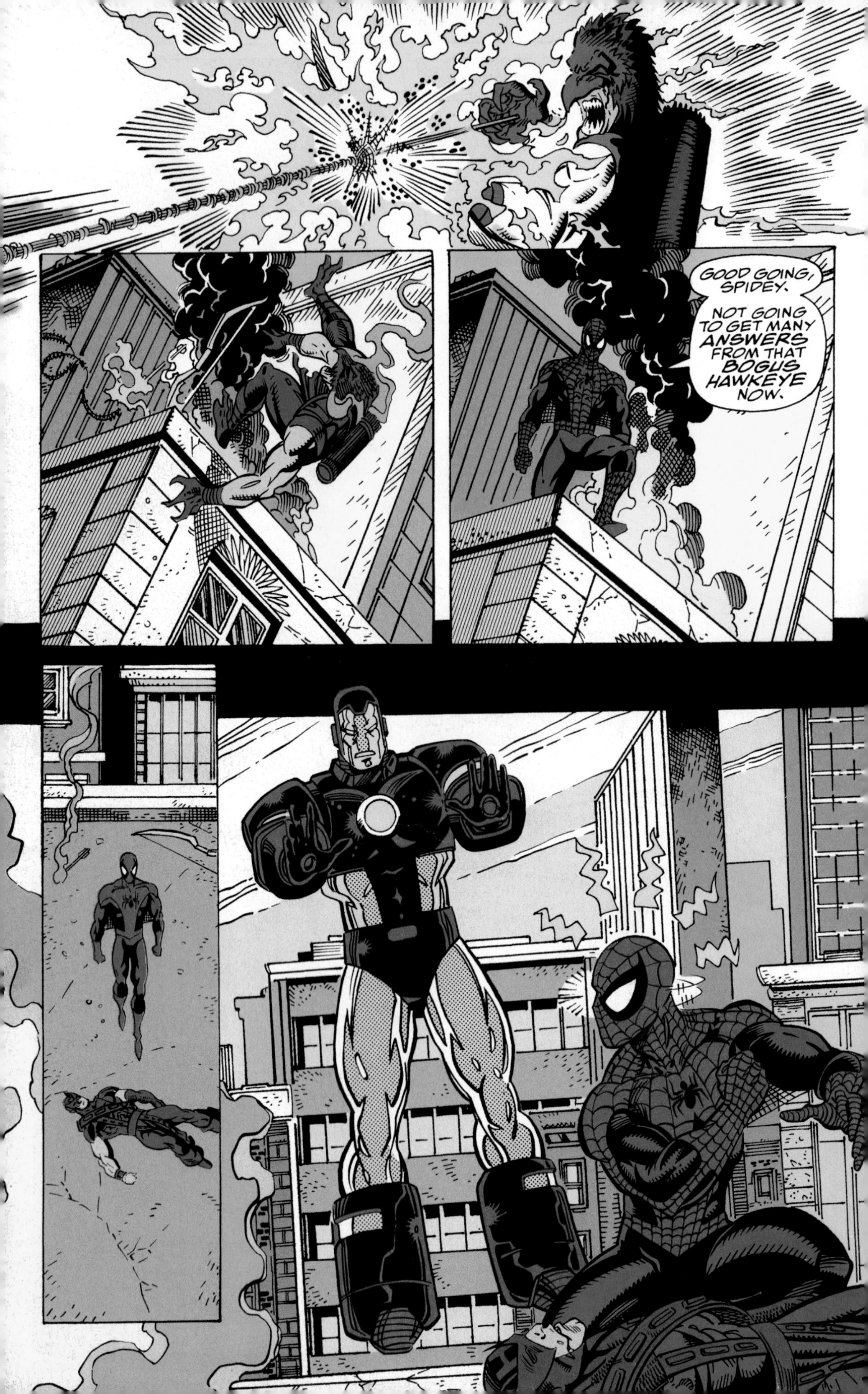
GOOD GOING, SPIDEY.
NOT GOING TO GET MANY ANSWERS FROM THAT BOGUS HAWKEYE NOW.

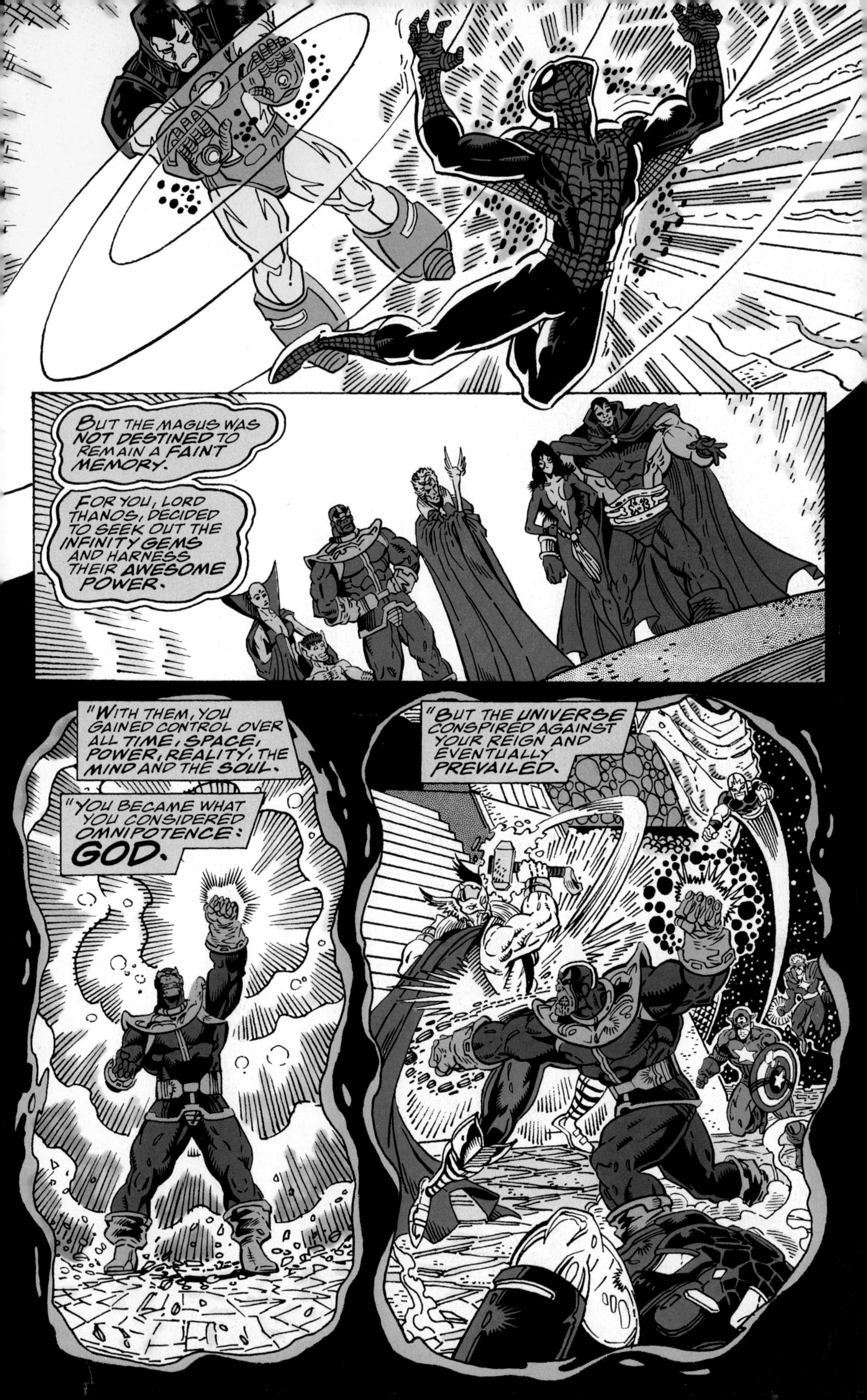
BUT THE MAGUS WAS NOT DESTINED TO REMAIN A FAINT MEMORY.
FOR YOU, LORD THANOS, DECIDED TO SEEK OUT THE INFINITY GEMS AND HARNESS THEIR AWESOME POWER.
"WITH THEM, YOU GAINED CONTROL OVER ALL TIME, SPACE, POWER, REALITY, THE MIND AND THE SOUL.
"YOU BECAME WHAT YOU CONSIDERED OMNIPOTENCE: GOD.
"BUT THE UNIVERSE CONSPIRED AGAINST YOUR REIGN AND EVENTUALLY PREVAILED.

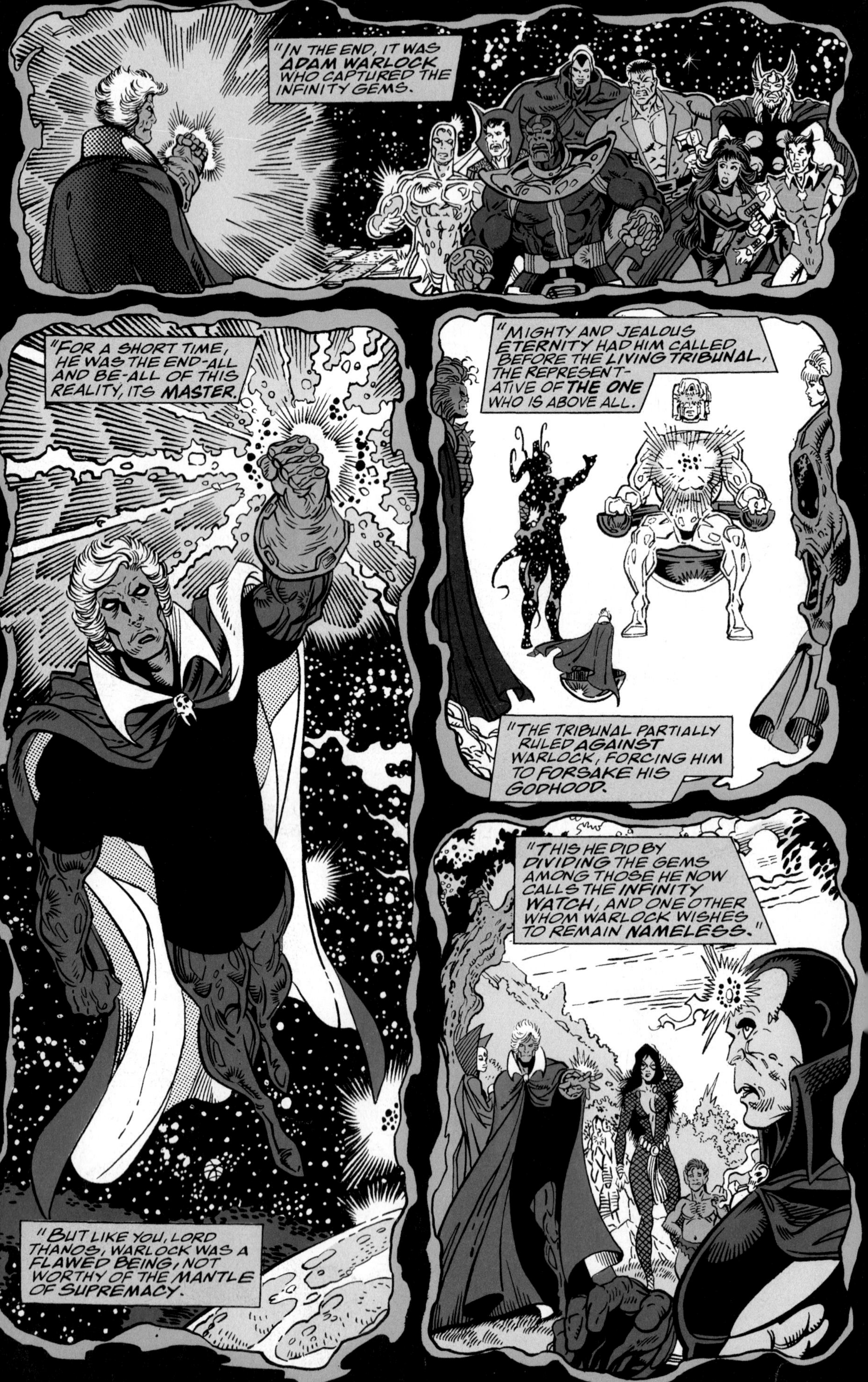
"IN THE END, IT WAS ADAM WARLOCK WHO CAPTURED THE INFINITY GEMS.
"FOR A SHORT TIME, HE WAS THE END-ALL AND BE-ALL OF THIS REALITY, ITS MASTER.
"BUT LIKE YOU, LORD THANOS, WARLOCK WAS A FLAWED BEING, NOT WORTHY OF THE MANTLE OF SUPREMACY.
"MIGHTY AND JEALOUS ETERNITY HAD HIM CALLED BEFORE THE LIVING TRIBUNAL, THE REPRESENT-ATIVE OF THE ONE WHO IS ABOVE ALL.
"THE TRIBUNAL PARTIALLY RULED AGAINST WARLOCK, FORCING HIM TO FORSAKE HIS GODHOOD.
"THIS HE DID BY DIVIDING THE GEMS AMONG THOSE HE NOW CALLS THE INFINITY WATCH, AND ONE OTHER WHOM WARLOCK WISHES TO REMAIN NAMELESS."

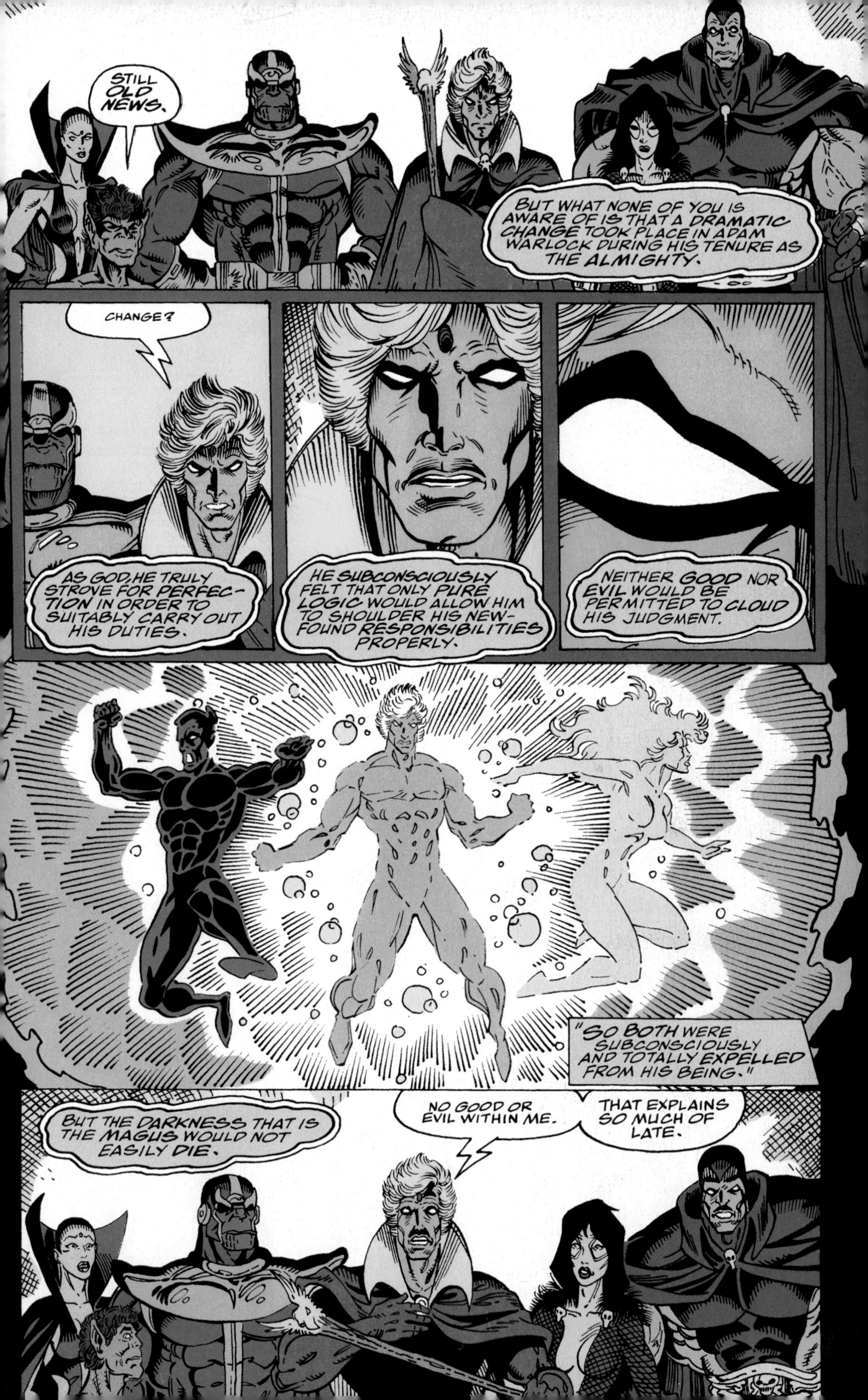
STILL OLD NEWS.
BUT WHAT NONE OF YOU IS AWARE OF IS THAT A DRAMATIC CHANGE TOOK PLACE IN ADAM WARLOCK DURING HIS TENURE AS THE ALMIGHTY.
CHANGE?
AS GOD, HE TRULY STROVE FOR PERFECTION IN ORDER TO SUITABLY CARRY OUT HIS DUTIES.
HE SUBCONSCIOUSLY FELT THAT ONLY PURE LOGIC WOULD ALLOW HIM TO SHOULDER HIS NEW-FOUND RESPONSIBILITIES PROPERLY.
NEITHER GOOD NOR EVIL WOULD BE PERMITTED TO CLOUD HIS JUDGMENT.
"SO BOTH WERE SUBCONSCIOUSLY AND TOTALLY EXPELLED FROM HIS BEING."
BUT THE DARKNESS THAT IS THE MAGUS WOULD NOT EASILY DIE.
NO GOOD OR EVIL WITHIN ME.
THAT EXPLAINS SO MUCH OF LATE.

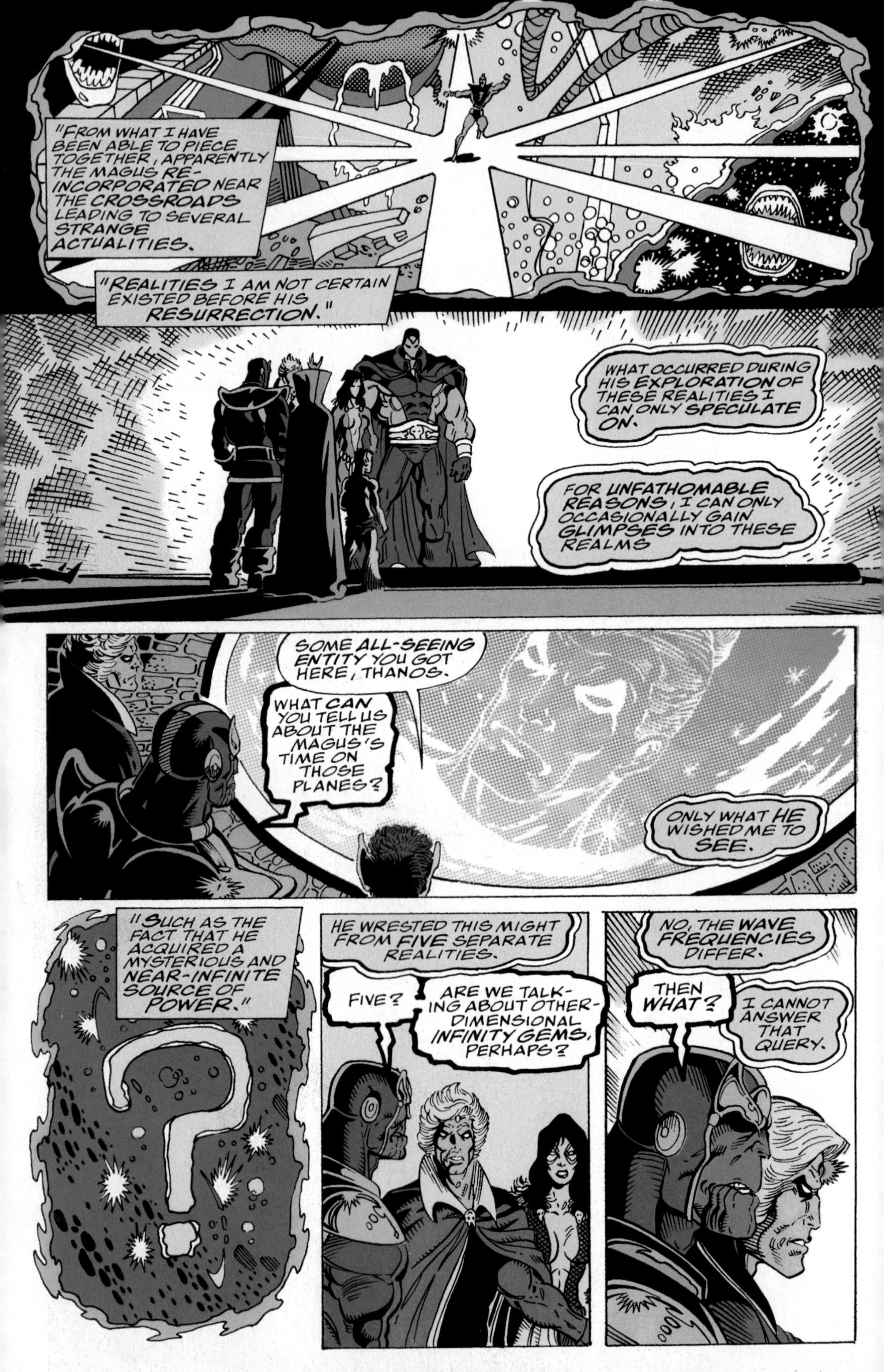
"FROM WHAT I HAVE BEEN ABLE TO PIECE TOGETHER, APPARENTLY THE MAGUS RE-INCORPORATED NEAR THE CROSSROADS LEADING TO SEVERAL STRANGE ACTUALITIES.
"REALITIES I AM NOT CERTAIN EXISTED BEFORE HIS RESURRECTION."
WHAT OCCURRED DURING HIS EXPLORATION OF THESE REALITIES I CAN ONLY SPECULATE ON.
FOR UNFATHOMABLE REASONS, I CAN ONLY OCCASIONALLY GAIN GLIMPSES INTO THESE REALMS
SOME ALL-SEEING ENTITY YOU GOT HERE, THANOS.
WHAT CAN YOU TELL US ABOUT THE MAGUS'S TIME ON THOSE PLANES?
ONLY WHAT HE WISHED ME TO SEE.
"SUCH AS THE FACT THAT HE ACQUIRED A MYSTERIOUS AND NEAR-INFINITE SOURCE OF POWER."
HE WRESTED THIS MIGHT FROM FIVE SEPARATE REALITIES.
FIVE?
ARE WE TALKING ABOUT OTHER-DIMENSIONAL INFINITY GEMS, PERHAPS?
NO, THE WAVE FREQUENCIES DIFFER.
THEN WHAT?
I CANNOT ANSWER THAT QUERY.

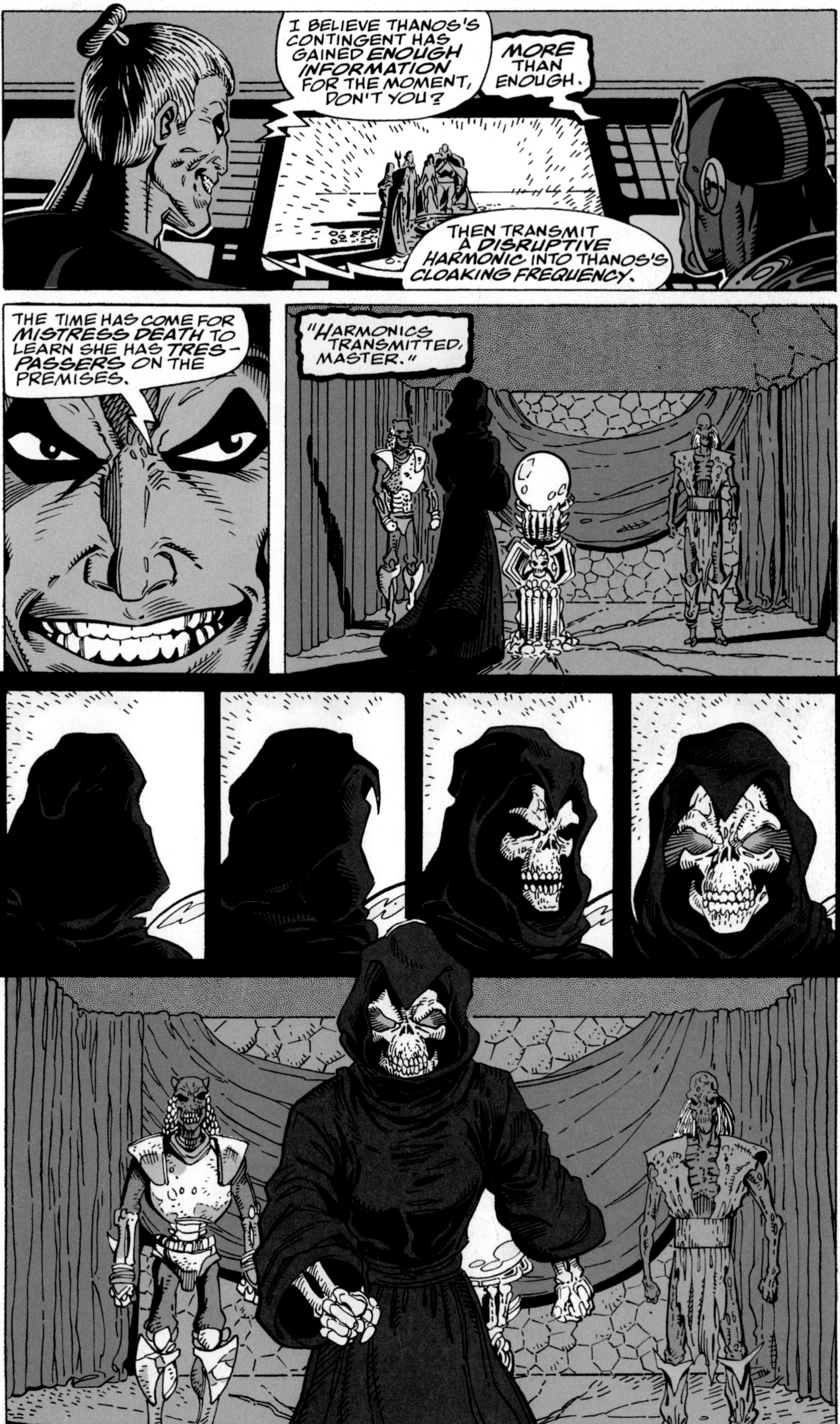
I BELIEVE THANOS'S CONTINGENT HAS GAINED ENOUGH INFORMATION FOR THE MOMENT, DON'T YOU?
MORE THAN ENOUGH.
THEN TRANSMIT A DISRUPTIVE HARMONIC INTO THANOS'S CLOAKING FREQUENCY.
THE TIME HAS COME FOR MISTRESS DEATH TO LEARN SHE HAS TRES-PASSERS ON THE PREMISES.
"HARMONICS TRANSMITTED, MASTER."

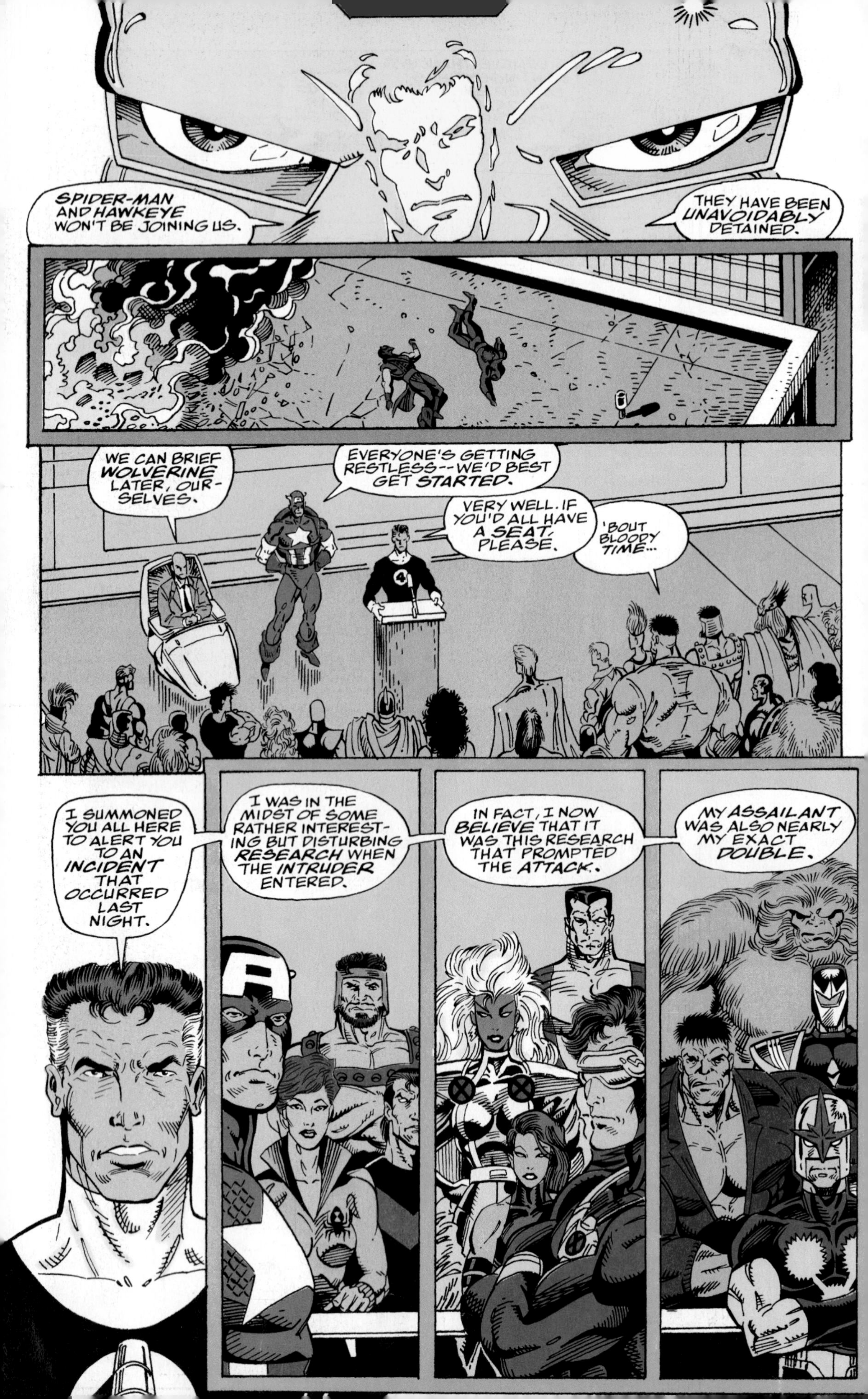
SPIDER-MAN AND HAWKEYE WON'T BE JOINING US.
THEY HAVE BEEN UNAVOIDABLY DETAINED.
WE CAN BRIEF WOLVERINE LATER, OUR-SELVES.
EVERYONE'S GETTING RESTLESS--WE'D BEST GET STARTED.
VERY WELL. IF YOU'D ALL HAVE A SEAT, PLEASE.
'BOUT BLOODY TIME...
I SUMMONED YOU ALL HERE TO ALERT YOU TO AN INCIDENT THAT OCCURRED LAST NIGHT.
I WAS IN THE MIDST OF SOME RATHER INTERESTING BUT DISTURBING RESEARCH WHEN THE INTRUDER ENTERED.
IN FACT, I NOW BELIEVE THAT IT WAS THIS RESEARCH THAT PROMPTED THE ATTACK.
MY ASSAILANT WAS ALSO NEARLY MY EXACT DOUBLE.

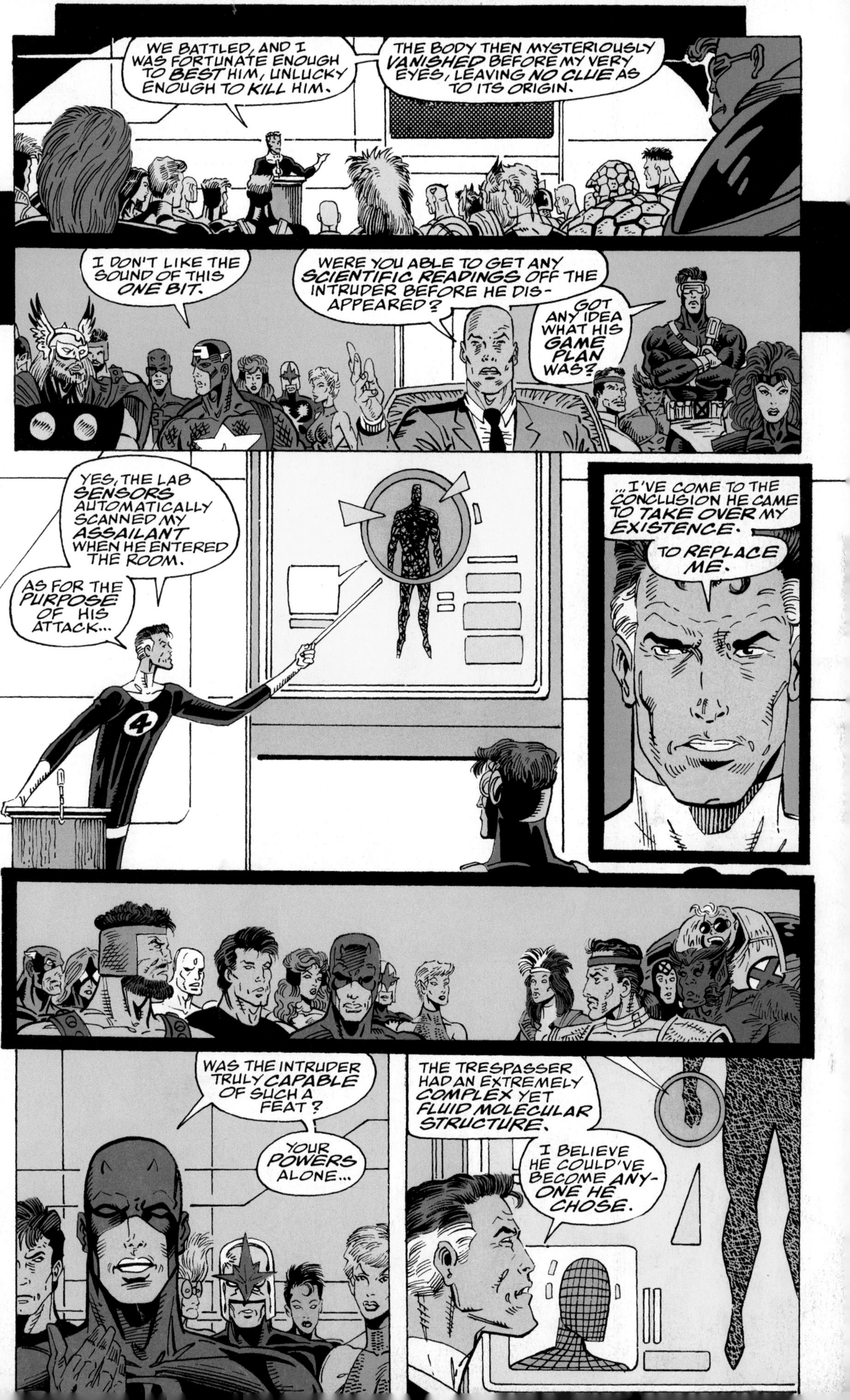
WE BATTLED, AND I WAS FORTUNATE ENOUGH TO BEST HIM, UNLUCKY ENOUGH TO KILL HIM.
THE BODY THEN MYSTERIOUSLY VANISHED BEFORE MY VERY EYES, LEAVING NO CLUE AS TO ITS ORIGIN.
I DON'T LIKE THE SOUND OF THIS ONE BIT.
WERE YOU ABLE TO GET ANY SCIENTIFIC READINGS OFF THE INTRUDER BEFORE HE DIS-APPEARED?
GOT ANY IDEA WHAT HIS GAME PLAN WAS?
YES, THE LAB SENSORS AUTOMATICALLY SCANNED MY ASSAILANT WHEN HE ENTERED THE ROOM.
AS FOR THE PURPOSE OF HIS ATTACK...
...I'VE COME TO THE CONCLUSION HE CAME TO TAKE OVER MY EXISTENCE.
TO REPLACE ME.
WAS THE INTRUDER TRULY CAPABLE OF SUCH A FEAT?
YOUR POWERS ALONE...
THE TRESPASSER HAD AN EXTREMELY COMPLEX YET FLUID MOLECULAR STRUCTURE.
I BELIEVE HE COULD'VE BECOME ANY-ONE HE CHOSE.

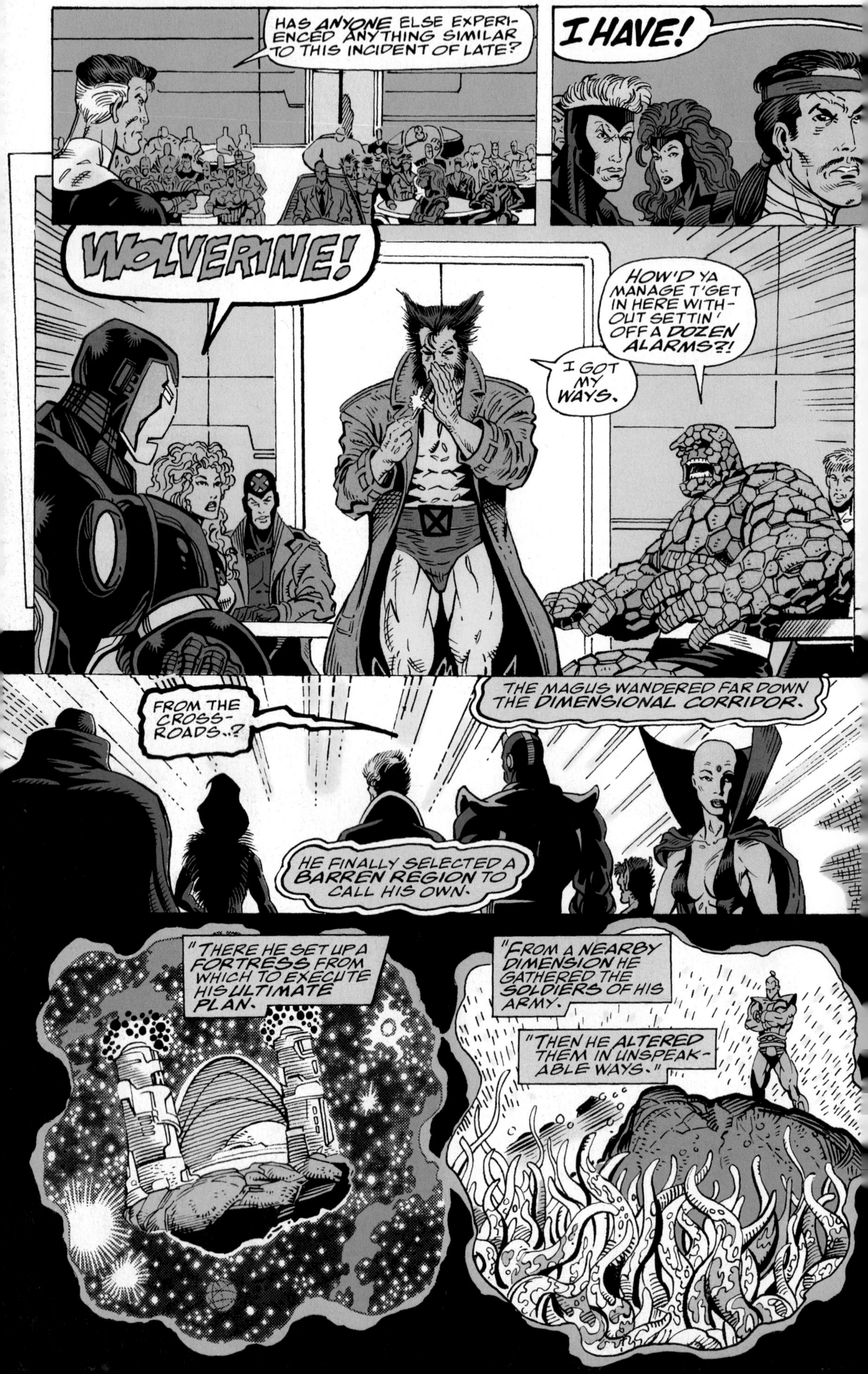
HAS ANYONE ELSE EXPERIENCED ANYTHING SIMILAR TO THIS INCIDENT OF LATE?
I HAVE!
WOLVERINE!
HOW'D YA MANAGE T'GET IN HERE WITHOUT SETTIN' OFF A DOZEN ALARMS?!
I GOT MY WAYS.
FROM THE CROSSROADS..?
THE MAGUS WANDERED FAR DOWN THE DIMENSIONAL CORRIDOR.
HE FINALLY SELECTED A BARREN REGION TO CALL HIS OWN.
"THERE HE SET UP A FORTRESS FROM WHICH TO EXECUTE HIS ULTIMATE PLAN.
"FROM A NEARBY DIMENSION HE GATHERED THE SOLDIERS OF HIS ARMY.
"THEN HE ALTERED THEM IN UNSPEAKABLE WAYS."

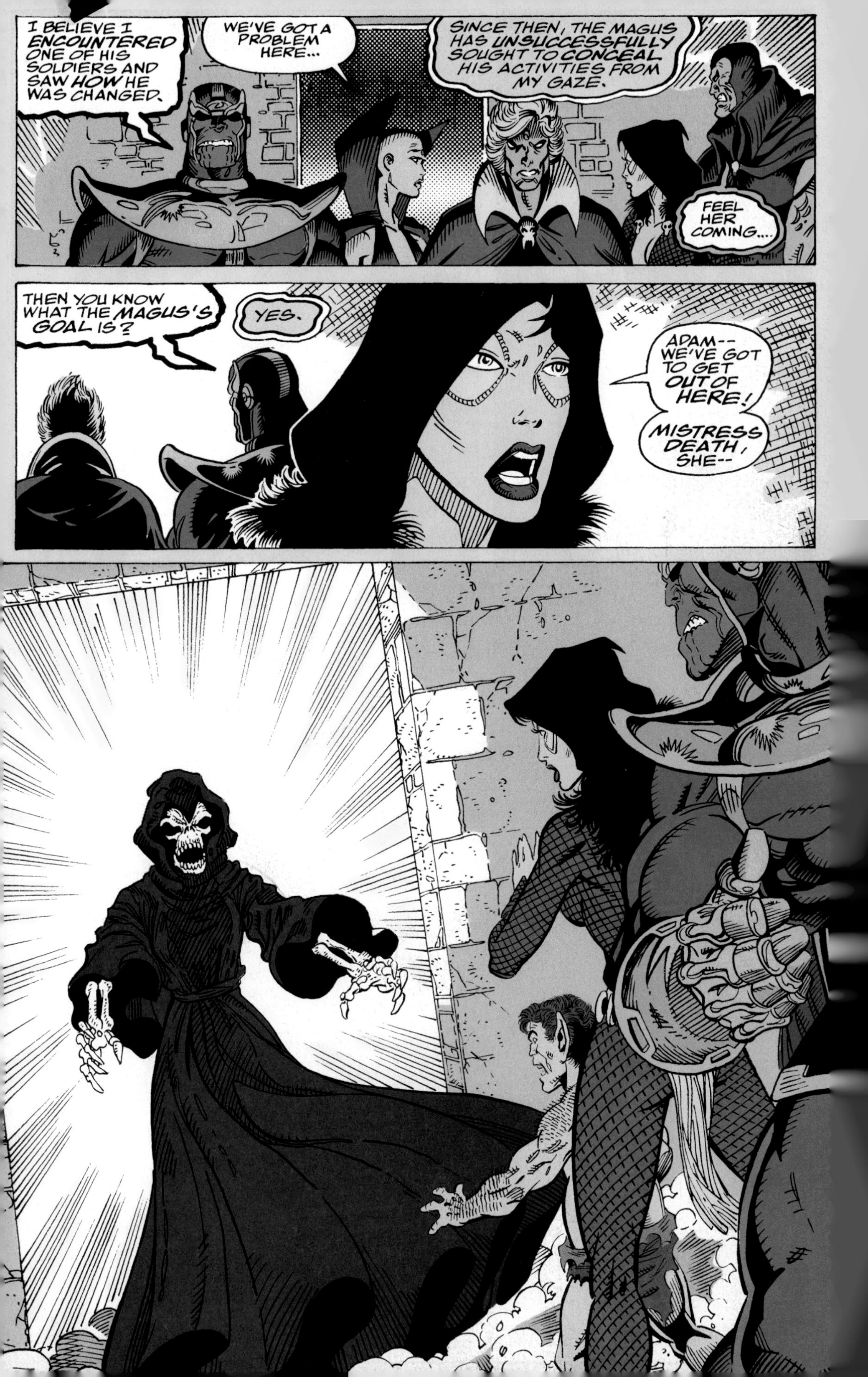
I BELIEVE I ENCOUNTERED ONE OF HIS SOLDIERS AND SAW HOW HE WAS CHANGED.
WE'VE GOT A PROBLEM HERE...
SINCE THEN, THE MAGUS HAS UNSUCCESSFULLY SOUGHT TO CONCEAL HIS ACTIVITIES FROM MY GAZE.
FEEL HER COMING...
THEN YOU KNOW WHAT THE MAGUS'S GOAL IS?
YES.
ADAM-- WE'VE GOT TO GET OUT OF HERE!
MISTRESS DEATH, SHE--

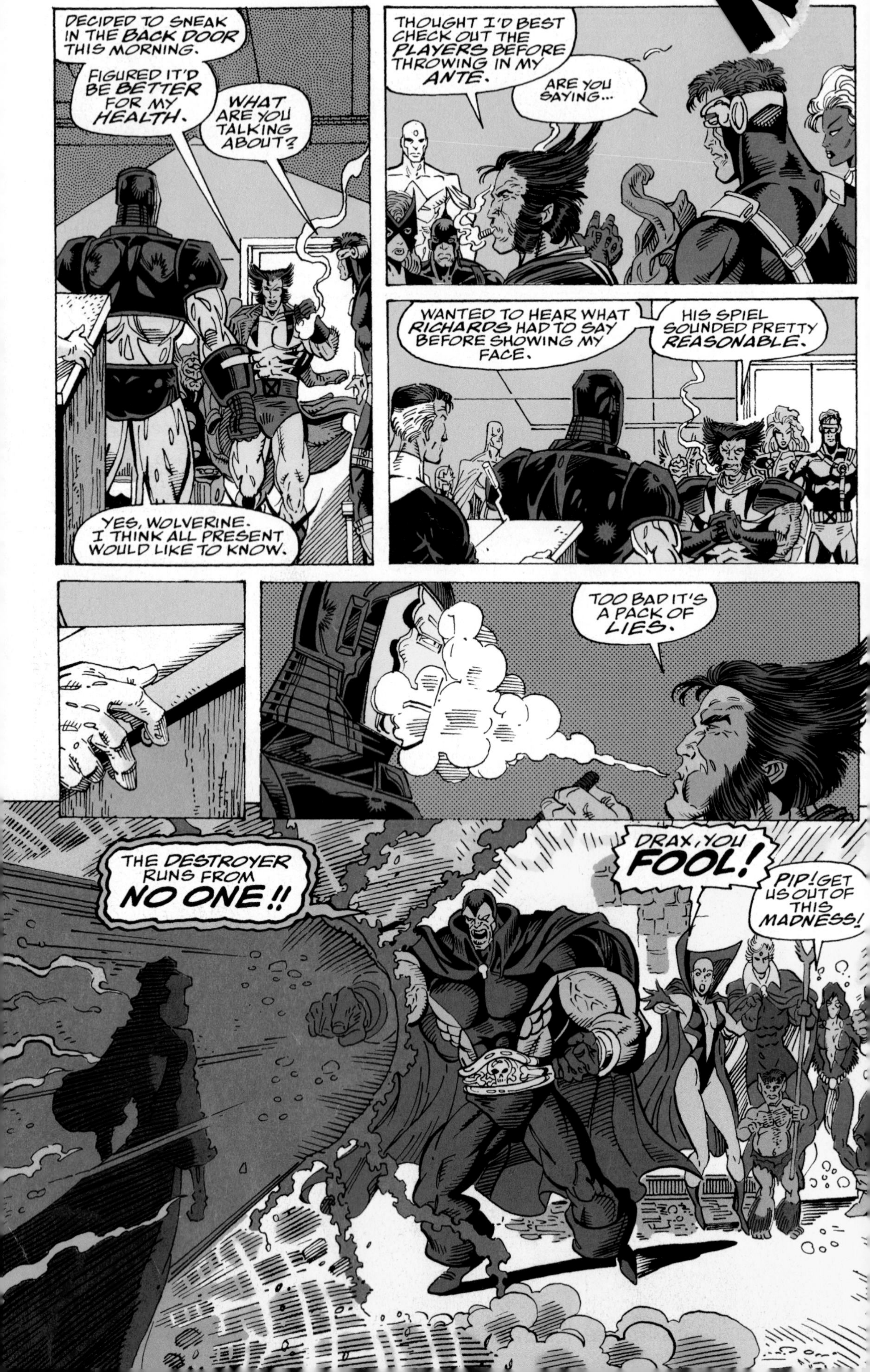
DECIDED TO SNEAK IN THE BACK DOOR THIS MORNING.
FIGURED IT'D BE BETTER FOR MY HEALTH.
WHAT ARE YOU TALKING ABOUT?
YES, WOLVERINE. I THINK ALL PRESENT WOULD LIKE TO KNOW.
THOUGHT I'D BEST CHECK OUT THE PLAYERS BEFORE THROWING IN MY ANTE.
ARE YOU SAYING...
WANTED TO HEAR WHAT RICHARDS HAD TO SAY BEFORE SHOWING MY FACE.
HIS SPIEL SOUNDED PRETTY REASONABLE.
TOO BAD IT'S A PACK OF LIES.
THE DESTROYER RUNS FROM NO ONE!!
DRAX, YOU FOOL!
PIP! GET US OUT OF THIS MADNESS!

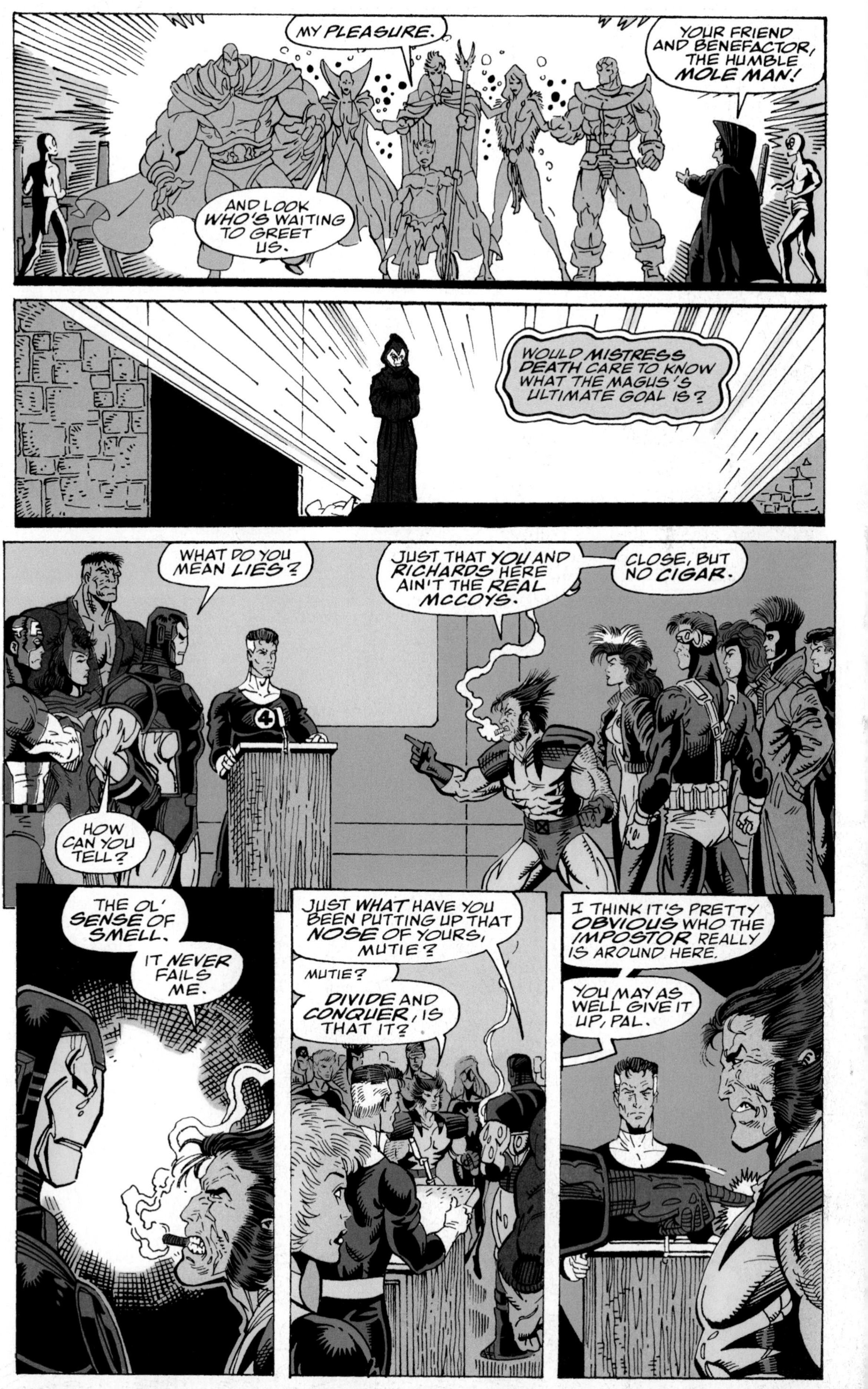
MY PLEASURE.
YOUR FRIEND AND BENEFACTOR, THE HUMBLE MOLE MAN!
AND LOOK WHO'S WAITING TO GREET US.
WOULD MISTRESS DEATH CARE TO KNOW WHAT THE MAGUS'S ULTIMATE GOAL IS?
WHAT DO YOU MEAN LIES?
JUST THAT YOU AND RICHARDS HERE AIN'T THE REAL McCOYS.
CLOSE, BUT NO CIGAR.
HOW CAN YOU TELL?
THE OL' SENSE OF SMELL.
IT NEVER FAILS ME.
JUST WHAT HAVE YOU BEEN PUTTING UP THAT NOSE OF YOURS, MUTIE?
MUTIE?
DIVIDE AND CONQUER, IS THAT IT?
I THINK IT'S PRETTY OBVIOUS WHO THE IMPOSTOR REALLY IS AROUND HERE.
YOU MAY AS WELL GIVE IT UP, PAL.

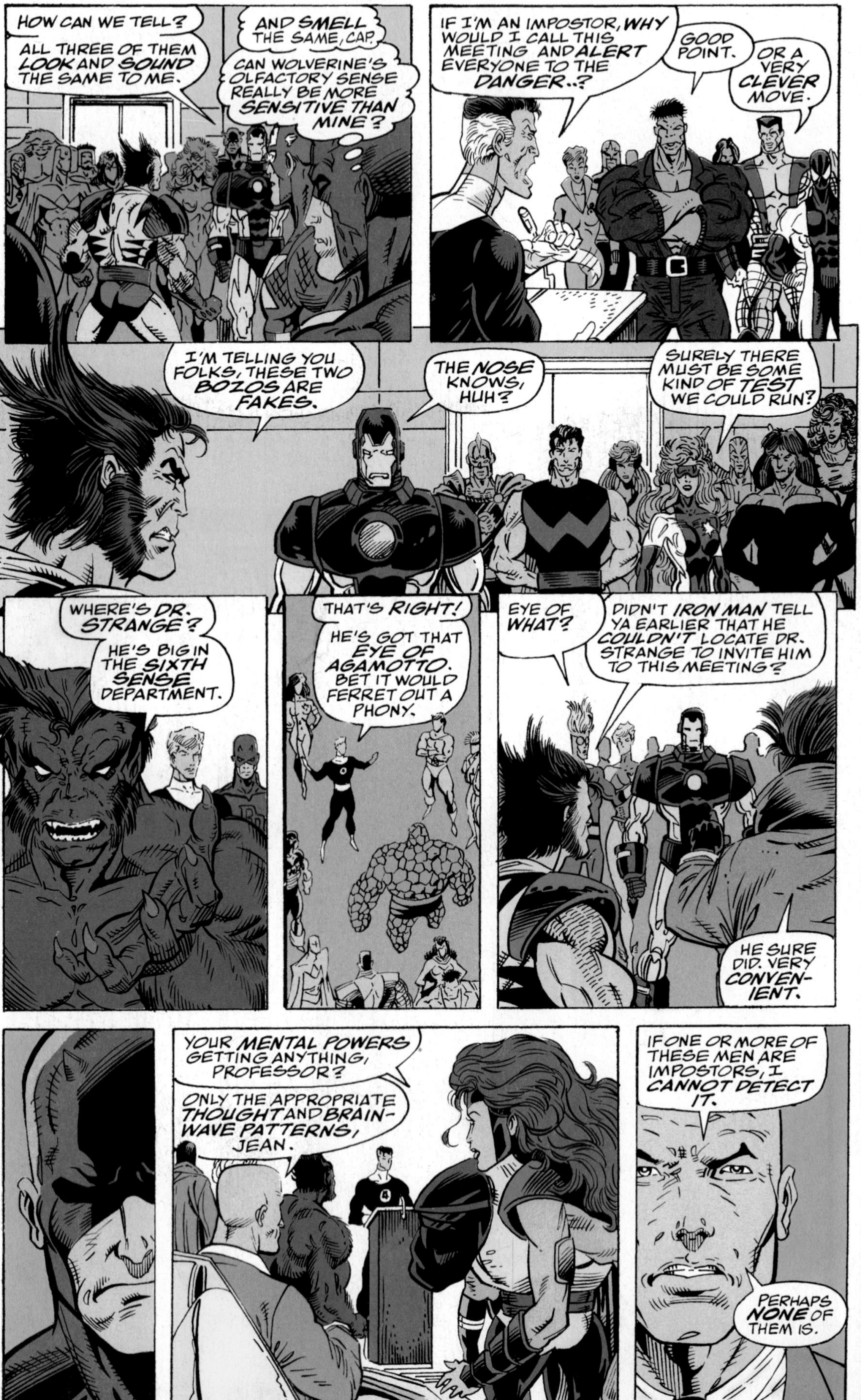
HOW CAN WE TELL?
ALL THREE OF THEM LOOK AND SOUND THE SAME TO ME.
AND SMELL THE SAME, CAP.
CAN WOLVERINE'S OLFACTORY SENSE REALLY BE MORE SENSITIVE THAN MINE?
IF I'M AN IMPOSTOR, WHY WOULD I CALL THIS MEETING AND ALERT EVERYONE TO THE DANGER..?
GOOD POINT.
OR A VERY CLEVER MOVE.
I'M TELLING YOU FOLKS, THESE TWO BOZOS ARE FAKES.
THE NOSE KNOWS, HUH?
SURELY THERE MUST BE SOME KIND OF TEST WE COULD RUN?
WHERE'S DR. STRANGE?
HE'S BIG IN THE SIXTH SENSE DEPARTMENT.
THAT'S RIGHT!
HE'S GOT THAT EYE OF AGAMOTTO. BET IT WOULD FERRET OUT A PHONY.
EYE OF WHAT?
DIDN'T IRON MAN TELL YA EARLIER THAT HE COULDN'T LOCATE DR. STRANGE TO INVITE HIM TO THIS MEETING?
HE SURE DID. VERY CONVEN-IENT.
YOUR MENTAL POWERS GETTING ANYTHING, PROFESSOR?
ONLY THE APPROPRIATE THOUGHT AND BRAIN-WAVE PATTERNS, JEAN.
IF ONE OR MORE OF THESE MEN ARE IMPOSTORS, I CANNOT DETECT IT.
PERHAPS NONE OF THEM IS.

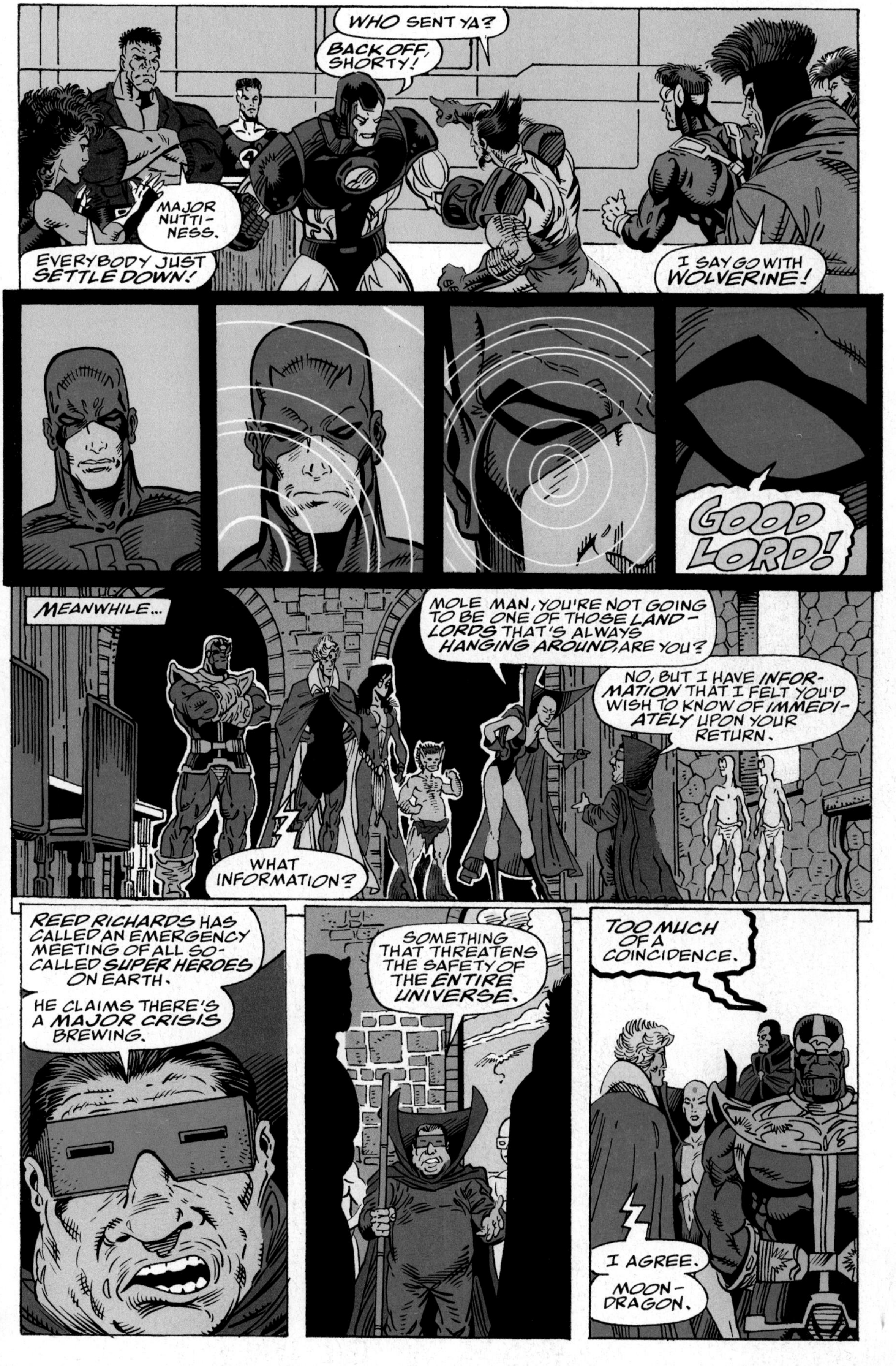

WHO SENT YA?
BACK OFF, SHORTY!
MAJOR NUTTI-NESS.
EVERYBODY JUST SETTLE DOWN!
I SAY GO WITH WOLVERINE!
GOOD LORD!
MEANWHILE...
MOLE MAN, YOU'RE NOT GOING TO BE ONE OF THOSE LAND-LORDS THAT'S ALWAYS HANGING AROUND, ARE YOU?
NO, BUT I HAVE INFOR-MATION THAT I FELT YOU'D WISH TO KNOW OF IMMEDI-ATELY UPON YOUR RETURN.
WHAT INFORMATION?
REED RICHARDS HAS CALLED AN EMERGENCY MEETING OF ALL SO-CALLED SUPER HEROES ON EARTH.
HE CLAIMS THERE'S A MAJOR CRISIS BREWING.
SOMETHING THAT THREATENS THE SAFETY OF THE ENTIRE UNIVERSE.
TOO MUCH OF A COINCIDENCE.
I AGREE.
MOON-DRAGON.

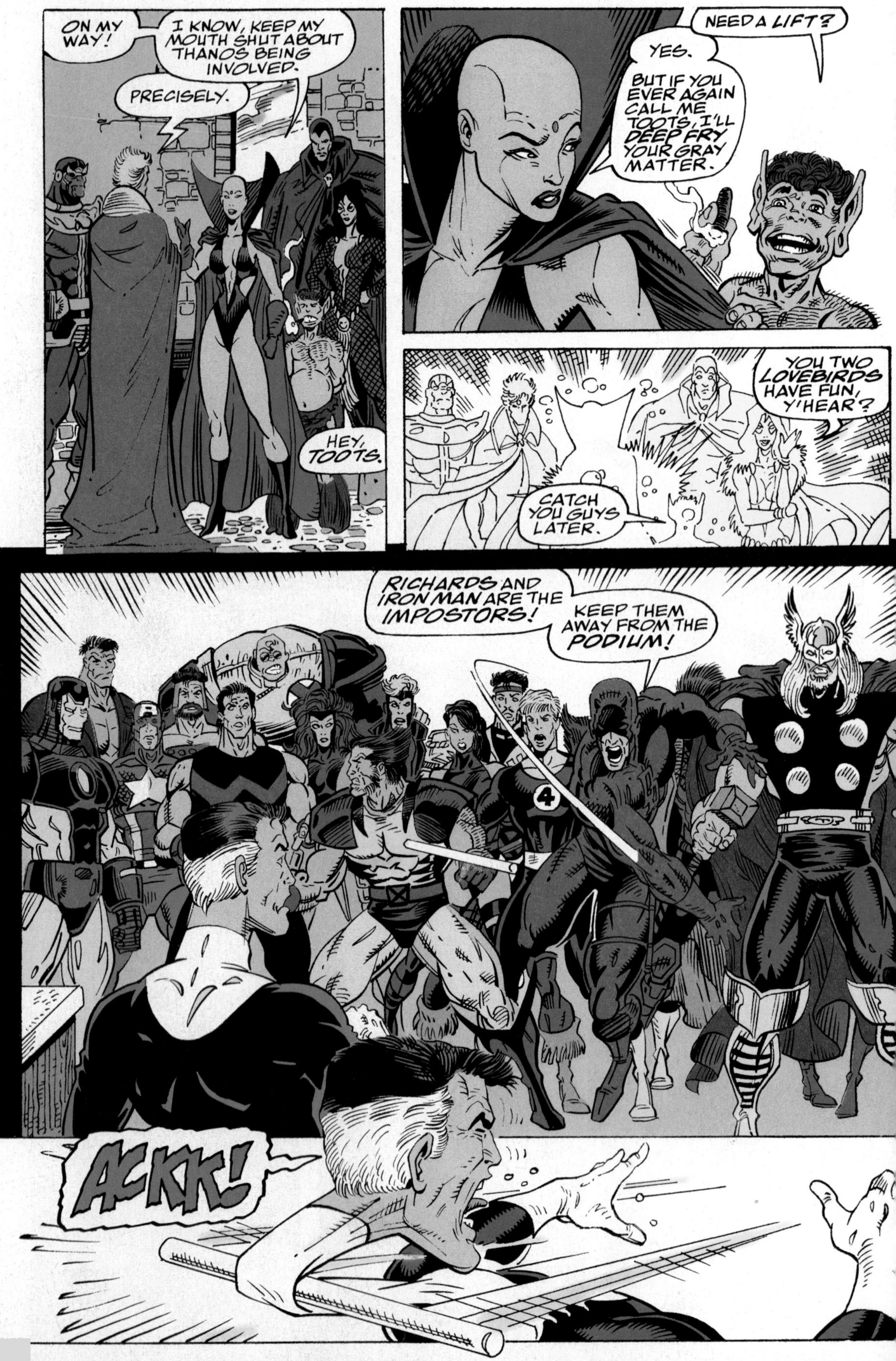
ON MY WAY!
I KNOW, KEEP MY MOUTH SHUT ABOUT THANOS BEING INVOLVED.
PRECISELY.
HEY, TOOTS.
NEED A LIFT?
YES.
BUT IF YOU EVER AGAIN CALL ME TOOTS, I'LL DEEP FRY YOUR GRAY MATTER.
YOU TWO LOVEBIRDS HAVE FUN, Y'HEAR?
CATCH YOU GUYS LATER.
RICHARDS AND IRON MAN ARE THE IMPOSTORS!
KEEP THEM AWAY FROM THE PODIUM!
ACKK!

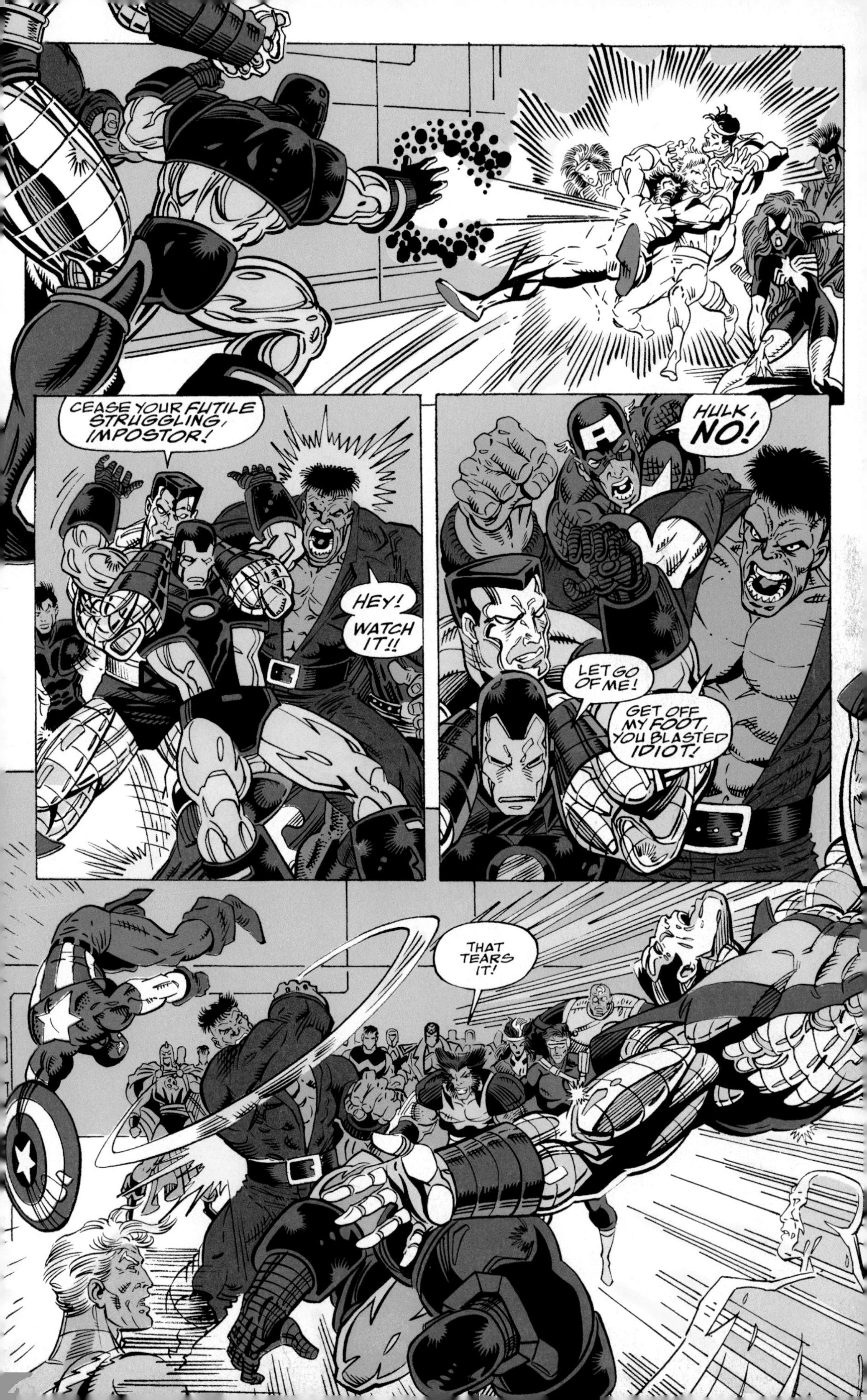
CEASE YOUR FUTILE STRUGGLING, IMPOSTOR!
HEY! WATCH IT!!
HULK, NO!
LET GO OF ME!
GET OFF MY FOOT, YOU BLASTED IDIOT!
THAT TEARS IT!

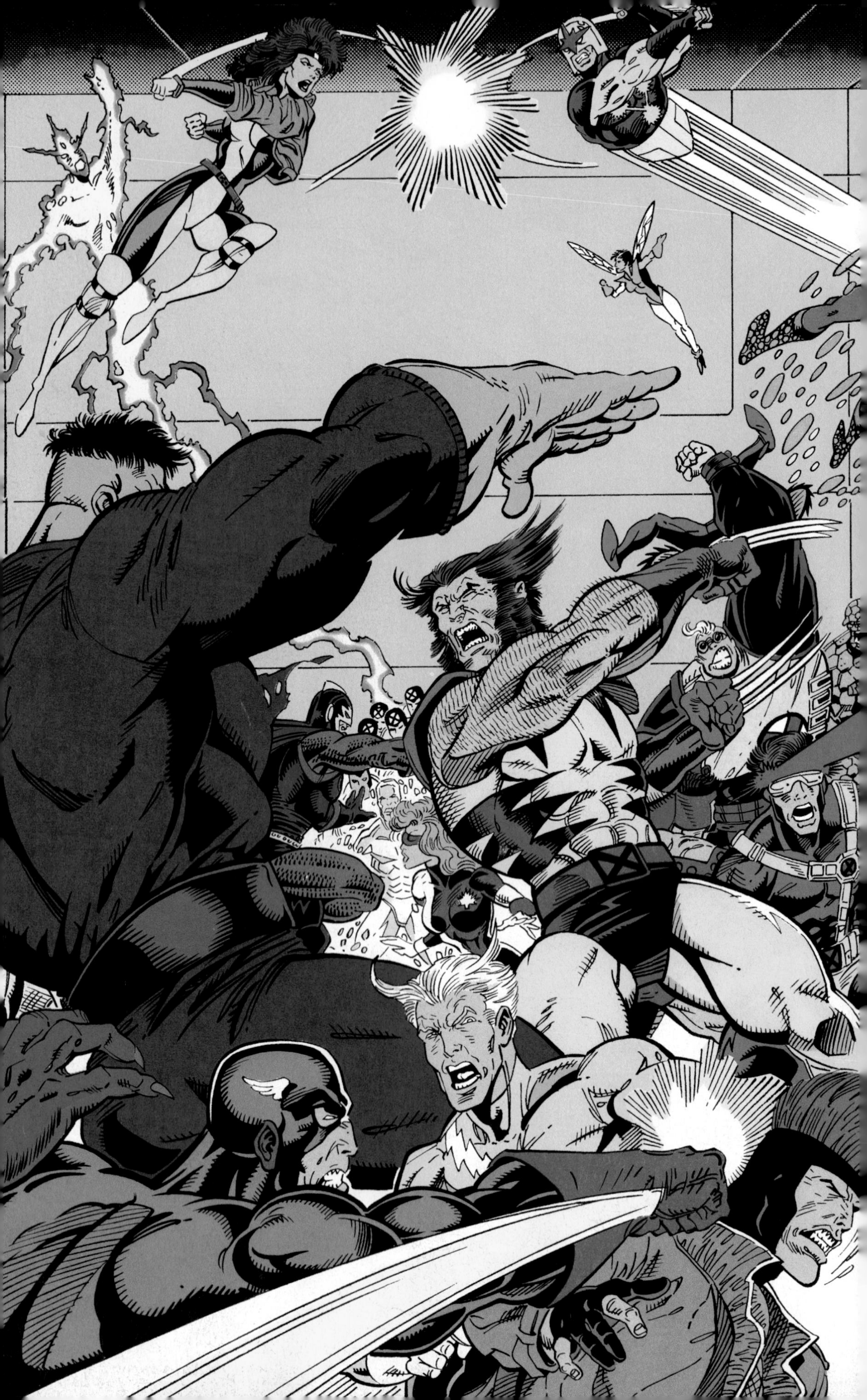

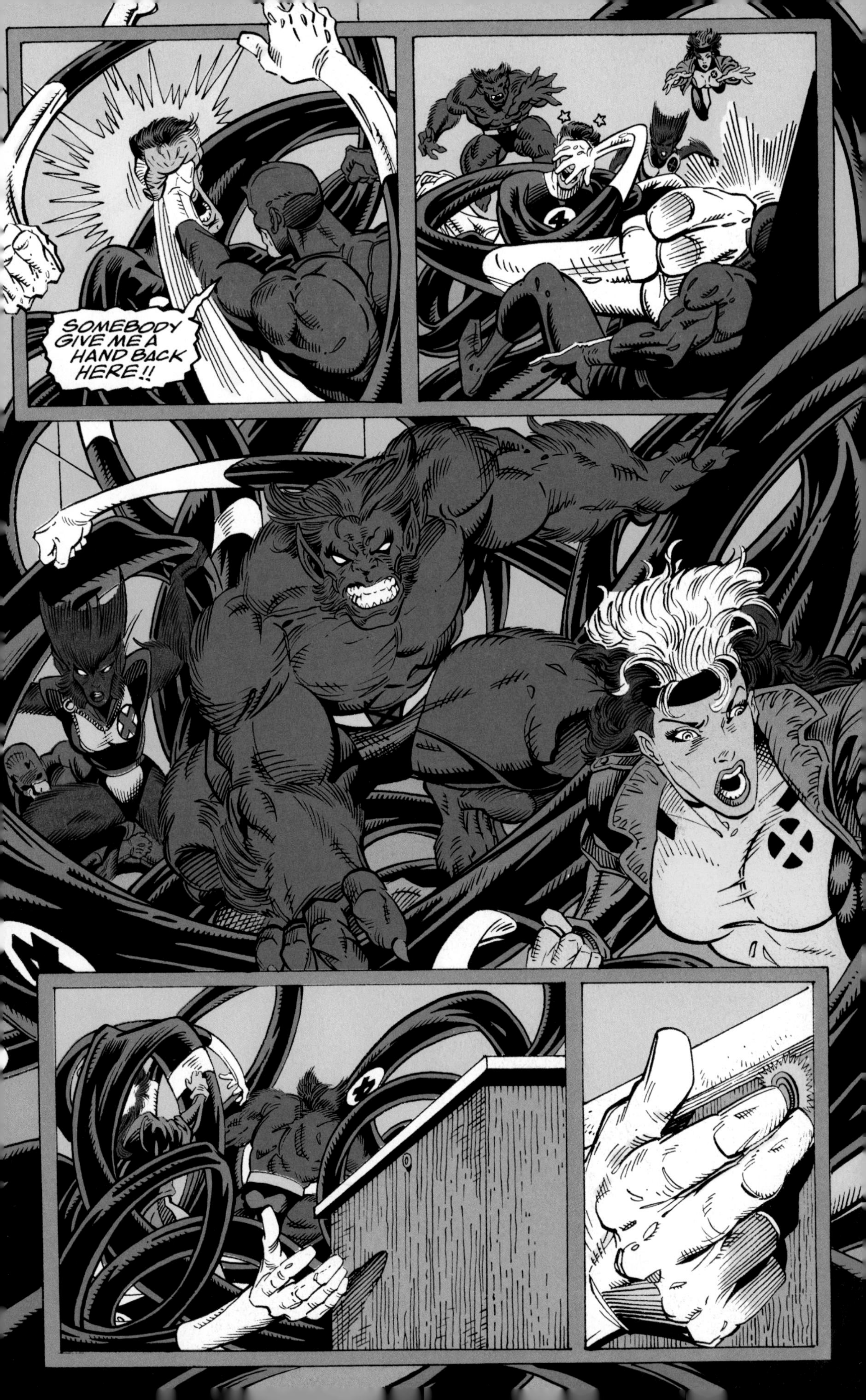
SOMEBODY GIVE ME A HAND BACK HERE!!

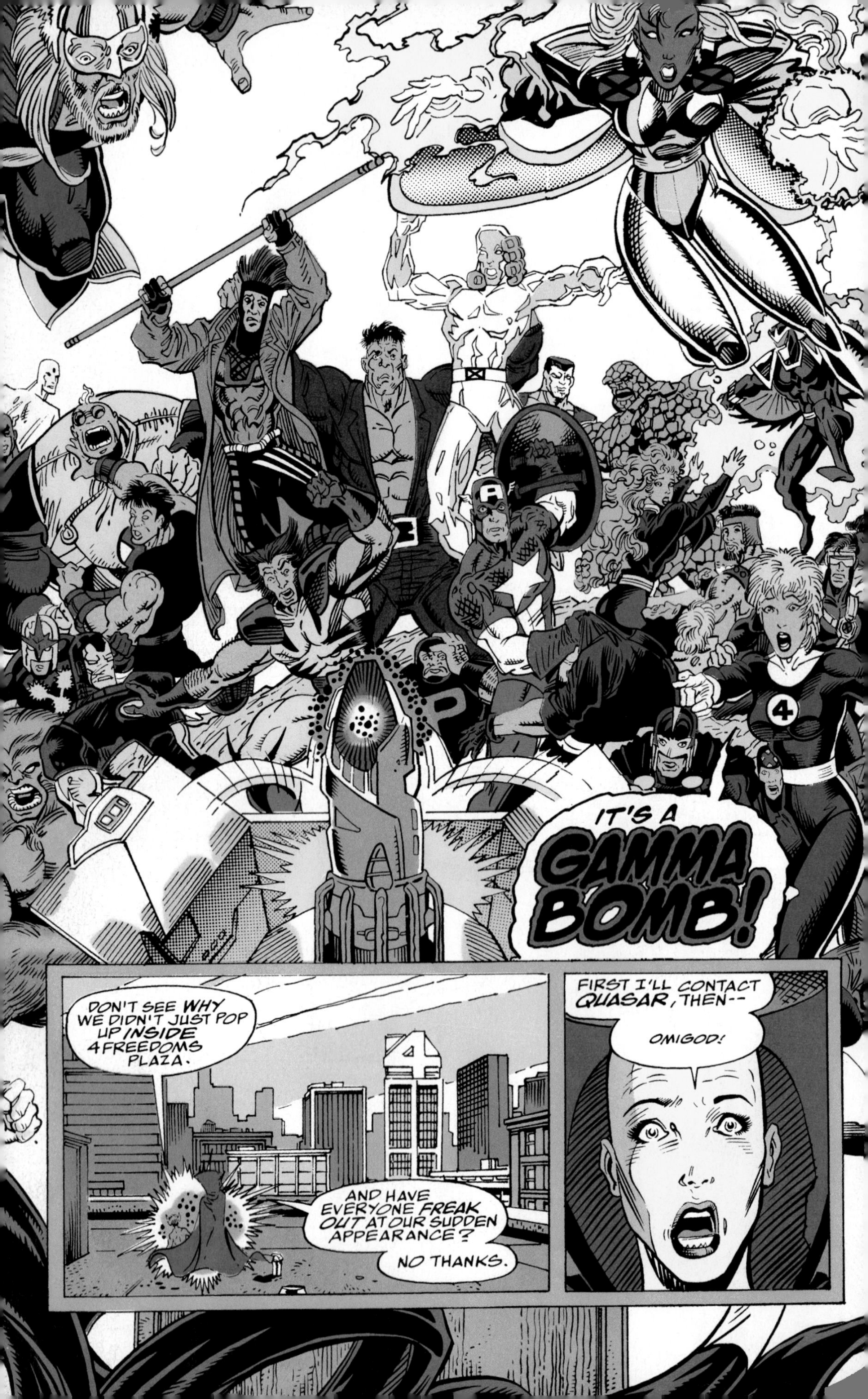
IT'S A GAMMA BOMB!
DON'T SEE WHY WE DIDN'T JUST POP UP INSIDE 4 FREEDOMS PLAZA.
AND HAVE EVERYONE FREAK OUT AT OUR SUDDEN APPEARANCE?
NO THANKS.
FIRST I'LL CONTACT QUASAR, THEN--
OMIGOD!

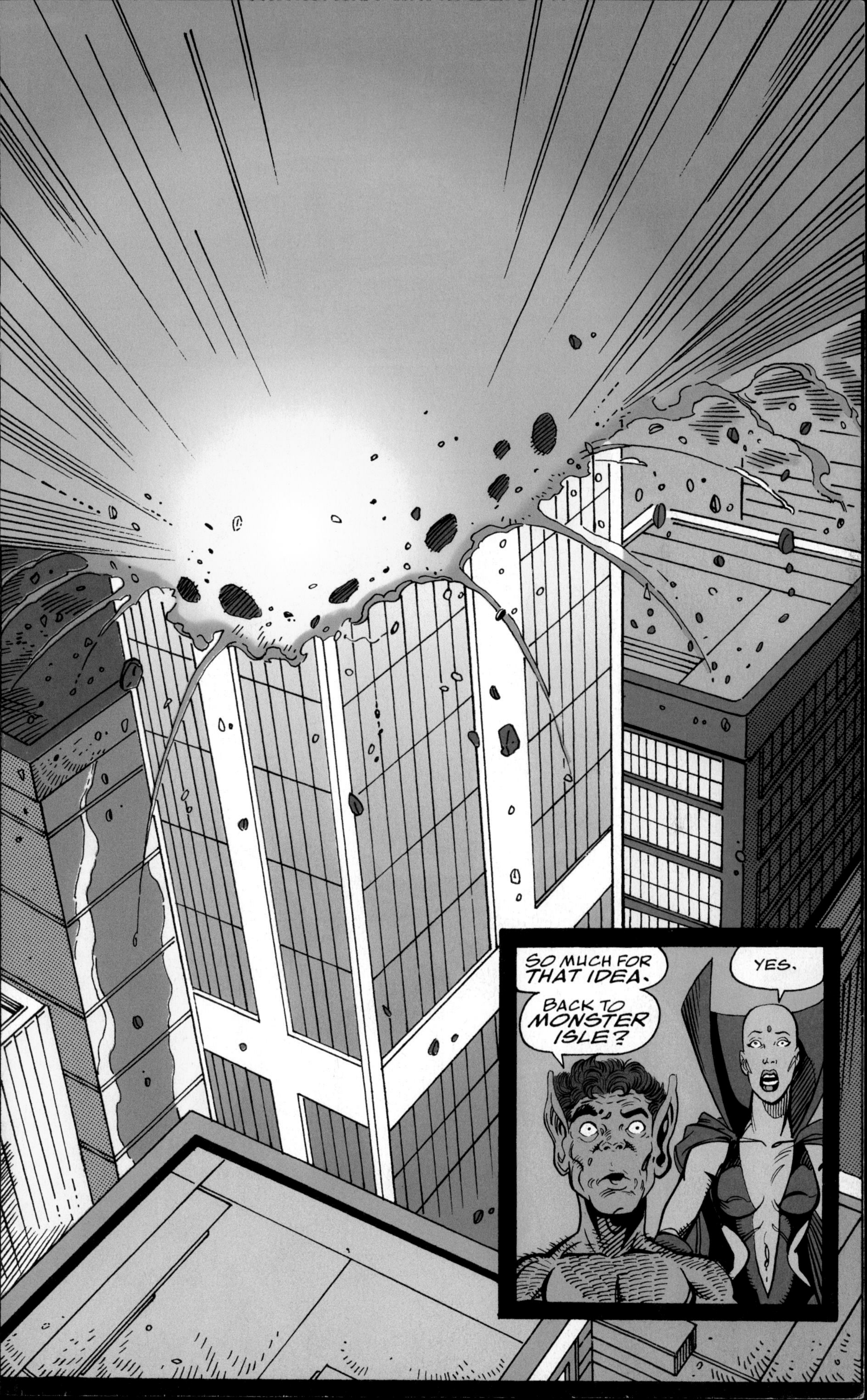
SO MUCH FOR THAT IDEA.
YES.
BACK TO MONSTER ISLE?

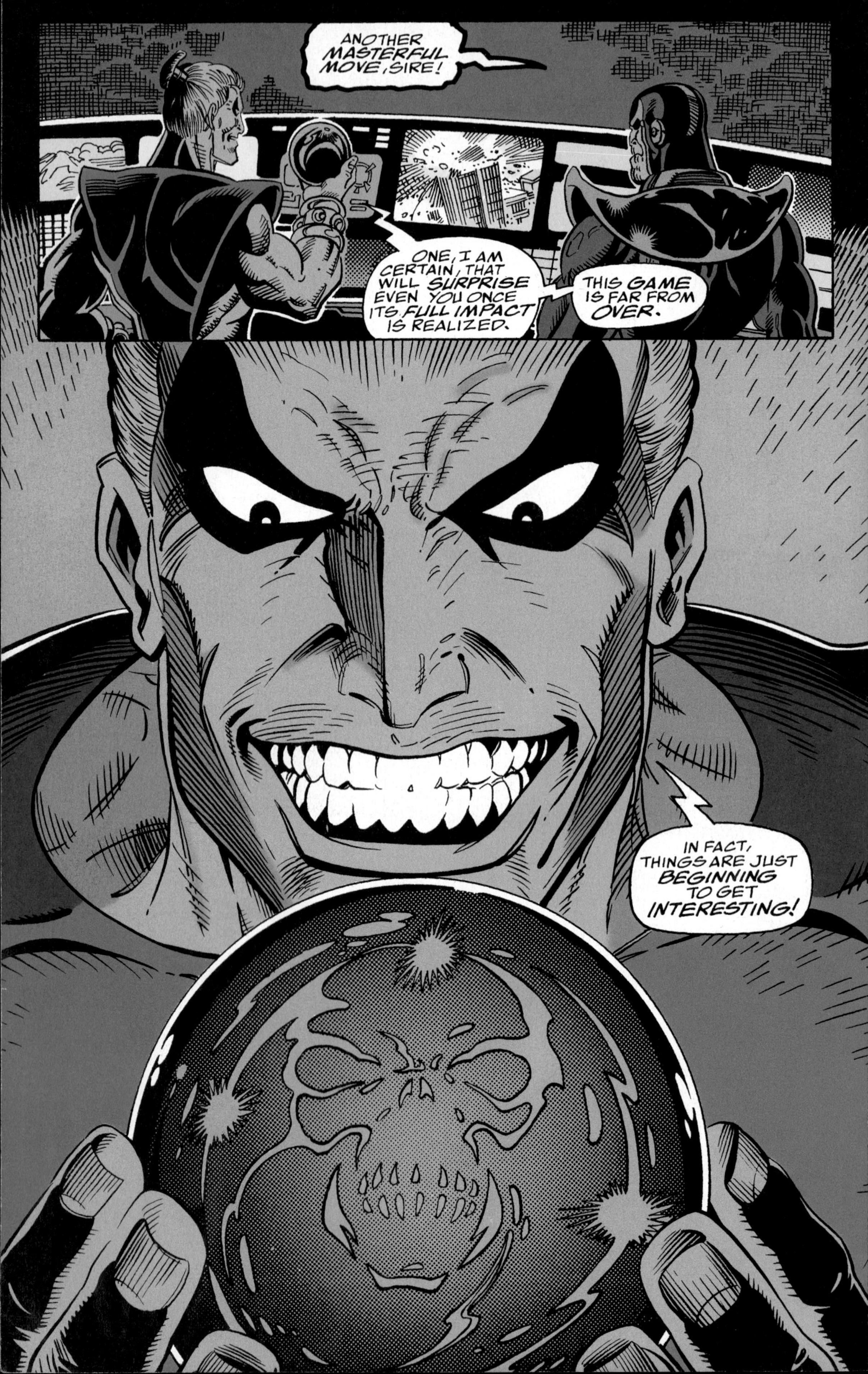

ANOTHER MASTERFUL MOVE, SIRE!
ONE, I AM CERTAIN, THAT WILL SURPRISE EVEN YOU ONCE ITS FULL IMPACT IS REALIZED.
THIS GAME IS FAR FROM OVER.
IN FACT, THINGS ARE JUST BEGINNING TO GET INTERESTING!

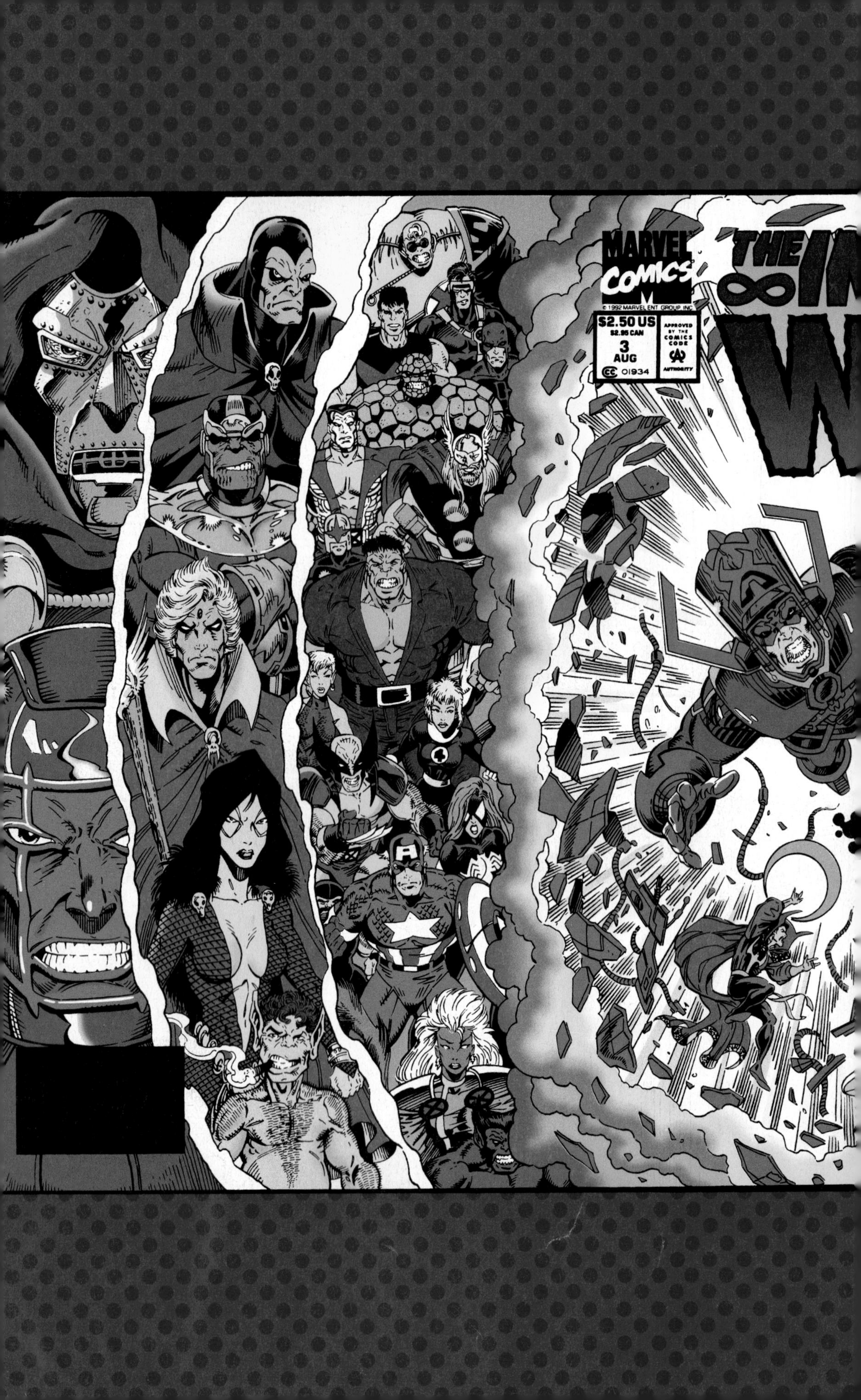

MARVEL COMICS
© 1992 MARVEL ENT. GROUP, INC.
$2.50 US
$2.95 CAN
3
AUG
01934
APPROVED BY THE COMICS CODE AUTHORITY

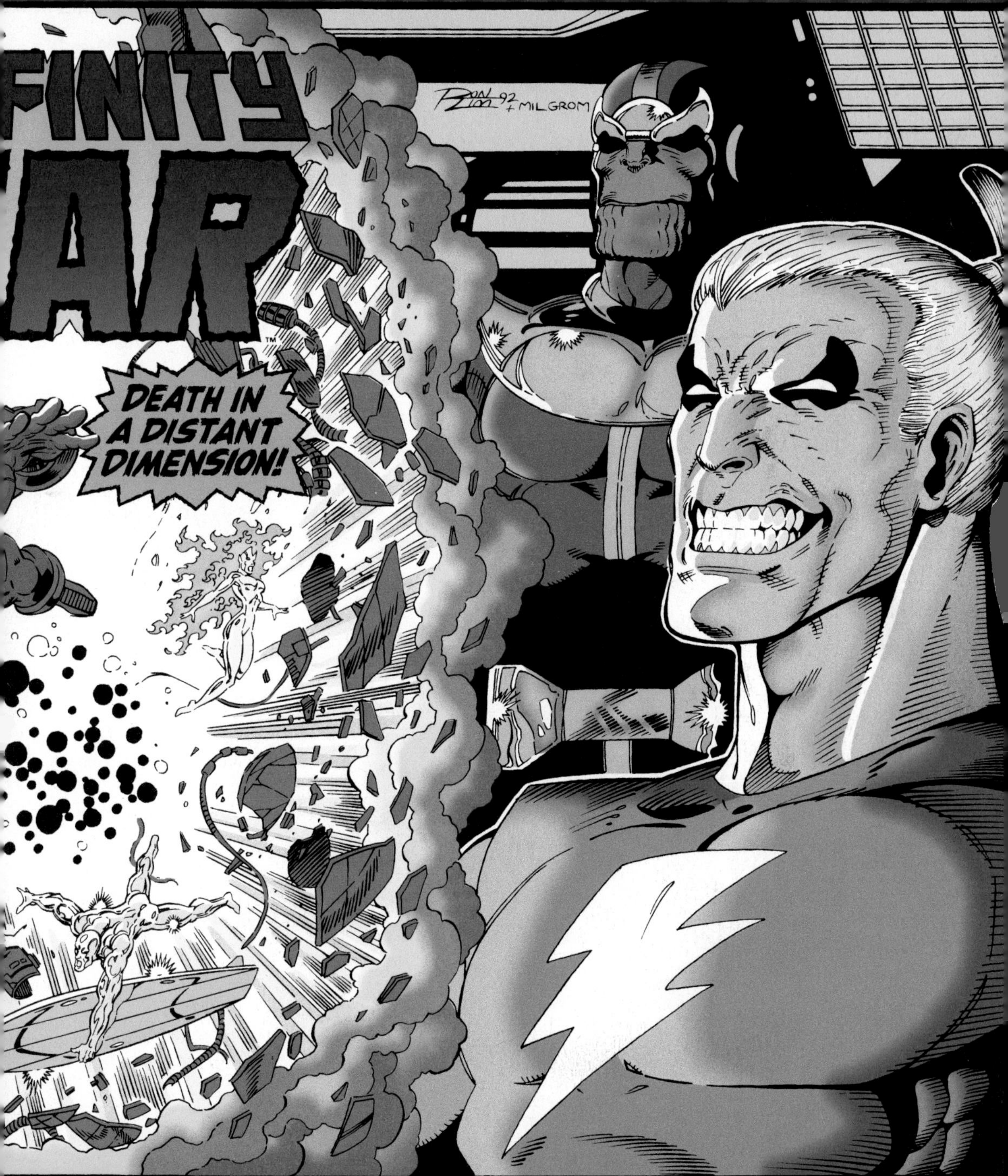
FINITY
AR
DEATH IN A DISTANT DIMENSION!
RON LIM '92 + MILGROM

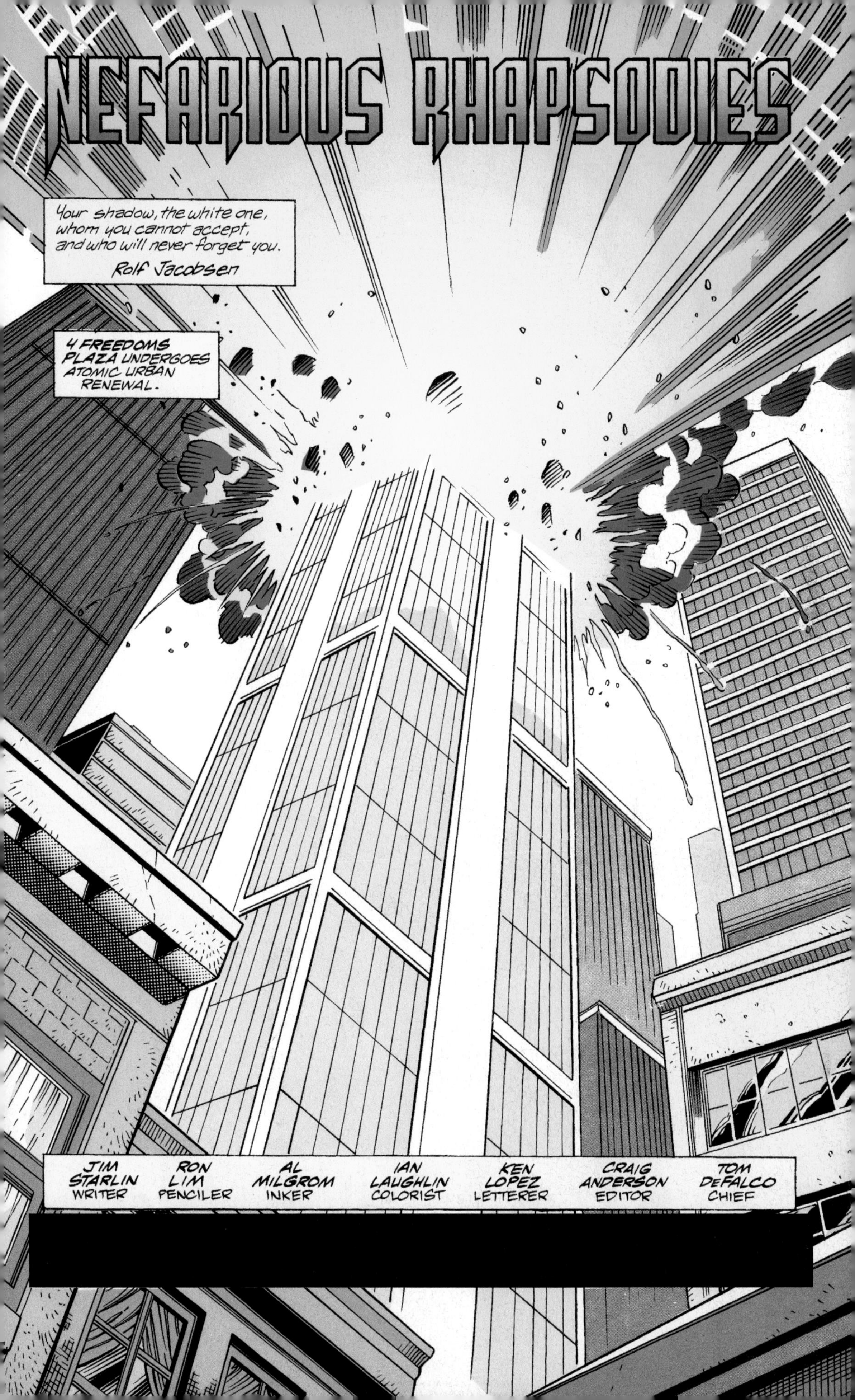
NEFARIOUS RHAPSODIES
Your shadow, the white one, whom you cannot accept, and who will never forget you.
Rolf Jacobsen
4 FREEDOMS PLAZA UNDERGOES ATOMIC URBAN RENEWAL.
JIM STARLIN WRITER
RON LIM PENCILER
AL MILGROM INKER
IAN LAUGHLIN COLORIST
KEN LOPEZ LETTERER
CRAIG ANDERSON EDITOR
TOM DeFALCO CHIEF
[redacted]

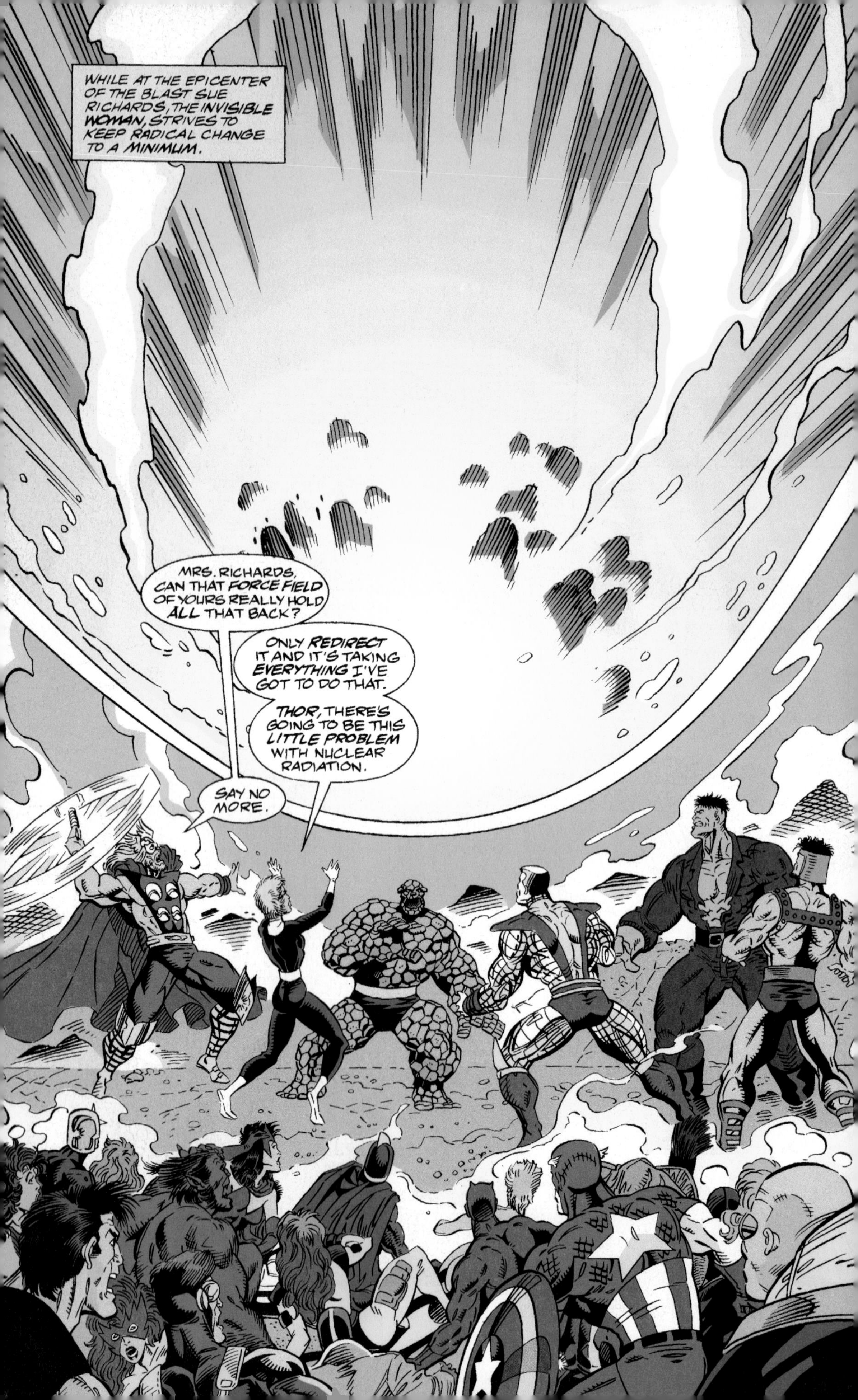
WHILE AT THE EPICENTER OF THE BLAST SUE RICHARDS, THE INVISIBLE WOMAN, STRIVES TO KEEP RADICAL CHANGE TO A MINIMUM.
MRS. RICHARDS, CAN THAT FORCE FIELD OF YOURS REALLY HOLD ALL THAT BACK?
ONLY REDIRECT IT AND IT'S TAKING EVERYTHING I'VE GOT TO DO THAT.
THOR, THERE'S GOING TO BE THIS LITTLE PROBLEM WITH NUCLEAR RADIATION.
SAY NO MORE.

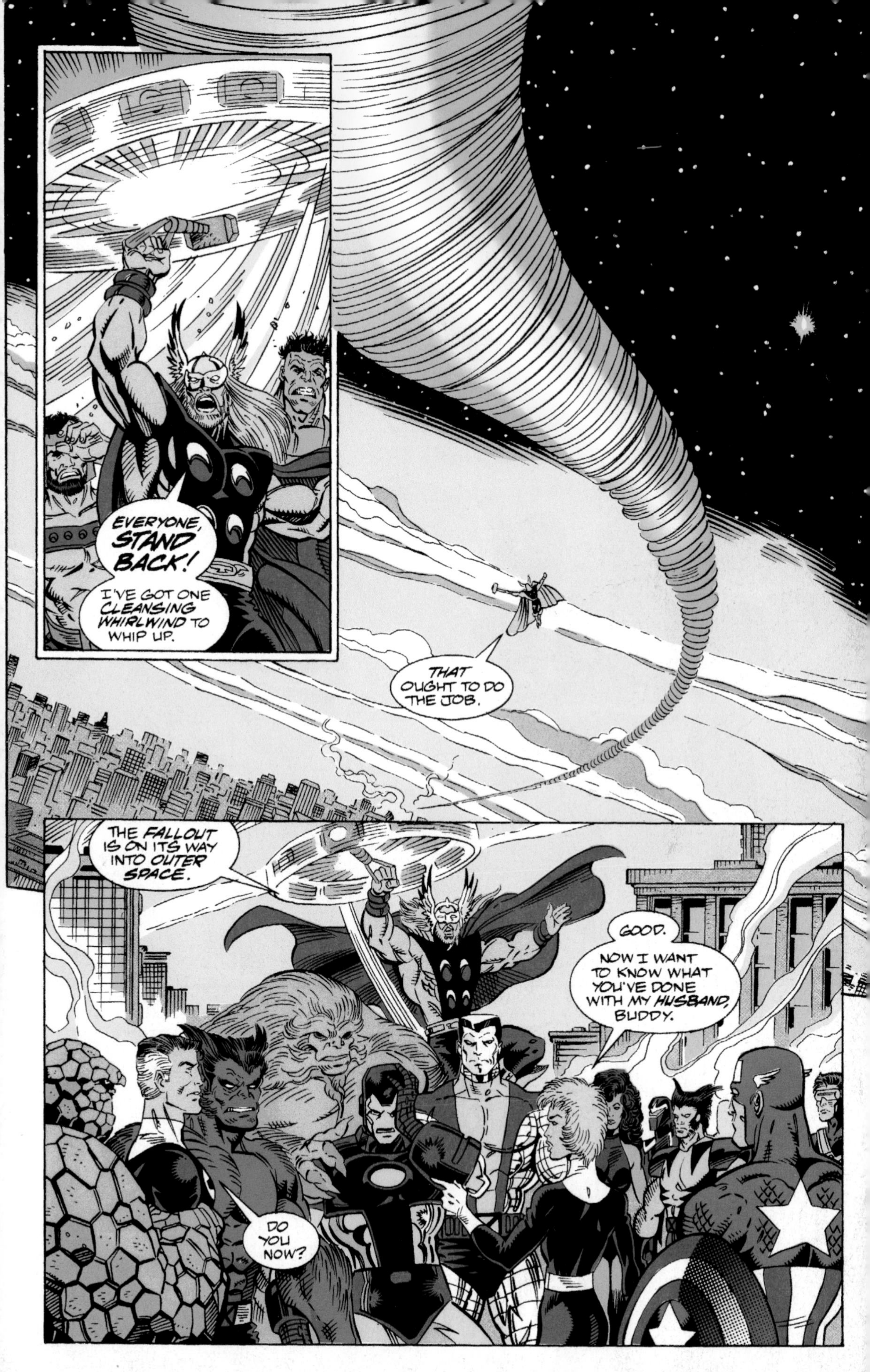
EVERYONE, STAND BACK!
I'VE GOT ONE CLEANSING WHIRLWIND TO WHIP UP.
THAT OUGHT TO DO THE JOB.
THE FALLOUT IS ON ITS WAY INTO OUTER SPACE.
GOOD.
NOW I WANT TO KNOW WHAT YOU'VE DONE WITH MY HUSBAND, BUDDY.
DO YOU NOW?

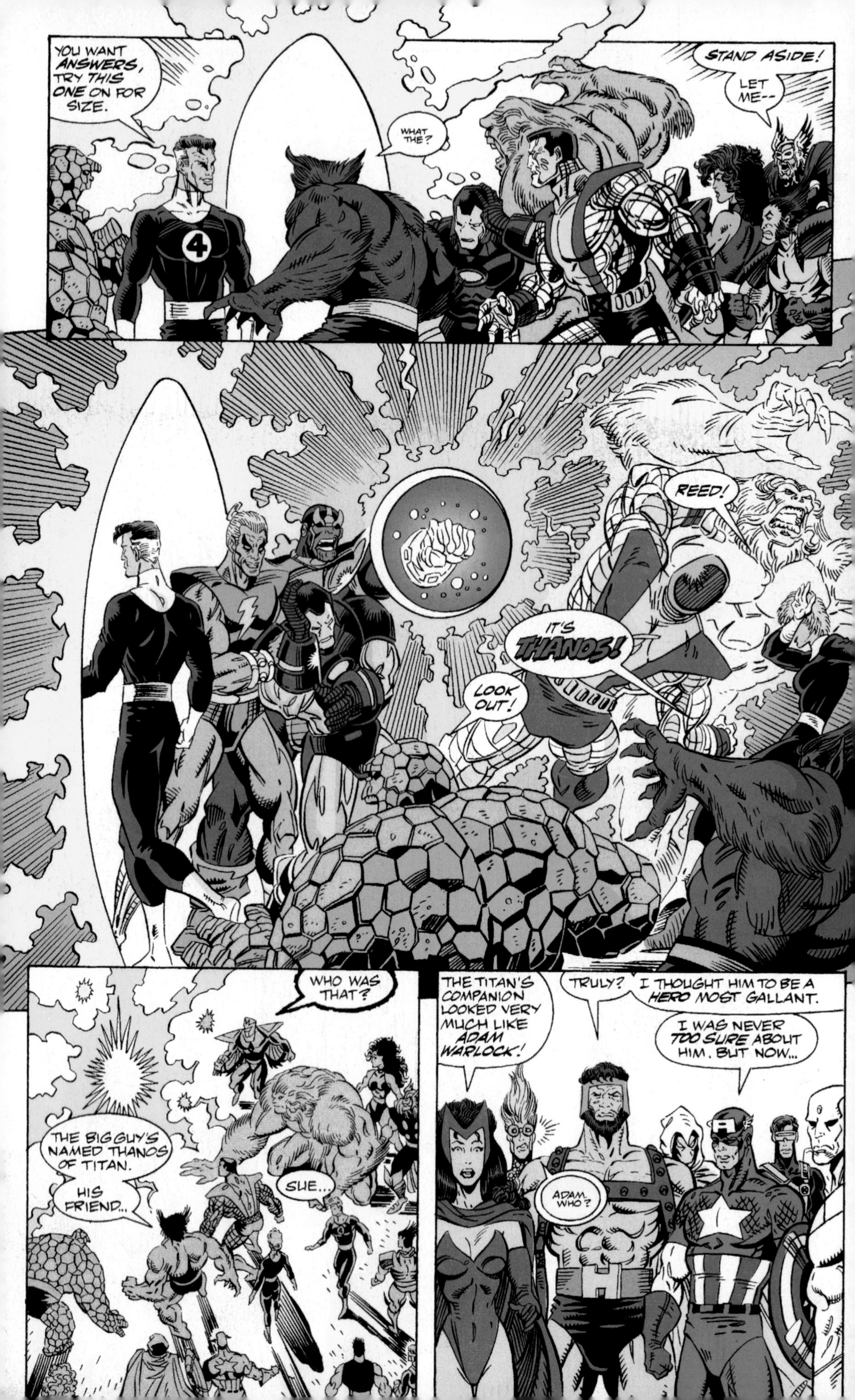
YOU WANT ANSWERS, TRY THIS ONE ON FOR SIZE.
WHAT THE?
STAND ASIDE!
LET ME--
REED!
IT'S THANOS!
LOOK OUT!
WHO WAS THAT?
THE BIG GUY'S NAMED THANOS OF TITAN.
HIS FRIEND...
SUE...
THE TITAN'S COMPANION LOOKED VERY MUCH LIKE ADAM WARLOCK!
TRULY?
I THOUGHT HIM TO BE A HERO MOST GALLANT.
I WAS NEVER TOO SURE ABOUT HIM. BUT NOW...
ADAM. WHO?

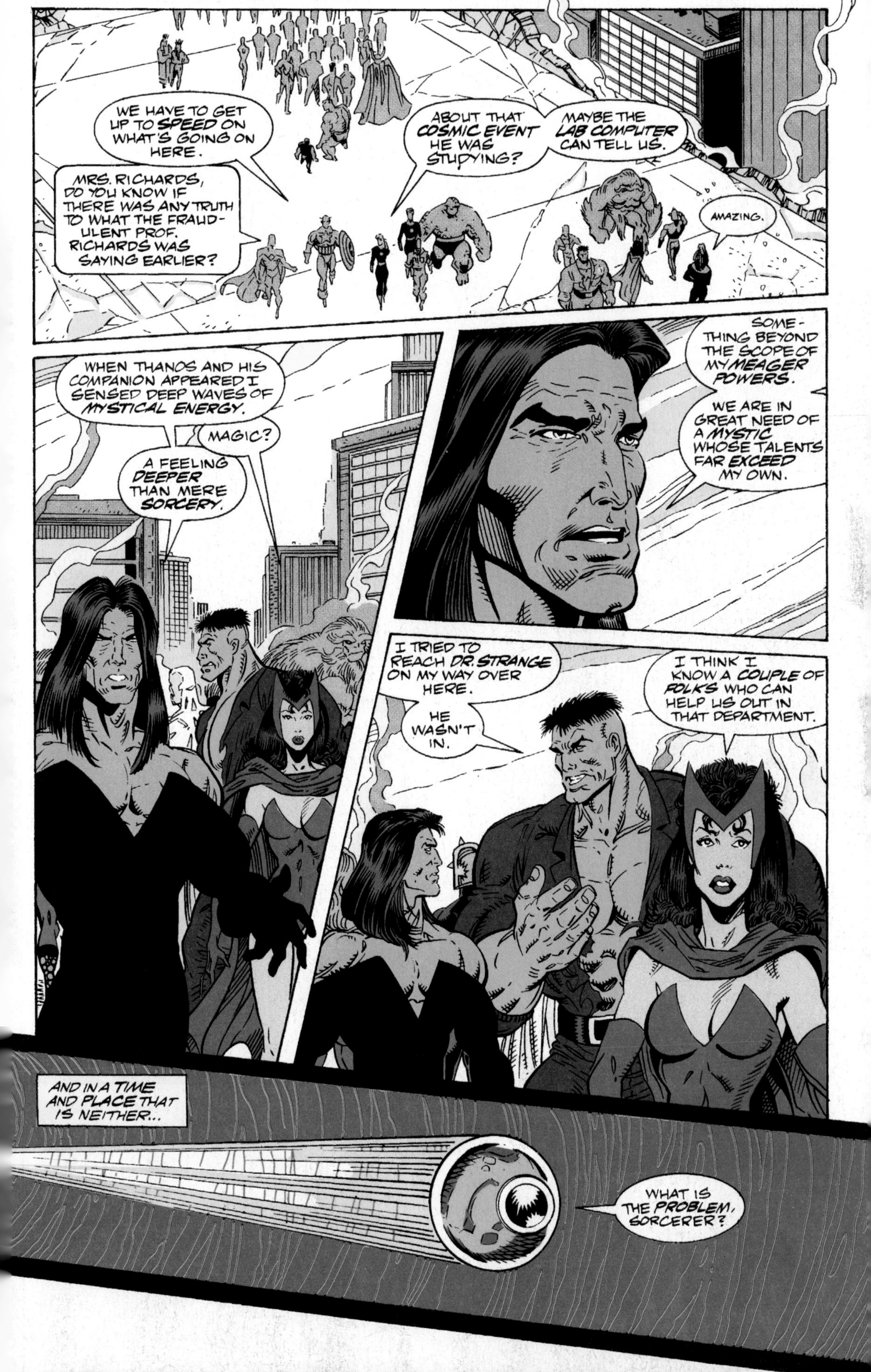
WE HAVE TO GET UP TO SPEED ON WHAT'S GOING ON HERE.
MRS. RICHARDS, DO YOU KNOW IF THERE WAS ANY TRUTH TO WHAT THE FRAUD-ULENT PROF. RICHARDS WAS SAYING EARLIER?
ABOUT THAT COSMIC EVENT HE WAS STUDYING?
MAYBE THE LAB COMPUTER CAN TELL US.
AMAZING.
WHEN THANOS AND HIS COMPANION APPEARED I SENSED DEEP WAVES OF MYSTICAL ENERGY.
MAGIC?
A FEELING DEEPER THAN MERE SORCERY.
SOME-THING BEYOND THE SCOPE OF MY MEAGER POWERS.
WE ARE IN GREAT NEED OF A MYSTIC WHOSE TALENTS FAR EXCEED MY OWN.
I TRIED TO REACH DR. STRANGE ON MY WAY OVER HERE.
HE WASN'T IN.
I THINK I KNOW A COUPLE OF FOLKS WHO CAN HELP US OUT IN THAT DEPARTMENT.
AND IN A TIME AND PLACE THAT IS NEITHER...
WHAT IS THE PROBLEM, SORCERER?

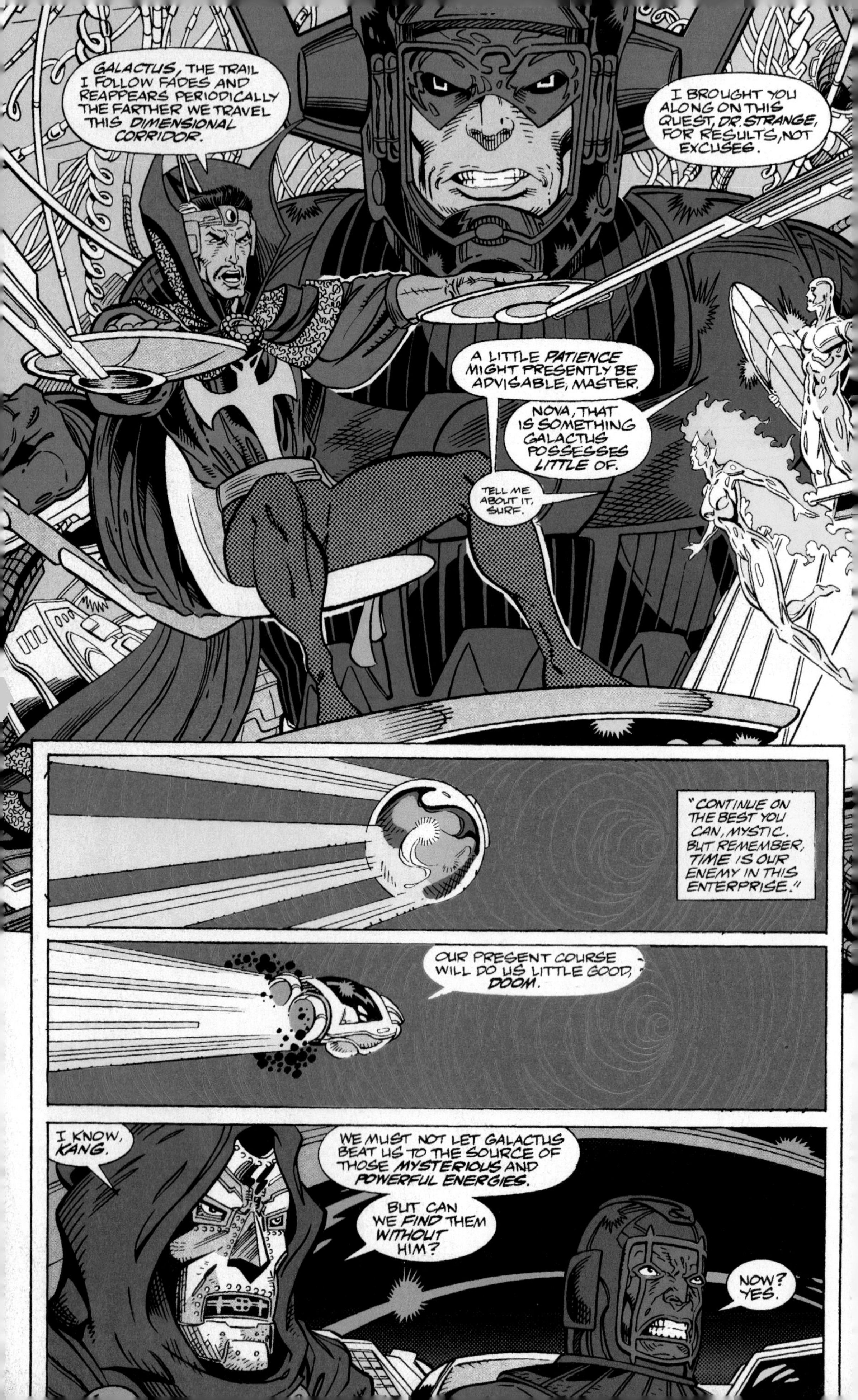
GALACTUS, THE TRAIL I FOLLOW FADES AND REAPPEARS PERIODICALLY THE FARTHER WE TRAVEL THIS DIMENSIONAL CORRIDOR.
I BROUGHT YOU ALONG ON THIS QUEST, DR. STRANGE, FOR RESULTS, NOT EXCUSES.
A LITTLE PATIENCE MIGHT PRESENTLY BE ADVISABLE, MASTER.
NOVA, THAT IS SOMETHING GALACTUS POSSESSES LITTLE OF.
TELL ME ABOUT IT, SURF.
"CONTINUE ON THE BEST YOU CAN, MYSTIC. BUT REMEMBER, TIME IS OUR ENEMY IN THIS ENTERPRISE."
OUR PRESENT COURSE WILL DO US LITTLE GOOD, DOOM.
I KNOW, KANG.
WE MUST NOT LET GALACTUS BEAT US TO THE SOURCE OF THOSE MYSTERIOUS AND POWERFUL ENERGIES.
BUT CAN WE FIND THEM WITHOUT HIM?
NOW? YES.

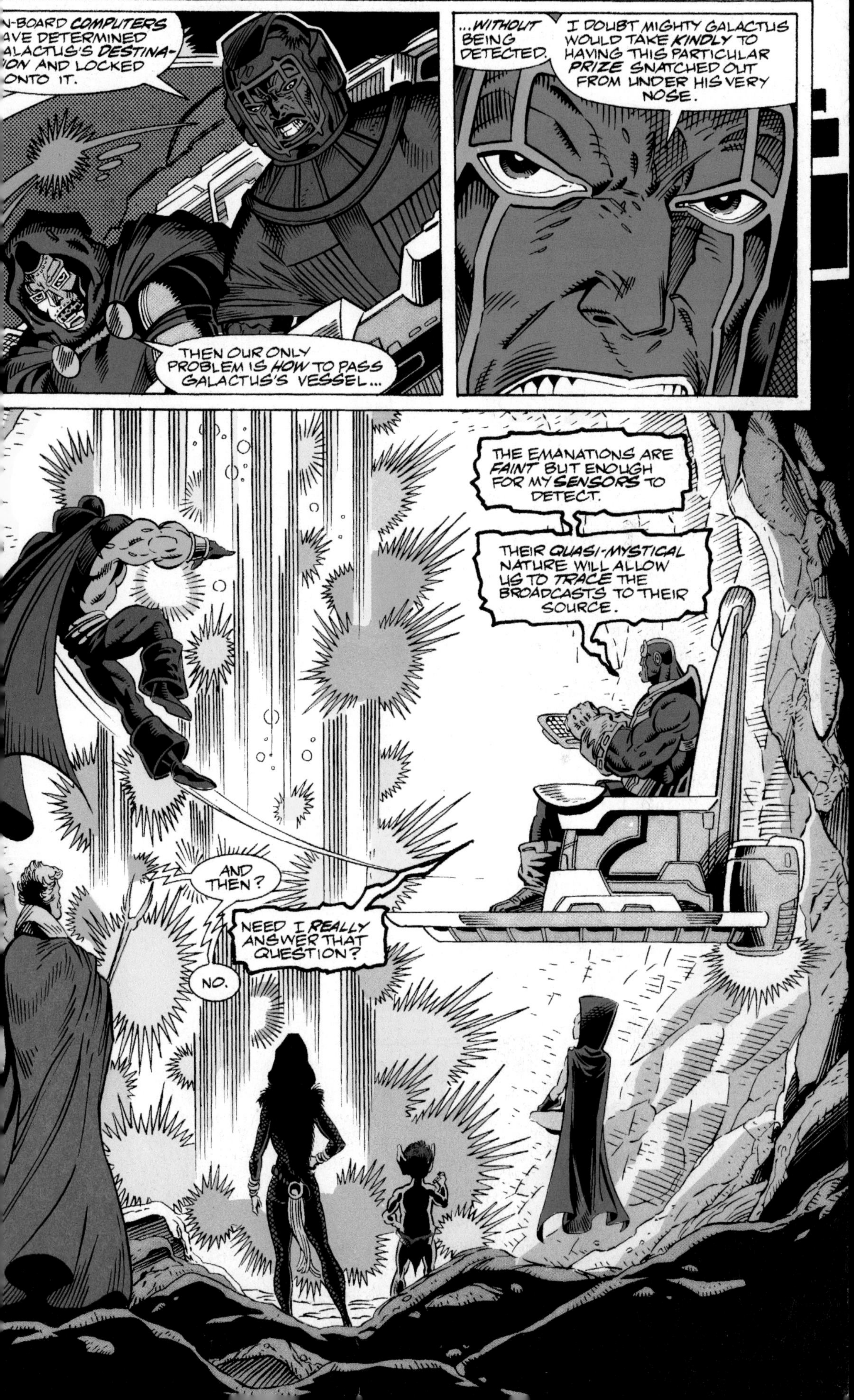

N-BOARD COMPUTERS AVE DETERMINED ALACTUS'S DESTINA-ION AND LOCKED ONTO IT.
THEN OUR ONLY PROBLEM IS HOW TO PASS GALACTUS'S VESSEL...
...WITHOUT BEING DETECTED.
I DOUBT MIGHTY GALACTUS WOULD TAKE KINDLY TO HAVING THIS PARTICULAR PRIZE SNATCHED OUT FROM UNDER HIS VERY NOSE.
THE EMANATIONS ARE FAINT BUT ENOUGH FOR MY SENSORS TO DETECT.
THEIR QUASI-MYSTICAL NATURE WILL ALLOW US TO TRACE THE BROADCASTS TO THEIR SOURCE.
AND THEN?
NEED I REALLY ANSWER THAT QUESTION?
NO.

IT IS MY GUESS THAT--

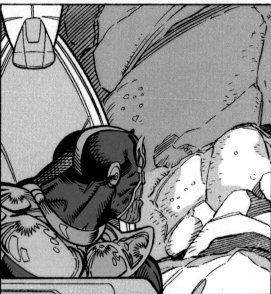

IS ANYTHING WRONG?

MANY THINGS, BUT *NOTHING* THAT NEED CONCERN *YOU* FOR THE MOMENT.

THEN LET US BE AWAY.

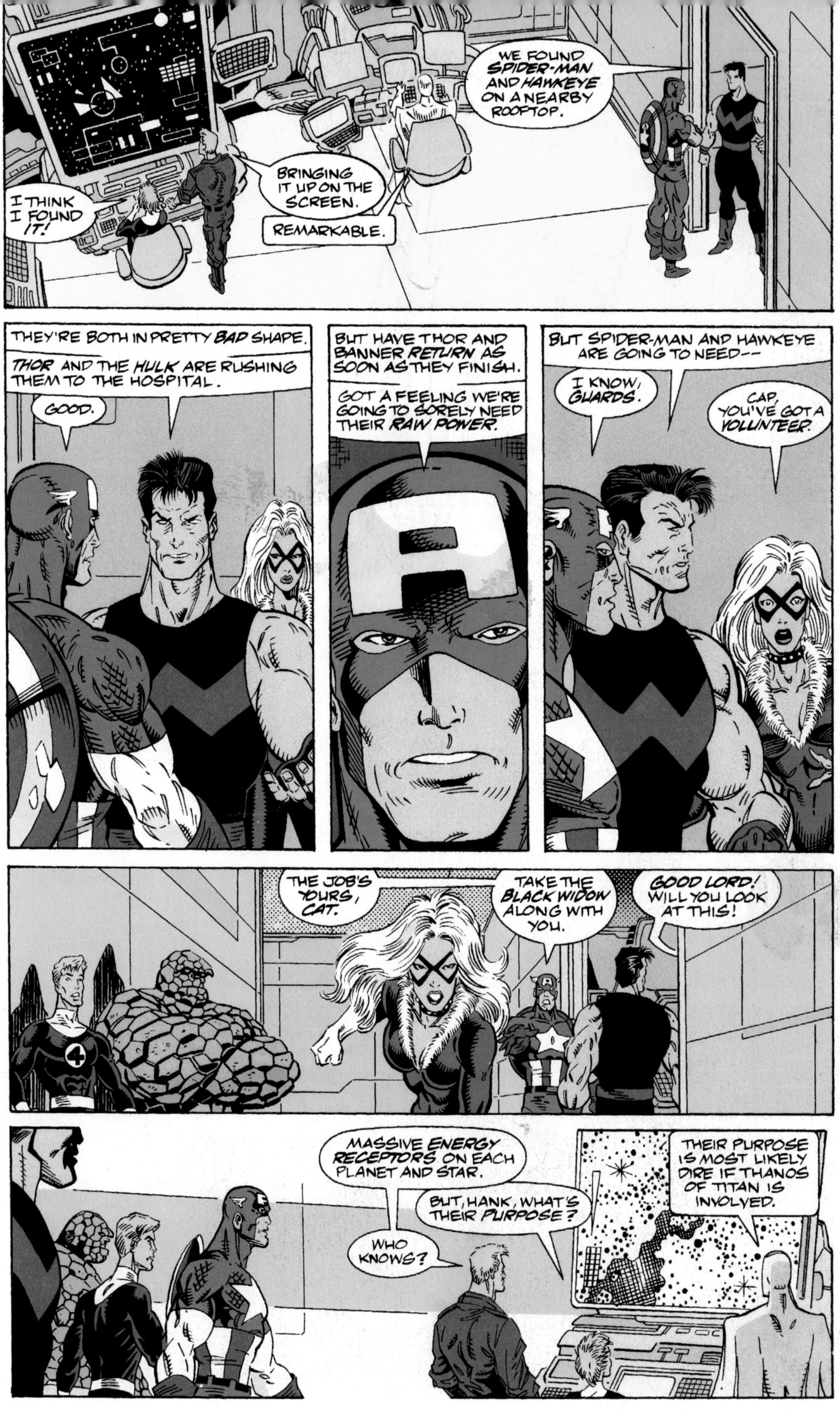
WE FOUND SPIDER-MAN AND HAWKEYE ON A NEARBY ROOFTOP.
I THINK I FOUND IT!
BRINGING IT UP ON THE SCREEN.
REMARKABLE.
THEY'RE BOTH IN PRETTY BAD SHAPE.
THOR AND THE HULK ARE RUSHING THEM TO THE HOSPITAL.
GOOD.
BUT HAVE THOR AND BANNER RETURN AS SOON AS THEY FINISH.
GOT A FEELING WE'RE GOING TO SORELY NEED THEIR RAW POWER.
BUT SPIDER-MAN AND HAWKEYE ARE GOING TO NEED--
I KNOW, GUARDS.
CAP, YOU'VE GOT A VOLUNTEER.
THE JOB'S YOURS, CAT.
TAKE THE BLACK WIDOW ALONG WITH YOU.
GOOD LORD! WILL YOU LOOK AT THIS!
MASSIVE ENERGY RECEPTORS ON EACH PLANET AND STAR.
BUT, HANK, WHAT'S THEIR PURPOSE?
WHO KNOWS?
THEIR PURPOSE IS MOST LIKELY DIRE IF THANOS OF TITAN IS INVOLVED.

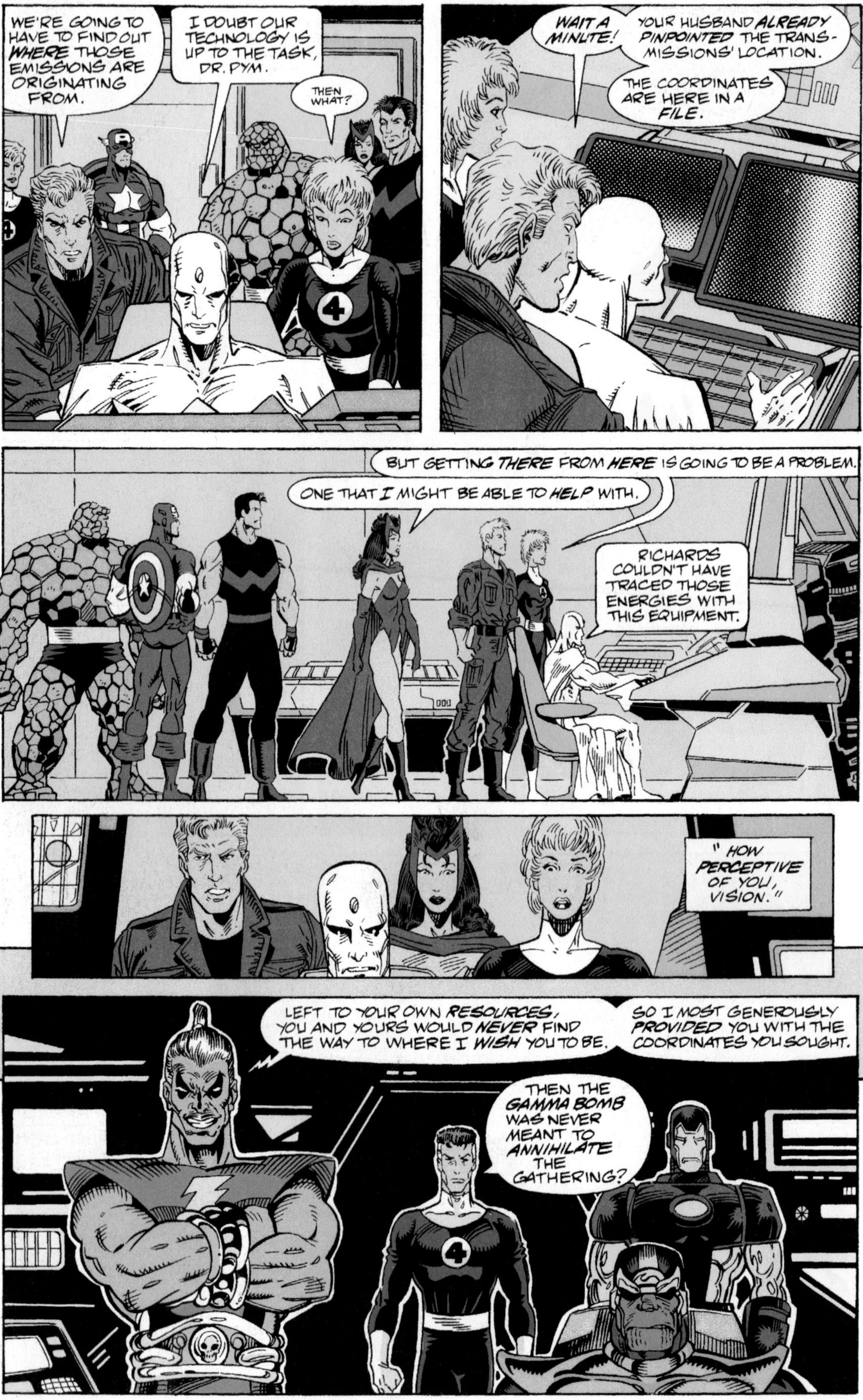

WE'RE GOING TO HAVE TO FIND OUT WHERE THOSE EMISSIONS ARE ORIGINATING FROM.
I DOUBT OUR TECHNOLOGY IS UP TO THE TASK, DR. PYM.
THEN WHAT?
WAIT A MINUTE!
YOUR HUSBAND ALREADY PINPOINTED THE TRANSMISSIONS' LOCATION.
THE COORDINATES ARE HERE IN A FILE.
BUT GETTING THERE FROM HERE IS GOING TO BE A PROBLEM.
ONE THAT I MIGHT BE ABLE TO HELP WITH.
RICHARDS COULDN'T HAVE TRACED THOSE ENERGIES WITH THIS EQUIPMENT.
"HOW PERCEPTIVE OF YOU, VISION."
LEFT TO YOUR OWN RESOURCES, YOU AND YOURS WOULD NEVER FIND THE WAY TO WHERE I WISH YOU TO BE.
SO I MOST GENEROUSLY PROVIDED YOU WITH THE COORDINATES YOU SOUGHT.
THEN THE GAMMA BOMB WAS NEVER MEANT TO ANNIHILATE THE GATHERING?

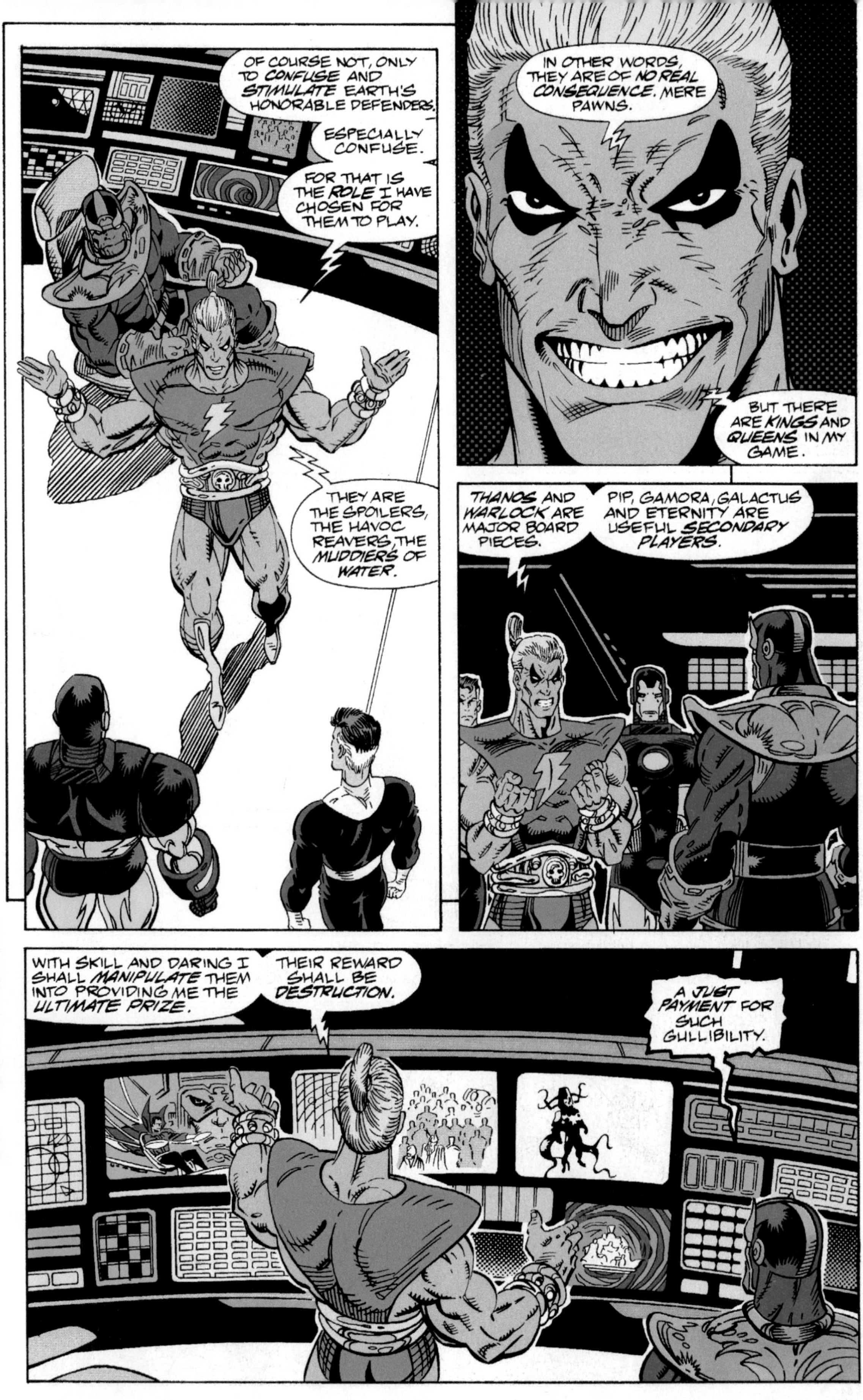
OF COURSE NOT, ONLY TO CONFUSE AND STIMULATE EARTH'S HONORABLE DEFENDERS.
ESPECIALLY CONFUSE.
FOR THAT IS THE ROLE I HAVE CHOSEN FOR THEM TO PLAY.
THEY ARE THE SPOILERS, THE HAVOC REAVERS, THE MUDDIERS OF WATER.
IN OTHER WORDS, THEY ARE OF NO REAL CONSEQUENCE. MERE PAWNS.
BUT THERE ARE KINGS AND QUEENS IN MY GAME.
THANOS AND WARLOCK ARE MAJOR BOARD PIECES.
PIP, GAMORA, GALACTUS AND ETERNITY ARE USEFUL SECONDARY PLAYERS.
WITH SKILL AND DARING I SHALL MANIPULATE THEM INTO PROVIDING ME THE ULTIMATE PRIZE.
THEIR REWARD SHALL BE DESTRUCTION.
A JUST PAYMENT FOR SUCH GULLIBILITY.

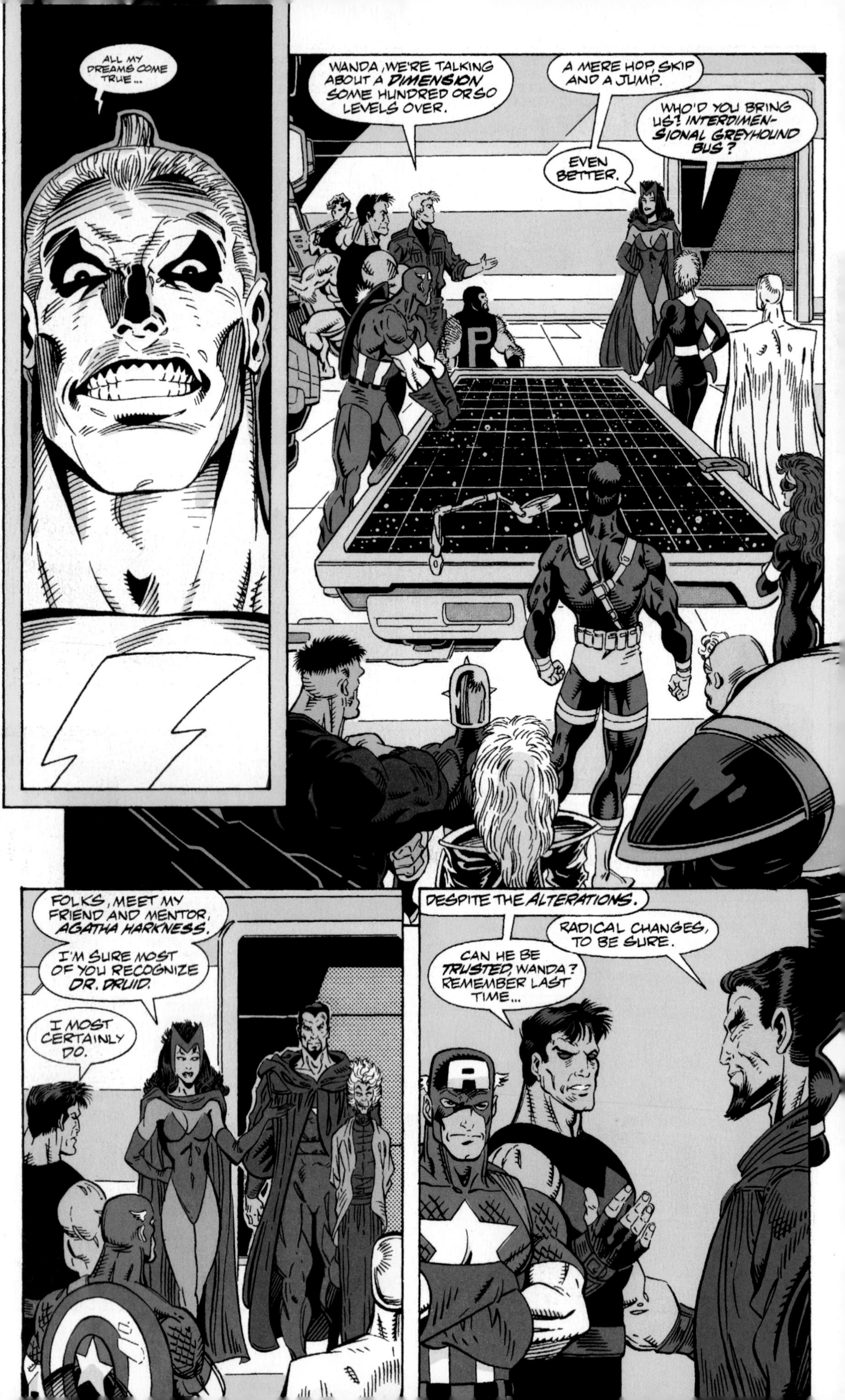

ALL MY DREAMS COME TRUE...
WANDA, WE'RE TALKING ABOUT A DIMENSION SOME HUNDRED OR SO LEVELS OVER.
A MERE HOP, SKIP AND A JUMP.
EVEN BETTER.
WHO'D YOU BRING US? INTERDIMENSIONAL GREYHOUND BUS?
FOLKS, MEET MY FRIEND AND MENTOR, AGATHA HARKNESS.
I'M SURE MOST OF YOU RECOGNIZE DR. DRUID.
I MOST CERTAINLY DO.
DESPITE THE ALTERATIONS.
CAN HE BE TRUSTED, WANDA? REMEMBER LAST TIME...
RADICAL CHANGES, TO BE SURE.

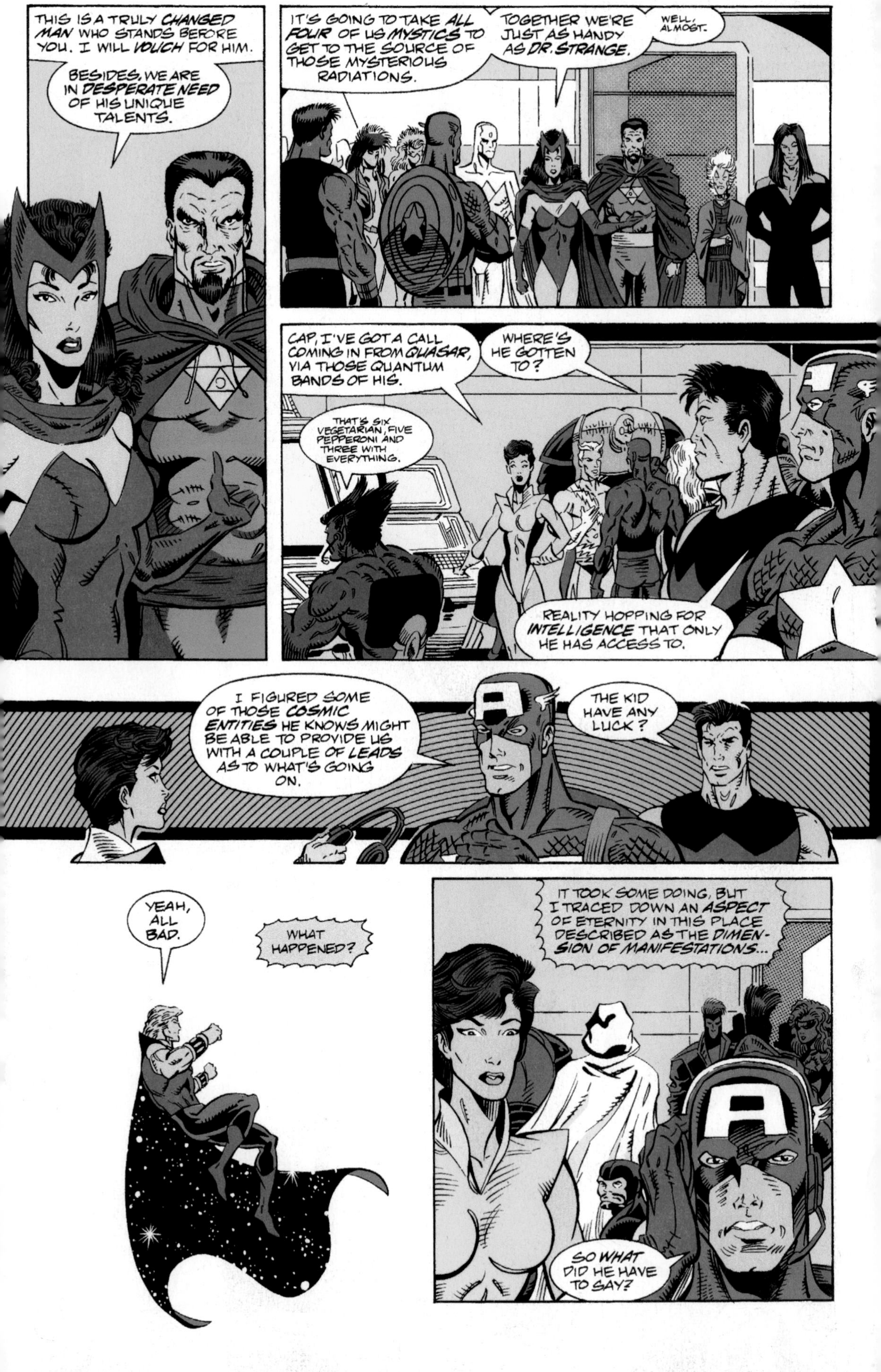
THIS IS A TRULY CHANGED MAN WHO STANDS BEFORE YOU. I WILL VOUCH FOR HIM.
BESIDES, WE ARE IN DESPERATE NEED OF HIS UNIQUE TALENTS.
IT'S GOING TO TAKE ALL FOUR OF US MYSTICS TO GET TO THE SOURCE OF THOSE MYSTERIOUS RADIATIONS.
TOGETHER WE'RE JUST AS HANDY AS DR. STRANGE.
WELL, ALMOST.
CAP, I'VE GOT A CALL COMING IN FROM QUASAR, VIA THOSE QUANTUM BANDS OF HIS.
WHERE'S HE GOTTEN TO?
THAT'S SIX VEGETARIAN, FIVE PEPPERONI AND THREE WITH EVERYTHING.
REALITY HOPPING FOR INTELLIGENCE THAT ONLY HE HAS ACCESS TO.
I FIGURED SOME OF THOSE COSMIC ENTITIES HE KNOWS MIGHT BE ABLE TO PROVIDE US WITH A COUPLE OF LEADS AS TO WHAT'S GOING ON.
THE KID HAVE ANY LUCK?
YEAH, ALL BAD.
WHAT HAPPENED?
IT TOOK SOME DOING, BUT I TRACED DOWN AN ASPECT OF ETERNITY IN THIS PLACE DESCRIBED AS THE DIMENSION OF MANIFESTATIONS...
SO WHAT DID HE HAVE TO SAY?

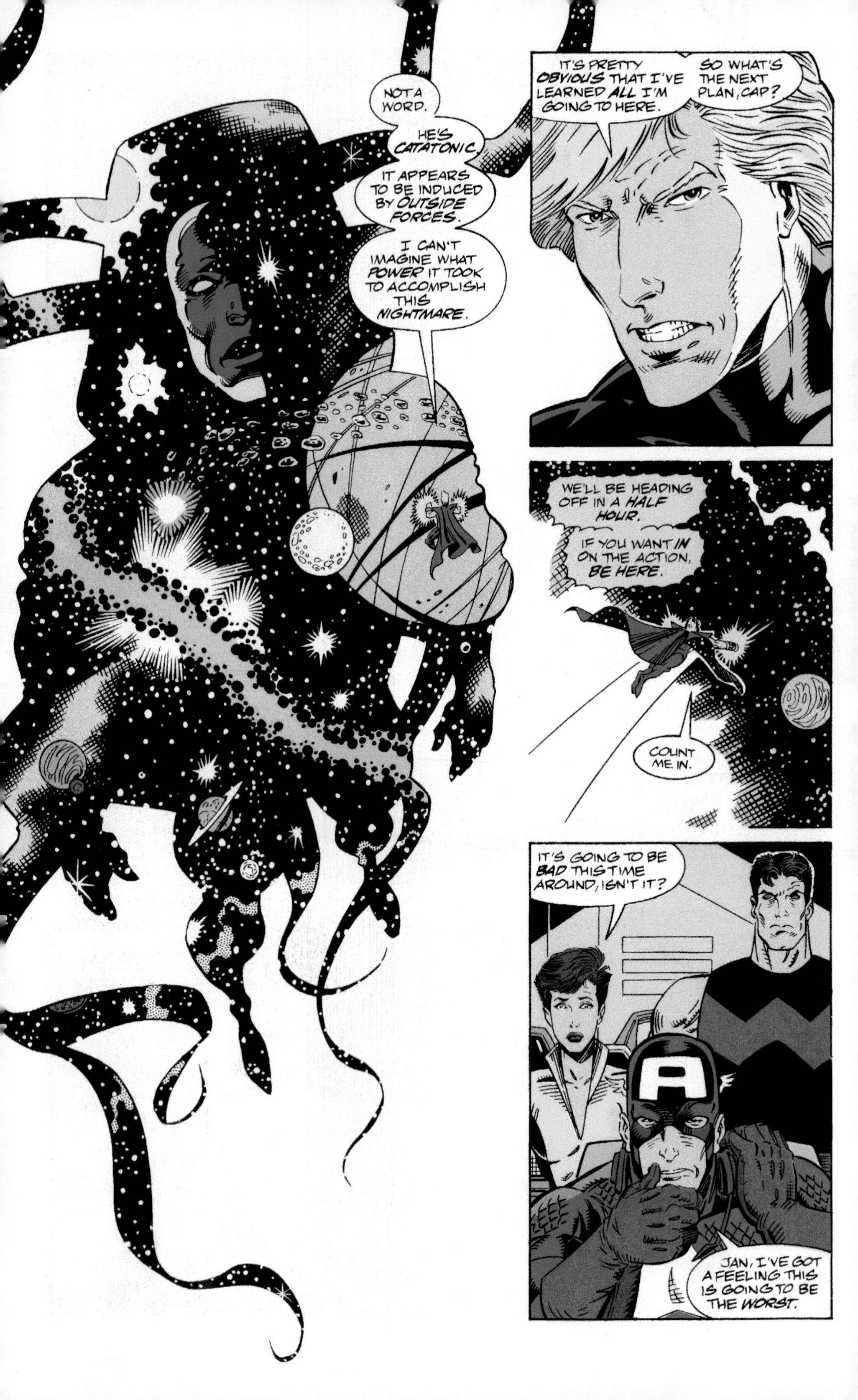
NOT A WORD.
HE'S CATATONIC.
IT APPEARS TO BE INDUCED BY OUTSIDE FORCES.
I CAN'T IMAGINE WHAT POWER IT TOOK TO ACCOMPLISH THIS NIGHTMARE.
IT'S PRETTY OBVIOUS THAT I'VE LEARNED ALL I'M GOING TO HERE.
SO WHAT'S THE NEXT PLAN, CAP?
WE'LL BE HEADING OFF IN A HALF HOUR.
IF YOU WANT IN ON THE ACTION, BE HERE.
COUNT ME IN.
IT'S GOING TO BE BAD THIS TIME AROUND, ISN'T IT?
JAN, I'VE GOT A FEELING THIS IS GOING TO BE THE WORST.

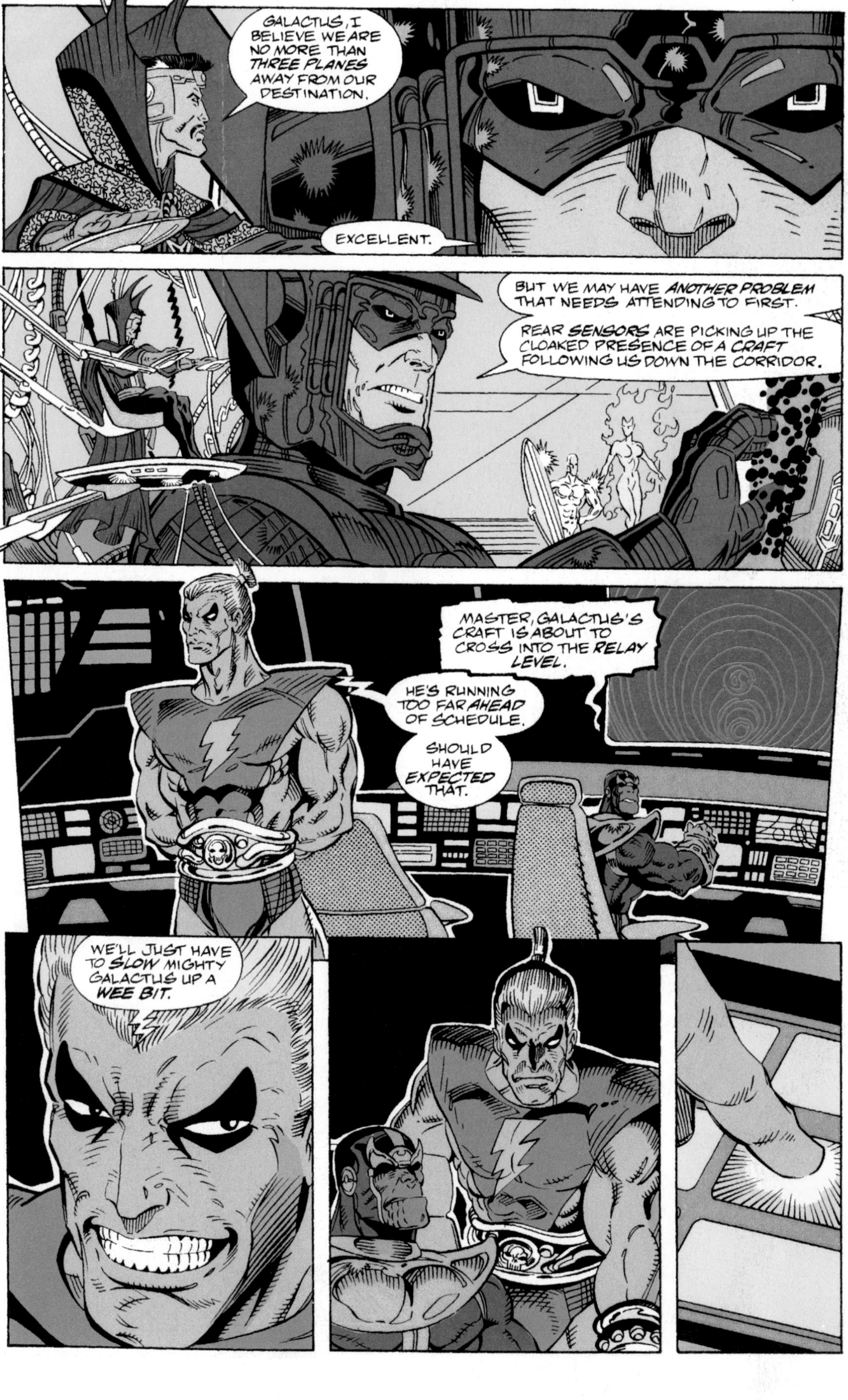
GALACTUS, I BELIEVE WE ARE NO MORE THAN THREE PLANES AWAY FROM OUR DESTINATION.
EXCELLENT.
BUT WE MAY HAVE ANOTHER PROBLEM THAT NEEDS ATTENDING TO FIRST.
REAR SENSORS ARE PICKING UP THE CLOAKED PRESENCE OF A CRAFT FOLLOWING US DOWN THE CORRIDOR.
MASTER, GALACTUS'S CRAFT IS ABOUT TO CROSS INTO THE RELAY LEVEL.
HE'S RUNNING TOO FAR AHEAD OF SCHEDULE.
SHOULD HAVE EXPECTED THAT.
WE'LL JUST HAVE TO SLOW MIGHTY GALACTUS UP A WEE BIT.

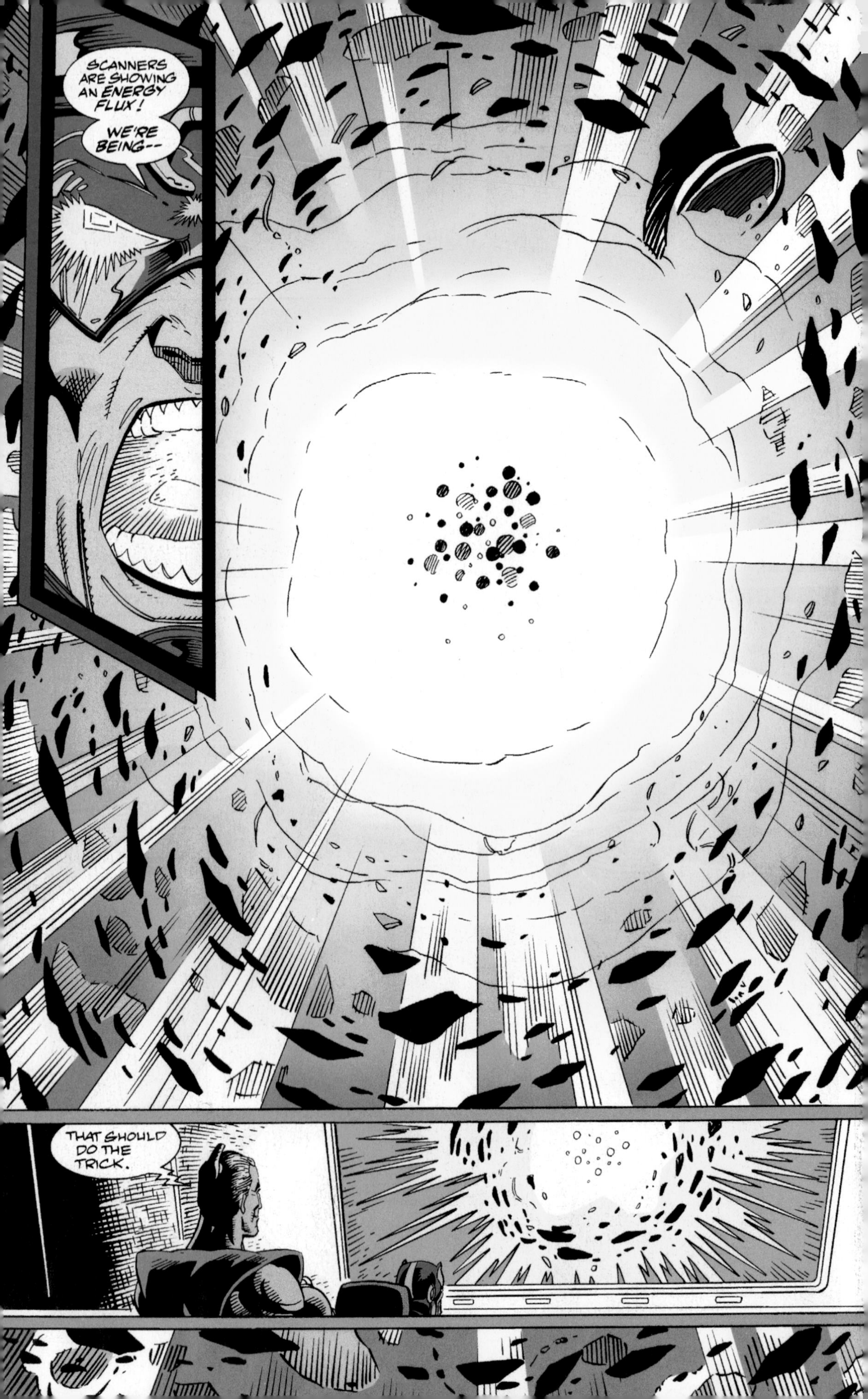
SCANNERS ARE SHOWING AN ENERGY FLUX!
WE'RE BEING--
THAT SHOULD DO THE TRICK.

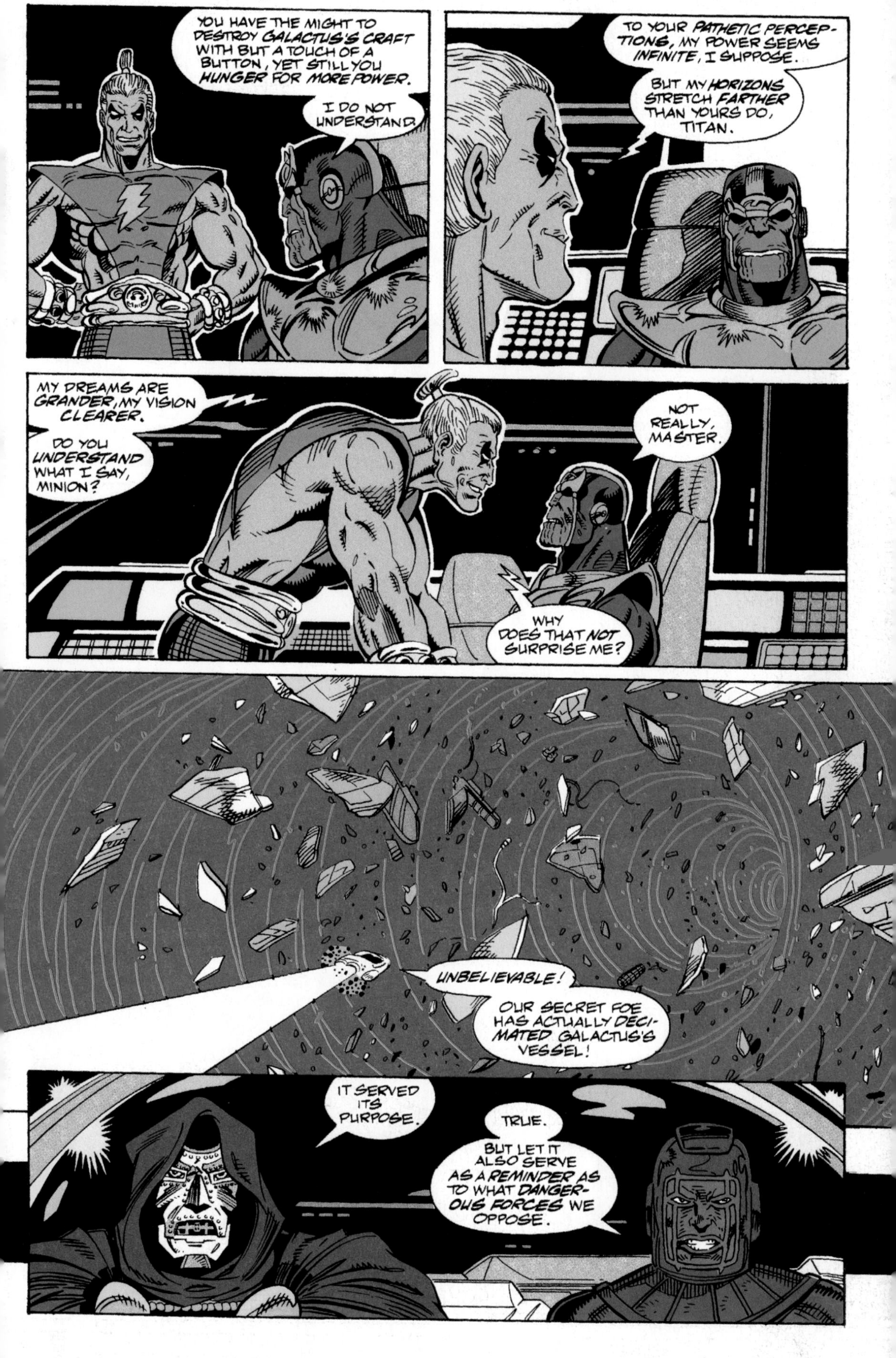
YOU HAVE THE MIGHT TO DESTROY GALACTUS'S CRAFT WITH BUT A TOUCH OF A BUTTON, YET STILL YOU HUNGER FOR MORE POWER.
I DO NOT UNDERSTAND.
TO YOUR PATHETIC PERCEPTIONS, MY POWER SEEMS INFINITE, I SUPPOSE.
BUT MY HORIZONS STRETCH FARTHER THAN YOURS DO, TITAN.
MY DREAMS ARE GRANDER, MY VISION CLEARER.
DO YOU UNDERSTAND WHAT I SAY, MINION?
NOT REALLY, MASTER.
WHY DOES THAT NOT SURPRISE ME?
UNBELIEVABLE!
OUR SECRET FOE HAS ACTUALLY DECIMATED GALACTUS'S VESSEL!
IT SERVED ITS PURPOSE.
TRUE.
BUT LET IT ALSO SERVE AS A REMINDER AS TO WHAT DANGEROUS FORCES WE OPPOSE.

THE *PRIZE* WILL SOON BE *OURS.*

AND THEN, DOOM, I SHALL, WITH DEEPLY FELT *SATISFACTION...*

"LET US NOW *CIRCUMVENT* BEFALLING THE SAME FATE."

...TERMINATE OUR PARTNERSHIP.

YOUR *TECHNOLOGY* I ENVY AND COVET, KANG, BUT YOU...

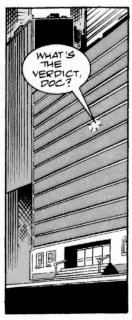

WHAT'S THE *VERDICT,* DOC?

A LITTLE *TIME* AND *TLC* AND THEY'LL BOTH BE AS *GOOD AS NEW.*

BUT THEY'RE...

...SEDATED. PAIN *KILLERS.*

LONG AS THAT'S THE *ONLY KILLERS* WE HAVE TO DEAL WITH.

YES, I IMAGINE BOTH MEN HAVE *ENEMIES* WHO WOULD...

...GET THEIR *BUTTS KICKED* IF THEY SHOW UP HERE TONIGHT.

OF COURSE. NOW IF YOU'LL EXCUSE ME. ROUNDS.

THANKS, DOC.

NOT CRAZY ABOUT BEING *RELEGATED* TO THE ROLE OF *NURSEMAID.*

ME NEITHER, BUT...

YEAH, IN A *CONFLICT* LIKE THE ONE BREWING...

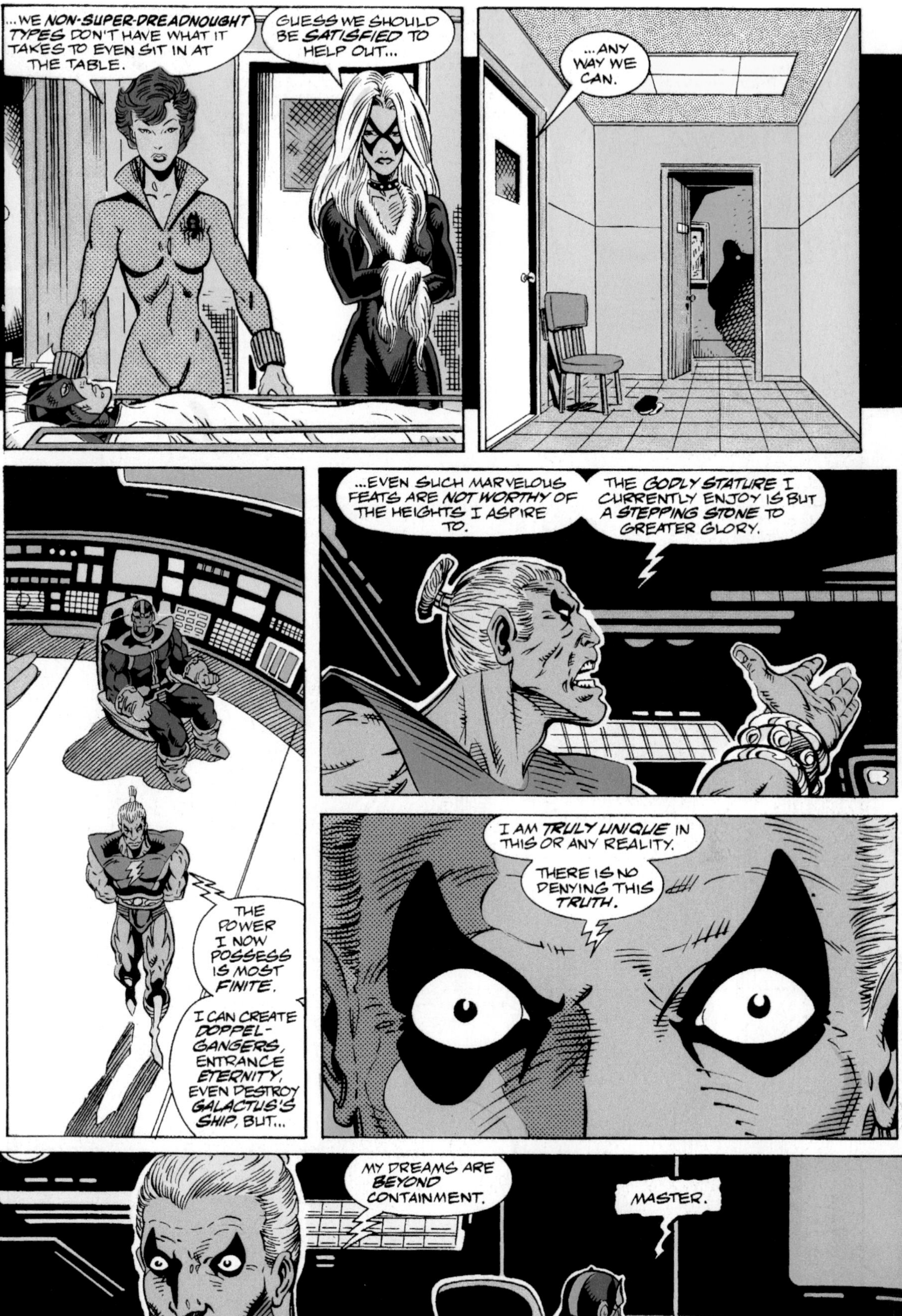
...WE NON-SUPER-DREADNOUGHT TYPES DON'T HAVE WHAT IT TAKES TO EVEN SIT IN AT THE TABLE.
GUESS WE SHOULD BE SATISFIED TO HELP OUT...
...ANY WAY WE CAN.
THE POWER I NOW POSSESS IS MOST FINITE.
I CAN CREATE DOPPEL-GANGERS, ENTRANCE ETERNITY, EVEN DESTROY GALACTUS'S SHIP, BUT...
...EVEN SUCH MARVELOUS FEATS ARE NOT WORTHY OF THE HEIGHTS I ASPIRE TO.
THE GODLY STATURE I CURRENTLY ENJOY IS BUT A STEPPING STONE TO GREATER GLORY.
I AM TRULY UNIQUE IN THIS OR ANY REALITY.
THERE IS NO DENYING THIS TRUTH.
MY DREAMS ARE BEYOND CONTAINMENT.
MASTER.

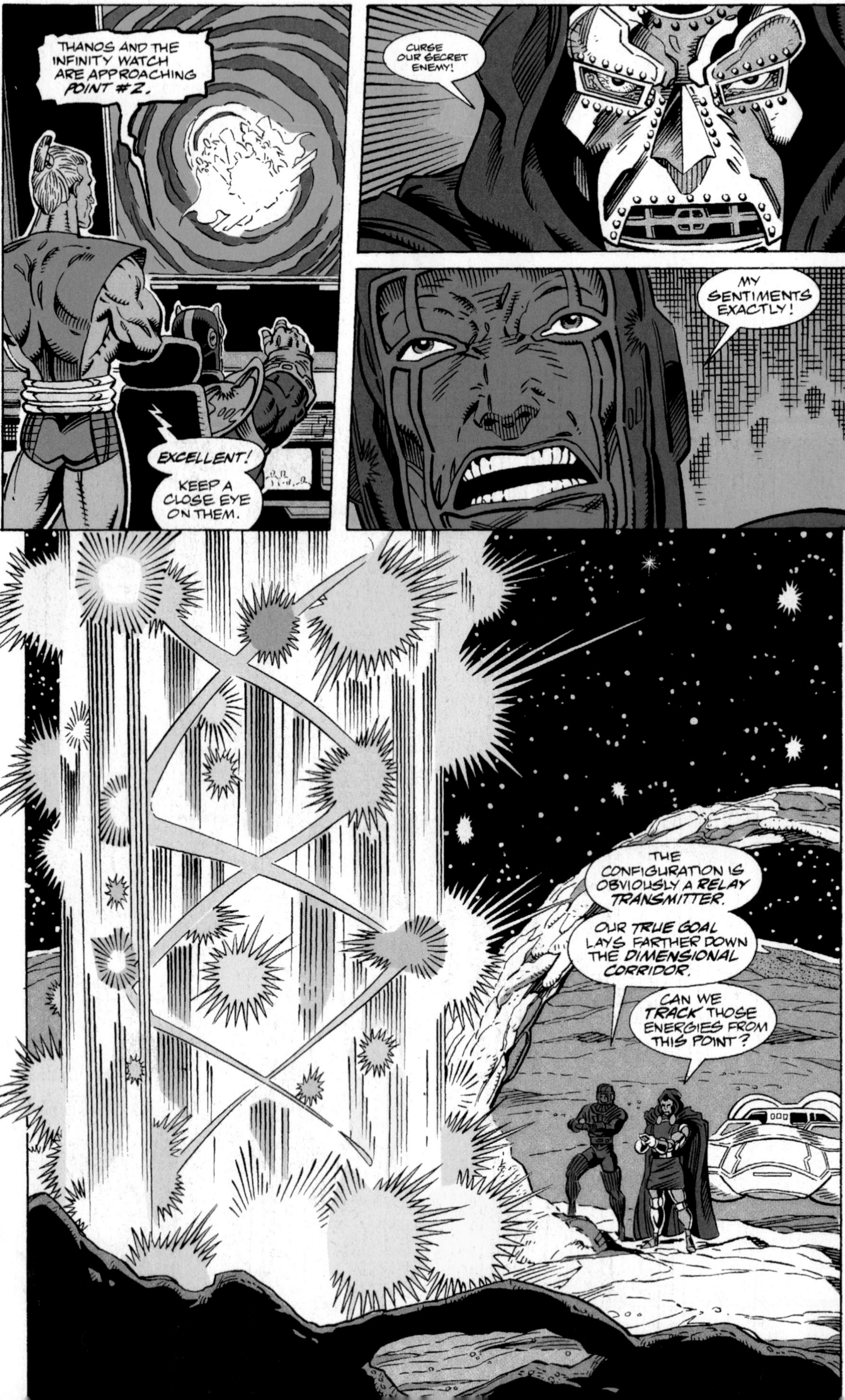
THANOS AND THE INFINITY WATCH ARE APPROACHING POINT #2.
EXCELLENT! KEEP A CLOSE EYE ON THEM.
CURSE OUR SECRET ENEMY!
MY SENTIMENTS EXACTLY!
THE CONFIGURATION IS OBVIOUSLY A RELAY TRANSMITTER.
OUR TRUE GOAL LAYS FARTHER DOWN THE DIMENSIONAL CORRIDOR.
CAN WE TRACK THOSE ENERGIES FROM THIS POINT?

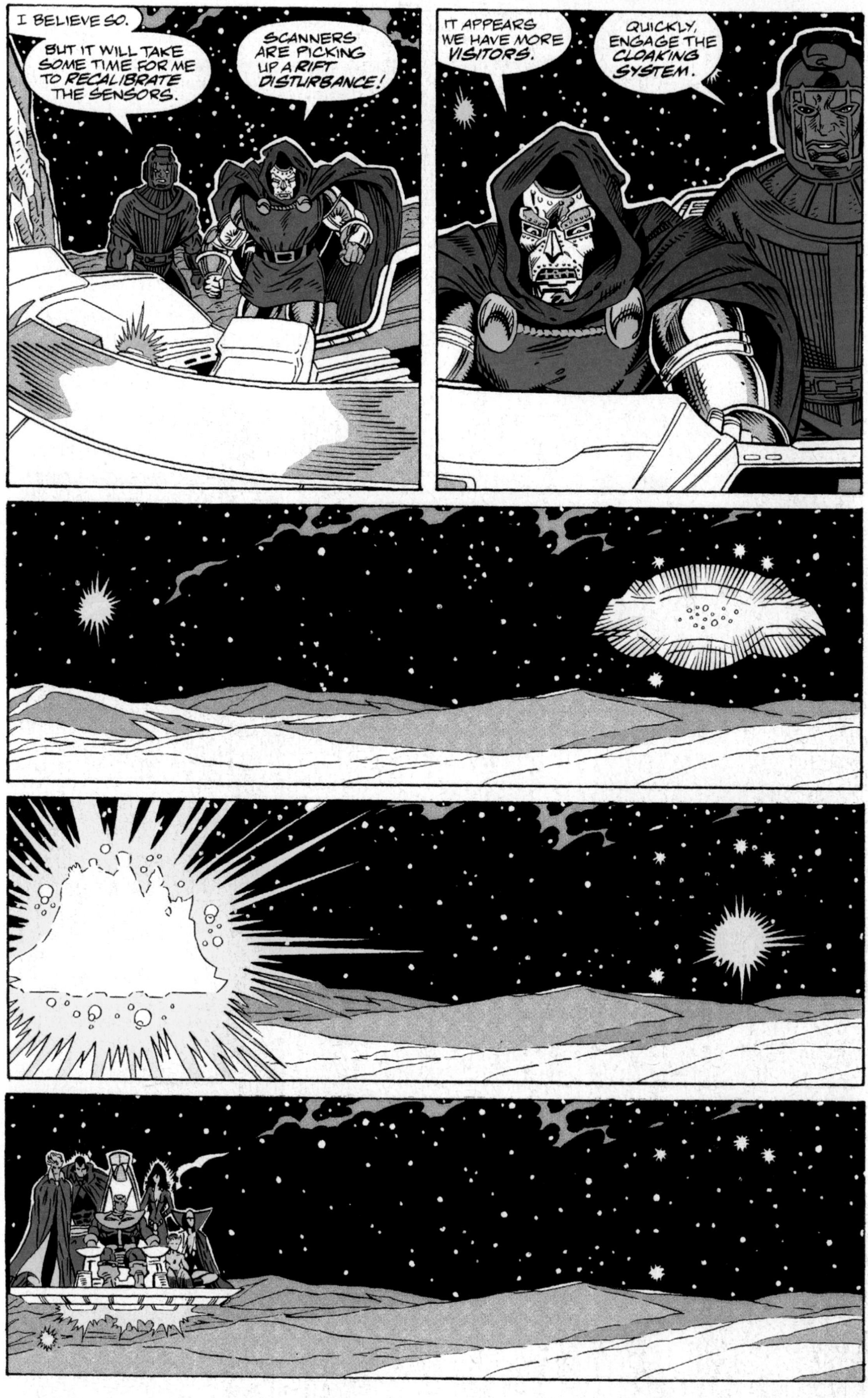
I BELIEVE SO.
BUT IT WILL TAKE SOME TIME FOR ME TO RECALIBRATE THE SENSORS.
SCANNERS ARE PICKING UP A RIFT DISTURBANCE!
IT APPEARS WE HAVE MORE VISITORS.
QUICKLY, ENGAGE THE CLOAKING SYSTEM.

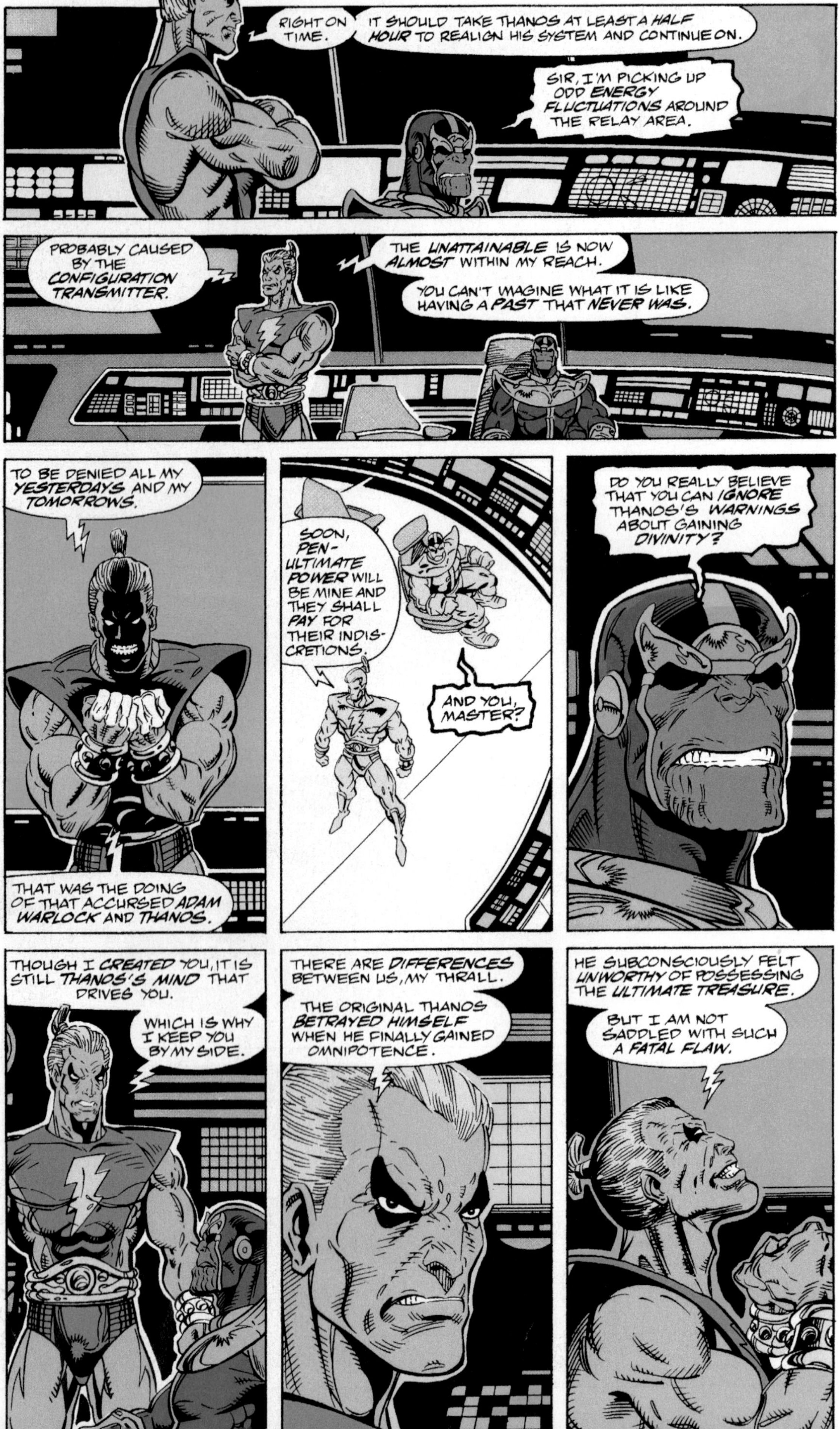
RIGHT ON TIME.
IT SHOULD TAKE THANOS AT LEAST A HALF HOUR TO REALIGN HIS SYSTEM AND CONTINUE ON.
SIR, I'M PICKING UP ODD ENERGY FLUCTUATIONS AROUND THE RELAY AREA.
PROBABLY CAUSED BY THE CONFIGURATION TRANSMITTER.
THE UNATTAINABLE IS NOW ALMOST WITHIN MY REACH.
YOU CAN'T IMAGINE WHAT IT IS LIKE HAVING A PAST THAT NEVER WAS.
TO BE DENIED ALL MY YESTERDAYS AND MY TOMORROWS.
THAT WAS THE DOING OF THAT ACCURSED ADAM WARLOCK AND THANOS.
SOON, PEN-ULTIMATE POWER WILL BE MINE AND THEY SHALL PAY FOR THEIR INDIS-CRETIONS.
AND YOU, MASTER?
DO YOU REALLY BELIEVE THAT YOU CAN IGNORE THANOS'S WARNINGS ABOUT GAINING DIVINITY?
THOUGH I CREATED YOU, IT IS STILL THANOS'S MIND THAT DRIVES YOU.
WHICH IS WHY I KEEP YOU BY MY SIDE.
THERE ARE DIFFERENCES BETWEEN US, MY THRALL.
THE ORIGINAL THANOS BETRAYED HIMSELF WHEN HE FINALLY GAINED OMNIPOTENCE.
HE SUBCONSCIOUSLY FELT UNWORTHY OF POSSESSING THE ULTIMATE TREASURE.
BUT I AM NOT SADDLED WITH SUCH A FATAL FLAW.

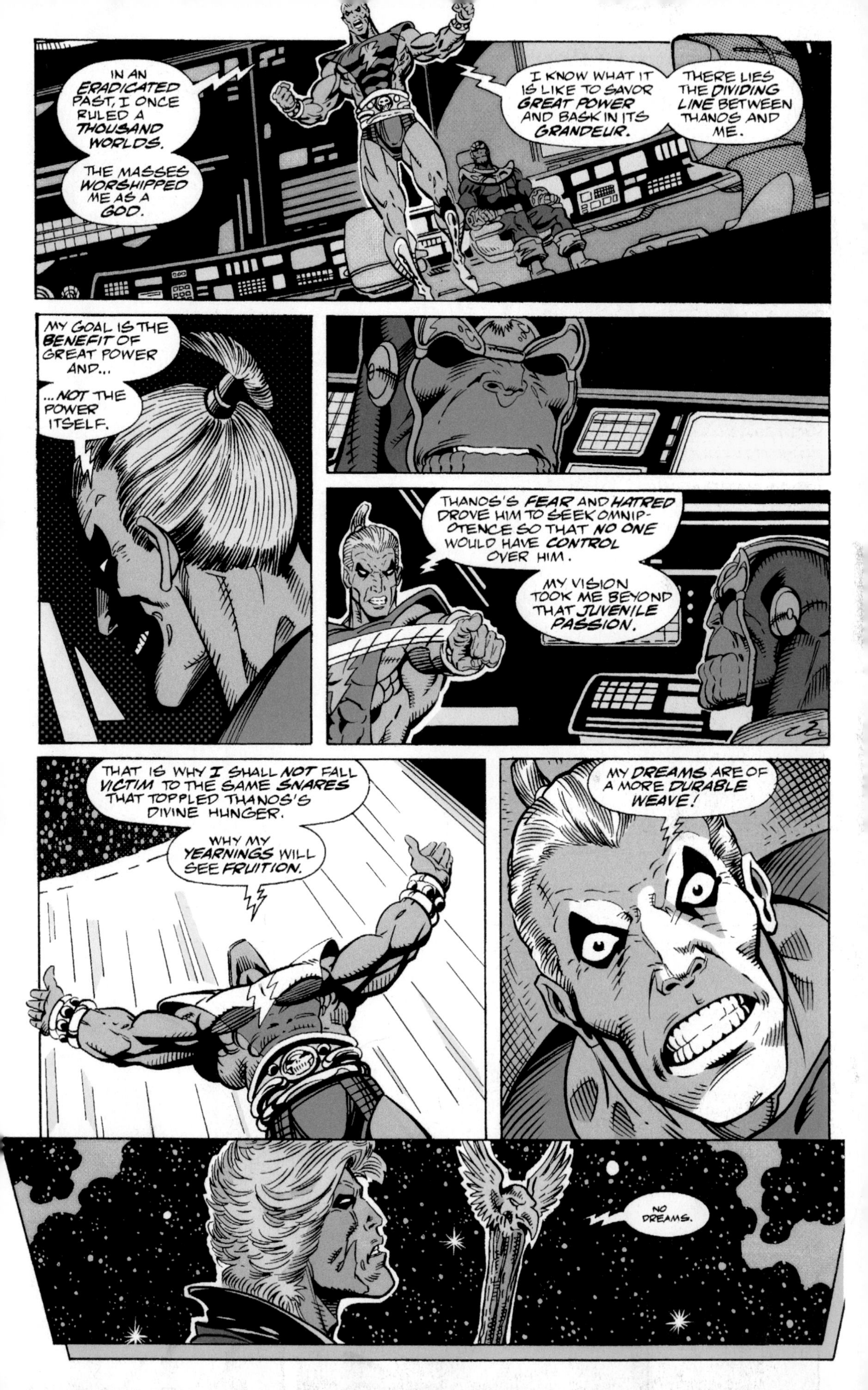
IN AN ERADICATED PAST, I ONCE RULED A THOUSAND WORLDS.
THE MASSES WORSHIPPED ME AS A GOD.
I KNOW WHAT IT IS LIKE TO SAVOR GREAT POWER AND BASK IN ITS GRANDEUR.
THERE LIES THE DIVIDING LINE BETWEEN THANOS AND ME.
MY GOAL IS THE BENEFIT OF GREAT POWER AND...
...NOT THE POWER ITSELF.
THANOS'S FEAR AND HATRED DROVE HIM TO SEEK OMNIP-OTENCE SO THAT NO ONE WOULD HAVE CONTROL OVER HIM.
MY VISION TOOK ME BEYOND THAT JUVENILE PASSION.
THAT IS WHY I SHALL NOT FALL VICTIM TO THE SAME SNARES THAT TOPPLED THANOS'S DIVINE HUNGER.
WHY MY YEARNINGS WILL SEE FRUITION.
MY DREAMS ARE OF A MORE DURABLE WEAVE!
NO DREAMS.

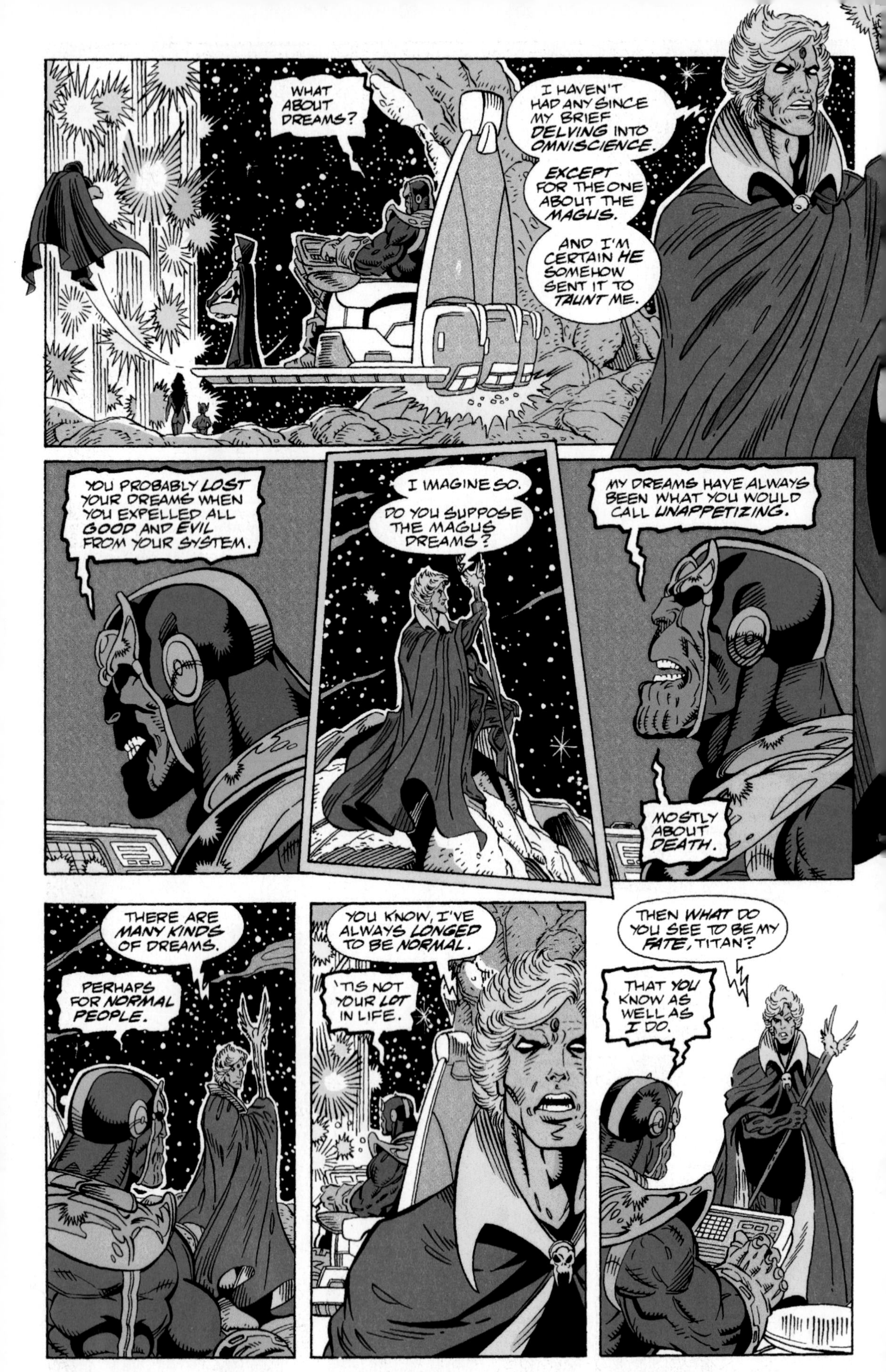
WHAT ABOUT DREAMS?
I HAVEN'T HAD ANY SINCE MY BRIEF DELVING INTO OMNISCIENCE.
EXCEPT FOR THE ONE ABOUT THE MAGUS.
AND I'M CERTAIN HE SOMEHOW SENT IT TO TAUNT ME.
YOU PROBABLY LOST YOUR DREAMS WHEN YOU EXPELLED ALL GOOD AND EVIL FROM YOUR SYSTEM.
I IMAGINE SO.
DO YOU SUPPOSE THE MAGUS DREAMS?
MY DREAMS HAVE ALWAYS BEEN WHAT YOU WOULD CALL UNAPPETIZING.
MOSTLY ABOUT DEATH.
THERE ARE MANY KINDS OF DREAMS.
PERHAPS FOR NORMAL PEOPLE.
YOU KNOW, I'VE ALWAYS LONGED TO BE NORMAL.
'TIS NOT YOUR LOT IN LIFE.
THEN WHAT DO YOU SEE TO BE MY FATE, TITAN?
THAT YOU KNOW AS WELL AS I DO.

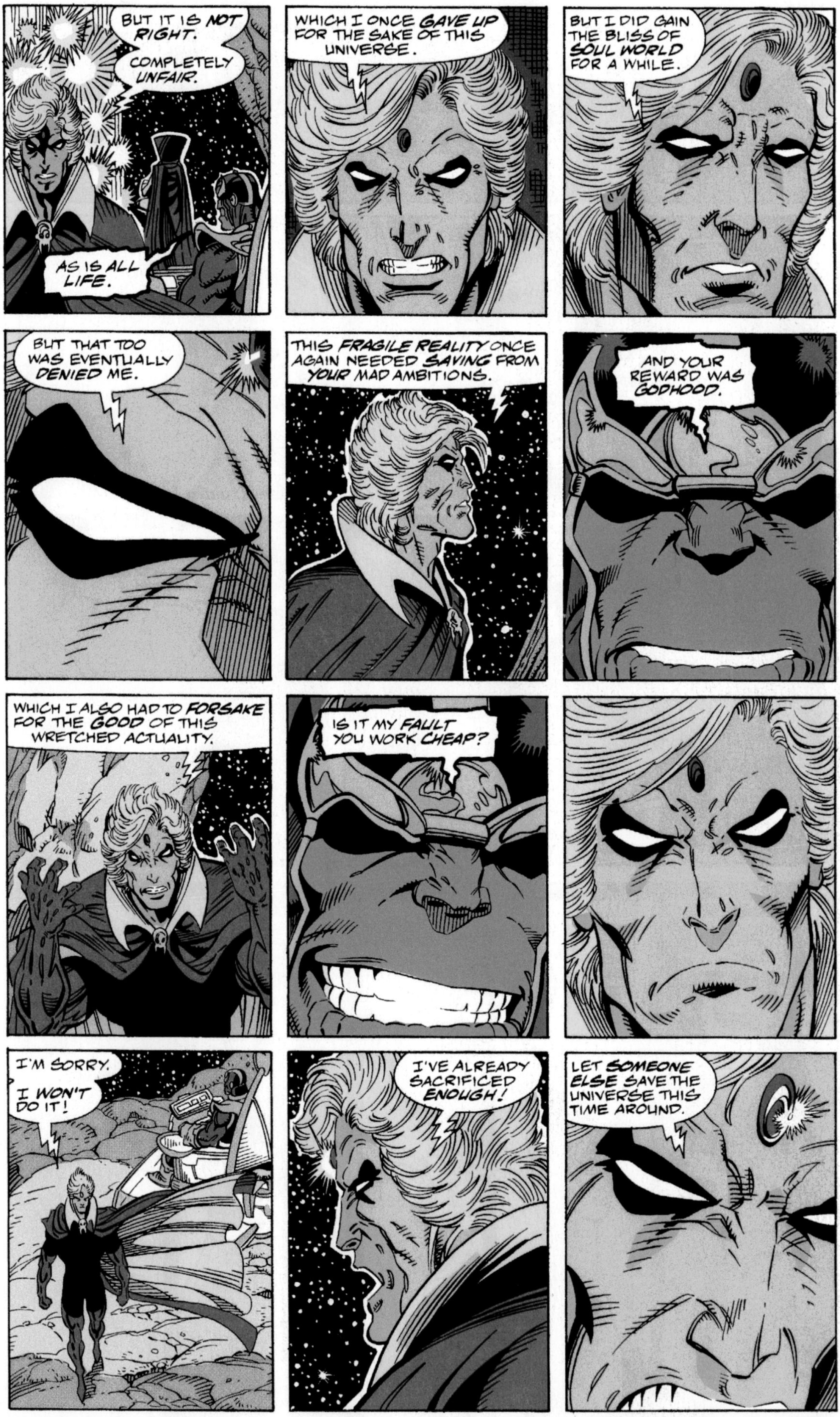
BUT IT IS NOT RIGHT.
COMPLETELY UNFAIR.
AS IS ALL LIFE.
WHICH I ONCE GAVE UP FOR THE SAKE OF THIS UNIVERSE.
BUT I DID GAIN THE BLISS OF SOUL WORLD FOR A WHILE.
BUT THAT TOO WAS EVENTUALLY DENIED ME.
THIS FRAGILE REALITY ONCE AGAIN NEEDED SAVING FROM YOUR MAD AMBITIONS.
AND YOUR REWARD WAS GODHOOD.
WHICH I ALSO HAD TO FORSAKE FOR THE GOOD OF THIS WRETCHED ACTUALITY.
IS IT MY FAULT YOU WORK CHEAP?
I'M SORRY.
I WON'T DO IT!
I'VE ALREADY SACRIFICED ENOUGH!
LET SOMEONE ELSE SAVE THE UNIVERSE THIS TIME AROUND.

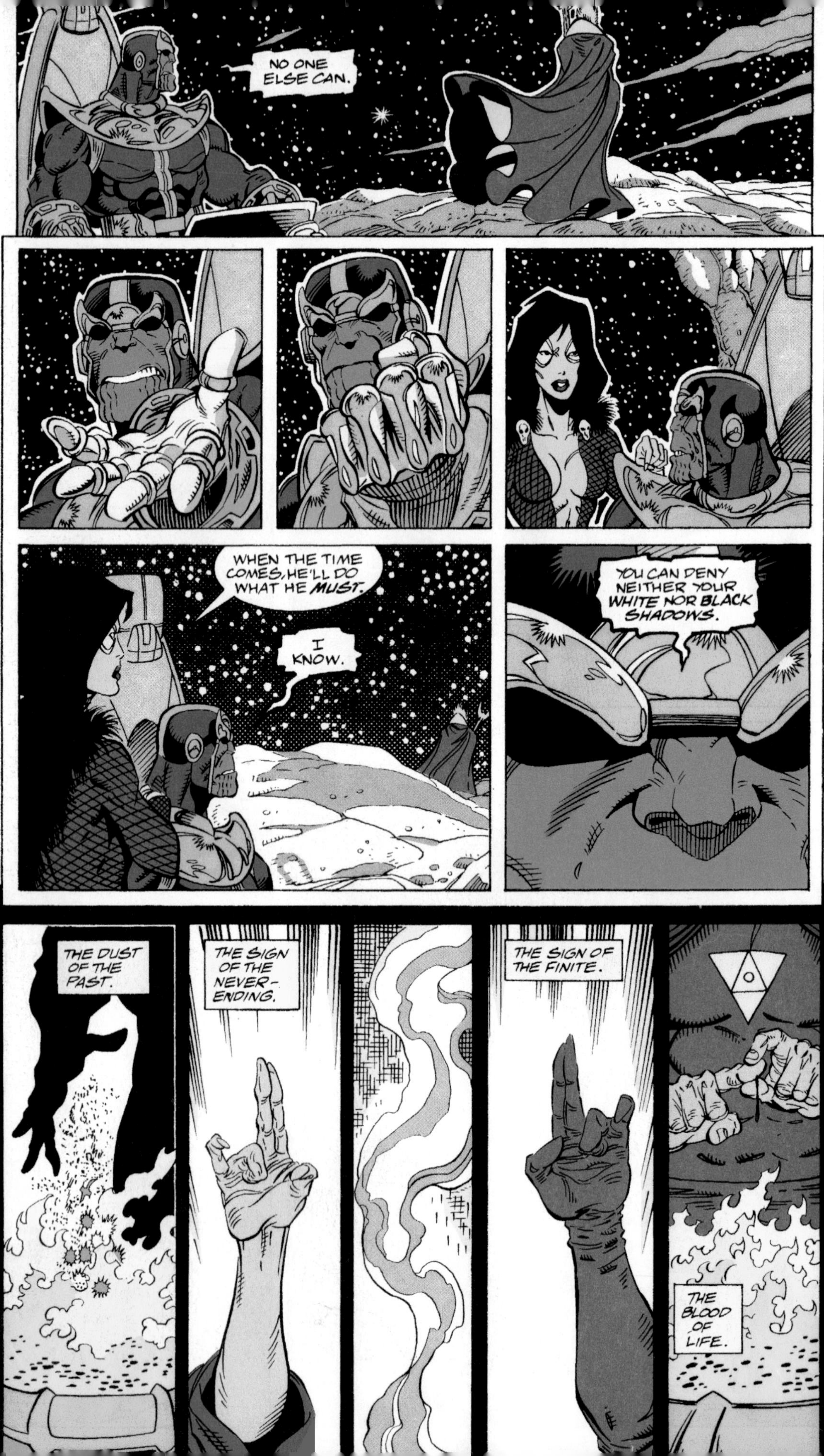
NO ONE ELSE CAN.
WHEN THE TIME COMES, HE'LL DO WHAT HE MUST.
I KNOW.
YOU CAN DENY NEITHER YOUR WHITE NOR BLACK SHADOWS.
THE DUST OF THE PAST.
THE SIGN OF THE NEVER-ENDING.
THE SIGN OF THE FINITE.
THE BLOOD OF LIFE.

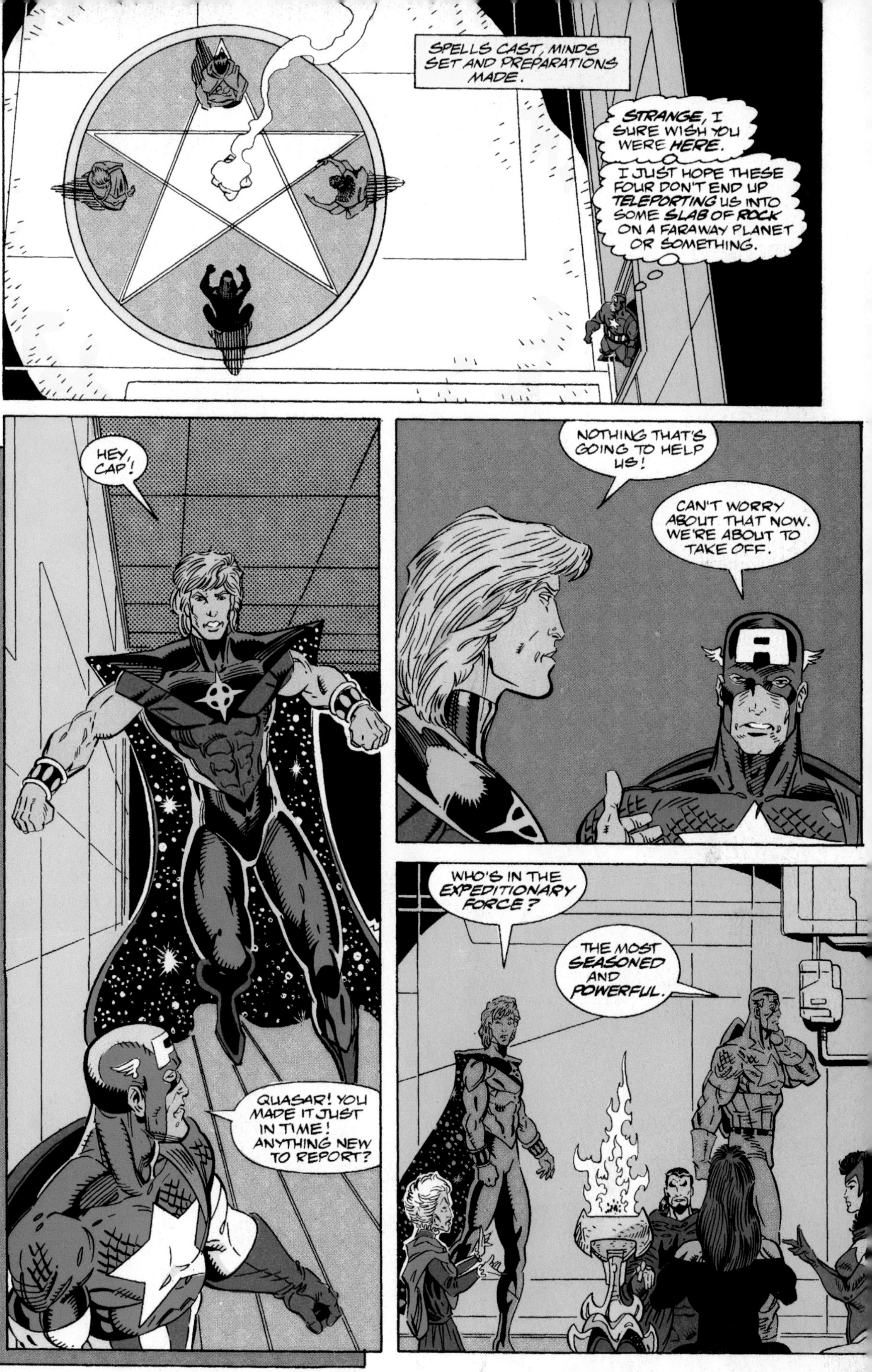
SPELLS CAST, MINDS SET AND PREPARATIONS MADE.
STRANGE, I SURE WISH YOU WERE HERE.
I JUST HOPE THESE FOUR DON'T END UP TELEPORTING US INTO SOME SLAB OF ROCK ON A FARAWAY PLANET OR SOMETHING.
HEY, CAP!
QUASAR! YOU MADE IT JUST IN TIME! ANYTHING NEW TO REPORT?
NOTHING THAT'S GOING TO HELP US!
CAN'T WORRY ABOUT THAT NOW. WE'RE ABOUT TO TAKE OFF.
WHO'S IN THE EXPEDITIONARY FORCE?
THE MOST SEASONED AND POWERFUL.

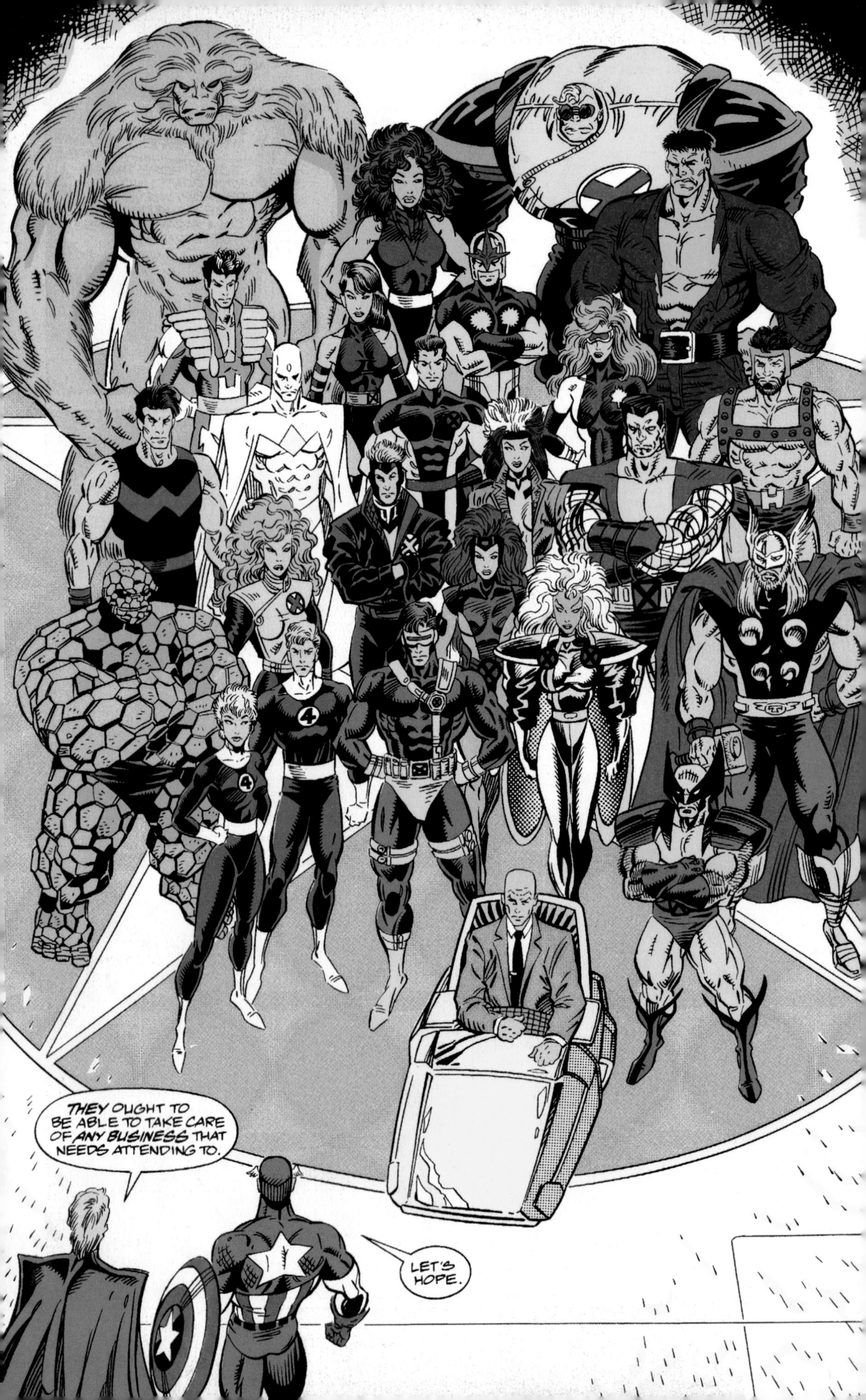
THEY OUGHT TO BE ABLE TO TAKE CARE OF ANY BUSINESS THAT NEEDS ATTENDING TO.
LET'S HOPE.

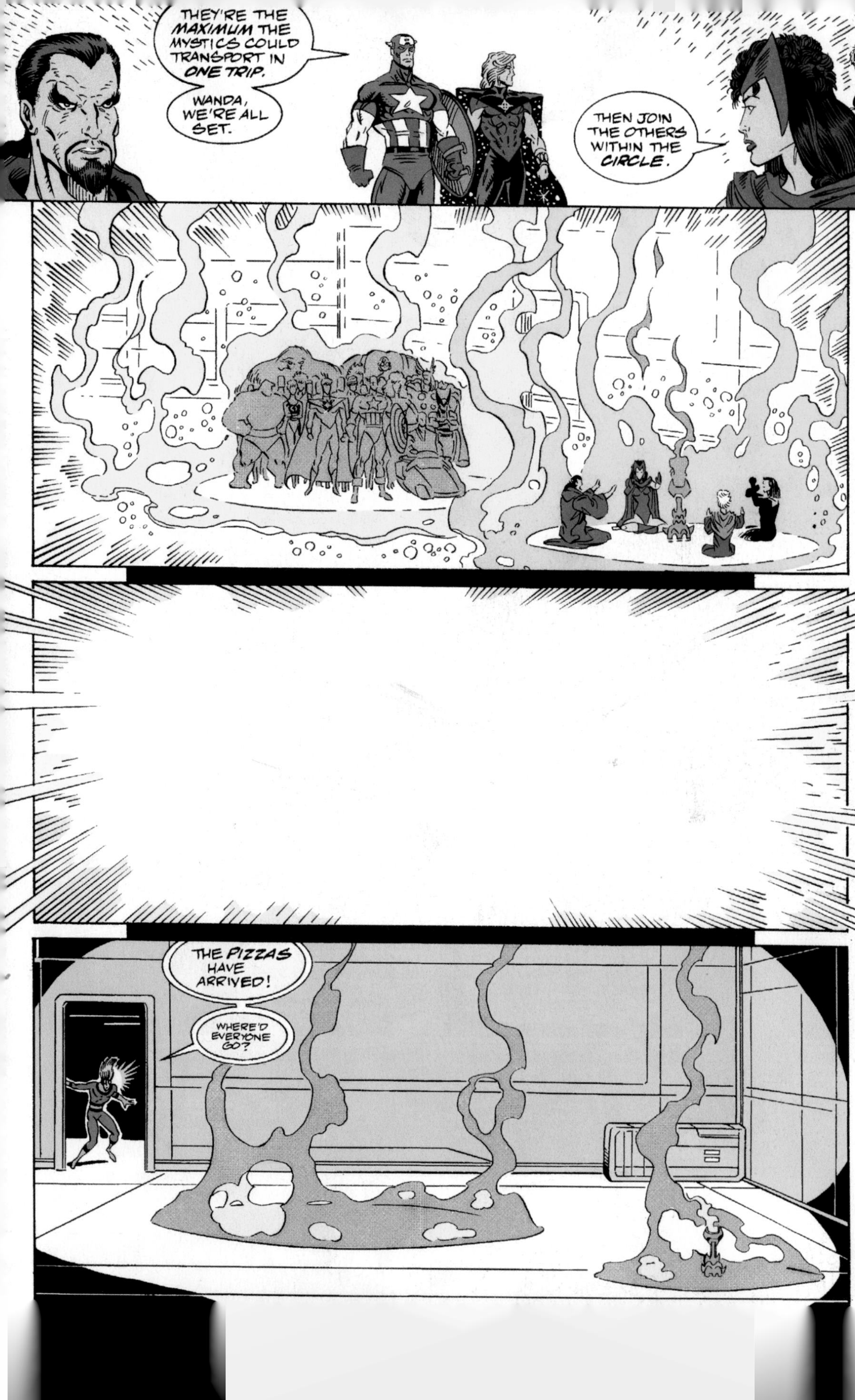
THEY'RE THE MAXIMUM THE MYSTICS COULD TRANSPORT IN ONE TRIP.
WANDA, WE'RE ALL SET.
THEN JOIN THE OTHERS WITHIN THE CIRCLE.
THE PIZZAS HAVE ARRIVED!
WHERE'D EVERYONE GO?

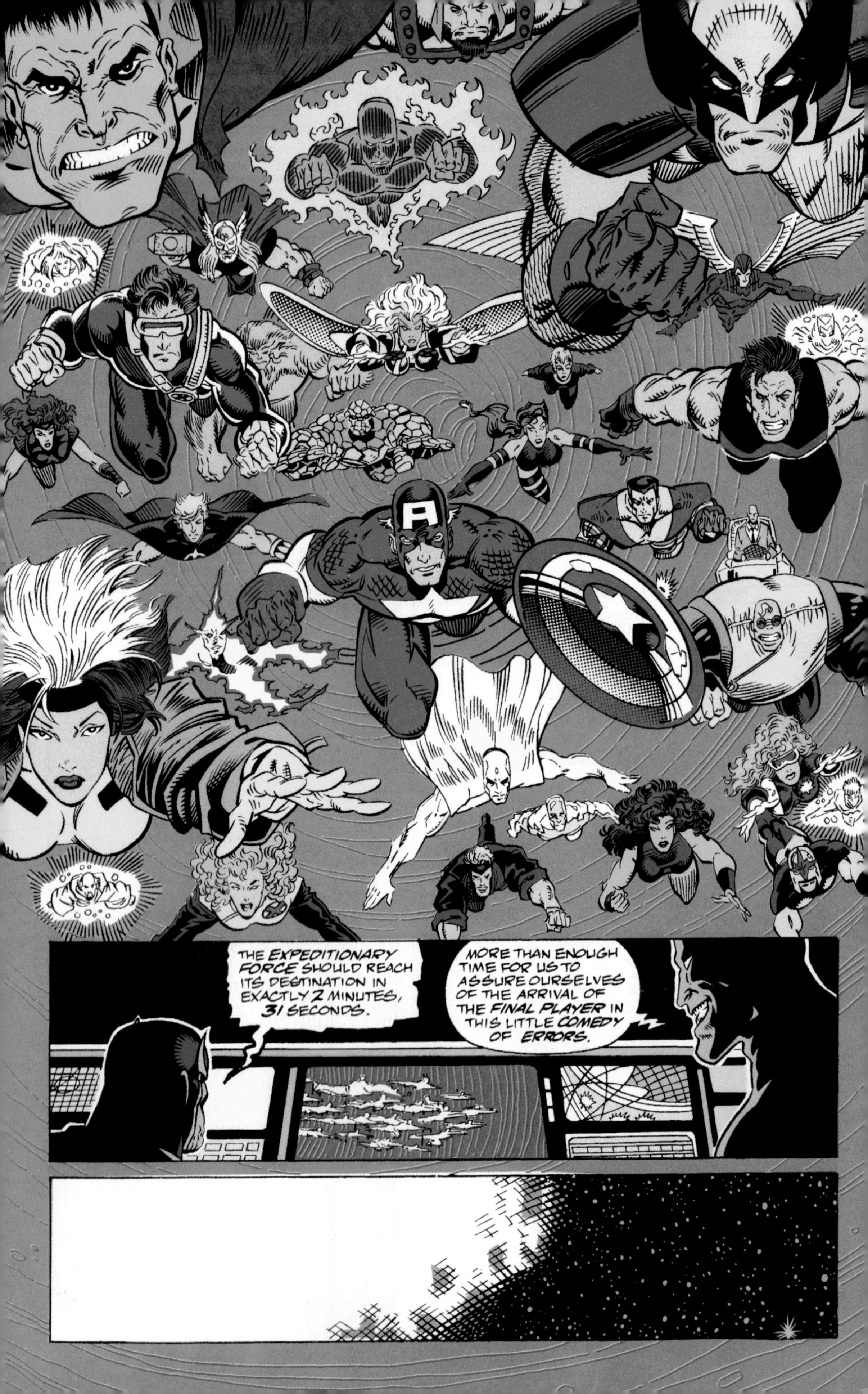
THE EXPEDITIONARY FORCE SHOULD REACH ITS DESTINATION IN EXACTLY 2 MINUTES, 31 SECONDS.
MORE THAN ENOUGH TIME FOR US TO ASSURE OURSELVES OF THE ARRIVAL OF THE FINAL PLAYER IN THIS LITTLE COMEDY OF ERRORS.

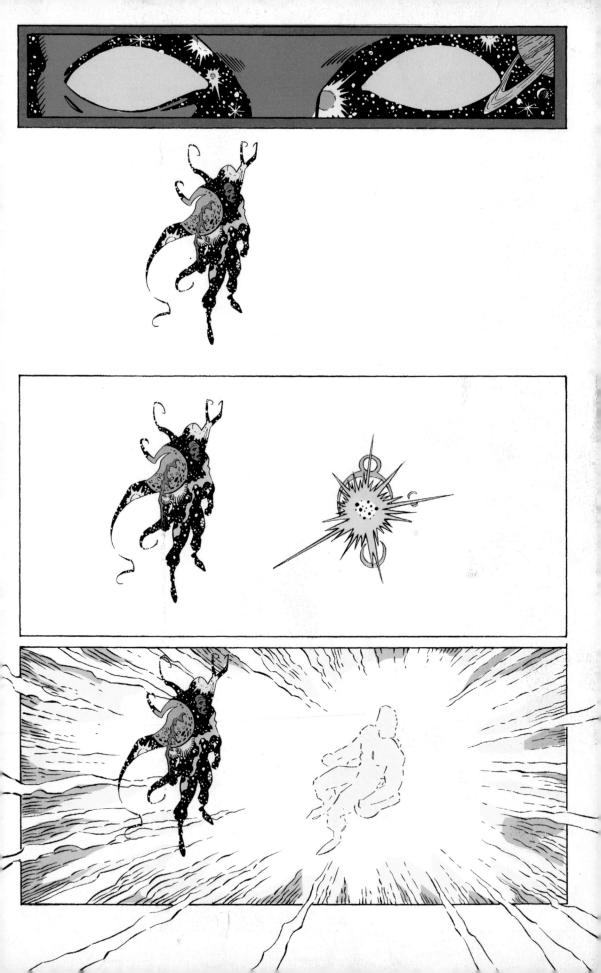

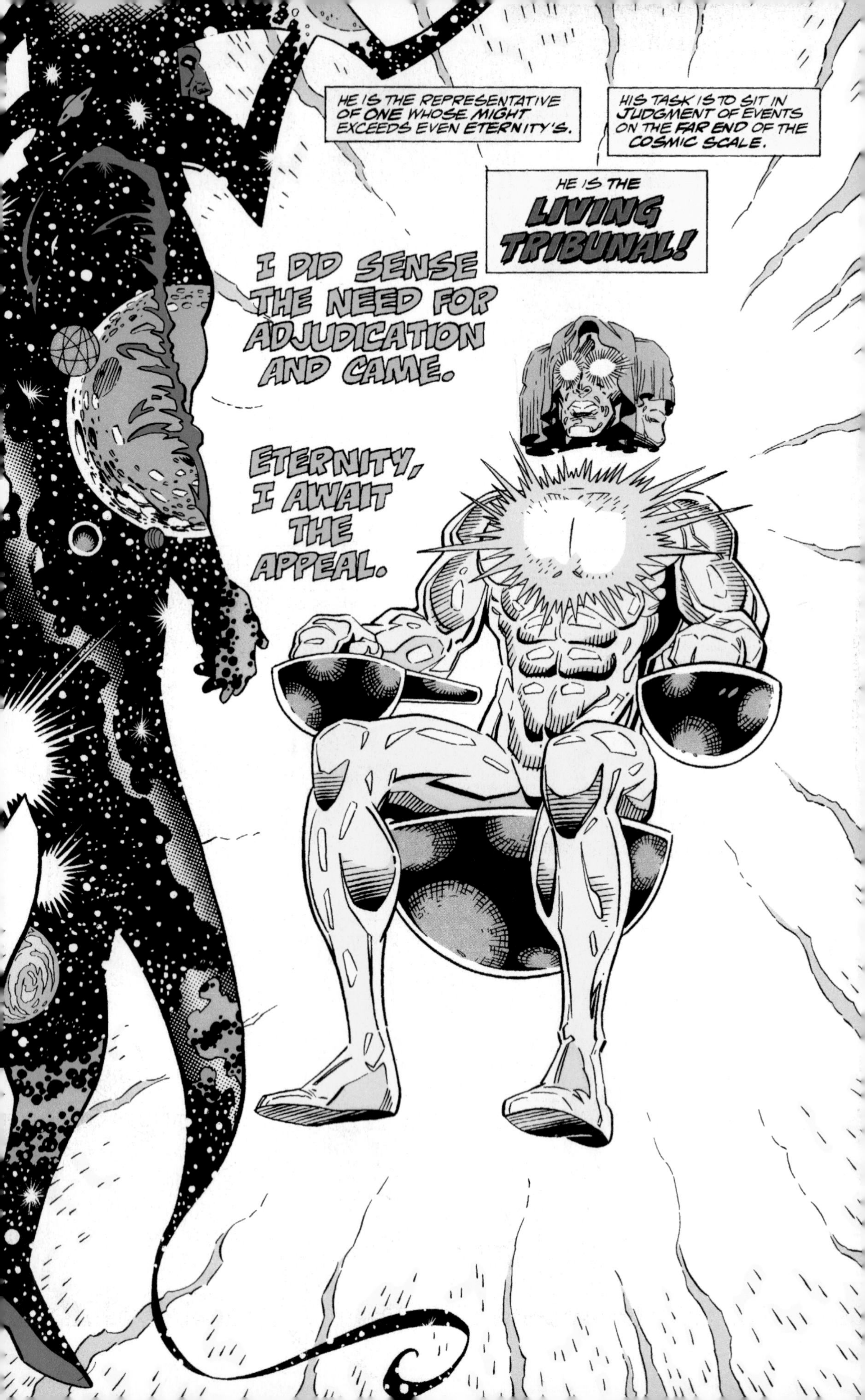
HE IS THE REPRESENTATIVE OF ONE WHOSE MIGHT EXCEEDS EVEN ETERNITY'S.
HIS TASK IS TO SIT IN JUDGMENT OF EVENTS ON THE FAR END OF THE COSMIC SCALE.
HE IS THE LIVING TRIBUNAL!
I DID SENSE THE NEED FOR ADJUDICATION AND CAME.
ETERNITY, I AWAIT THE APPEAL.

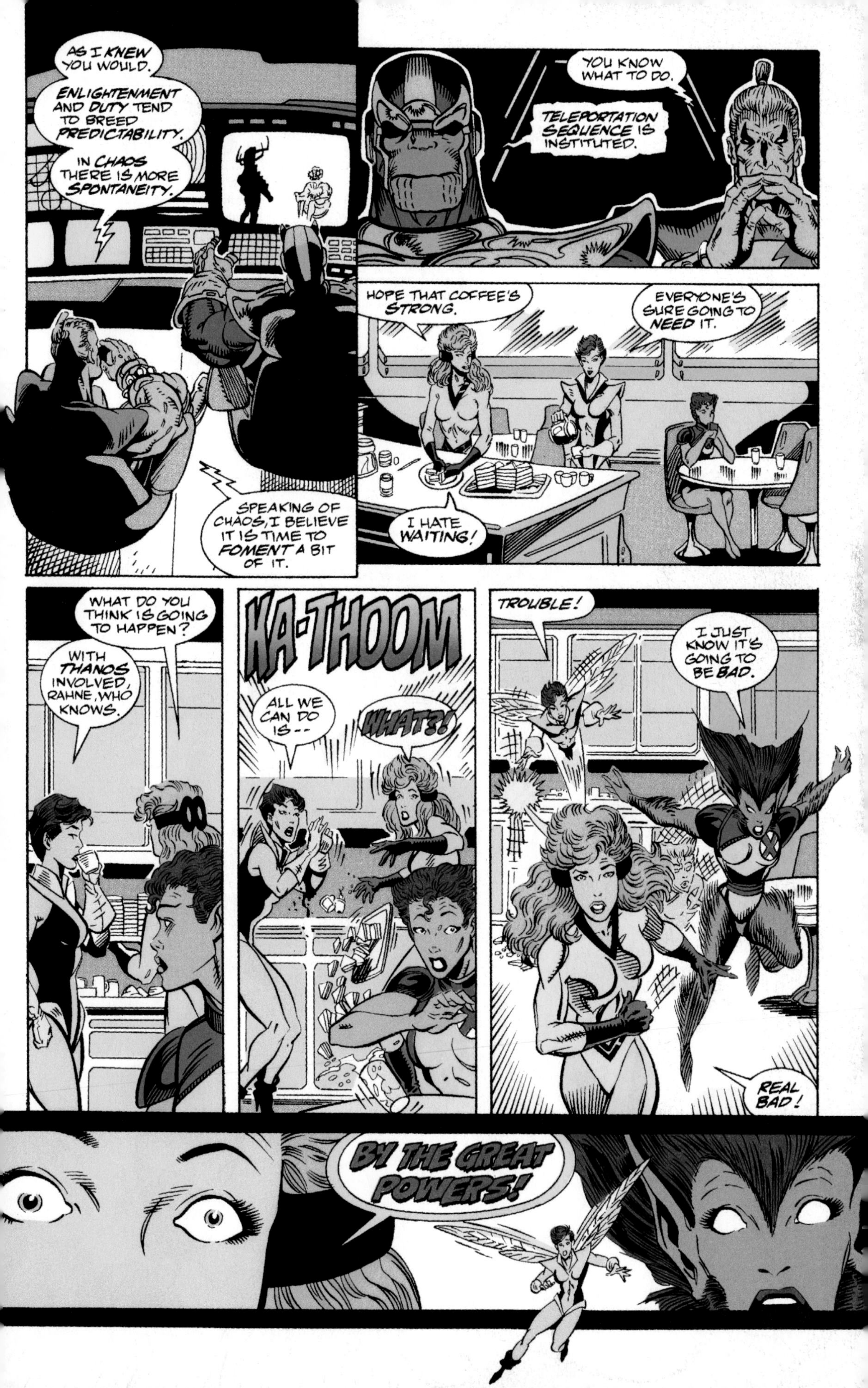

AS I KNEW YOU WOULD.
ENLIGHTENMENT AND DUTY TEND TO BREED PREDICTABILITY.
IN CHAOS THERE IS MORE SPONTANEITY.
YOU KNOW WHAT TO DO.
TELEPORTATION SEQUENCE IS INSTITUTED.
SPEAKING OF CHAOS, I BELIEVE IT IS TIME TO FOMENT A BIT OF IT.
HOPE THAT COFFEE'S STRONG.
EVERYONE'S SURE GOING TO NEED IT.
I HATE WAITING!
WHAT DO YOU THINK IS GOING TO HAPPEN?
WITH THANOS INVOLVED, RAHNE, WHO KNOWS.
KA-THOOM
ALL WE CAN DO IS--
WHAT?!
TROUBLE!
I JUST KNOW IT'S GOING TO BE BAD.
REAL BAD!
BY THE GREAT POWERS!

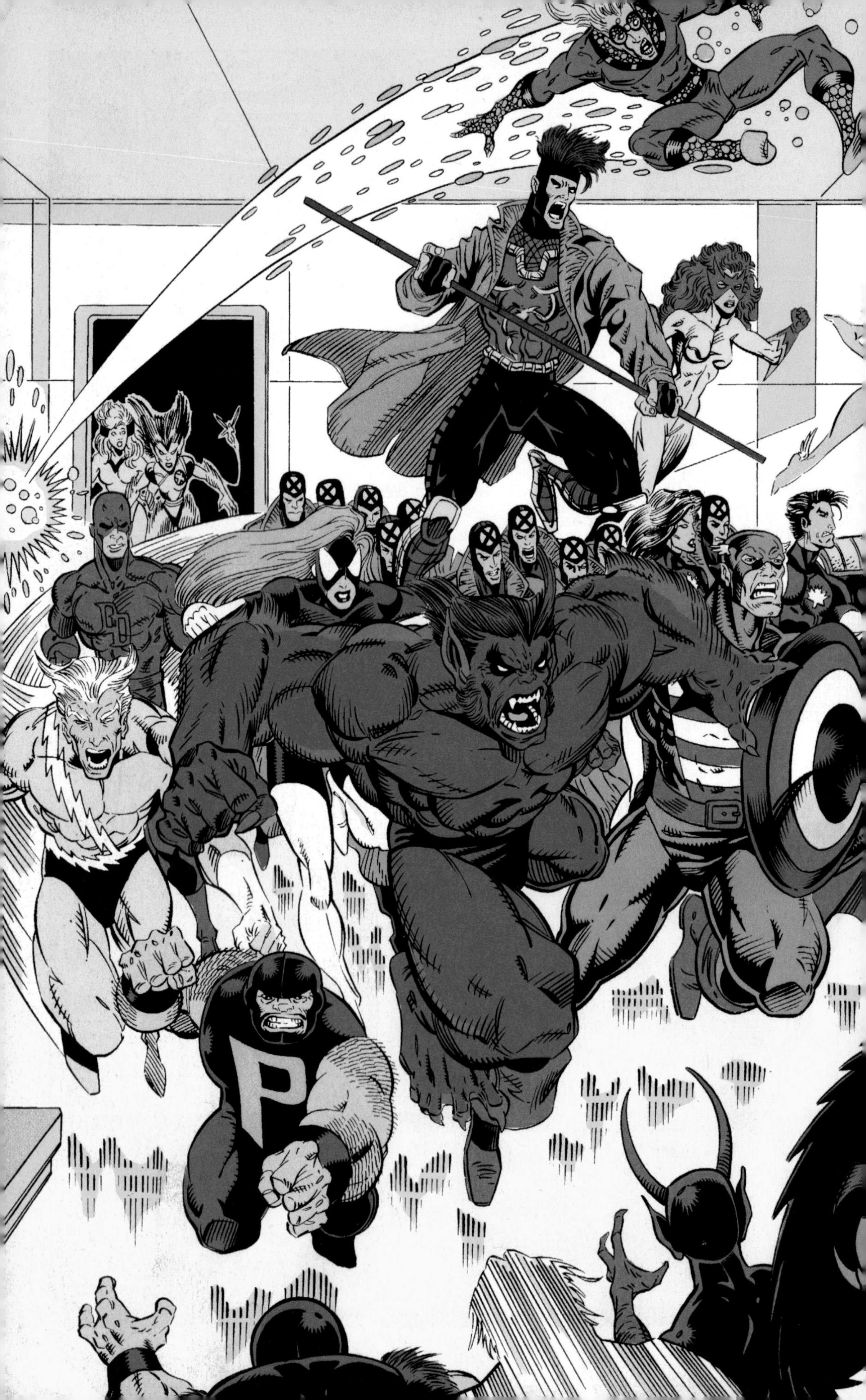

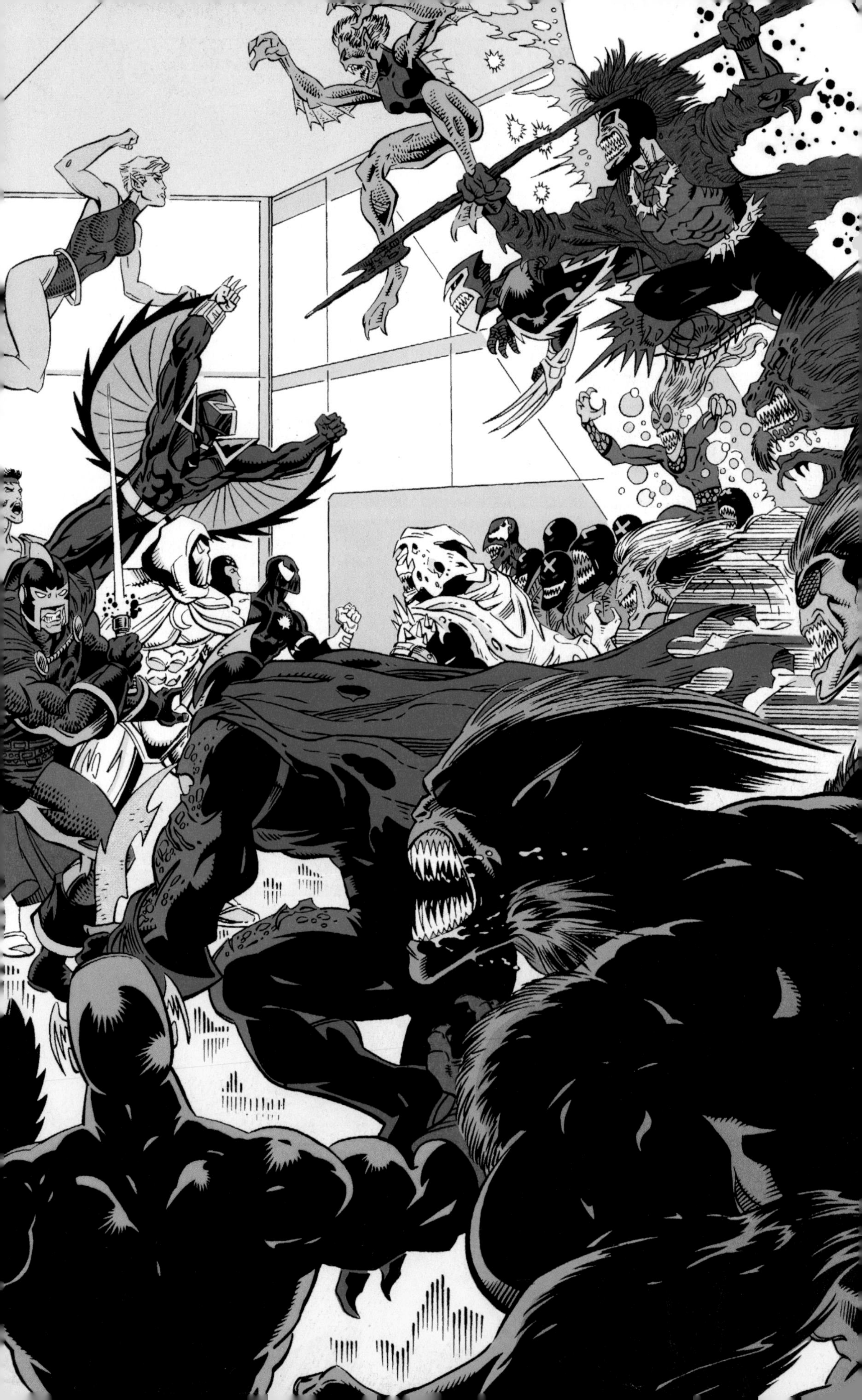

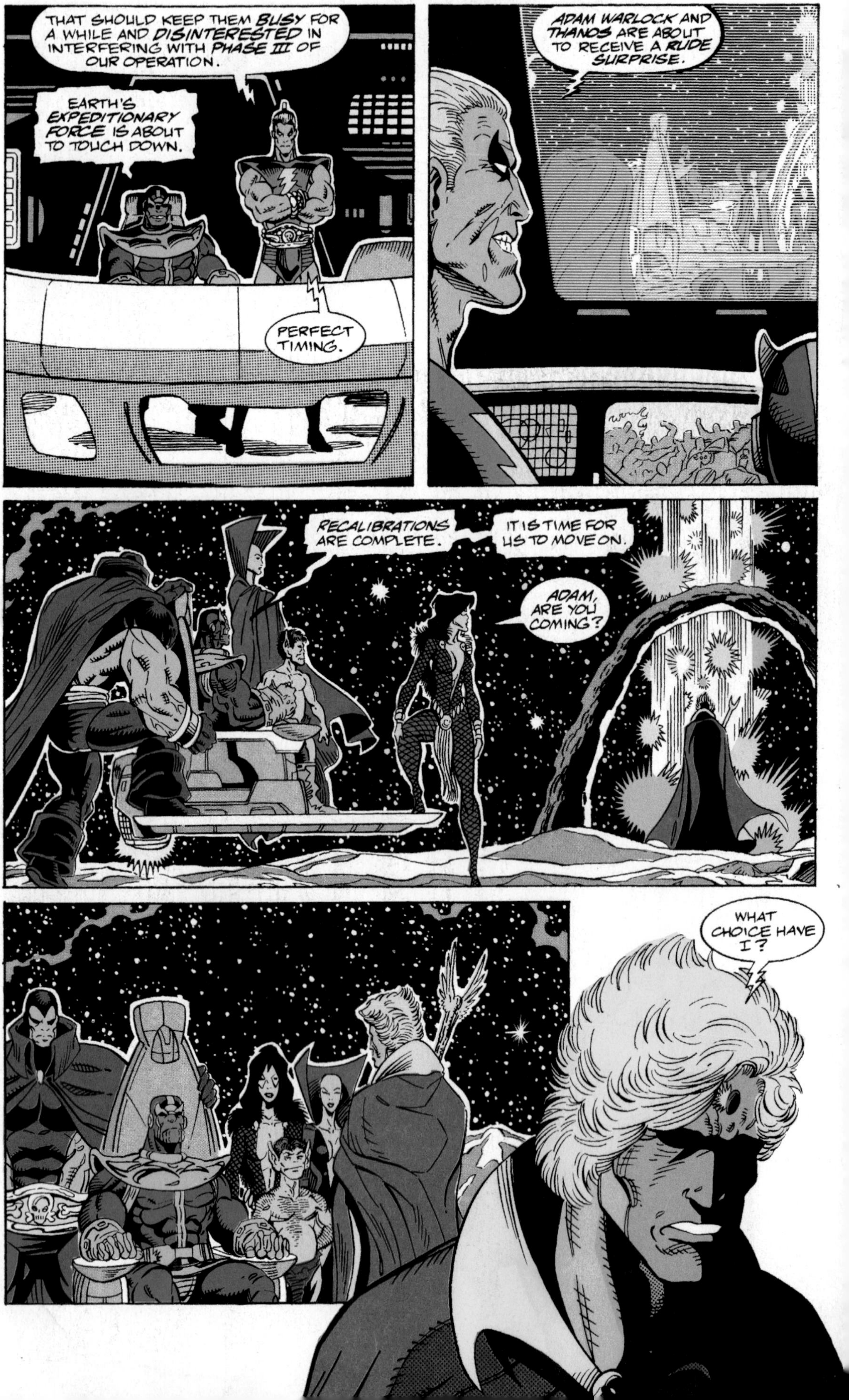
THAT SHOULD KEEP THEM BUSY FOR A WHILE AND DISINTERESTED IN INTERFERING WITH PHASE III OF OUR OPERATION.
EARTH'S EXPEDITIONARY FORCE IS ABOUT TO TOUCH DOWN.
PERFECT TIMING.
ADAM WARLOCK AND THANOS ARE ABOUT TO RECEIVE A RUDE SURPRISE.
RECALIBRATIONS ARE COMPLETE.
IT IS TIME FOR US TO MOVE ON.
ADAM, ARE YOU COMING?
WHAT CHOICE HAVE I?

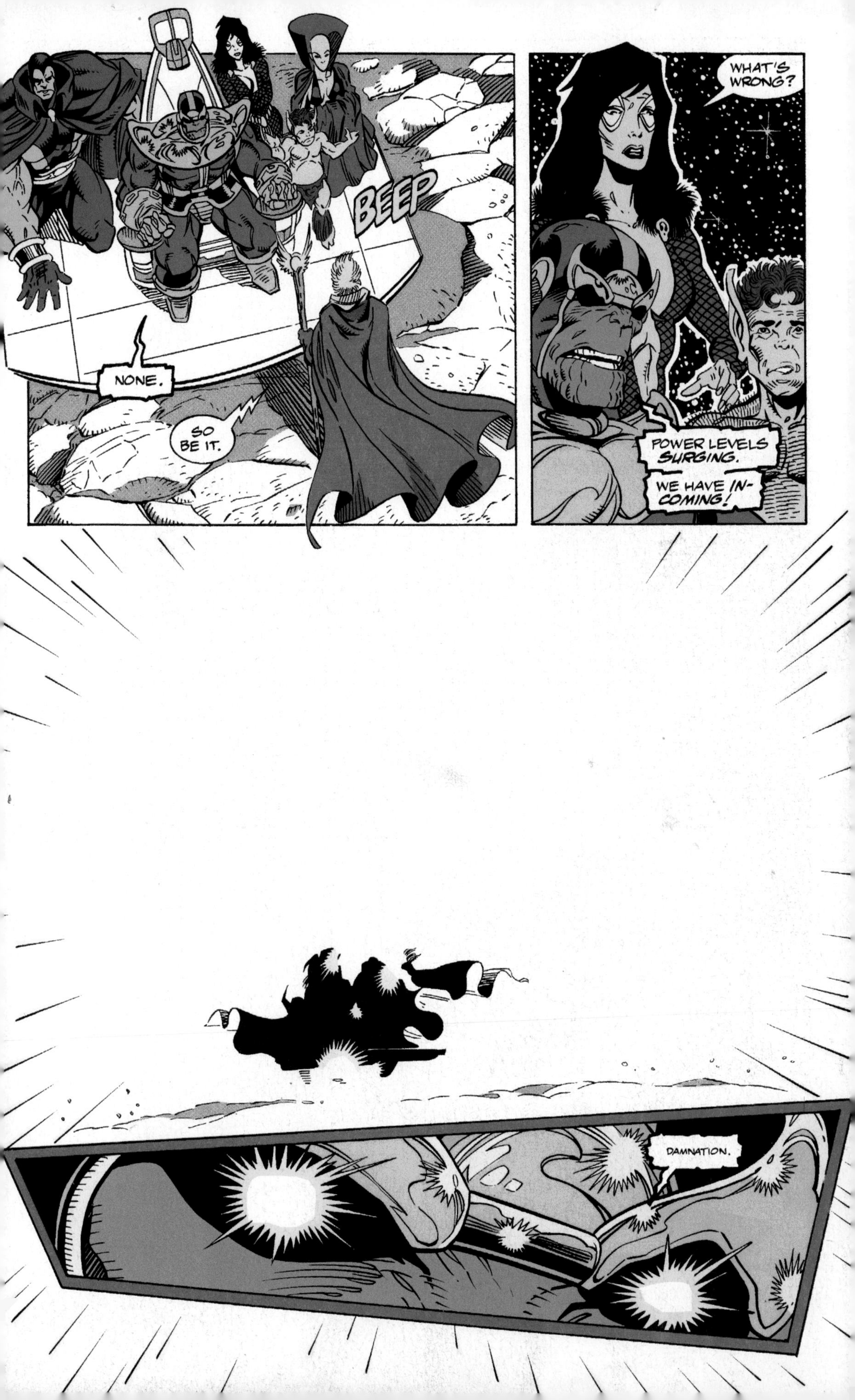
BEEP
NONE.
SO BE IT.
WHAT'S WRONG?
POWER LEVELS SURGING.
WE HAVE INCOMING!
DAMNATION.

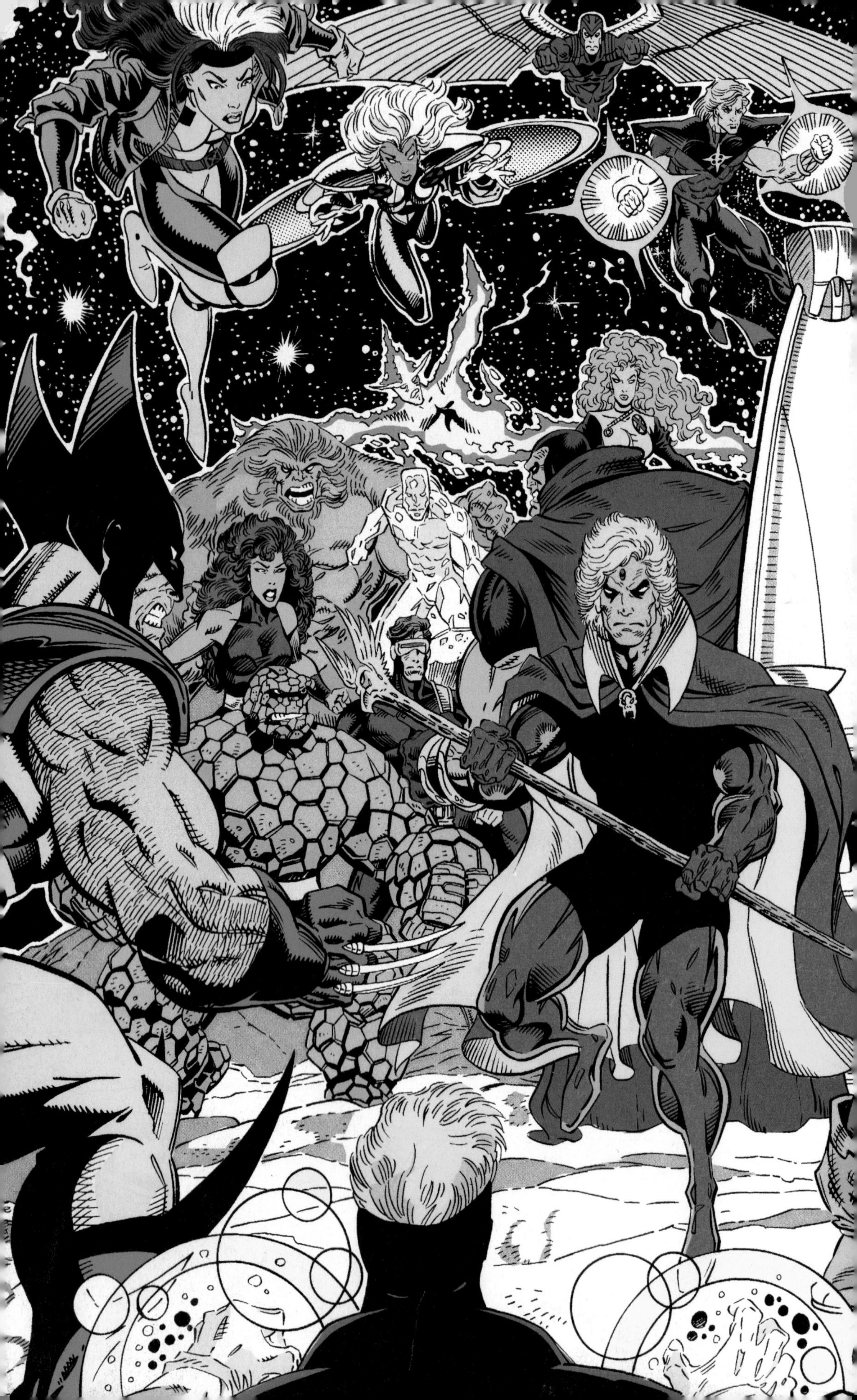

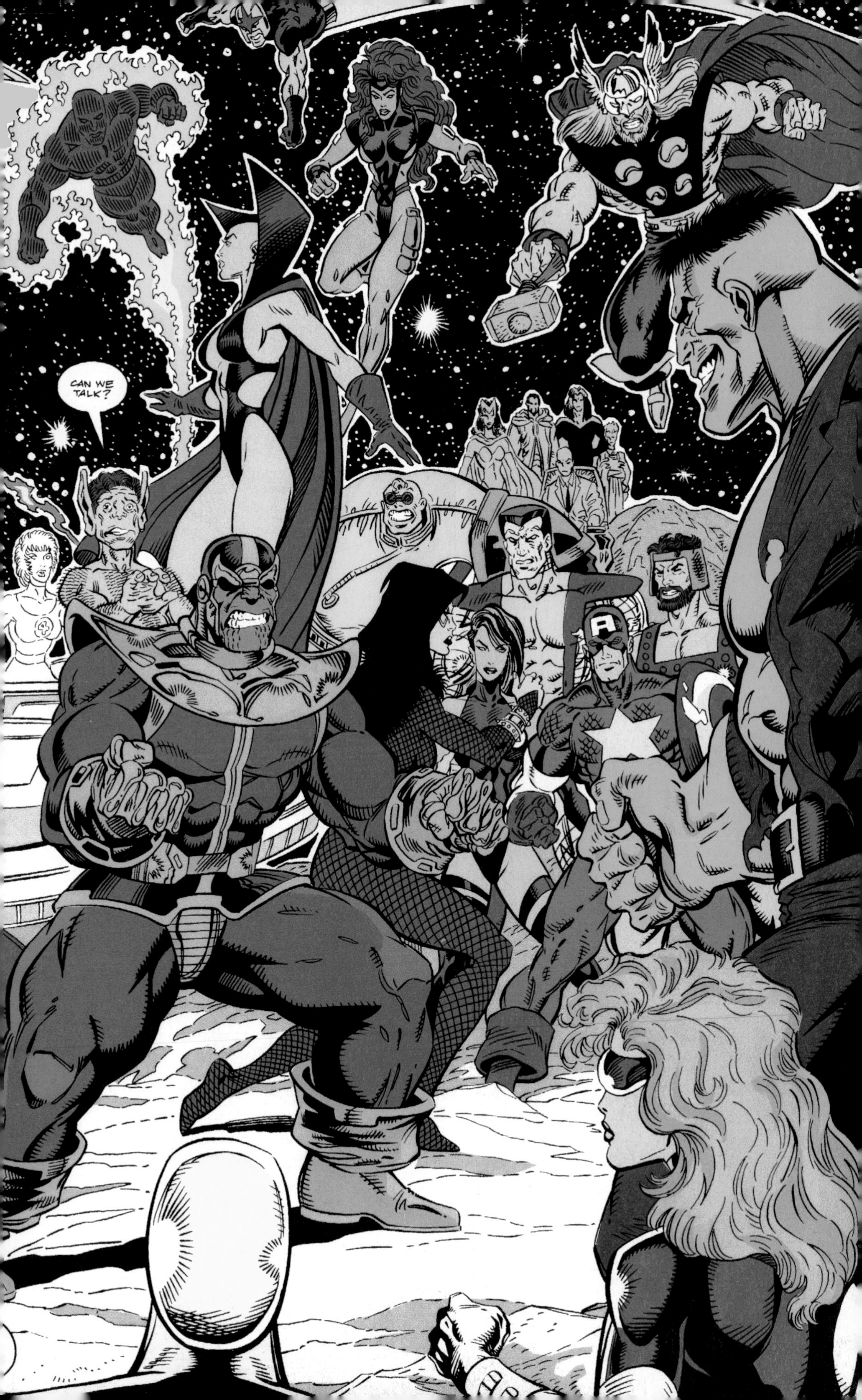
CAN WE TALK?

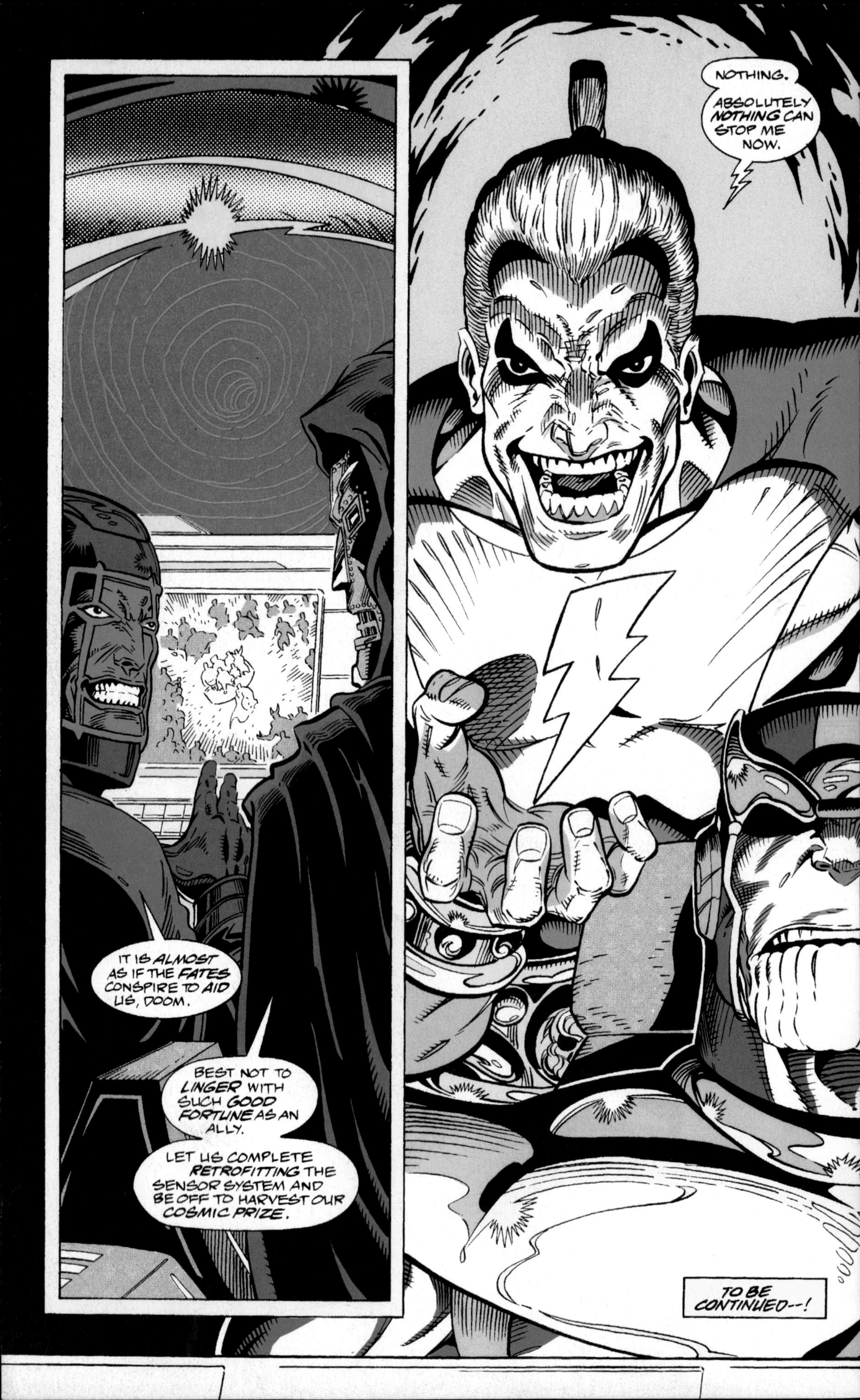
IT IS ALMOST AS IF THE FATES CONSPIRE TO AID US, DOOM.
BEST NOT TO LINGER WITH SUCH GOOD FORTUNE AS AN ALLY.
LET US COMPLETE RETROFITTING THE SENSOR SYSTEM AND BE OFF TO HARVEST OUR COSMIC PRIZE.
NOTHING.
ABSOLUTELY NOTHING CAN STOP ME NOW.
TO BE CONTINUED--!

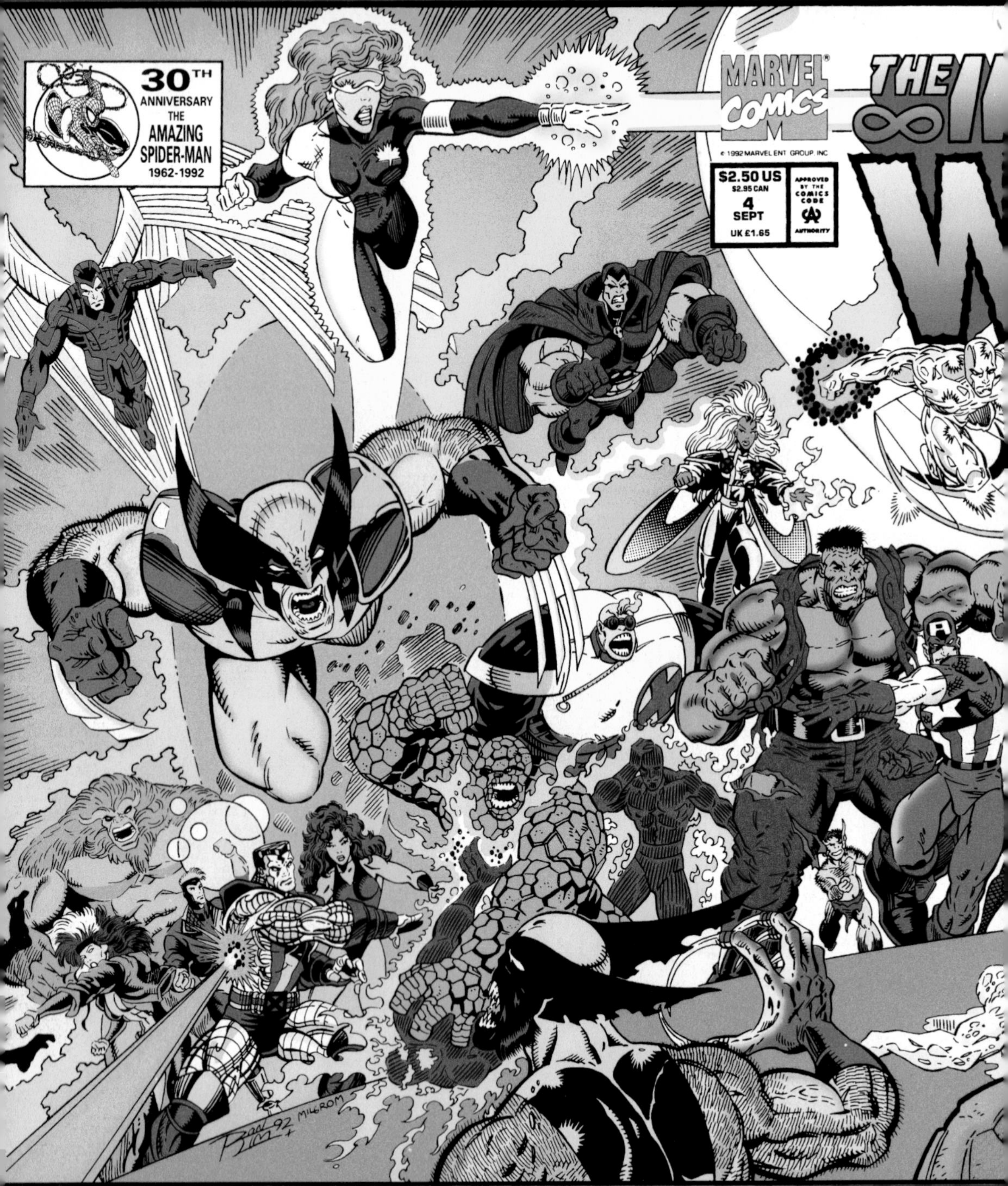
30TH ANNIVERSARY
THE AMAZING SPIDER-MAN
1962-1992
MARVEL COMICS
© 1992 MARVEL ENT. GROUP, INC.
$2.50 US
$2.95 CAN
4
SEPT
UK £1.65
APPROVED BY THE COMICS CODE AUTHORITY
THE

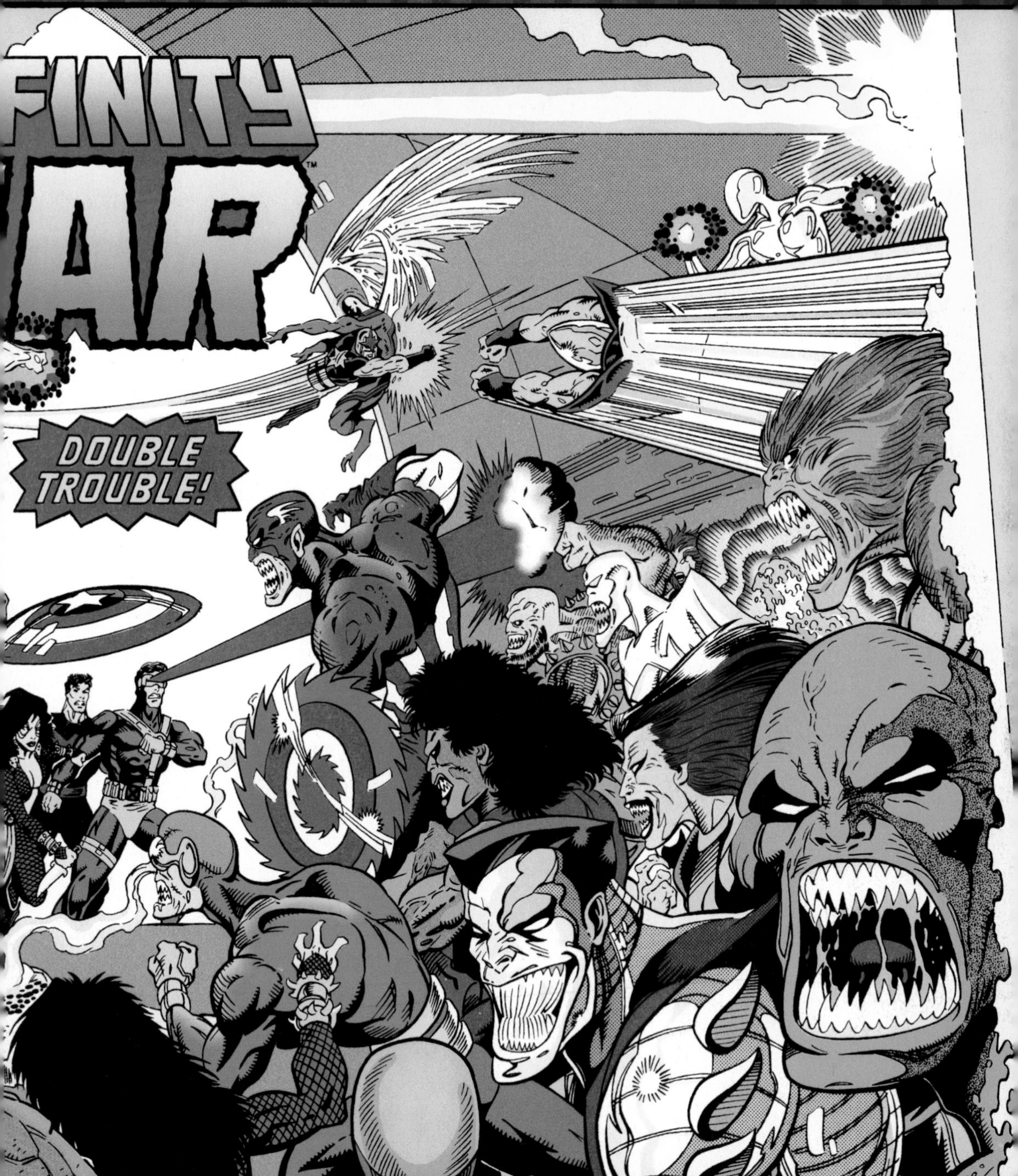
FINITY
AR
DOUBLE TROUBLE!

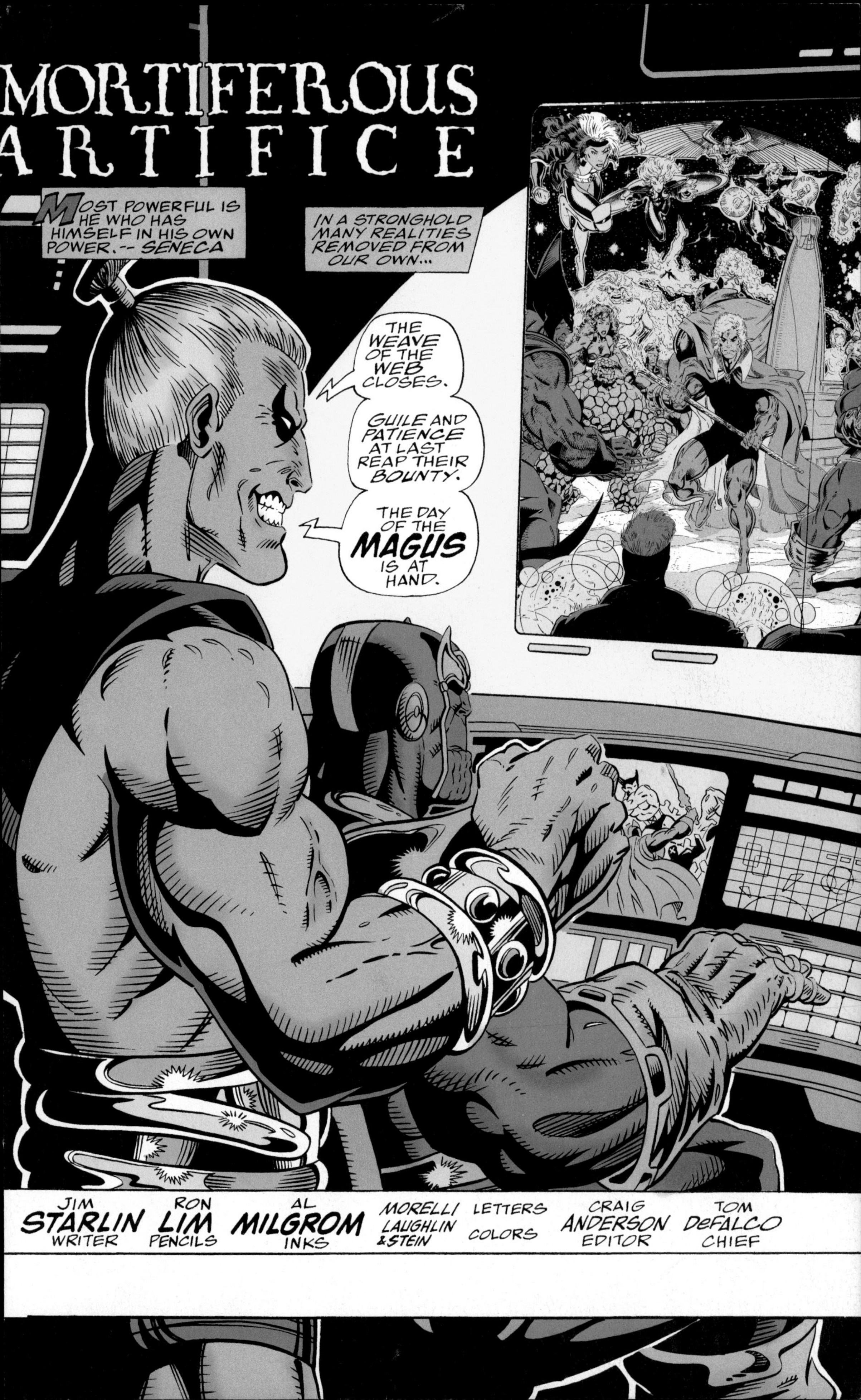
MORTIFEROUS ARTIFICE
MOST POWERFUL IS HE WHO HAS HIMSELF IN HIS OWN POWER. -- SENECA
IN A STRONGHOLD MANY REALITIES REMOVED FROM OUR OWN...
THE WEAVE OF THE WEB CLOSES.
GUILE AND PATIENCE AT LAST REAP THEIR BOUNTY.
THE DAY OF THE MAGUS IS AT HAND.
JIM STARLIN WRITER
RON LIM PENCILS
AL MILGROM INKS
MORELLI LETTERS
LAUGHLIN & STEIN COLORS
CRAIG ANDERSON EDITOR
TOM DeFALCO CHIEF

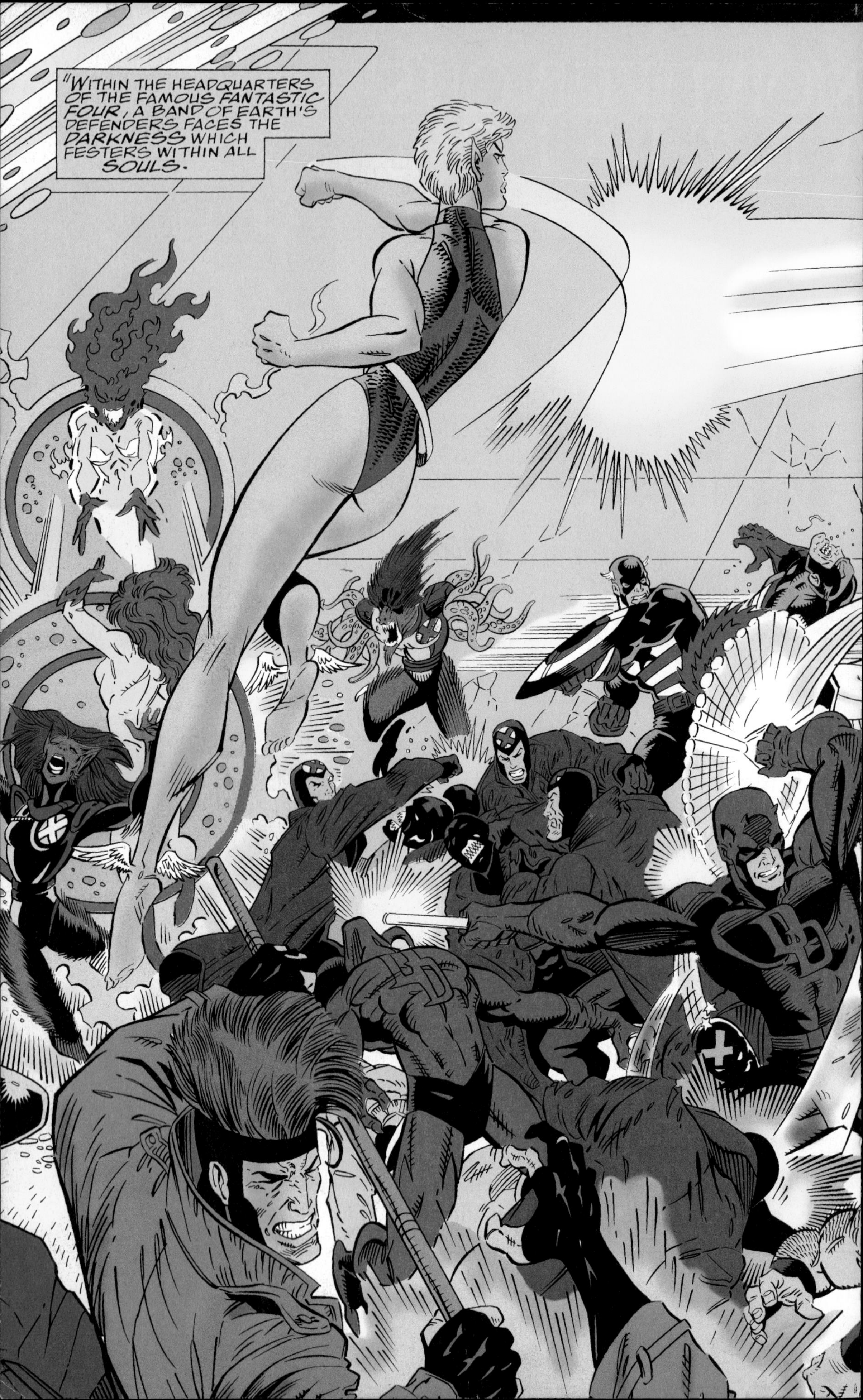
"WITHIN THE HEADQUARTERS OF THE FAMOUS FANTASTIC FOUR, A BAND OF EARTH'S DEFENDERS FACES THE DARKNESS WHICH FESTERS WITHIN ALL SOULS.

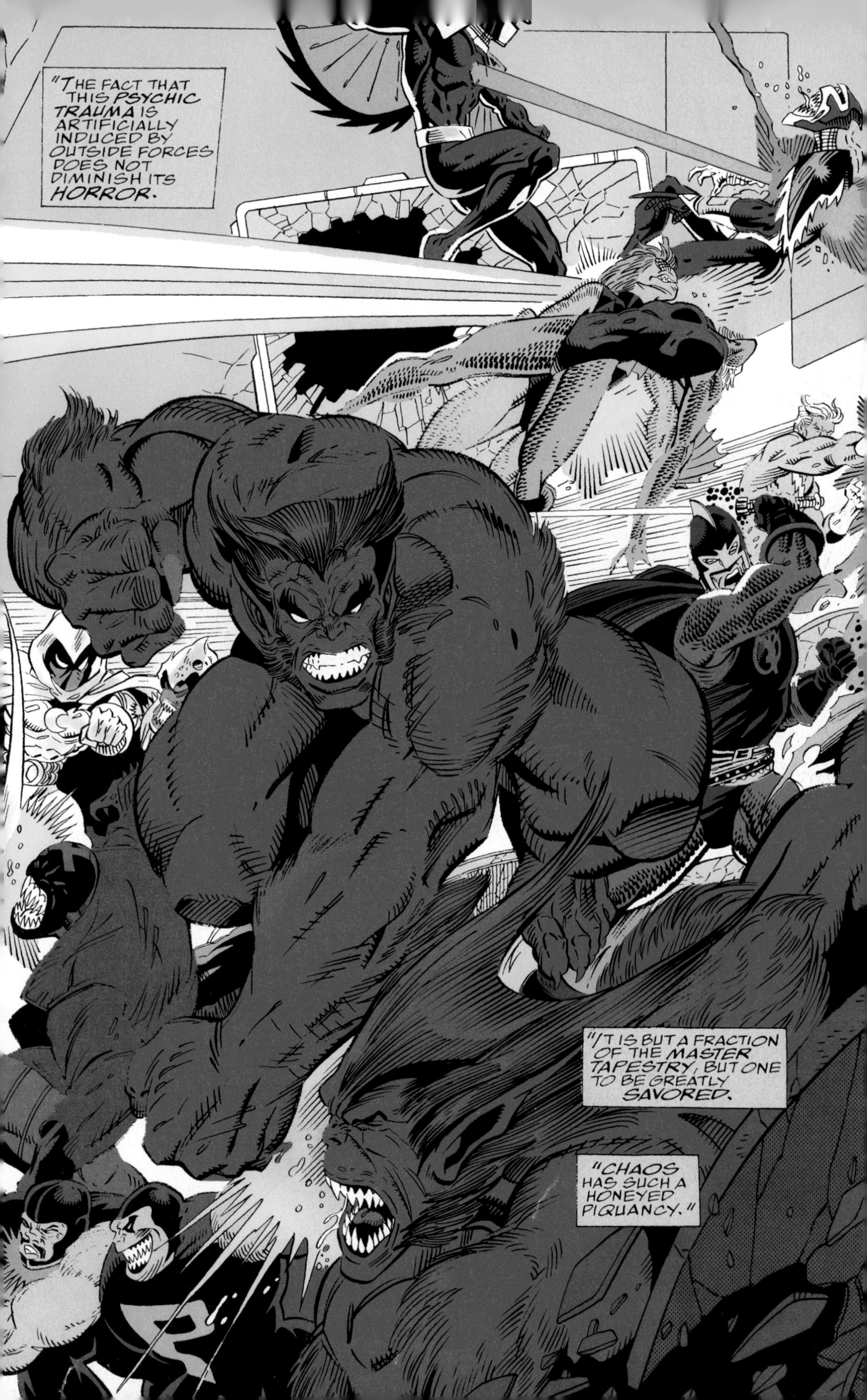
"THE FACT THAT THIS PSYCHIC TRAUMA IS ARTIFICIALLY INDUCED BY OUTSIDE FORCES DOES NOT DIMINISH ITS HORROR.
"IT IS BUT A FRACTION OF THE MASTER TAPESTRY, BUT ONE TO BE GREATLY SAVORED.
"CHAOS HAS SUCH A HONEYED PIQUANCY."

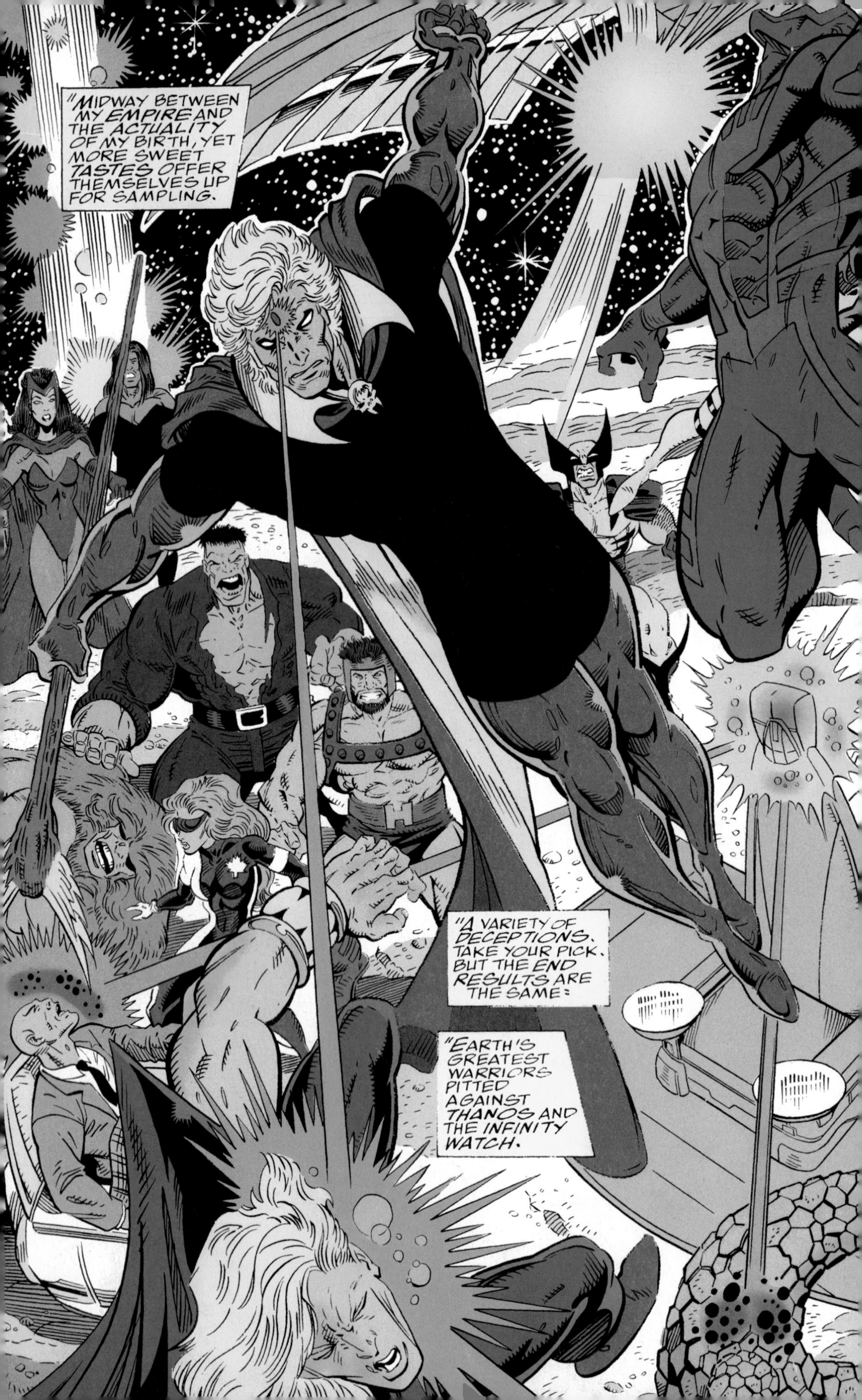
"MIDWAY BETWEEN MY EMPIRE AND THE ACTUALITY OF MY BIRTH, YET MORE SWEET TASTES OFFER THEMSELVES UP FOR SAMPLING.
"A VARIETY OF DECEPTIONS. TAKE YOUR PICK. BUT THE END RESULTS ARE THE SAME:
"EARTH'S GREATEST WARRIORS PITTED AGAINST THANOS AND THE INFINITY WATCH.

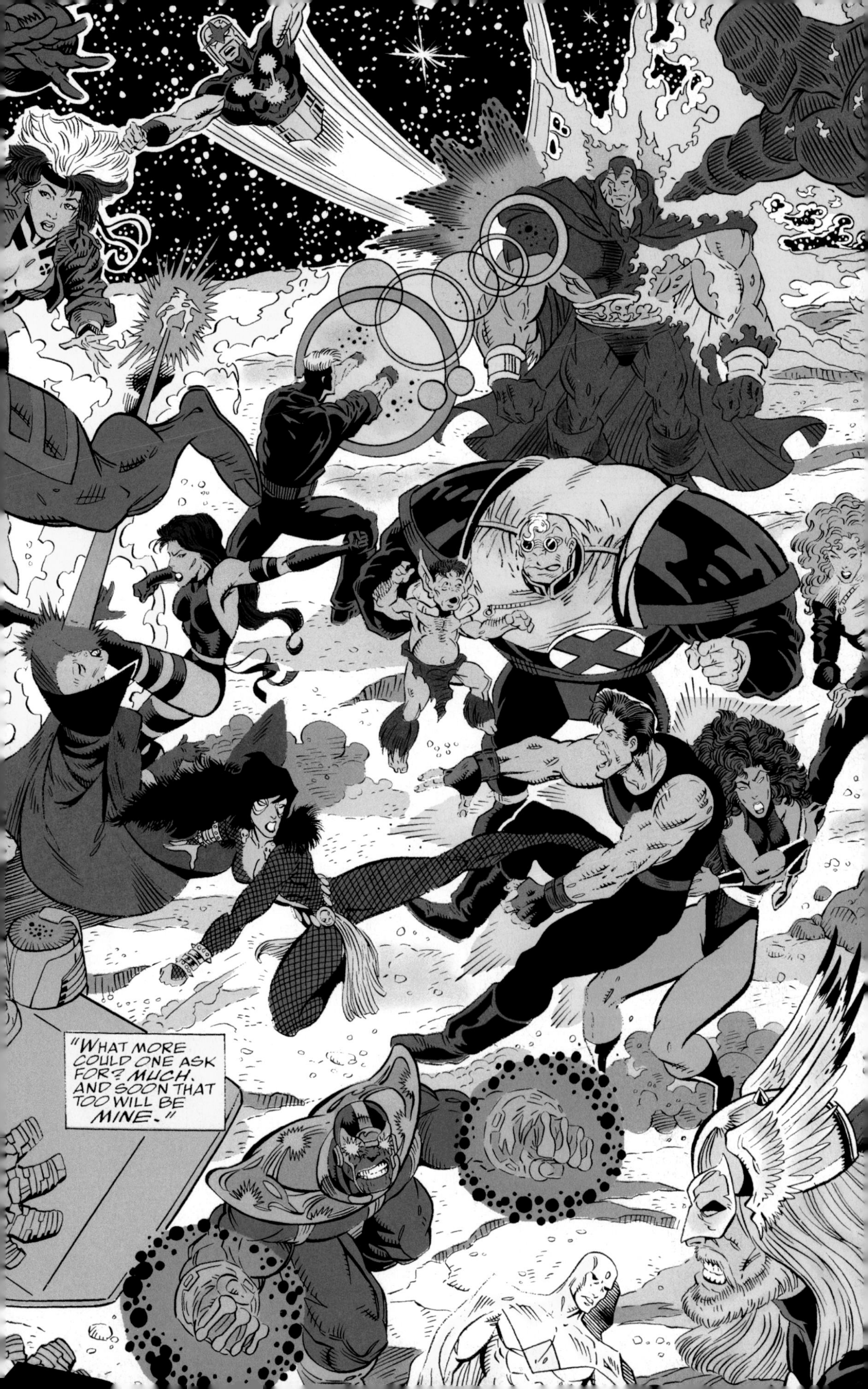
"WHAT MORE COULD ONE ASK FOR? MUCH. AND SOON THAT TOO WILL BE MINE."

HOW GOES IT WITH *PHASE III* OF THE OPERATION, MY *THRALL?*

HARMONICS CONTINUE TO BUILD.

DESIRED LEVELS OF CONCENTRATION ARE *IMMINENT.*

APPRISE ME INSTANTLY OF *FRUITION.*

KANG, COMPUTERS SHOW THAT OUR *FINAL DESTINATION* IS A MERE THREE DIMENSIONAL SEQUENCES AWAY.

I KNOW...

...YOU PRIMITIVE *CRETIN!*

I MAY HAVE INITIALLY NEEDED *DOOM'S DATA* TO BEGIN THIS QUEST AND HE HAS BEEN OF SOME *ASSISTANCE* SINCE, BUT...

...HIS *MEDIEVAL MANNERS* GRATE ON MY NERVES.

THE TIME TO *DISPOSE* OF HIM CAN'T COME SOON ENOUGH.

PREPARE TO *WARP.*

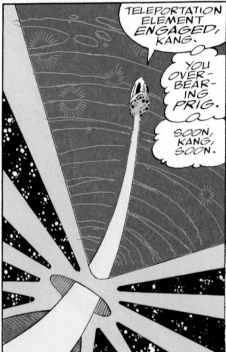

TELEPORTATION ELEMENT *ENGAGED,* KANG.

YOU OVER-BEAR-ING *PRIG.*

SOON, KANG, SOON.

I HAVE ONCE AGAIN PICKED UP THAT *SCANNER ABERRATION,* MASTER.

I THINK--

FORGET IT!

THE TIME HAS COME TO CHECK ON *GALACTUS'S CONTINGENT.*

THEY WILL SOON ONCE AGAIN BE *NEEDED* ON STAGE.

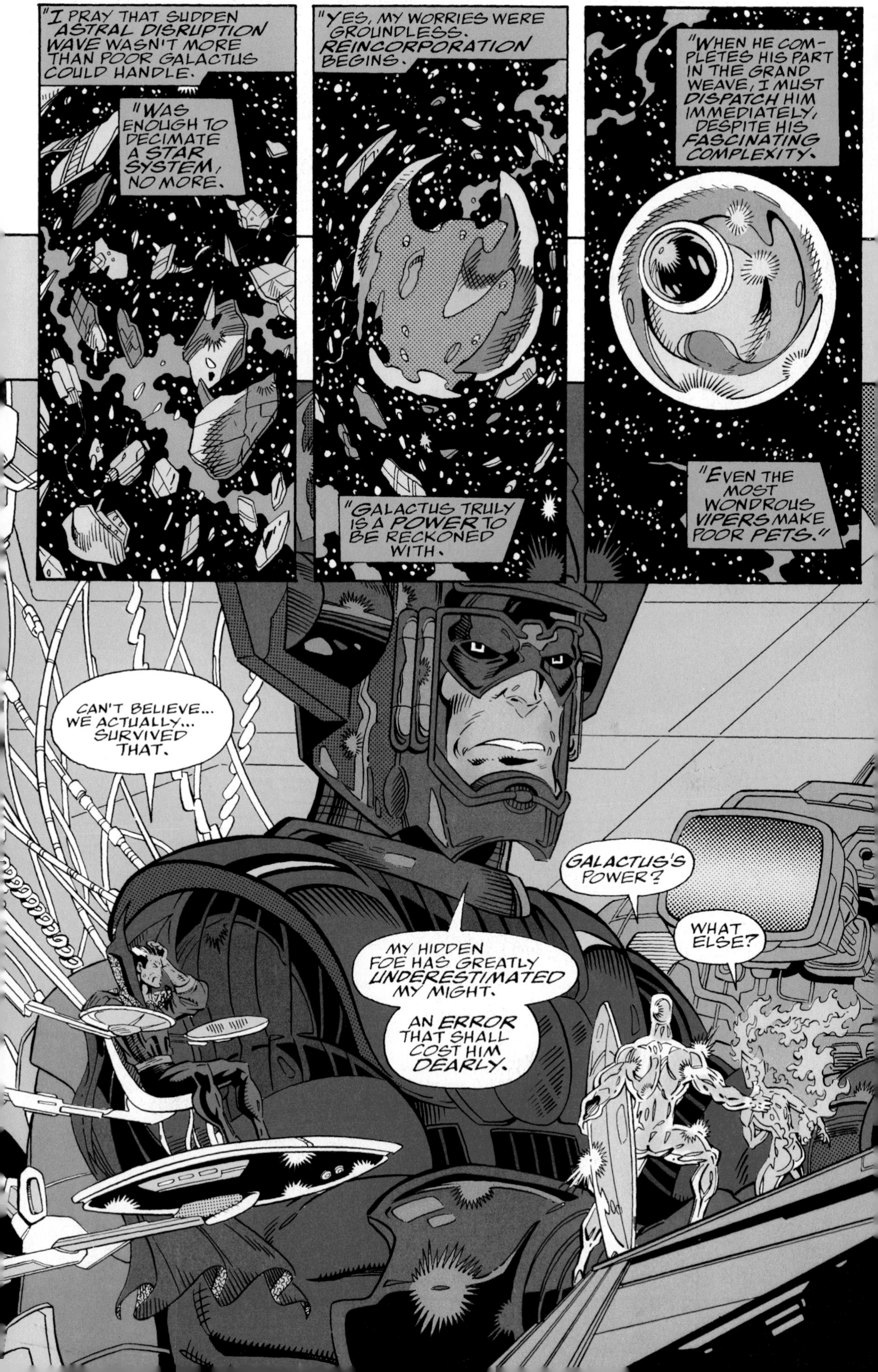

"I PRAY THAT SUDDEN ASTRAL DISRUPTION WAVE WASN'T MORE THAN POOR GALACTUS COULD HANDLE.
"WAS ENOUGH TO DECIMATE A STAR SYSTEM, NO MORE.
"YES, MY WORRIES WERE GROUNDLESS. REINCORPORATION BEGINS.
"GALACTUS TRULY IS A POWER TO BE RECKONED WITH.
"WHEN HE COMPLETES HIS PART IN THE GRAND WEAVE, I MUST DISPATCH HIM IMMEDIATELY, DESPITE HIS FASCINATING COMPLEXITY.
"EVEN THE MOST WONDROUS VIPERS MAKE POOR PETS."
CAN'T BELIEVE... WE ACTUALLY... SURVIVED THAT.
GALACTUS'S POWER?
WHAT ELSE?
MY HIDDEN FOE HAS GREATLY UNDERESTIMATED MY MIGHT.
AN ERROR THAT SHALL COST HIM DEARLY.

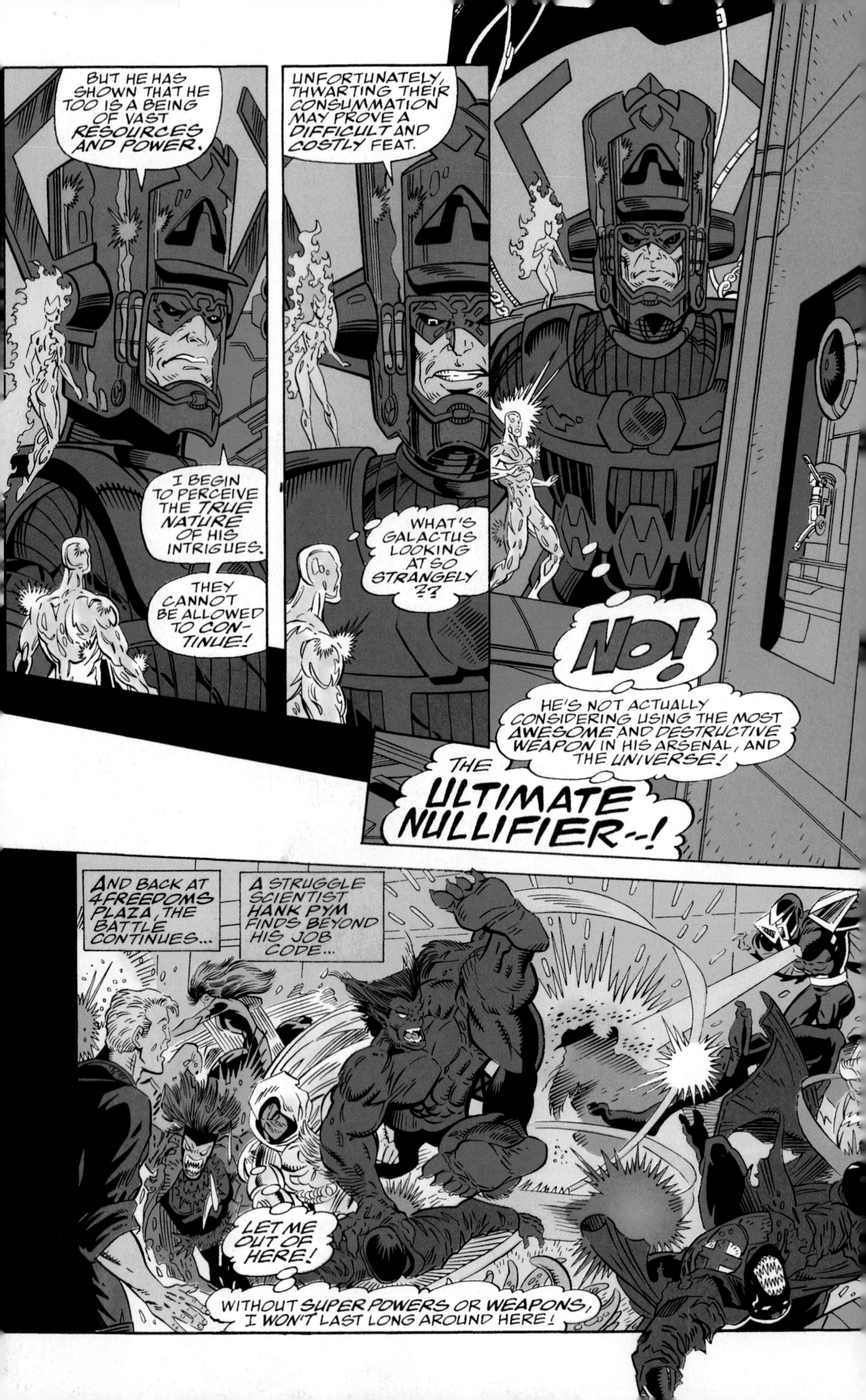

BUT HE HAS SHOWN THAT HE TOO IS A BEING OF VAST RESOURCES AND POWER.
I BEGIN TO PERCEIVE THE TRUE NATURE OF HIS INTRIGUES.
THEY CANNOT BE ALLOWED TO CONTINUE!
UNFORTUNATELY, THWARTING THEIR CONSUMMATION MAY PROVE A DIFFICULT AND COSTLY FEAT.
WHAT'S GALACTUS LOOKING AT SO STRANGELY ??
NO!
HE'S NOT ACTUALLY CONSIDERING USING THE MOST AWESOME AND DESTRUCTIVE WEAPON IN HIS ARSENAL, AND THE UNIVERSE!
THE ULTIMATE NULLIFIER--!
AND BACK AT 4 FREEDOMS PLAZA, THE BATTLE CONTINUES...
A STRUGGLE SCIENTIST HANK PYM FINDS BEYOND HIS JOB CODE...
LET ME OUT OF HERE!
WITHOUT SUPER POWERS OR WEAPONS, I WON'T LAST LONG AROUND HERE!

LET THE *TIGHTS*-AND-*MUSCLE CROWD* WORK IT OUT BETWEEN THEM-SELVES.

I'M TAKING A *POWDER* INTO THE *COMPUTER ROOM* UNTIL THIS RUCKUS IS SETTLED!

SAY WHAT...?

NEW *TELEMETRY* COMING IN ON RICHARDS' SCANNERS.

INCREDIBLE!

THEY'RE PICKING UP ENERGY BROAD-CASTS TO EVERY STAR SYSTEM IN THE MILKY WAY GALAXY!

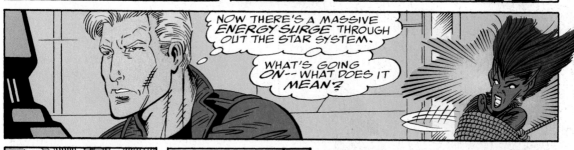

NOW THERE'S A MASSIVE *ENERGY SURGE* THROUGH OUT THE STAR SYSTEM.

WHAT'S GOING *ON*-- WHAT DOES IT *MEAN?*

THERE'S A *SHIFT* IN THE SURGE'S *VIBRATORY PATTERN!*

APPEARS TO BE *MYRIAD* PEAKS AND *DIPS* WITHIN THE *HARMONIC STRUCTURE* ITSELF.

THE BROADCAST IS OBVIOUSLY TRYING TO MATCH *FREQUENCIES* WITH AN EXISTING PATTERN.

IT'S ALMOST AS IF IT WERE...

GOOD LORD!

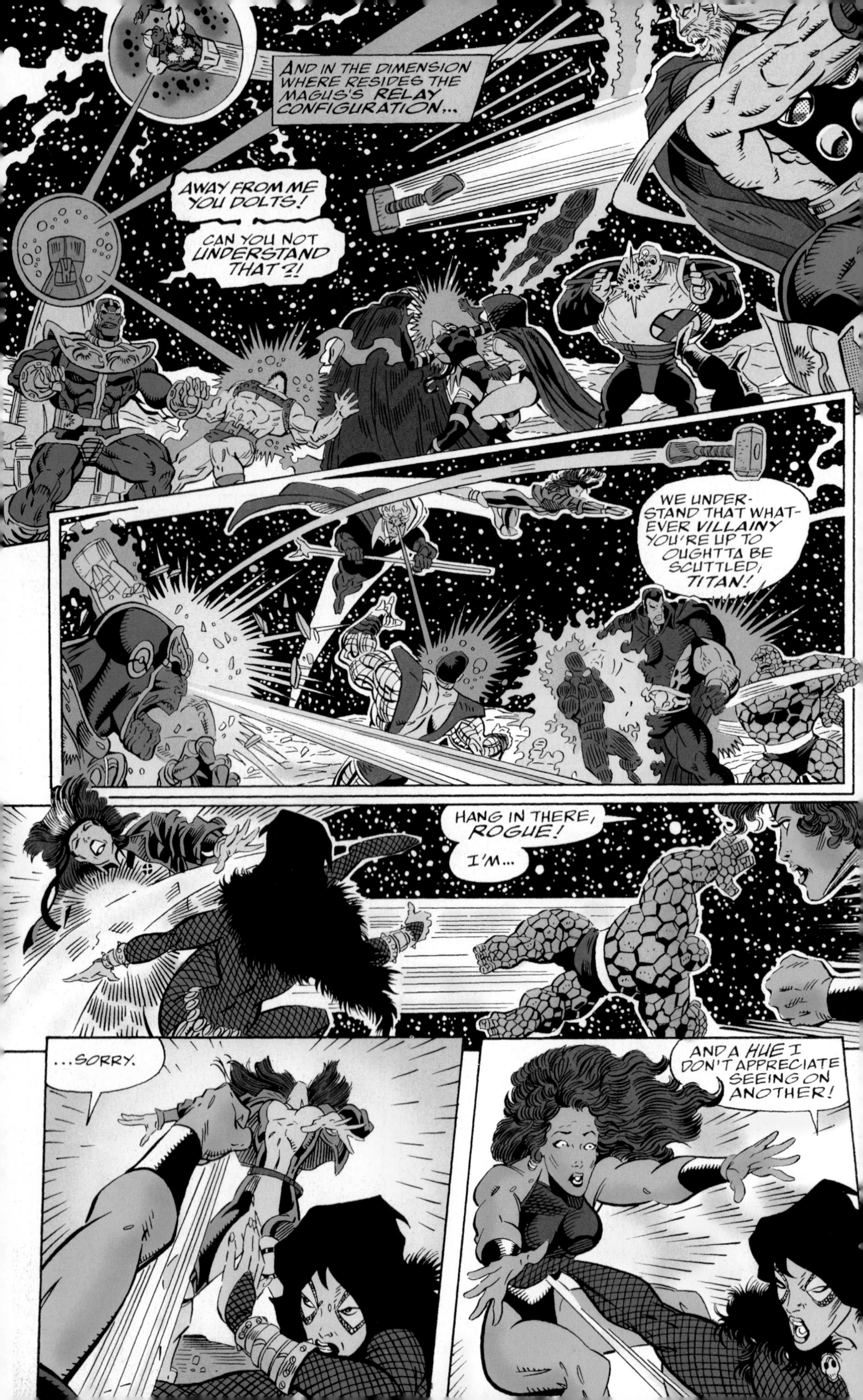
AND IN THE DIMENSION WHERE RESIDES THE MAGUS'S RELAY CONFIGURATION...
AWAY FROM ME YOU DOLTS!
CAN YOU NOT UNDERSTAND THAT?!
WE UNDERSTAND THAT WHATEVER VILLAINY YOU'RE UP TO OUGHTTA BE SCUTTLED, TITAN!
HANG IN THERE, ROGUE!
I'M...
...SORRY.
AND A HUE I DON'T APPRECIATE SEEING ON ANOTHER!

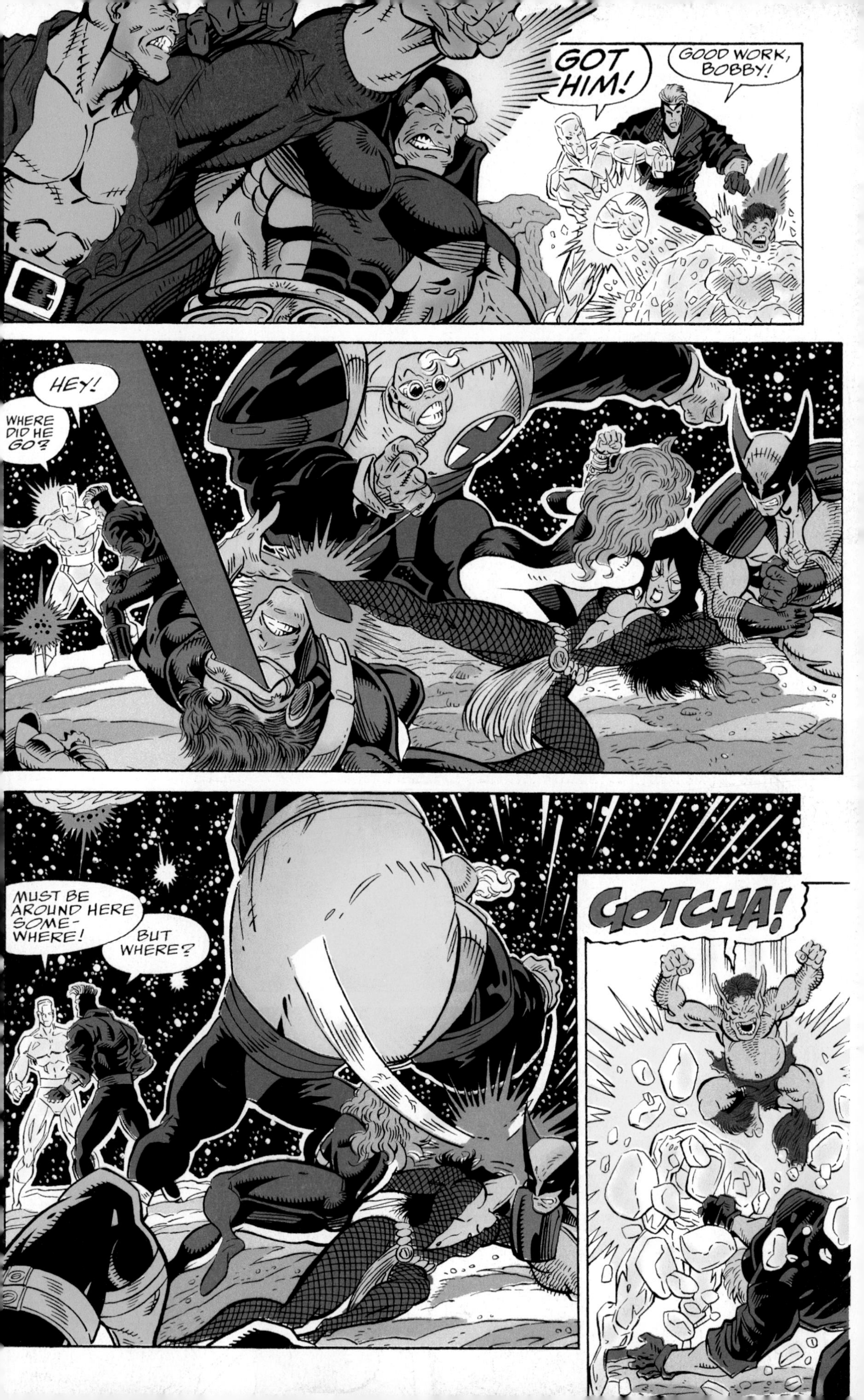
GOT HIM!
GOOD WORK, BOBBY!
HEY!
WHERE DID HE GO?
MUST BE AROUND HERE SOME-WHERE!
BUT WHERE?
GOTCHA!

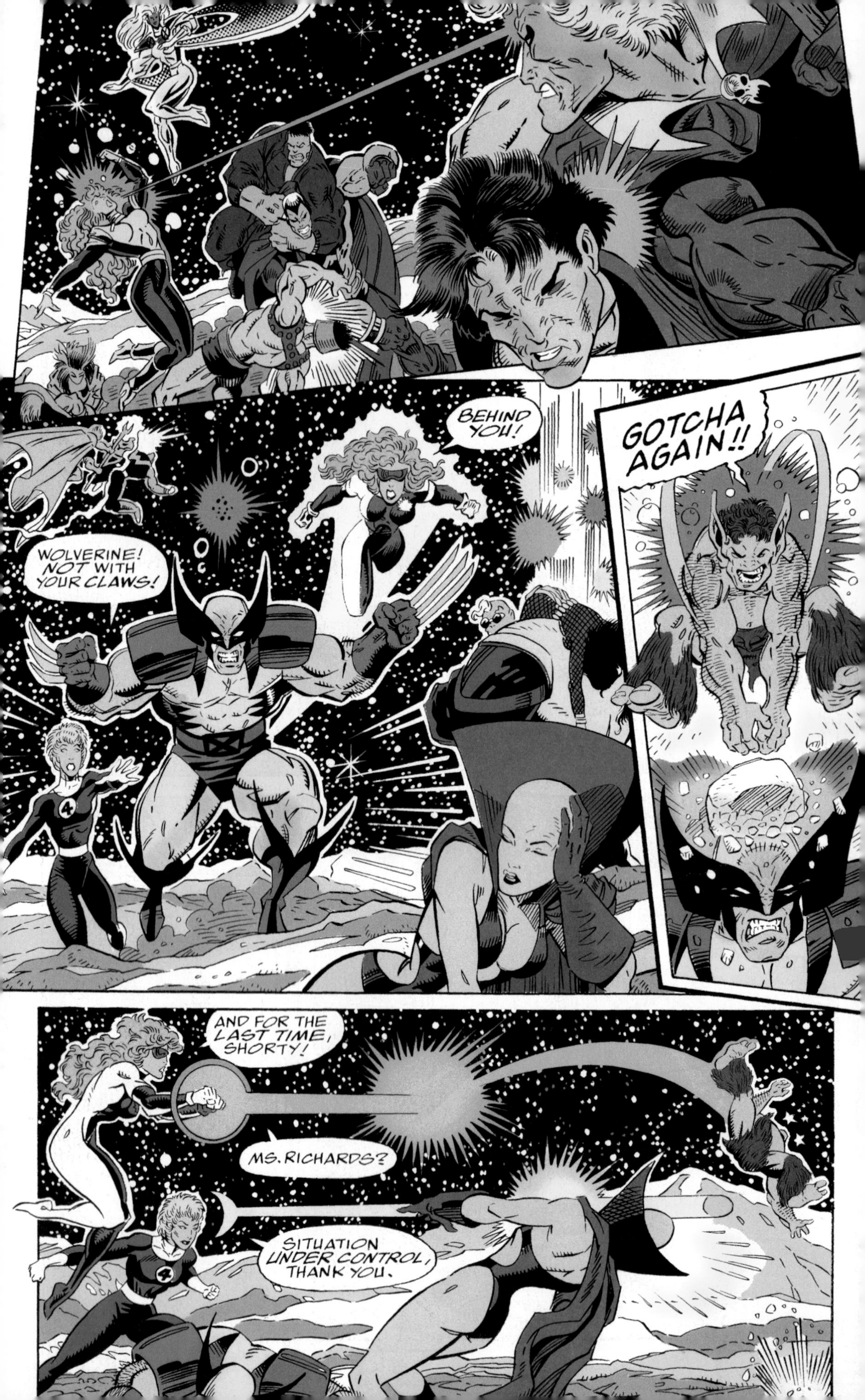
BEHIND YOU!
GOTCHA AGAIN!!
WOLVERINE! NOT WITH YOUR CLAWS!
AND FOR THE LAST TIME, SHORTY!
MS. RICHARDS?
SITUATION UNDER CONTROL, THANK YOU.

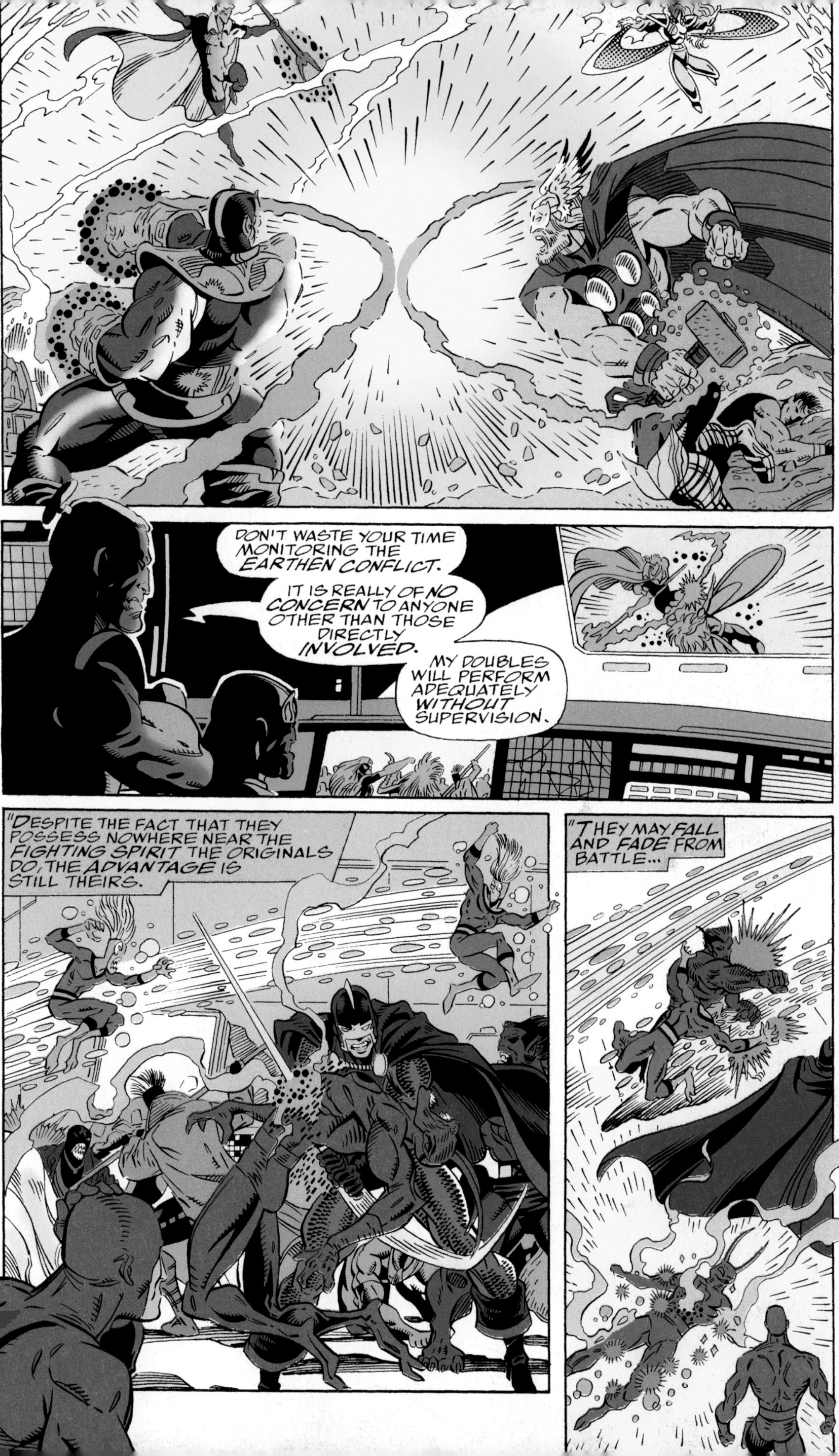

DON'T WASTE YOUR TIME MONITORING THE EARTHEN CONFLICT.
IT IS REALLY OF NO CONCERN TO ANYONE OTHER THAN THOSE DIRECTLY INVOLVED.
MY DOUBLES WILL PERFORM ADEQUATELY WITHOUT SUPERVISION.
"DESPITE THE FACT THAT THEY POSSESS NOWHERE NEAR THE FIGHTING SPIRIT THE ORIGINALS DO, THE ADVANTAGE IS STILL THEIRS.
"THEY MAY FALL AND FADE FROM BATTLE...

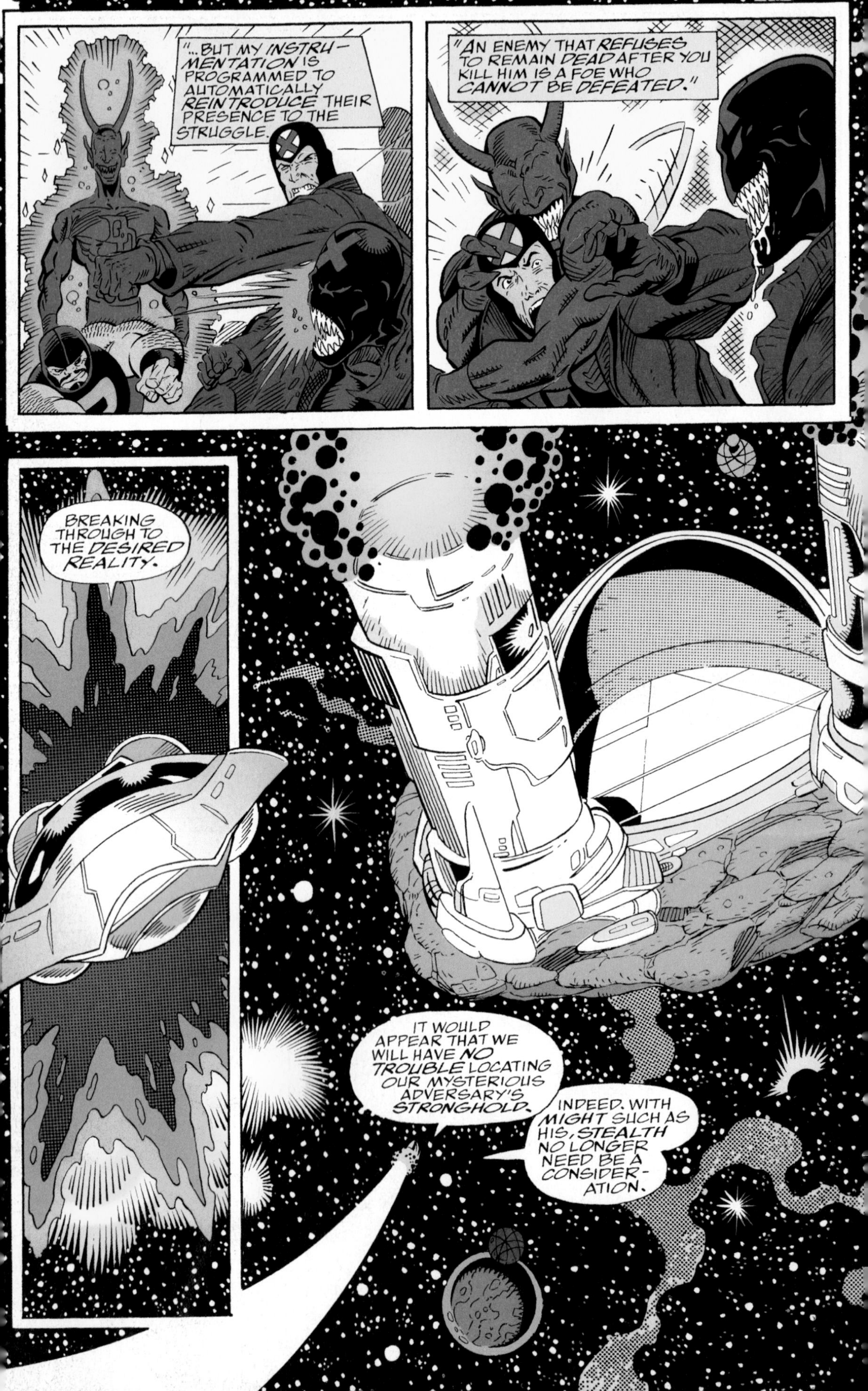
"...BUT MY INSTRUMENTATION IS PROGRAMMED TO AUTOMATICALLY REINTRODUCE THEIR PRESENCE TO THE STRUGGLE.
"AN ENEMY THAT REFUSES TO REMAIN DEAD AFTER YOU KILL HIM IS A FOE WHO CANNOT BE DEFEATED."
BREAKING THROUGH TO THE DESIRED REALITY.
IT WOULD APPEAR THAT WE WILL HAVE NO TROUBLE LOCATING OUR MYSTERIOUS ADVERSARY'S STRONGHOLD.
INDEED. WITH MIGHT SUCH AS HIS, STEALTH NO LONGER NEED BE A CONSIDERATION.

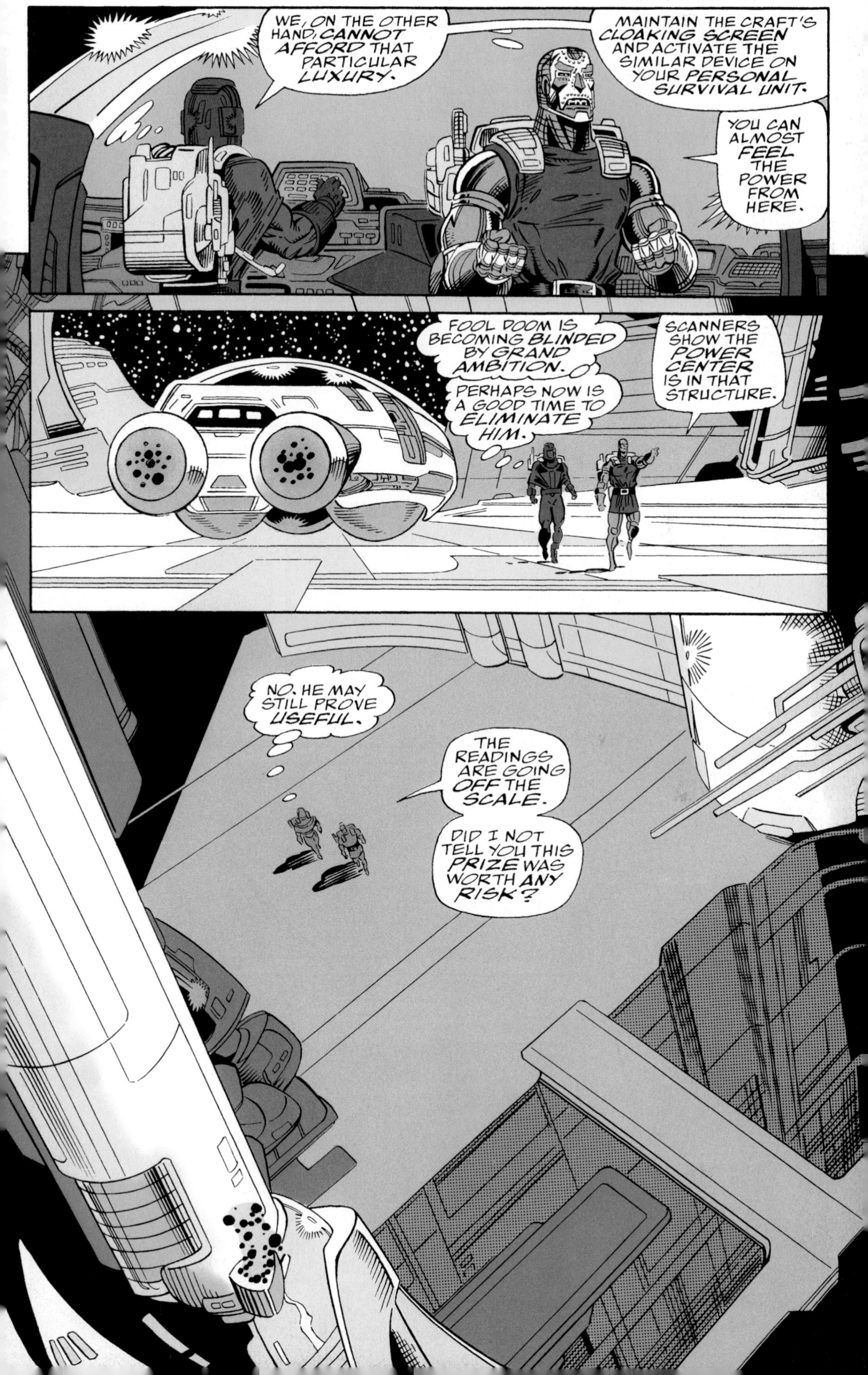
WE, ON THE OTHER HAND, CANNOT AFFORD THAT PARTICULAR LUXURY.
MAINTAIN THE CRAFT'S CLOAKING SCREEN AND ACTIVATE THE SIMILAR DEVICE ON YOUR PERSONAL SURVIVAL UNIT.
YOU CAN ALMOST FEEL THE POWER FROM HERE.
FOOL DOOM IS BECOMING BLINDED BY GRAND AMBITION.
PERHAPS NOW IS A GOOD TIME TO ELIMINATE HIM.
SCANNERS SHOW THE POWER CENTER IS IN THAT STRUCTURE.
NO. HE MAY STILL PROVE USEFUL.
THE READINGS ARE GOING OFF THE SCALE.
DID I NOT TELL YOU THIS PRIZE WAS WORTH ANY RISK?

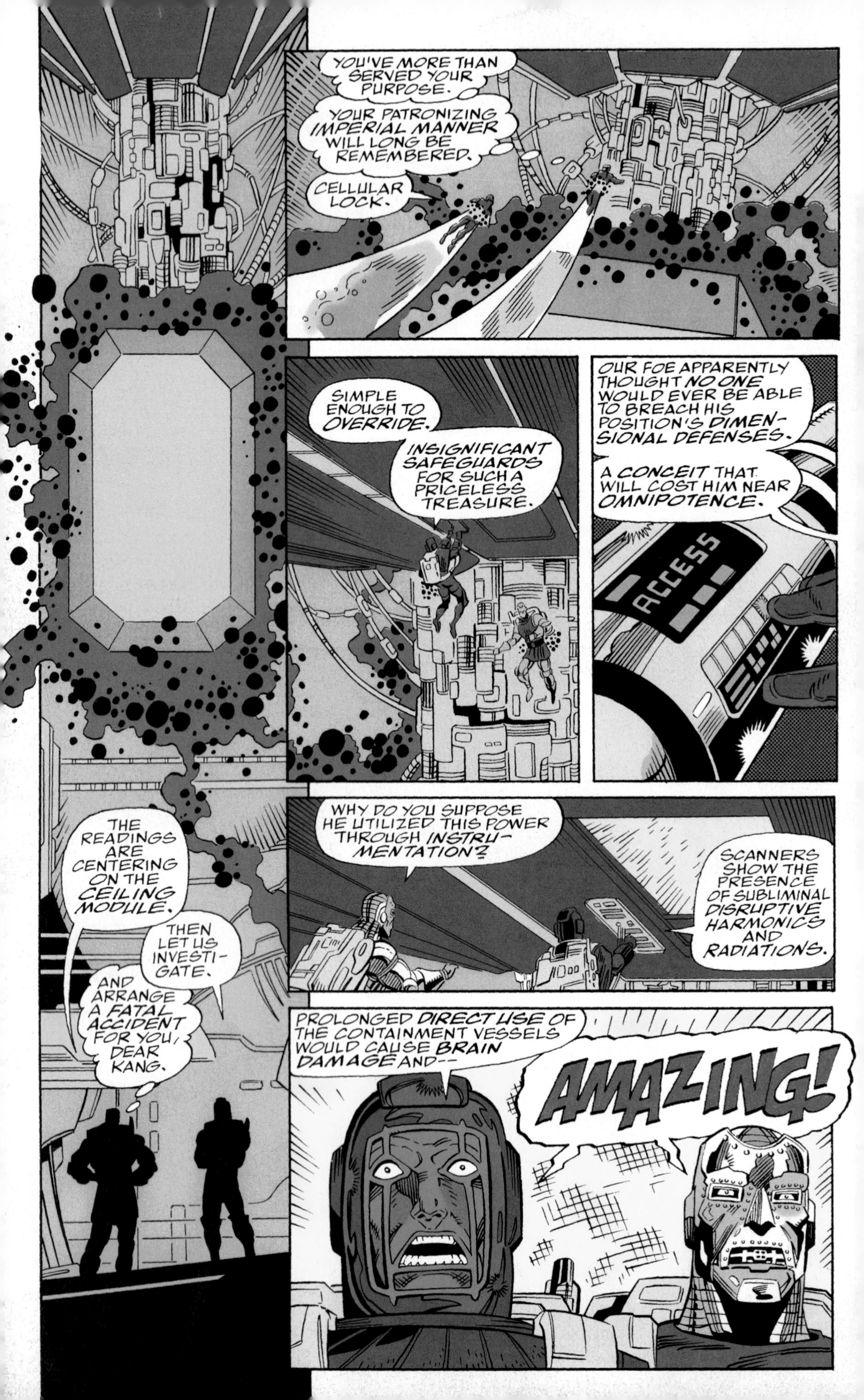
YOU'VE MORE THAN SERVED YOUR PURPOSE.
YOUR PATRONIZING IMPERIAL MANNER WILL LONG BE REMEMBERED.
CELLULAR LOCK.
SIMPLE ENOUGH TO OVERRIDE.
INSIGNIFICANT SAFEGUARDS FOR SUCH A PRICELESS TREASURE.
OUR FOE APPARENTLY THOUGHT NO ONE WOULD EVER BE ABLE TO BREACH HIS POSITION'S DIMENSIONAL DEFENSES.
A CONCEIT THAT WILL COST HIM NEAR OMNIPOTENCE.
ACCESS
THE READINGS ARE CENTERING ON THE CEILING MODULE.
THEN LET US INVESTIGATE.
AND ARRANGE A FATAL ACCIDENT FOR YOU, DEAR KANG.
WHY DO YOU SUPPOSE HE UTILIZED THIS POWER THROUGH INSTRUMENTATION?
SCANNERS SHOW THE PRESENCE OF SUBLIMINAL DISRUPTIVE HARMONICS AND RADIATIONS.
PROLONGED DIRECT USE OF THE CONTAINMENT VESSELS WOULD CAUSE BRAIN DAMAGE AND--
AMAZING!

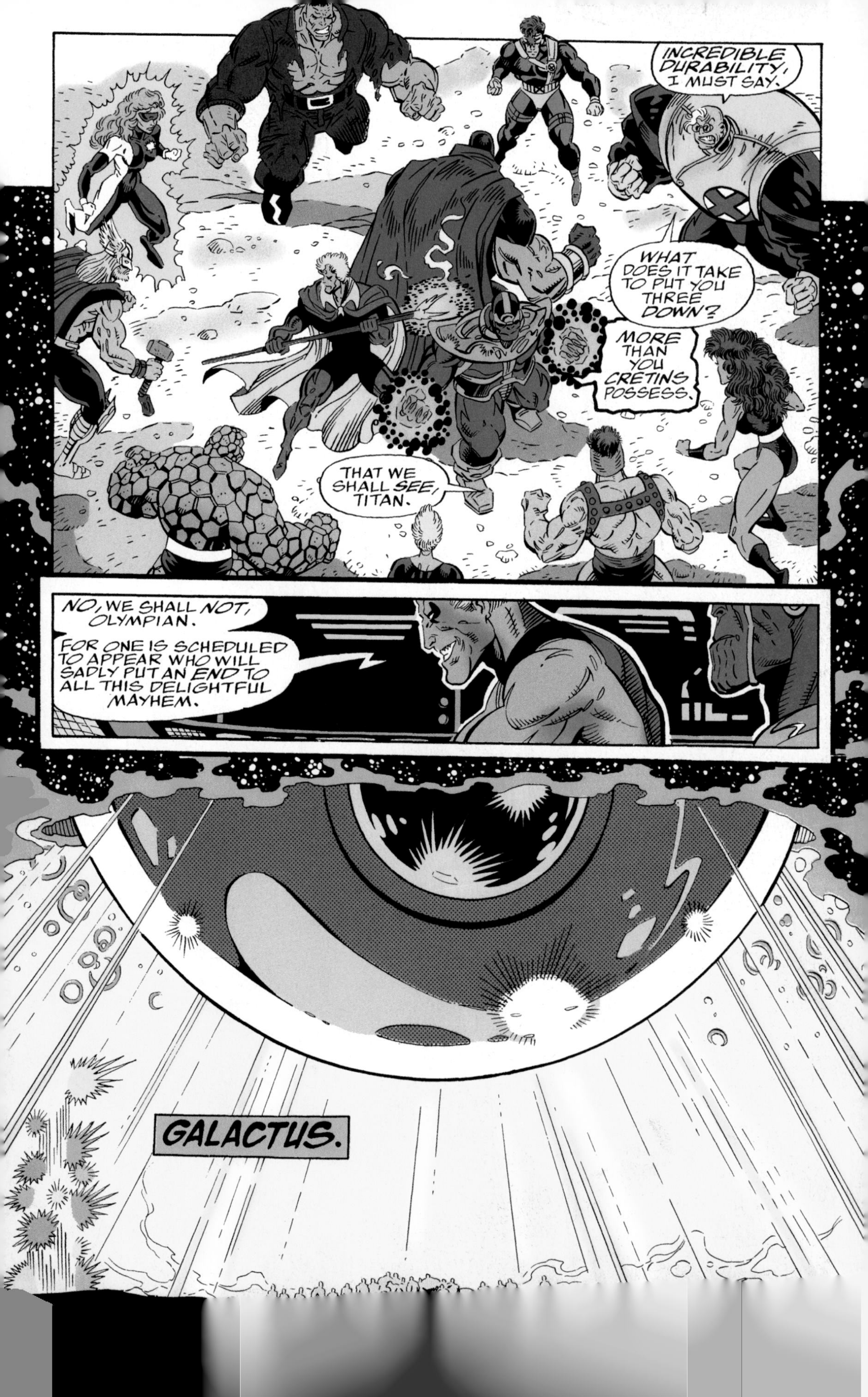
INCREDIBLE DURABILITY, I MUST SAY.
WHAT DOES IT TAKE TO PUT YOU THREE DOWN?
MORE THAN YOU CRETINS POSSESS.
THAT WE SHALL SEE, TITAN.
NO, WE SHALL NOT, OLYMPIAN.
FOR ONE IS SCHEDULED TO APPEAR WHO WILL SADLY PUT AN END TO ALL THIS DELIGHTFUL MAYHEM.
GALACTUS.

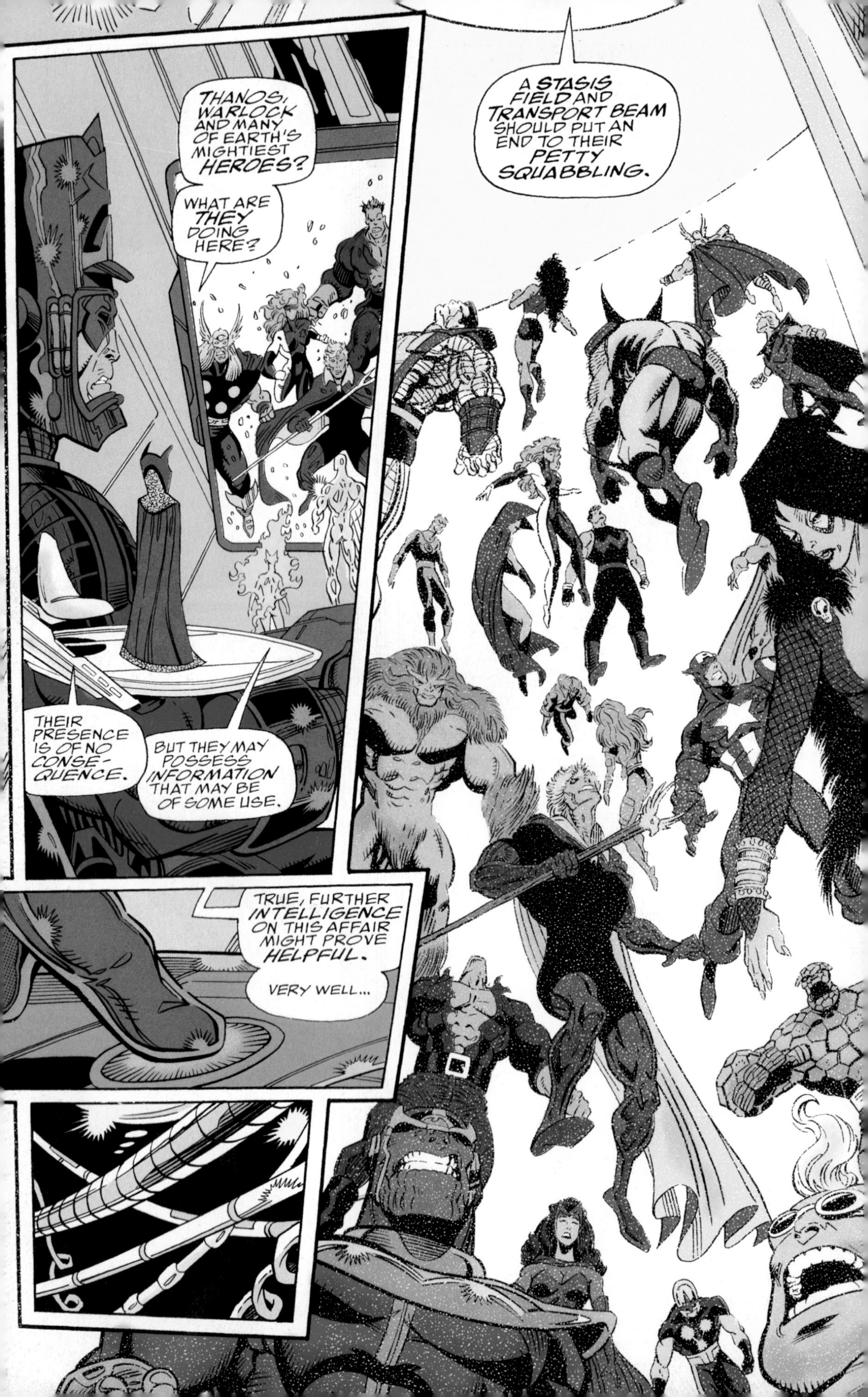
THANOS, WARLOCK AND MANY OF EARTH'S MIGHTIEST HEROES?
WHAT ARE THEY DOING HERE?
THEIR PRESENCE IS OF NO CONSE-QUENCE.
BUT THEY MAY POSSESS INFORMATION THAT MAY BE OF SOME USE.
A STASIS FIELD AND TRANSPORT BEAM SHOULD PUT AN END TO THEIR PETTY SQUABBLING.
TRUE, FURTHER INTELLIGENCE ON THIS AFFAIR MIGHT PROVE HELPFUL.
VERY WELL...

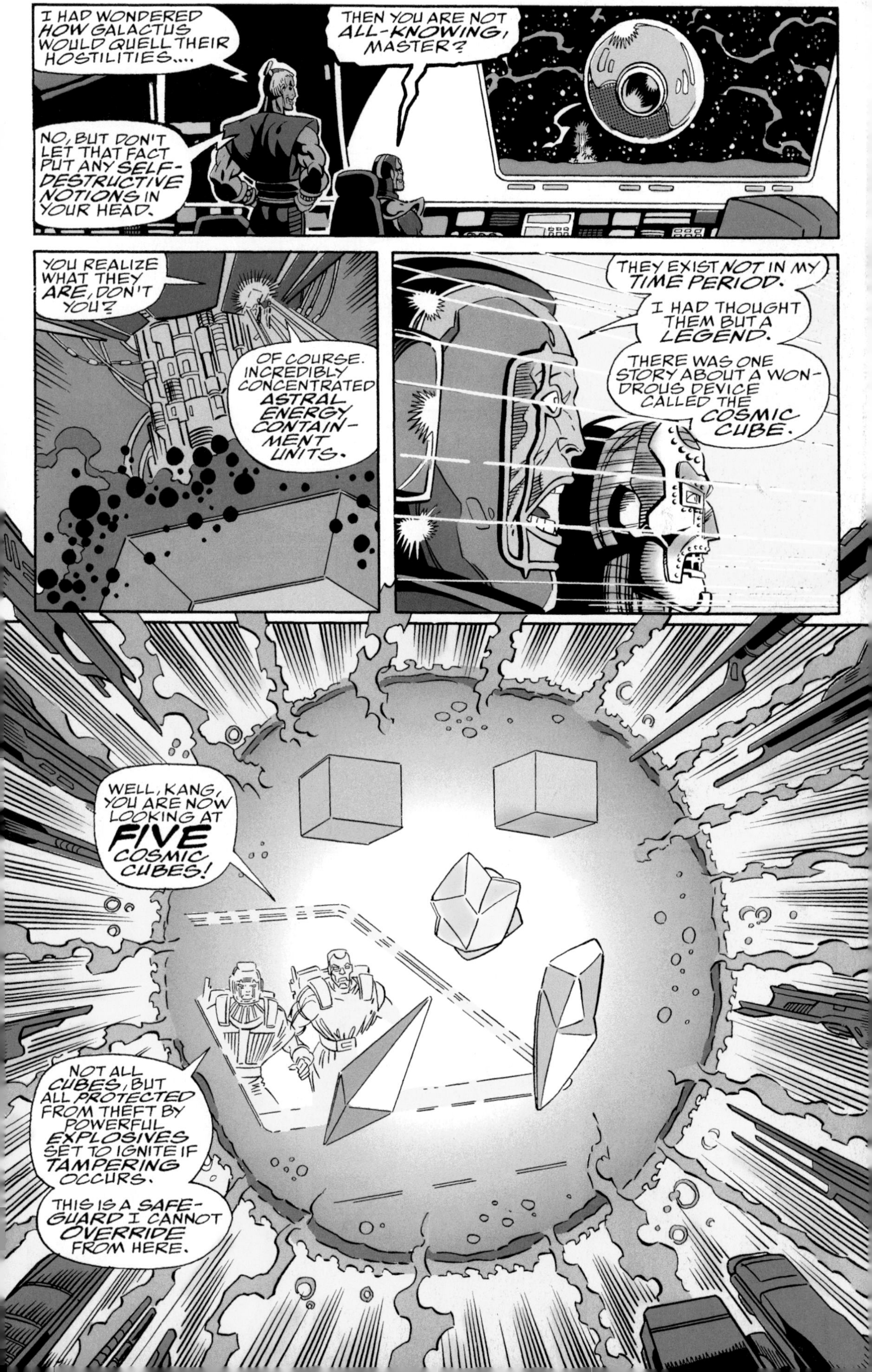
I HAD WONDERED HOW GALACTUS WOULD QUELL THEIR HOSTILITIES....
THEN YOU ARE NOT ALL-KNOWING, MASTER?
NO, BUT DON'T LET THAT FACT PUT ANY SELF-DESTRUCTIVE NOTIONS IN YOUR HEAD.
YOU REALIZE WHAT THEY ARE, DON'T YOU?
OF COURSE. INCREDIBLY CONCENTRATED ASTRAL ENERGY CONTAINMENT UNITS.
THEY EXIST NOT IN MY TIME PERIOD.
I HAD THOUGHT THEM BUT A LEGEND.
THERE WAS ONE STORY ABOUT A WONDROUS DEVICE CALLED THE COSMIC CUBE.
WELL, KANG, YOU ARE NOW LOOKING AT FIVE COSMIC CUBES!
NOT ALL CUBES, BUT ALL PROTECTED FROM THEFT BY POWERFUL EXPLOSIVES SET TO IGNITE IF TAMPERING OCCURS.
THIS IS A SAFEGUARD I CANNOT OVERRIDE FROM HERE.

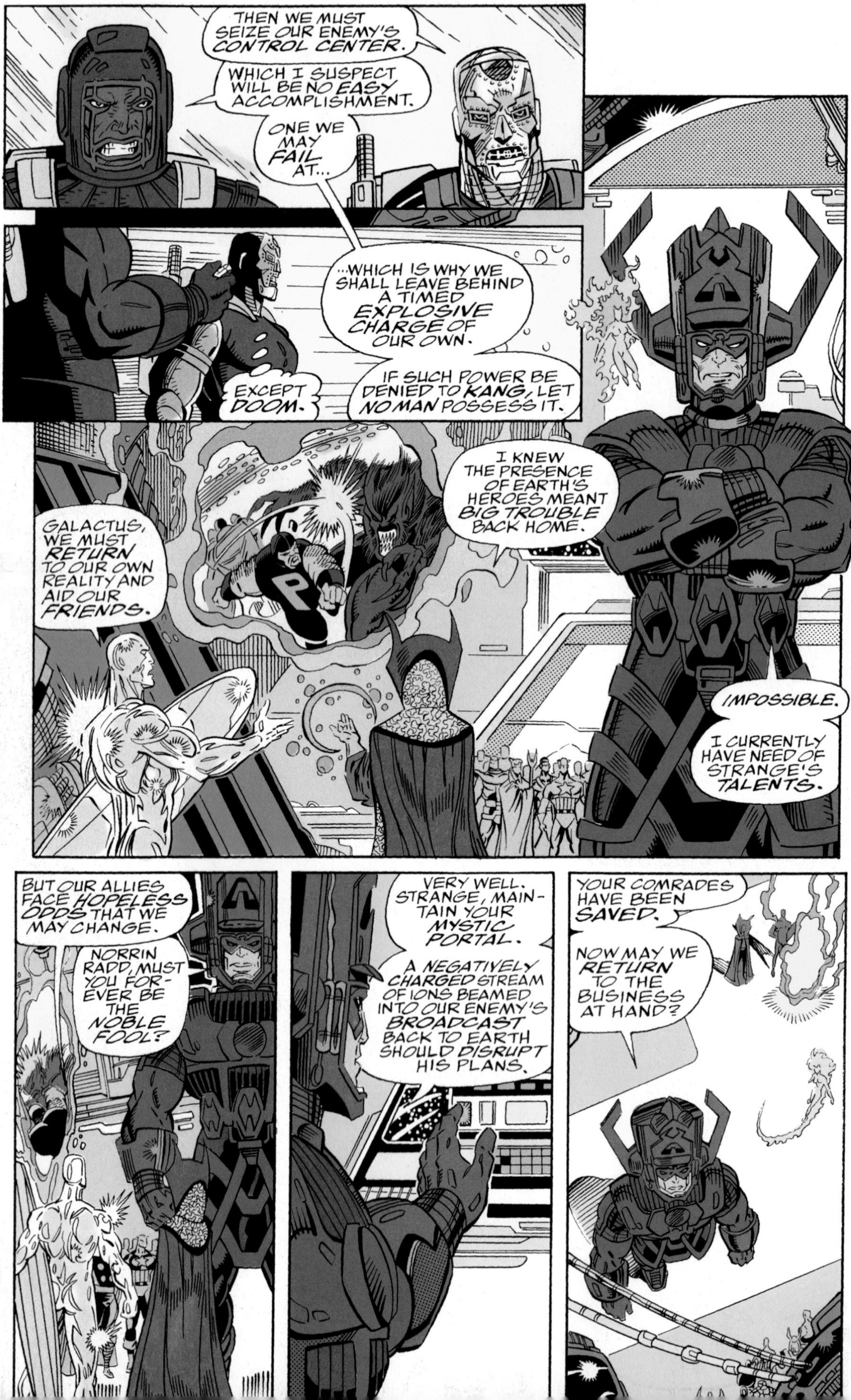
THEN WE MUST SEIZE OUR ENEMY'S CONTROL CENTER.
WHICH I SUSPECT WILL BE NO EASY ACCOMPLISHMENT.
ONE WE MAY FAIL AT...
...WHICH IS WHY WE SHALL LEAVE BEHIND A TIMED EXPLOSIVE CHARGE OF OUR OWN.
EXCEPT DOOM.
IF SUCH POWER BE DENIED TO KANG, LET NO MAN POSSESS IT.
GALACTUS, WE MUST RETURN TO OUR OWN REALITY AND AID OUR FRIENDS.
I KNEW THE PRESENCE OF EARTH'S HEROES MEANT BIG TROUBLE BACK HOME.
IMPOSSIBLE.
I CURRENTLY HAVE NEED OF STRANGE'S TALENTS.
BUT OUR ALLIES FACE HOPELESS ODDS THAT WE MAY CHANGE.
NORRIN RADD, MUST YOU FOREVER BE THE NOBLE FOOL?
VERY WELL. STRANGE, MAINTAIN YOUR MYSTIC PORTAL.
A NEGATIVELY CHARGED STREAM OF IONS BEAMED INTO OUR ENEMY'S BROADCAST BACK TO EARTH SHOULD DISRUPT HIS PLANS.
YOUR COMRADES HAVE BEEN SAVED.
NOW MAY WE RETURN TO THE BUSINESS AT HAND?

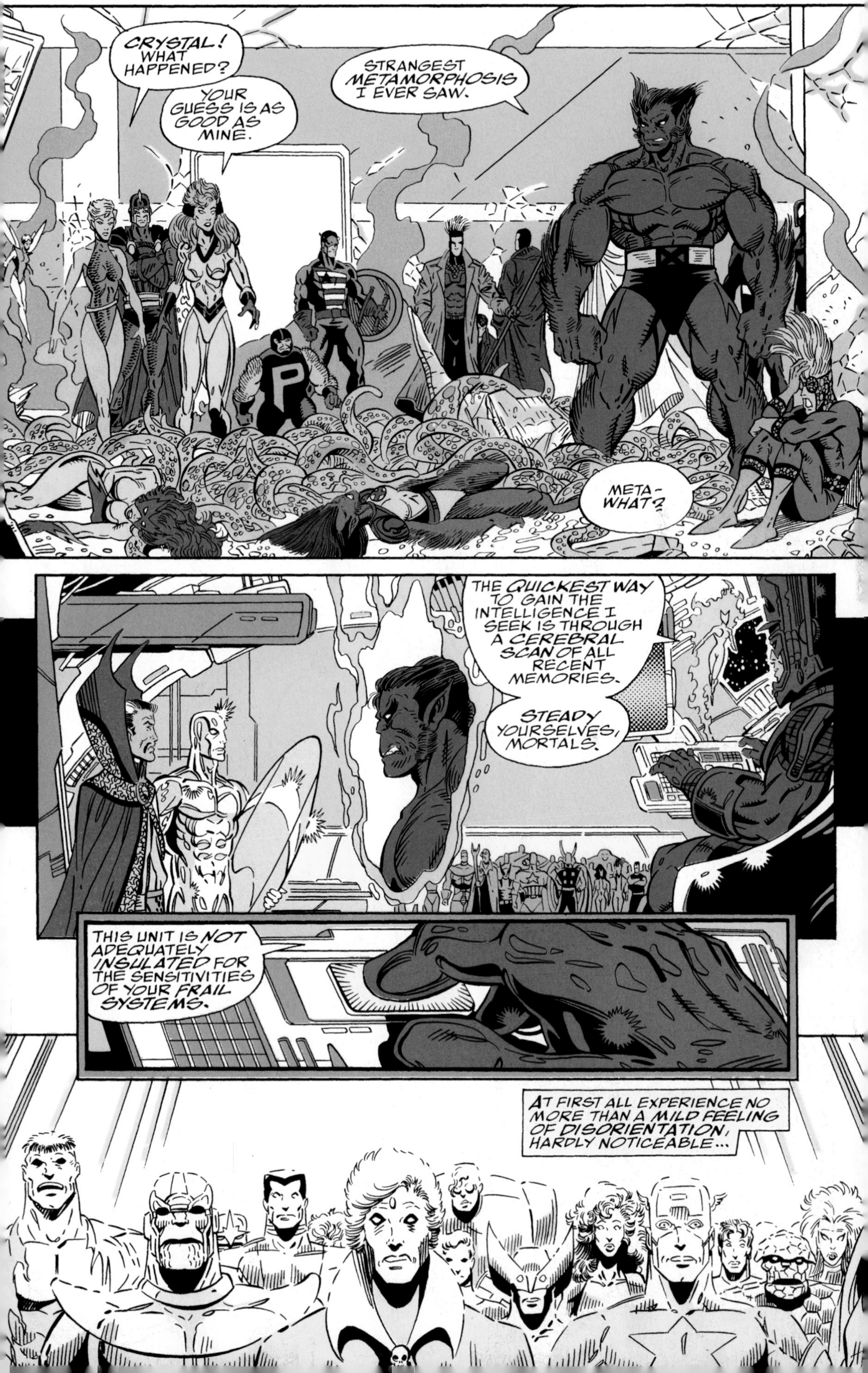
CRYSTAL! WHAT HAPPENED?
YOUR GUESS IS AS GOOD AS MINE.
STRANGEST METAMORPHOSIS I EVER SAW.
META-WHAT?
THE QUICKEST WAY TO GAIN THE INTELLIGENCE I SEEK IS THROUGH A CEREBRAL SCAN OF ALL RECENT MEMORIES.
STEADY YOURSELVES, MORTALS.
THIS UNIT IS NOT ADEQUATELY INSULATED FOR THE SENSITIVITIES OF YOUR FRAIL SYSTEMS.
AT FIRST ALL EXPERIENCE NO MORE THAN A MILD FEELING OF DISORIENTATION, HARDLY NOTICEABLE...

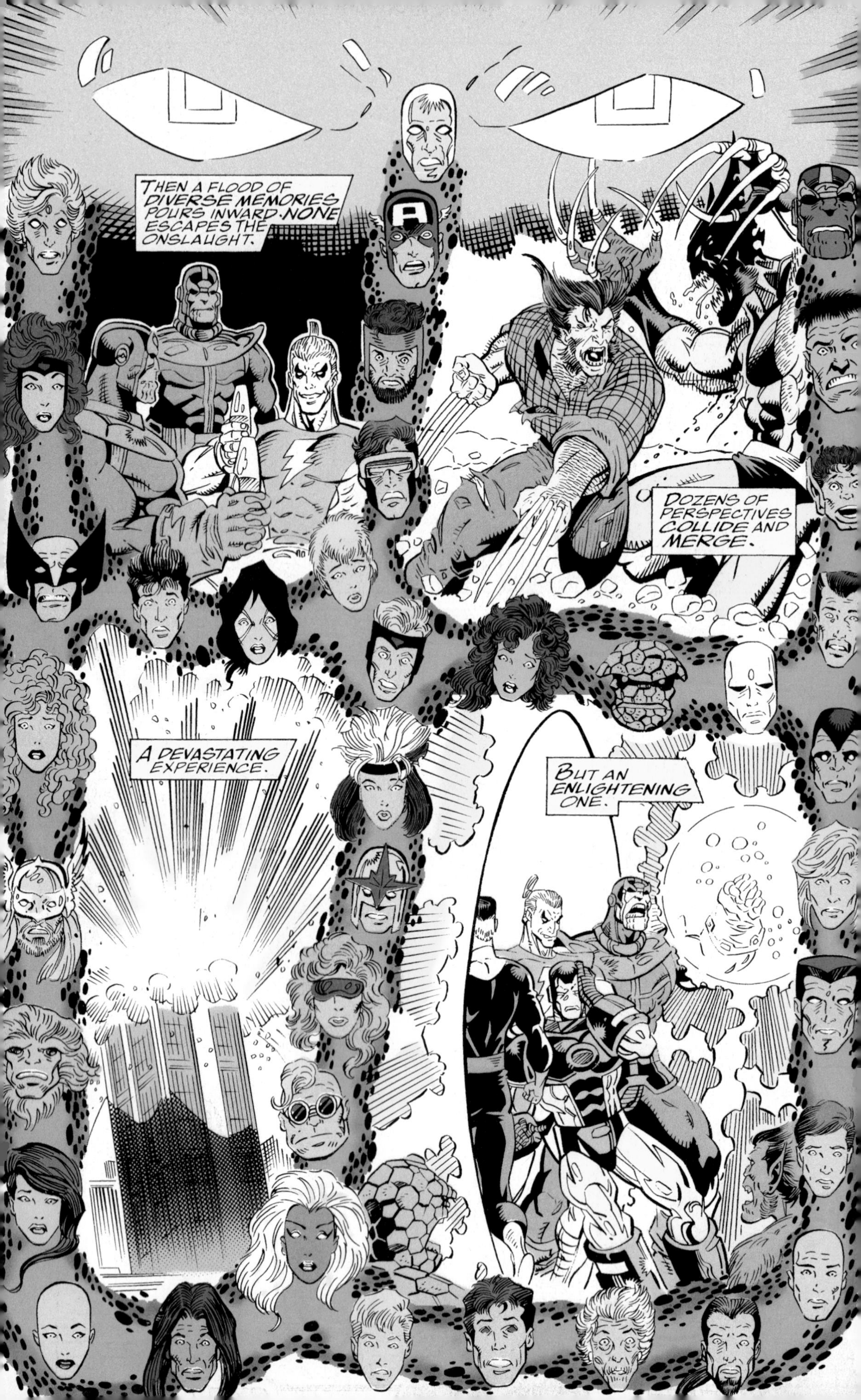
THEN A FLOOD OF DIVERSE MEMORIES POURS INWARD. NONE ESCAPES THE ONSLAUGHT.
DOZENS OF PERSPECTIVES COLLIDE AND MERGE.
A DEVASTATING EXPERIENCE.
BUT AN ENLIGHTENING ONE.

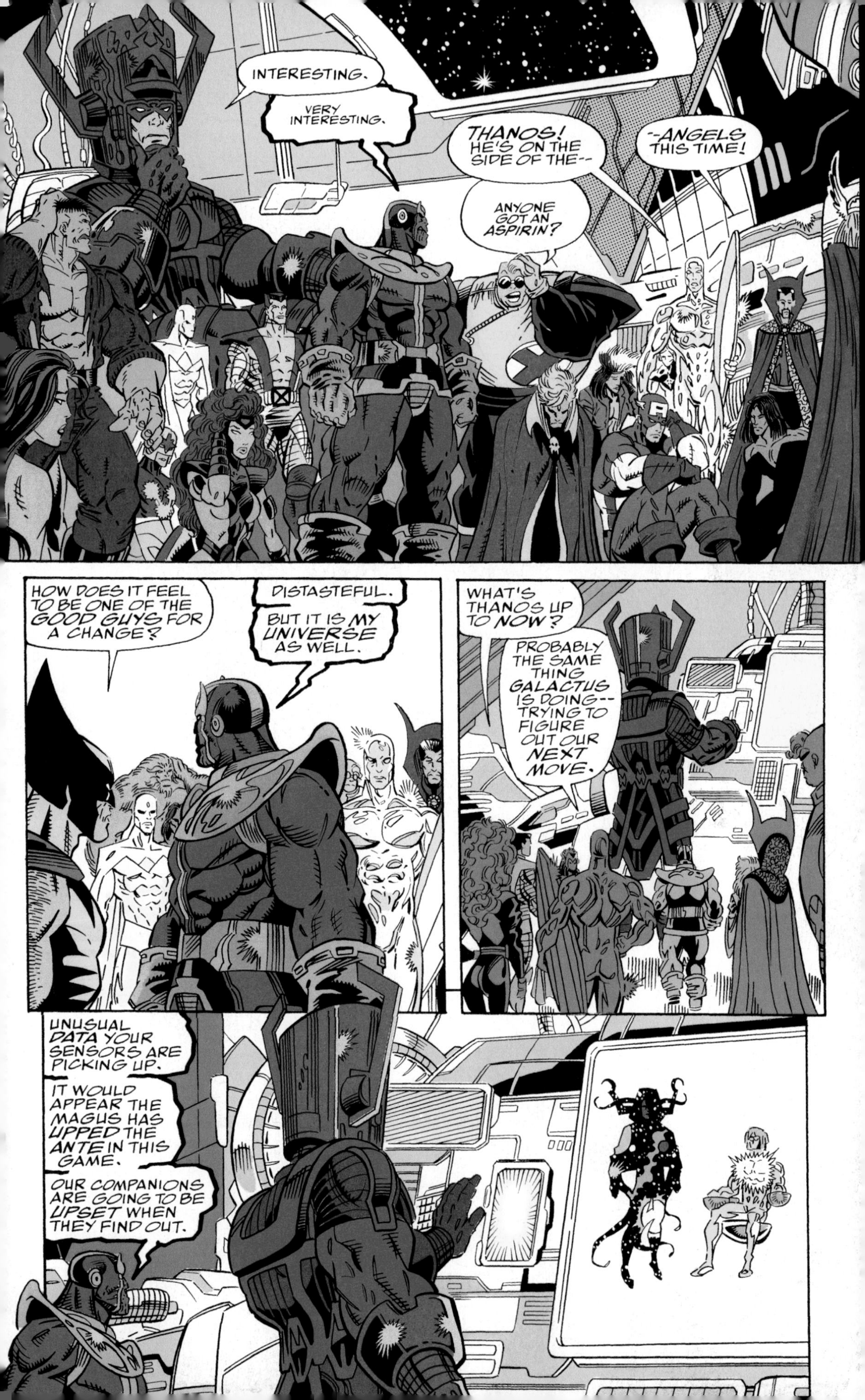

INTERESTING.
VERY INTERESTING.
THANOS! HE'S ON THE SIDE OF THE--
--ANGELS THIS TIME!
ANYONE GOT AN ASPIRIN?
HOW DOES IT FEEL TO BE ONE OF THE GOOD GUYS FOR A CHANGE?
DISTASTEFUL.
BUT IT IS MY UNIVERSE AS WELL.
WHAT'S THANOS UP TO NOW?
PROBABLY THE SAME THING GALACTUS IS DOING-- TRYING TO FIGURE OUT OUR NEXT MOVE.
UNUSUAL DATA YOUR SENSORS ARE PICKING UP.
IT WOULD APPEAR THE MAGUS HAS UPPED THE ANTE IN THIS GAME.
OUR COMPANIONS ARE GOING TO BE UPSET WHEN THEY FIND OUT.

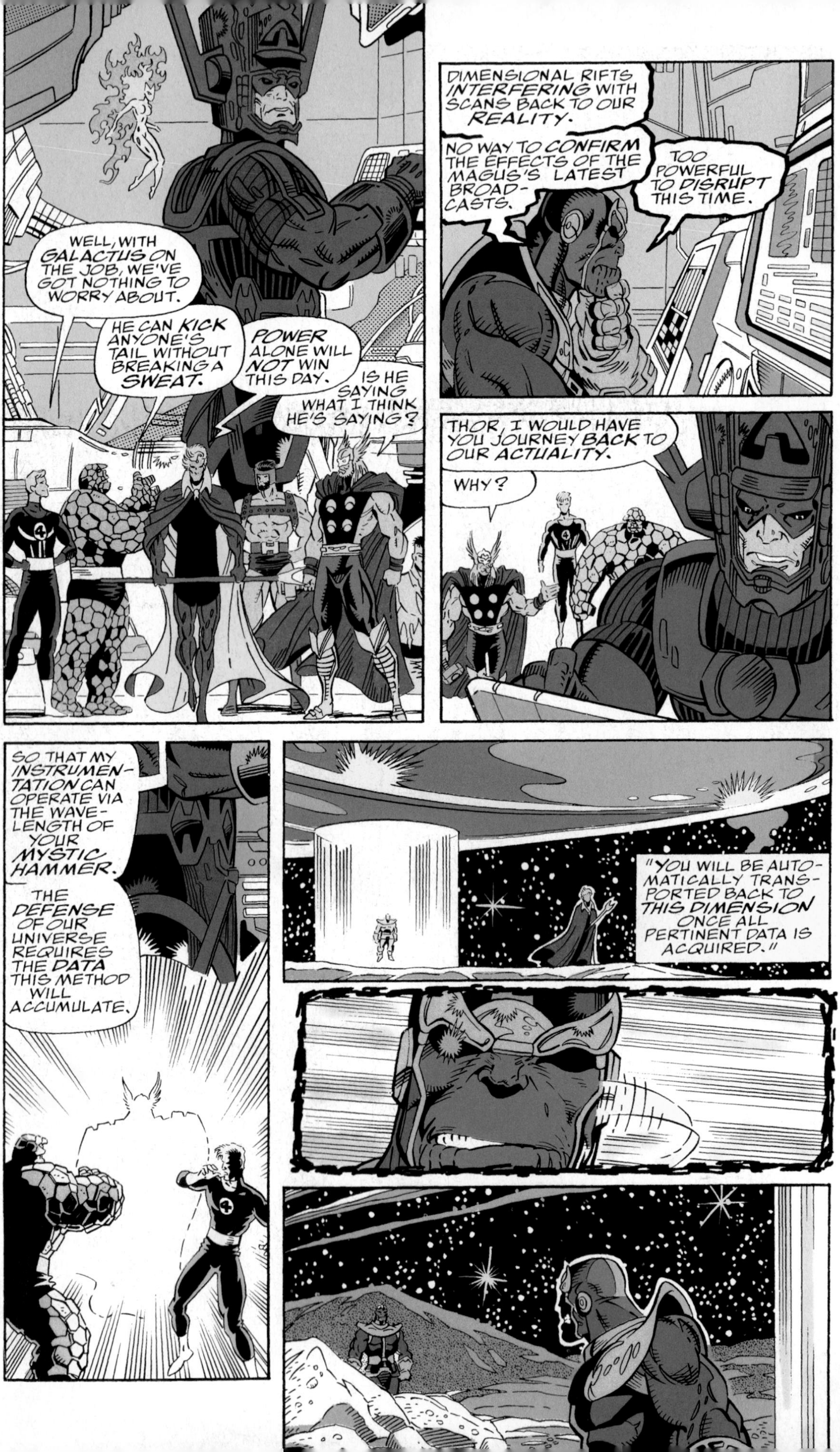

WELL, WITH GALACTUS ON THE JOB, WE'VE GOT NOTHING TO WORRY ABOUT.
HE CAN KICK ANYONE'S TAIL WITHOUT BREAKING A SWEAT.
POWER ALONE WILL NOT WIN THIS DAY.
IS HE SAYING WHAT I THINK HE'S SAYING?
DIMENSIONAL RIFTS INTERFERING WITH SCANS BACK TO OUR REALITY.
NO WAY TO CONFIRM THE EFFECTS OF THE MAGUS'S LATEST BROAD-CASTS.
TOO POWERFUL TO DISRUPT THIS TIME.
THOR, I WOULD HAVE YOU JOURNEY BACK TO OUR ACTUALITY.
WHY?
SO THAT MY INSTRUMEN-TATION CAN OPERATE VIA THE WAVE-LENGTH OF YOUR MYSTIC HAMMER.
THE DEFENSE OF OUR UNIVERSE REQUIRES THE DATA THIS METHOD WILL ACCUMULATE.
"YOU WILL BE AUTO-MATICALLY TRANS-PORTED BACK TO THIS DIMENSION ONCE ALL PERTINENT DATA IS ACQUIRED."

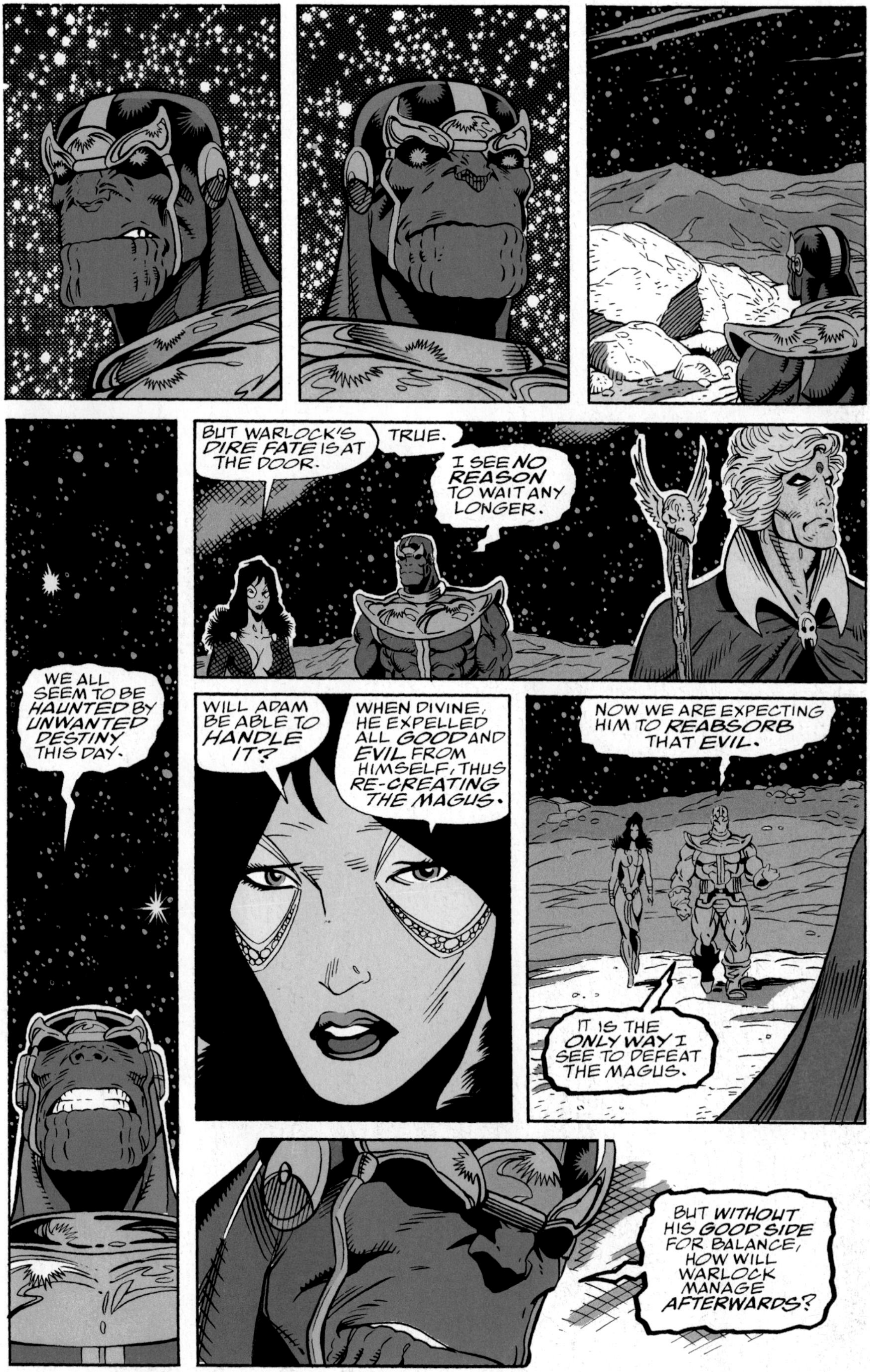
BUT WARLOCK'S DIRE FATE IS AT THE DOOR.
TRUE.
I SEE NO REASON TO WAIT ANY LONGER.
WE ALL SEEM TO BE HAUNTED BY UNWANTED DESTINY THIS DAY.
WILL ADAM BE ABLE TO HANDLE IT?
WHEN DIVINE, HE EXPELLED ALL GOOD AND EVIL FROM HIMSELF, THUS RE-CREATING THE MAGUS.
NOW WE ARE EXPECTING HIM TO REABSORB THAT EVIL.
IT IS THE ONLY WAY I SEE TO DEFEAT THE MAGUS.
BUT WITHOUT HIS GOOD SIDE FOR BALANCE, HOW WILL WARLOCK MANAGE AFTERWARDS?

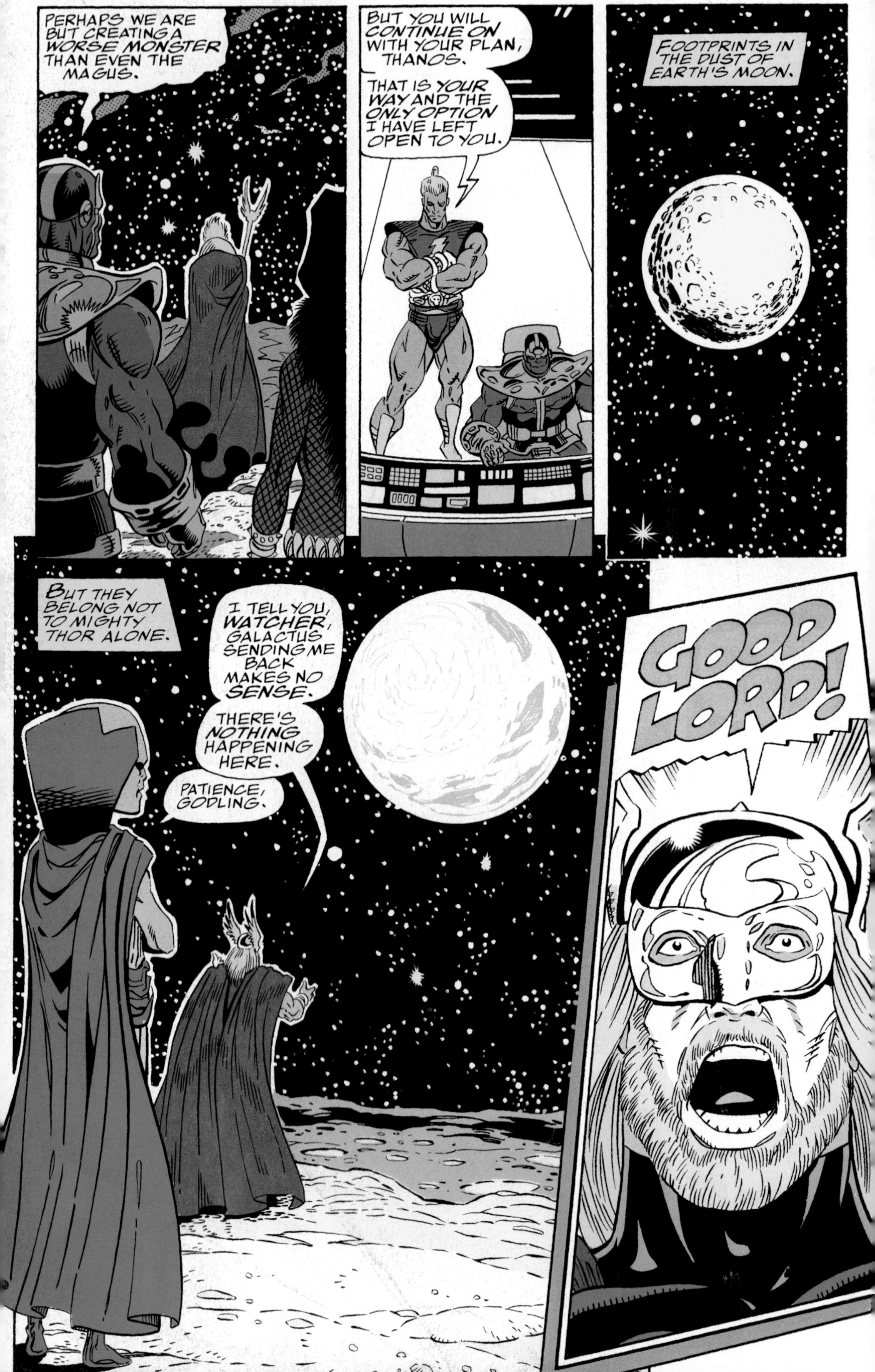
PERHAPS WE ARE BUT CREATING A WORSE MONSTER THAN EVEN THE MAGUS.
BUT YOU WILL CONTINUE ON WITH YOUR PLAN, THANOS.
THAT IS YOUR WAY AND THE ONLY OPTION I HAVE LEFT OPEN TO YOU.
FOOTPRINTS IN THE DUST OF EARTH'S MOON.
BUT THEY BELONG NOT TO MIGHTY THOR ALONE.
I TELL YOU, WATCHER, GALACTUS SENDING ME BACK MAKES NO SENSE.
THERE'S NOTHING HAPPENING HERE.
PATIENCE, GODLING.
GOOD LORD!

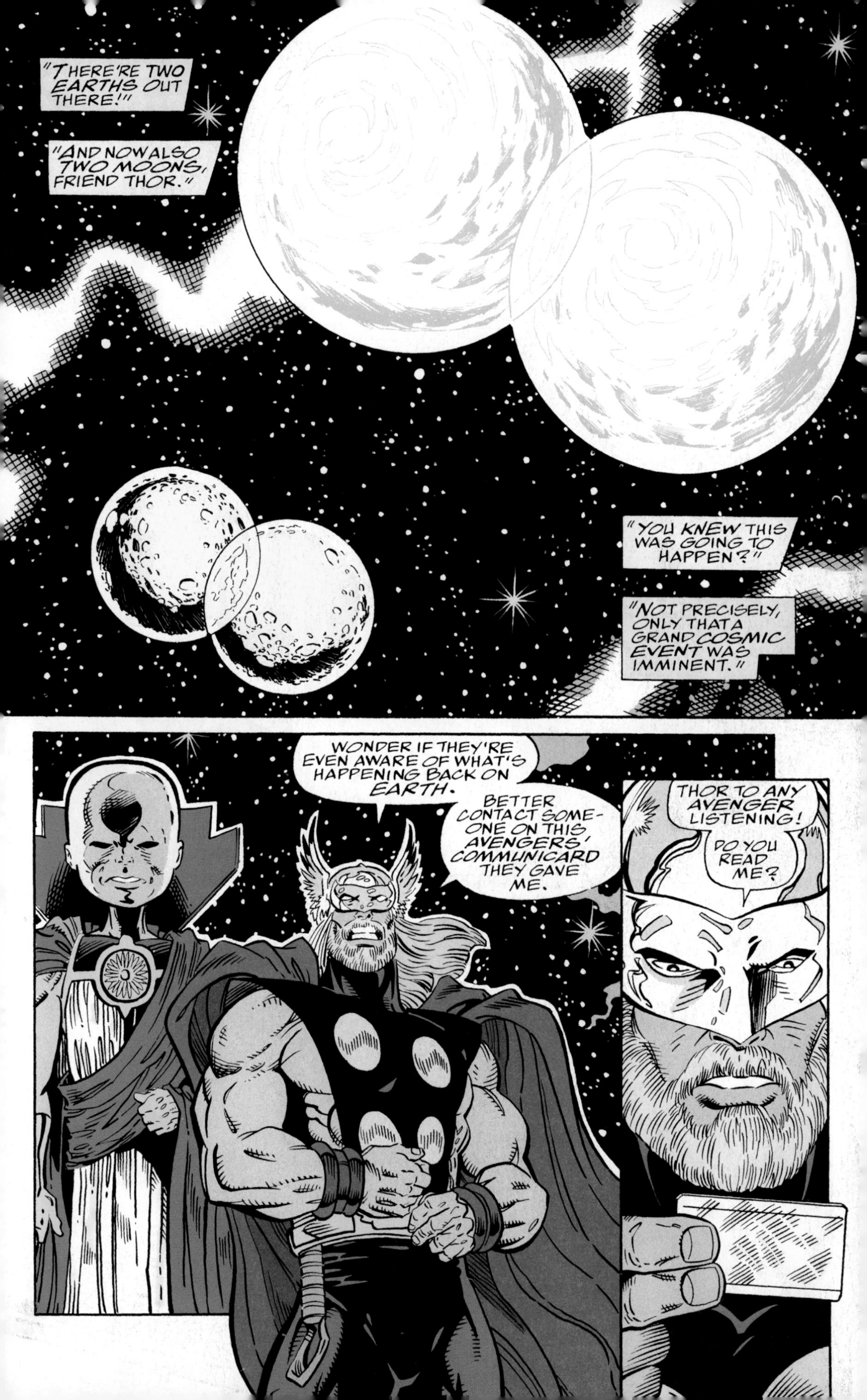
"THERE'RE TWO EARTHS OUT THERE!"
"AND NOW ALSO TWO MOONS, FRIEND THOR."
"YOU KNEW THIS WAS GOING TO HAPPEN?"
"NOT PRECISELY, ONLY THAT A GRAND COSMIC EVENT WAS IMMINENT."
WONDER IF THEY'RE EVEN AWARE OF WHAT'S HAPPENING BACK ON EARTH.
BETTER CONTACT SOME-ONE ON THIS AVENGERS' COMMUNICARD THEY GAVE ME.
THOR TO ANY AVENGER LISTENING!
DO YOU READ ME?

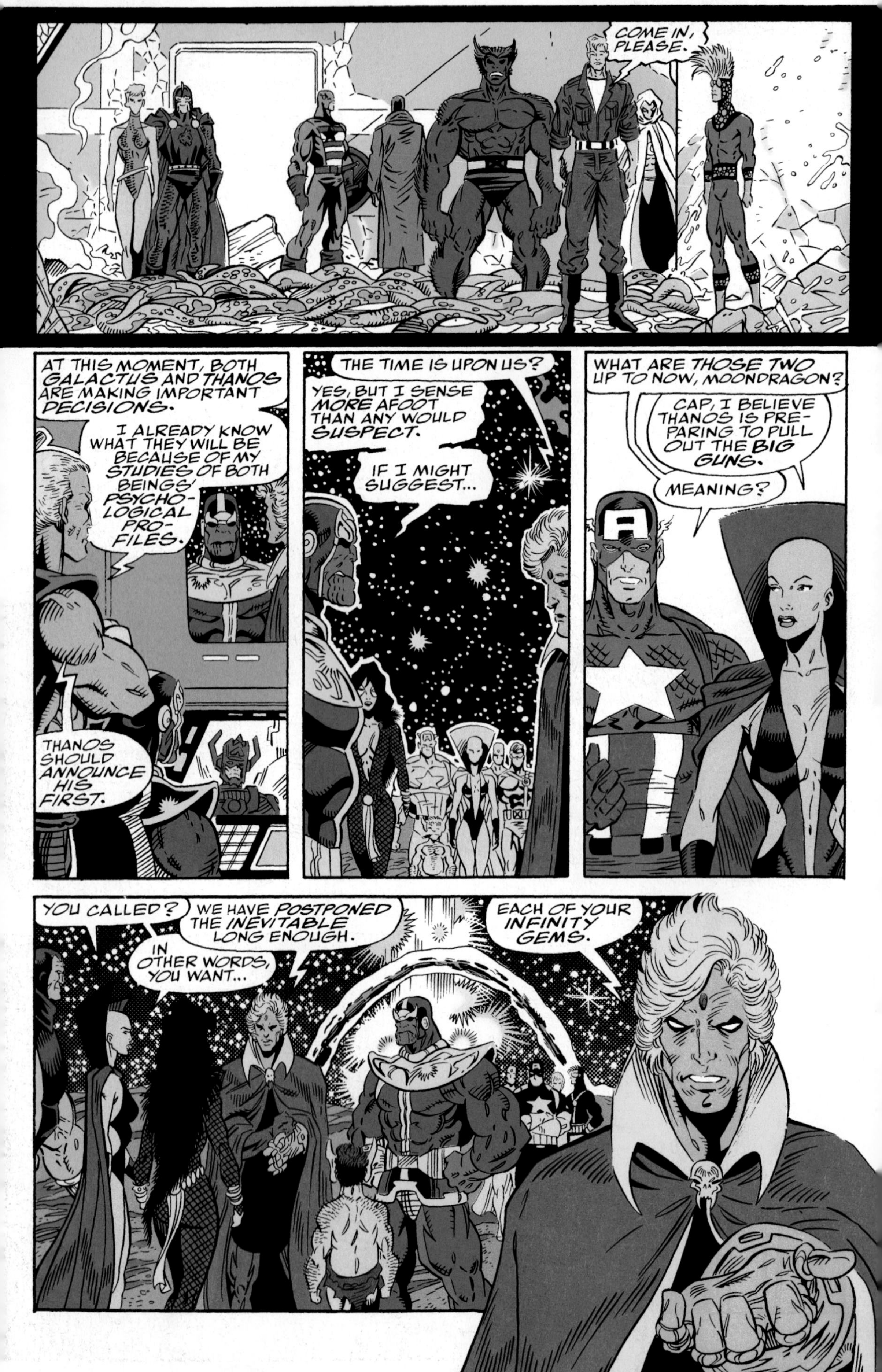
COME IN, PLEASE.
AT THIS MOMENT, BOTH GALACTUS AND THANOS ARE MAKING IMPORTANT DECISIONS.
I ALREADY KNOW WHAT THEY WILL BE BECAUSE OF MY STUDIES OF BOTH BEINGS' PSYCHOLOGICAL PROFILES.
THANOS SHOULD ANNOUNCE HIS FIRST.
THE TIME IS UPON US?
YES, BUT I SENSE MORE AFOOT THAN ANY WOULD SUSPECT.
IF I MIGHT SUGGEST...
WHAT ARE THOSE TWO UP TO NOW, MOONDRAGON?
CAP, I BELIEVE THANOS IS PREPARING TO PULL OUT THE BIG GUNS.
MEANING?
YOU CALLED?
WE HAVE POSTPONED THE INEVITABLE LONG ENOUGH.
IN OTHER WORDS, YOU WANT...
EACH OF YOUR INFINITY GEMS.

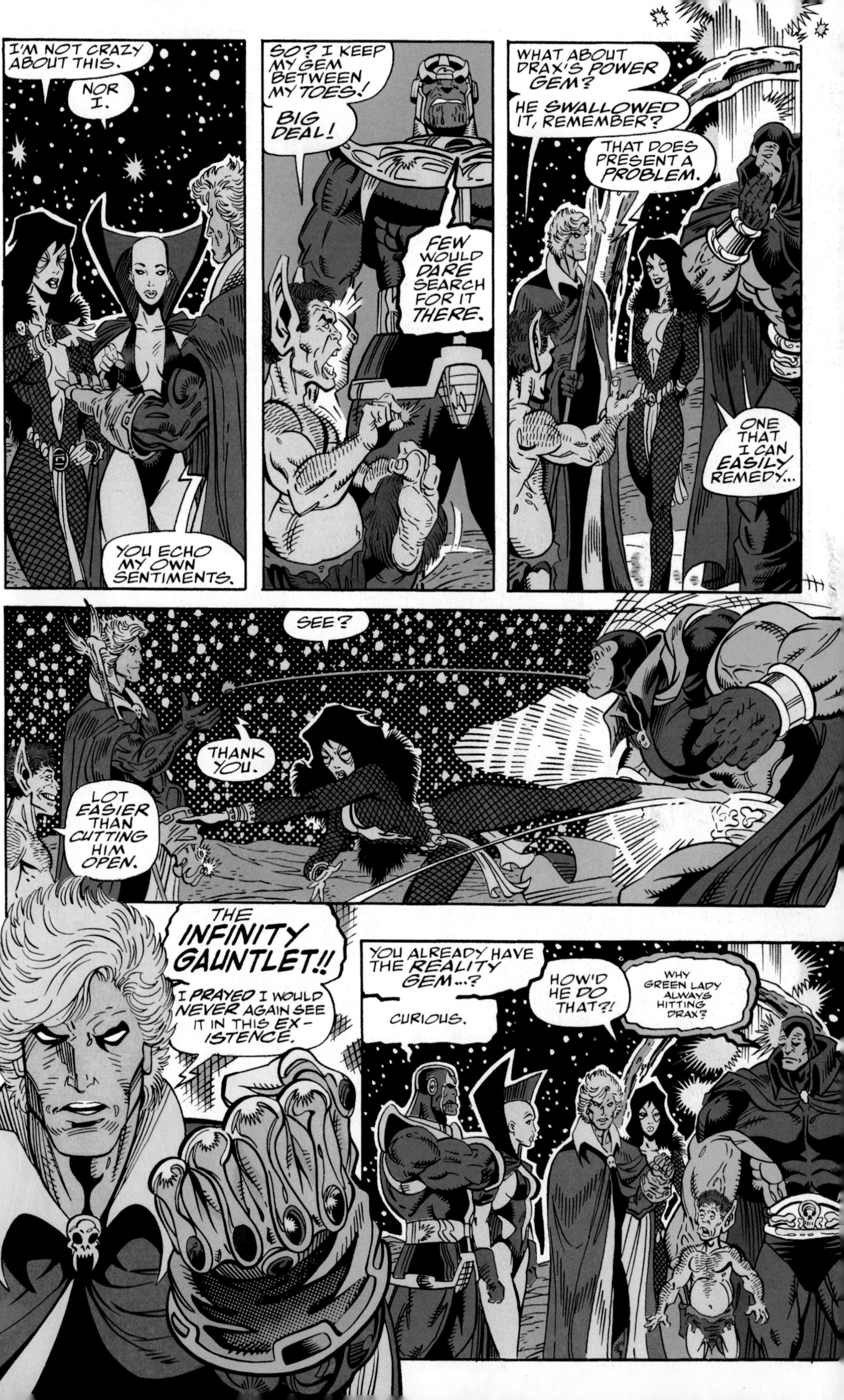
I'M NOT CRAZY ABOUT THIS.
NOR I.
YOU ECHO MY OWN SENTIMENTS.
SO? I KEEP MY GEM BETWEEN MY TOES!
BIG DEAL!
FEW WOULD DARE SEARCH FOR IT THERE.
WHAT ABOUT DRAX'S POWER GEM?
HE SWALLOWED IT, REMEMBER?
THAT DOES PRESENT A PROBLEM.
ONE THAT I CAN EASILY REMEDY...
SEE?
THANK YOU.
LOT EASIER THAN CUTTING HIM OPEN.
THE INFINITY GAUNTLET!!
I PRAYED I WOULD NEVER AGAIN SEE IT IN THIS EX-ISTENCE.
YOU ALREADY HAVE THE REALITY GEM...?
CURIOUS.
HOW'D HE DO THAT?!
WHY GREEN LADY ALWAYS HITTING DRAX?

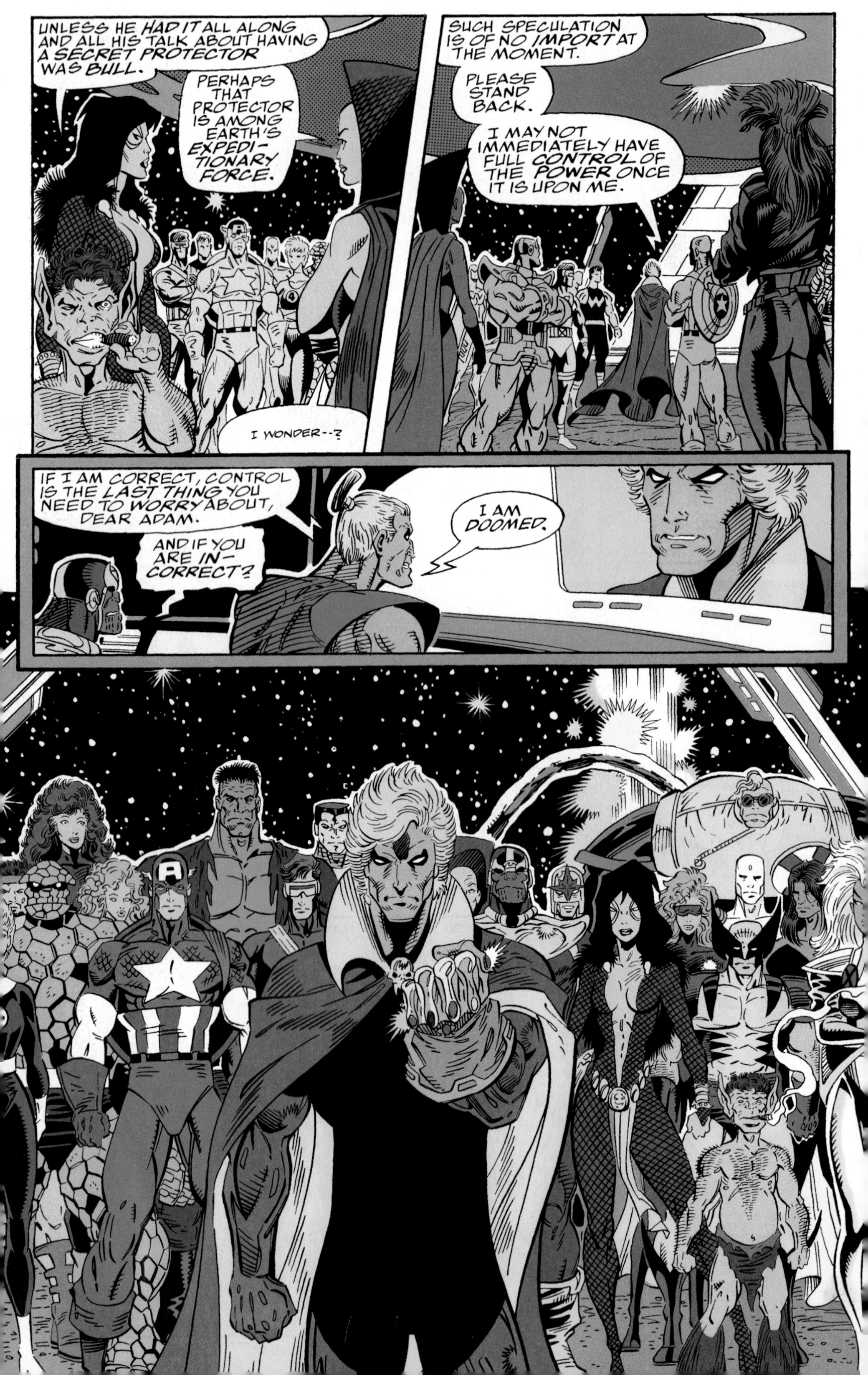
UNLESS HE HAD IT ALL ALONG AND ALL HIS TALK ABOUT HAVING A SECRET PROTECTOR WAS BULL.
PERHAPS THAT PROTECTOR IS AMONG EARTH'S EXPEDITIONARY FORCE.
I WONDER--?
SUCH SPECULATION IS OF NO IMPORT AT THE MOMENT.
PLEASE STAND BACK.
I MAY NOT IMMEDIATELY HAVE FULL CONTROL OF THE POWER ONCE IT IS UPON ME.
IF I AM CORRECT, CONTROL IS THE LAST THING YOU NEED TO WORRY ABOUT, DEAR ADAM.
AND IF YOU ARE INCORRECT?
I AM DOOMED.

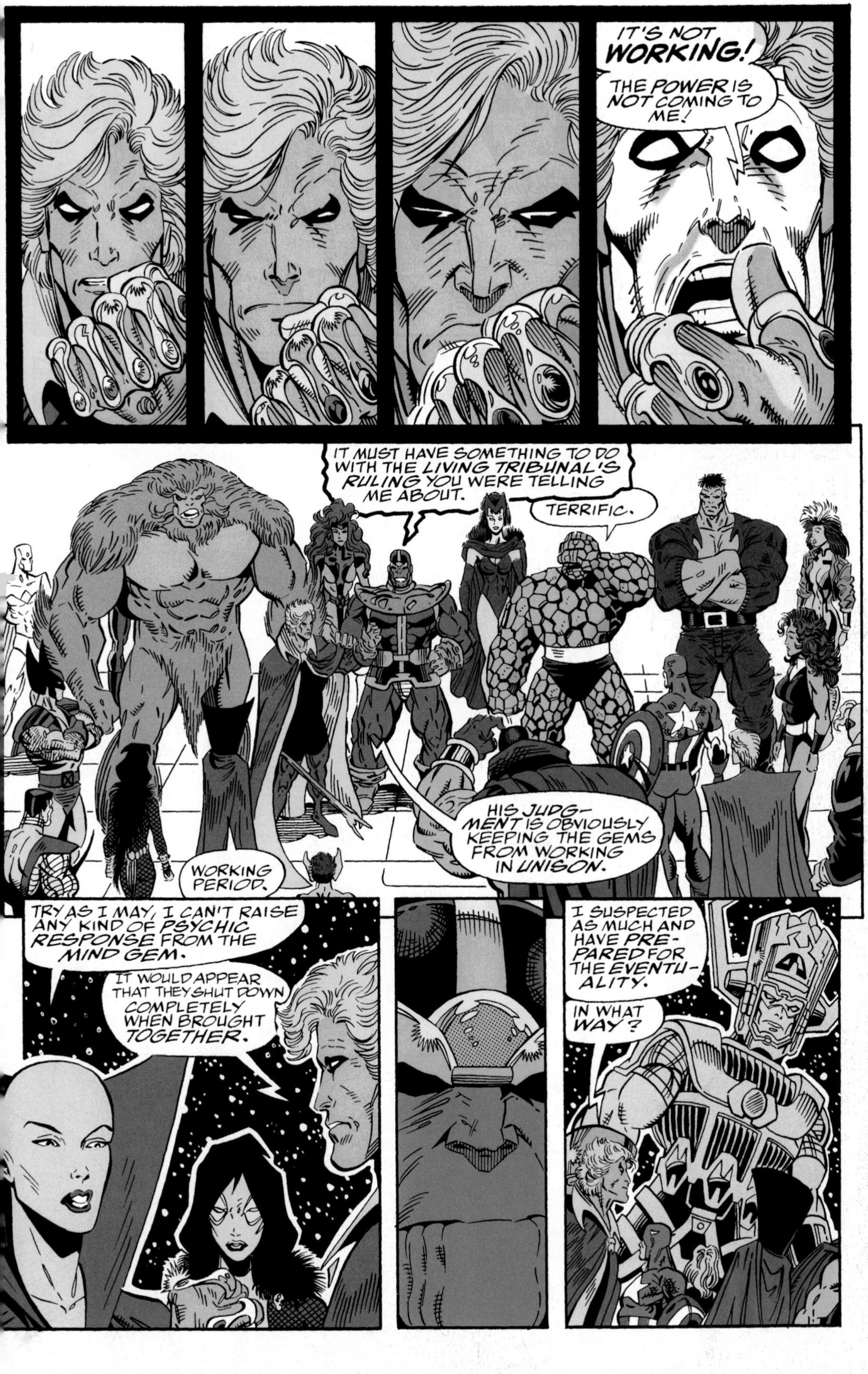
IT'S NOT WORKING!
THE POWER IS NOT COMING TO ME!
IT MUST HAVE SOMETHING TO DO WITH THE LIVING TRIBUNAL'S RULING YOU WERE TELLING ME ABOUT.
TERRIFIC.
HIS JUDG-MENT IS OBVIOUSLY KEEPING THE GEMS FROM WORKING IN UNISON.
WORKING PERIOD.
TRY AS I MAY, I CAN'T RAISE ANY KIND OF PSYCHIC RESPONSE FROM THE MIND GEM.
IT WOULD APPEAR THAT THEY SHUT DOWN COMPLETELY WHEN BROUGHT TOGETHER.
I SUSPECTED AS MUCH AND HAVE PRE-PARED FOR THE EVENTU-ALITY.
IN WHAT WAY?

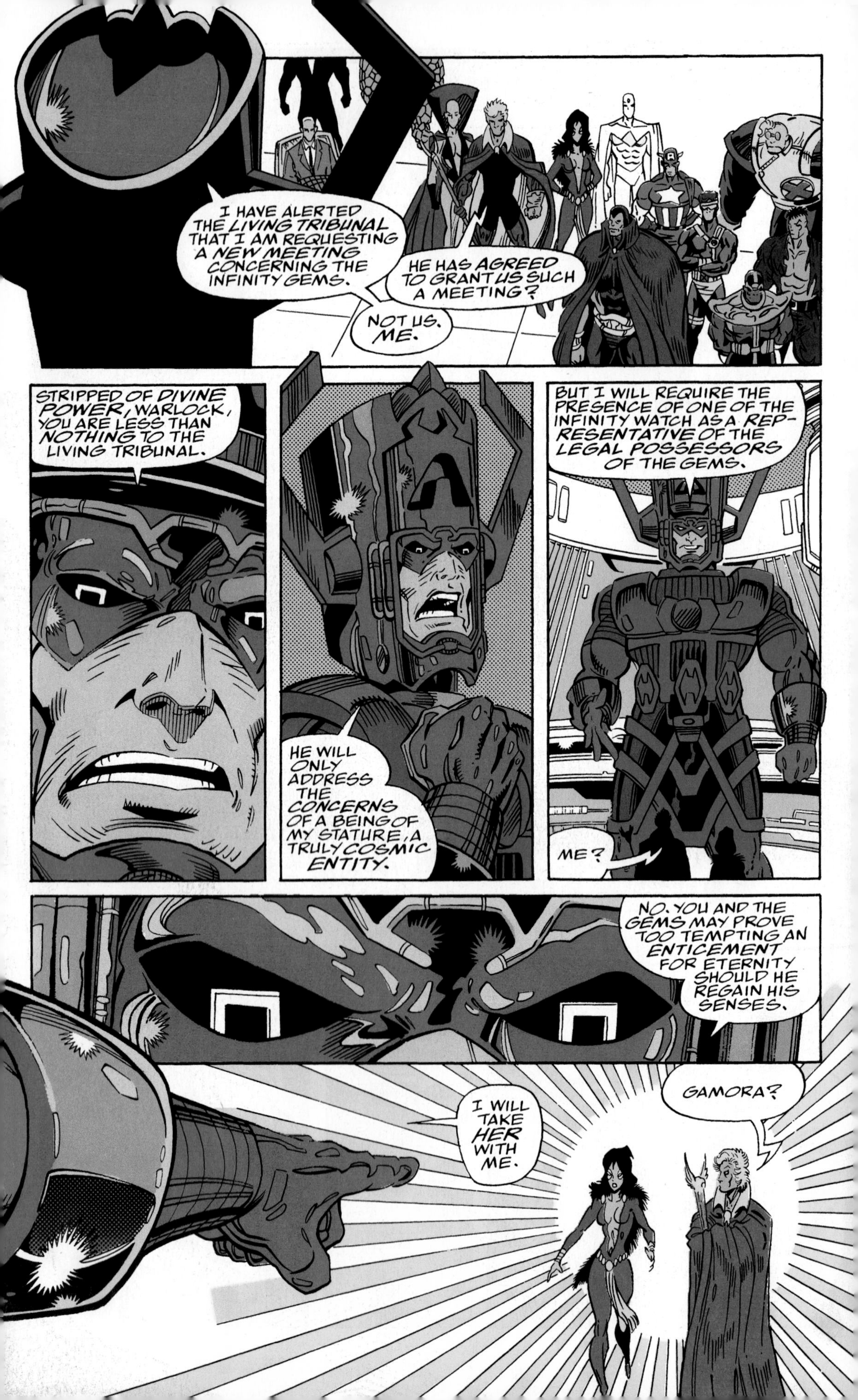

I HAVE ALERTED THE LIVING TRIBUNAL THAT I AM REQUESTING A NEW MEETING CONCERNING THE INFINITY GEMS.
HE HAS AGREED TO GRANT US SUCH A MEETING?
NOT US. ME.
STRIPPED OF DIVINE POWER, WARLOCK, YOU ARE LESS THAN NOTHING TO THE LIVING TRIBUNAL.
HE WILL ONLY ADDRESS THE CONCERNS OF A BEING OF MY STATURE, A TRULY COSMIC ENTITY.
BUT I WILL REQUIRE THE PRESENCE OF ONE OF THE INFINITY WATCH AS A REPRESENTATIVE OF THE LEGAL POSSESSORS OF THE GEMS.
ME?
NO. YOU AND THE GEMS MAY PROVE TOO TEMPTING AN ENTICEMENT FOR ETERNITY SHOULD HE REGAIN HIS SENSES.
I WILL TAKE HER WITH ME.
GAMORA?

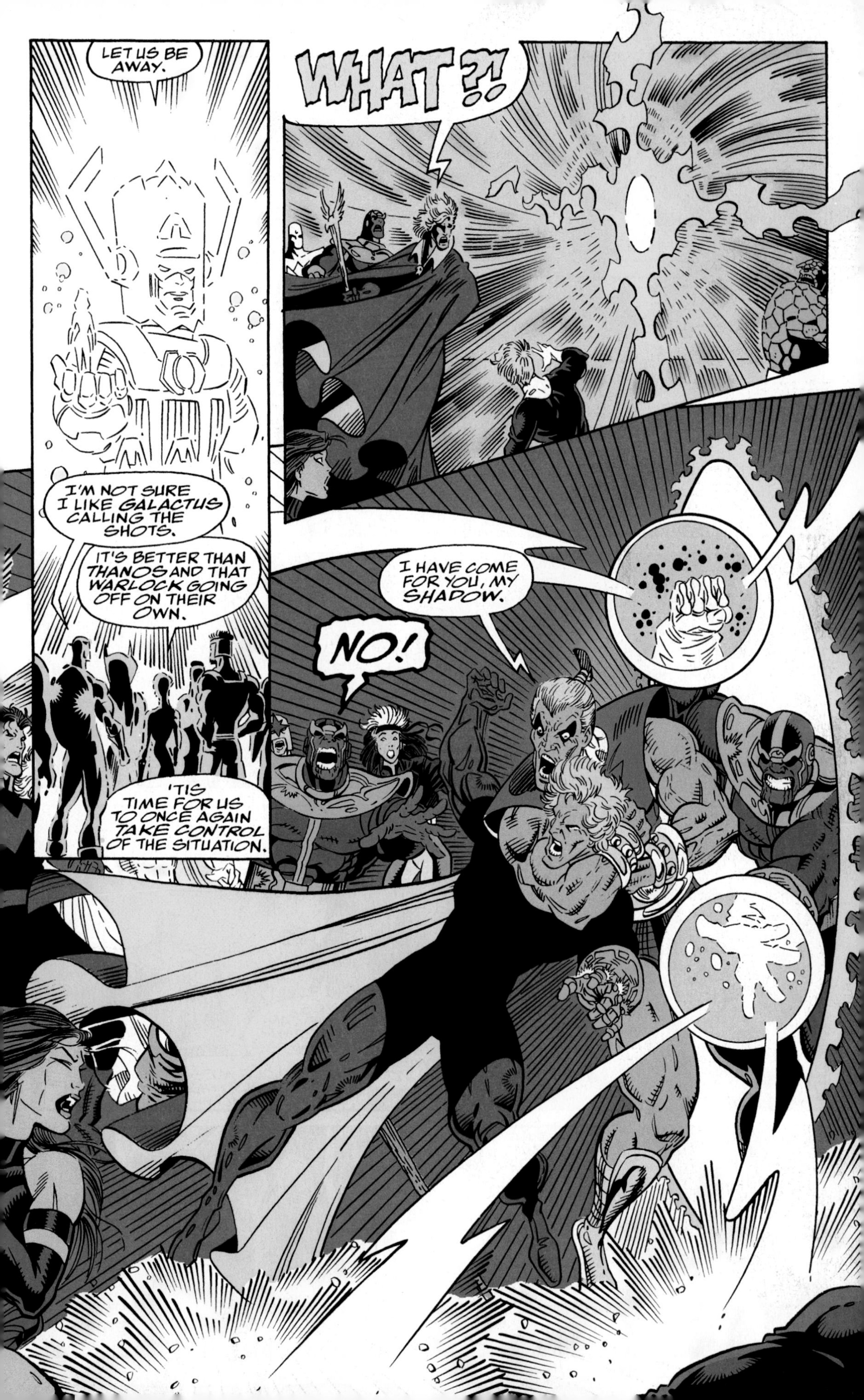
LET US BE AWAY.
WHAT ?!
I'M NOT SURE I LIKE GALACTUS CALLING THE SHOTS.
IT'S BETTER THAN THANOS AND THAT WARLOCK GOING OFF ON THEIR OWN.
'TIS TIME FOR US TO ONCE AGAIN TAKE CONTROL OF THE SITUATION.
I HAVE COME FOR YOU, MY SHADOW.
NO!

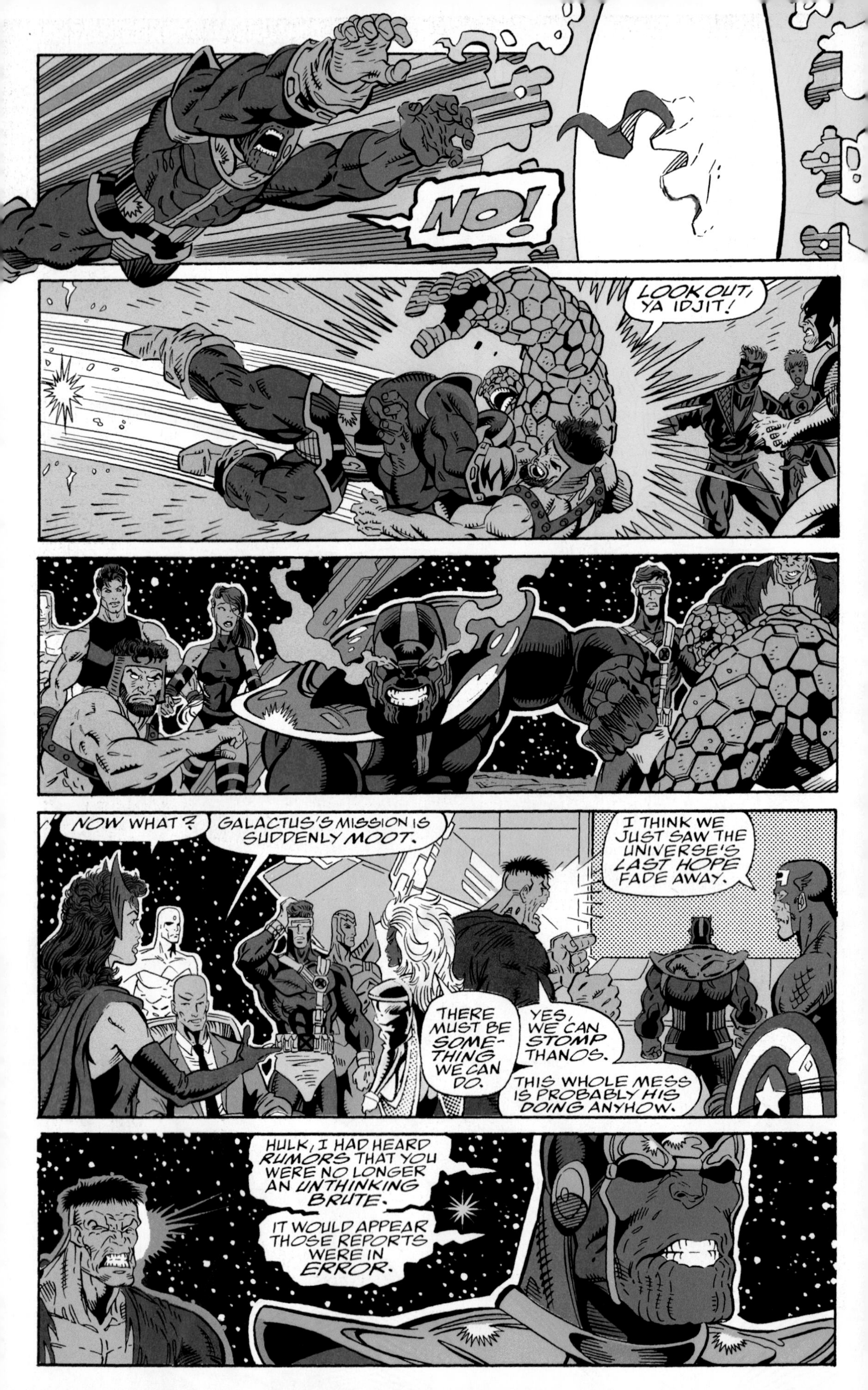
NO!
LOOK OUT, YA IDJIT!
NOW WHAT?
GALACTUS'S MISSION IS SUDDENLY MOOT.
I THINK WE JUST SAW THE UNIVERSE'S LAST HOPE FADE AWAY.
THERE MUST BE SOME-THING WE CAN DO.
YES, WE CAN STOMP THANOS.
THIS WHOLE MESS IS PROBABLY HIS DOING ANYHOW.
HULK, I HAD HEARD RUMORS THAT YOU WERE NO LONGER AN UNTHINKING BRUTE.
IT WOULD APPEAR THOSE REPORTS WERE IN ERROR.

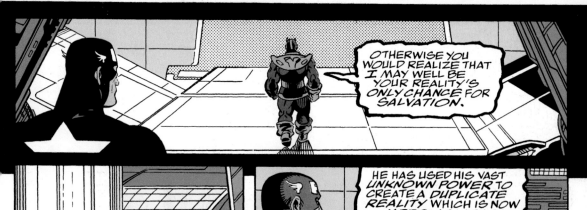

OTHERWISE YOU WOULD REALIZE THAT I MAY WELL BE YOUR REALITY'S ONLY CHANCE FOR SALVATION.

HE HAS USED HIS VAST *UNKNOWN* POWER TO CREATE A *DUPLICATE REALITY* WHICH IS NOW *MERGING* WITH THE *ORIGINAL.*

WHEN THAT MERGER IS *COMPLETE,* THE GALAXY WILL BE TOTALLY IN HIS *THRALL!*

THANKS FOR THE *OFFER,* THANOS.

BUT *YOUR* KIND OF HELP WE CAN DO *WITHOUT.*

HAVE IT YOUR WAY, THEN.

BUT YOU MAY BE *INTERESTED* IN LEARNING THAT THE *MAGUS* IS IN THE PROCESS OF TAKING OVER THE ENTIRE *MILKY WAY* GALAXY.

AS ARE THE *DOPPELGANGERS* THAT DEFEATED YOUR *LOST FRIENDS.*

AND BY THE WAY, EVERYONE BACK ON *EARTH* AND THE REST OF THE GALAXY ARE *ENTRANCED.*

IT IS TO MAKE THE TAKEOVER GO MORE *SMOOTHLY.*

HOW DO YOU--

FROM THE *TELEMETRY* BEING TRANSMITTED THROUGH *THOR'S HAMMER.*

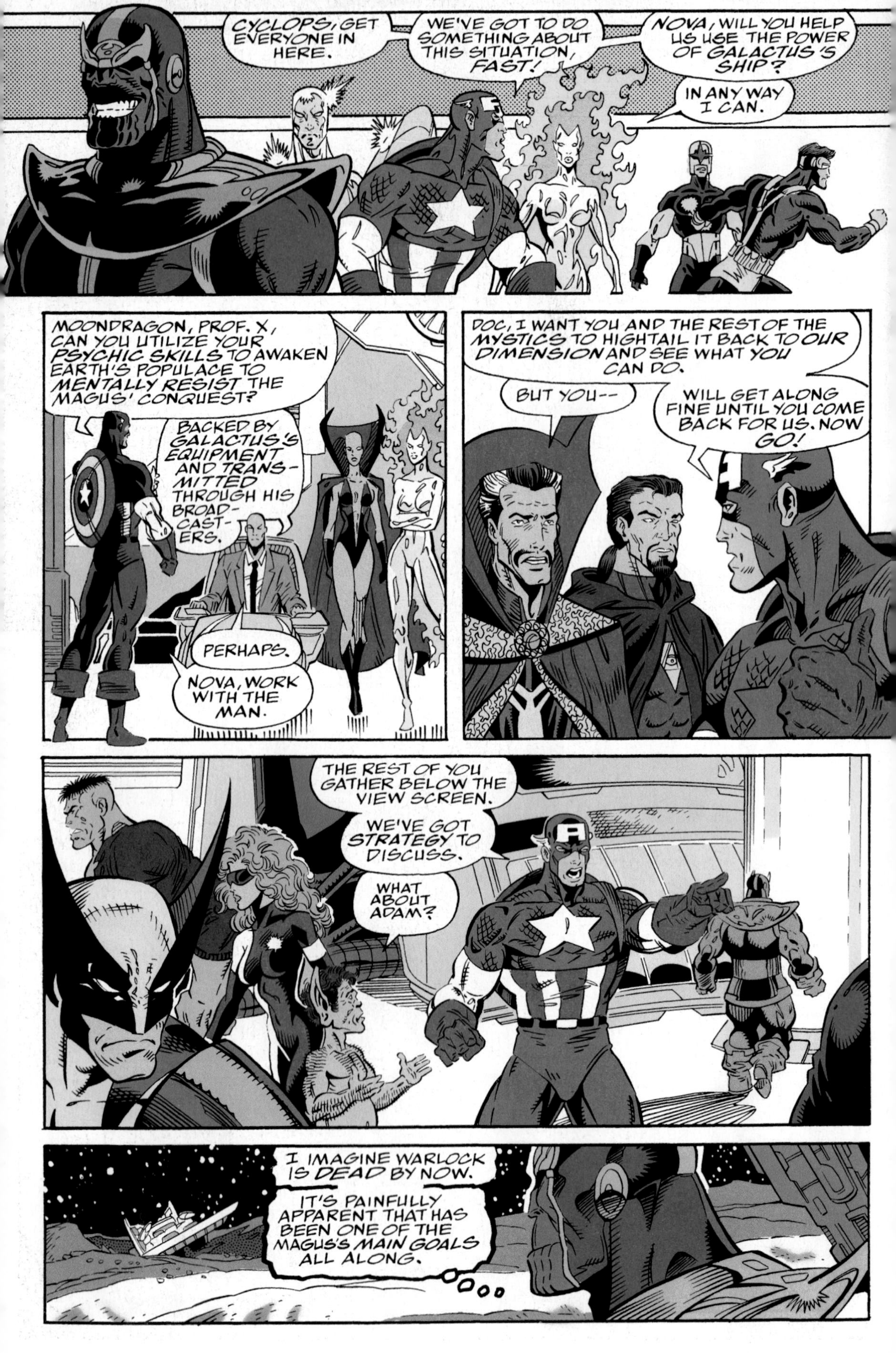
CYCLOPS, GET EVERYONE IN HERE.
WE'VE GOT TO DO SOMETHING ABOUT THIS SITUATION, FAST!
NOVA, WILL YOU HELP US USE THE POWER OF GALACTUS'S SHIP?
IN ANY WAY I CAN.
MOONDRAGON, PROF. X, CAN YOU UTILIZE YOUR PSYCHIC SKILLS TO AWAKEN EARTH'S POPULACE TO MENTALLY RESIST THE MAGUS' CONQUEST?
BACKED BY GALACTUS'S EQUIPMENT AND TRANSMITTED THROUGH HIS BROADCASTERS.
PERHAPS.
NOVA, WORK WITH THE MAN.
DOC, I WANT YOU AND THE REST OF THE MYSTICS TO HIGHTAIL IT BACK TO OUR DIMENSION AND SEE WHAT YOU CAN DO.
BUT YOU--
WILL GET ALONG FINE UNTIL YOU COME BACK FOR US. NOW GO!
THE REST OF YOU GATHER BELOW THE VIEW SCREEN.
WE'VE GOT STRATEGY TO DISCUSS.
WHAT ABOUT ADAM?
I IMAGINE WARLOCK IS DEAD BY NOW.
IT'S PAINFULLY APPARENT THAT HAS BEEN ONE OF THE MAGUS'S MAIN GOALS ALL ALONG.

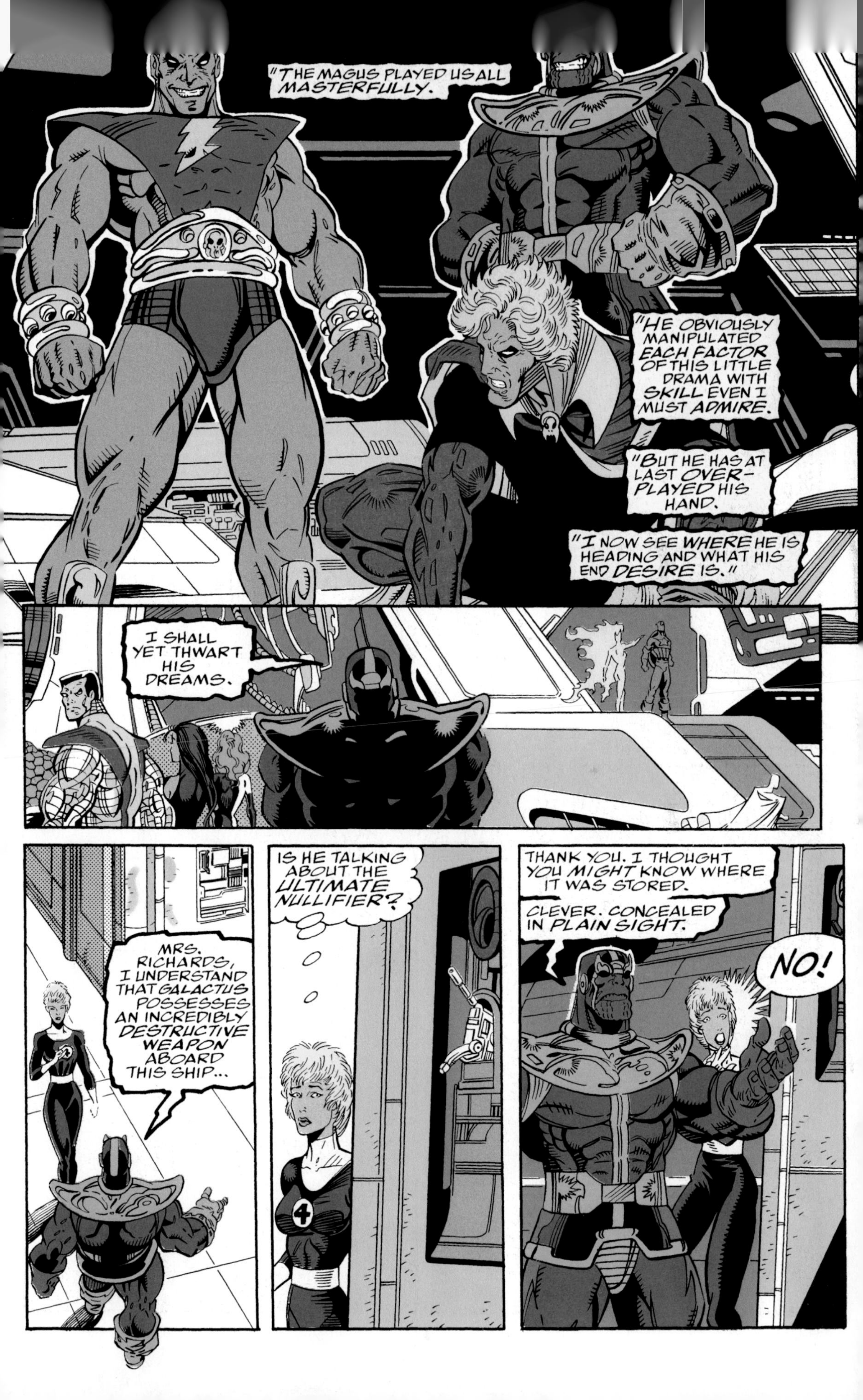

"THE MAGUS PLAYED US ALL MASTERFULLY.
"HE OBVIOUSLY MANIPULATED EACH FACTOR OF THIS LITTLE DRAMA WITH SKILL EVEN I MUST ADMIRE.
"BUT HE HAS AT LAST OVER-PLAYED HIS HAND.
"I NOW SEE WHERE HE IS HEADING AND WHAT HIS END DESIRE IS."
I SHALL YET THWART HIS DREAMS.
MRS. RICHARDS, I UNDERSTAND THAT GALACTUS POSSESSES AN INCREDIBLY DESTRUCTIVE WEAPON ABOARD THIS SHIP...
IS HE TALKING ABOUT THE ULTIMATE NULLIFIER?
THANK YOU. I THOUGHT YOU MIGHT KNOW WHERE IT WAS STORED.
CLEVER. CONCEALED IN PLAIN SIGHT.
NO!

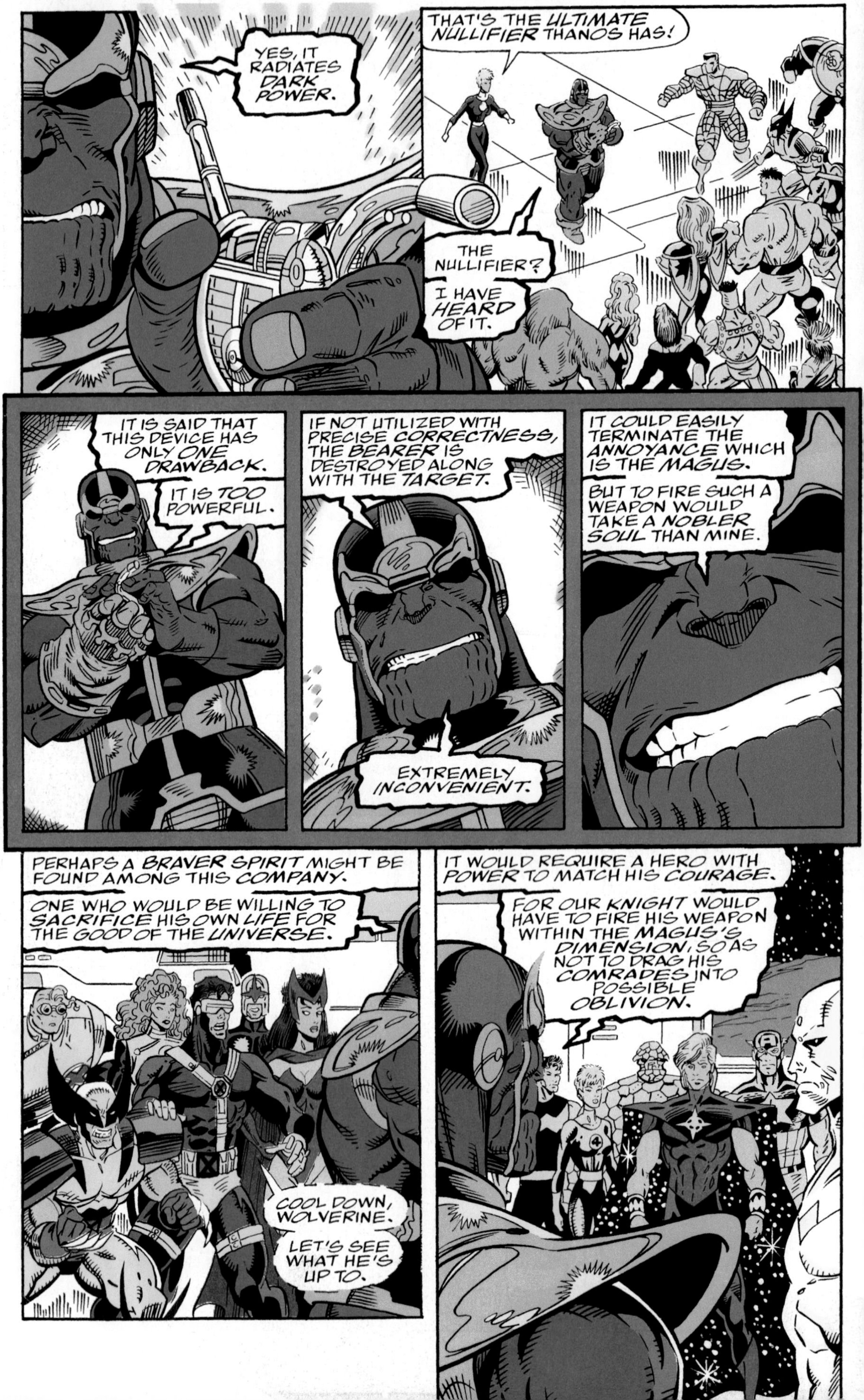
YES, IT RADIATES DARK POWER.
THAT'S THE ULTIMATE NULLIFIER THANOS HAS!
THE NULLIFIER? I HAVE HEARD OF IT.
IT IS SAID THAT THIS DEVICE HAS ONLY ONE DRAWBACK.
IT IS TOO POWERFUL.
IF NOT UTILIZED WITH PRECISE CORRECTNESS, THE BEARER IS DESTROYED ALONG WITH THE TARGET.
EXTREMELY INCONVENIENT.
IT COULD EASILY TERMINATE THE ANNOYANCE WHICH IS THE MAGUS.
BUT TO FIRE SUCH A WEAPON WOULD TAKE A NOBLER SOUL THAN MINE.
PERHAPS A BRAVER SPIRIT MIGHT BE FOUND AMONG THIS COMPANY.
ONE WHO WOULD BE WILLING TO SACRIFICE HIS OWN LIFE FOR THE GOOD OF THE UNIVERSE.
COOL DOWN, WOLVERINE.
LET'S SEE WHAT HE'S UP TO.
IT WOULD REQUIRE A HERO WITH POWER TO MATCH HIS COURAGE.
FOR OUR KNIGHT WOULD HAVE TO FIRE HIS WEAPON WITHIN THE MAGUS'S DIMENSION, SO AS NOT TO DRAG HIS COMRADES INTO POSSIBLE OBLIVION.

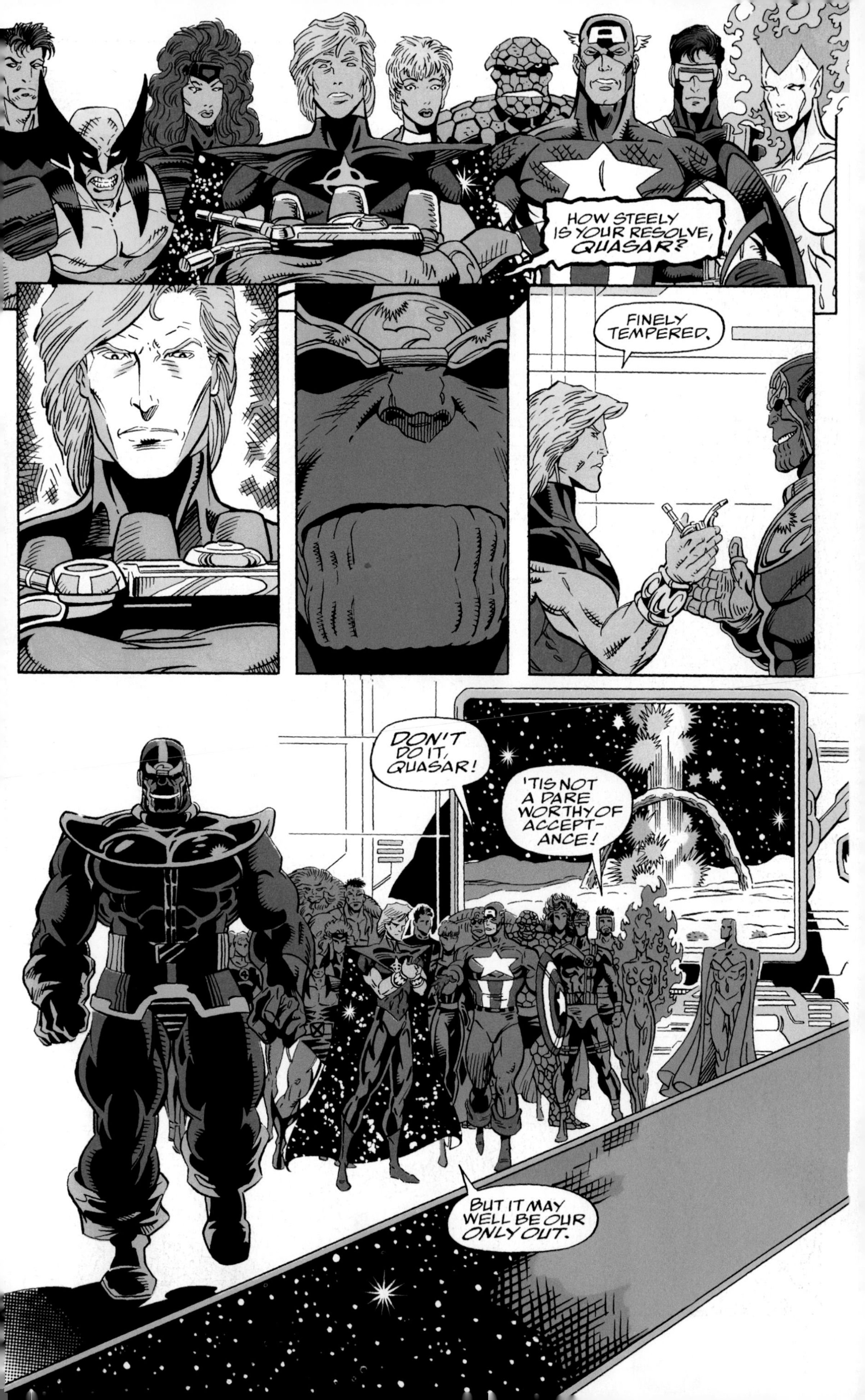
HOW STEELY IS YOUR RESOLVE, QUASAR?
FINELY TEMPERED.
DON'T DO IT, QUASAR!
'TIS NOT A DARE WORTHY OF ACCEPT-ANCE!
BUT IT MAY WELL BE OUR ONLY OUT.

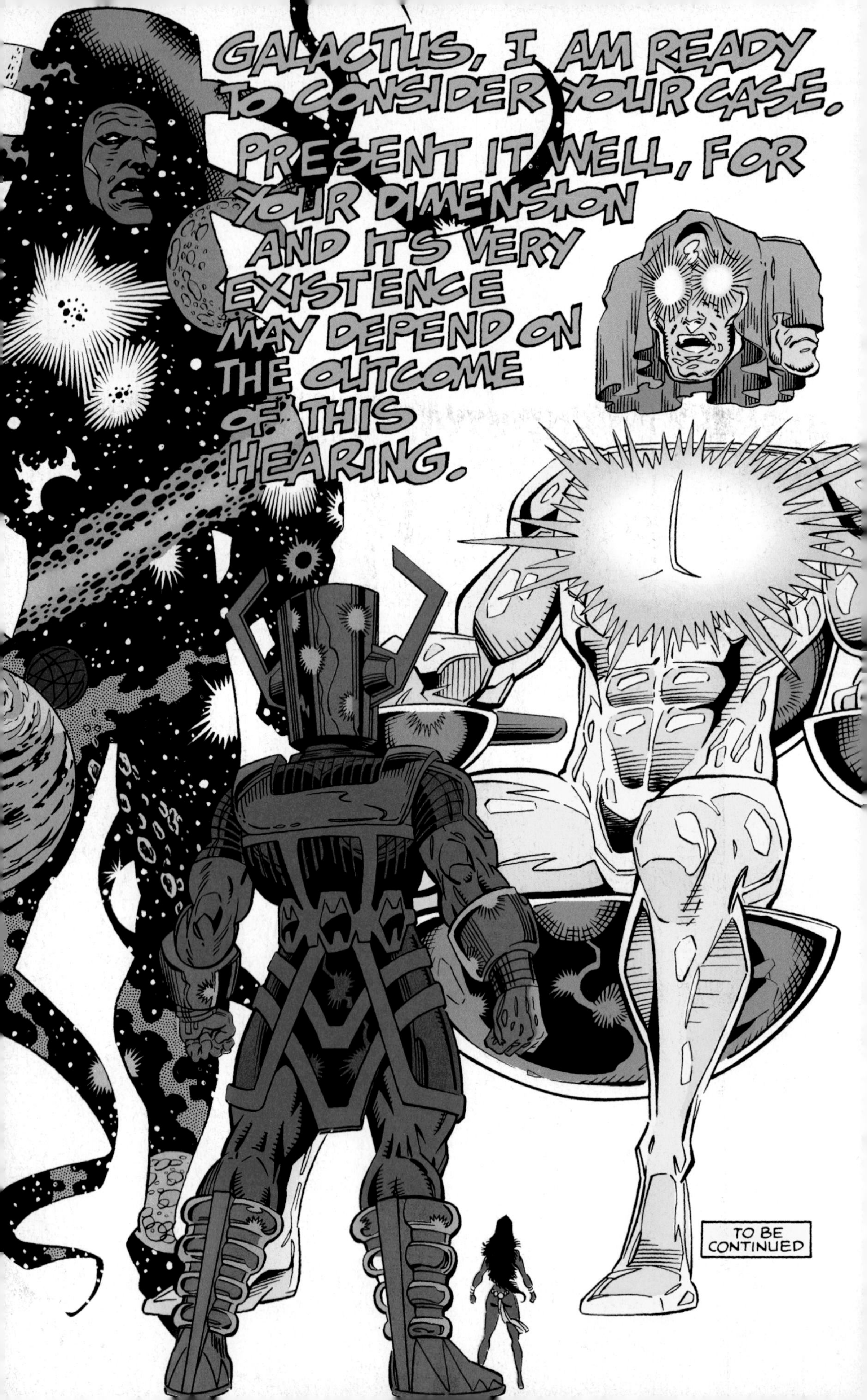
GALACTUS, I AM READY TO CONSIDER YOUR CASE.
PRESENT IT WELL, FOR YOUR DIMENSION AND ITS VERY EXISTENCE MAY DEPEND ON THE OUTCOME OF THIS HEARING.
TO BE CONTINUED

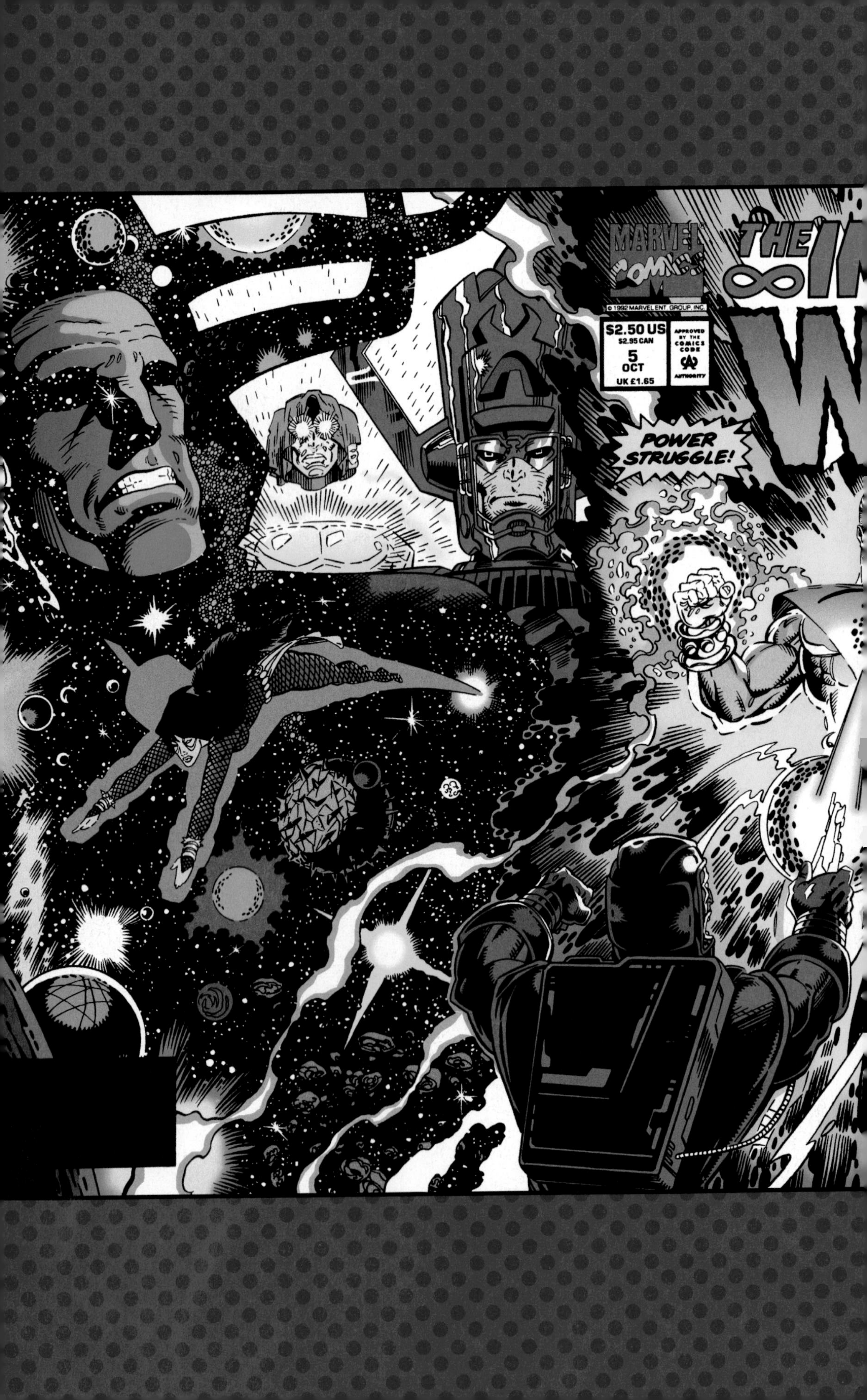
MARVEL COMICS
THE
© 1992 MARVEL ENT. GROUP, INC.
$2.50 US
$2.95 CAN
5
OCT
UK £1.65
APPROVED BY THE COMICS CODE AUTHORITY
POWER STRUGGLE!

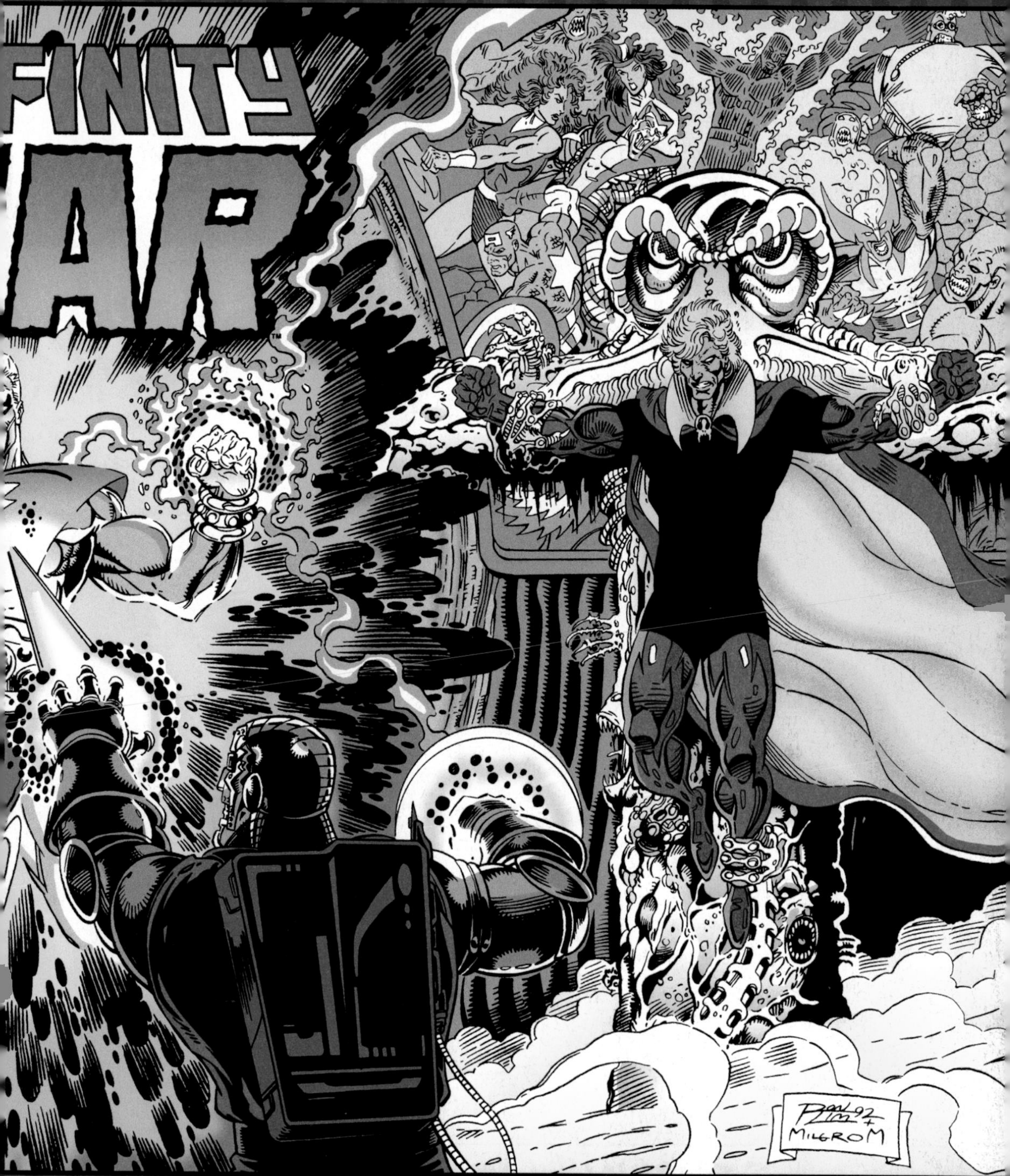
FINITY
AR
MILGROM

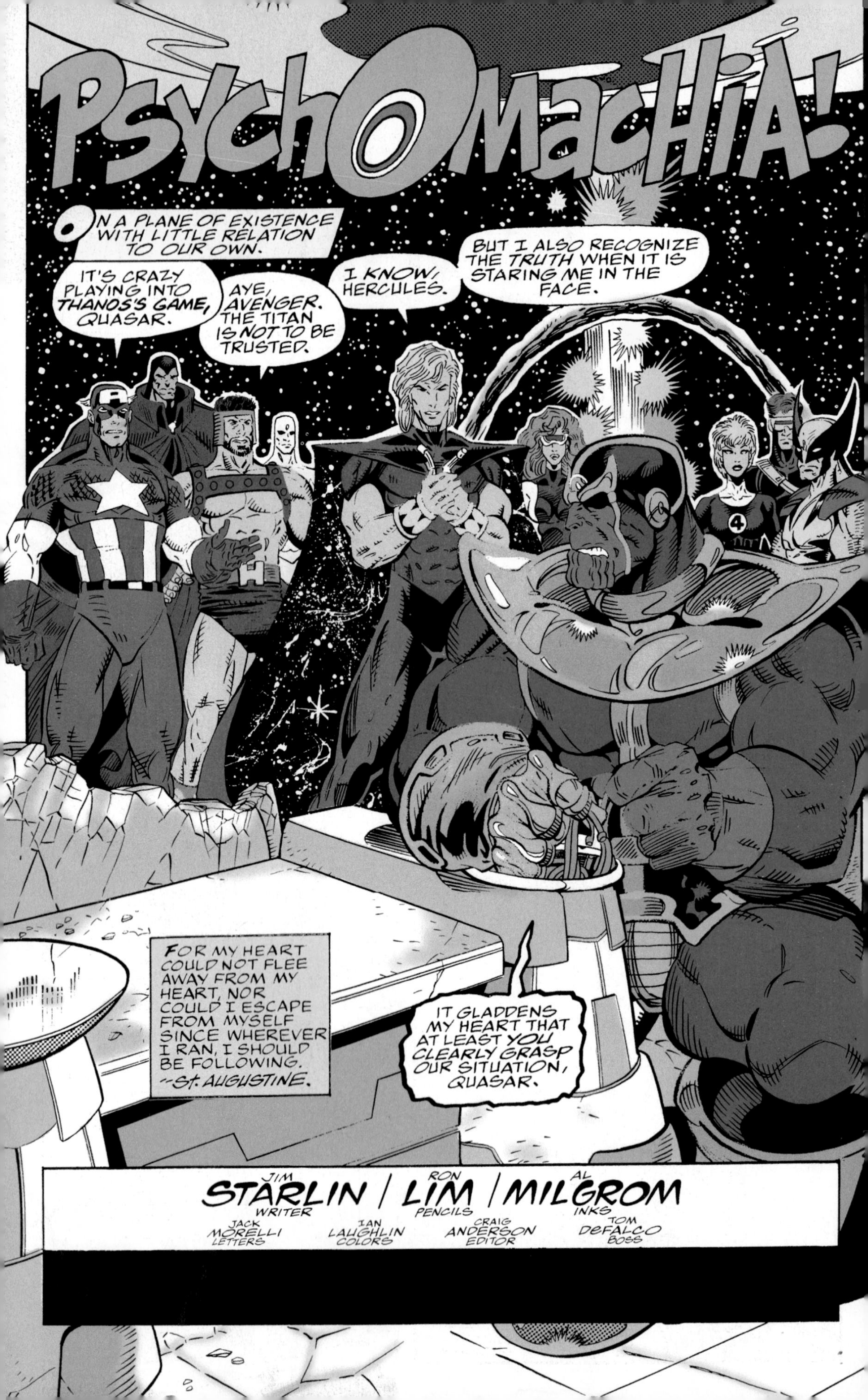
PSYCHOMACHIA!
ON A PLANE OF EXISTENCE WITH LITTLE RELATION TO OUR OWN.
IT'S CRAZY PLAYING INTO THANOS'S GAME, QUASAR.
AYE, AVENGER. THE TITAN IS NOT TO BE TRUSTED.
I KNOW, HERCULES.
BUT I ALSO RECOGNIZE THE TRUTH WHEN IT IS STARING ME IN THE FACE.
FOR MY HEART COULD NOT FLEE AWAY FROM MY HEART, NOR COULD I ESCAPE FROM MYSELF SINCE WHEREVER I RAN, I SHOULD BE FOLLOWING. --ST. AUGUSTINE.
IT GLADDENS MY HEART THAT AT LEAST YOU CLEARLY GRASP OUR SITUATION, QUASAR.
JIM STARLIN WRITER / RON LIM PENCILS / AL MILGROM INKS
JACK MORELLI LETTERS
IAN LAUGHLIN COLORS
CRAIG ANDERSON EDITOR
TOM DeFALCO BOSS

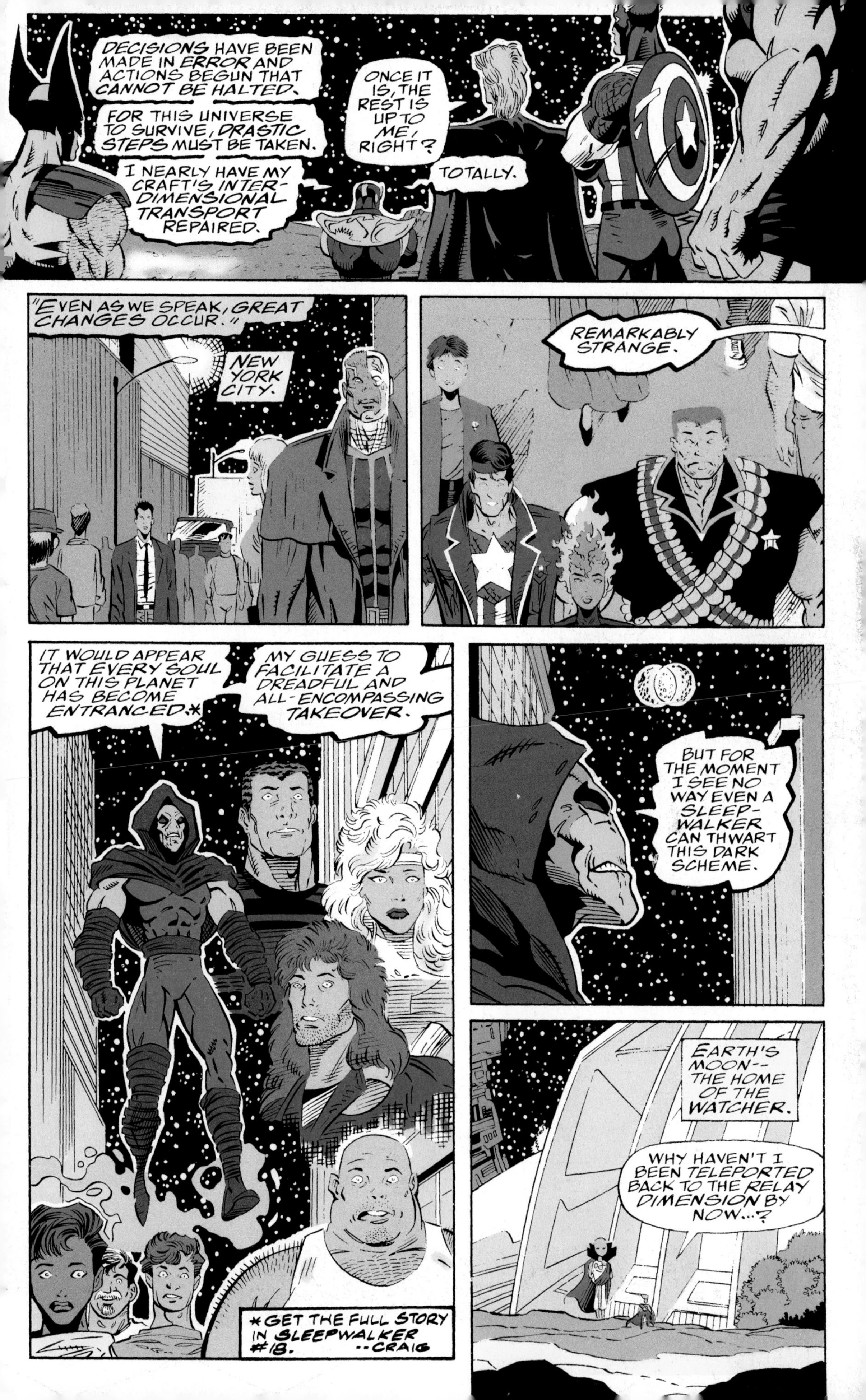
DECISIONS HAVE BEEN MADE IN ERROR AND ACTIONS BEGUN THAT CANNOT BE HALTED.
FOR THIS UNIVERSE TO SURVIVE, DRASTIC STEPS MUST BE TAKEN.
I NEARLY HAVE MY CRAFT'S INTER-DIMENSIONAL TRANSPORT REPAIRED.
ONCE IT IS, THE REST IS UP TO ME, RIGHT?
TOTALLY.
"EVEN AS WE SPEAK, GREAT CHANGES OCCUR."
NEW YORK CITY.
REMARKABLY STRANGE.
IT WOULD APPEAR THAT EVERY SOUL ON THIS PLANET HAS BECOME ENTRANCED.*
MY GUESS TO FACILITATE A DREADFUL AND ALL-ENCOMPASSING TAKEOVER.
*GET THE FULL STORY IN SLEEPWALKER #18. --CRAIG
BUT FOR THE MOMENT I SEE NO WAY EVEN A SLEEP-WALKER CAN THWART THIS DARK SCHEME.
EARTH'S MOON--THE HOME OF THE WATCHER.
WHY HAVEN'T I BEEN TELEPORTED BACK TO THE RELAY DIMENSION BY NOW...?

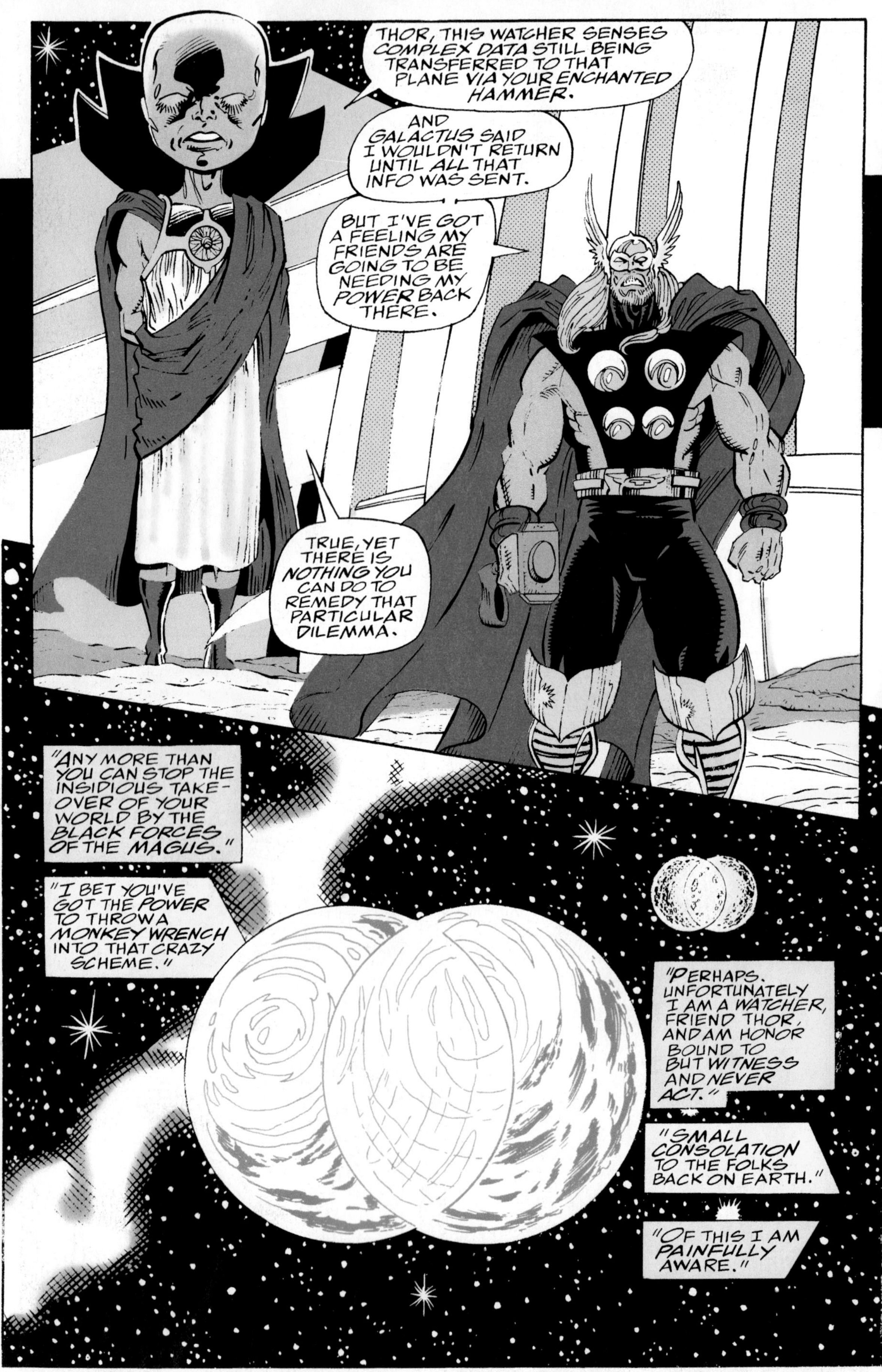
THOR, THIS WATCHER SENSES COMPLEX DATA STILL BEING TRANSFERRED TO THAT PLANE VIA YOUR ENCHANTED HAMMER.
AND GALACTUS SAID I WOULDN'T RETURN UNTIL ALL THAT INFO WAS SENT.
BUT I'VE GOT A FEELING MY FRIENDS ARE GOING TO BE NEEDING MY POWER BACK THERE.
TRUE, YET THERE IS NOTHING YOU CAN DO TO REMEDY THAT PARTICULAR DILEMMA.
"ANY MORE THAN YOU CAN STOP THE INSIDIOUS TAKE-OVER OF YOUR WORLD BY THE BLACK FORCES OF THE MAGUS."
"I BET YOU'VE GOT THE POWER TO THROW A MONKEY WRENCH INTO THAT CRAZY SCHEME."
"PERHAPS. UNFORTUNATELY I AM A WATCHER, FRIEND THOR, AND AM HONOR BOUND TO BUT WITNESS AND NEVER ACT."
"SMALL CONSOLATION TO THE FOLKS BACK ON EARTH."
"OF THIS I AM PAINFULLY AWARE."

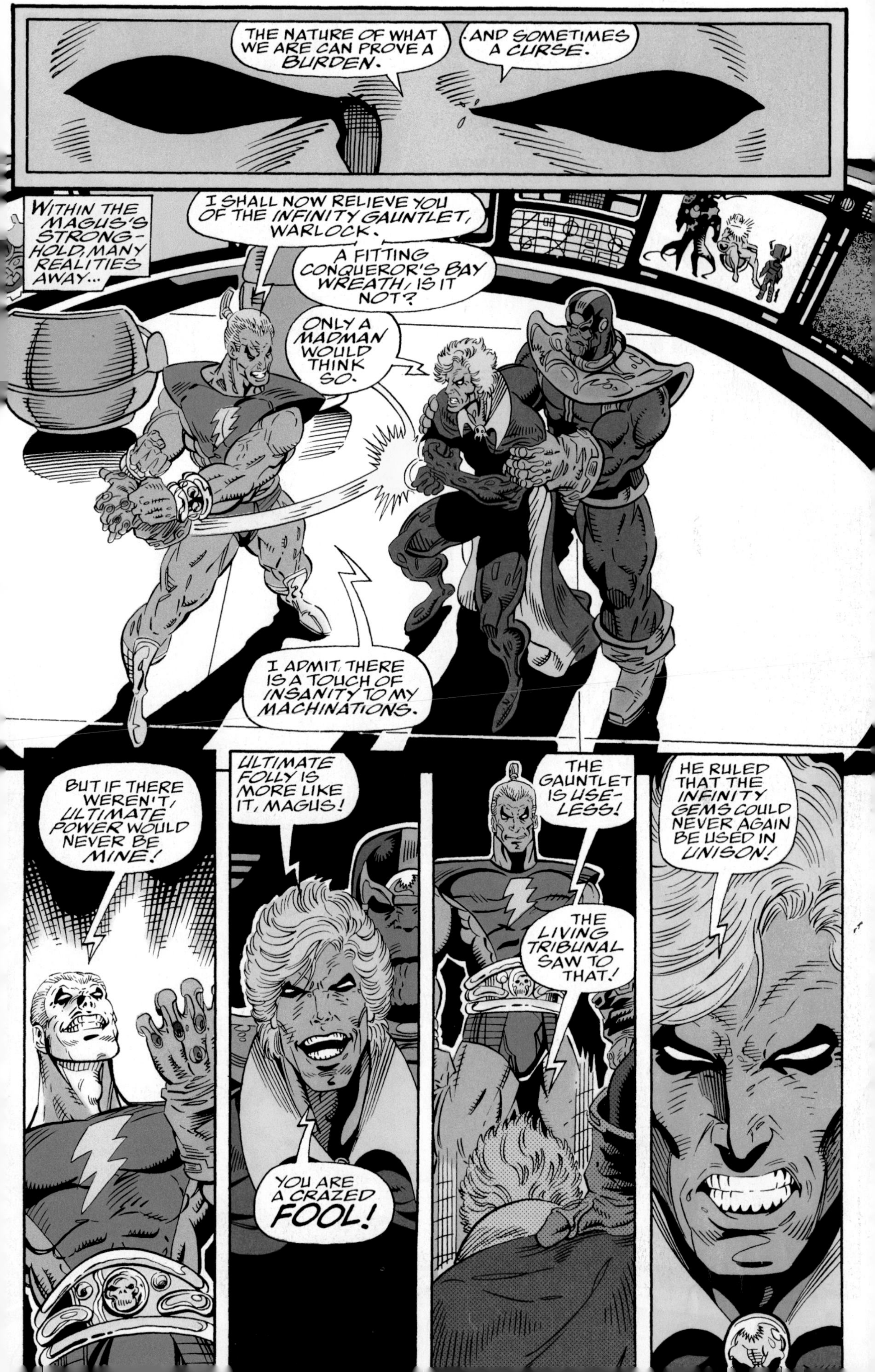

THE NATURE OF WHAT WE ARE CAN PROVE A BURDEN.
.AND SOMETIMES A CURSE.
WITHIN THE MAGUS'S STRONG-HOLD, MANY REALITIES AWAY...
I SHALL NOW RELIEVE YOU OF THE INFINITY GAUNTLET, WARLOCK.
A FITTING CONQUEROR'S BAY WREATH, IS IT NOT?
ONLY A MADMAN WOULD THINK SO.
I ADMIT, THERE IS A TOUCH OF INSANITY TO MY MACHINATIONS.
BUT IF THERE WEREN'T, ULTIMATE POWER WOULD NEVER BE MINE!
ULTIMATE FOLLY IS MORE LIKE IT, MAGUS!
YOU ARE A CRAZED FOOL!
THE GAUNTLET IS USE-LESS!
THE LIVING TRIBUNAL SAW TO THAT!
HE RULED THAT THE INFINITY GEMS COULD NEVER AGAIN BE USED IN UNISON!

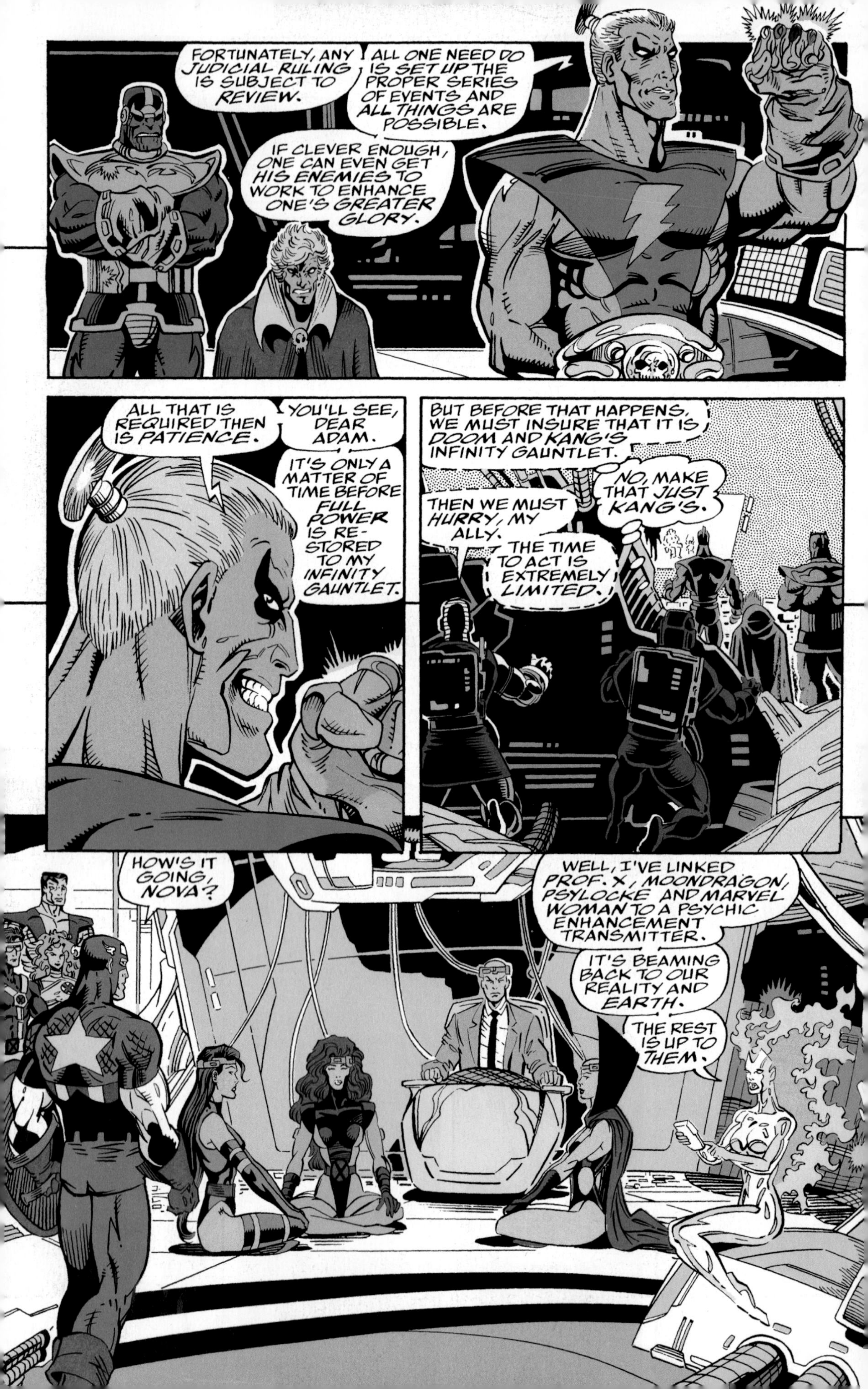
FORTUNATELY, ANY JUDICIAL RULING IS SUBJECT TO REVIEW.
ALL ONE NEED DO IS SET UP THE PROPER SERIES OF EVENTS AND ALL THINGS ARE POSSIBLE.
IF CLEVER ENOUGH, ONE CAN EVEN GET HIS ENEMIES TO WORK TO ENHANCE ONE'S GREATER GLORY.
ALL THAT IS REQUIRED THEN IS PATIENCE.
YOU'LL SEE, DEAR ADAM.
IT'S ONLY A MATTER OF TIME BEFORE FULL POWER IS RESTORED TO MY INFINITY GAUNTLET.
BUT BEFORE THAT HAPPENS, WE MUST INSURE THAT IT IS DOOM AND KANG'S INFINITY GAUNTLET.
NO, MAKE THAT JUST KANG'S.
THEN WE MUST HURRY, MY ALLY.
THE TIME TO ACT IS EXTREMELY LIMITED.
HOW'S IT GOING, NOVA?
WELL, I'VE LINKED PROF. X, MOONDRAGON, PSYLOCKE AND MARVEL WOMAN TO A PSYCHIC ENHANCEMENT TRANSMITTER.
IT'S BEAMING BACK TO OUR REALITY AND EARTH.
THE REST IS UP TO THEM.

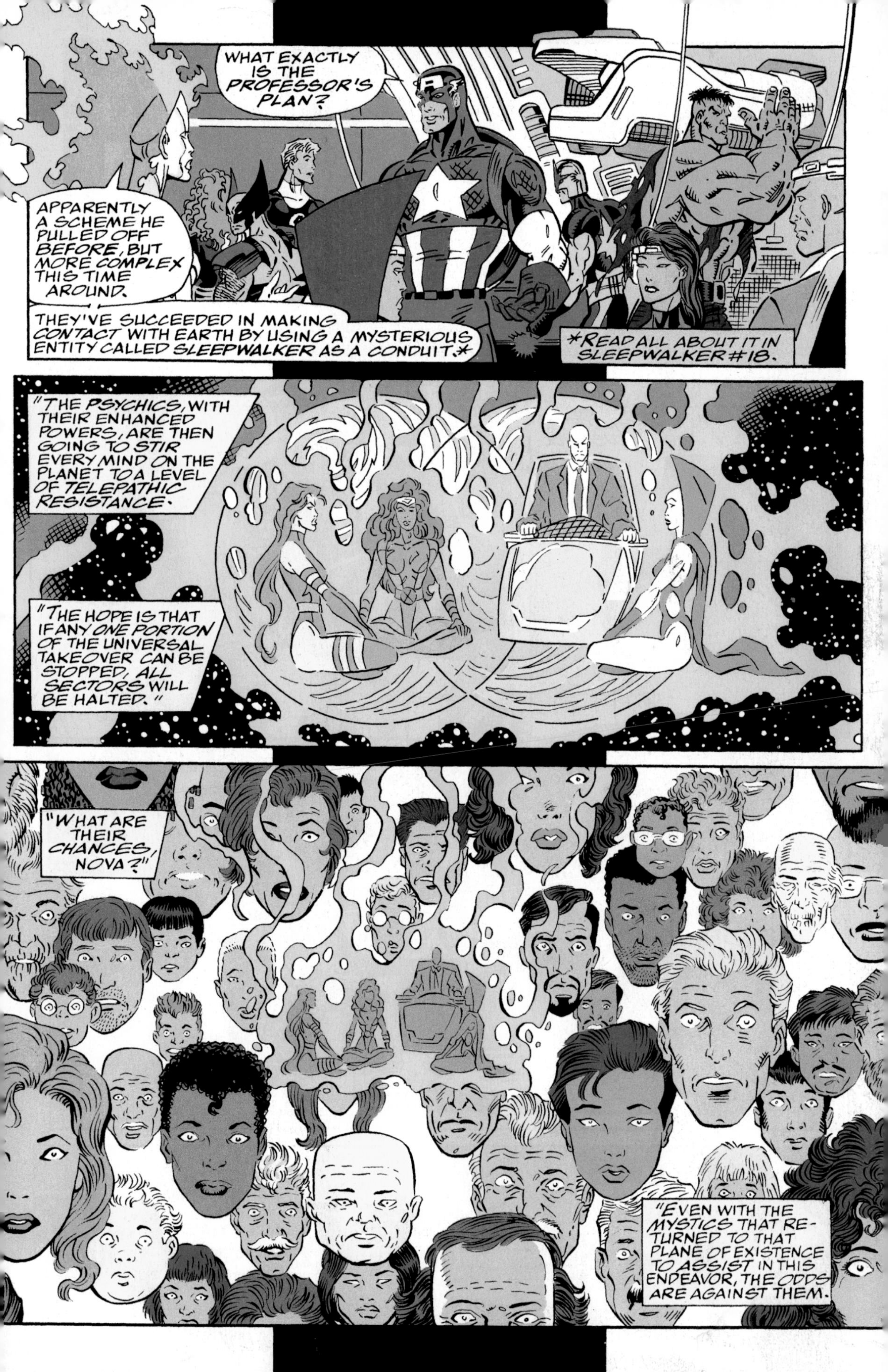
WHAT EXACTLY IS THE PROFESSOR'S PLAN?
APPARENTLY A SCHEME HE PULLED OFF BEFORE, BUT MORE COMPLEX THIS TIME AROUND.
THEY'VE SUCCEEDED IN MAKING CONTACT WITH EARTH BY USING A MYSTERIOUS ENTITY CALLED SLEEPWALKER AS A CONDUIT.*
*READ ALL ABOUT IT IN SLEEPWALKER #18.
"THE PSYCHICS, WITH THEIR ENHANCED POWERS, ARE THEN GOING TO STIR EVERY MIND ON THE PLANET TO A LEVEL OF TELEPATHIC RESISTANCE.
"THE HOPE IS THAT IF ANY ONE PORTION OF THE UNIVERSAL TAKEOVER CAN BE STOPPED, ALL SECTORS WILL BE HALTED."
"WHAT ARE THEIR CHANCES, NOVA?"
"EVEN WITH THE MYSTICS THAT RE-TURNED TO THAT PLANE OF EXISTENCE TO ASSIST IN THIS ENDEAVOR, THE ODDS ARE AGAINST THEM.

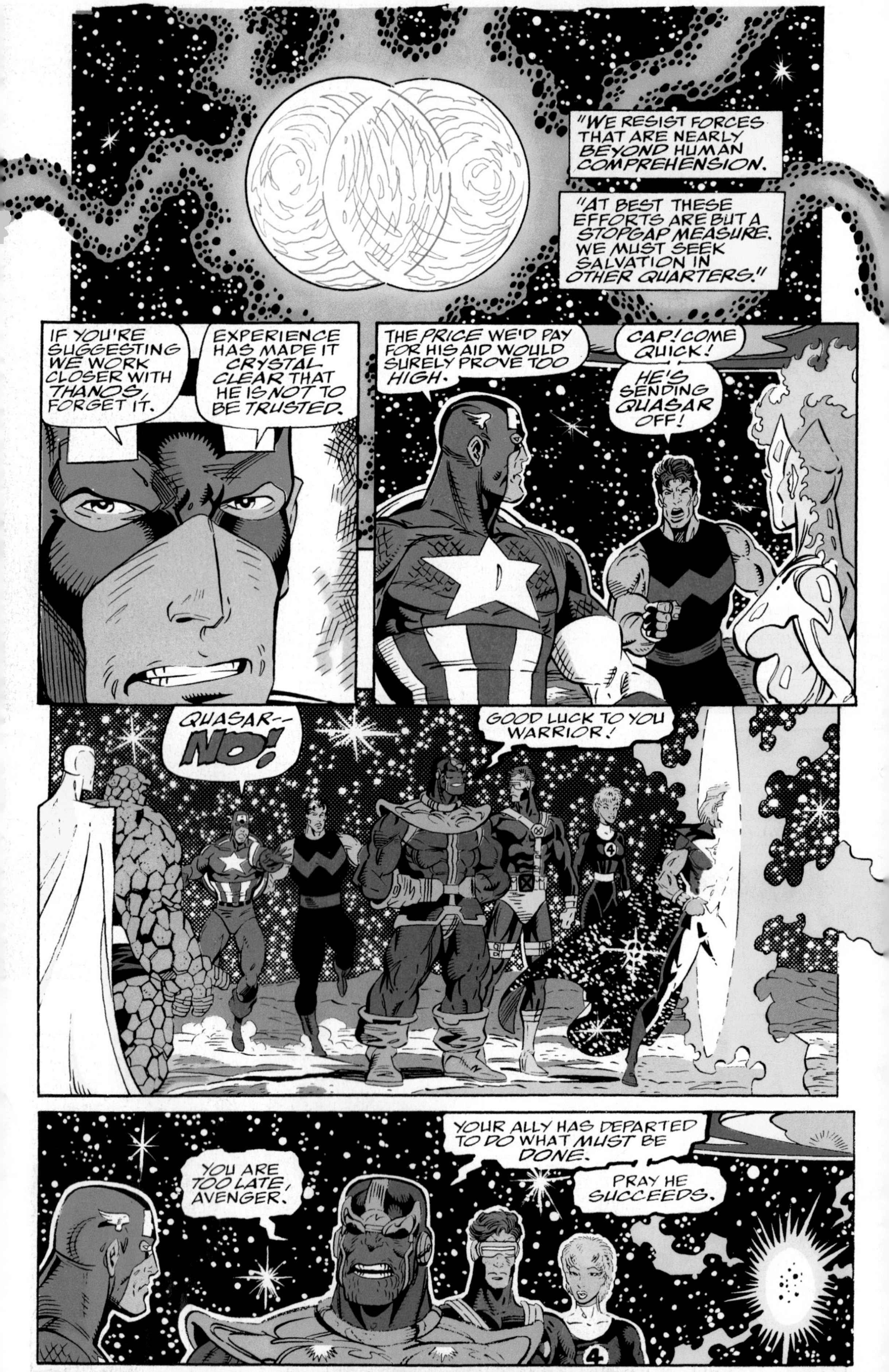
"WE RESIST FORCES THAT ARE NEARLY BEYOND HUMAN COMPREHENSION.
"AT BEST THESE EFFORTS ARE BUT A STOPGAP MEASURE. WE MUST SEEK SALVATION IN OTHER QUARTERS."
IF YOU'RE SUGGESTING WE WORK CLOSER WITH THANOS, FORGET IT.
EXPERIENCE HAS MADE IT CRYSTAL CLEAR THAT HE IS NOT TO BE TRUSTED.
THE PRICE WE'D PAY FOR HIS AID WOULD SURELY PROVE TOO HIGH.
CAP! COME QUICK!
HE'S SENDING QUASAR OFF!
QUASAR-- NO!
GOOD LUCK TO YOU WARRIOR!
YOU ARE TOO LATE, AVENGER.
YOUR ALLY HAS DEPARTED TO DO WHAT MUST BE DONE.
PRAY HE SUCCEEDS.

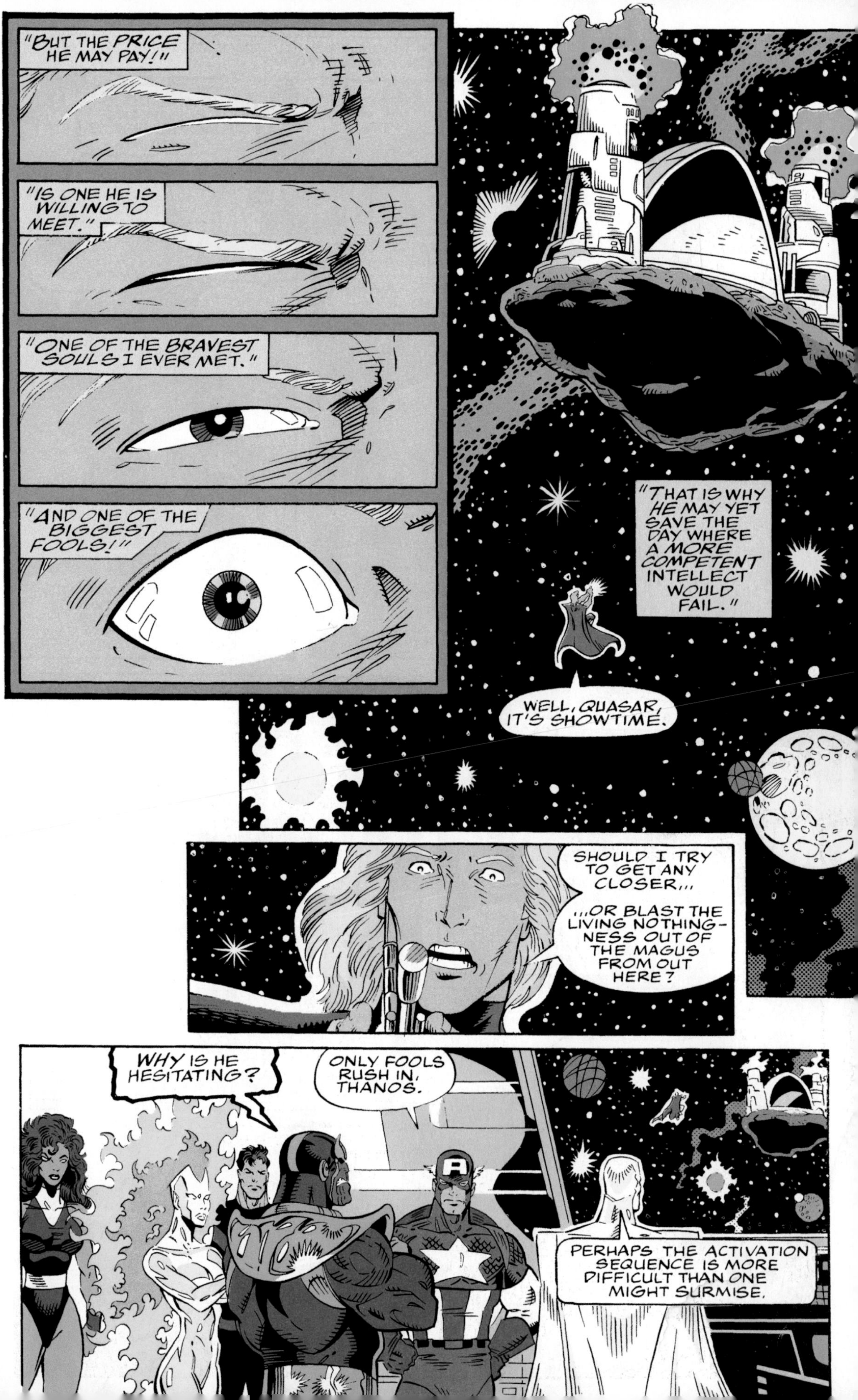
"BUT THE PRICE HE MAY PAY!"
"IS ONE HE IS WILLING TO MEET."
"ONE OF THE BRAVEST SOULS I EVER MET."
"AND ONE OF THE BIGGEST FOOLS!"
"THAT IS WHY HE MAY YET SAVE THE DAY WHERE A MORE COMPETENT INTELLECT WOULD FAIL."
WELL, QUASAR, IT'S SHOWTIME.
SHOULD I TRY TO GET ANY CLOSER...
...OR BLAST THE LIVING NOTHINGNESS OUT OF THE MAGUS FROM OUT HERE?
WHY IS HE HESITATING?
ONLY FOOLS RUSH IN, THANOS.
PERHAPS THE ACTIVATION SEQUENCE IS MORE DIFFICULT THAN ONE MIGHT SURMISE.

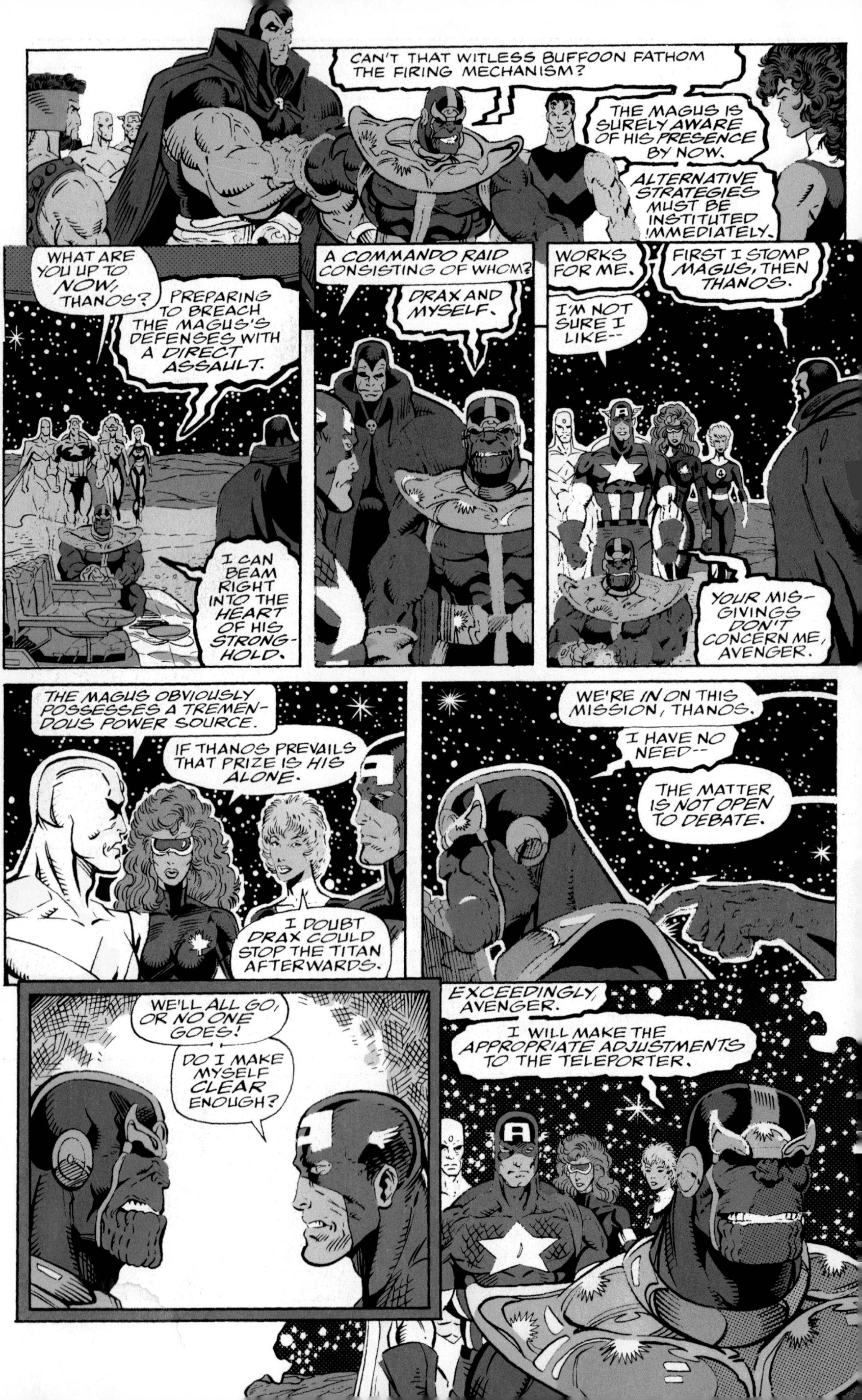
CAN'T THAT WITLESS BUFFOON FATHOM THE FIRING MECHANISM?
THE MAGUS IS SURELY AWARE OF HIS PRESENCE BY NOW.
ALTERNATIVE STRATEGIES MUST BE INSTITUTED IMMEDIATELY.
WHAT ARE YOU UP TO NOW, THANOS?
PREPARING TO BREACH THE MAGUS'S DEFENSES WITH A DIRECT ASSAULT.
I CAN BEAM RIGHT INTO THE HEART OF HIS STRONGHOLD.
A COMMANDO RAID CONSISTING OF WHOM?
DRAX AND MYSELF.
WORKS FOR ME.
FIRST I STOMP MAGUS, THEN THANOS.
I'M NOT SURE I LIKE--
YOUR MISGIVINGS DON'T CONCERN ME, AVENGER.
THE MAGUS OBVIOUSLY POSSESSES A TREMENDOUS POWER SOURCE.
IF THANOS PREVAILS THAT PRIZE IS HIS ALONE.
I DOUBT DRAX COULD STOP THE TITAN AFTERWARDS.
WE'RE IN ON THIS MISSION, THANOS.
I HAVE NO NEED--
THE MATTER IS NOT OPEN TO DEBATE.
WE'LL ALL GO, OR NO ONE GOES!
DO I MAKE MYSELF CLEAR ENOUGH?
EXCEEDINGLY, AVENGER.
I WILL MAKE THE APPROPRIATE ADJUSTMENTS TO THE TELEPORTER.

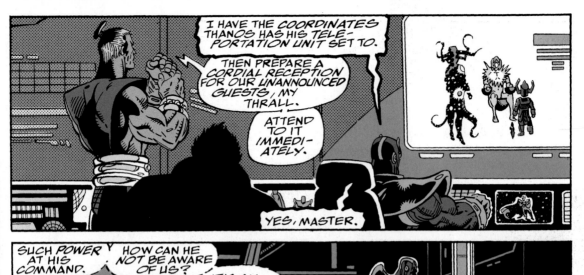

I HAVE THE *COORDINATES* THANOS HAS HIS TELE-PORTATION UNIT SET TO.

THEN PREPARE A *CORDIAL* RECEPTION FOR OUR *UNANNOUNCED* GUESTS, MY *THRALL.*

ATTEND TO IT IMMEDI-ATELY.

YES, MASTER.

SUCH *POWER* AT HIS COMMAND.

HOW CAN HE *NOT* BE AWARE OF US?

IT'S ALL A MATTER OF *FOCUS.*

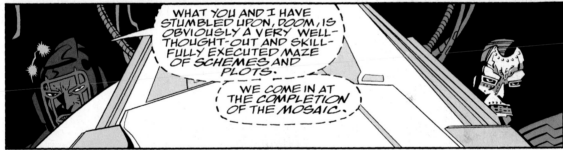

WHAT YOU AND I HAVE *STUMBLED* UPON, DOOM, IS OBVIOUSLY A VERY WELL-THOUGHT-OUT AND SKILL-FULLY EXECUTED MAZE OF *SCHEMES* AND *PLOTS.*

WE COME IN AT THE *COMPLETION* OF THE *MOSAIC.*

FORTUNATELY FOR US, THE *CRAFTSMAN* IS SO ABSORBED IN HIS *WORK* THE OUTSIDE WORLD NO LONGER MATTERS TO HIM.

OUR ENEMY IS NOT AWARE OF US BECAUSE WE WERE NEVER *PART* OF HIS PLAN.

HE HASN'T *SPOTTED* US BECAUSE HE ISN'T *LOOKING* FOR US.

A *FATAL FLAW* IN THE DESIGN.

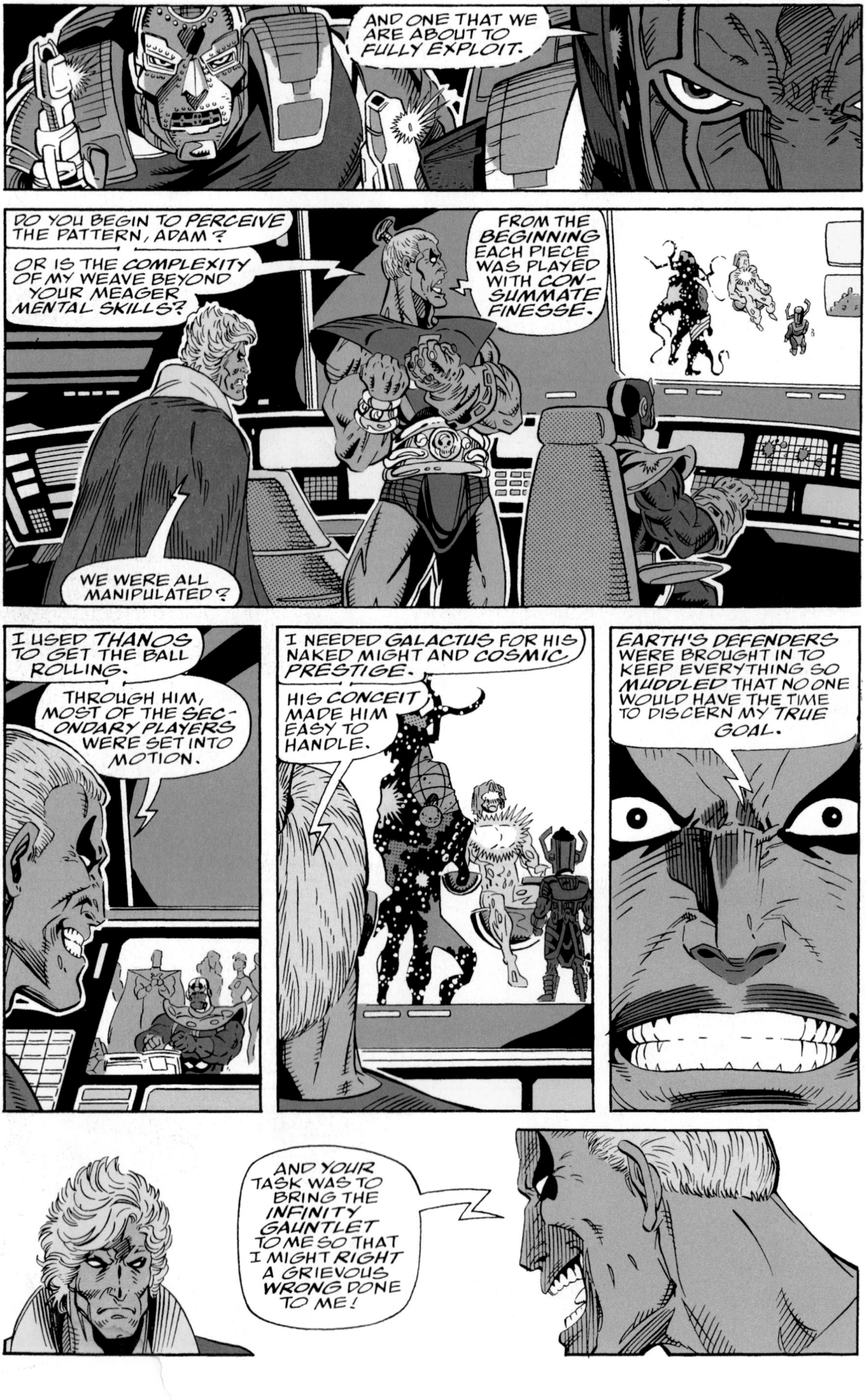
AND ONE THAT WE ARE ABOUT TO FULLY EXPLOIT.
DO YOU BEGIN TO PERCEIVE THE PATTERN, ADAM?
OR IS THE COMPLEXITY OF MY WEAVE BEYOND YOUR MEAGER MENTAL SKILLS?
FROM THE BEGINNING EACH PIECE WAS PLAYED WITH CON-SUMMATE FINESSE.
WE WERE ALL MANIPULATED?
I USED THANOS TO GET THE BALL ROLLING.
THROUGH HIM, MOST OF THE SEC-ONDARY PLAYERS WERE SET INTO MOTION.
I NEEDED GALACTUS FOR HIS NAKED MIGHT AND COSMIC PRESTIGE.
HIS CONCEIT MADE HIM EASY TO HANDLE.
EARTH'S DEFENDERS WERE BROUGHT IN TO KEEP EVERYTHING SO MUDDLED THAT NO ONE WOULD HAVE THE TIME TO DISCERN MY TRUE GOAL.
AND YOUR TASK WAS TO BRING THE INFINITY GAUNTLET TO ME SO THAT I MIGHT RIGHT A GRIEVOUS WRONG DONE TO ME!

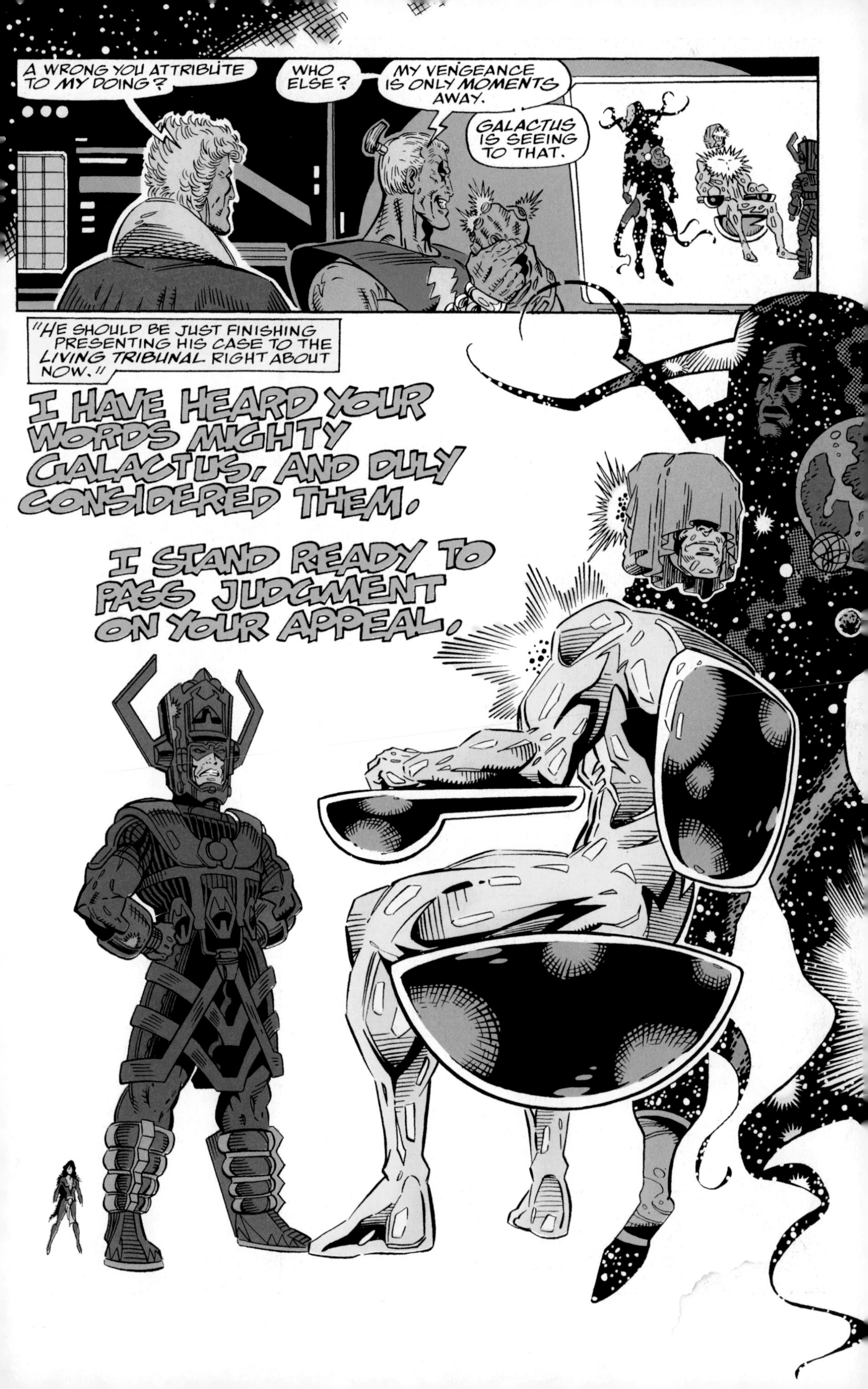

A WRONG YOU ATTRIBUTE TO MY DOING?
WHO ELSE?
MY VENGEANCE IS ONLY MOMENTS AWAY.
GALACTUS IS SEEING TO THAT.
"HE SHOULD BE JUST FINISHING PRESENTING HIS CASE TO THE LIVING TRIBUNAL RIGHT ABOUT NOW."
I HAVE HEARD YOUR WORDS MIGHTY GALACTUS, AND DULY CONSIDERED THEM.
I STAND READY TO PASS JUDGMENT ON YOUR APPEAL.

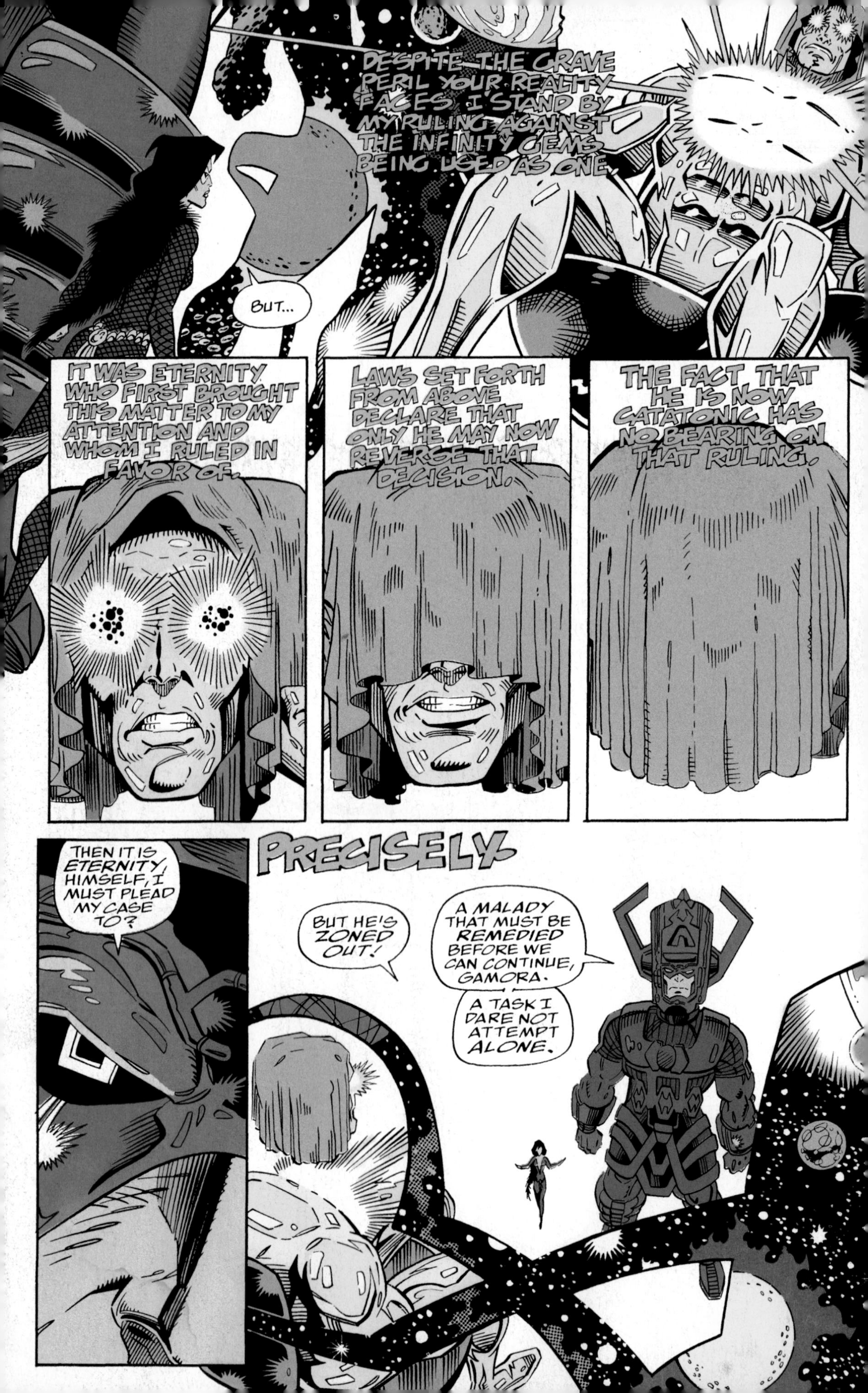
DESPITE THE GRAVE PERIL YOUR REALITY FACES, I STAND BY MY RULING AGAINST THE INFINITY GEMS BEING USED AS ONE.
BUT...
IT WAS ETERNITY WHO FIRST BROUGHT THIS MATTER TO MY ATTENTION AND WHOM I RULED IN FAVOR OF.
LAWS SET FORTH FROM ABOVE DECLARE THAT ONLY HE MAY NOW REVERSE THAT DECISION.
THE FACT THAT HE IS NOW CATATONIC HAS NO BEARING ON THAT RULING.
THEN IT IS ETERNITY, HIMSELF, I MUST PLEAD MY CASE TO?
PRECISELY.
BUT HE'S ZONED OUT!
A MALADY THAT MUST BE REMEDIED BEFORE WE CAN CONTINUE, GAMORA.
A TASK I DARE NOT ATTEMPT ALONE.

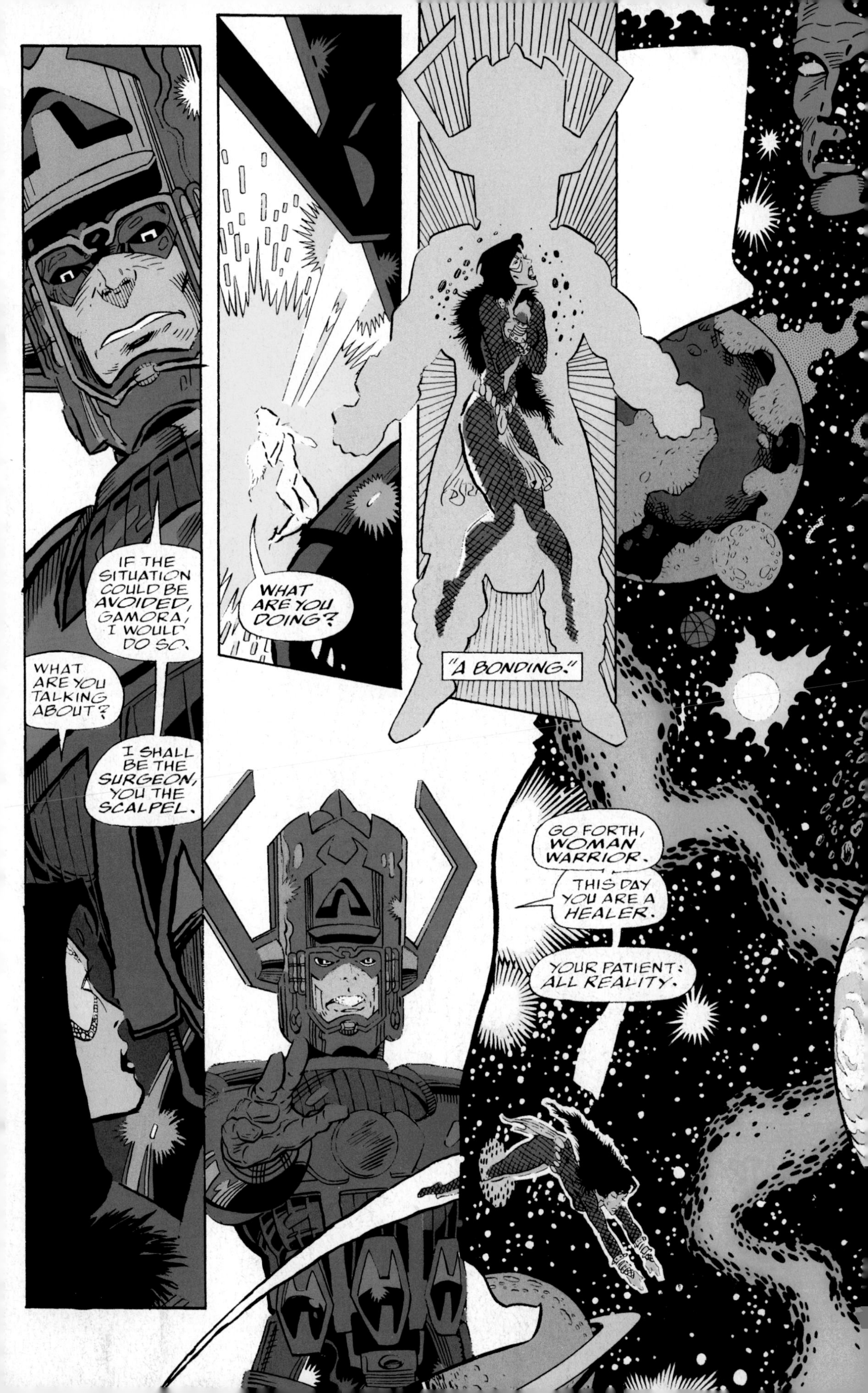
IF THE SITUATION COULD BE AVOIDED, GAMORA, I WOULD DO SO.
WHAT ARE YOU TALKING ABOUT?
I SHALL BE THE SURGEON, YOU THE SCALPEL.
WHAT ARE YOU DOING?
"A BONDING."
GO FORTH, WOMAN WARRIOR.
THIS DAY YOU ARE A HEALER.
YOUR PATIENT: ALL REALITY.

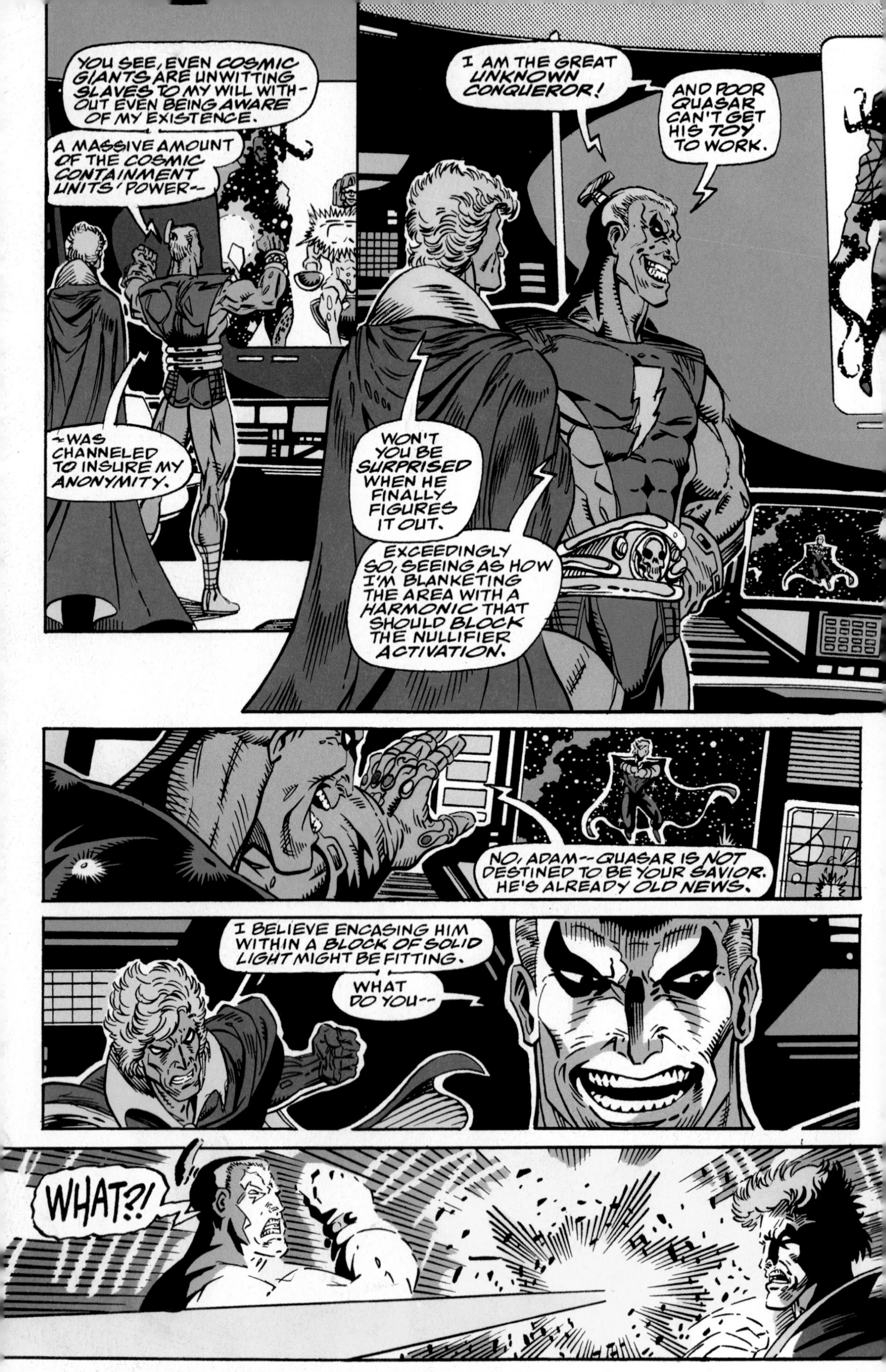
YOU SEE, EVEN COSMIC GIANTS ARE UNWITTING SLAVES TO MY WILL WITH-OUT EVEN BEING AWARE OF MY EXISTENCE.
A MASSIVE AMOUNT OF THE COSMIC CONTAINMENT UNITS' POWER--
--WAS CHANNELED TO INSURE MY ANONYMITY.
I AM THE GREAT UNKNOWN CONQUEROR!
AND POOR QUASAR CAN'T GET HIS TOY TO WORK.
WON'T YOU BE SURPRISED WHEN HE FINALLY FIGURES IT OUT.
EXCEEDINGLY SO, SEEING AS HOW I'M BLANKETING THE AREA WITH A HARMONIC THAT SHOULD BLOCK THE NULLIFIER ACTIVATION.
NO, ADAM--QUASAR IS NOT DESTINED TO BE YOUR SAVIOR. HE'S ALREADY OLD NEWS.
I BELIEVE ENCASING HIM WITHIN A BLOCK OF SOLID LIGHT MIGHT BE FITTING.
WHAT DO YOU--
WHAT?!

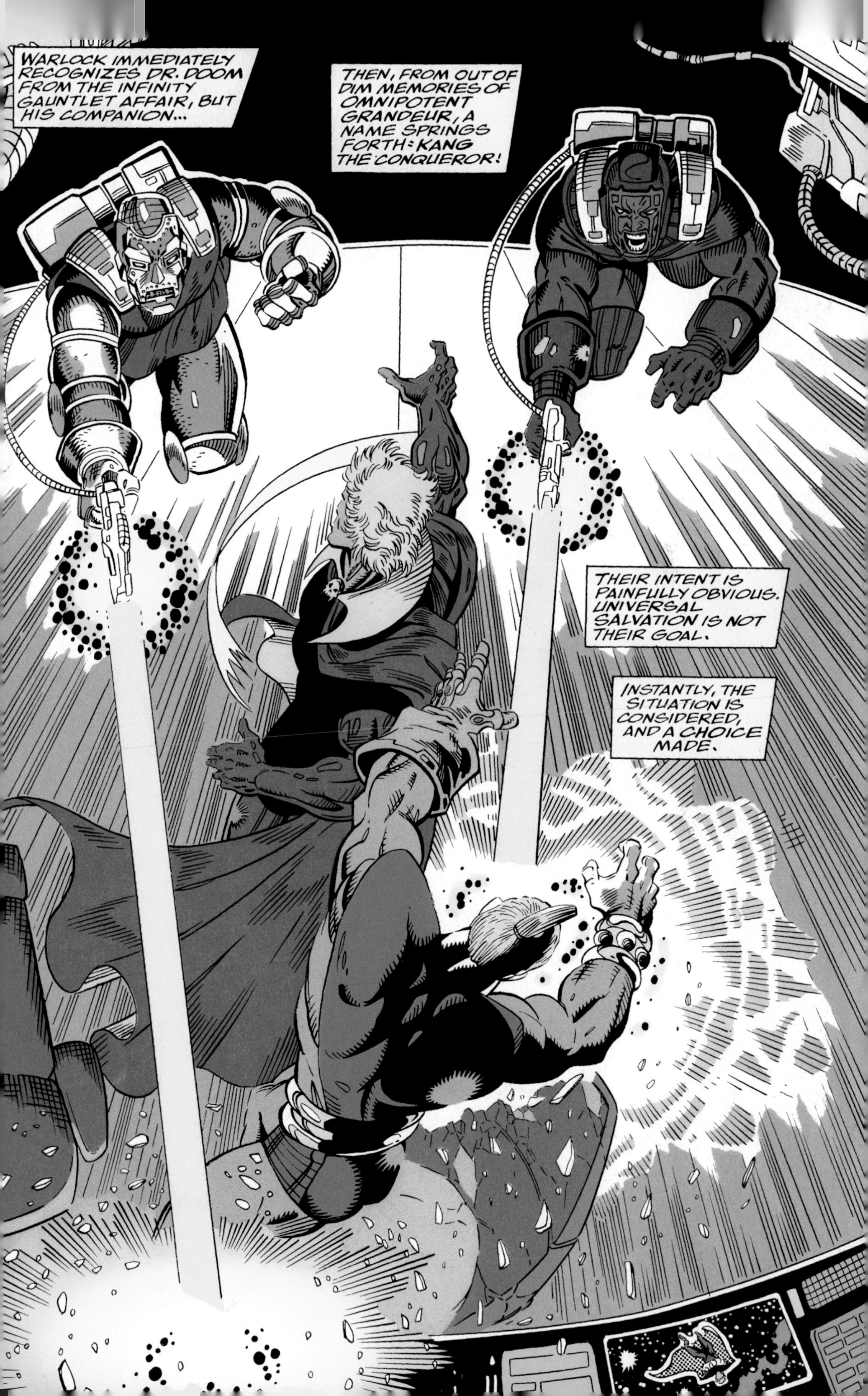
WARLOCK IMMEDIATELY RECOGNIZES DR. DOOM FROM THE INFINITY GAUNTLET AFFAIR, BUT HIS COMPANION...
THEN, FROM OUT OF DIM MEMORIES OF OMNIPOTENT GRANDEUR, A NAME SPRINGS FORTH: KANG THE CONQUEROR!
THEIR INTENT IS PAINFULLY OBVIOUS. UNIVERSAL SALVATION IS NOT THEIR GOAL.
INSTANTLY, THE SITUATION IS CONSIDERED, AND A CHOICE MADE.

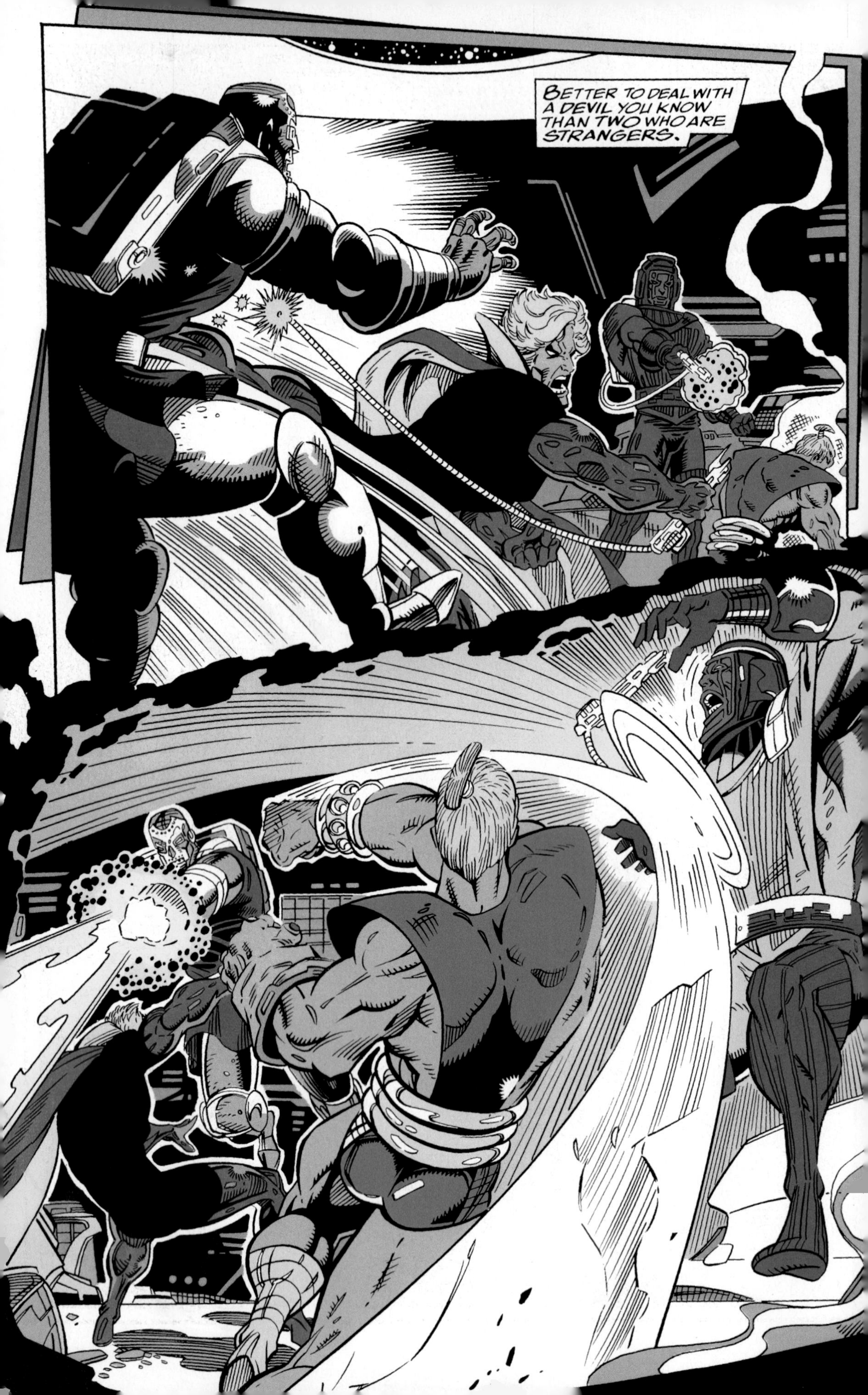
BETTER TO DEAL WITH A DEVIL YOU KNOW THAN TWO WHO ARE STRANGERS.

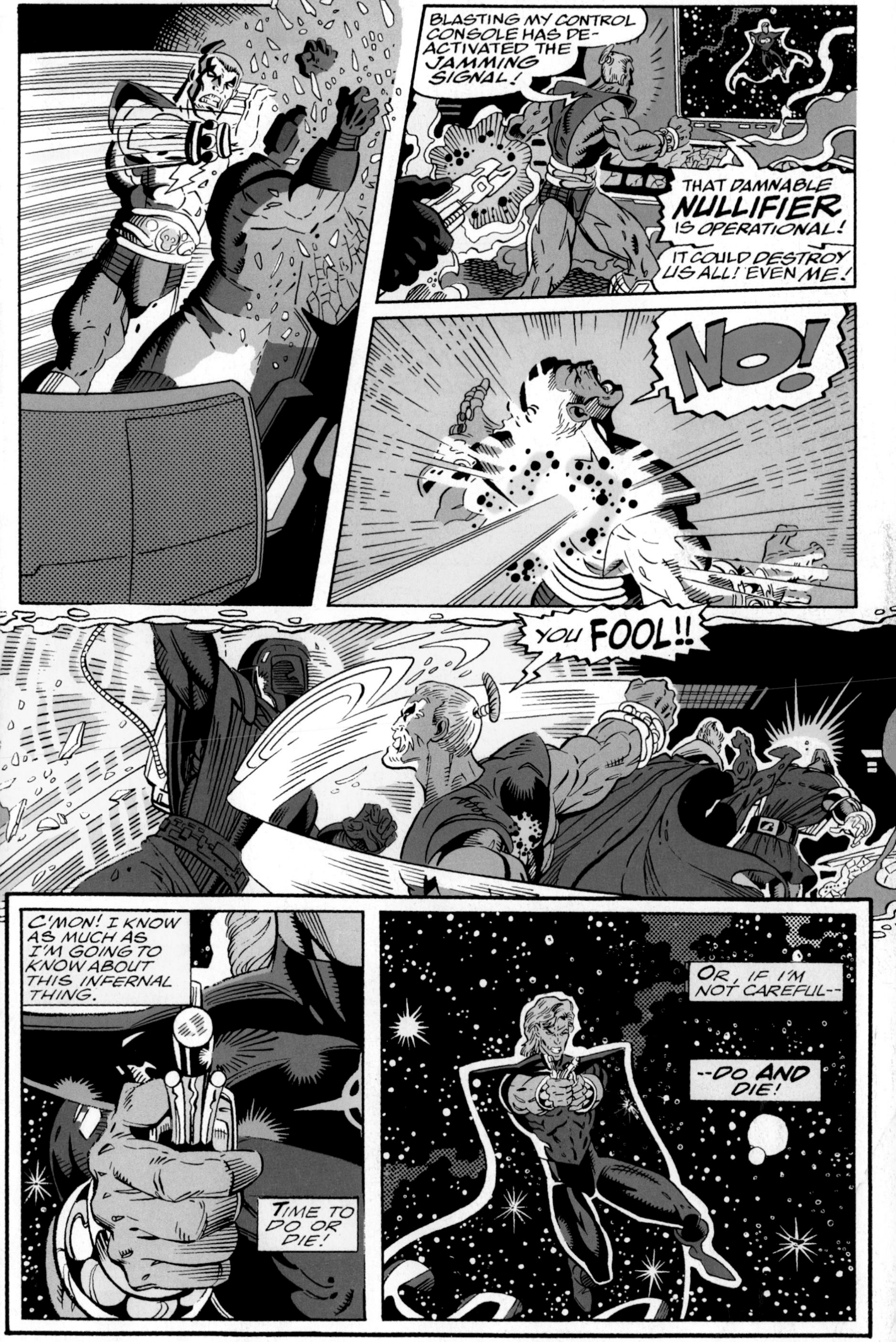
BLASTING MY CONTROL CONSOLE HAS DE-ACTIVATED THE JAMMING SIGNAL!
THAT DAMNABLE NULLIFIER IS OPERATIONAL!
IT COULD DESTROY US ALL! EVEN ME!
NO!
YOU FOOL!!
C'MON! I KNOW AS MUCH AS I'M GOING TO KNOW ABOUT THIS INFERNAL THING.
TIME TO DO OR DIE!
OR, IF I'M NOT CAREFUL--
--DO AND DIE!

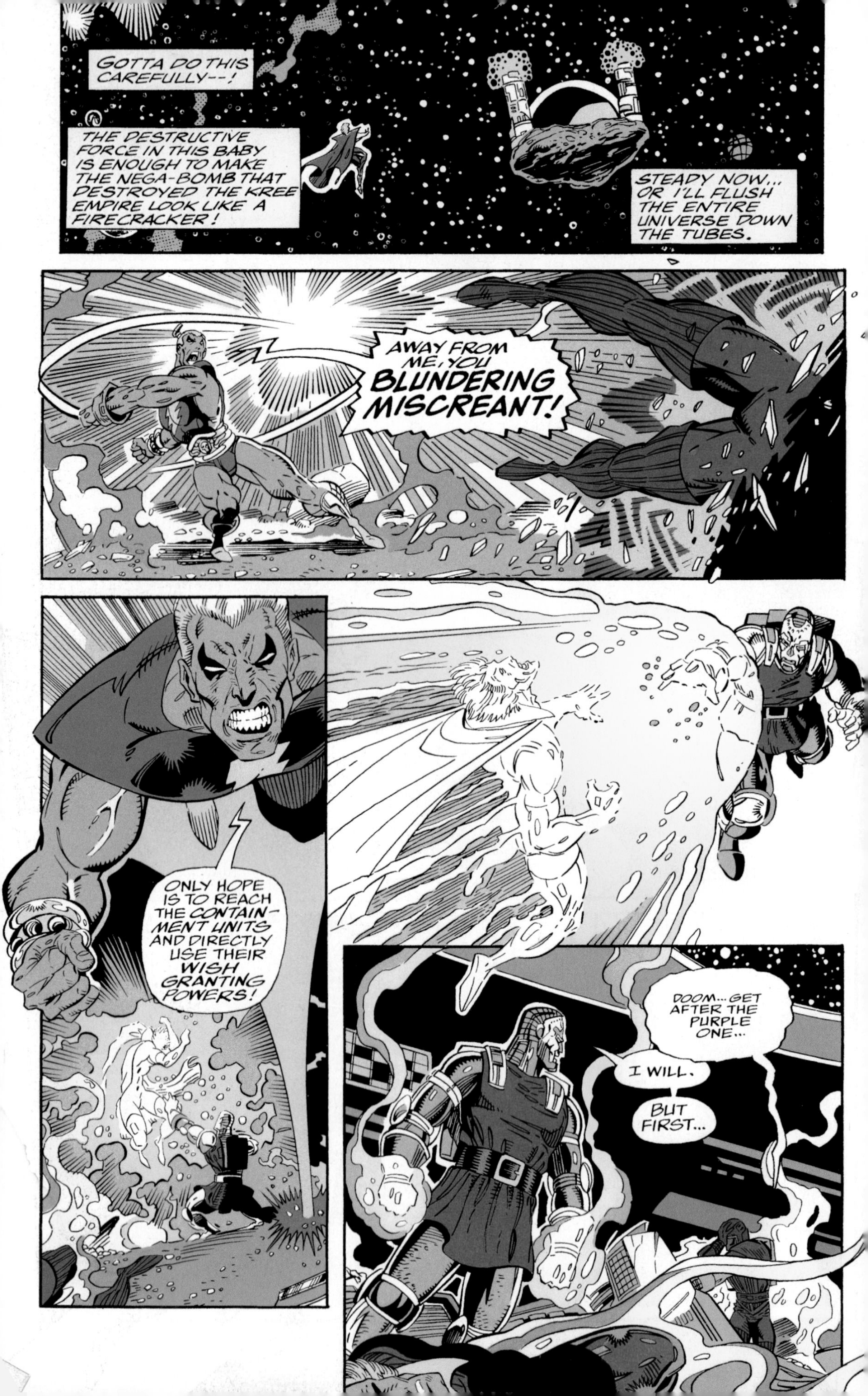
GOTTA DO THIS CAREFULLY--!
THE DESTRUCTIVE FORCE IN THIS BABY IS ENOUGH TO MAKE THE NEGA-BOMB THAT DESTROYED THE KREE EMPIRE LOOK LIKE A FIRECRACKER!
STEADY NOW... OR I'LL FLUSH THE ENTIRE UNIVERSE DOWN THE TUBES.
AWAY FROM ME, YOU BLUNDERING MISCREANT!
ONLY HOPE IS TO REACH THE CONTAINMENT UNITS AND DIRECTLY USE THEIR WISH GRANTING POWERS!
DOOM... GET AFTER THE PURPLE ONE...
I WILL.
BUT FIRST...

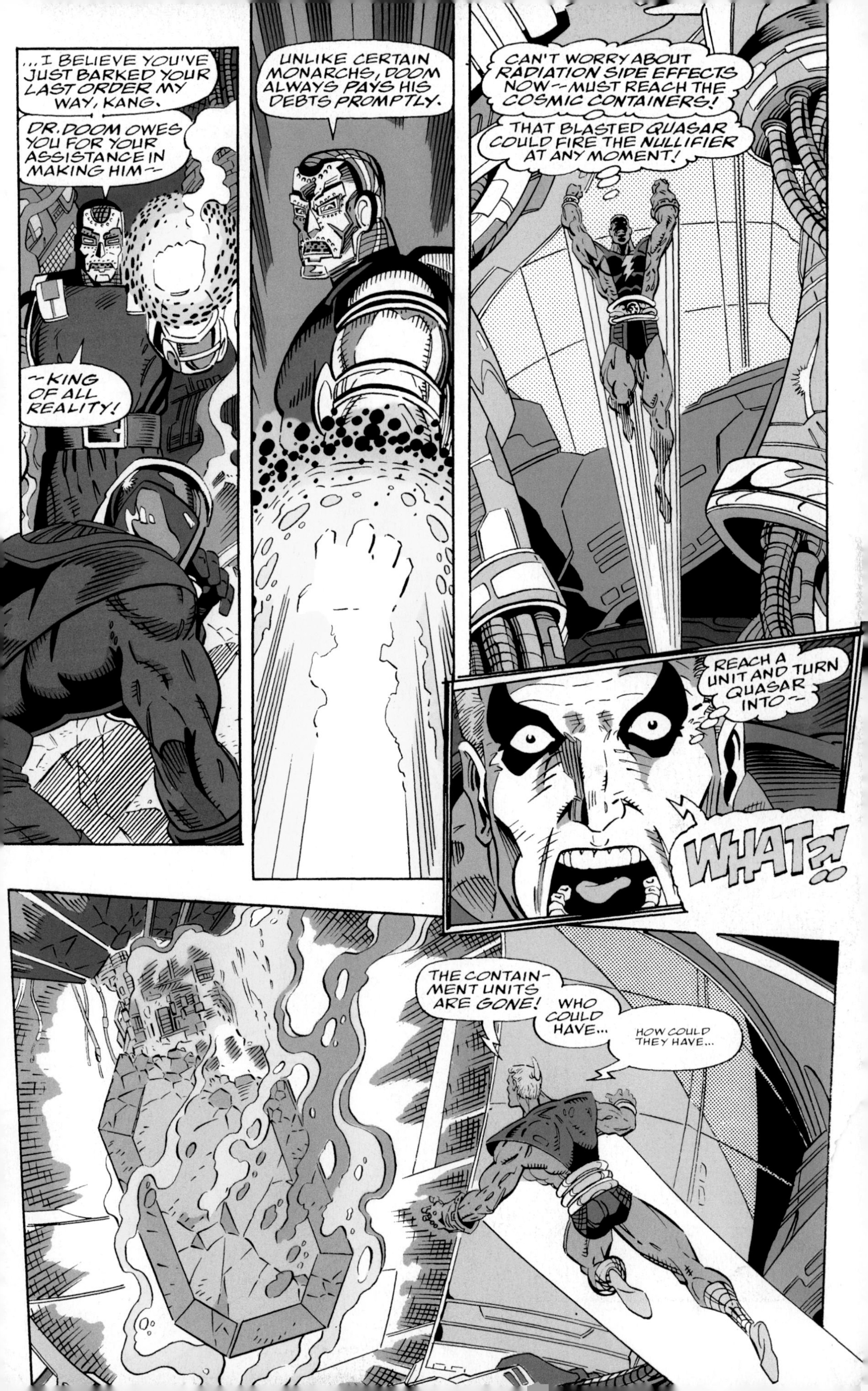
...I BELIEVE YOU'VE JUST BARKED YOUR LAST ORDER MY WAY, KANG.
DR. DOOM OWES YOU FOR YOUR ASSISTANCE IN MAKING HIM--
--KING OF ALL REALITY!
UNLIKE CERTAIN MONARCHS, DOOM ALWAYS PAYS HIS DEBTS PROMPTLY.
CAN'T WORRY ABOUT RADIATION SIDE EFFECTS NOW--MUST REACH THE COSMIC CONTAINERS!
THAT BLASTED QUASAR COULD FIRE THE NULLIFIER AT ANY MOMENT!
REACH A UNIT AND TURN QUASAR INTO--
WHAT?!
THE CONTAINMENT UNITS ARE GONE!
WHO COULD HAVE...
HOW COULD THEY HAVE...

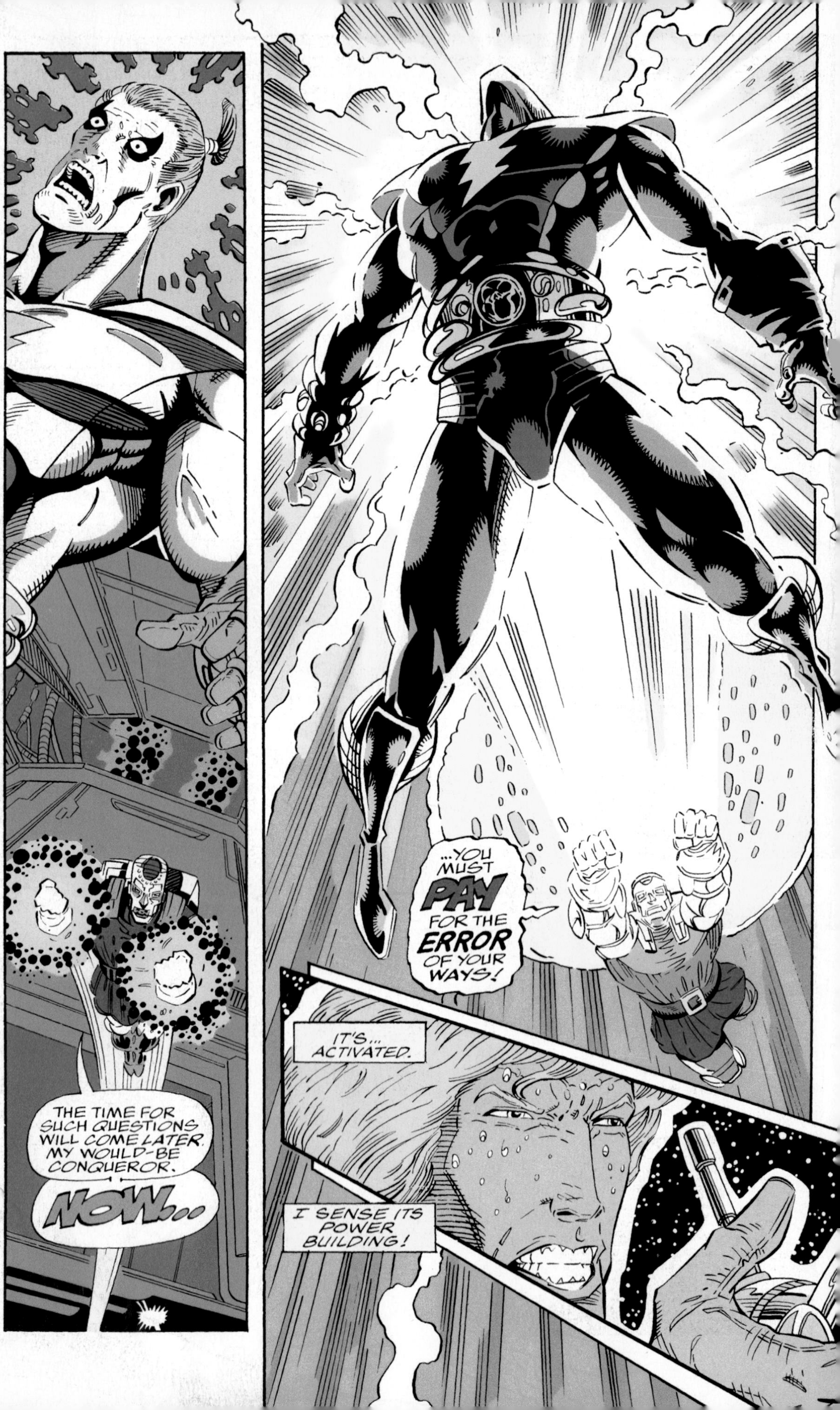
THE TIME FOR SUCH QUESTIONS WILL COME LATER, MY WOULD-BE CONQUEROR.
NOW...
...YOU MUST PAY FOR THE ERROR OF YOUR WAYS!
IT'S... ACTIVATED.
I SENSE ITS POWER BUILDING!

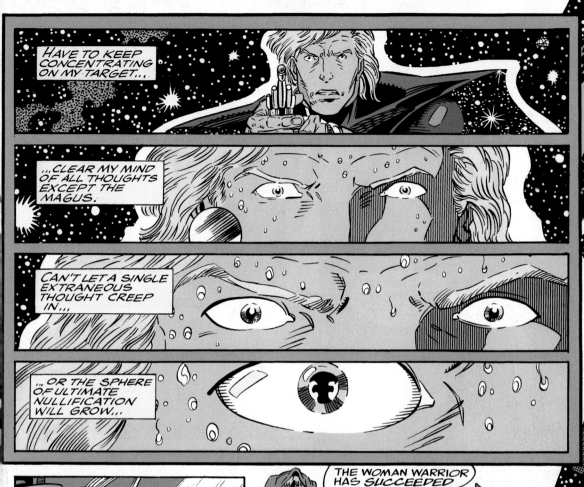

HAVE TO KEEP CONCENTRATING ON MY TARGET...

...CLEAR MY MIND OF ALL THOUGHTS EXCEPT THE MAGUS.

CAN'T LET A SINGLE EXTRANEOUS THOUGHT CREEP IN...

... OR THE SPHERE OF ULTIMATE NULLIFICATION WILL GROW...

...AND MUSHROOM OUT OF MY CONTROL!

THE WOMAN WARRIOR HAS SUCCEEDED IN HER QUEST.

BLAST YOU, GALACTUS!

YOU *USED* ME!!

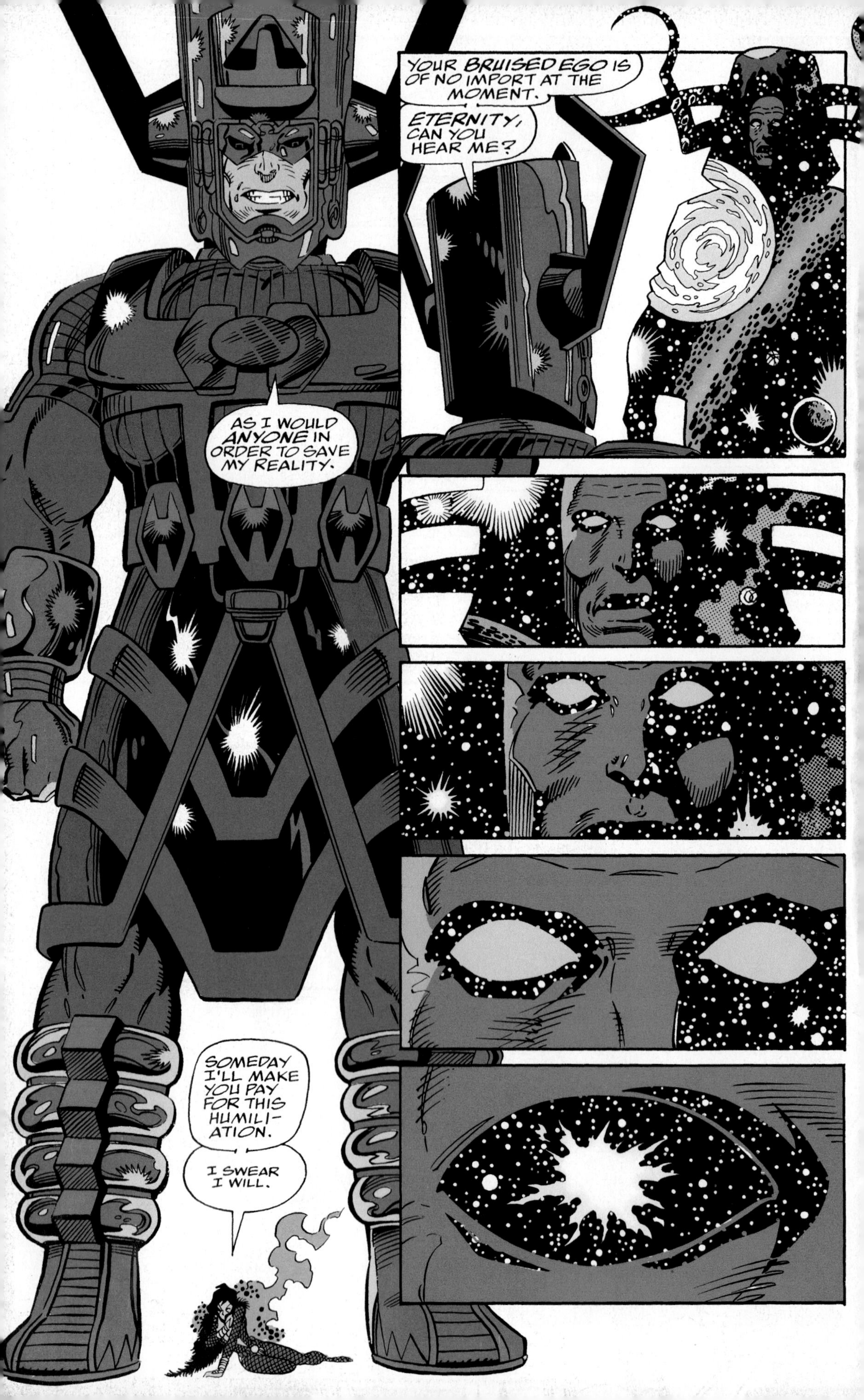
AS I WOULD ANYONE IN ORDER TO SAVE MY REALITY.
SOMEDAY I'LL MAKE YOU PAY FOR THIS HUMILI-ATION.
I SWEAR I WILL.
YOUR BRUISED EGO IS OF NO IMPORT AT THE MOMENT.
ETERNITY, CAN YOU HEAR ME?

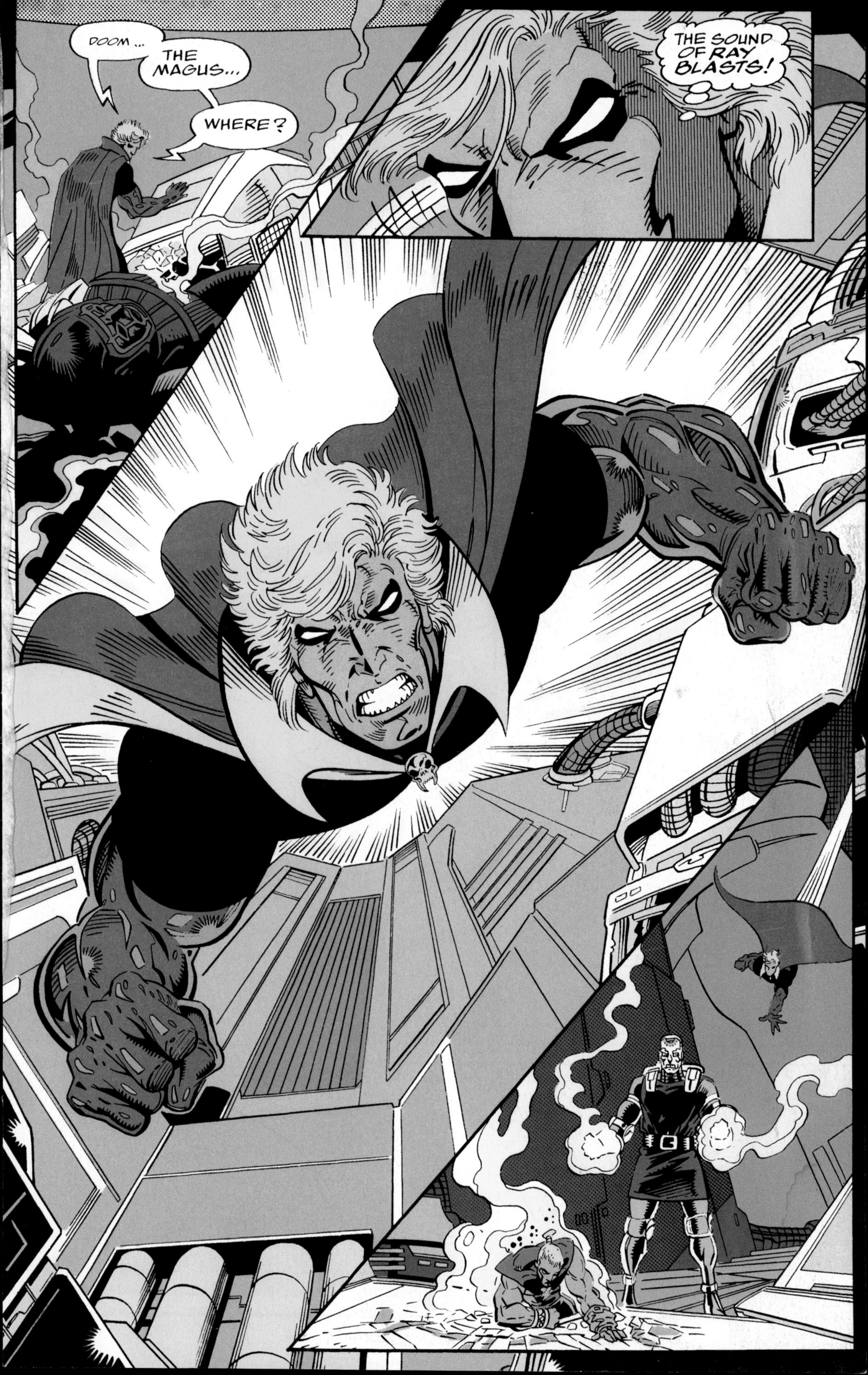
DOOM... THE MAGUS...
WHERE?
THE SOUND OF RAY BLASTS!

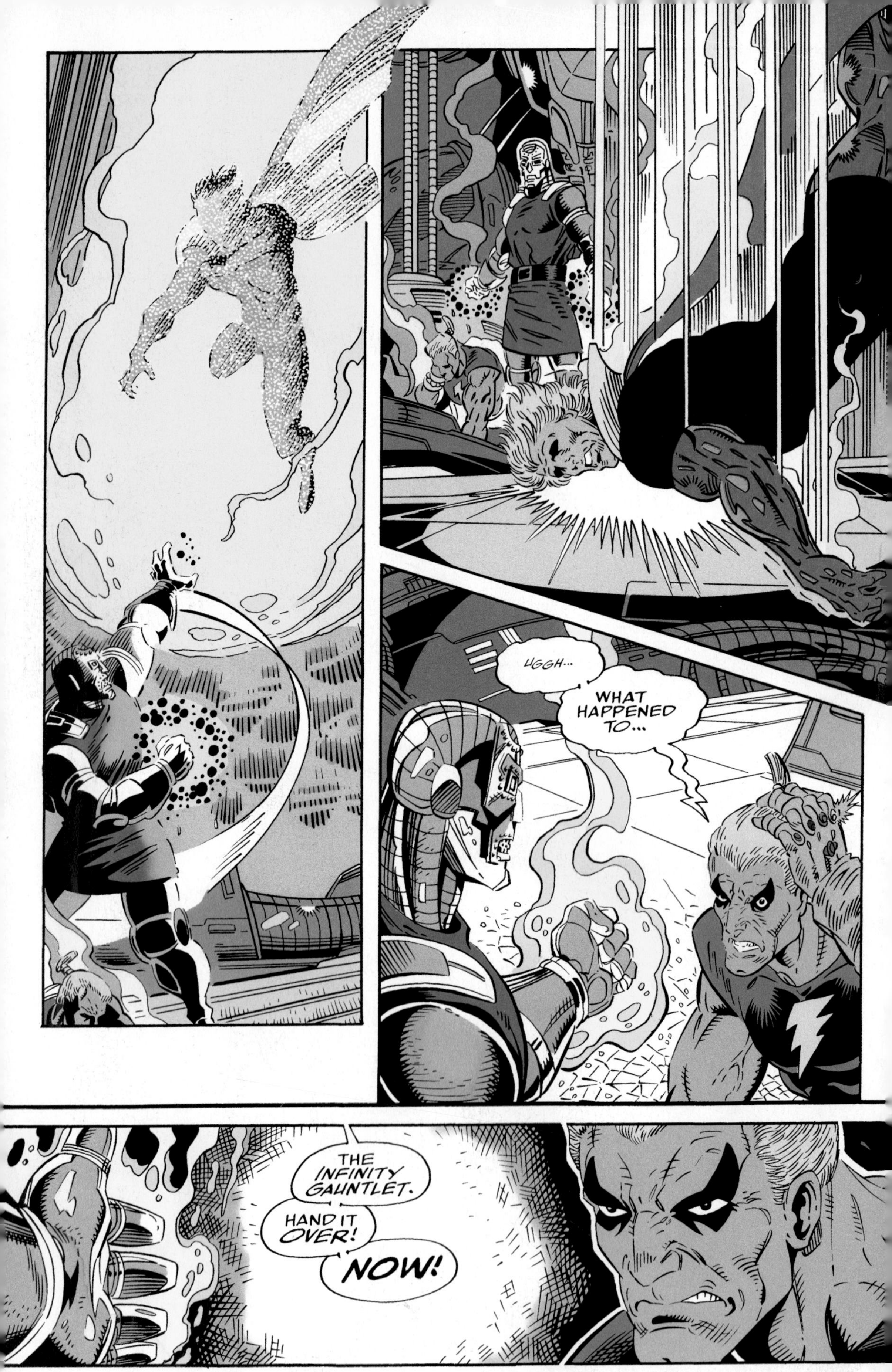
UGGH...
WHAT HAPPENED TO...
THE INFINITY GAUNTLET.
HAND IT OVER!
NOW!

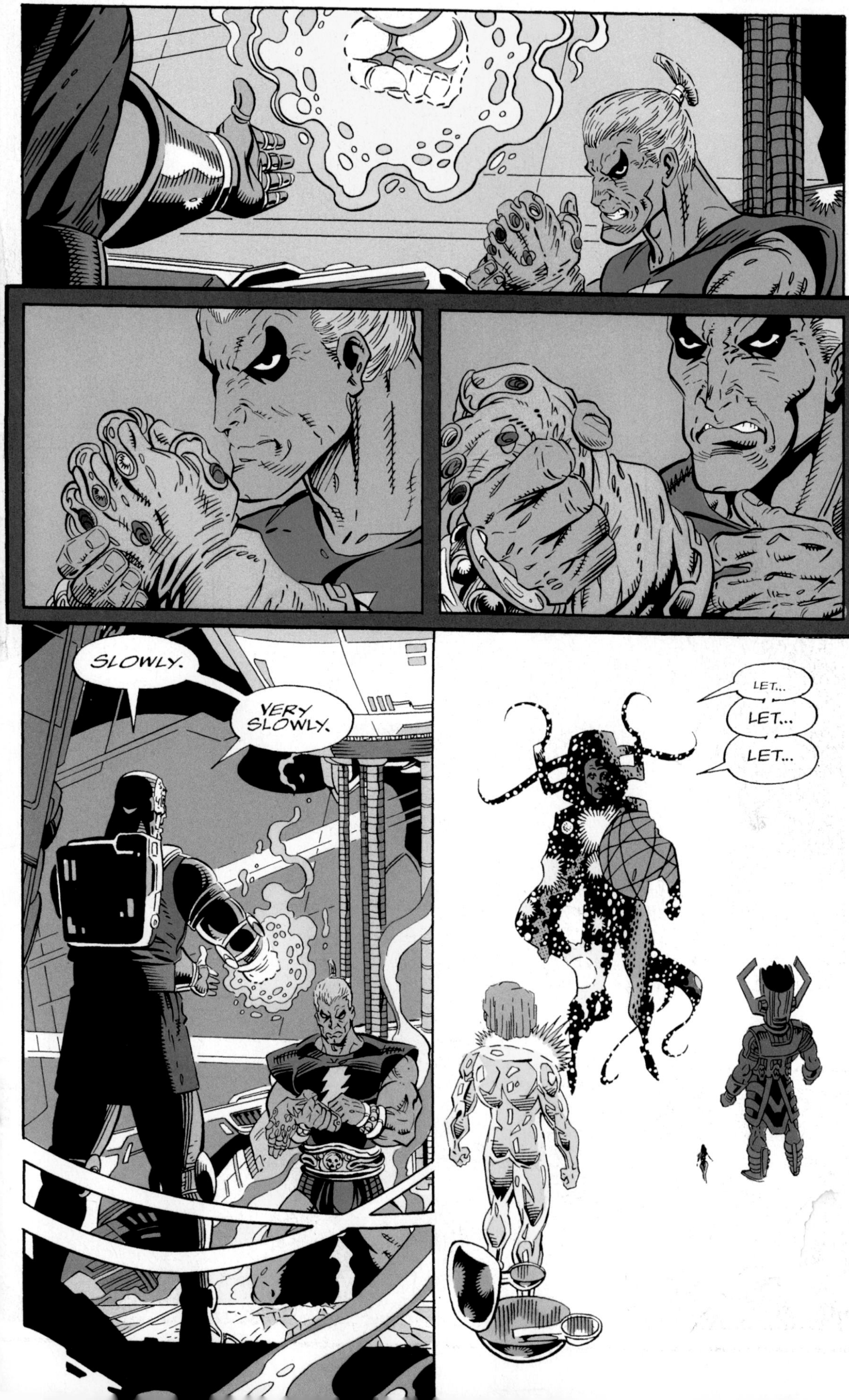
SLOWLY.
VERY SLOWLY.
LET...
LET...
LET...

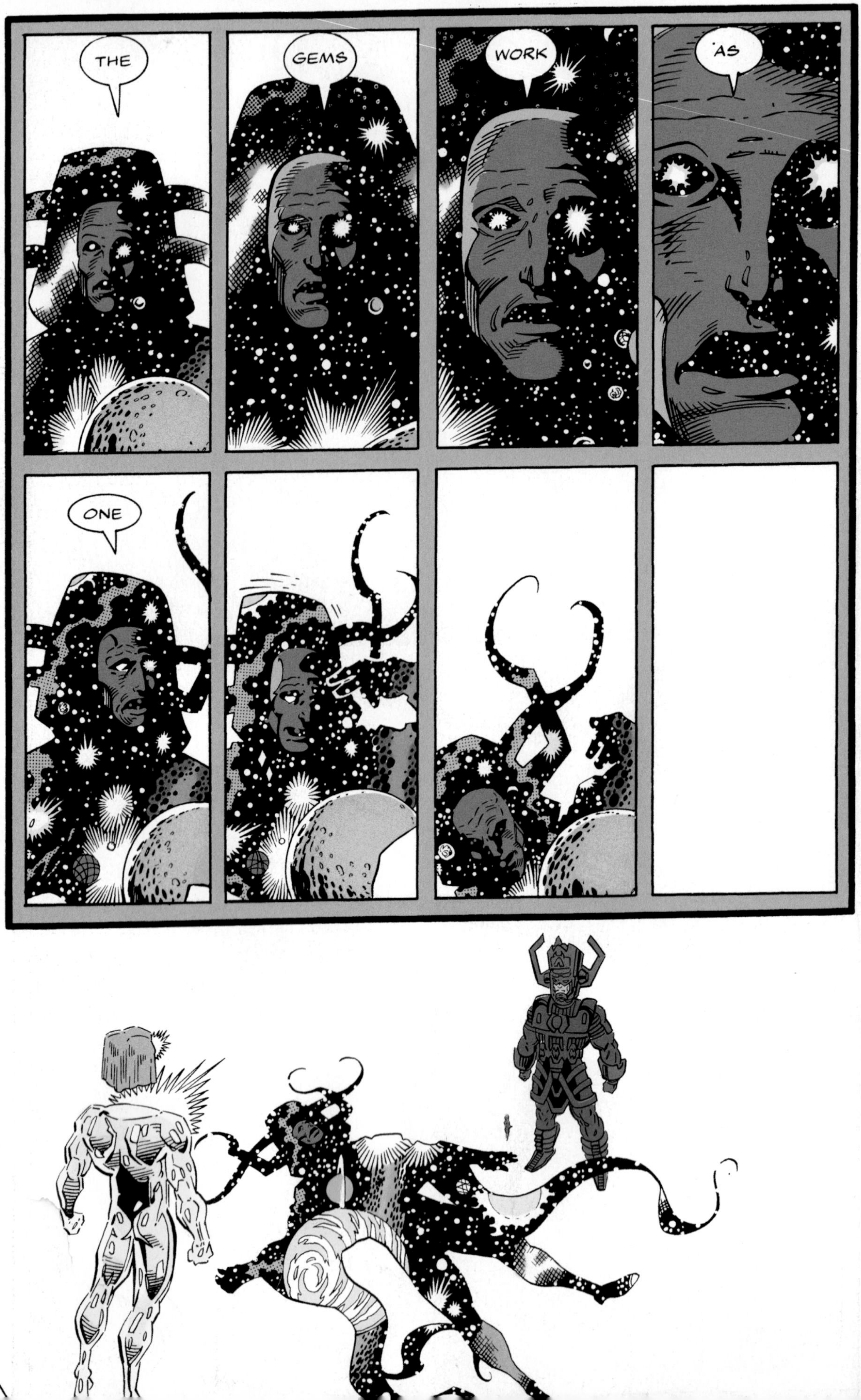
THE
GEMS
WORK
AS
ONE

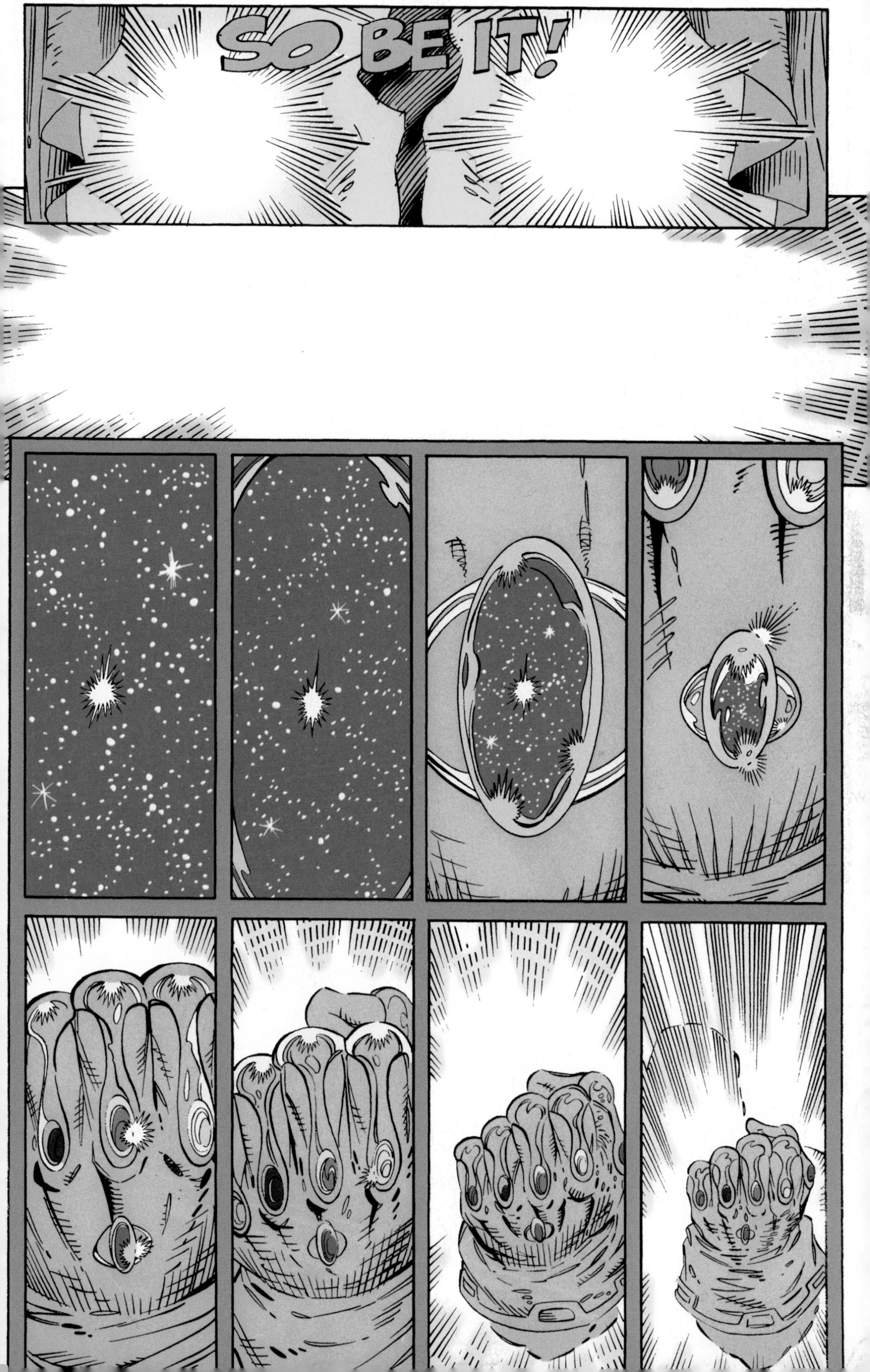
SO BE IT!

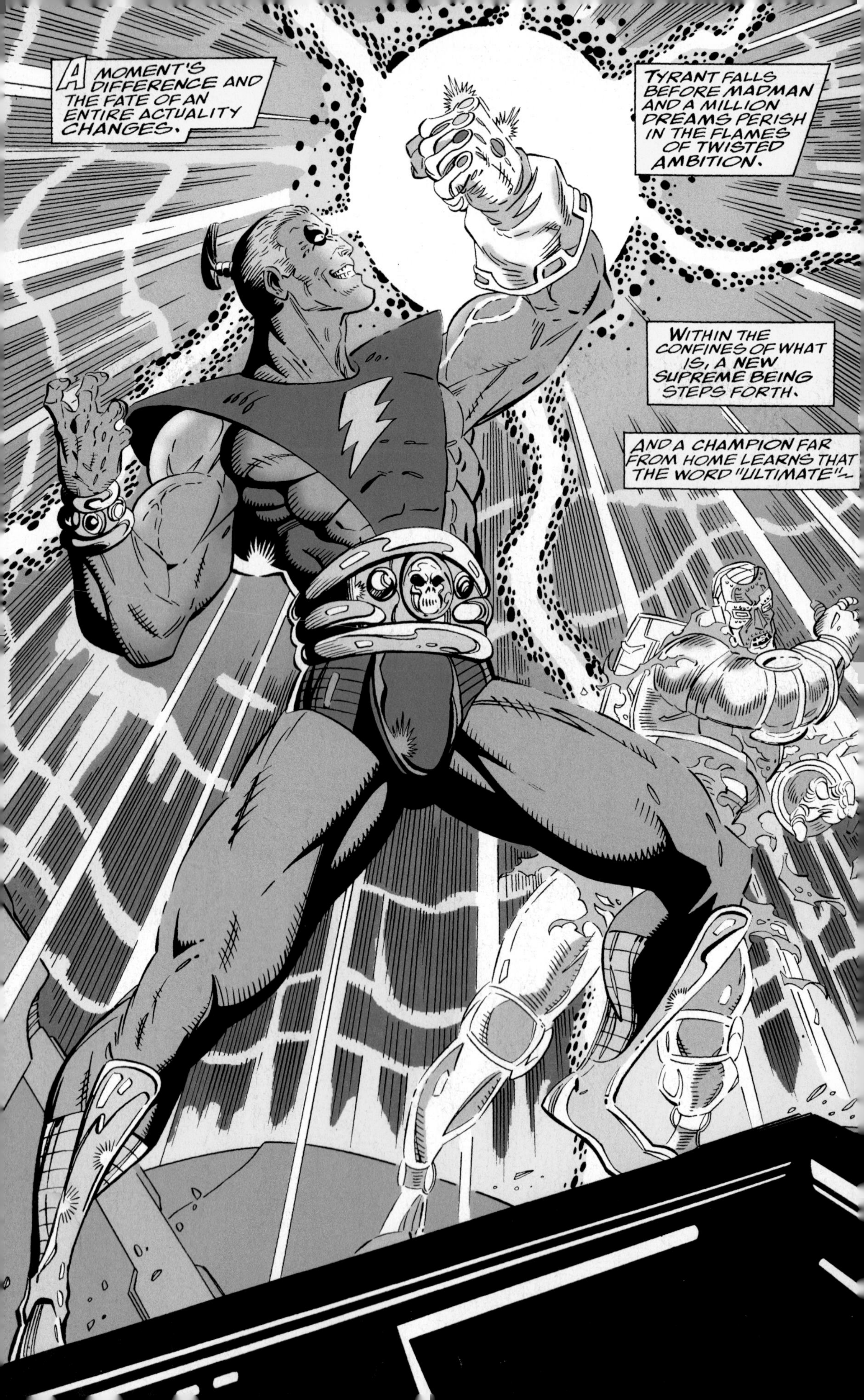
A MOMENT'S DIFFERENCE AND THE FATE OF AN ENTIRE ACTUALITY CHANGES.
TYRANT FALLS BEFORE MADMAN AND A MILLION DREAMS PERISH IN THE FLAMES OF TWISTED AMBITION.
WITHIN THE CONFINES OF WHAT IS, A NEW SUPREME BEING STEPS FORTH.
AND A CHAMPION FAR FROM HOME LEARNS THAT THE WORD "ULTIMATE"--

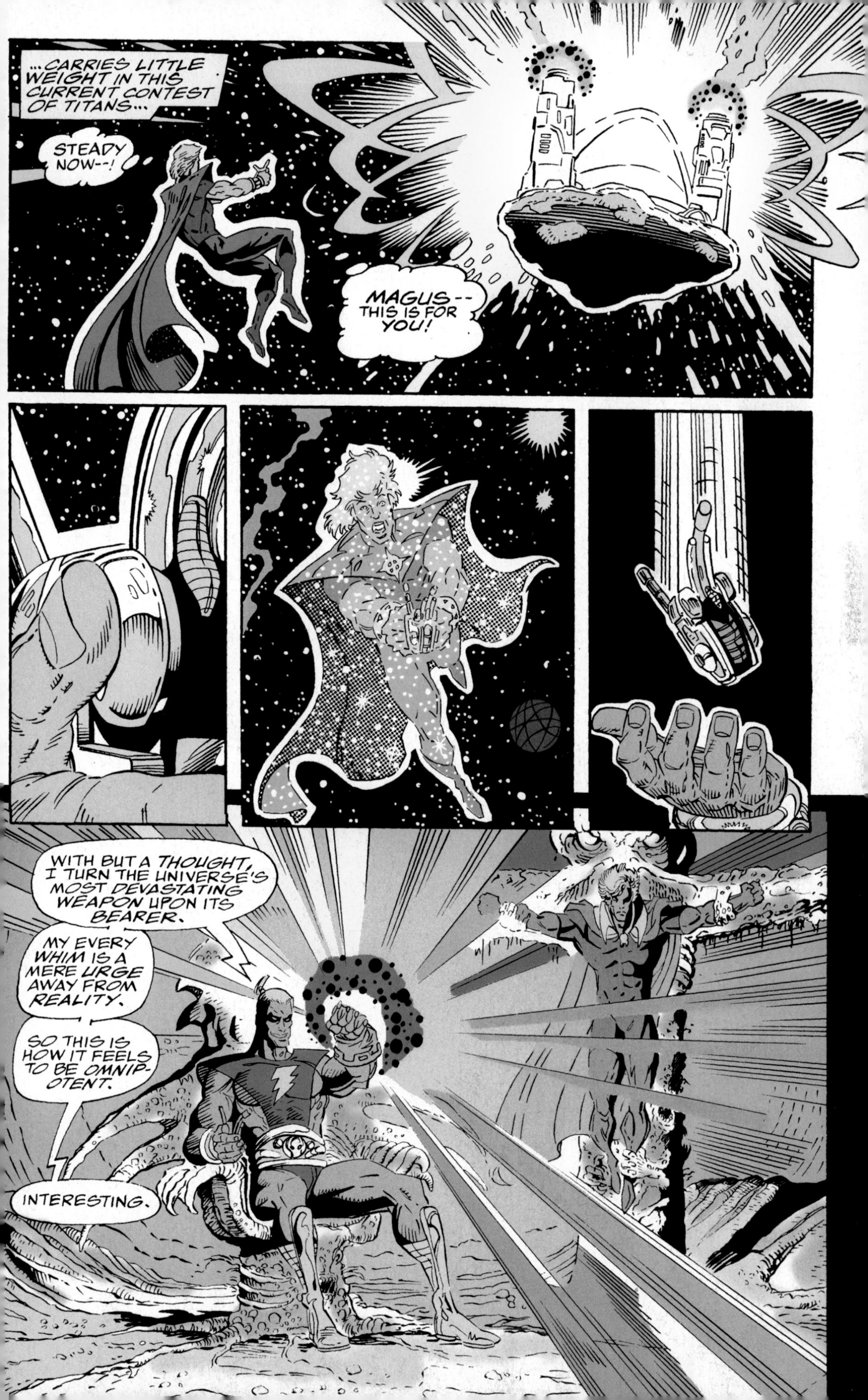
...CARRIES LITTLE WEIGHT IN THIS CURRENT CONTEST OF TITANS...
STEADY NOW--!
MAGUS-- THIS IS FOR YOU!
WITH BUT A THOUGHT, I TURN THE UNIVERSE'S MOST DEVASTATING WEAPON UPON ITS BEARER.
MY EVERY WHIM IS A MERE URGE AWAY FROM REALITY.
SO THIS IS HOW IT FEELS TO BE OMNIPOTENT.
INTERESTING.

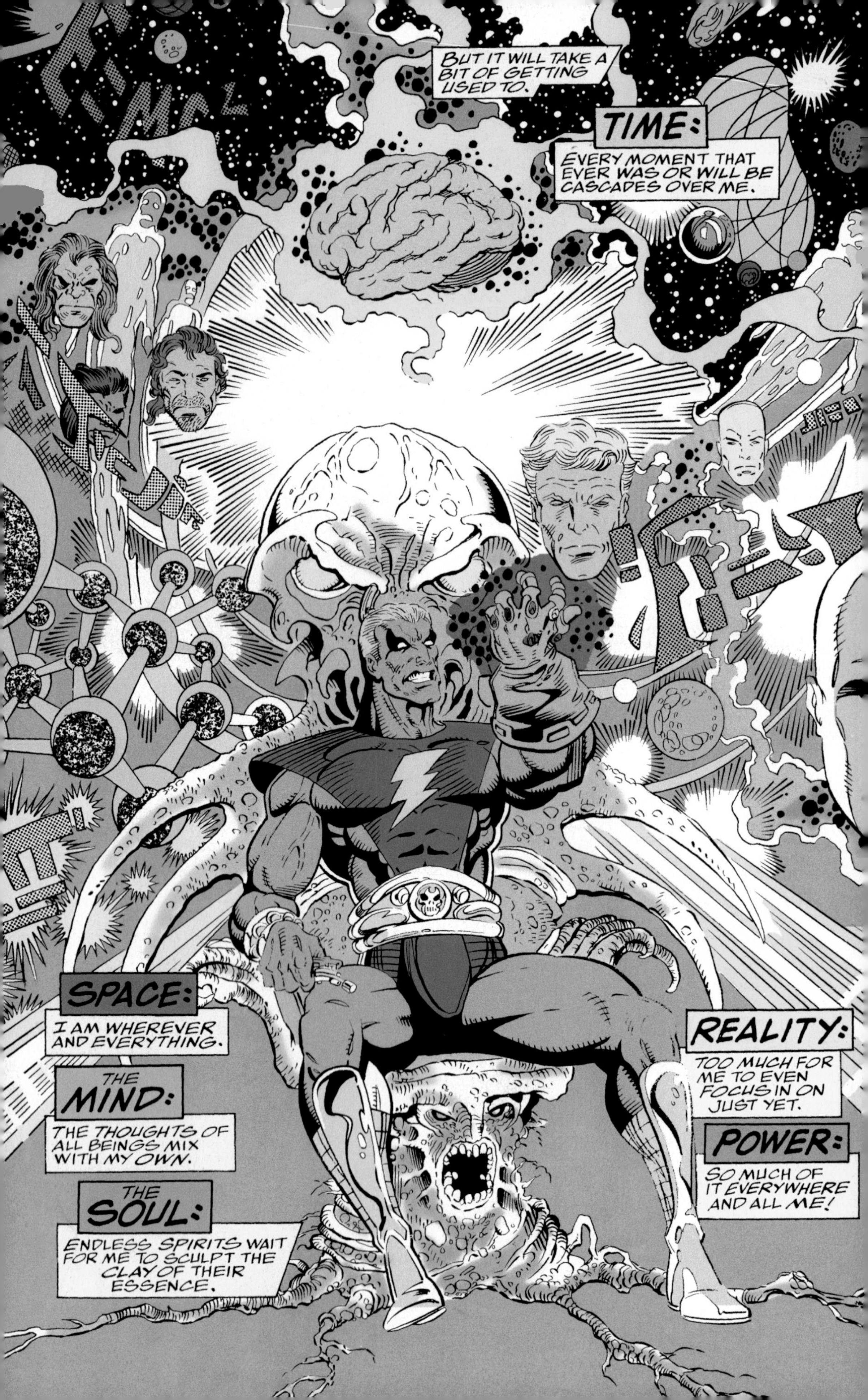
BUT IT WILL TAKE A BIT OF GETTING USED TO.
TIME:
EVERY MOMENT THAT EVER WAS OR WILL BE CASCADES OVER ME.
SPACE:
I AM WHEREVER AND EVERYTHING.
THE MIND:
THE THOUGHTS OF ALL BEINGS MIX WITH MY OWN.
THE SOUL:
ENDLESS SPIRITS WAIT FOR ME TO SCULPT THE CLAY OF THEIR ESSENCE.
REALITY:
TOO MUCH FOR ME TO EVEN FOCUS IN ON JUST YET.
POWER:
SO MUCH OF IT EVERYWHERE AND ALL ME!

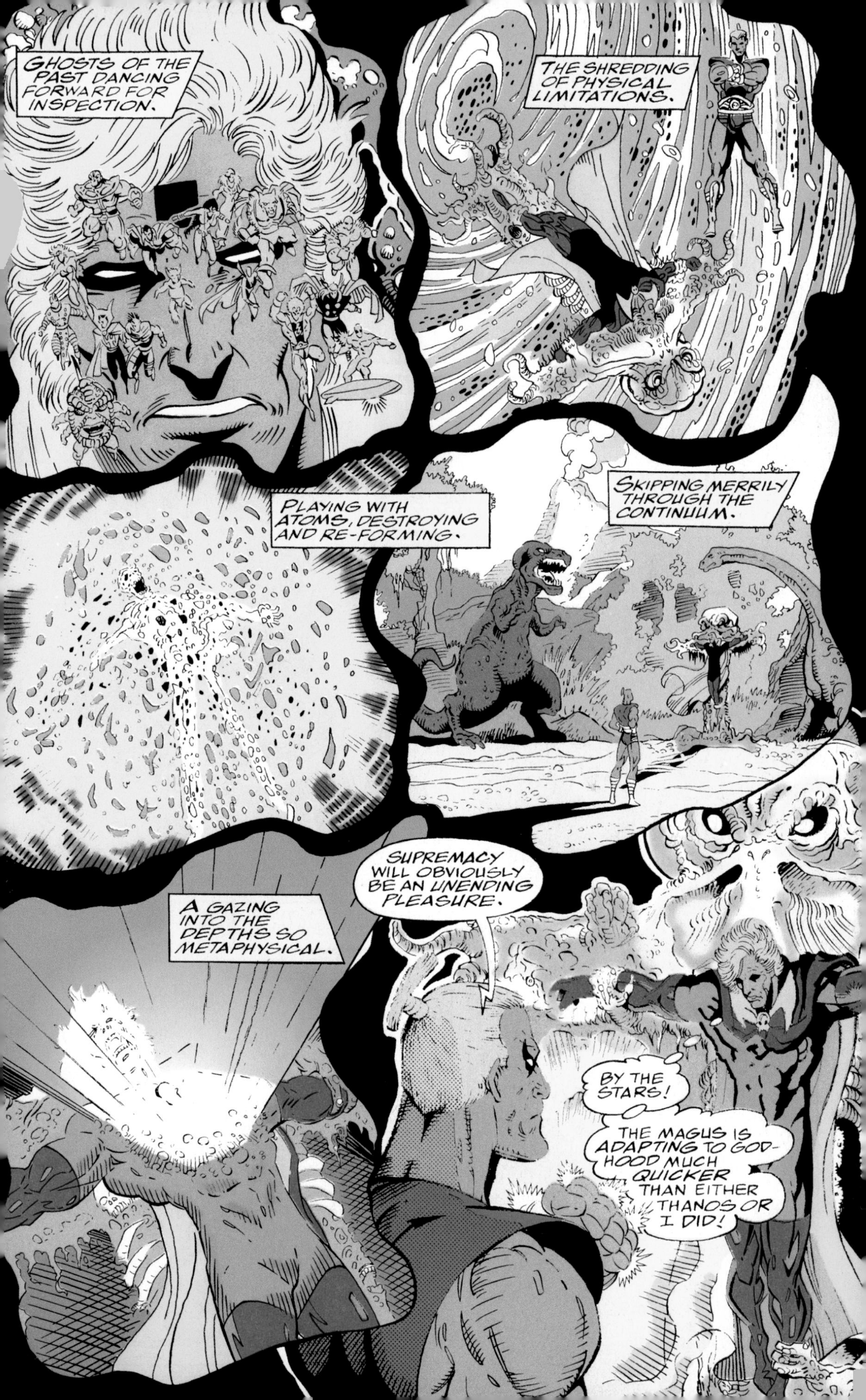
GHOSTS OF THE PAST DANCING FORWARD FOR INSPECTION.
THE SHREDDING OF PHYSICAL LIMITATIONS.
PLAYING WITH ATOMS, DESTROYING AND RE-FORMING.
SKIPPING MERRILY THROUGH THE CONTINUUM.
A GAZING INTO THE DEPTHS SO METAPHYSICAL.
SUPREMACY WILL OBVIOUSLY BE AN UNENDING PLEASURE.
BY THE STARS!
THE MAGUS IS ADAPTING TO GOD-HOOD MUCH QUICKER THAN EITHER THANOS OR I DID!

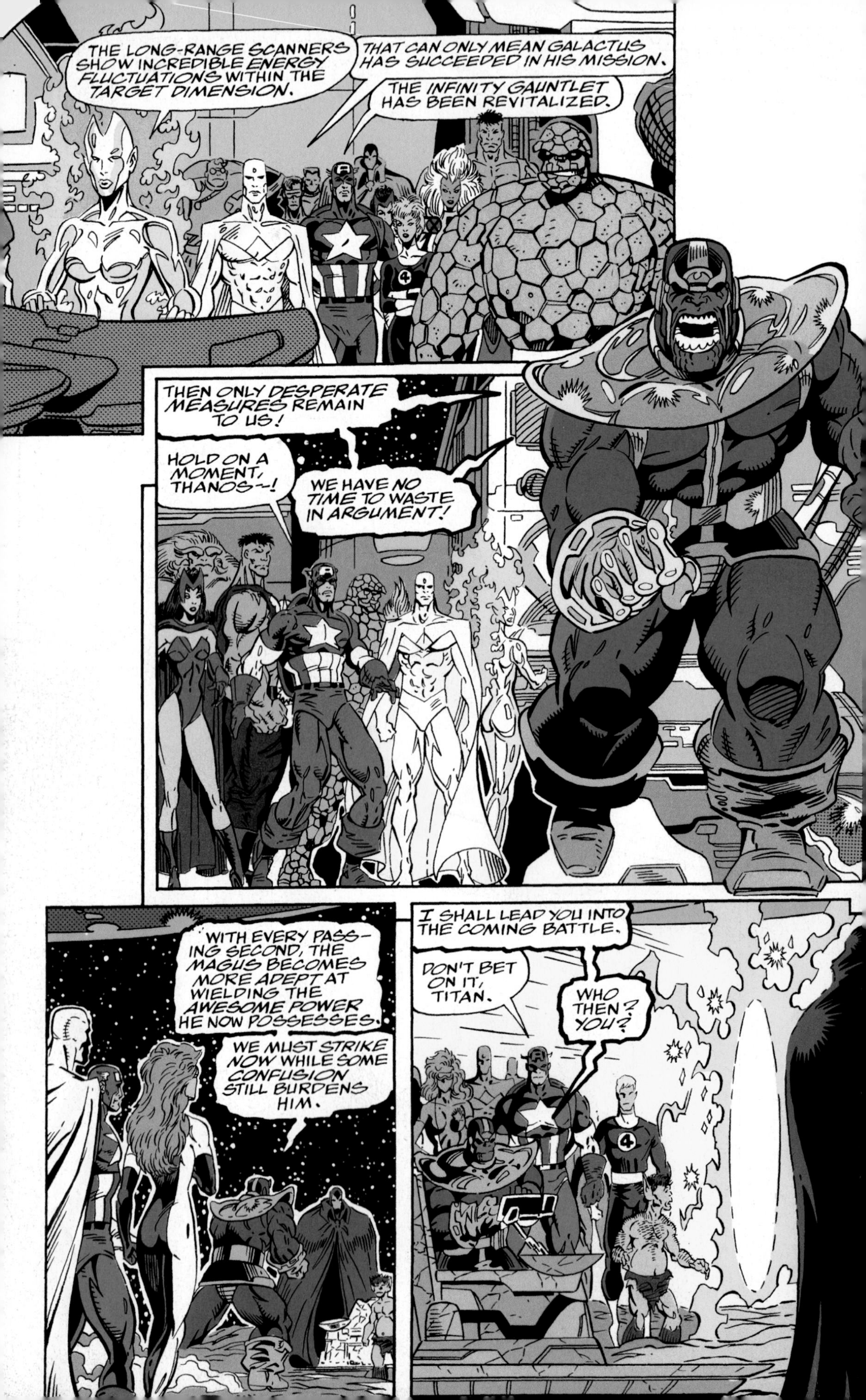
THE LONG-RANGE SCANNERS SHOW INCREDIBLE ENERGY FLUCTUATIONS WITHIN THE TARGET DIMENSION.
THAT CAN ONLY MEAN GALACTUS HAS SUCCEEDED IN HIS MISSION.
THE INFINITY GAUNTLET HAS BEEN REVITALIZED.
THEN ONLY DESPERATE MEASURES REMAIN TO US!
HOLD ON A MOMENT, THANOS--!
WE HAVE NO TIME TO WASTE IN ARGUMENT!
WITH EVERY PASSING SECOND, THE MAGUS BECOMES MORE ADEPT AT WIELDING THE AWESOME POWER HE NOW POSSESSES.
WE MUST STRIKE NOW WHILE SOME CONFUSION STILL BURDENS HIM.
I SHALL LEAD YOU INTO THE COMING BATTLE.
DON'T BET ON IT, TITAN.
WHO THEN? YOU?

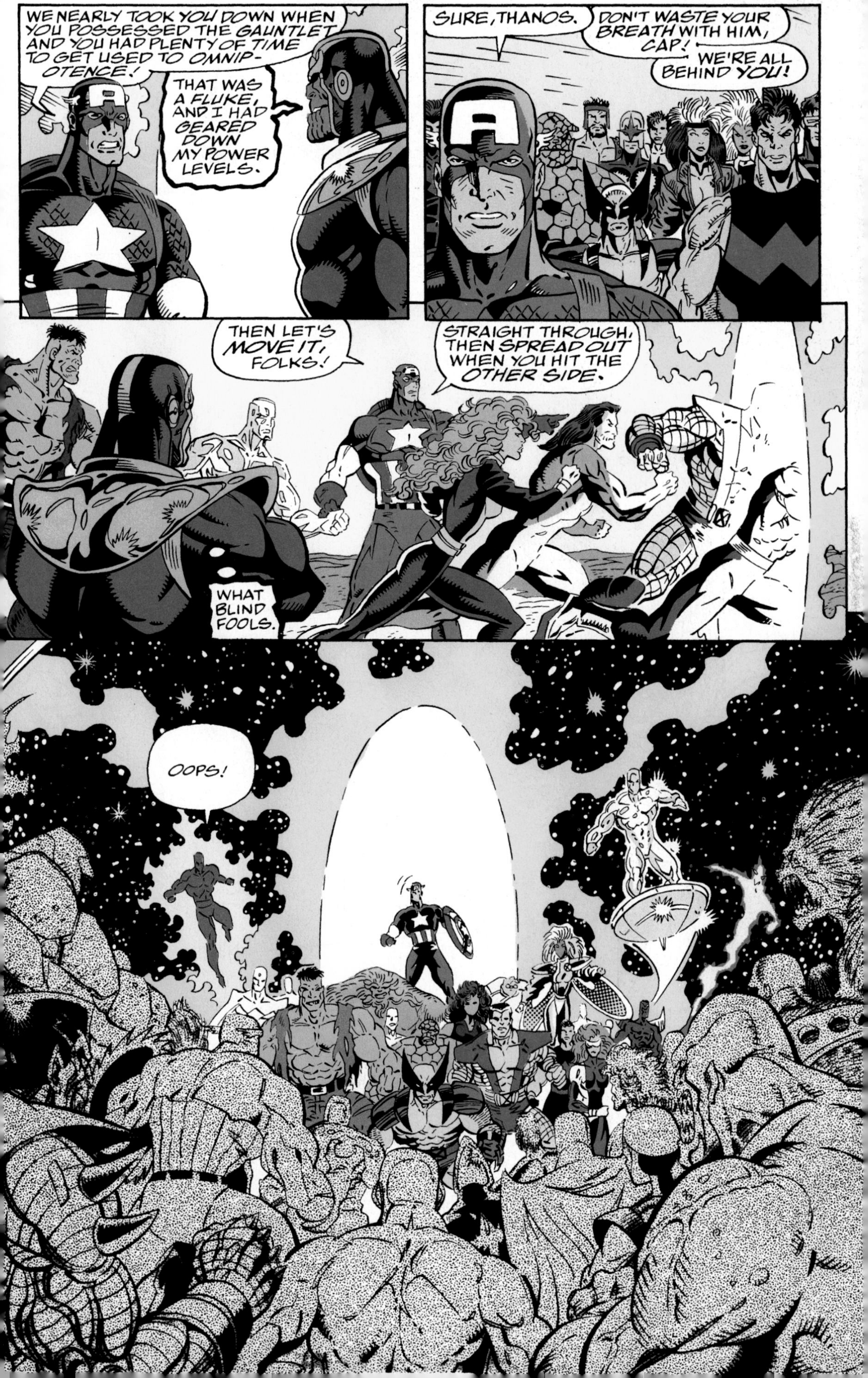
WE NEARLY TOOK YOU DOWN WHEN YOU POSSESSED THE GAUNTLET AND YOU HAD PLENTY OF TIME TO GET USED TO OMNIPOTENCE!
THAT WAS A FLUKE, AND I HAD GEARED DOWN MY POWER LEVELS.
SURE, THANOS.
DON'T WASTE YOUR BREATH WITH HIM, CAP!
WE'RE ALL BEHIND YOU!
THEN LET'S MOVE IT, FOLKS!
STRAIGHT THROUGH, THEN SPREAD OUT WHEN YOU HIT THE OTHER SIDE.
WHAT BLIND FOOLS.
OOPS!

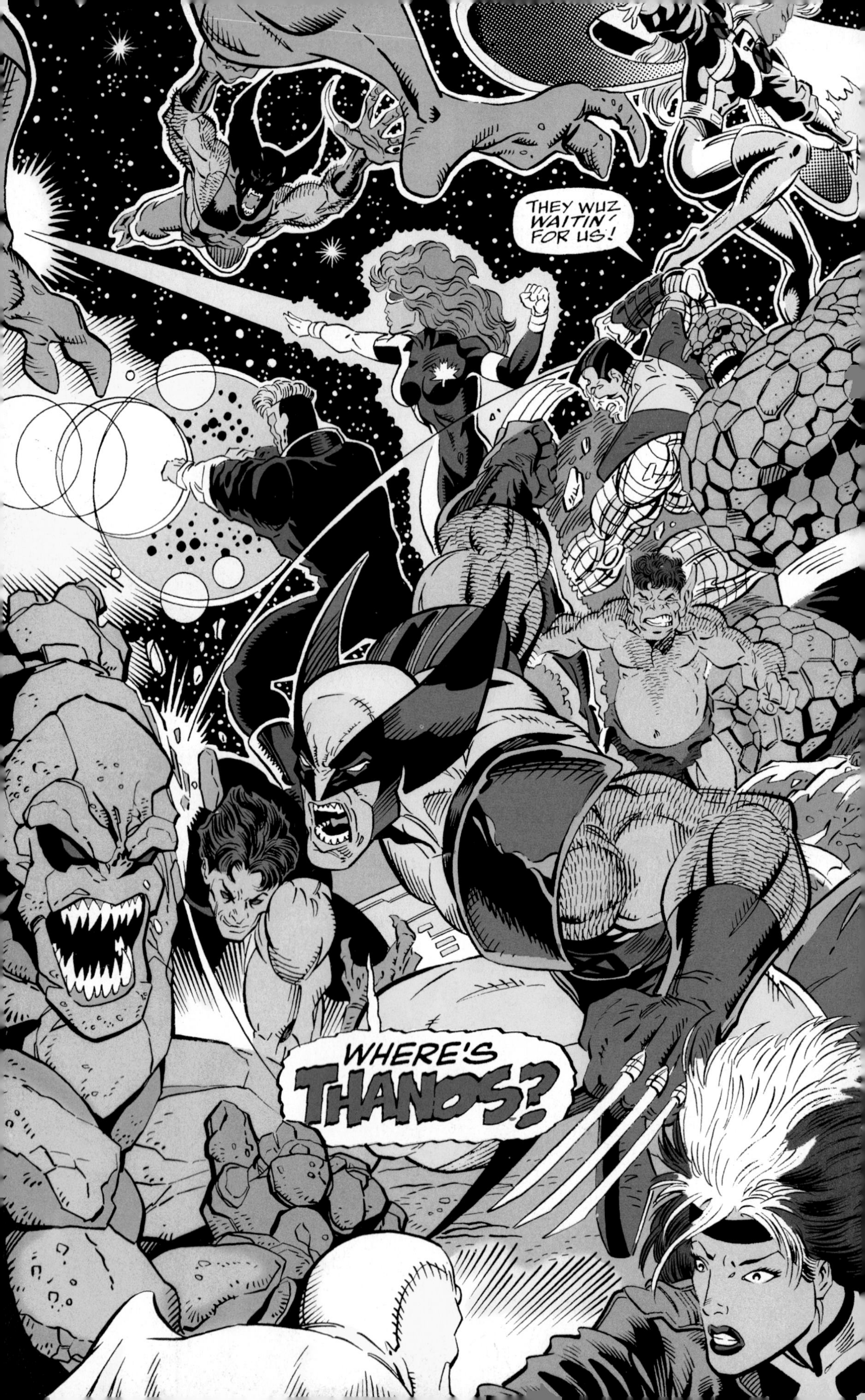
THEY WUZ WAITIN' FOR US!
WHERE'S THANOS?

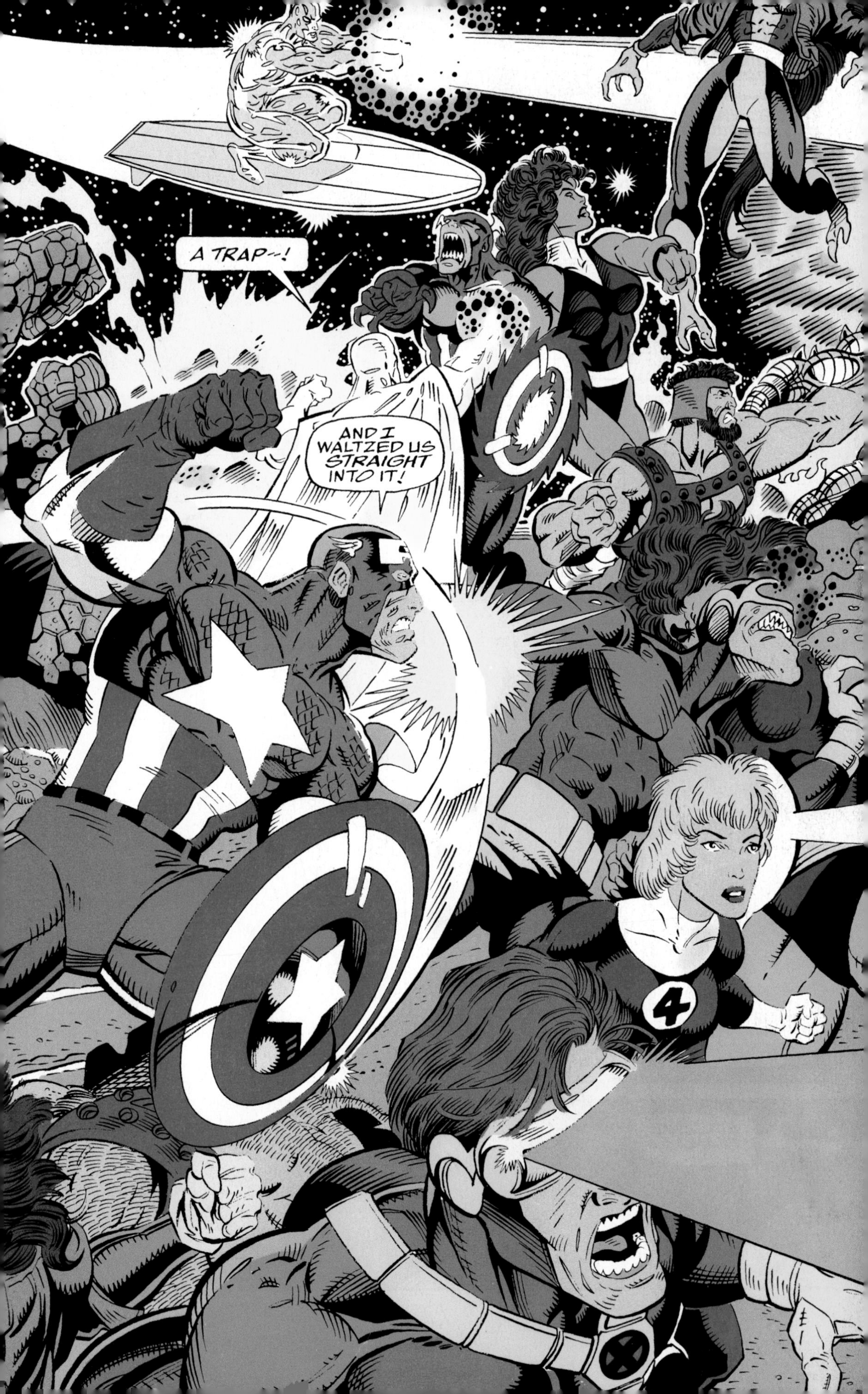
A TRAP--!
AND I WALTZED US STRAIGHT INTO IT!

YES, BLIND FOOLS TO THINK I WOULD *LEAD* THEM TO ANYTHING OTHER THAN BLOODY SLAUGHTER.

SO EASILY MANIPULATED.

THE SPECIES WILL BE BETTER OFF *WITHOUT* THEM.

AND WHILE THEY KEEP THE MAGUS'S FORCES BUSY OUT IN THE STRONGHOLD'S COURTYARD, I'LL RESET THE TELEPORTER'S COORDINATES TO...

...DEPOSIT ME JUST *OUTSIDE* THE MAGUS'S CONTROL ROOM.

THE FLEDGLING GOD SHOULD STILL BE VULNERABLE TO A CAREFULLY AIMED AND UNEXPECTED LASER CHARGE.

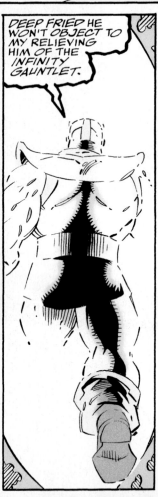

DEEP FRIED HE WON'T OBJECT TO MY RELIEVING HIM OF THE INFINITY GAUNTLET.

MUST MOVE *QUICKLY*--

I CAN--

WELCOME, THANOS.

YOU?

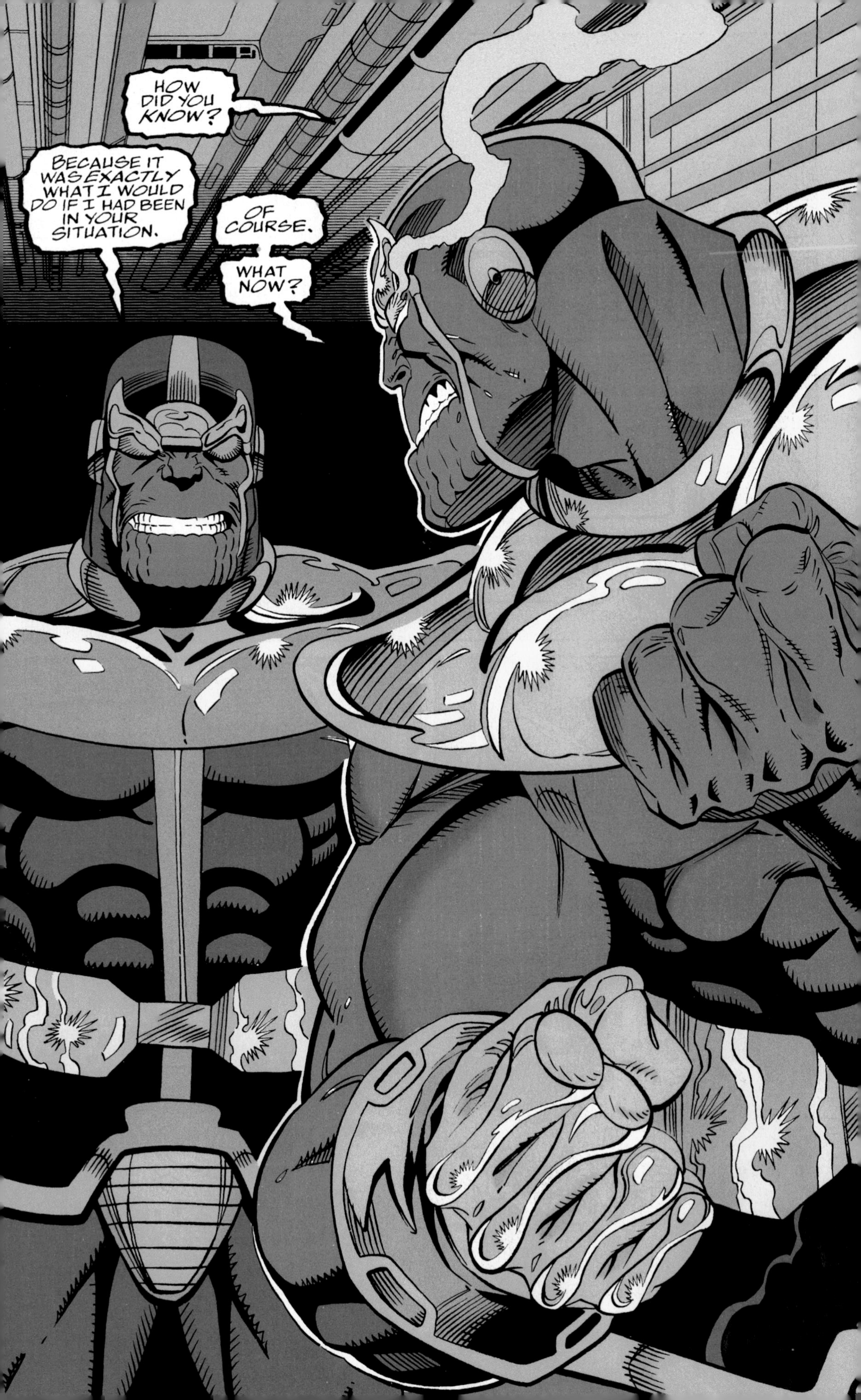
HOW DID YOU KNOW?
BECAUSE IT WAS EXACTLY WHAT I WOULD DO IF I HAD BEEN IN YOUR SITUATION.
OF COURSE.
WHAT NOW?

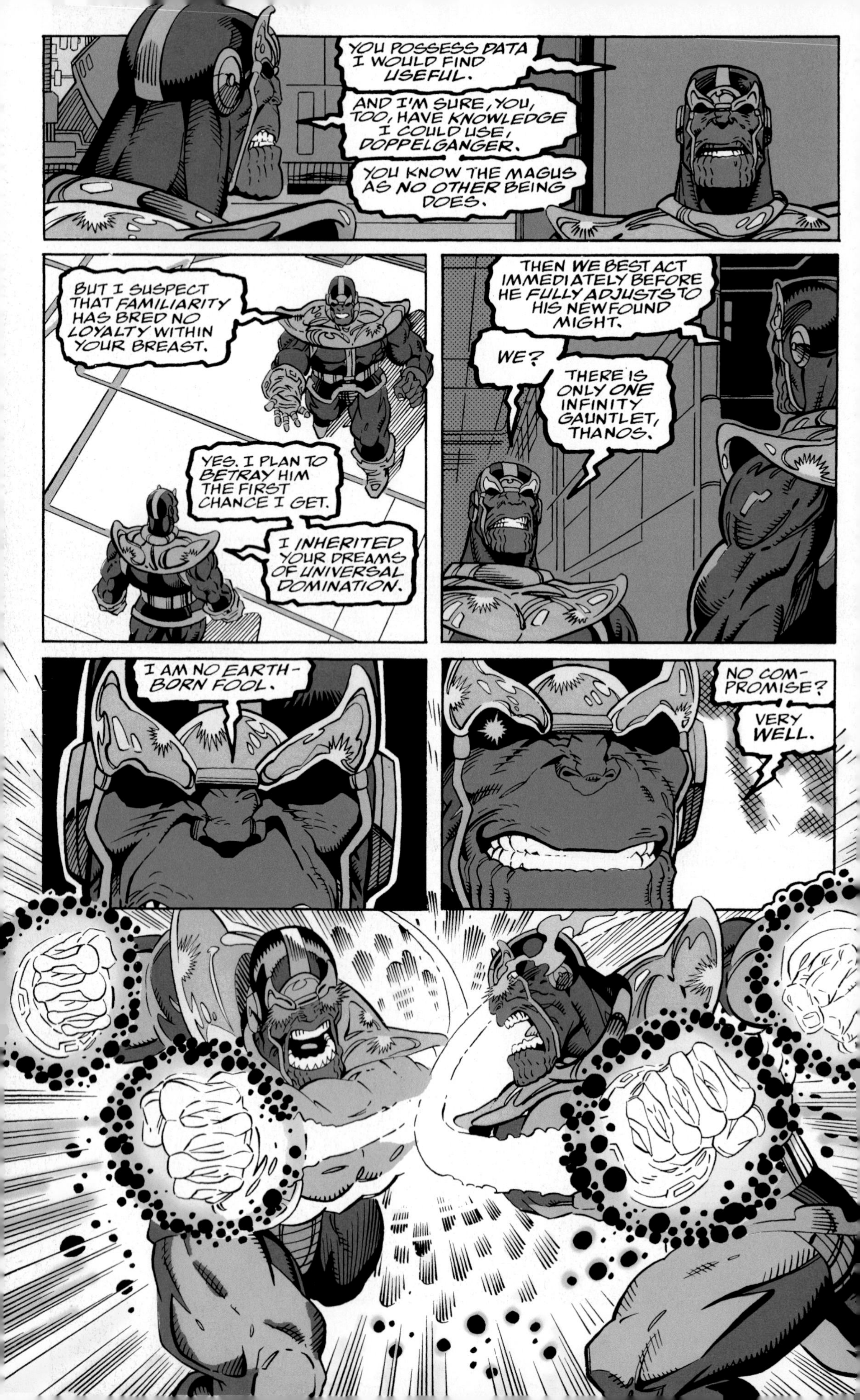
YOU POSSESS DATA I WOULD FIND USEFUL.
AND I'M SURE, YOU, TOO, HAVE KNOWLEDGE I COULD USE, DOPPELGANGER.
YOU KNOW THE MAGUS AS NO OTHER BEING DOES.
BUT I SUSPECT THAT FAMILIARITY HAS BRED NO LOYALTY WITHIN YOUR BREAST.
YES. I PLAN TO BETRAY HIM THE FIRST CHANCE I GET.
I INHERITED YOUR DREAMS OF UNIVERSAL DOMINATION.
THEN WE BEST ACT IMMEDIATELY BEFORE HE FULLY ADJUSTS TO HIS NEWFOUND MIGHT.
WE?
THERE IS ONLY ONE INFINITY GAUNTLET, THANOS.
I AM NO EARTH-BORN FOOL.
NO COM-PROMISE?
VERY WELL.

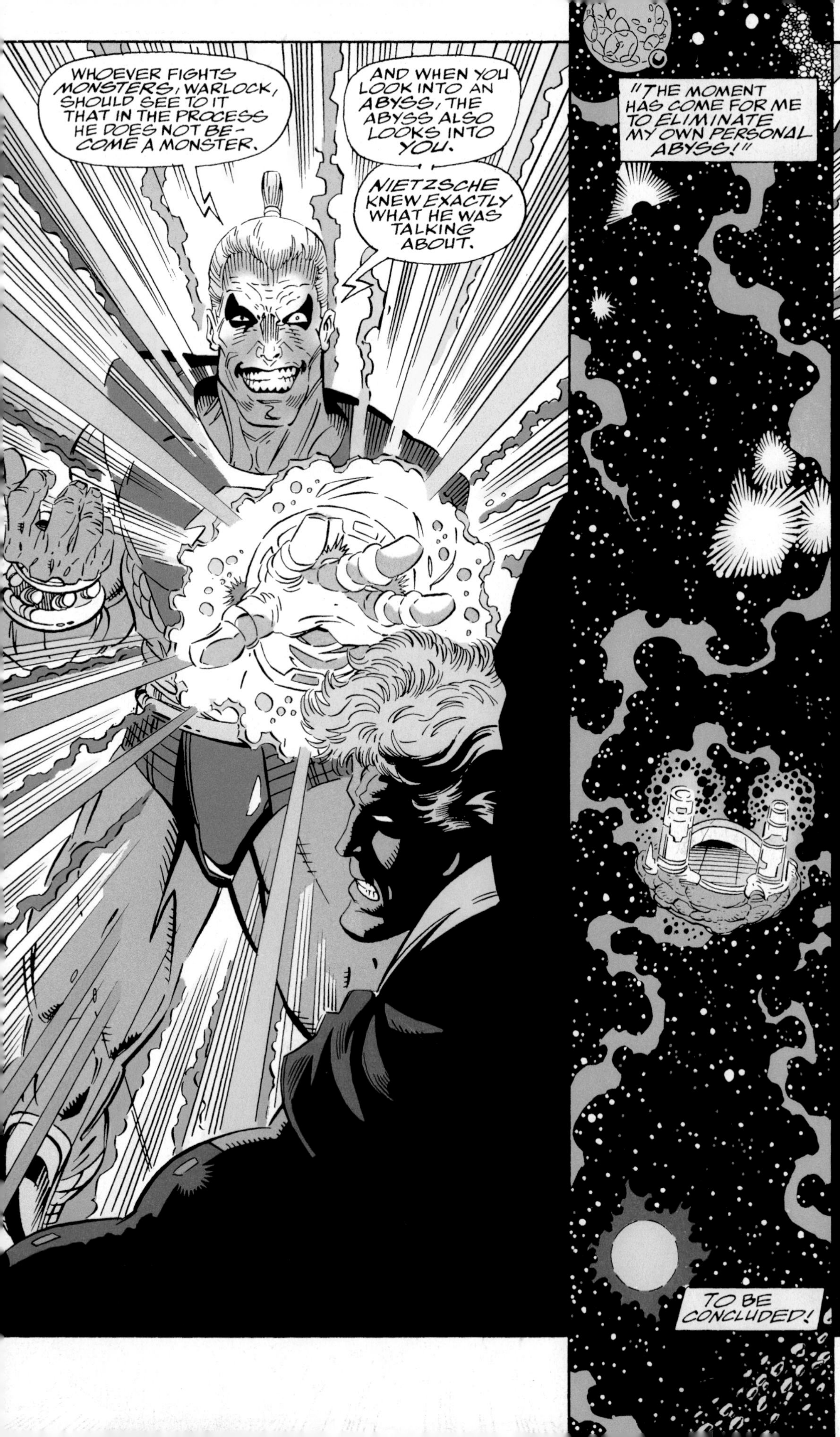
WHOEVER FIGHTS MONSTERS, WARLOCK, SHOULD SEE TO IT THAT IN THE PROCESS HE DOES NOT BE- COME A MONSTER.
AND WHEN YOU LOOK INTO AN ABYSS, THE ABYSS ALSO LOOKS INTO YOU.
NIETZSCHE KNEW EXACTLY WHAT HE WAS TALKING ABOUT.
"THE MOMENT HAS COME FOR ME TO ELIMINATE MY OWN PERSONAL ABYSS!"
TO BE CONCLUDED!

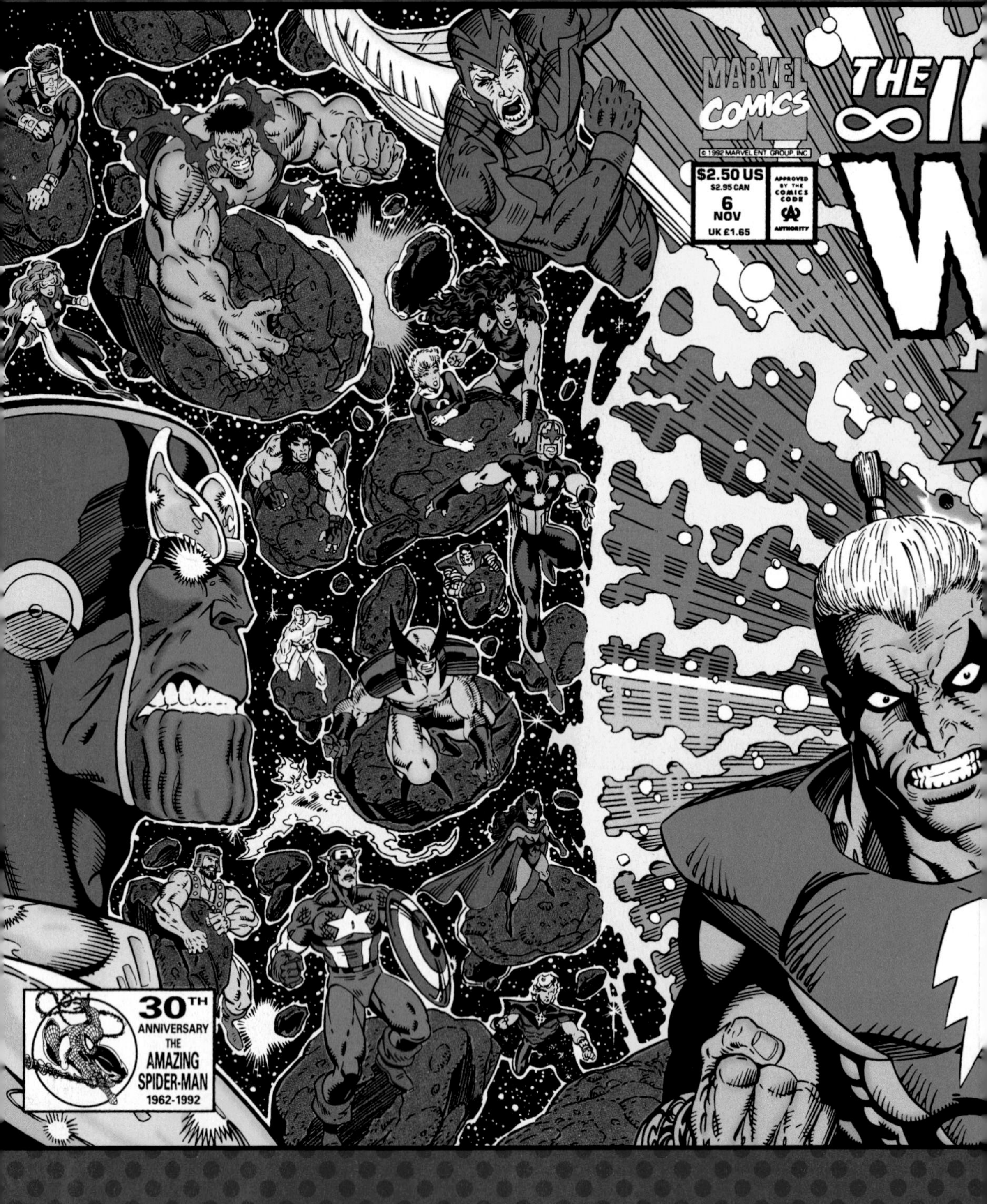
MARVEL COMICS
© 1992 MARVEL ENT. GROUP INC.
THE
$2.50 US
$2.95 CAN
6
NOV
UK £1.65
APPROVED BY THE COMICS CODE AUTHORITY
30TH
ANNIVERSARY
THE
AMAZING
SPIDER-MAN
1962-1992

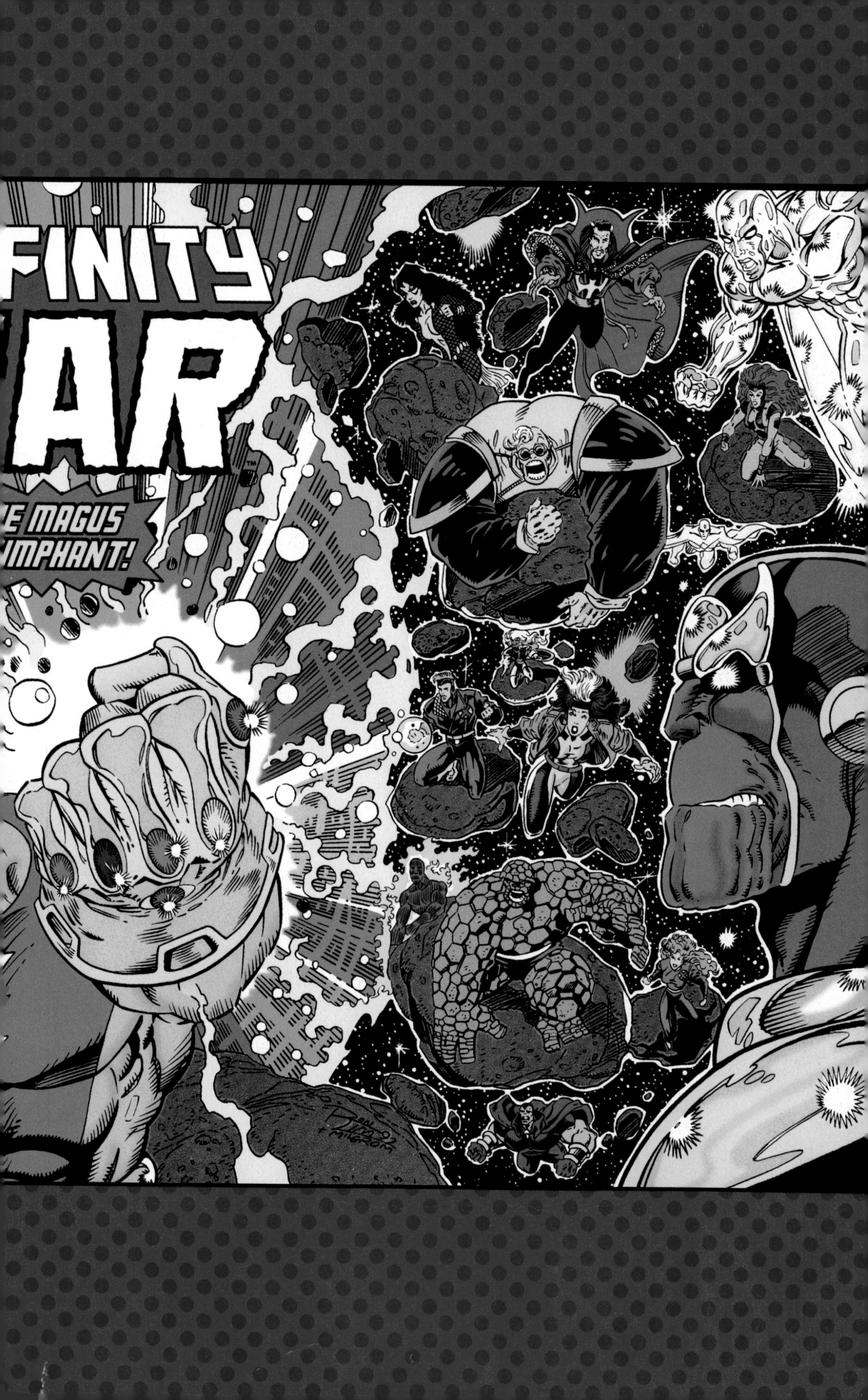

FINITY
AR
E MAGUS
UMPHANT!

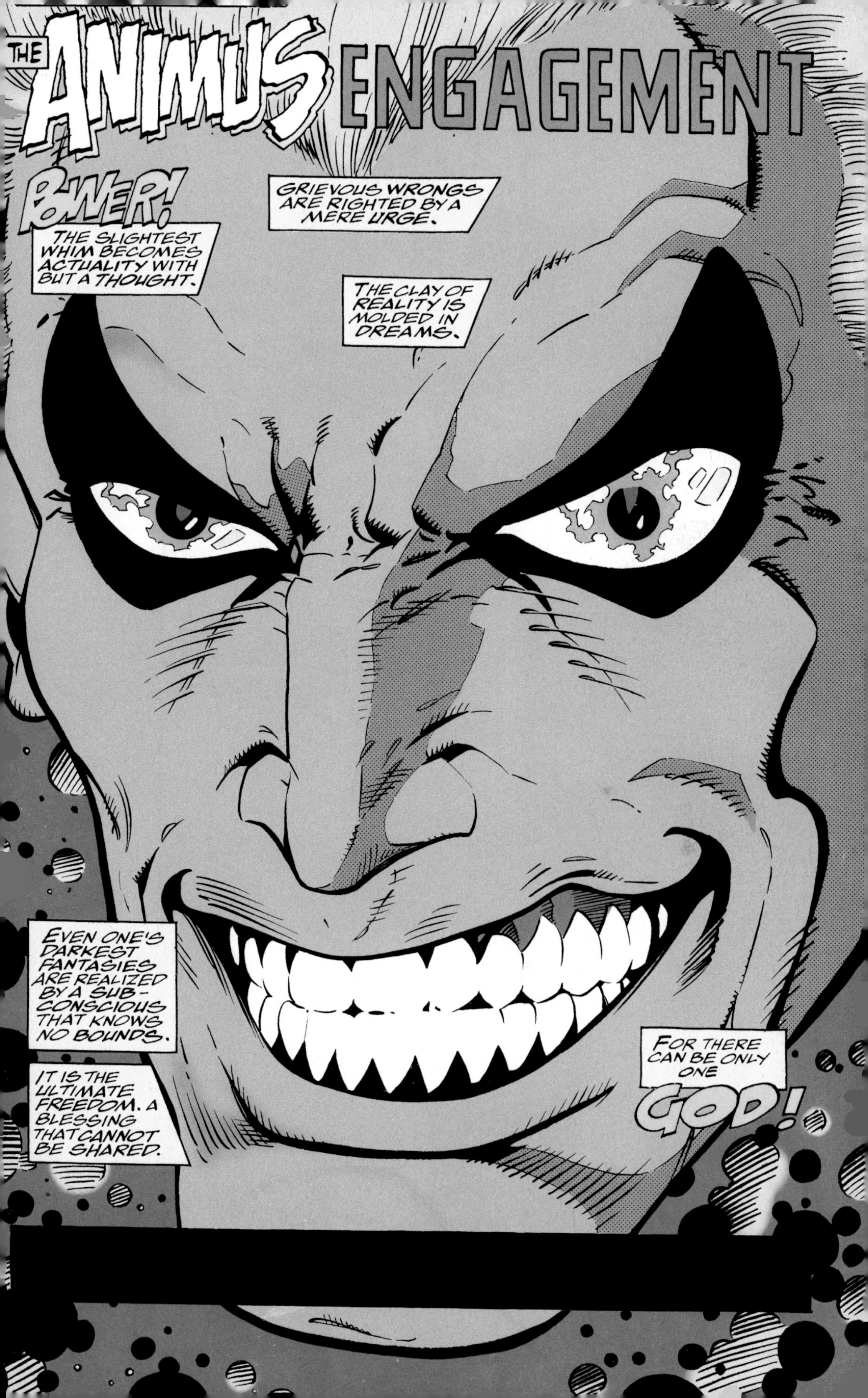
THE ANIMUS ENGAGEMENT
POWER!
THE SLIGHTEST WHIM BECOMES ACTUALITY WITH BUT A THOUGHT.
GRIEVOUS WRONGS ARE RIGHTED BY A MERE URGE.
THE CLAY OF REALITY IS MOLDED IN DREAMS.
EVEN ONE'S DARKEST FANTASIES ARE REALIZED BY A SUB-CONSCIOUS THAT KNOWS NO BOUNDS.
IT IS THE ULTIMATE FREEDOM. A BLESSING THAT CANNOT BE SHARED.
FOR THERE CAN BE ONLY ONE
GOD!
[redacted]

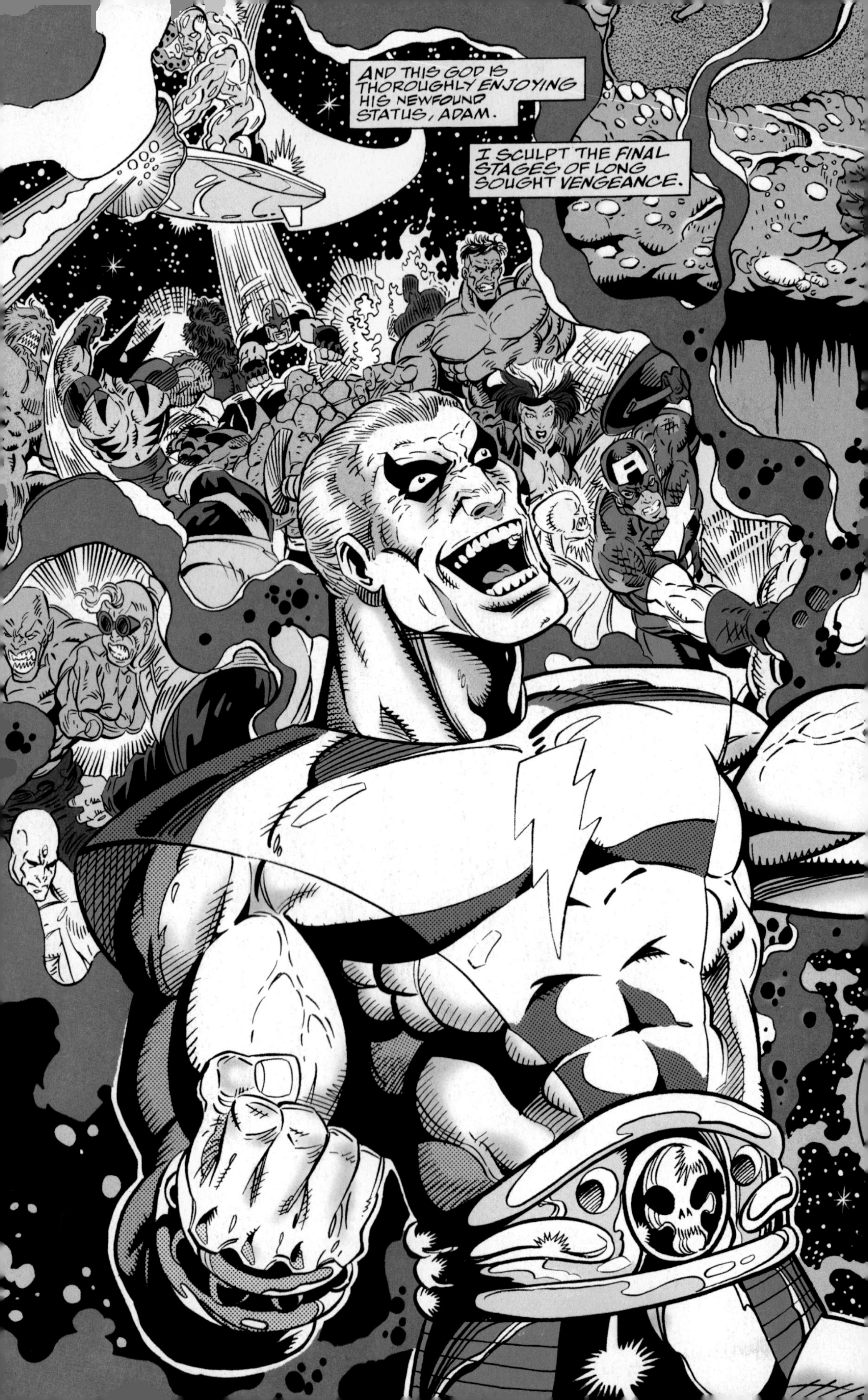
AND THIS GOD IS THOROUGHLY ENJOYING HIS NEWFOUND STATUS, ADAM.
I SCULPT THE FINAL STAGES OF LONG SOUGHT VENGEANCE.

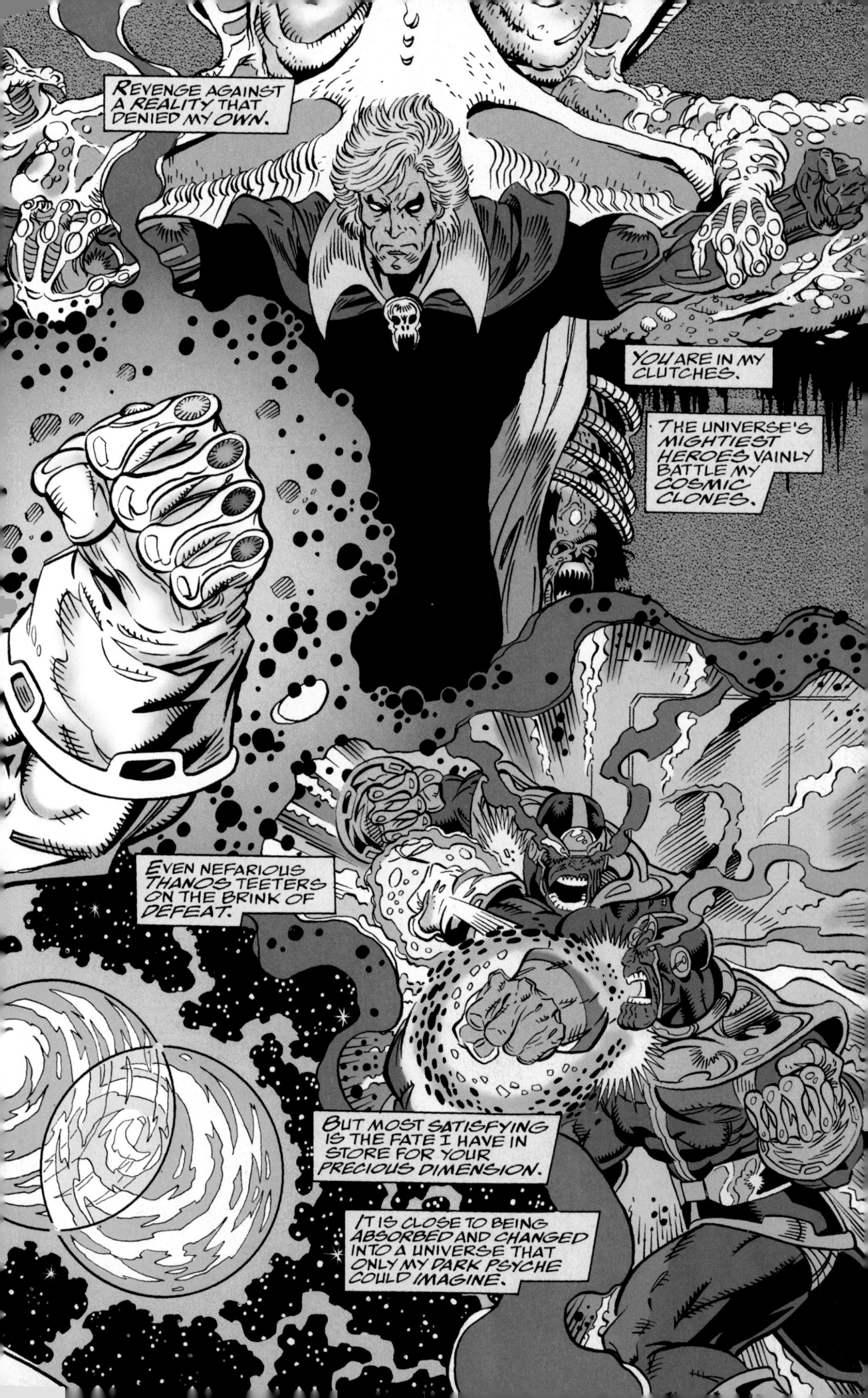
REVENGE AGAINST A REALITY THAT DENIED MY OWN.
YOU ARE IN MY CLUTCHES.
THE UNIVERSE'S MIGHTIEST HEROES VAINLY BATTLE MY COSMIC CLONES.
EVEN NEFARIOUS THANOS TEETERS ON THE BRINK OF DEFEAT.
BUT MOST SATISFYING IS THE FATE I HAVE IN STORE FOR YOUR PRECIOUS DIMENSION.
IT IS CLOSE TO BEING ABSORBED AND CHANGED INTO A UNIVERSE THAT ONLY MY DARK PSYCHE COULD IMAGINE.

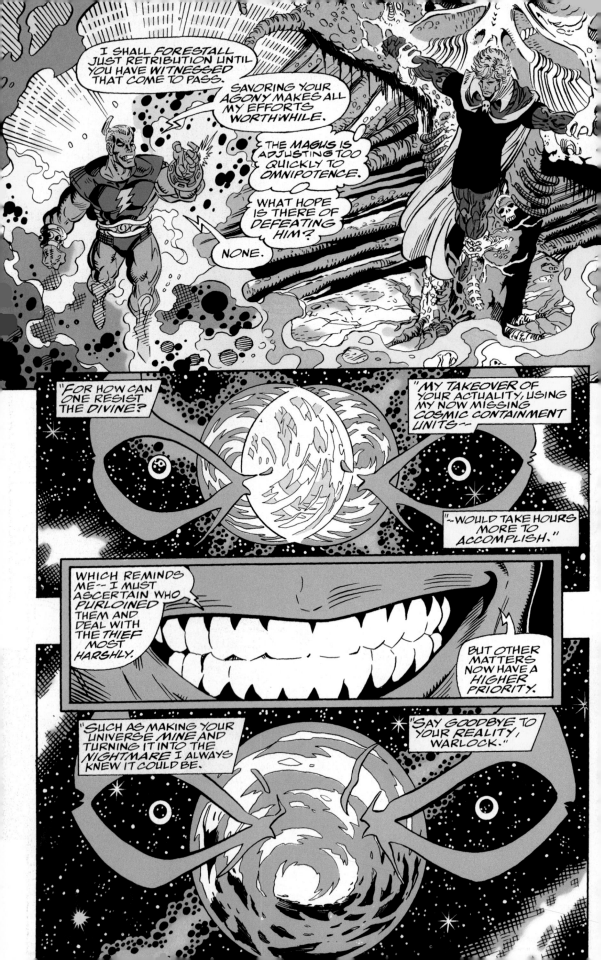

I SHALL FORESTALL JUST RETRIBUTION UNTIL YOU HAVE WITNESSED THAT COME TO PASS.

SAVORING YOUR AGONY MAKES ALL MY EFFORTS WORTHWHILE.

THE MAGUS IS ADJUSTING TOO QUICKLY TO OMNIPOTENCE.

WHAT HOPE IS THERE OF DEFEATING HIM?

NONE.

"FOR HOW CAN ONE RESIST THE DIVINE?"

"MY TAKEOVER OF YOUR ACTUALITY, USING MY NOW MISSING COSMIC CONTAINMENT UNITS--

"--WOULD TAKE HOURS MORE TO ACCOMPLISH."

WHICH REMINDS ME-- I MUST ASCERTAIN WHO PURLOINED THEM AND DEAL WITH THE THIEF MOST HARSHLY.

BUT OTHER MATTERS NOW HAVE A HIGHER PRIORITY.

"SUCH AS MAKING YOUR UNIVERSE MINE AND TURNING IT INTO THE NIGHTMARE I ALWAYS KNEW IT COULD BE.

"SAY GOODBYE TO YOUR REALITY, WARLOCK."

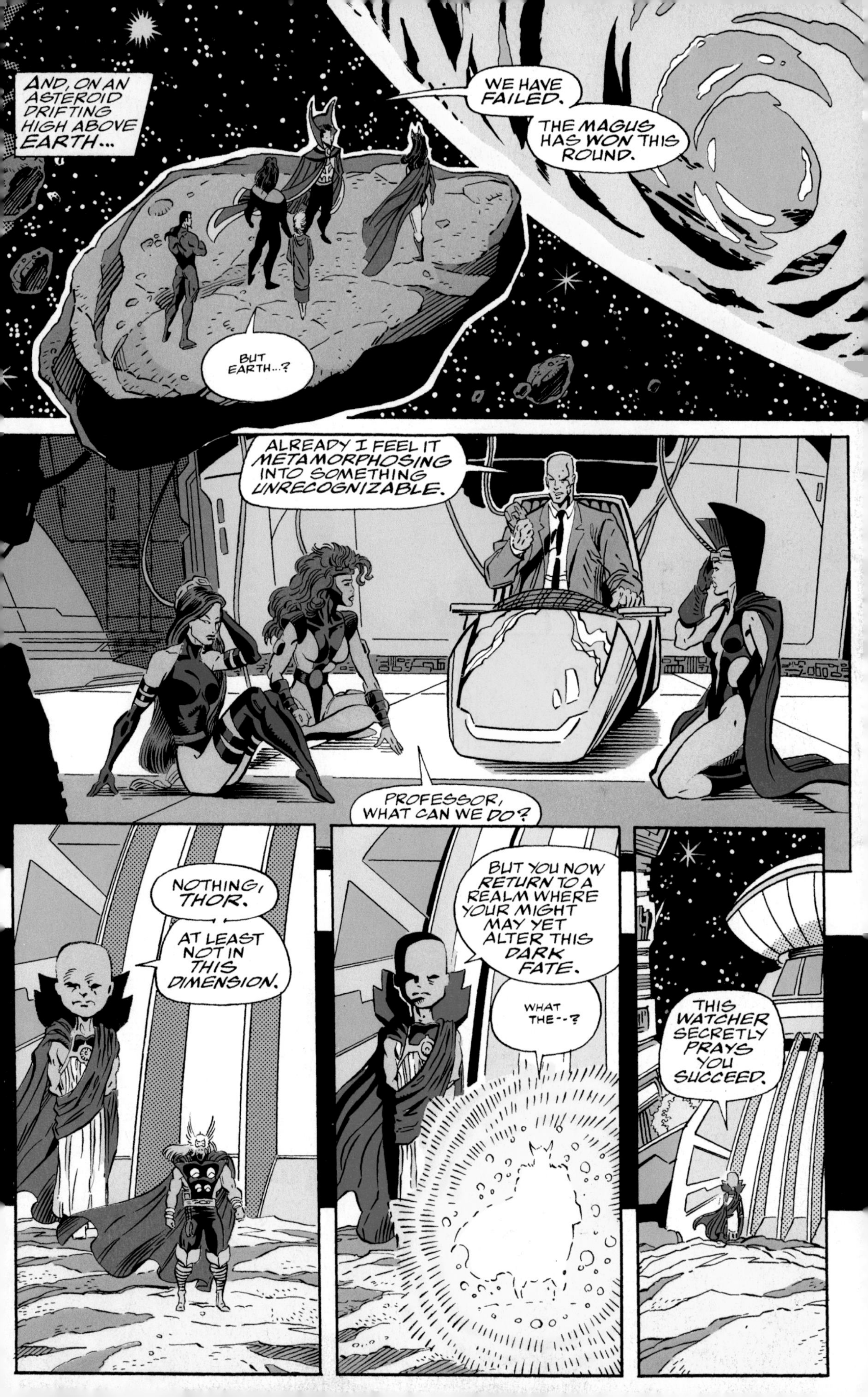
AND, ON AN ASTEROID DRIFTING HIGH ABOVE EARTH...
WE HAVE FAILED.
THE MAGUS HAS WON THIS ROUND.
BUT EARTH...?
ALREADY I FEEL IT METAMORPHOSING INTO SOMETHING UNRECOGNIZABLE.
PROFESSOR, WHAT CAN WE DO?
NOTHING, THOR.
AT LEAST NOT IN THIS DIMENSION.
BUT YOU NOW RETURN TO A REALM WHERE YOUR MIGHT MAY YET ALTER THIS DARK FATE.
WHAT THE--?
THIS WATCHER SECRETLY PRAYS YOU SUCCEED.

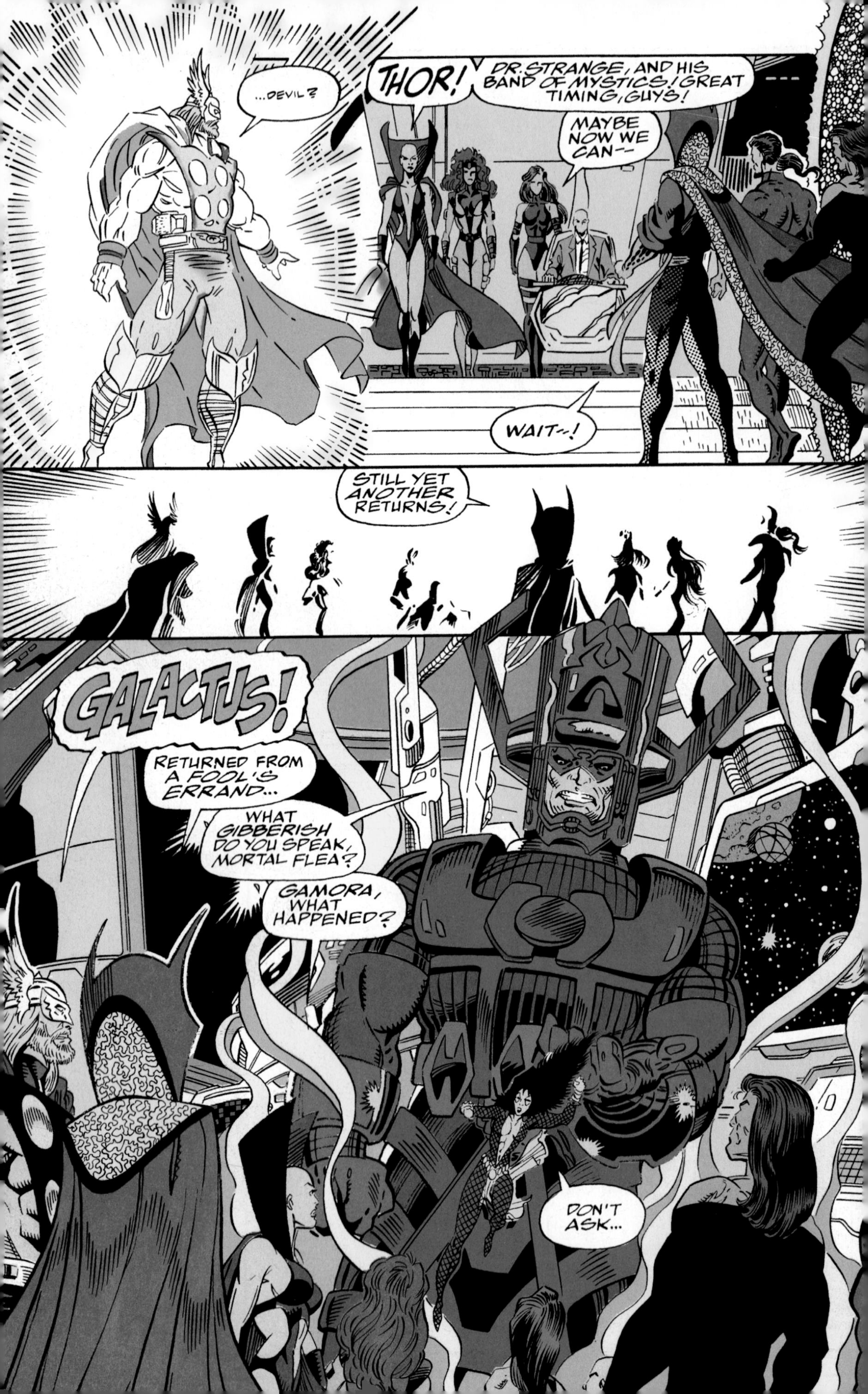
...DEVIL?
THOR!
DR. STRANGE, AND HIS BAND OF MYSTICS! GREAT TIMING, GUYS!
MAYBE NOW WE CAN--
WAIT--!
STILL YET ANOTHER RETURNS!
GALACTUS!
RETURNED FROM A FOOL'S ERRAND...
WHAT GIBBERISH DO YOU SPEAK, MORTAL FLEA?
GAMORA, WHAT HAPPENED?
DON'T ASK...

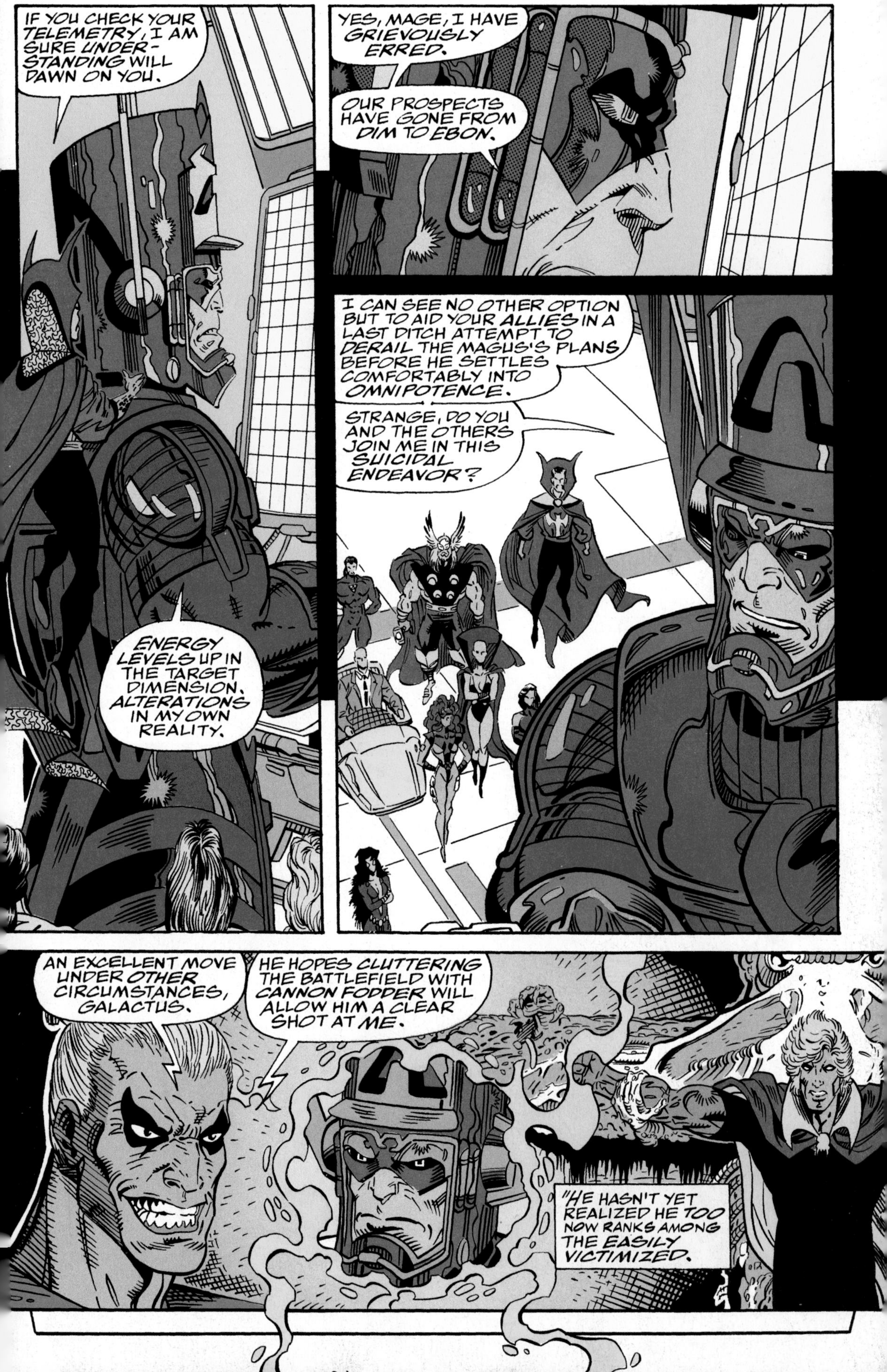
IF YOU CHECK YOUR TELEMETRY, I AM SURE UNDER-STANDING WILL DAWN ON YOU.
ENERGY LEVELS UP IN THE TARGET DIMENSION. ALTERATIONS IN MY OWN REALITY.
YES, MAGE, I HAVE GRIEVOUSLY ERRED.
OUR PROSPECTS HAVE GONE FROM DIM TO EBON.
I CAN SEE NO OTHER OPTION BUT TO AID YOUR ALLIES IN A LAST DITCH ATTEMPT TO DERAIL THE MAGUS'S PLANS BEFORE HE SETTLES COMFORTABLY INTO OMNIPOTENCE.
STRANGE, DO YOU AND THE OTHERS JOIN ME IN THIS SUICIDAL ENDEAVOR?
AN EXCELLENT MOVE UNDER OTHER CIRCUMSTANCES, GALACTUS.
HE HOPES CLUTTERING THE BATTLEFIELD WITH CANNON FODDER WILL ALLOW HIM A CLEAR SHOT AT ME.
"HE HASN'T YET REALIZED HE TOO NOW RANKS AMONG THE EASILY VICTIMIZED.

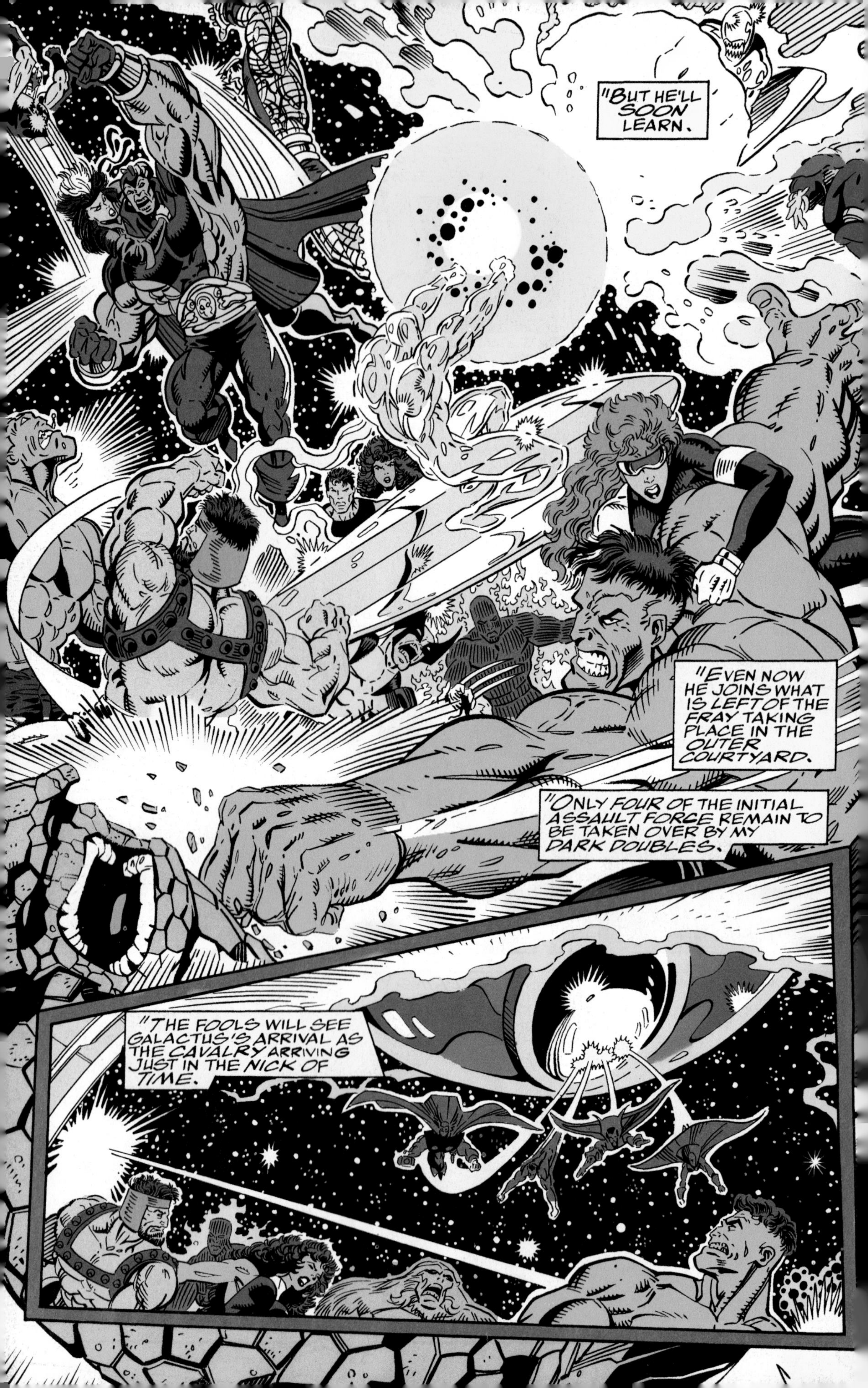
"BUT HE'LL SOON LEARN.
"EVEN NOW HE JOINS WHAT IS LEFT OF THE FRAY TAKING PLACE IN THE OUTER COURTYARD.
"ONLY FOUR OF THE INITIAL ASSAULT FORCE REMAIN TO BE TAKEN OVER BY MY DARK DOUBLES.
"THE FOOLS WILL SEE GALACTUS'S ARRIVAL AS THE CAVALRY ARRIVING JUST IN THE NICK OF TIME.

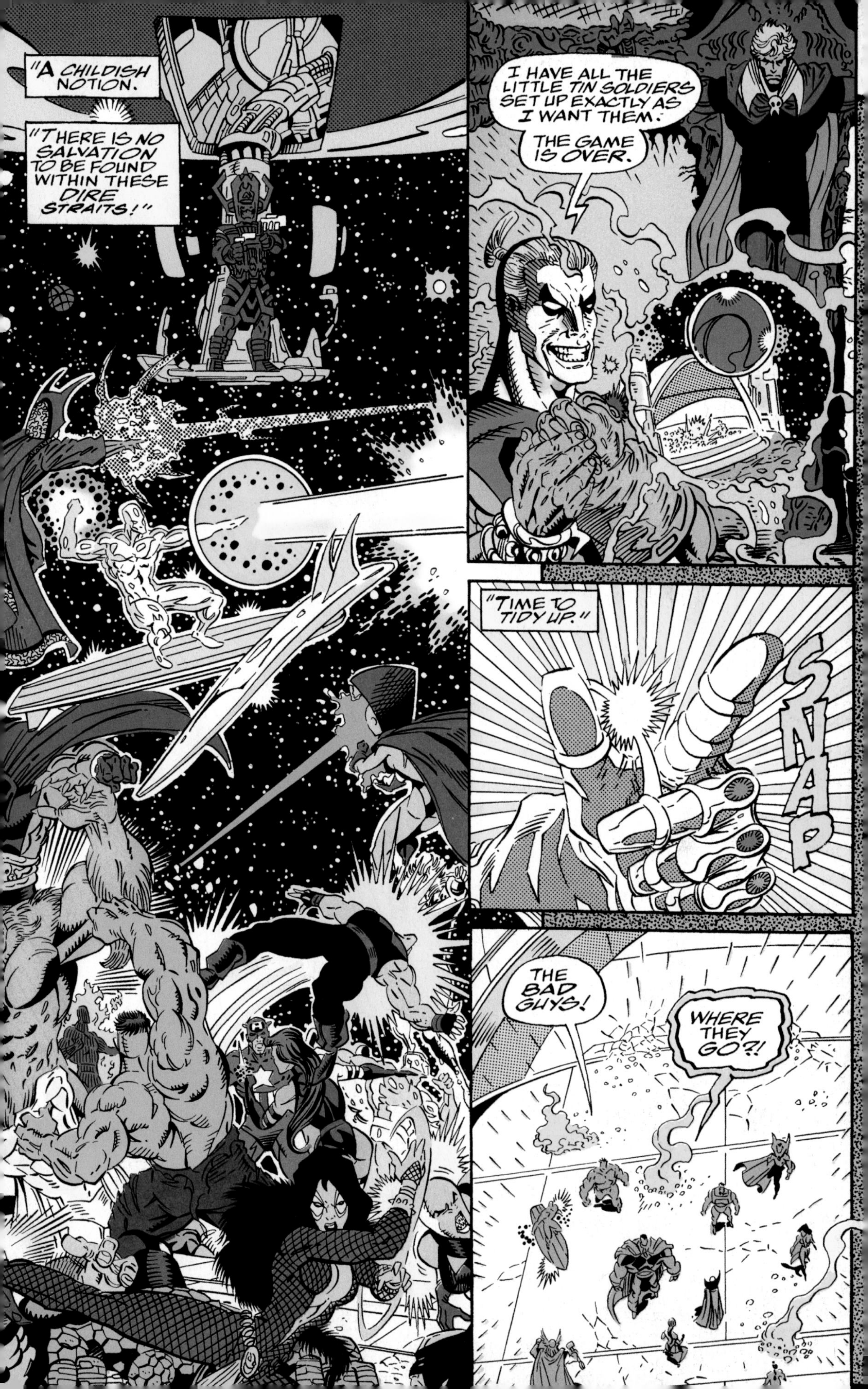
"A CHILDISH NOTION.
"THERE IS NO SALVATION TO BE FOUND WITHIN THESE DIRE STRAITS!"
I HAVE ALL THE LITTLE TIN SOLDIERS SET UP EXACTLY AS I WANT THEM.
THE GAME IS OVER.
"TIME TO TIDY UP."
SNAP
THE BAD GUYS!
WHERE THEY GO?!

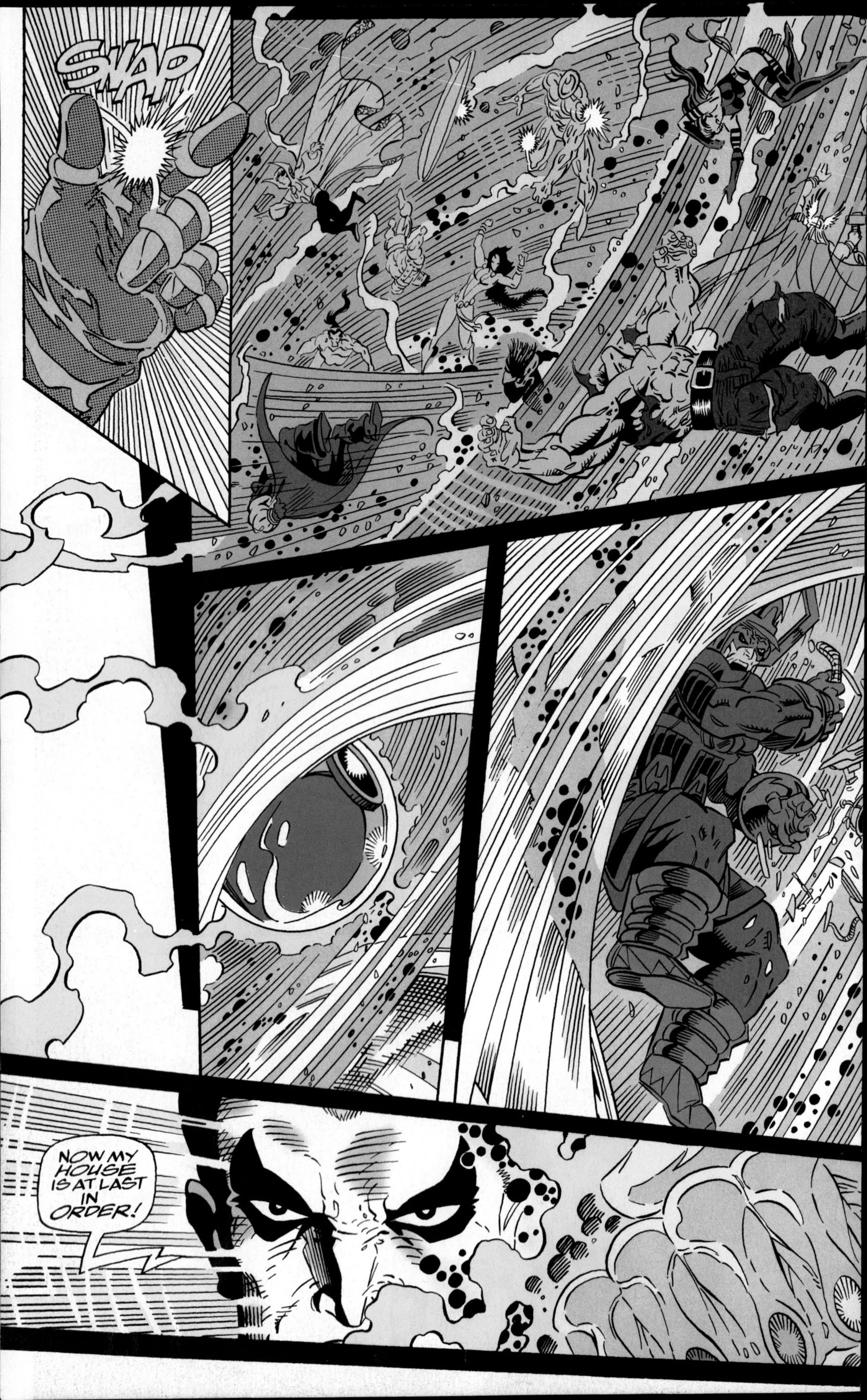
SNAP
NOW MY HOUSE IS AT LAST IN ORDER!

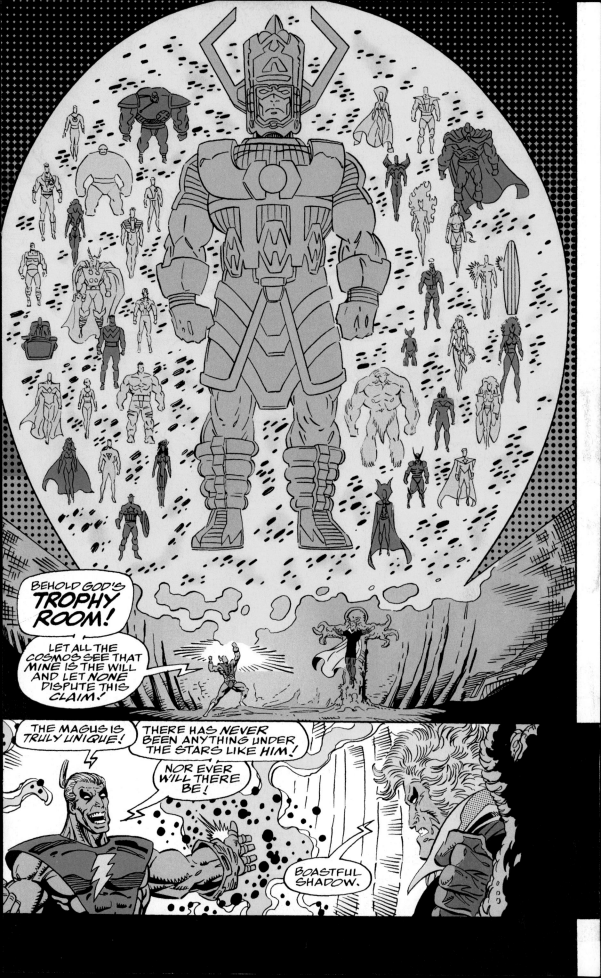

BEHOLD GOD'S **TROPHY ROOM!**

LET ALL THE COSMOS SEE THAT MINE IS THE WILL AND LET *NONE* DISPUTE THIS CLAIM!

THE MAGUS IS *TRULY UNIQUE!*

THERE HAS *NEVER* BEEN ANYTHING UNDER THE STARS LIKE *HIM!*

NOR EVER *WILL THERE BE!*

BOASTFUL SHADOW.

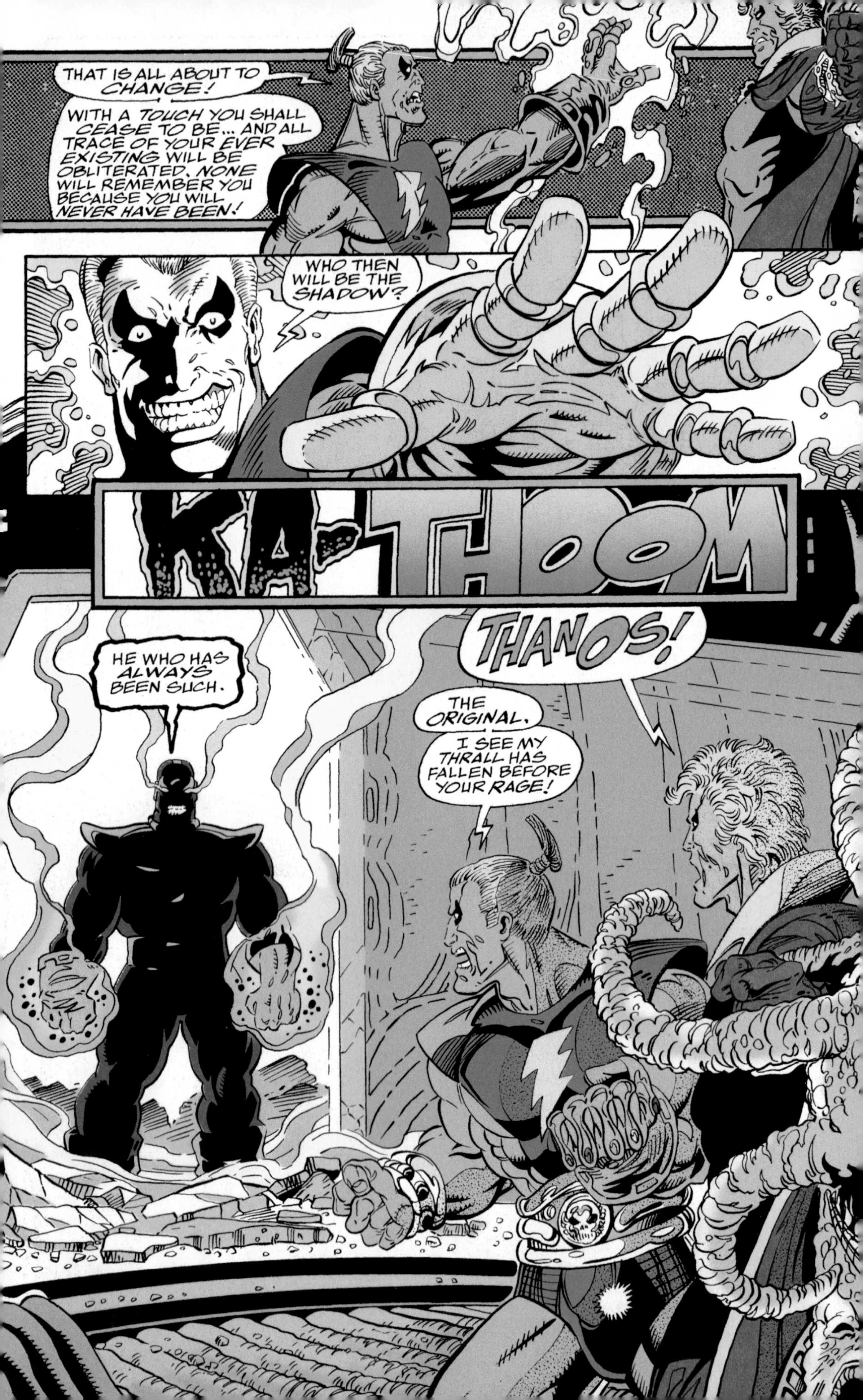
THAT IS ALL ABOUT TO CHANGE!
WITH A TOUCH YOU SHALL CEASE TO BE... AND ALL TRACE OF YOUR EVER EXISTING WILL BE OBLITERATED. NONE WILL REMEMBER YOU BECAUSE YOU WILL NEVER HAVE BEEN!
WHO THEN WILL BE THE SHADOW?
KA-THOOM
THANOS!
HE WHO HAS ALWAYS BEEN SUCH.
THE ORIGINAL. I SEE MY THRALL HAS FALLEN BEFORE YOUR RAGE!

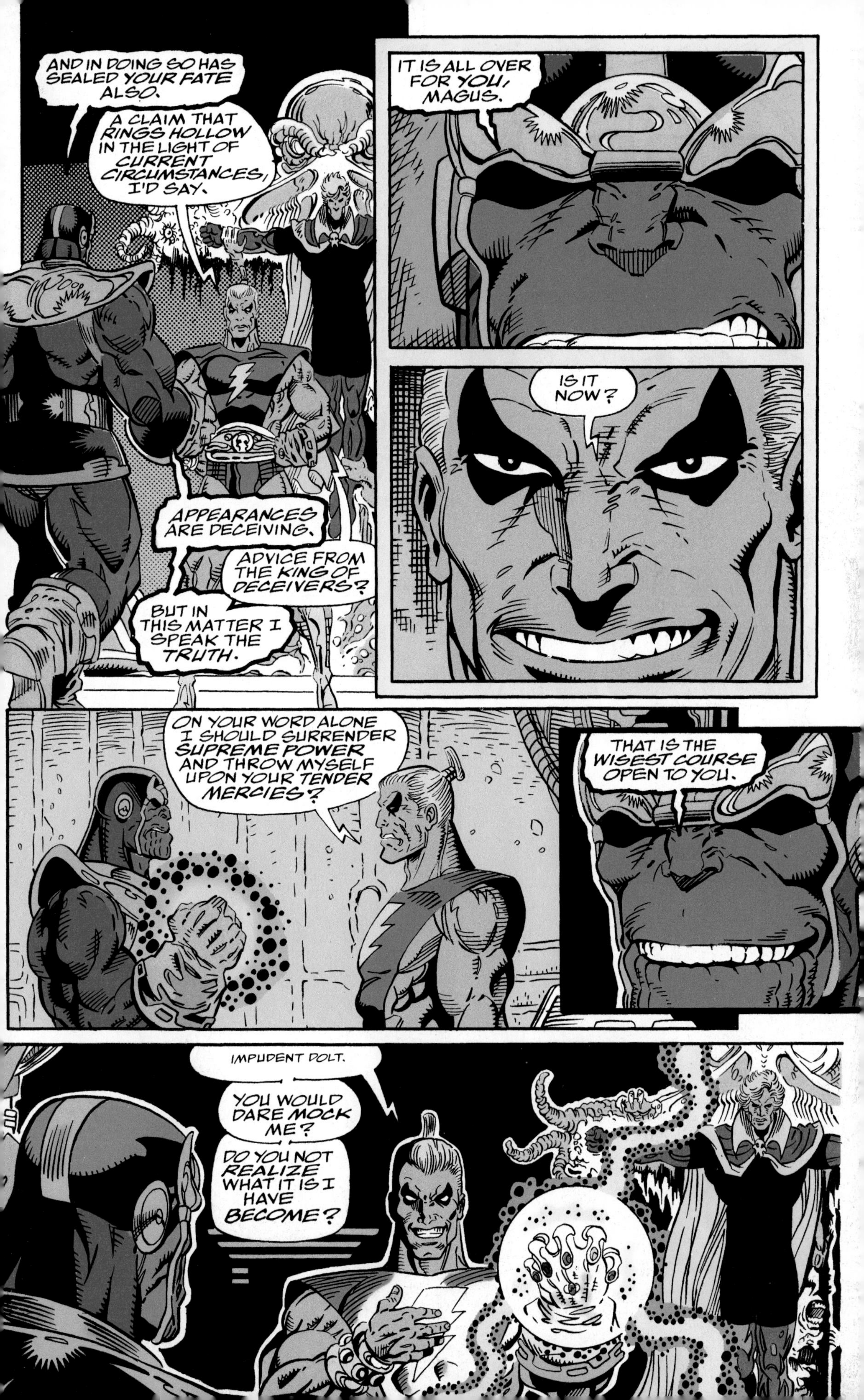
AND IN DOING SO HAS SEALED YOUR FATE ALSO.
A CLAIM THAT RINGS HOLLOW IN THE LIGHT OF CURRENT CIRCUMSTANCES, I'D SAY.
APPEARANCES ARE DECEIVING.
ADVICE FROM THE KING OF DECEIVERS?
BUT IN THIS MATTER I SPEAK THE TRUTH.
IT IS ALL OVER FOR YOU, MAGUS.
IS IT NOW?
ON YOUR WORD ALONE I SHOULD SURRENDER SUPREME POWER AND THROW MYSELF UPON YOUR TENDER MERCIES?
THAT IS THE WISEST COURSE OPEN TO YOU.
IMPUDENT DOLT.
YOU WOULD DARE MOCK ME?
DO YOU NOT REALIZE WHAT IT IS I HAVE BECOME?

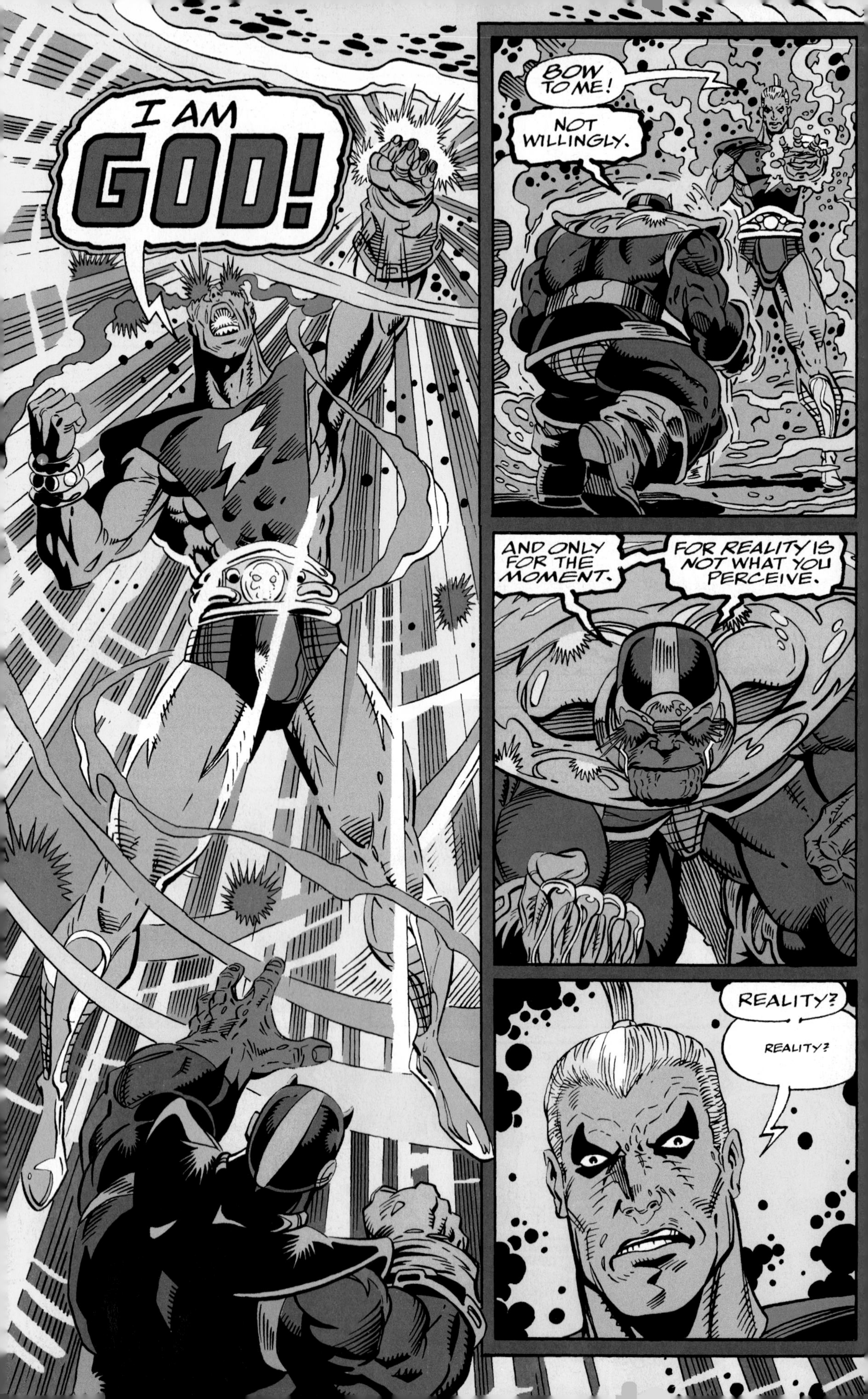
I AM GOD!
BOW TO ME!
NOT WILLINGLY.
AND ONLY FOR THE MOMENT.
FOR REALITY IS NOT WHAT YOU PERCEIVE.
REALITY?
REALITY?

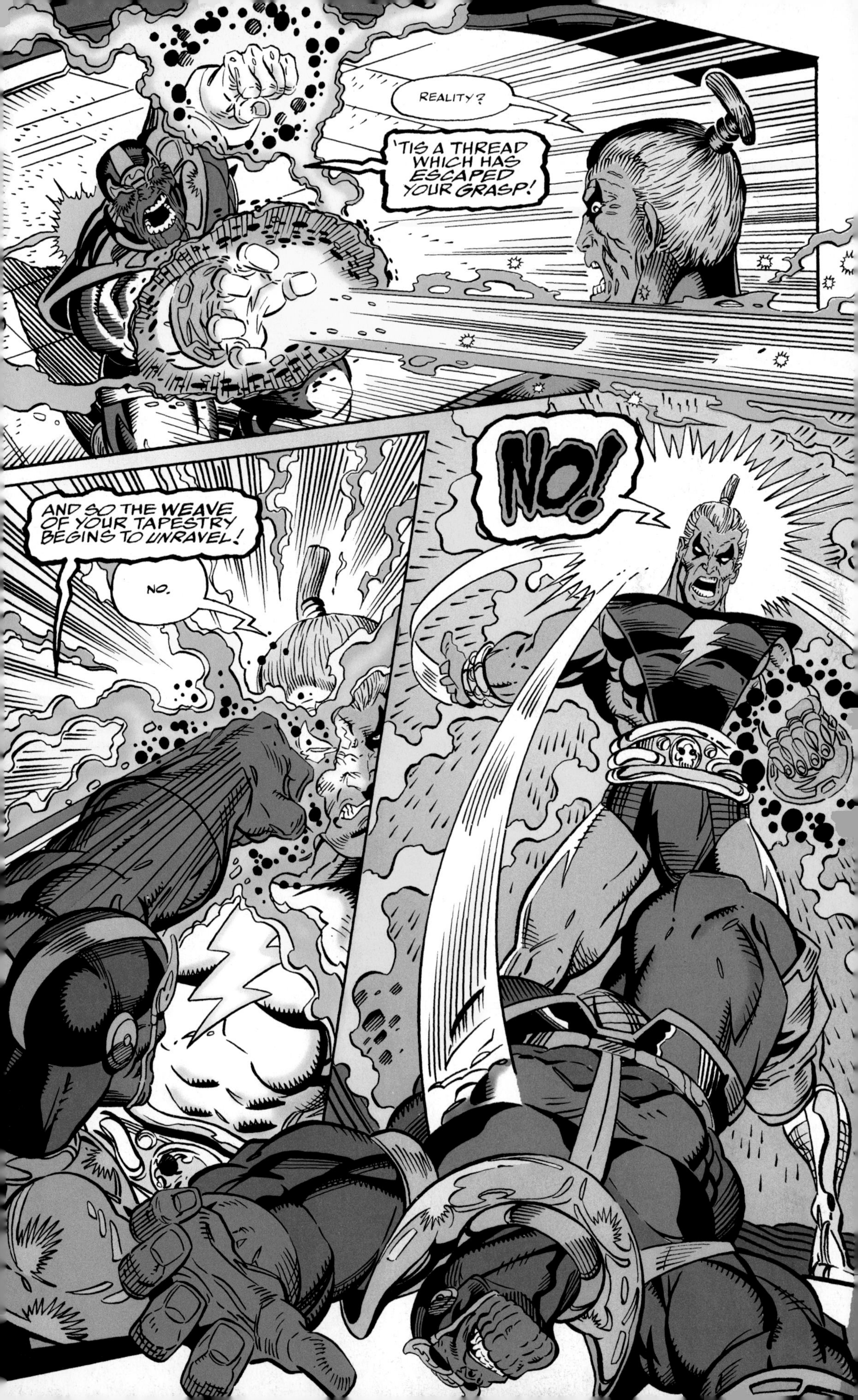
REALITY?
'TIS A THREAD WHICH HAS ESCAPED YOUR GRASP!
AND SO THE WEAVE OF YOUR TAPESTRY BEGINS TO UNRAVEL!
NO.
NO!

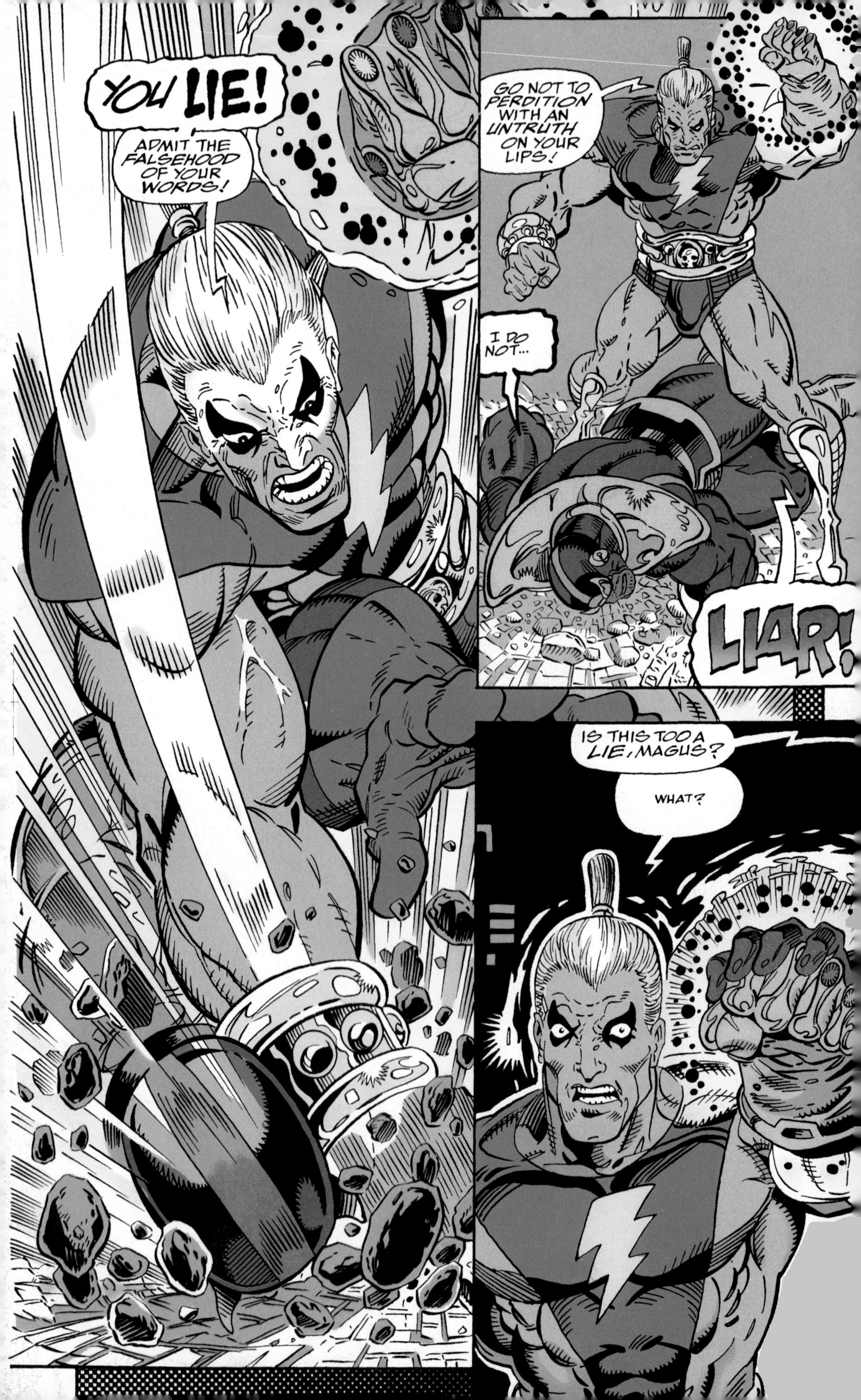
YOU LIE!
ADMIT THE FALSEHOOD OF YOUR WORDS!
GO NOT TO PERDITION WITH AN UNTRUTH ON YOUR LIPS!
I DO NOT...
LIAR!
IS THIS TOO A LIE, MAGUS?
WHAT?

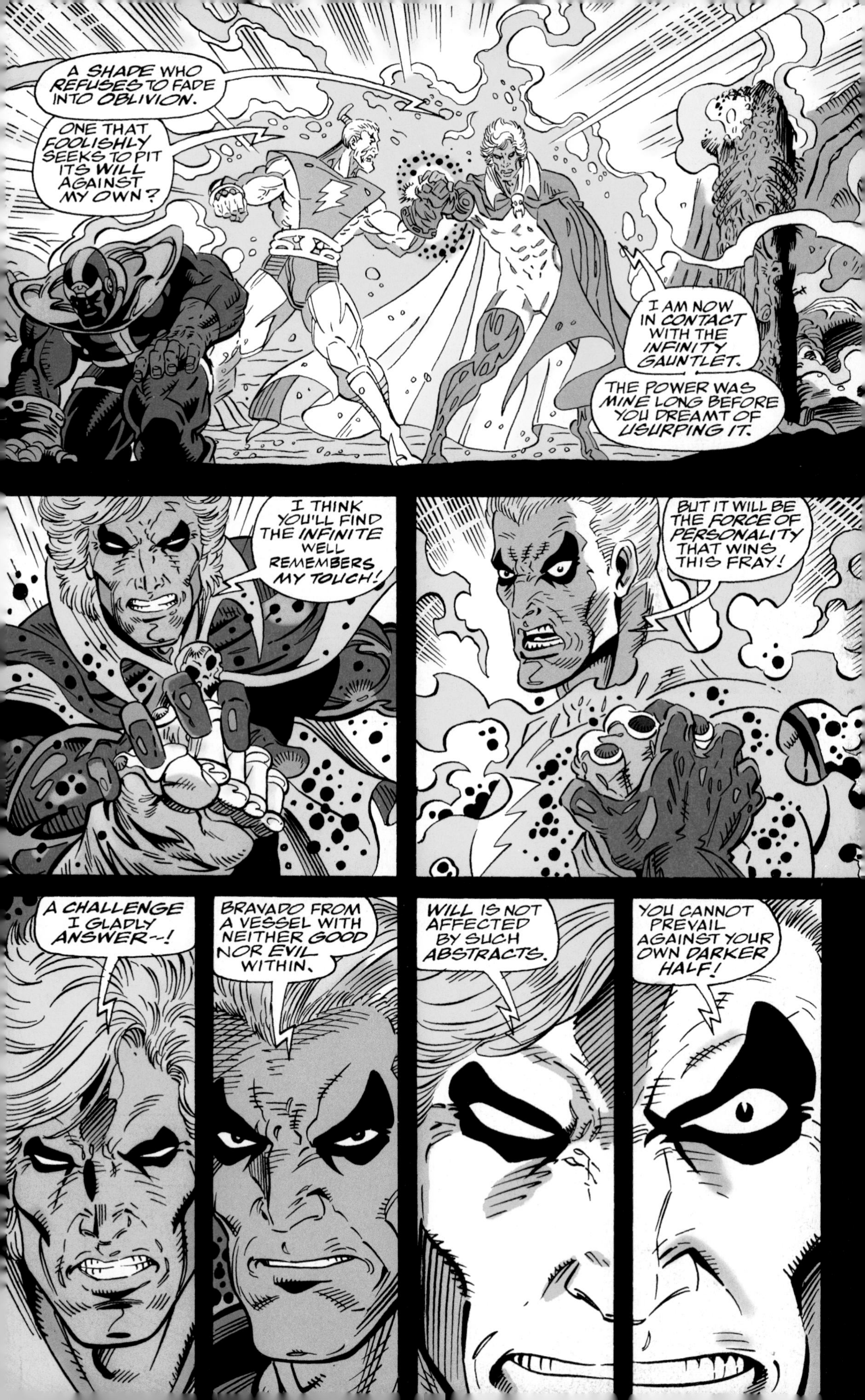
A SHADE WHO REFUSES TO FADE INTO OBLIVION.
ONE THAT FOOLISHLY SEEKS TO PIT ITS WILL AGAINST MY OWN?
I AM NOW IN CONTACT WITH THE INFINITY GAUNTLET.
THE POWER WAS MINE LONG BEFORE YOU DREAMT OF USURPING IT.
I THINK YOU'LL FIND THE INFINITE WELL REMEMBERS MY TOUCH!
BUT IT WILL BE THE FORCE OF PERSONALITY THAT WINS THIS FRAY!
A CHALLENGE I GLADLY ANSWER--!
BRAVADO FROM A VESSEL WITH NEITHER GOOD NOR EVIL WITHIN.
WILL IS NOT AFFECTED BY SUCH ABSTRACTS.
YOU CANNOT PREVAIL AGAINST YOUR OWN DARKER HALF!

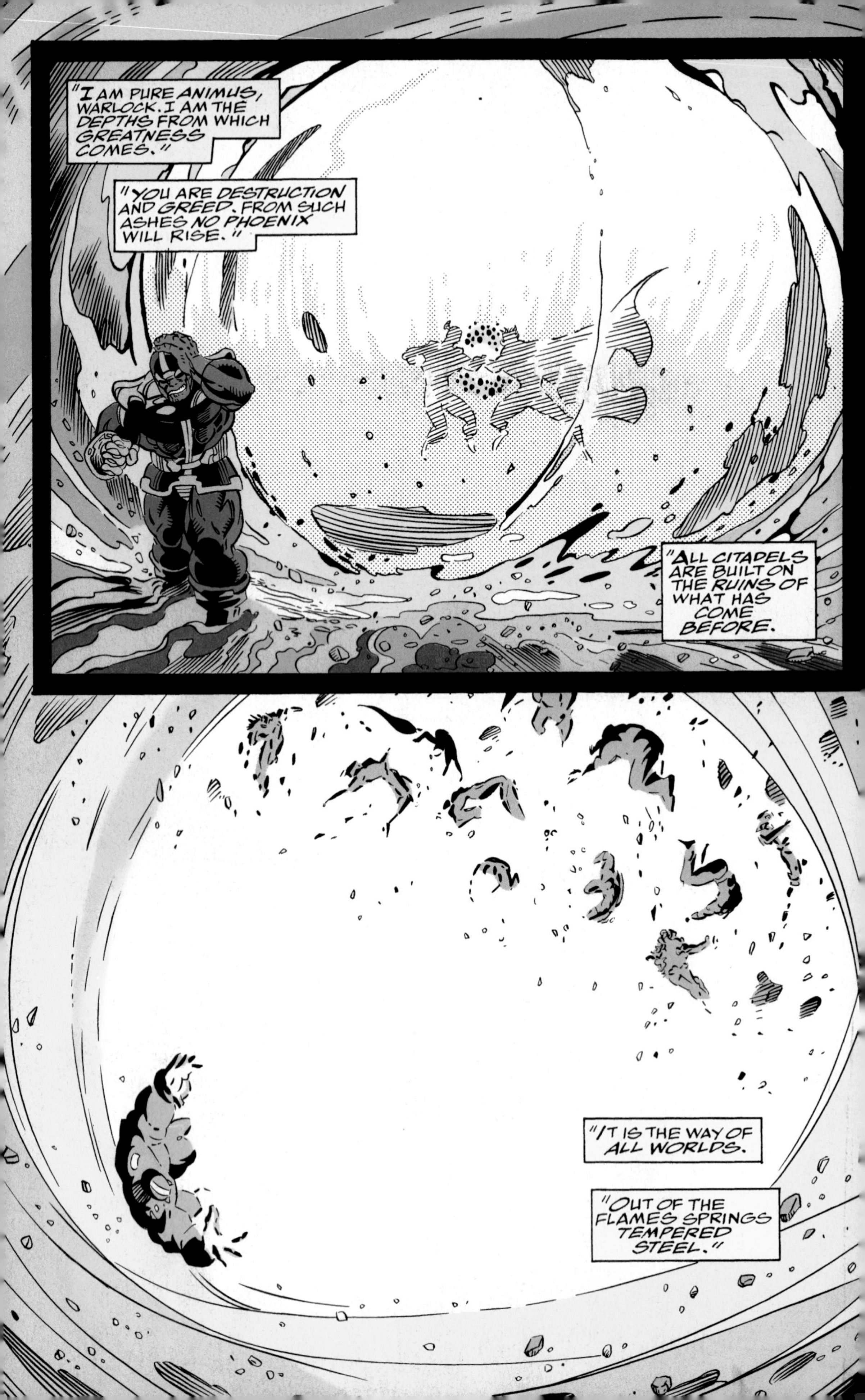
"I AM PURE ANIMUS, WARLOCK. I AM THE DEPTHS FROM WHICH GREATNESS COMES."
"YOU ARE DESTRUCTION AND GREED. FROM SUCH ASHES NO PHOENIX WILL RISE."
"ALL CITADELS ARE BUILT ON THE RUINS OF WHAT HAS COME BEFORE.
"IT IS THE WAY OF ALL WORLDS.
"OUT OF THE FLAMES SPRINGS TEMPERED STEEL."

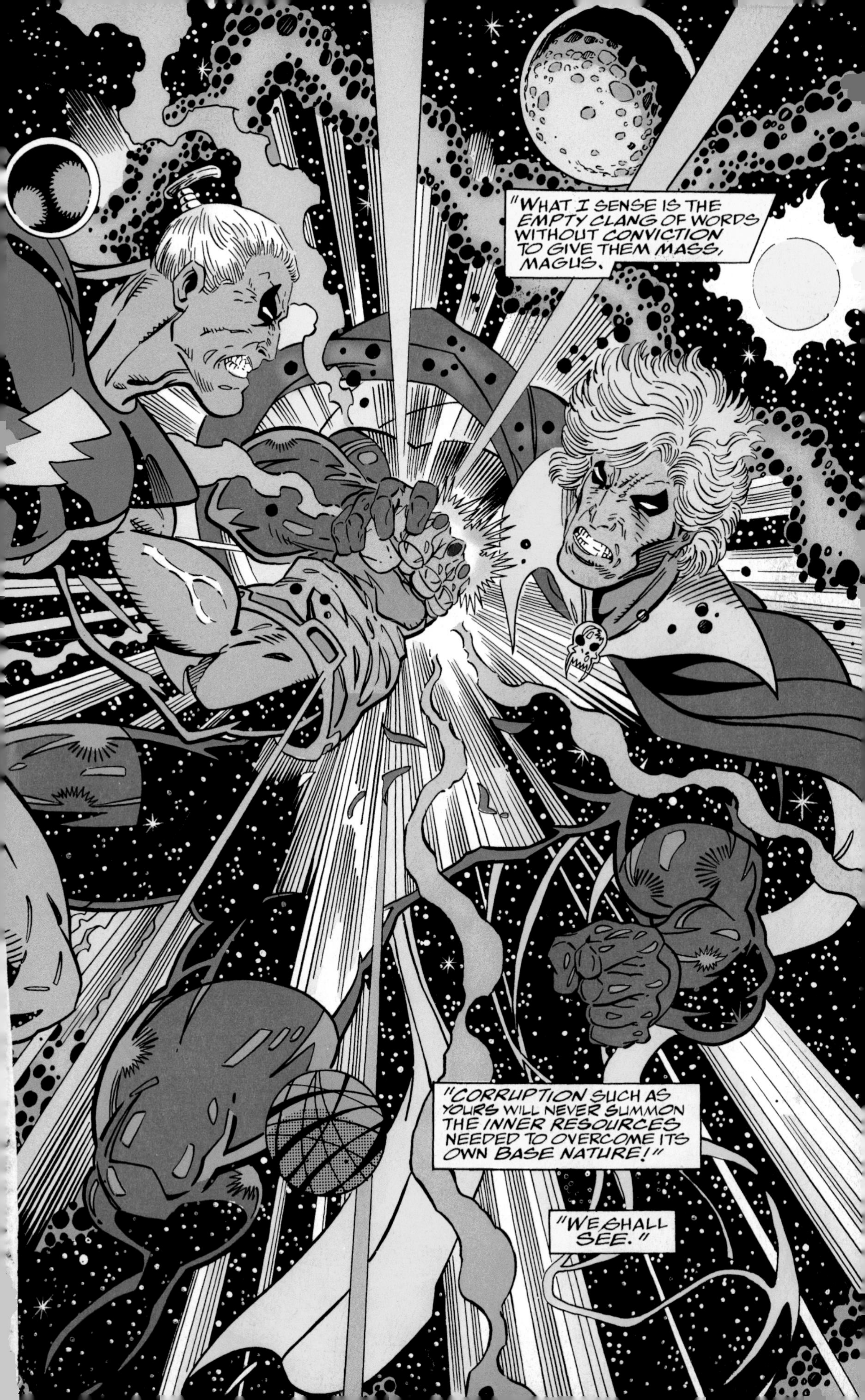
"WHAT I SENSE IS THE EMPTY CLANG OF WORDS WITHOUT CONVICTION TO GIVE THEM MASS, MAGUS.
"CORRUPTION SUCH AS YOURS WILL NEVER SUMMON THE INNER RESOURCES NEEDED TO OVERCOME ITS OWN BASE NATURE!"
"WE SHALL SEE."

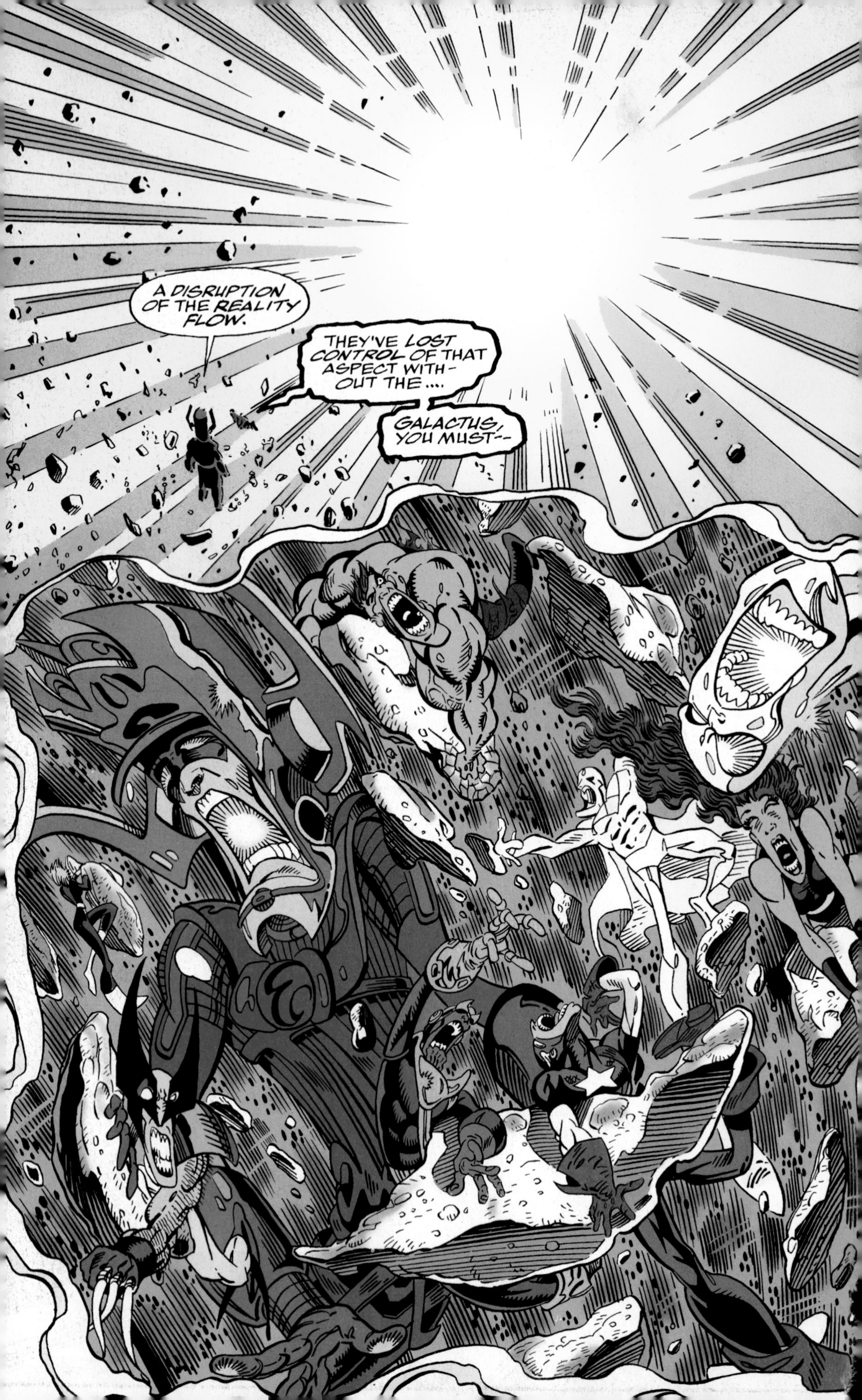
A DISRUPTION OF THE REALITY FLOW.
THEY'VE LOST CONTROL OF THAT ASPECT WITH-OUT THE....
GALACTUS, YOU MUST--

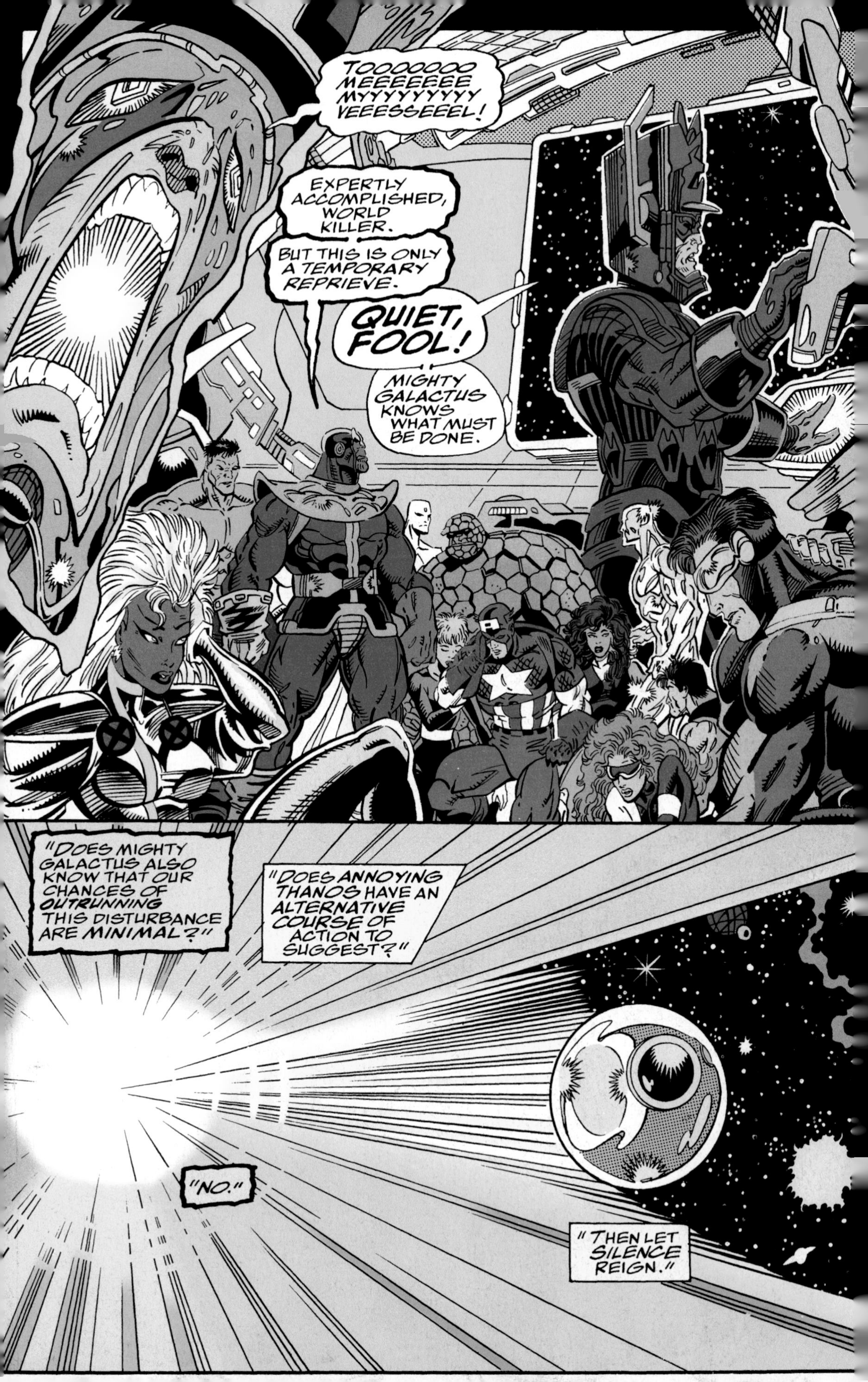
TOOOOOOO MEEEEEEE MYYYYYYYYY VEEESSEEEL!
EXPERTLY ACCOMPLISHED, WORLD KILLER.
BUT THIS IS ONLY A TEMPORARY REPRIEVE.
QUIET, FOOL!
MIGHTY GALACTUS KNOWS WHAT MUST BE DONE.
"DOES MIGHTY GALACTUS ALSO KNOW THAT OUR CHANCES OF OUTRUNNING THIS DISTURBANCE ARE MINIMAL?"
"DOES ANNOYING THANOS HAVE AN ALTERNATIVE COURSE OF ACTION TO SUGGEST?"
"NO."
"THEN LET SILENCE REIGN."

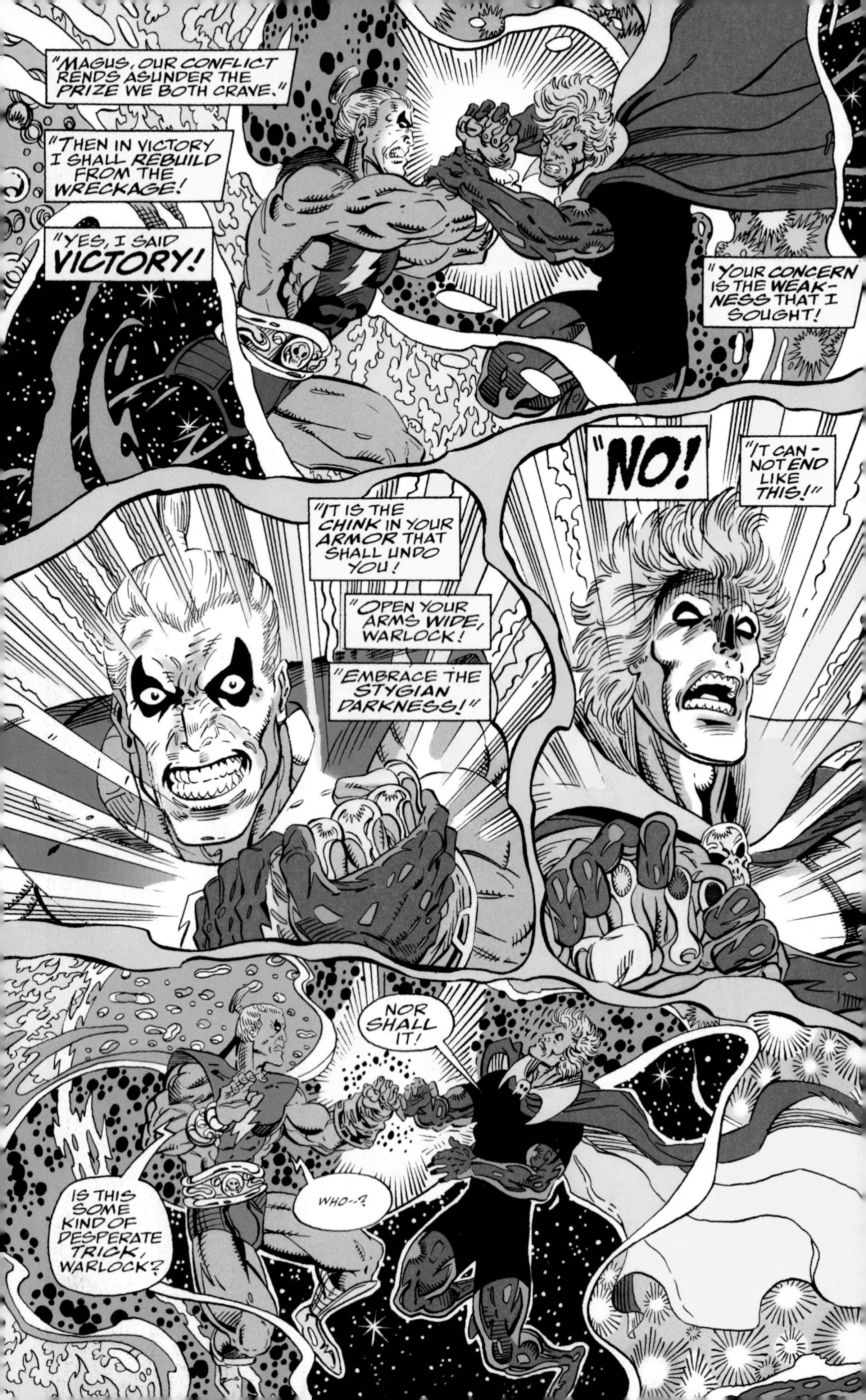
"MAGUS, OUR CONFLICT RENDS ASUNDER THE PRIZE WE BOTH CRAVE."
"THEN IN VICTORY I SHALL REBUILD FROM THE WRECKAGE!
"YES, I SAID VICTORY!
"YOUR CONCERN IS THE WEAKNESS THAT I SOUGHT!
"IT IS THE CHINK IN YOUR ARMOR THAT SHALL UNDO YOU!
"OPEN YOUR ARMS WIDE, WARLOCK!
"EMBRACE THE STYGIAN DARKNESS!"
"NO!
"IT CANNOT END LIKE THIS!"
NOR SHALL IT!
IS THIS SOME KIND OF DESPERATE TRICK, WARLOCK?
WHO--?

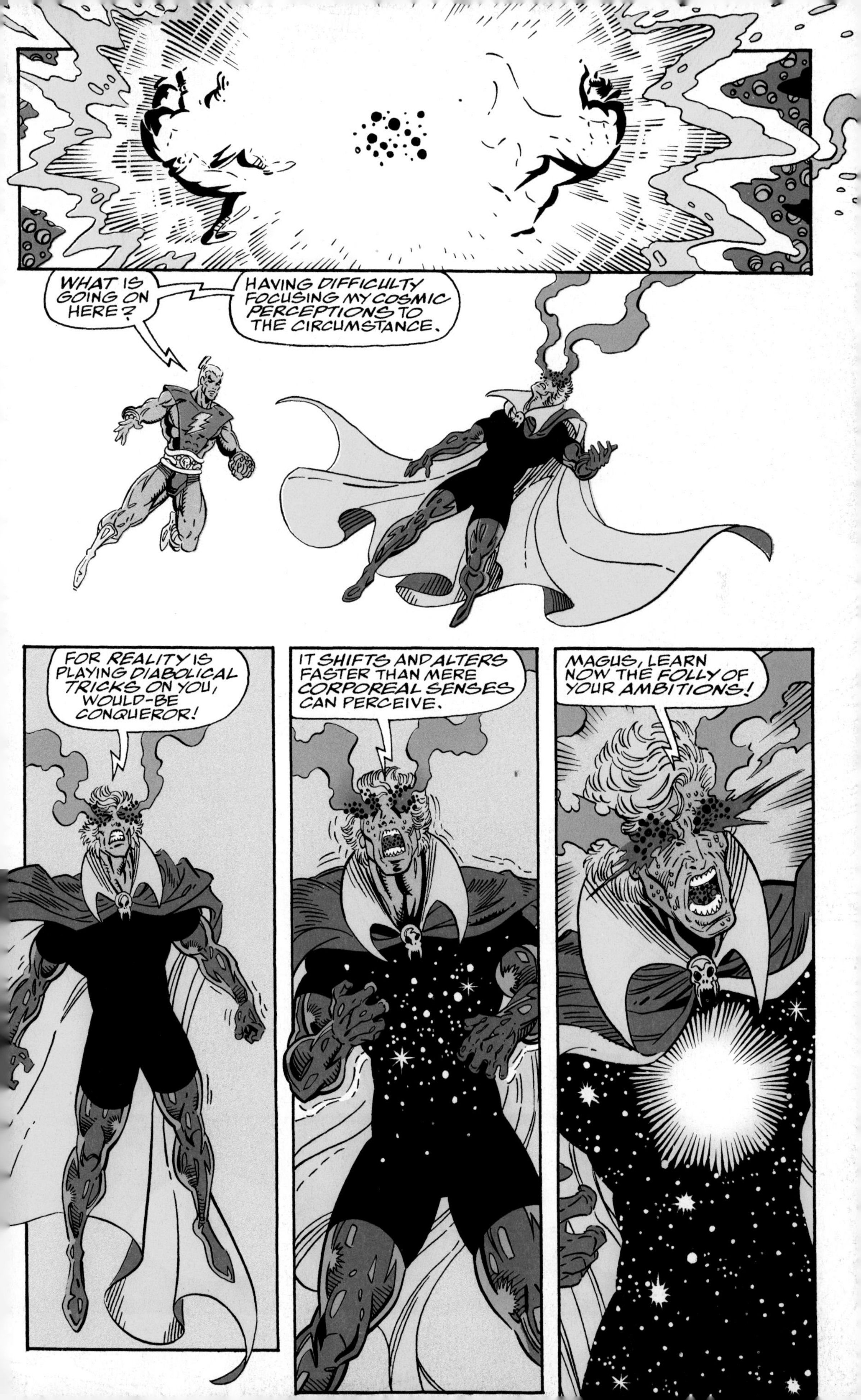
WHAT IS GOING ON HERE?
HAVING DIFFICULTY FOCUSING MY COSMIC PERCEPTIONS TO THE CIRCUMSTANCE.
FOR REALITY IS PLAYING DIABOLICAL TRICKS ON YOU, WOULD-BE CONQUEROR!
IT SHIFTS AND ALTERS FASTER THAN MERE CORPOREAL SENSES CAN PERCEIVE.
MAGUS, LEARN NOW THE FOLLY OF YOUR AMBITIONS!

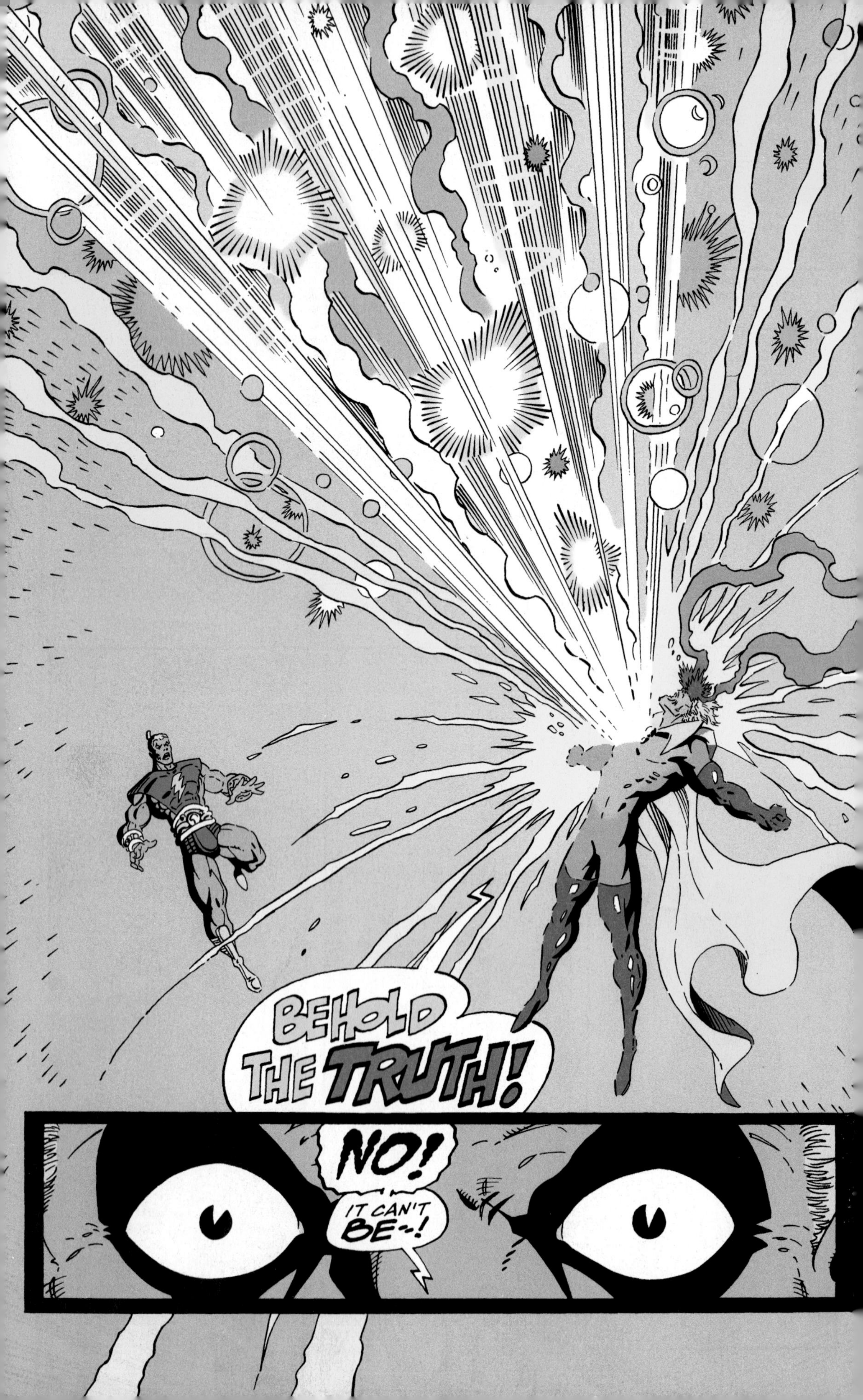
BEHOLD THE TRUTH!
NO! IT CAN'T BE--!

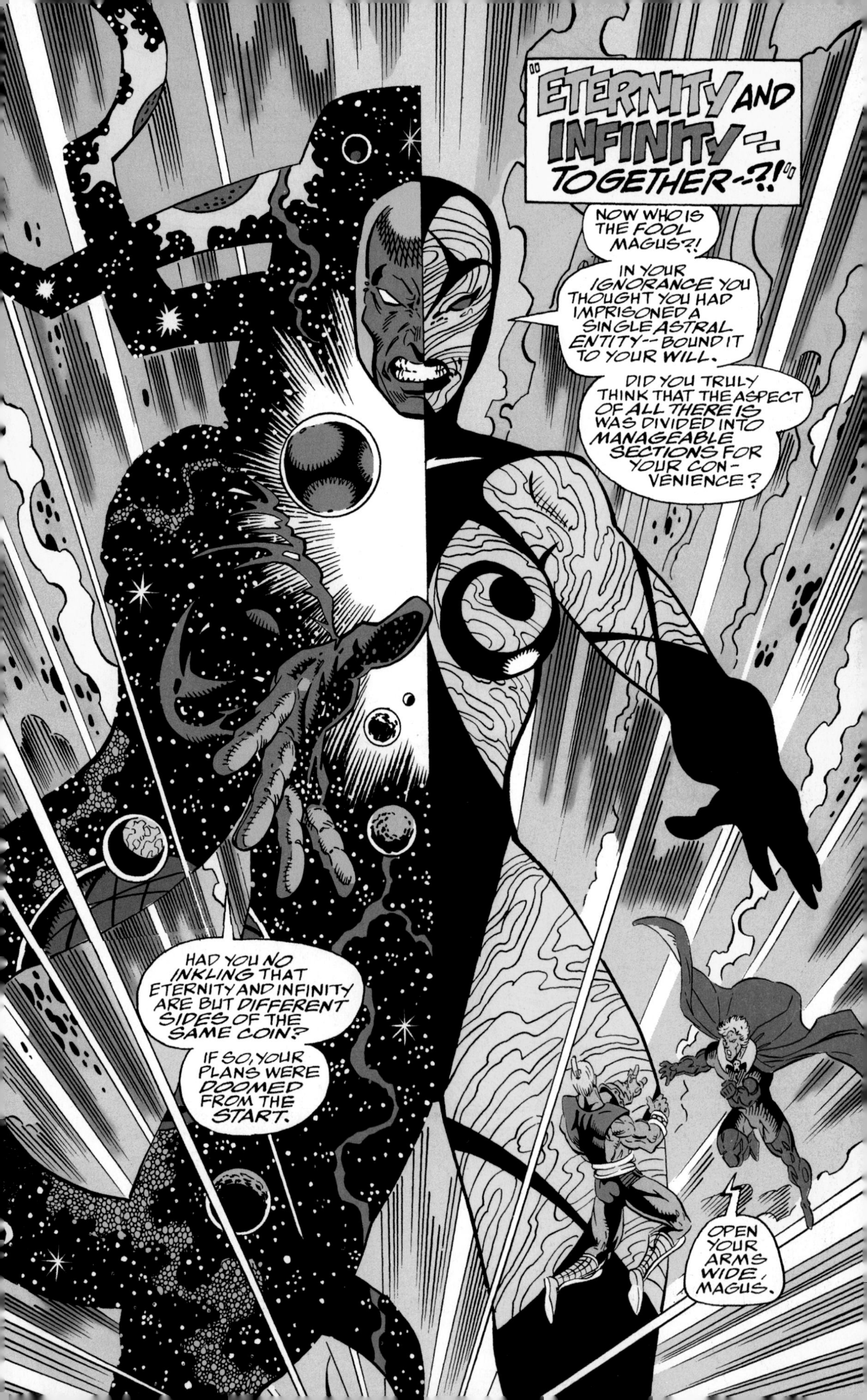
"ETERNITY AND INFINITY -- TOGETHER --?!"
NOW WHO IS THE FOOL MAGUS?!
IN YOUR IGNORANCE YOU THOUGHT YOU HAD IMPRISONED A SINGLE ASTRAL ENTITY -- BOUND IT TO YOUR WILL.
DID YOU TRULY THINK THAT THE ASPECT OF ALL THERE IS WAS DIVIDED INTO MANAGEABLE SECTIONS FOR YOUR CONVENIENCE?
HAD YOU NO INKLING THAT ETERNITY AND INFINITY ARE BUT DIFFERENT SIDES OF THE SAME COIN?
IF SO, YOUR PLANS WERE DOOMED FROM THE START.
OPEN YOUR ARMS WIDE, MAGUS.

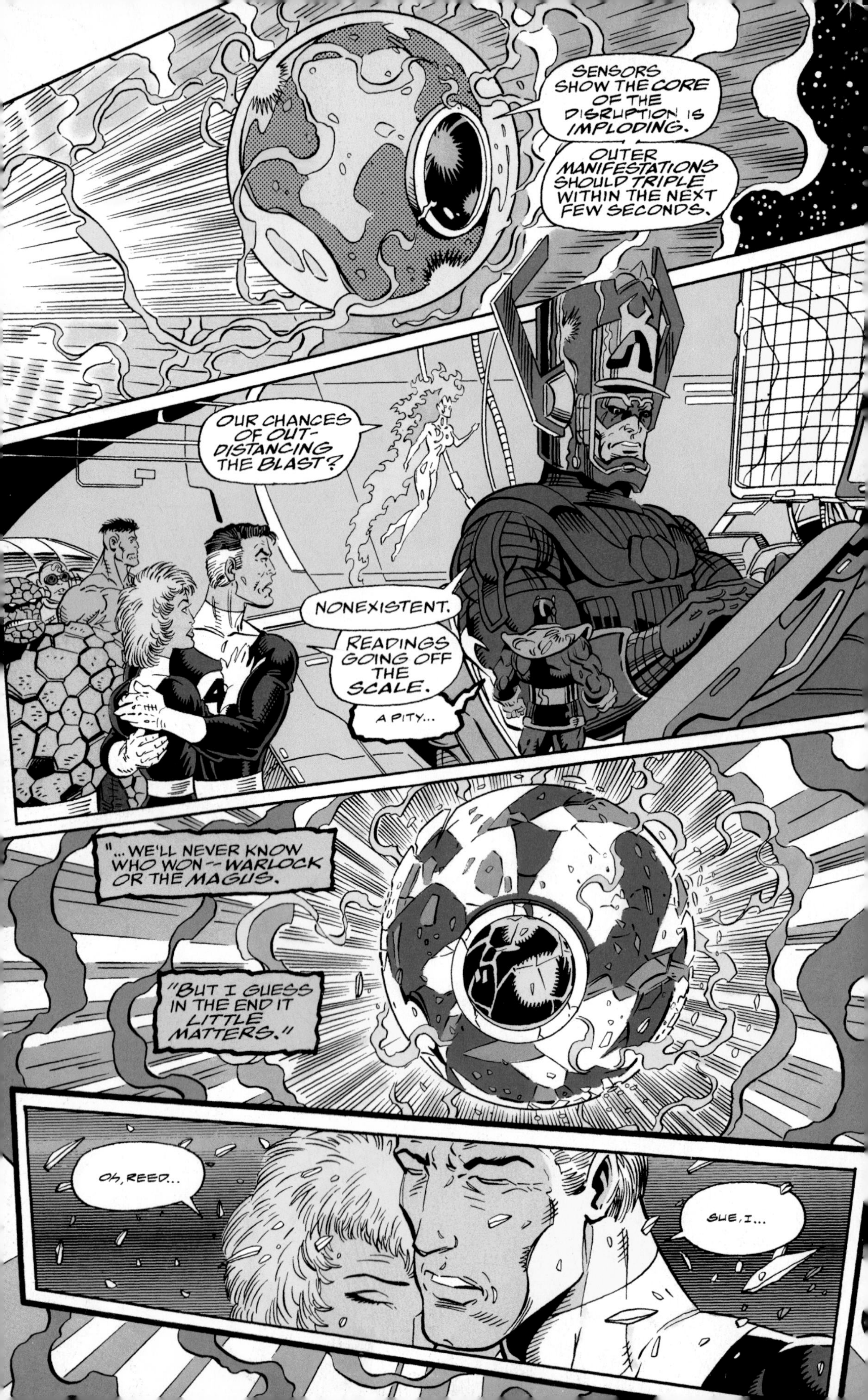
SENSORS SHOW THE CORE OF THE DISRUPTION IS IMPLODING.
OUTER MANIFESTATIONS SHOULD TRIPLE WITHIN THE NEXT FEW SECONDS.
OUR CHANCES OF OUT-DISTANCING THE BLAST?
NONEXISTENT.
READINGS GOING OFF THE SCALE.
A PITY...
"...WE'LL NEVER KNOW WHO WON--WARLOCK OR THE MAGUS.
"BUT I GUESS IN THE END IT LITTLE MATTERS."
OH, REED...
SUE, I...

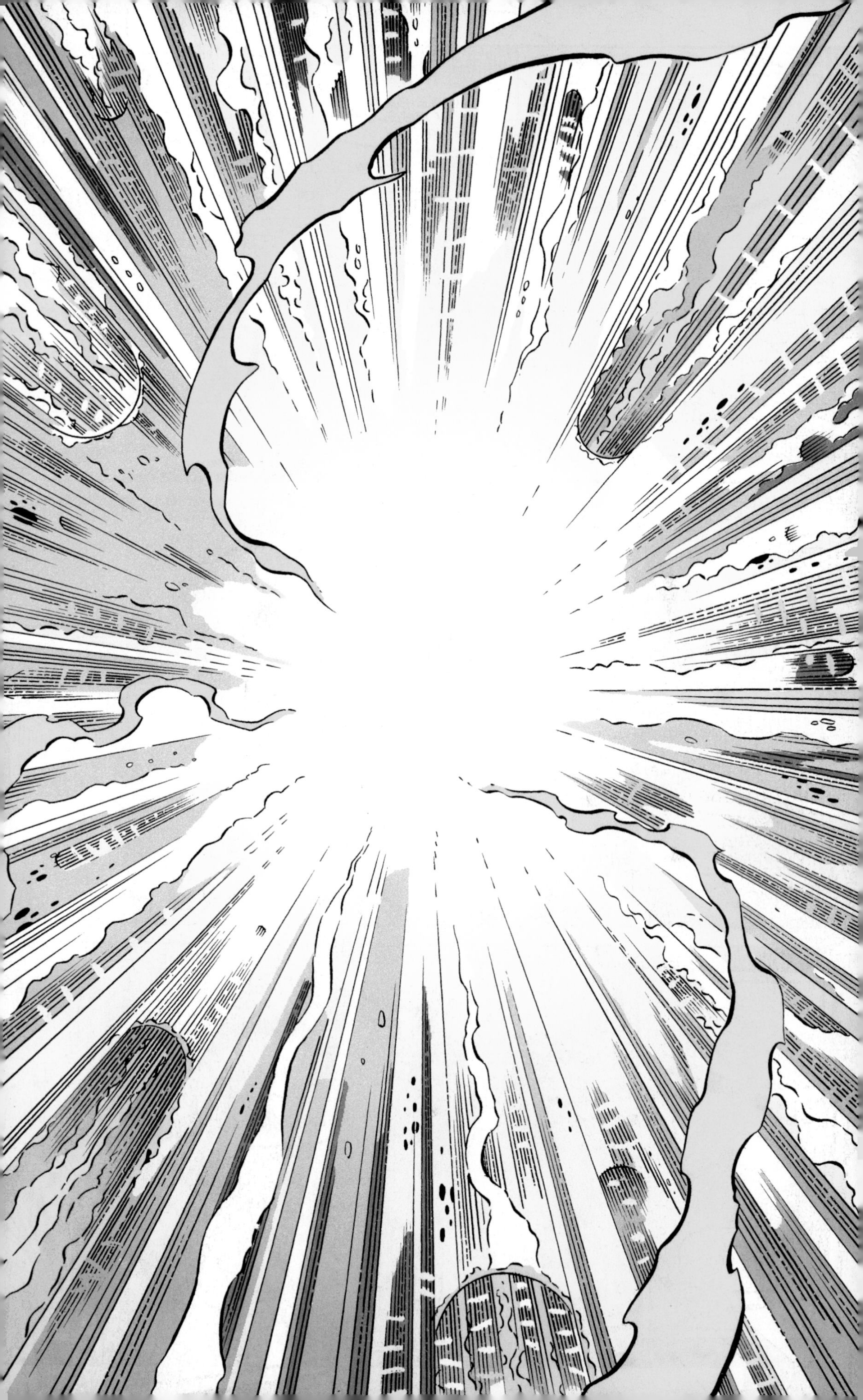

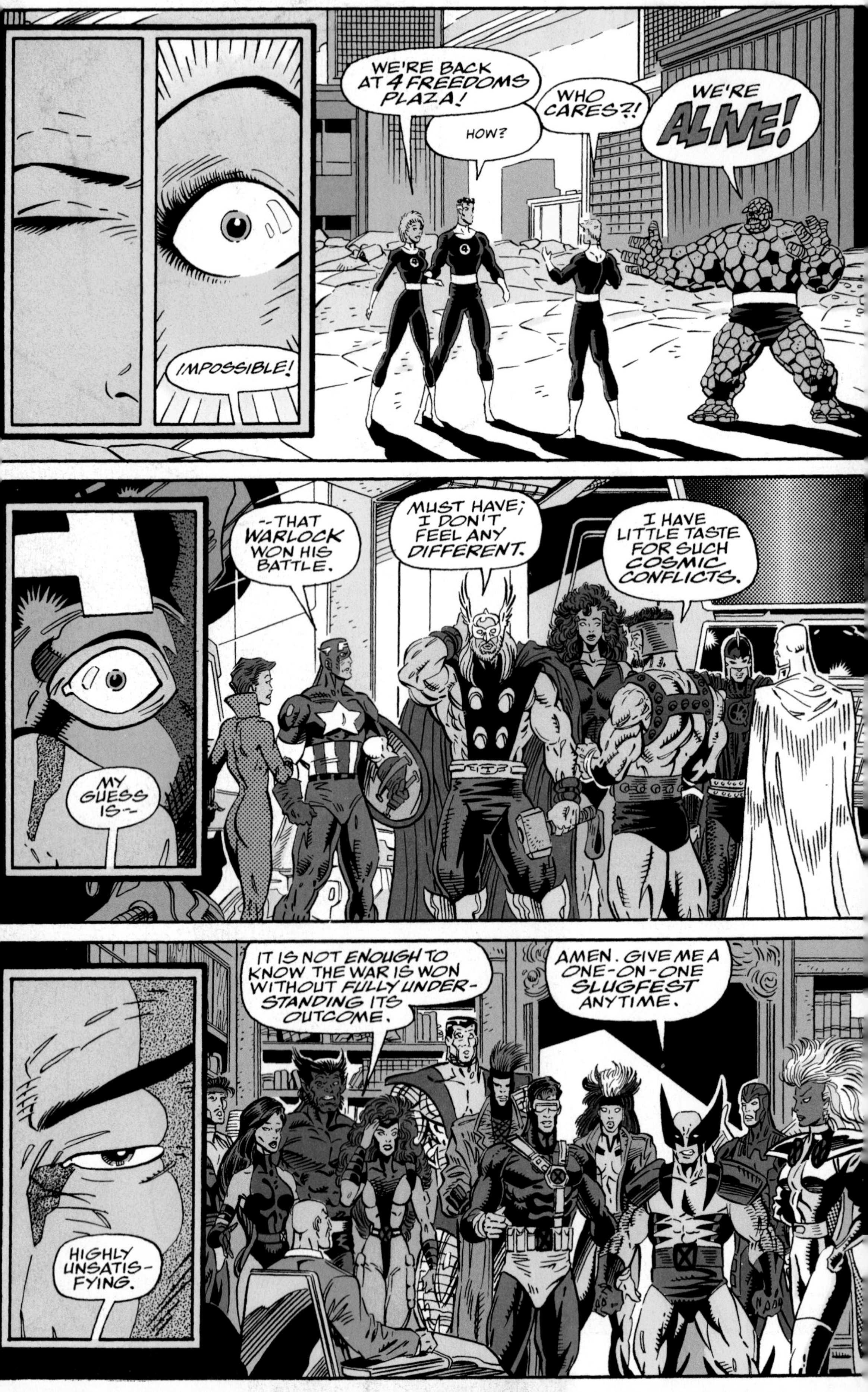
IMPOSSIBLE!
WE'RE BACK AT 4 FREEDOMS PLAZA!
HOW?
WHO CARES?!
WE'RE ALIVE!
MY GUESS IS--
--THAT WARLOCK WON HIS BATTLE.
MUST HAVE; I DON'T FEEL ANY DIFFERENT.
I HAVE LITTLE TASTE FOR SUCH COSMIC CONFLICTS.
HIGHLY UNSATIS-FYING.
IT IS NOT ENOUGH TO KNOW THE WAR IS WON WITHOUT FULLY UNDER-STANDING ITS OUTCOME.
AMEN. GIVE ME A ONE-ON-ONE SLUGFEST ANYTIME.

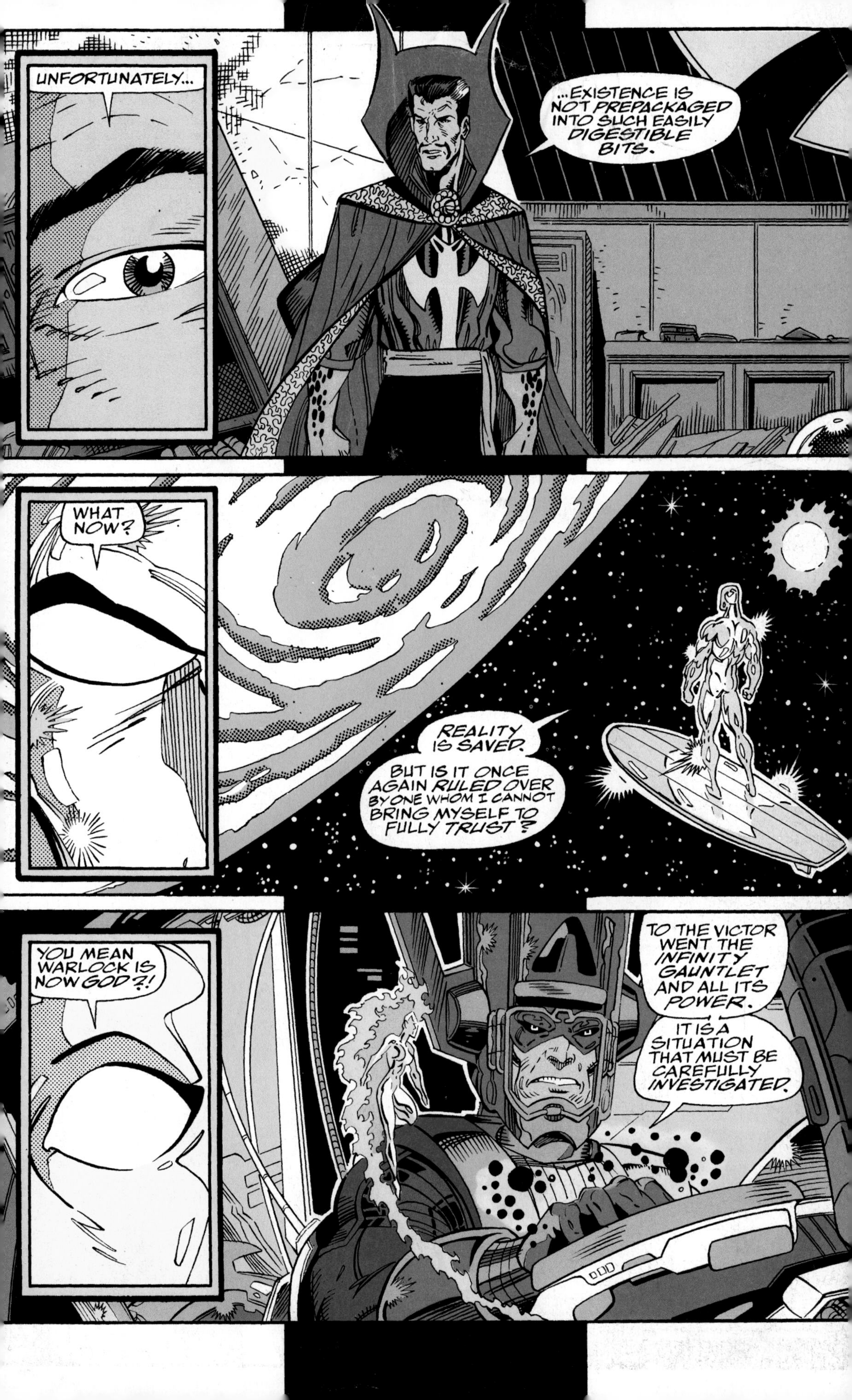
UNFORTUNATELY...
...EXISTENCE IS NOT PREPACKAGED INTO SUCH EASILY DIGESTIBLE BITS.
WHAT NOW?
REALITY IS SAVED.
BUT IS IT ONCE AGAIN RULED OVER BY ONE WHOM I CANNOT BRING MYSELF TO FULLY TRUST?
YOU MEAN WARLOCK IS NOW GOD?!
TO THE VICTOR WENT THE INFINITY GAUNTLET AND ALL ITS POWER.
IT IS A SITUATION THAT MUST BE CAREFULLY INVESTIGATED.

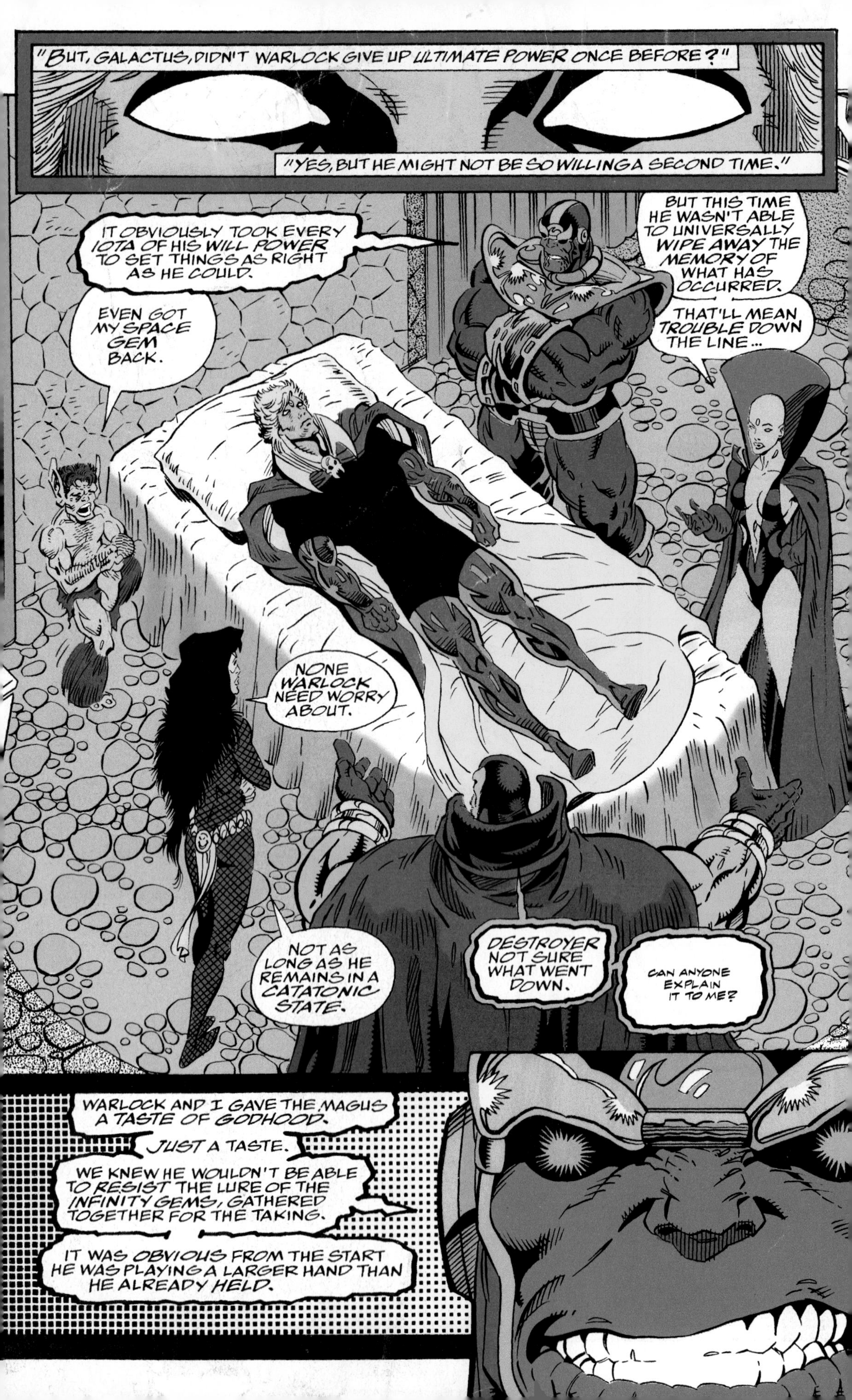
"BUT, GALACTUS, DIDN'T WARLOCK GIVE UP ULTIMATE POWER ONCE BEFORE?"
"YES, BUT HE MIGHT NOT BE SO WILLING A SECOND TIME."
IT OBVIOUSLY TOOK EVERY IOTA OF HIS WILL POWER TO SET THINGS AS RIGHT AS HE COULD.
BUT THIS TIME HE WASN'T ABLE TO UNIVERSALLY WIPE AWAY THE MEMORY OF WHAT HAS OCCURRED.
THAT'LL MEAN TROUBLE DOWN THE LINE...
EVEN GOT MY SPACE GEM BACK.
NONE WARLOCK NEED WORRY ABOUT.
NOT AS LONG AS HE REMAINS IN A CATATONIC STATE.
DESTROYER NOT SURE WHAT WENT DOWN.
CAN ANYONE EXPLAIN IT TO ME?
WARLOCK AND I GAVE THE MAGUS A TASTE OF GODHOOD.
JUST A TASTE.
WE KNEW HE WOULDN'T BE ABLE TO RESIST THE LURE OF THE INFINITY GEMS, GATHERED TOGETHER FOR THE TAKING.
IT WAS OBVIOUS FROM THE START HE WAS PLAYING A LARGER HAND THAN HE ALREADY HELD.

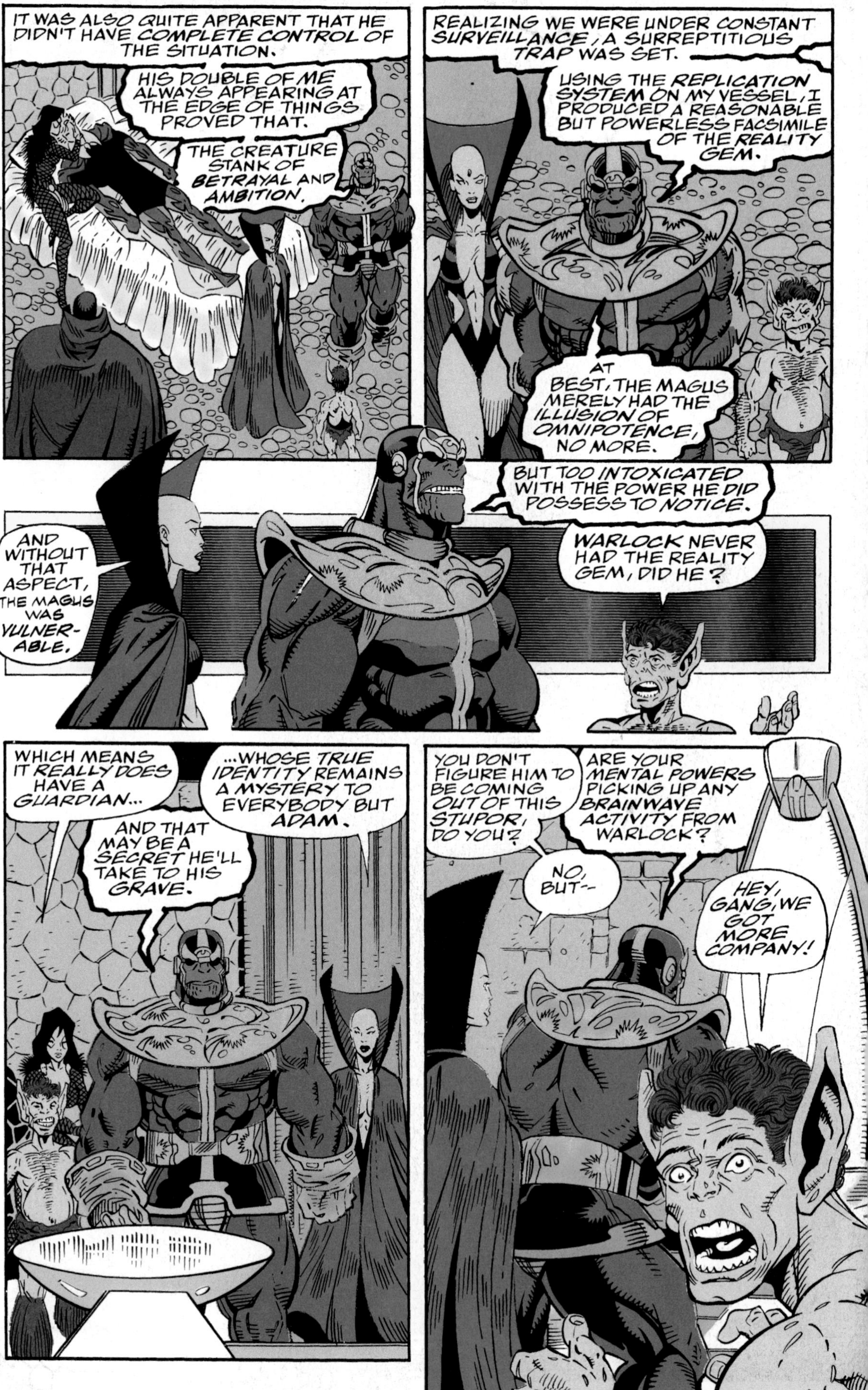
IT WAS ALSO QUITE APPARENT THAT HE DIDN'T HAVE COMPLETE CONTROL OF THE SITUATION.
HIS DOUBLE OF ME ALWAYS APPEARING AT THE EDGE OF THINGS PROVED THAT.
THE CREATURE STANK OF BETRAYAL AND AMBITION.
REALIZING WE WERE UNDER CONSTANT SURVEILLANCE, A SURREPTITIOUS TRAP WAS SET.
USING THE REPLICATION SYSTEM ON MY VESSEL, I PRODUCED A REASONABLE BUT POWERLESS FACSIMILE OF THE REALITY GEM.
AT BEST, THE MAGUS MERELY HAD THE ILLUSION OF OMNIPOTENCE, NO MORE.
BUT TOO INTOXICATED WITH THE POWER HE DID POSSESS TO NOTICE.
AND WITHOUT THAT ASPECT, THE MAGUS WAS VULNER-ABLE.
WARLOCK NEVER HAD THE REALITY GEM, DID HE?
WHICH MEANS IT REALLY DOES HAVE A GUARDIAN...
...WHOSE TRUE IDENTITY REMAINS A MYSTERY TO EVERYBODY BUT ADAM.
AND THAT MAY BE A SECRET HE'LL TAKE TO HIS GRAVE.
YOU DON'T FIGURE HIM TO BE COMING OUT OF THIS STUPOR, DO YOU?
ARE YOUR MENTAL POWERS PICKING UP ANY BRAINWAVE ACTIVITY FROM WARLOCK?
NO, BUT--
HEY, GANG, WE GOT MORE COMPANY!

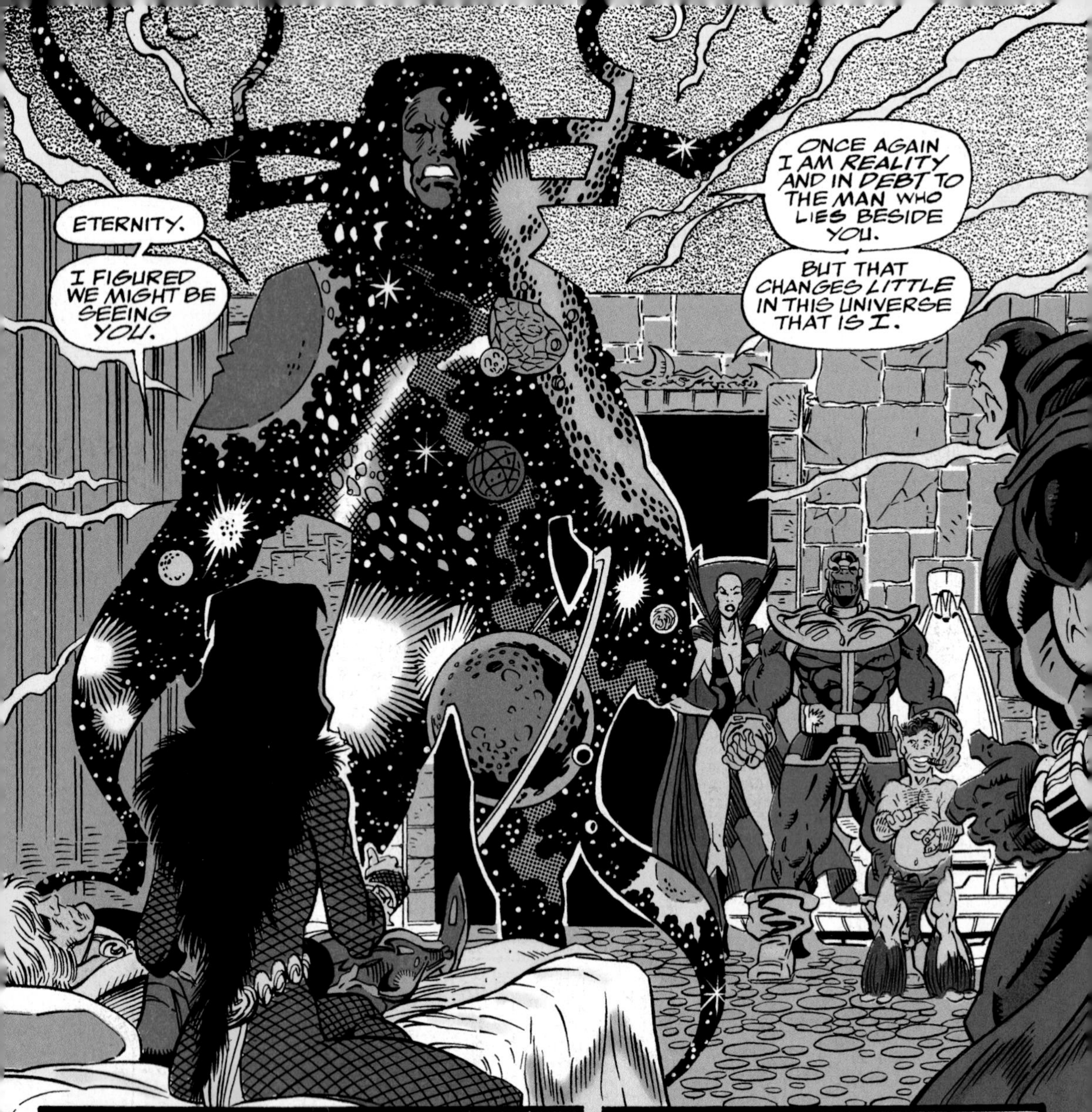
ETERNITY.
I FIGURED WE MIGHT BE SEEING YOU.
ONCE AGAIN I AM REALITY AND IN DEBT TO THE MAN WHO LIES BESIDE YOU.
BUT THAT CHANGES LITTLE IN THIS UNIVERSE THAT IS I.

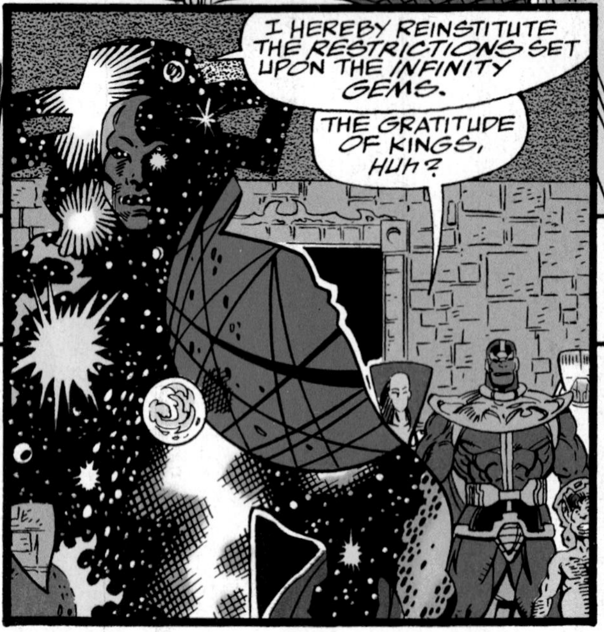
I HEREBY REINSTITUTE THE RESTRICTIONS SET UPON THE INFINITY GEMS.
THE GRATITUDE OF KINGS, HUH?

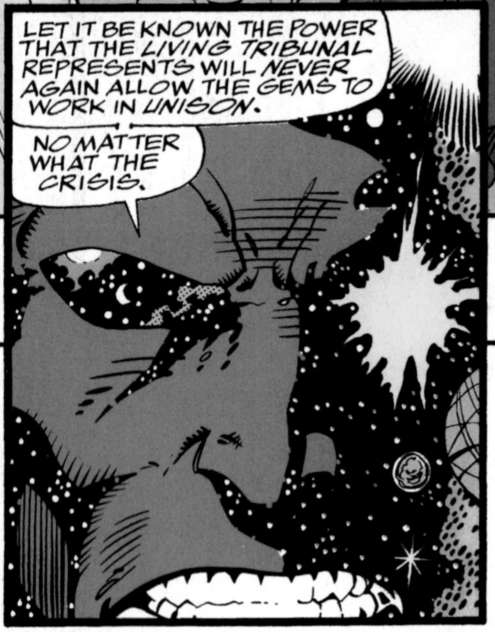
LET IT BE KNOWN THE POWER THAT THE LIVING TRIBUNAL REPRESENTS WILL NEVER AGAIN ALLOW THE GEMS TO WORK IN UNISON.
NO MATTER WHAT THE CRISIS.

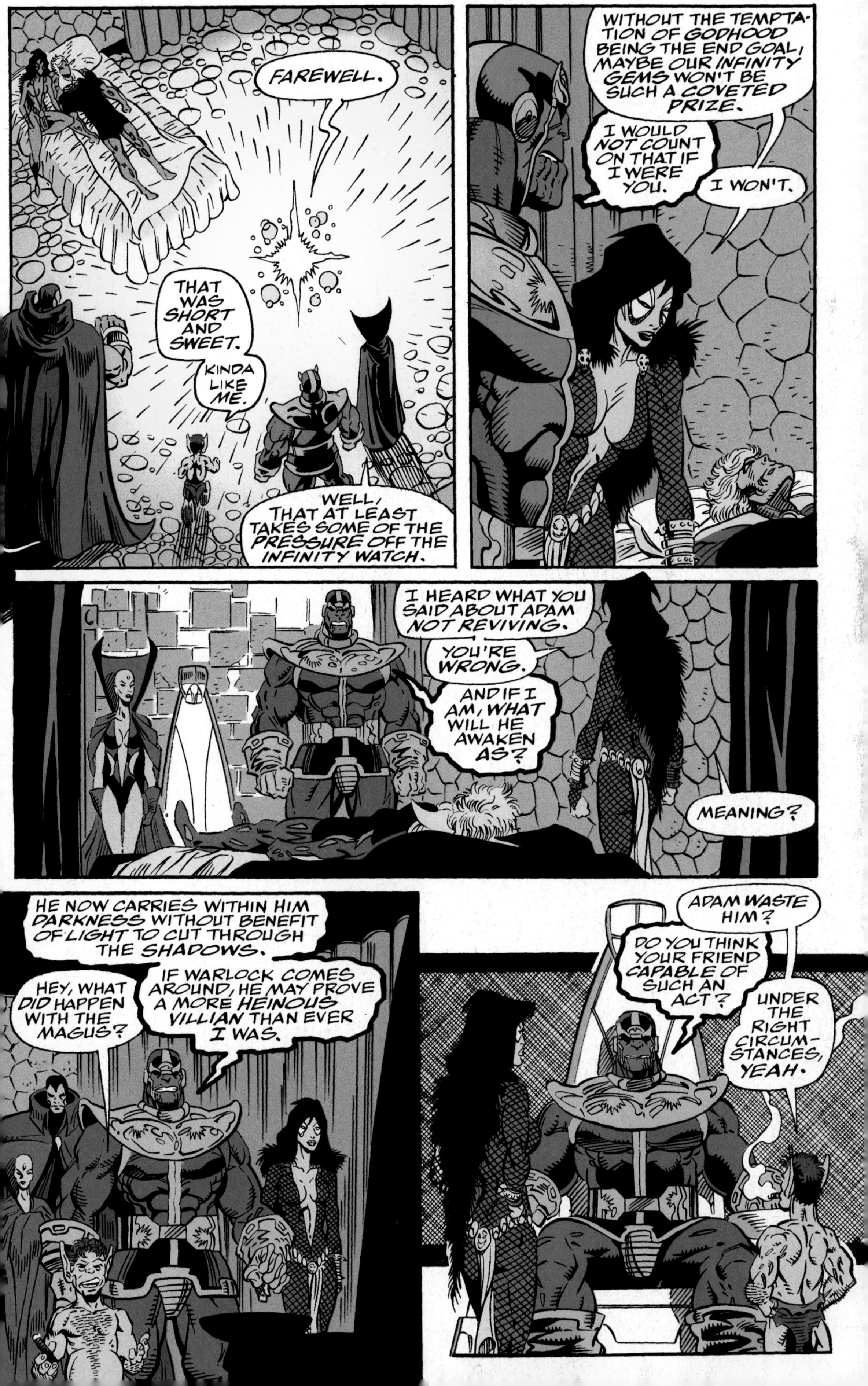
FAREWELL.
THAT WAS SHORT AND SWEET.
KINDA LIKE ME.
WELL, THAT AT LEAST TAKES SOME OF THE PRESSURE OFF THE INFINITY WATCH.
WITHOUT THE TEMPTATION OF GODHOOD BEING THE END GOAL, MAYBE OUR INFINITY GEMS WON'T BE SUCH A COVETED PRIZE.
I WOULD NOT COUNT ON THAT IF I WERE YOU.
I WON'T.
I HEARD WHAT YOU SAID ABOUT ADAM NOT REVIVING.
YOU'RE WRONG.
AND IF I AM, WHAT WILL HE AWAKEN AS?
MEANING?
HE NOW CARRIES WITHIN HIM DARKNESS WITHOUT BENEFIT OF LIGHT TO CUT THROUGH THE SHADOWS.
IF WARLOCK COMES AROUND, HE MAY PROVE A MORE HEINOUS VILLIAN THAN EVER I WAS.
HEY, WHAT DID HAPPEN WITH THE MAGUS?
ADAM WASTE HIM?
DO YOU THINK YOUR FRIEND CAPABLE OF SUCH AN ACT?
UNDER THE RIGHT CIRCUMSTANCES, YEAH.

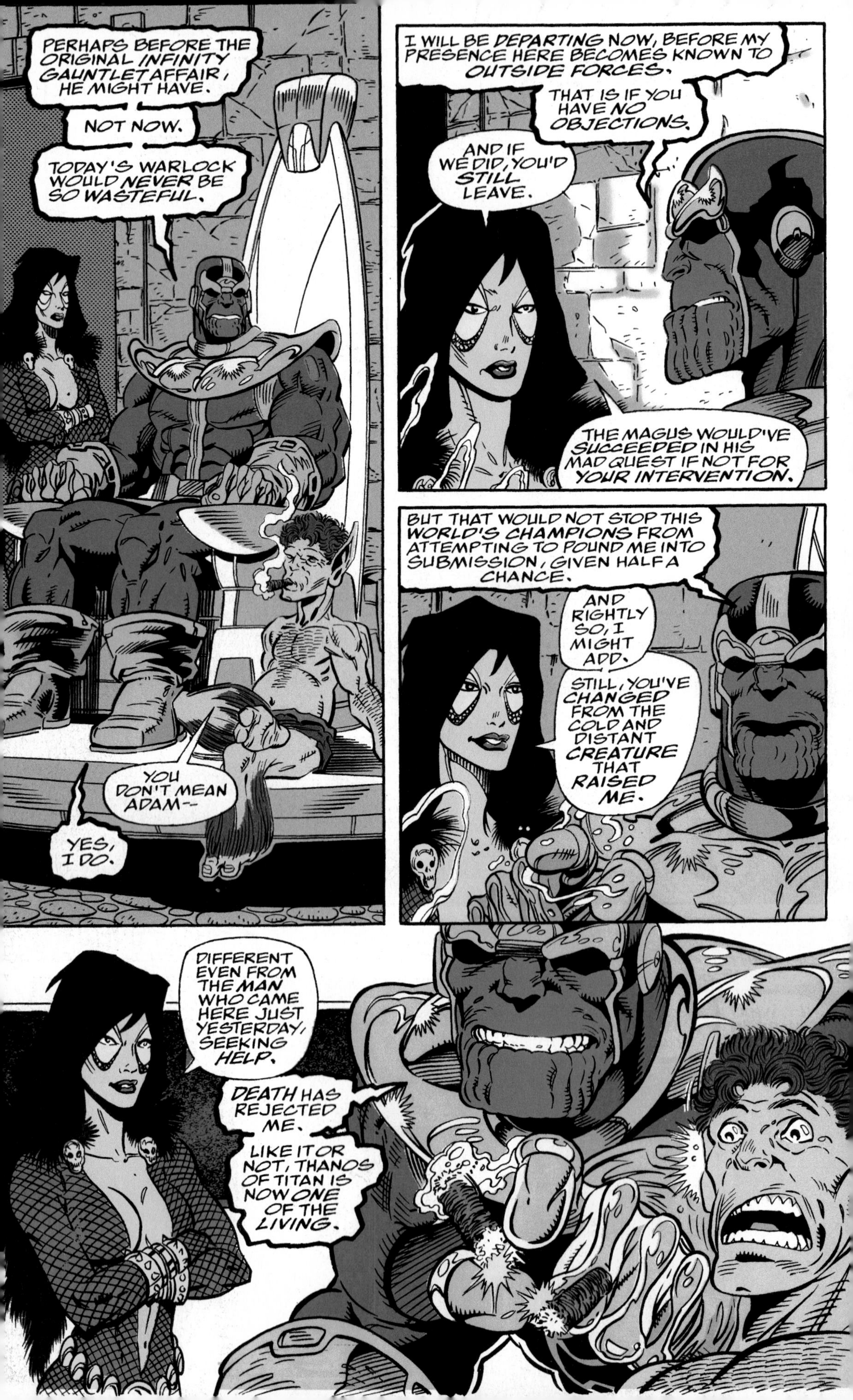

PERHAPS BEFORE THE ORIGINAL INFINITY GAUNTLET AFFAIR, HE MIGHT HAVE.
NOT NOW.
TODAY'S WARLOCK WOULD NEVER BE SO WASTEFUL.
YOU DON'T MEAN ADAM--
YES, I DO.
I WILL BE DEPARTING NOW, BEFORE MY PRESENCE HERE BECOMES KNOWN TO OUTSIDE FORCES.
THAT IS IF YOU HAVE NO OBJECTIONS.
AND IF WE DID, YOU'D STILL LEAVE.
THE MAGUS WOULD'VE SUCCEEDED IN HIS MAD QUEST IF NOT FOR YOUR INTERVENTION.
BUT THAT WOULD NOT STOP THIS WORLD'S CHAMPIONS FROM ATTEMPTING TO POUND ME INTO SUBMISSION, GIVEN HALF A CHANCE.
AND RIGHTLY SO, I MIGHT ADD.
STILL, YOU'VE CHANGED FROM THE COLD AND DISTANT CREATURE THAT RAISED ME.
DIFFERENT EVEN FROM THE MAN WHO CAME HERE JUST YESTERDAY, SEEKING HELP.
DEATH HAS REJECTED ME.
LIKE IT OR NOT, THANOS OF TITAN IS NOW ONE OF THE LIVING.

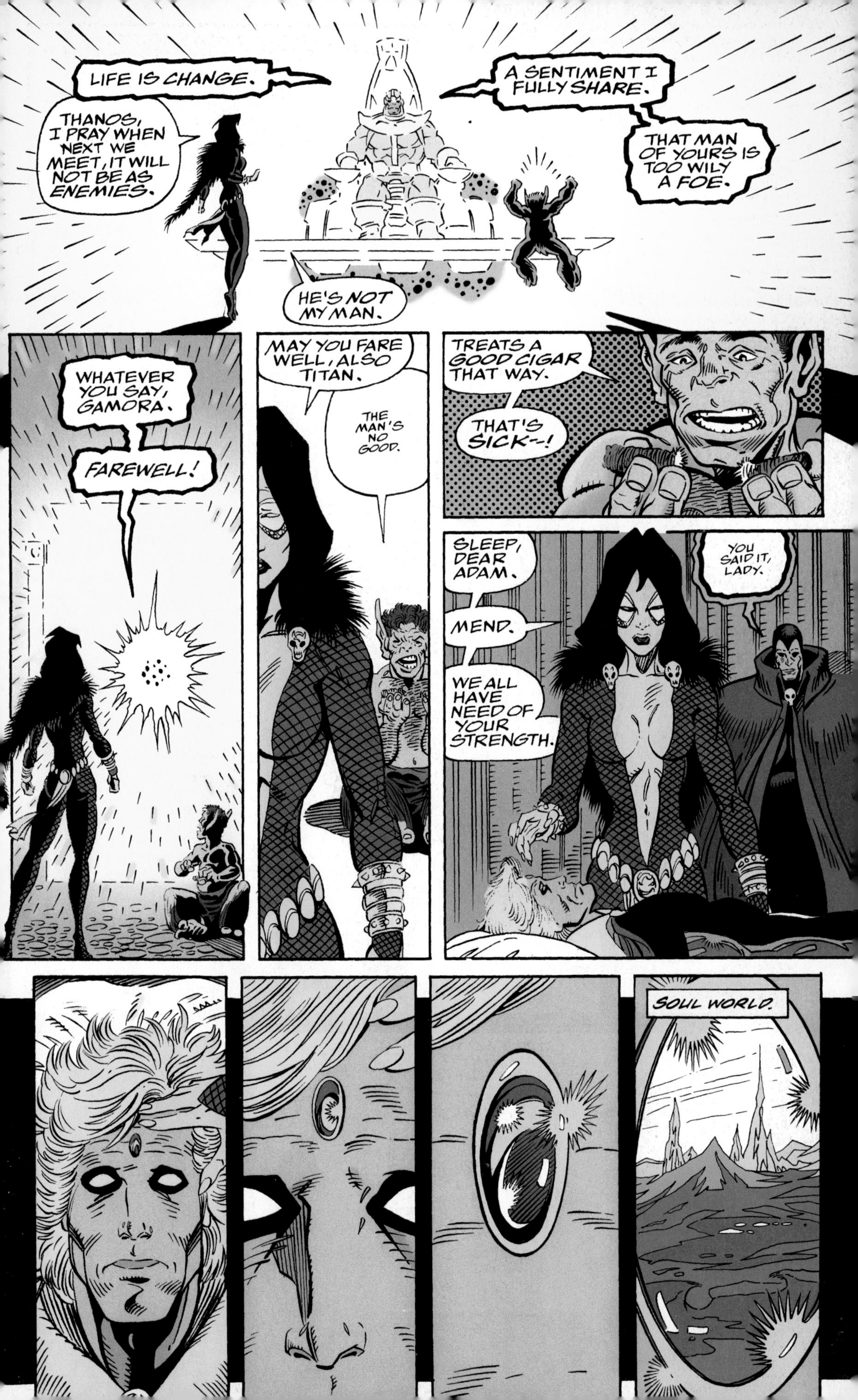
LIFE IS CHANGE.
THANOS, I PRAY WHEN NEXT WE MEET, IT WILL NOT BE AS ENEMIES.
A SENTIMENT I FULLY SHARE.
THAT MAN OF YOURS IS TOO WILY A FOE.
HE'S NOT MY MAN.
WHATEVER YOU SAY, GAMORA.
FAREWELL!
MAY YOU FARE WELL, ALSO TITAN.
THE MAN'S NO GOOD.
TREATS A GOOD CIGAR THAT WAY.
THAT'S SICK--!
SLEEP, DEAR ADAM.
MEND.
WE ALL HAVE NEED OF YOUR STRENGTH.
YOU SAID IT, LADY.
SOUL WORLD.

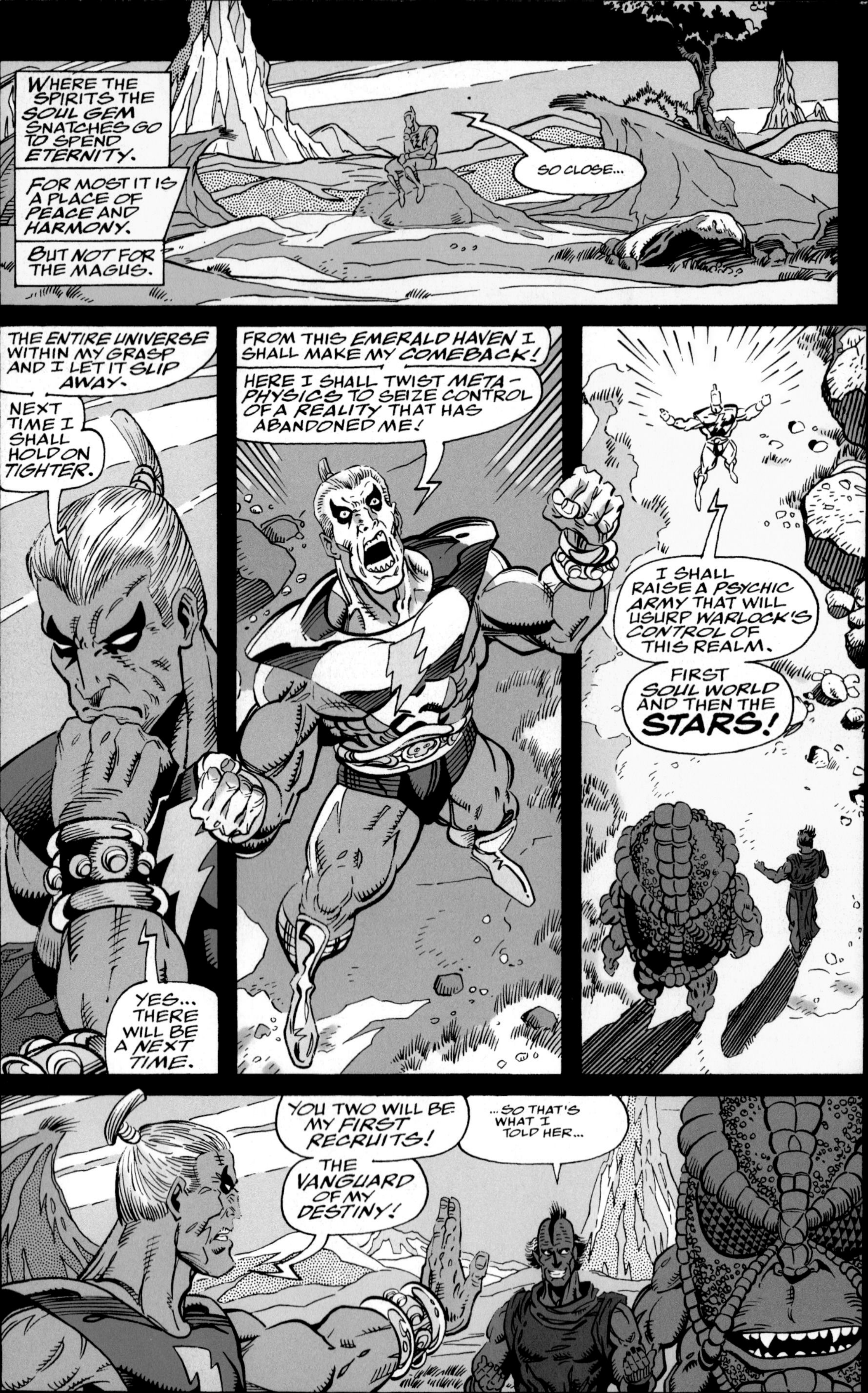
WHERE THE SPIRITS THE SOUL GEM SNATCHES GO TO SPEND ETERNITY.
FOR MOST IT IS A PLACE OF PEACE AND HARMONY.
BUT NOT FOR THE MAGUS.
SO CLOSE...
THE ENTIRE UNIVERSE WITHIN MY GRASP AND I LET IT SLIP AWAY.
NEXT TIME I SHALL HOLD ON TIGHTER.
YES... THERE WILL BE A NEXT TIME.
FROM THIS EMERALD HAVEN I SHALL MAKE MY COMEBACK!
HERE I SHALL TWIST META-PHYSICS TO SEIZE CONTROL OF A REALITY THAT HAS ABANDONED ME!
I SHALL RAISE A PSYCHIC ARMY THAT WILL USURP WARLOCK'S CONTROL OF THIS REALM.
FIRST SOUL WORLD AND THEN THE STARS!
YOU TWO WILL BE MY FIRST RECRUITS!
THE VANGUARD OF MY DESTINY!
...SO THAT'S WHAT I TOLD HER...

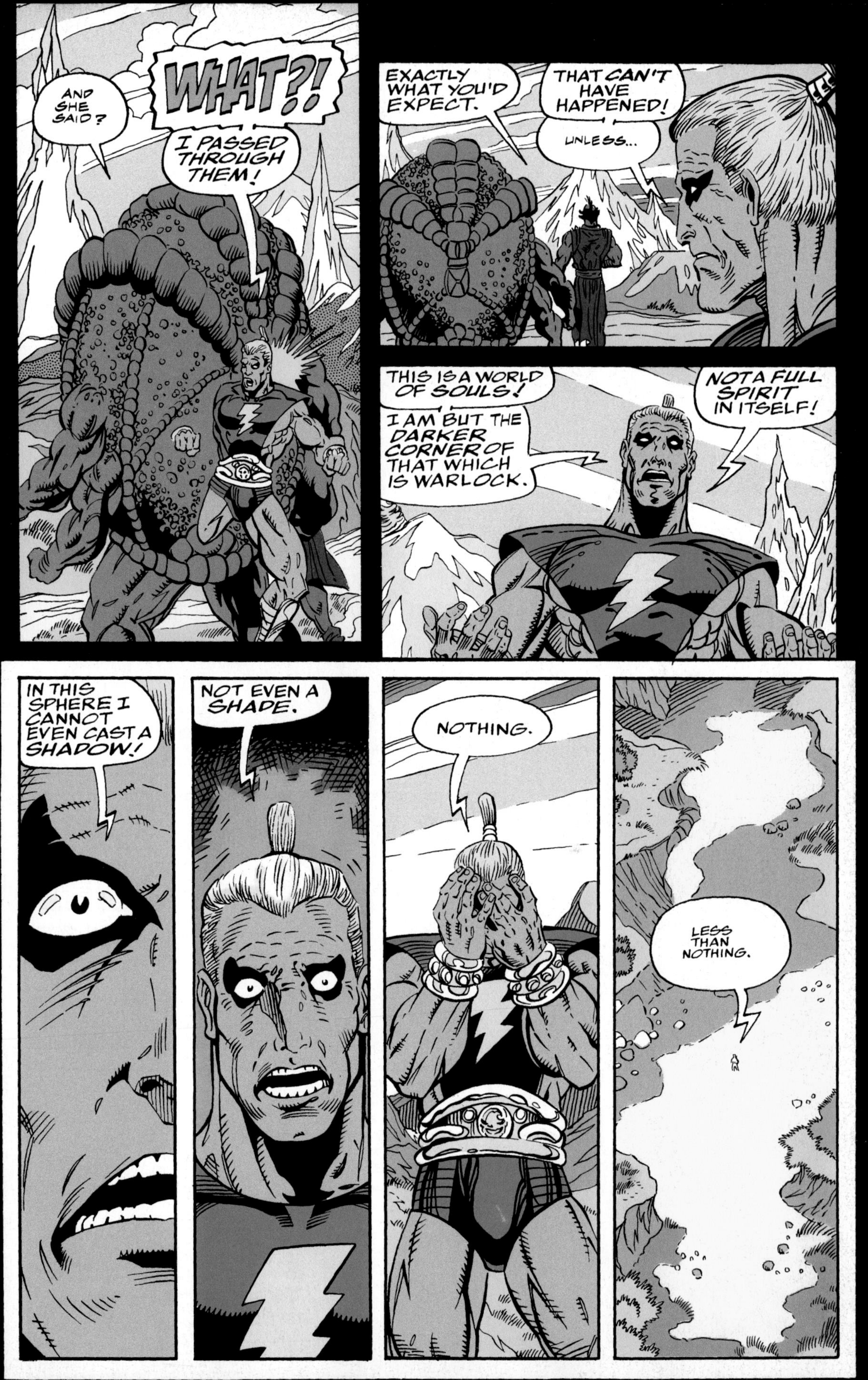
AND SHE SAID?
WHAT?!
I PASSED THROUGH THEM!
EXACTLY WHAT YOU'D EXPECT.
THAT CAN'T HAVE HAPPENED!
UNLESS...
THIS IS A WORLD OF SOULS!
I AM BUT THE DARKER CORNER OF THAT WHICH IS WARLOCK.
NOT A FULL SPIRIT IN ITSELF!
IN THIS SPHERE I CANNOT EVEN CAST A SHADOW!
NOT EVEN A SHADE.
NOTHING.
LESS THAN NOTHING.

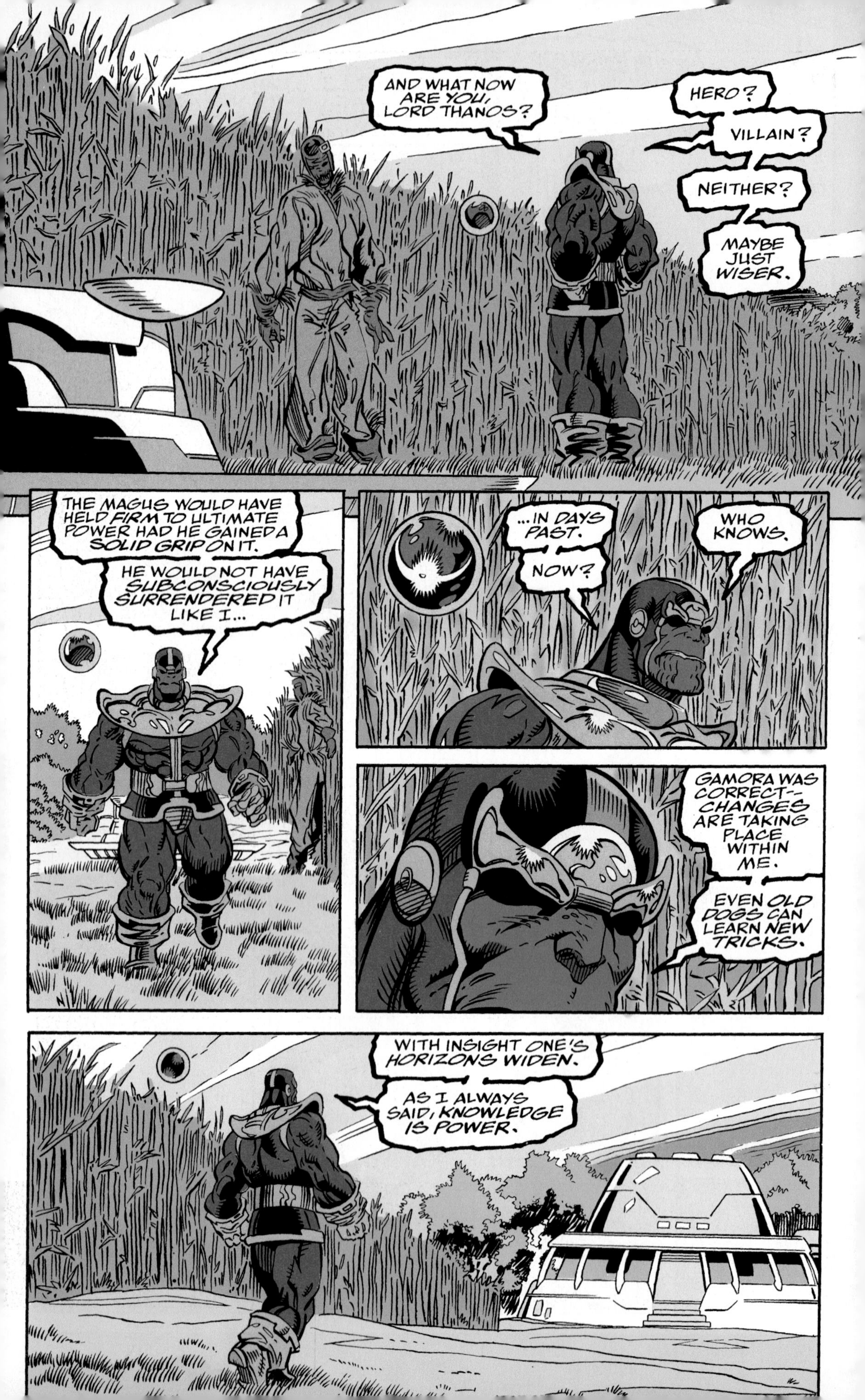
AND WHAT NOW ARE YOU, LORD THANOS?
HERO?
VILLAIN?
NEITHER?
MAYBE JUST WISER.
THE MAGUS WOULD HAVE HELD FIRM TO ULTIMATE POWER HAD HE GAINED A SOLID GRIP ON IT.
HE WOULD NOT HAVE SUBCONSCIOUSLY SURRENDERED IT LIKE I...
...IN DAYS PAST.
NOW?
WHO KNOWS.
GAMORA WAS CORRECT-- CHANGES ARE TAKING PLACE WITHIN ME.
EVEN OLD DOGS CAN LEARN NEW TRICKS.
WITH INSIGHT ONE'S HORIZONS WIDEN.
AS I ALWAYS SAID, KNOWLEDGE IS POWER.

LESSONS LEARNED: THE ONE *TRUE* VICTORY.

PERHAPS NOW THANOS COULD *RETAIN* ULTIMATE POWER WERE HE TO *GAIN* IT AGAIN.

BUT DO I STILL *CRAVE* SUCH AN *EXOTIC DISH?*

I SUSPECT *FUTURE* EVENTS WILL ANSWER THAT RHETORICAL QUERY.

YET, STILL OTHER, MORE *PRESSING* QUESTIONS REMAIN.

THE MOST IMPORTANT BEING *WHO* STOLE THE MAGUS'S COSMIC CONTAINMENT UNITS?

IN THE RUSH OF *VICTORY* AND ITS ACCOMPANYING *BEDLAM,* I DOUBT THAT ANY BUT I HAVE GIVEN THIS MYSTERY MUCH *THOUGHT.*

I CAN THINK OF ONLY ONE VIABLE *SUSPECT.*

THE MAGUS WAS CREATED WHEN WARLOCK USED THE INFINITY GEMS TO EXPEL ALL *GOOD* AND *EVIL* FROM HIS SELF TO BE-COME A BETTER SUPREME BEING.

ALL *GOOD* AND *EVIL...*

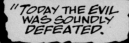

"TODAY THE EVIL WAS SOUNDLY DEFEATED.

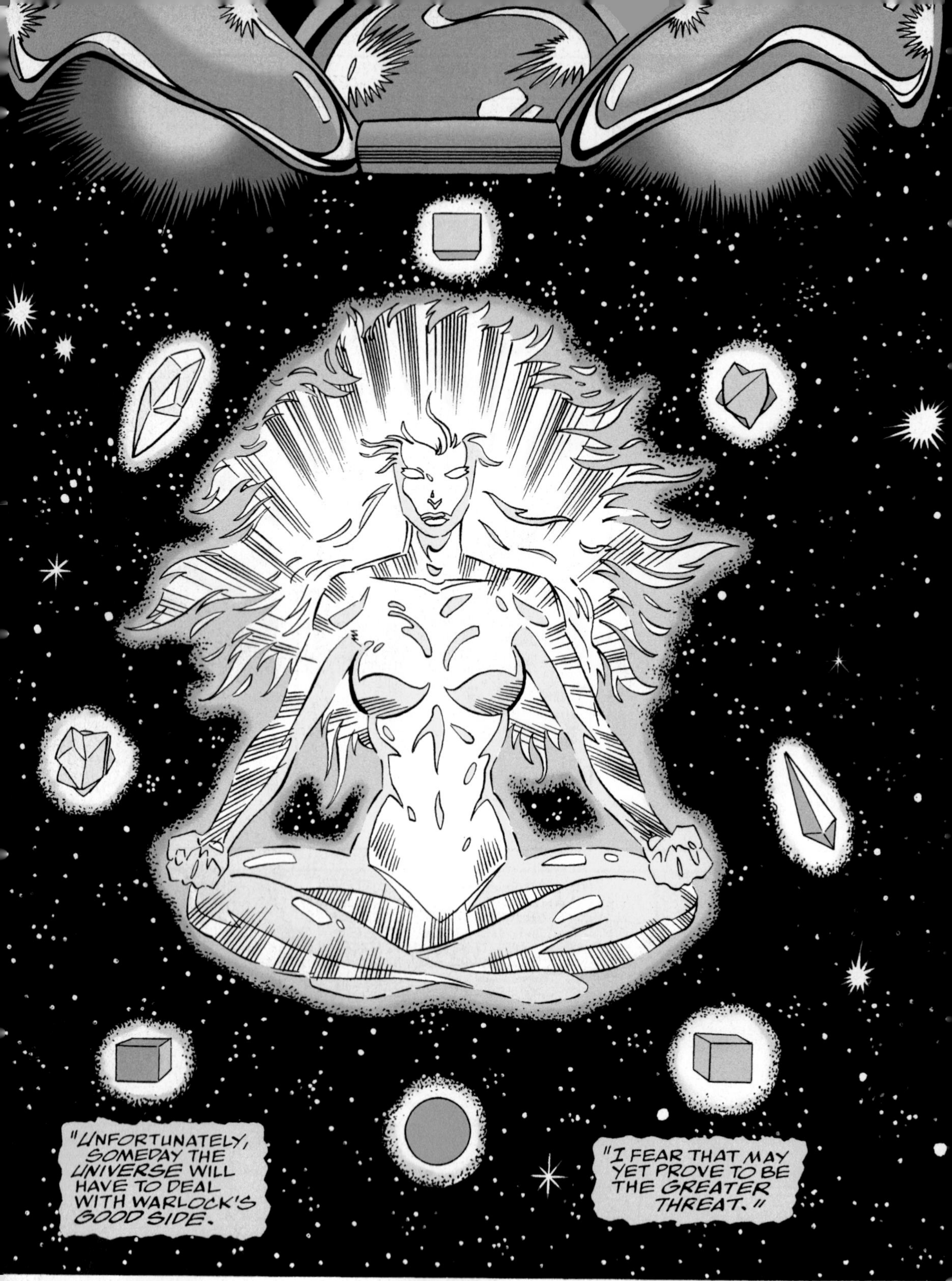
"UNFORTUNATELY, SOMEDAY THE UNIVERSE WILL HAVE TO DEAL WITH WARLOCK'S GOOD SIDE.
"I FEAR THAT MAY YET PROVE TO BE THE GREATER THREAT."

JIM STARLIN
WRITER

RON LIM
PENCILER

AL MILGROM
INKER

IAN LAUGHLIN
COLORIST

JACK MORELLI
LETTERER

CRAIG ANDERSON
EDITOR

TOM DEFALCO
EDITOR IN CHIEF

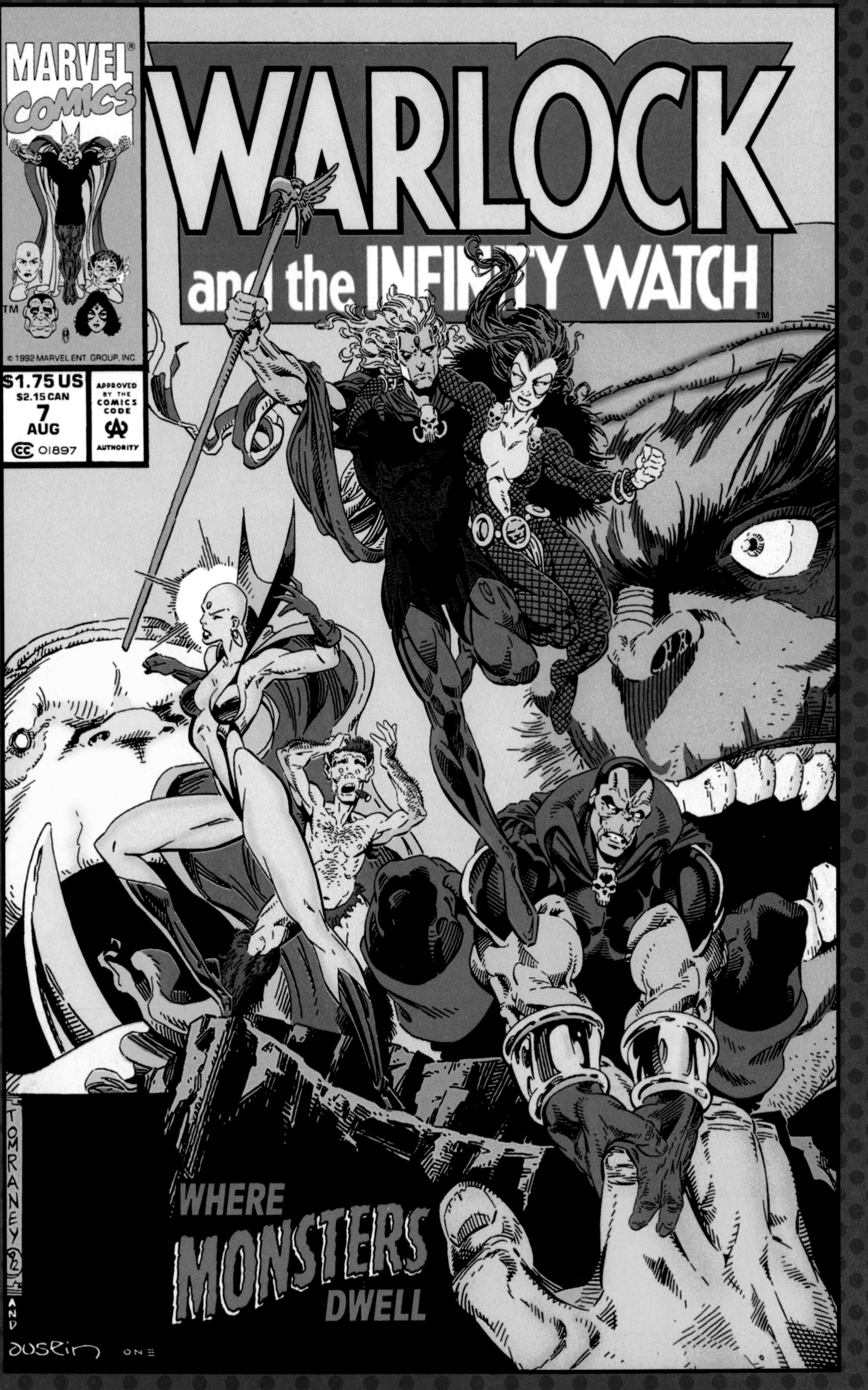

MARVEL COMICS
WARLOCK and the INFINITY WATCH
TM
© 1992 MARVEL ENT. GROUP, INC.
$1.75 US
$2.15 CAN
7
AUG
CC 01897
APPROVED BY THE COMICS CODE AUTHORITY
TOM RANEY 92
AND
austin
WHERE MONSTERS DWELL

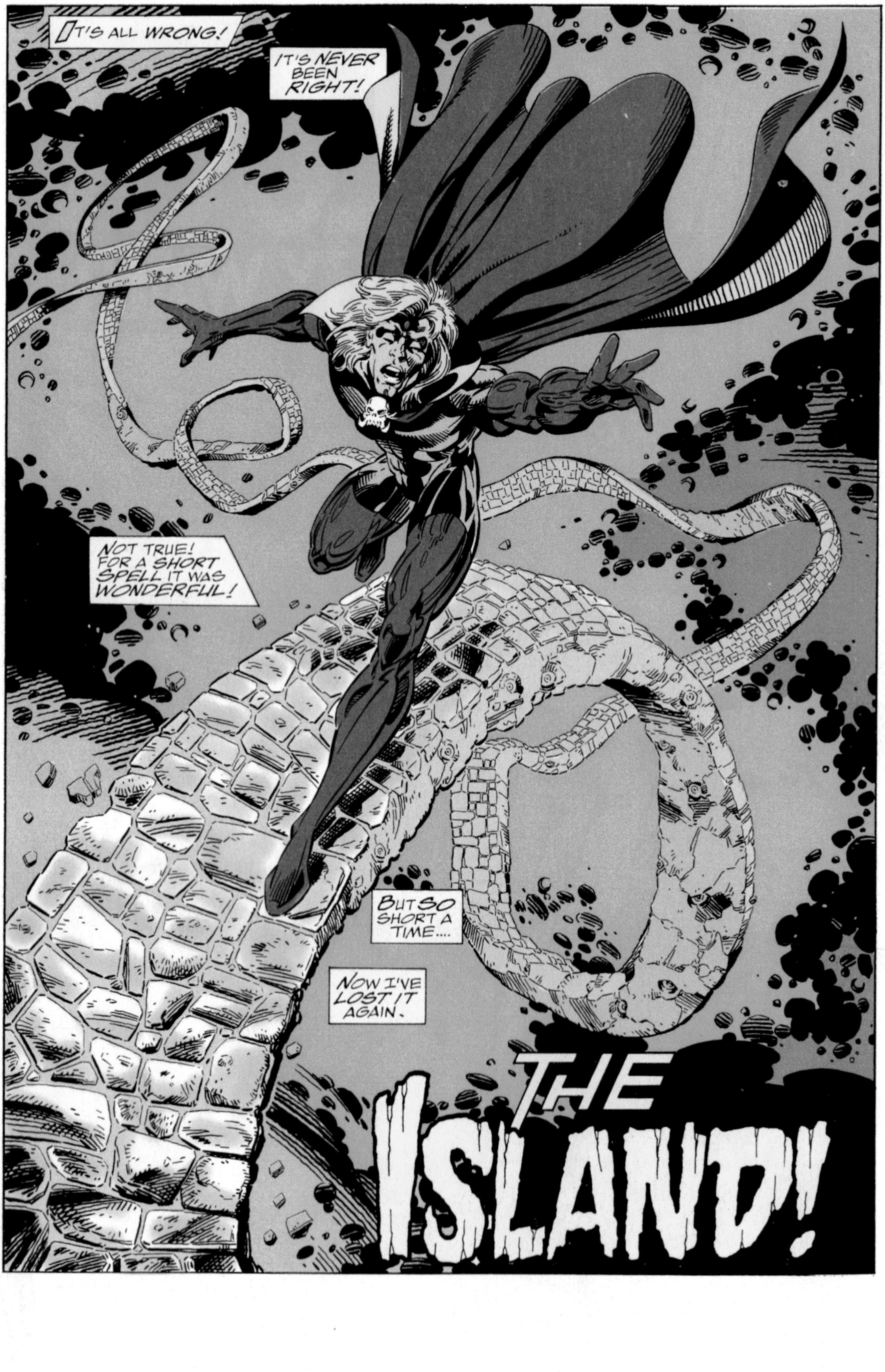
IT'S ALL WRONG!
IT'S NEVER BEEN RIGHT!
NOT TRUE! FOR A SHORT SPELL IT WAS WONDERFUL!
BUT SO SHORT A TIME....
NOW I'VE LOST IT AGAIN.
THE ISLAND!

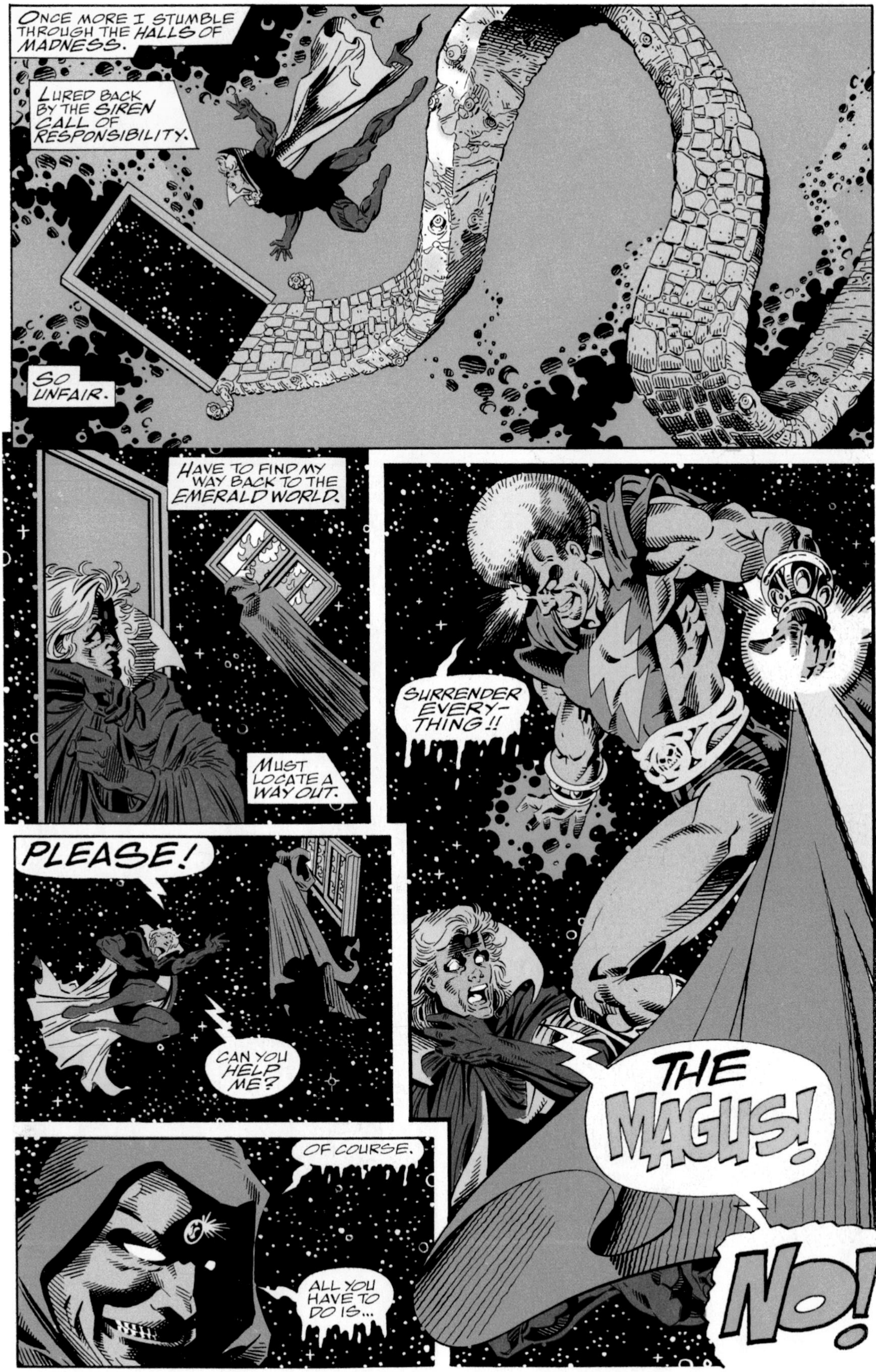

ONCE MORE I STUMBLE THROUGH THE HALLS OF MADNESS.
LURED BACK BY THE SIREN CALL OF RESPONSIBILITY.
SO UNFAIR.
HAVE TO FIND MY WAY BACK TO THE EMERALD WORLD.
MUST LOCATE A WAY OUT.
PLEASE!
CAN YOU HELP ME?
OF COURSE.
ALL YOU HAVE TO DO IS...
SURRENDER EVERY-THING!!
THE MAGUS!
NO!

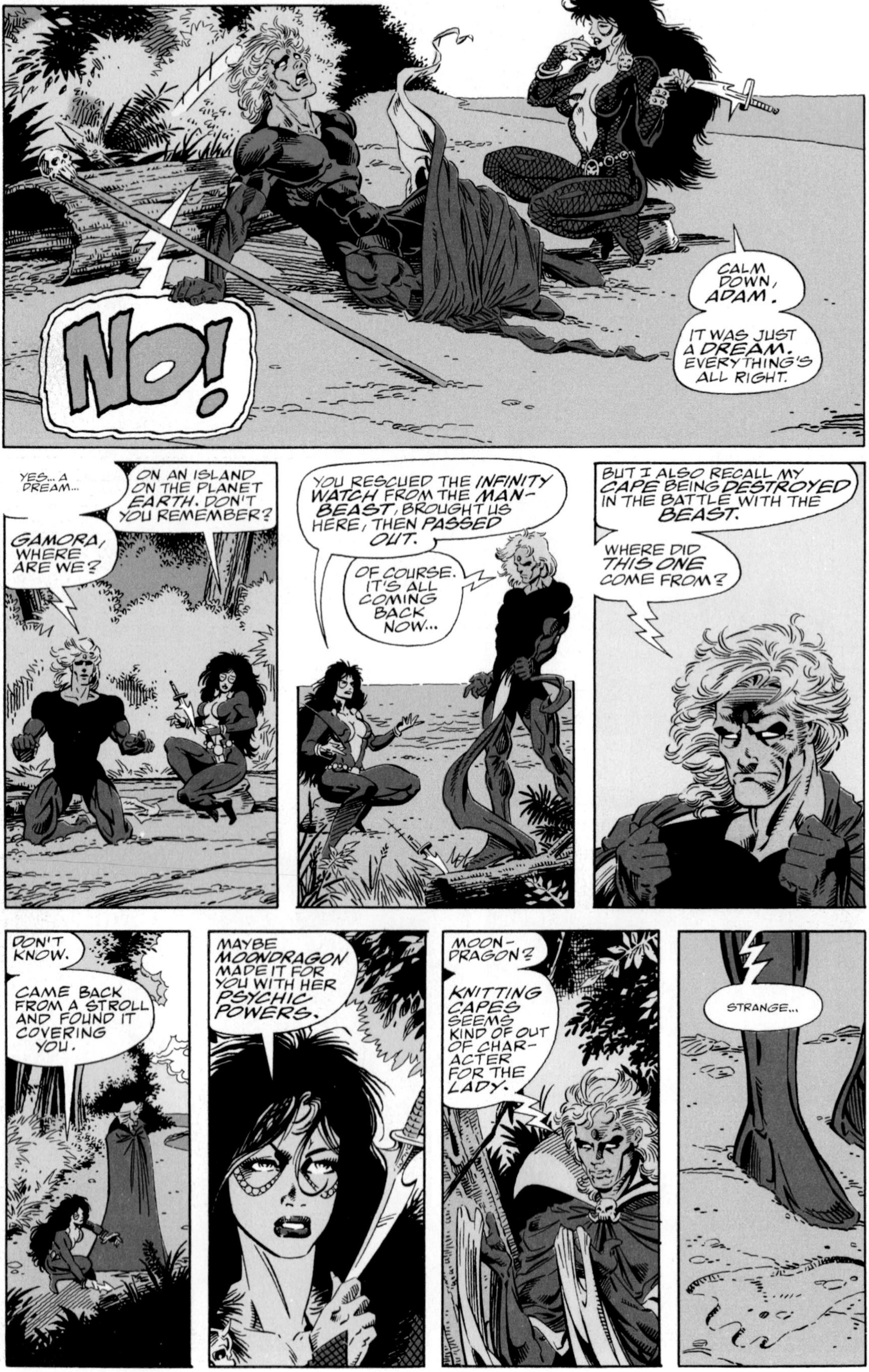
NO!
CALM DOWN, ADAM.
IT WAS JUST A DREAM. EVERYTHING'S ALL RIGHT.
YES... A DREAM...
GAMORA, WHERE ARE WE?
ON AN ISLAND ON THE PLANET EARTH. DON'T YOU REMEMBER?
YOU RESCUED THE INFINITY WATCH FROM THE MAN-BEAST, BROUGHT US HERE, THEN PASSED OUT.
OF COURSE. IT'S ALL COMING BACK NOW...
BUT I ALSO RECALL MY CAPE BEING DESTROYED IN THE BATTLE WITH THE BEAST.
WHERE DID THIS ONE COME FROM?
DON'T KNOW.
CAME BACK FROM A STROLL AND FOUND IT COVERING YOU.
MAYBE MOONDRAGON MADE IT FOR YOU WITH HER PSYCHIC POWERS.
MOON-DRAGON?
KNITTING CAPES SEEMS KIND OF OUT OF CHAR-ACTER FOR THE LADY.
STRANGE...

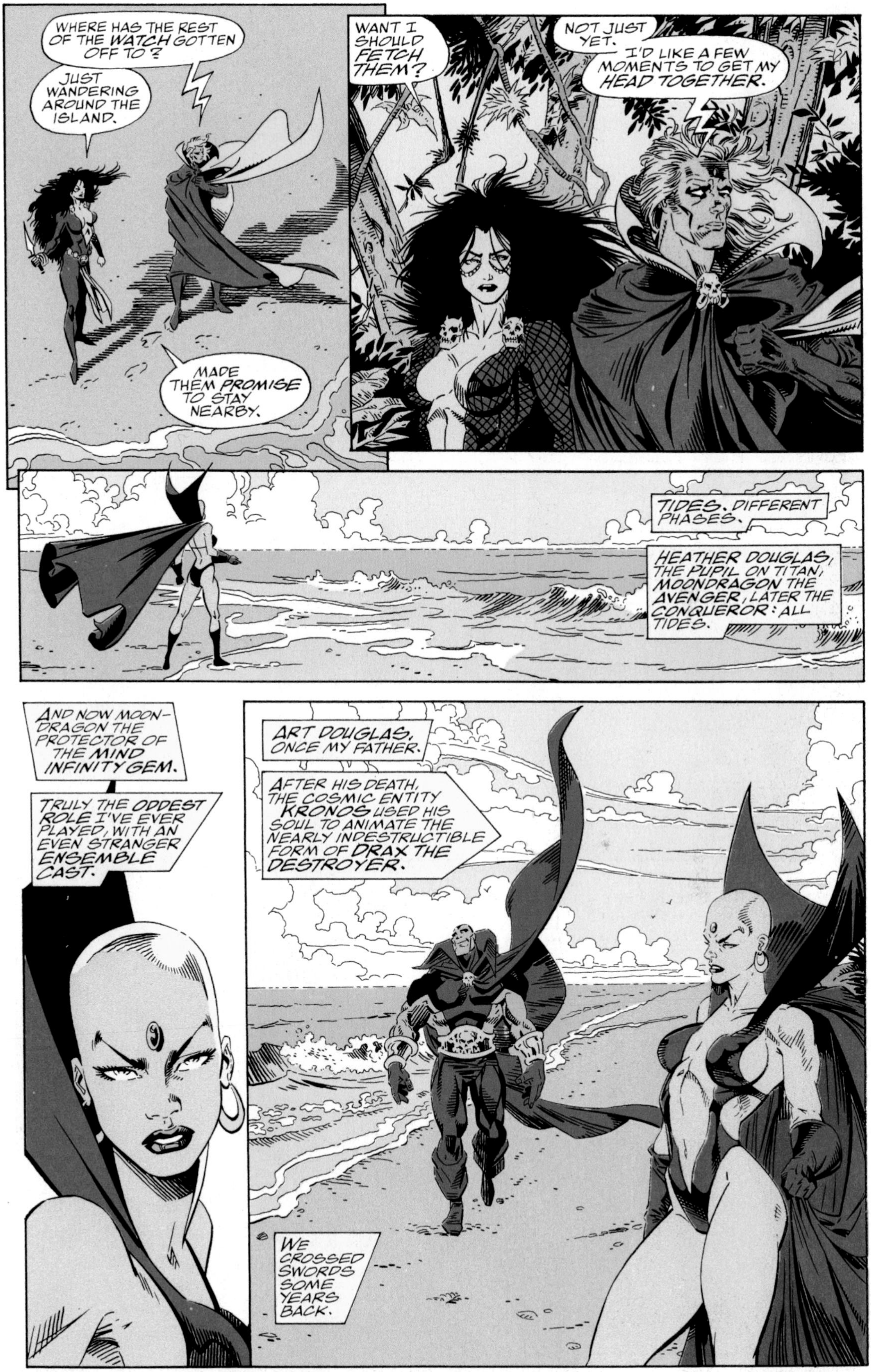

WHERE HAS THE REST OF THE WATCH GOTTEN OFF TO?
JUST WANDERING AROUND THE ISLAND.
MADE THEM PROMISE TO STAY NEARBY.
WANT I SHOULD FETCH THEM?
NOT JUST YET.
I'D LIKE A FEW MOMENTS TO GET MY HEAD TOGETHER.
TIDES. DIFFERENT PHASES.
HEATHER DOUGLAS, THE PUPIL ON TITAN, MOONDRAGON THE AVENGER, LATER THE CONQUEROR: ALL TIDES.
AND NOW MOON-DRAGON THE PROTECTOR OF THE MIND INFINITY GEM.
TRULY THE ODDEST ROLE I'VE EVER PLAYED, WITH AN EVEN STRANGER ENSEMBLE CAST.
ART DOUGLAS, ONCE MY FATHER.
AFTER HIS DEATH, THE COSMIC ENTITY KRONOS USED HIS SOUL TO ANIMATE THE NEARLY INDESTRUCTIBLE FORM OF DRAX THE DESTROYER.
WE CROSSED SWORDS SOME YEARS BACK.

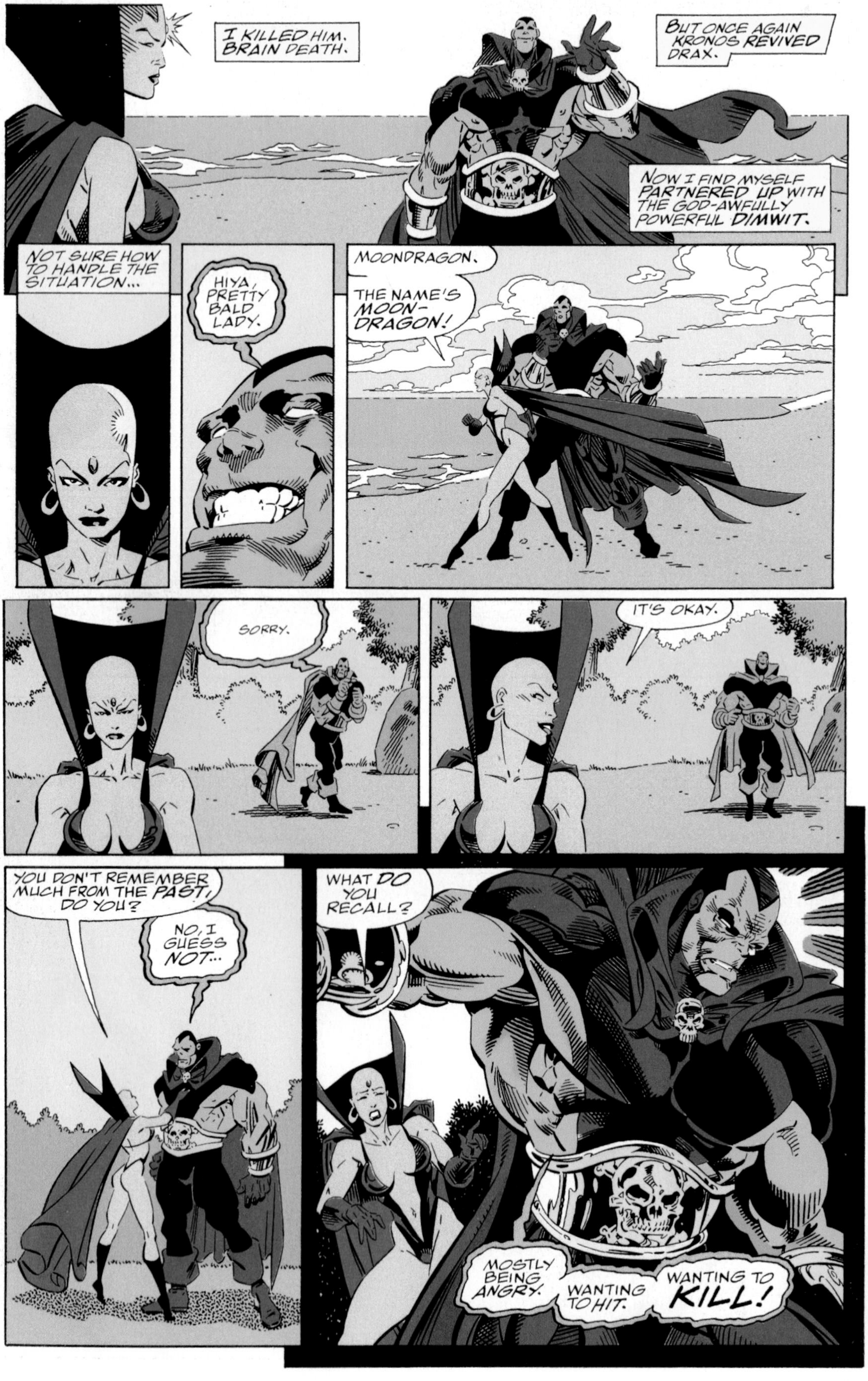
I KILLED HIM. BRAIN DEATH.
BUT ONCE AGAIN KRONOS REVIVED DRAX.
NOW I FIND MYSELF PARTNERED UP WITH THE GOD-AWFULLY POWERFUL DIMWIT.
NOT SURE HOW TO HANDLE THE SITUATION...
HIYA, PRETTY BALD LADY.
MOONDRAGON.
THE NAME'S MOON-DRAGON!
SORRY.
IT'S OKAY.
YOU DON'T REMEMBER MUCH FROM THE PAST, DO YOU?
NO, I GUESS NOT...
WHAT DO YOU RECALL?
MOSTLY BEING ANGRY.
WANTING TO HIT.
WANTING TO KILL!

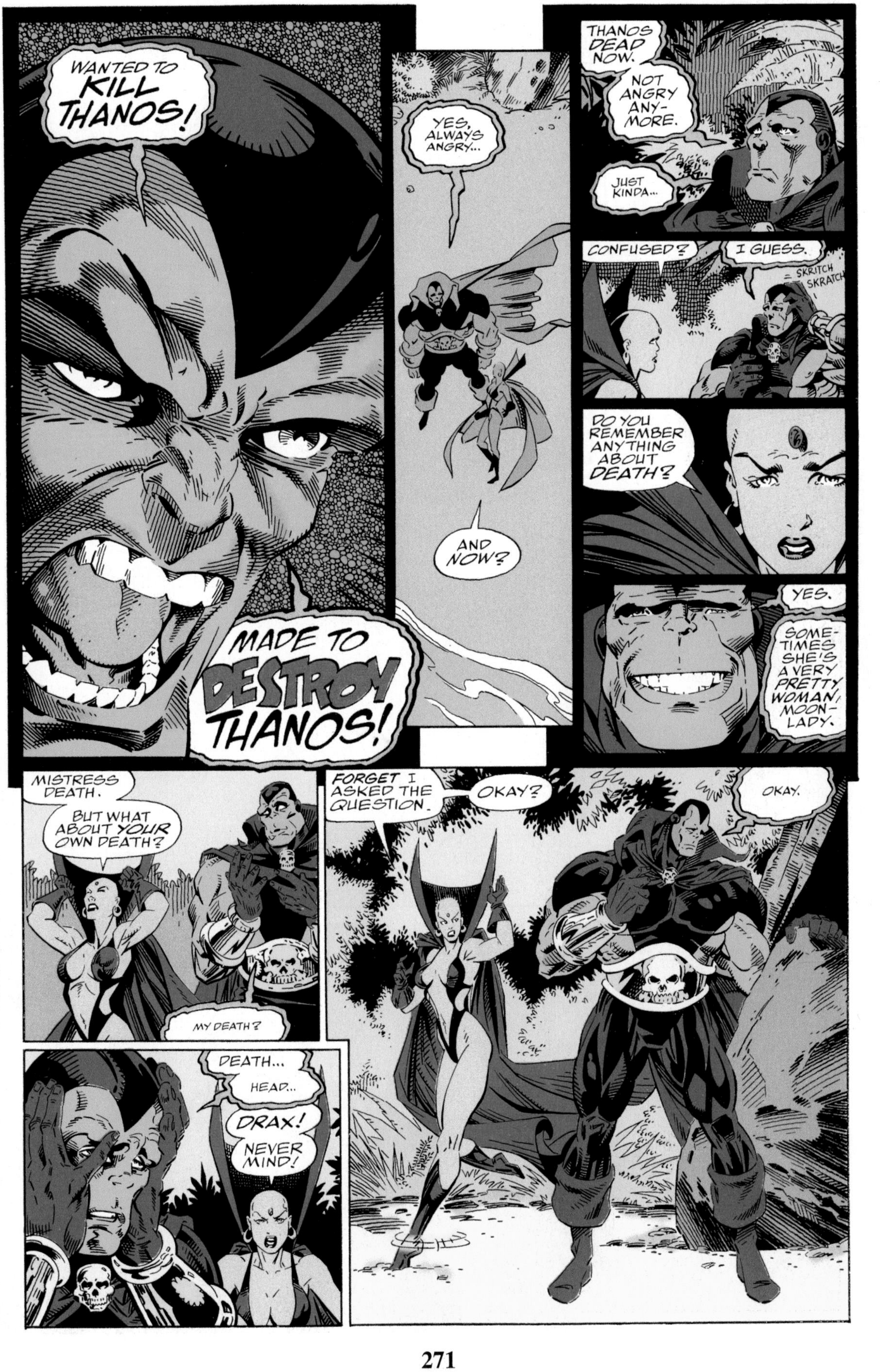
WANTED TO KILL THANOS!
MADE TO DESTROY THANOS!
YES, ALWAYS ANGRY...
AND NOW?
THANOS DEAD NOW.
NOT ANGRY ANY-MORE.
JUST KINDA...
CONFUSED?
I GUESS.
SKRITCH SKRATCH
DO YOU REMEMBER ANYTHING ABOUT DEATH?
YES.
SOME-TIMES SHE'S A VERY PRETTY WOMAN, MOON-LADY.
MISTRESS DEATH.
BUT WHAT ABOUT YOUR OWN DEATH?
MY DEATH?
DEATH...
HEAD...
DRAX!
NEVER MIND!
FORGET I ASKED THE QUESTION.
OKAY?
OKAY.

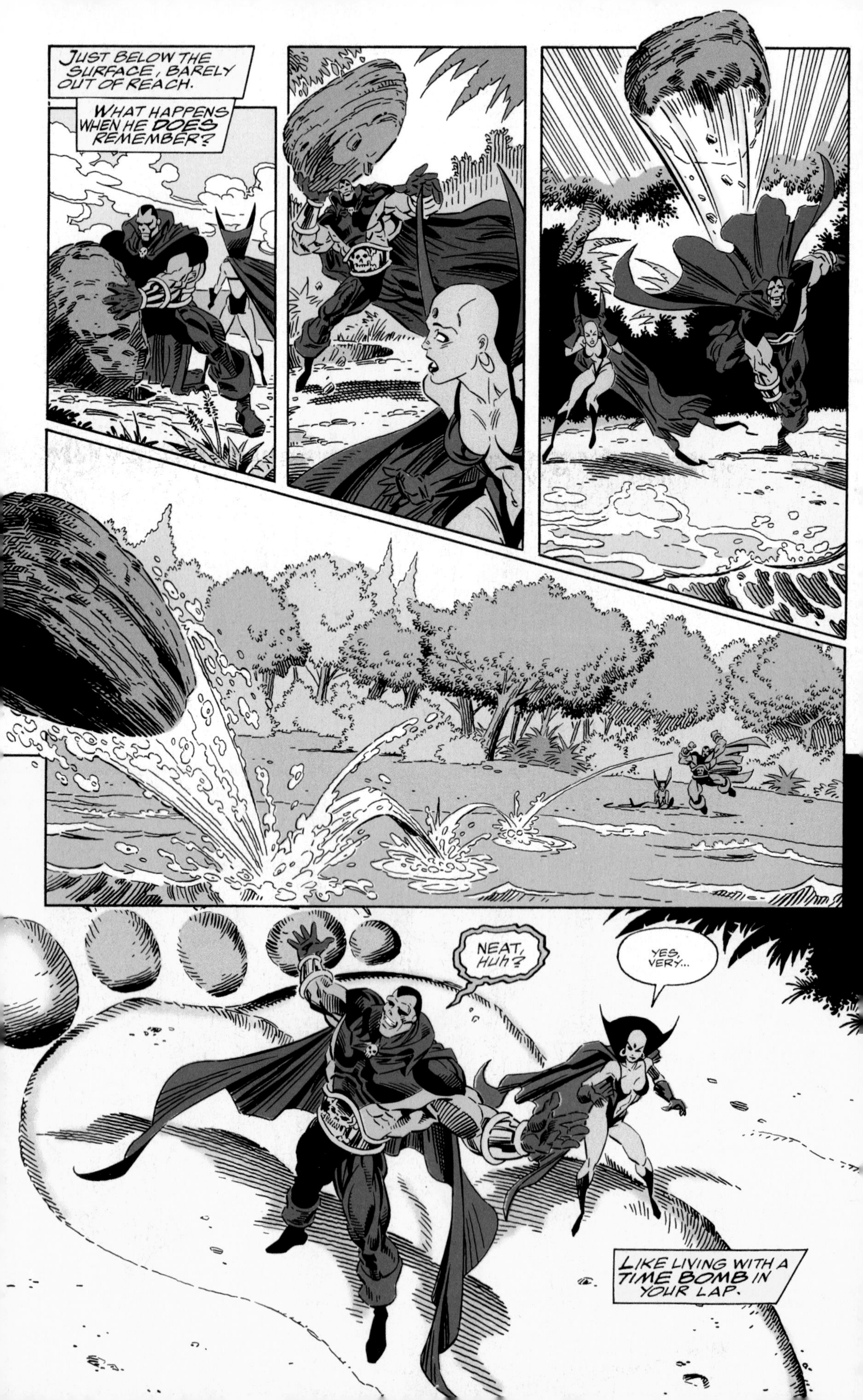
JUST BELOW THE SURFACE, BARELY OUT OF REACH.
WHAT HAPPENS WHEN HE DOES REMEMBER?
NEAT, HUH?
YES, VERY...
LIKE LIVING WITH A TIME BOMB IN YOUR LAP.

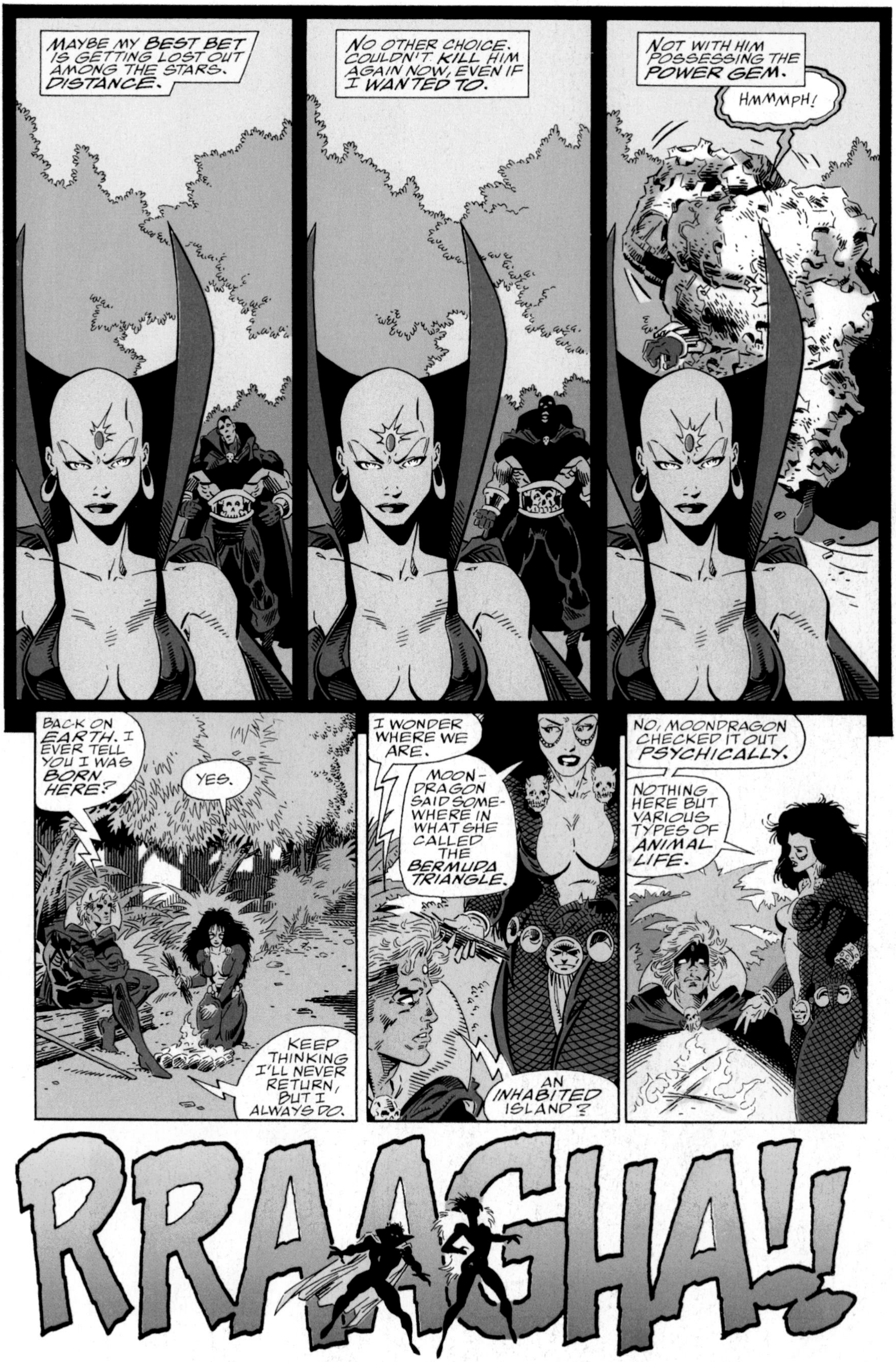
MAYBE MY BEST BET IS GETTING LOST OUT AMONG THE STARS. DISTANCE.
NO OTHER CHOICE. COULDN'T KILL HIM AGAIN NOW, EVEN IF I WANTED TO.
NOT WITH HIM POSSESSING THE POWER GEM.
HMMMPH!
BACK ON EARTH. I EVER TELL YOU I WAS BORN HERE?
YES.
KEEP THINKING I'LL NEVER RETURN, BUT I ALWAYS DO.
I WONDER WHERE WE ARE.
MOONDRAGON SAID SOMEWHERE IN WHAT SHE CALLED THE BERMUDA TRIANGLE.
AN INHABITED ISLAND?
NO, MOONDRAGON CHECKED IT OUT PSYCHICALLY.
NOTHING HERE BUT VARIOUS TYPES OF ANIMAL LIFE.
RRAAGHA!!

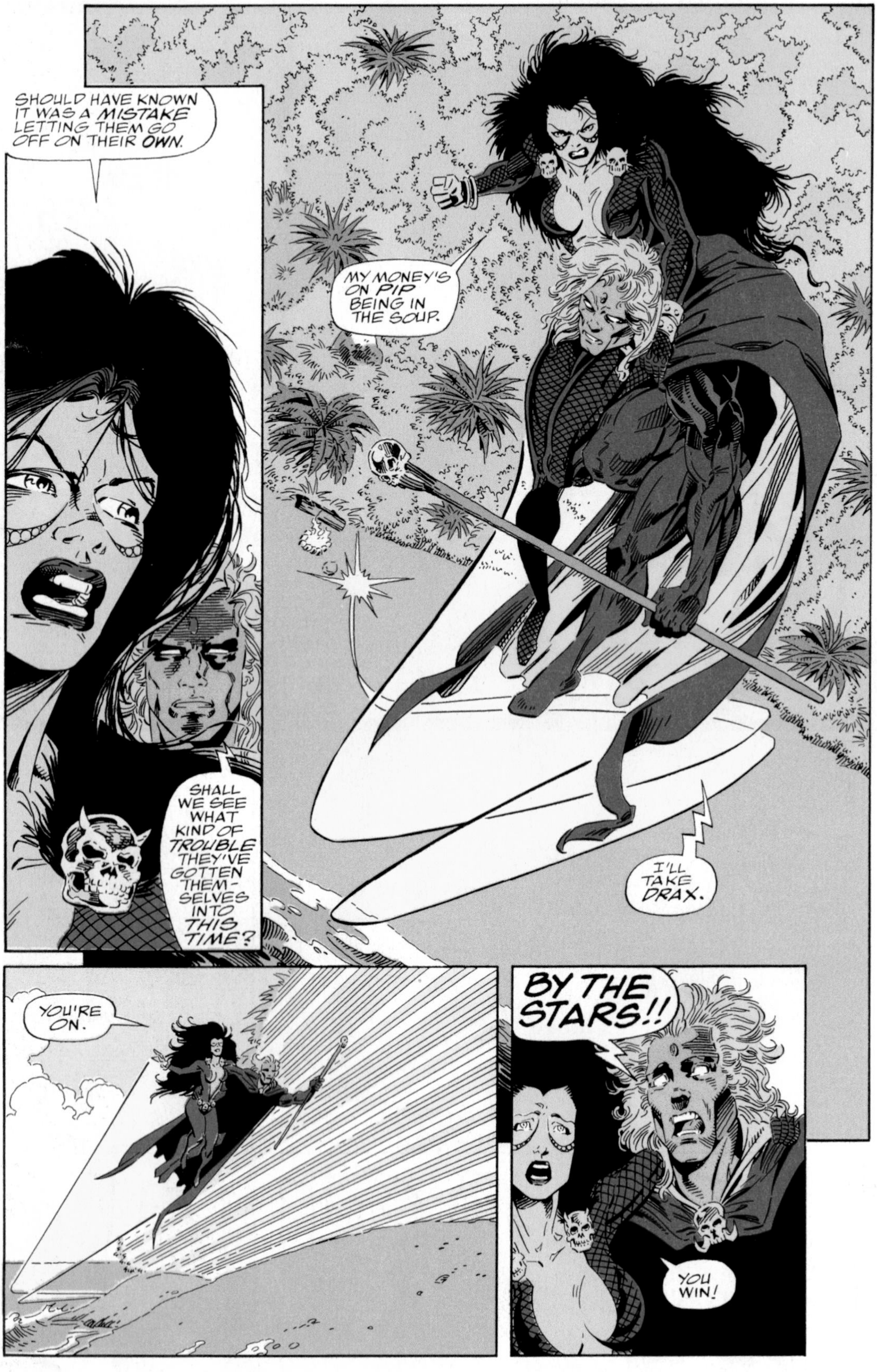

SHOULD HAVE KNOWN IT WAS A MISTAKE LETTING THEM GO OFF ON THEIR OWN.
MY MONEY'S ON PIP BEING IN THE SOUP.
SHALL WE SEE WHAT KIND OF TROUBLE THEY'VE GOTTEN THEM-SELVES INTO THIS TIME?
I'LL TAKE DRAX.
YOU'RE ON.
BY THE STARS!!
YOU WIN!

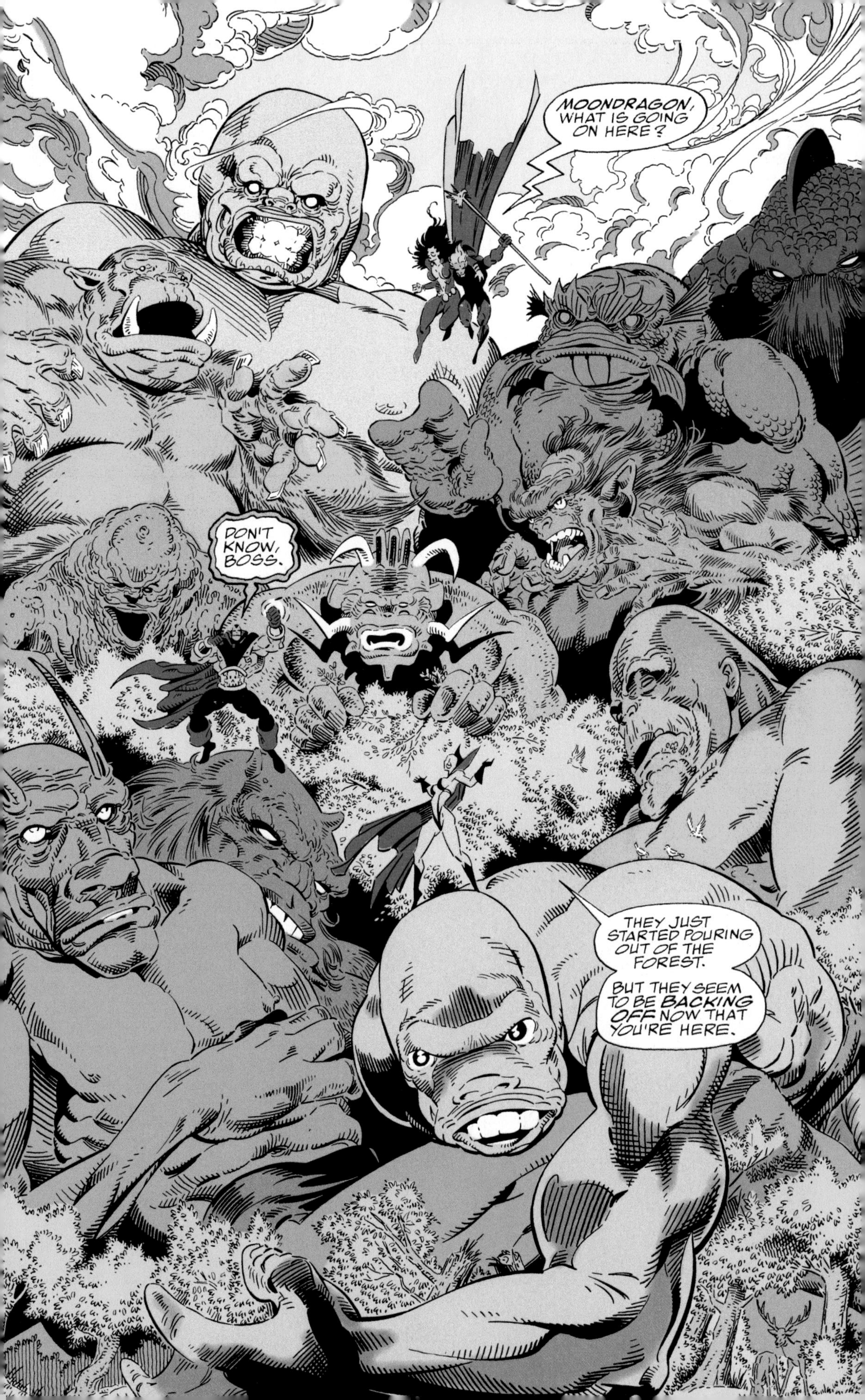
MOONDRAGON, WHAT IS GOING ON HERE?
DON'T KNOW, BOSS.
THEY JUST STARTED POURING OUT OF THE FOREST.
BUT THEY SEEM TO BE BACKING OFF NOW THAT YOU'RE HERE.

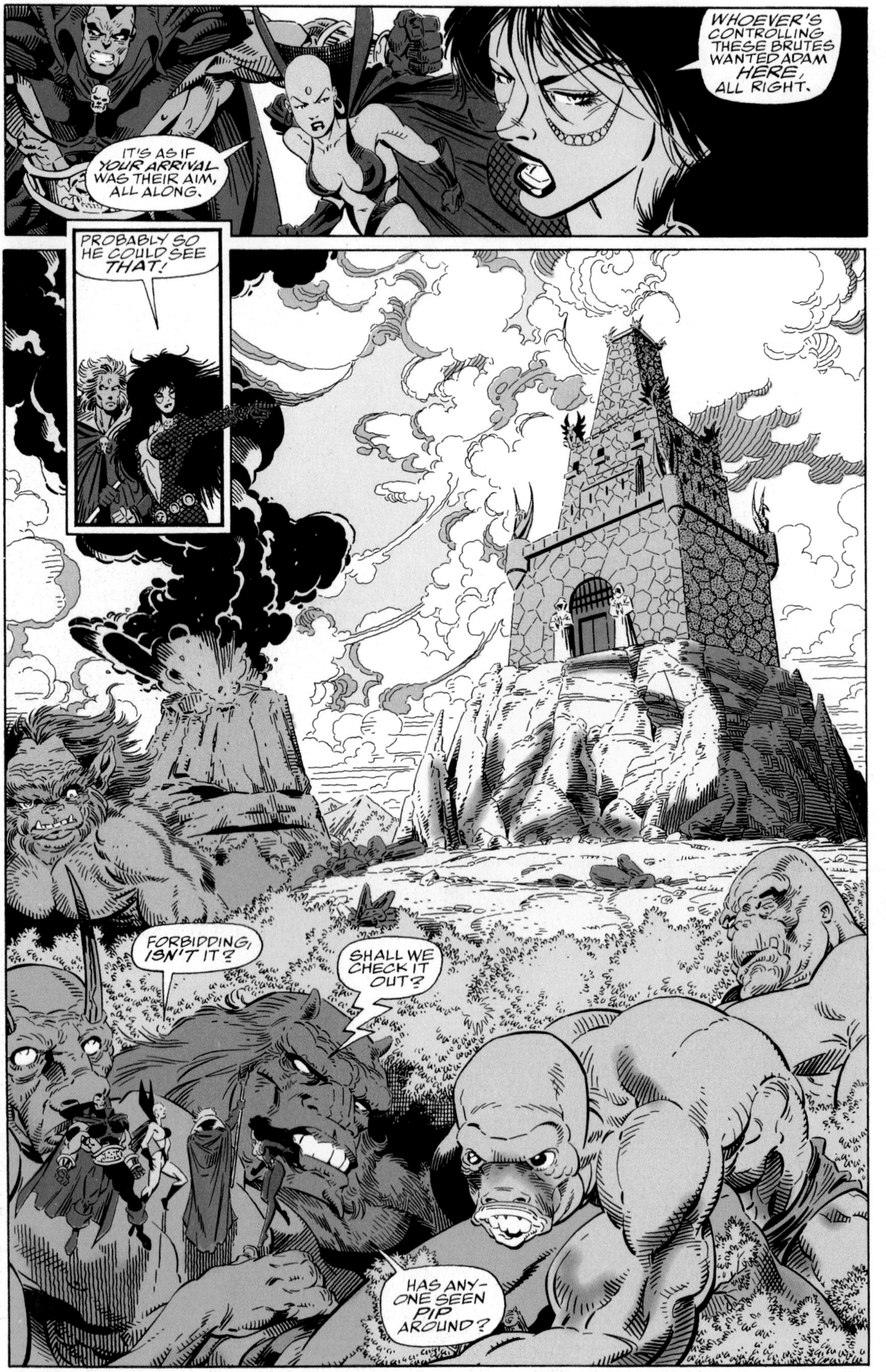
WHOEVER'S CONTROLLING THESE BRUTES WANTED ADAM HERE, ALL RIGHT.
IT'S AS IF YOUR ARRIVAL WAS THEIR AIM, ALL ALONG.
PROBABLY SO HE COULD SEE THAT!
FORBIDDING, ISN'T IT?
SHALL WE CHECK IT OUT?
HAS ANY-ONE SEEN PIP AROUND?

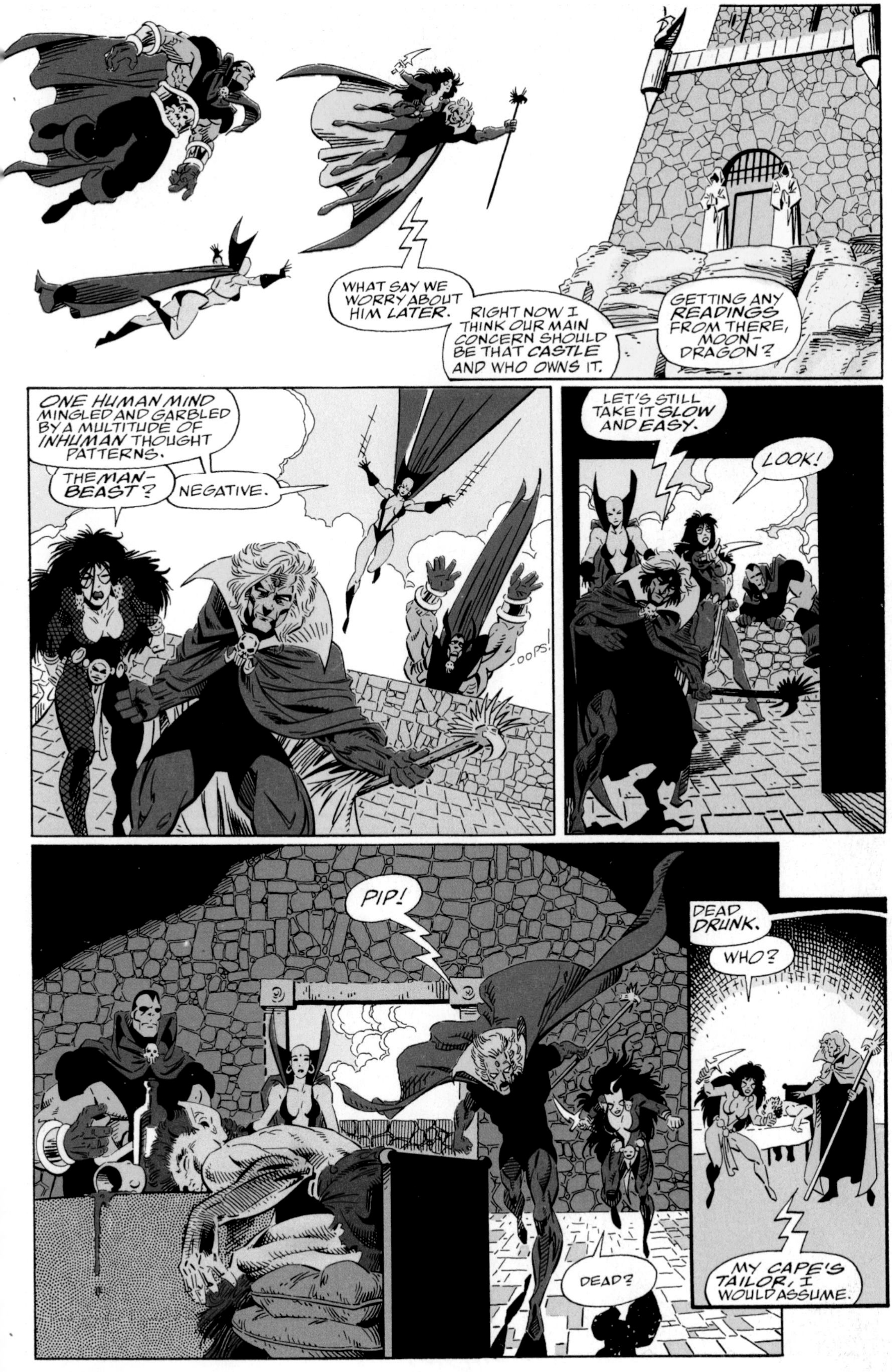
WHAT SAY WE WORRY ABOUT HIM LATER.
RIGHT NOW I THINK OUR MAIN CONCERN SHOULD BE THAT CASTLE AND WHO OWNS IT.
GETTING ANY READINGS FROM THERE, MOON-DRAGON?
ONE HUMAN MIND MINGLED AND GARBLED BY A MULTITUDE OF INHUMAN THOUGHT PATTERNS.
THE MAN-BEAST?
NEGATIVE.
-OOPS!
LET'S STILL TAKE IT SLOW AND EASY.
LOOK!
PIP!
DEAD?
DEAD DRUNK.
WHO?
MY CAPE'S TAILOR, I WOULD ASSUME.

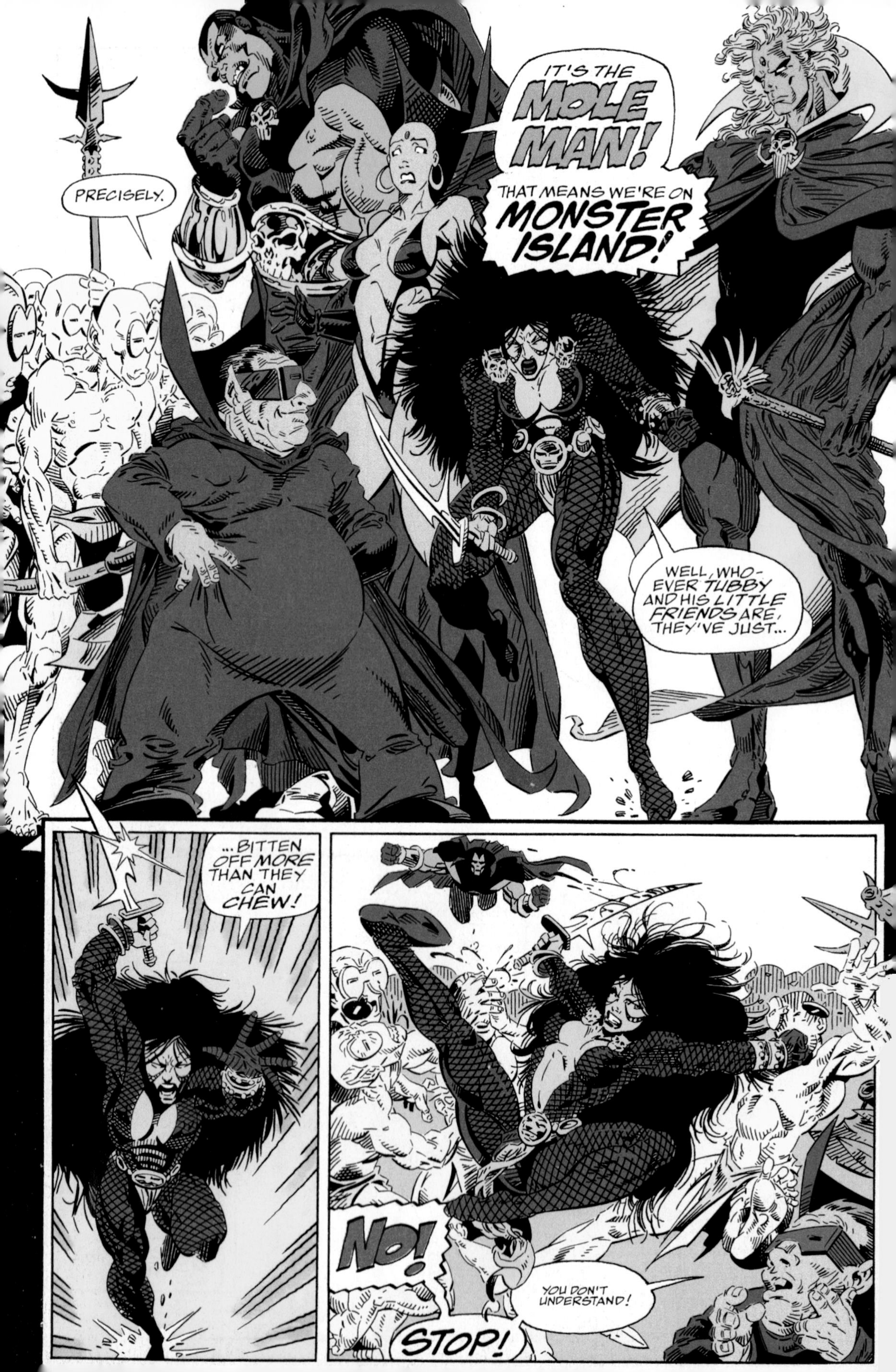
IT'S THE MOLE MAN!
THAT MEANS WE'RE ON MONSTER ISLAND!
PRECISELY.
WELL, WHO-EVER TUBBY AND HIS LITTLE FRIENDS ARE, THEY'VE JUST...
...BITTEN OFF MORE THAN THEY CAN CHEW!
NO!
YOU DON'T UNDERSTAND!
STOP!

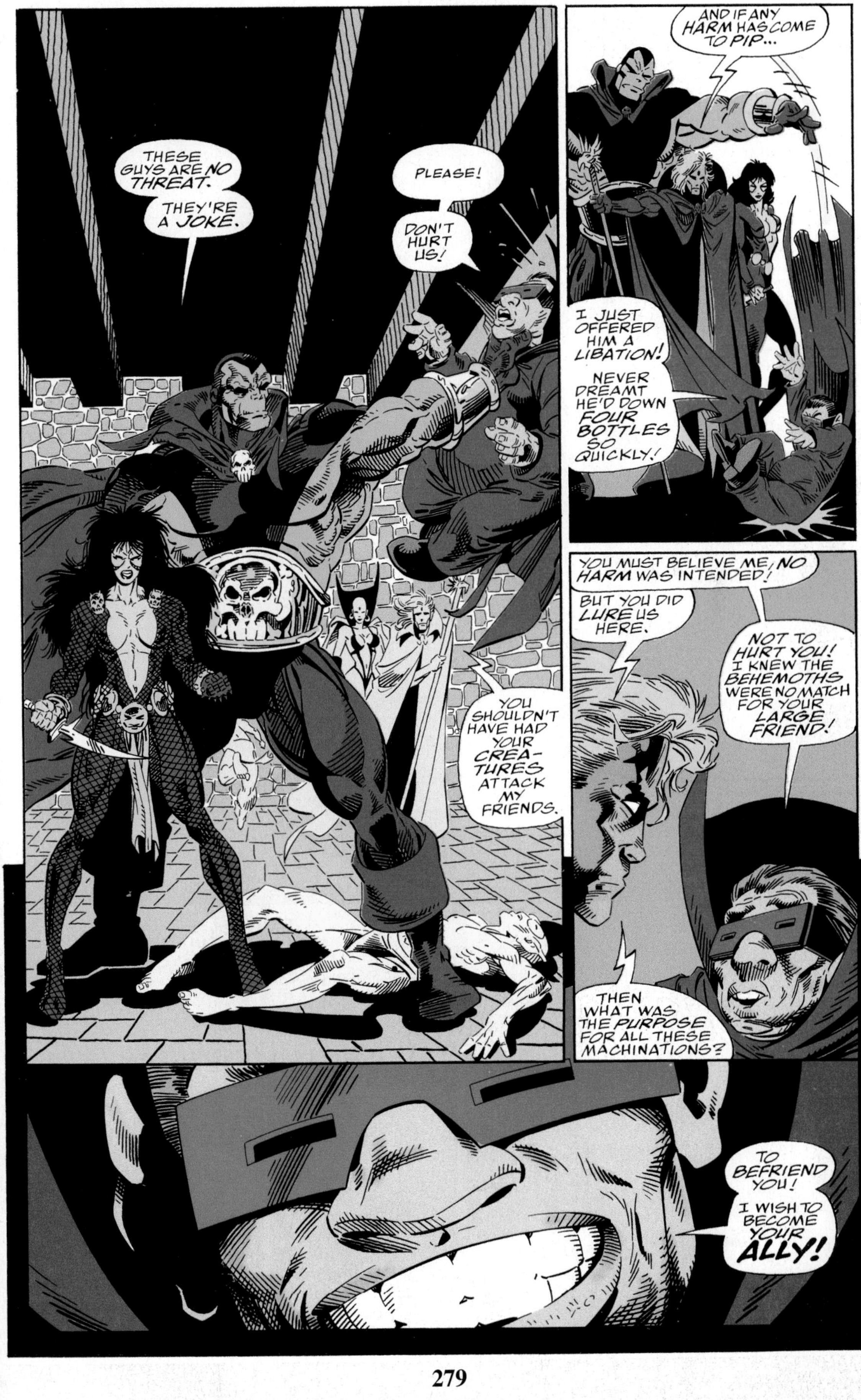
THESE GUYS ARE NO THREAT.
THEY'RE A JOKE.
PLEASE!
DON'T HURT US!
YOU SHOULDN'T HAVE HAD YOUR CREA-TURES ATTACK MY FRIENDS.
AND IF ANY HARM HAS COME TO PIP...
I JUST OFFERED HIM A LIBATION!
NEVER DREAMT HE'D DOWN FOUR BOTTLES SO QUICKLY!
YOU MUST BELIEVE ME, NO HARM WAS INTENDED!
BUT YOU DID LURE US HERE.
NOT TO HURT YOU! I KNEW THE BEHEMOTHS WERE NO MATCH FOR YOUR LARGE FRIEND!
THEN WHAT WAS THE PURPOSE FOR ALL THESE MACHINATIONS?
TO BEFRIEND YOU!
I WISH TO BECOME YOUR ALLY!

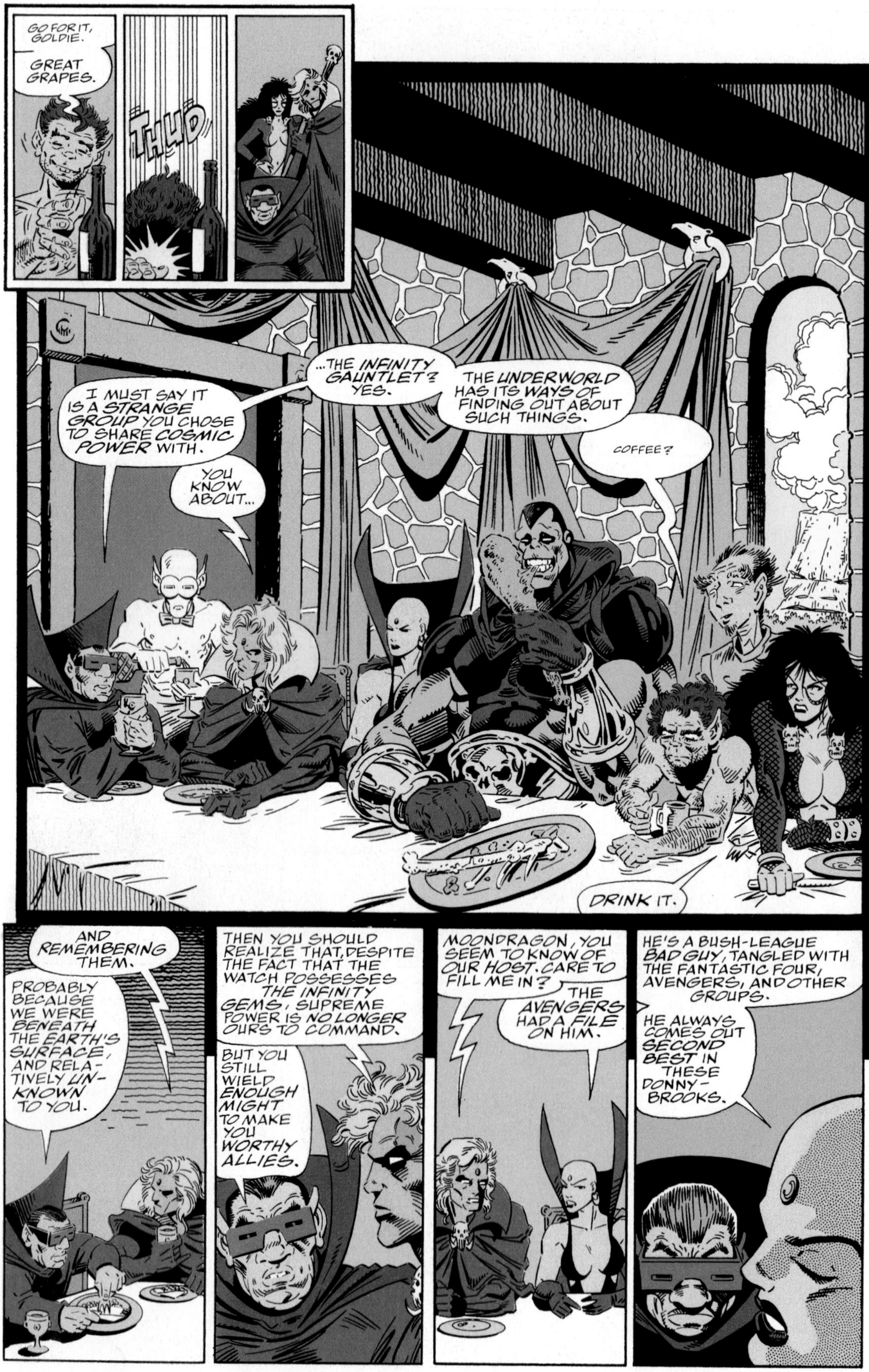
GO FOR IT, GOLDIE.
GREAT GRAPES.
THUD
I MUST SAY IT IS A STRANGE GROUP YOU CHOSE TO SHARE COSMIC POWER WITH.
YOU KNOW ABOUT...
...THE INFINITY GAUNTLET? YES.
THE UNDERWORLD HAS ITS WAYS OF FINDING OUT ABOUT SUCH THINGS.
COFFEE?
DRINK IT.
AND REMEMBERING THEM.
PROBABLY BECAUSE WE WERE BENEATH THE EARTH'S SURFACE, AND RELATIVELY UNKNOWN TO YOU.
THEN YOU SHOULD REALIZE THAT, DESPITE THE FACT THAT THE WATCH POSSESSES THE INFINITY GEMS, SUPREME POWER IS NO LONGER OURS TO COMMAND.
BUT YOU STILL WIELD ENOUGH MIGHT TO MAKE YOU WORTHY ALLIES.
MOONDRAGON, YOU SEEM TO KNOW OF OUR HOST. CARE TO FILL ME IN?
THE AVENGERS HAD A FILE ON HIM.
HE'S A BUSH-LEAGUE BAD GUY, TANGLED WITH THE FANTASTIC FOUR, AVENGERS, AND OTHER GROUPS.
HE ALWAYS COMES OUT SECOND BEST IN THESE DONNYBROOKS.

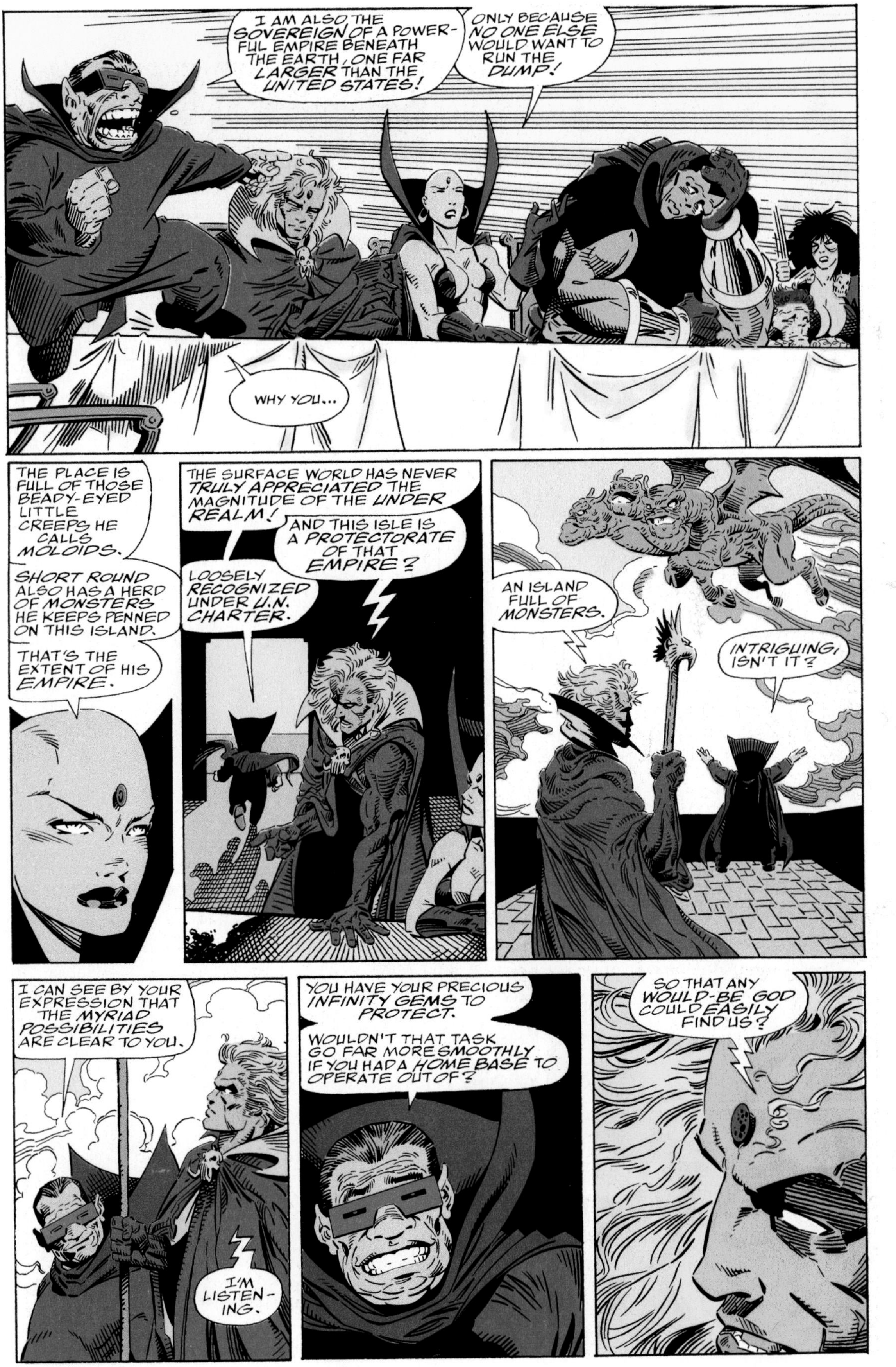

I AM ALSO THE SOVEREIGN OF A POWERFUL EMPIRE BENEATH THE EARTH, ONE FAR LARGER THAN THE UNITED STATES!
ONLY BECAUSE NO ONE ELSE WOULD WANT TO RUN THE DUMP!
WHY YOU...
THE PLACE IS FULL OF THOSE BEADY-EYED LITTLE CREEPS HE CALLS MOLOIDS.
SHORT ROUND ALSO HAS A HERD OF MONSTERS HE KEEPS PENNED ON THIS ISLAND.
THAT'S THE EXTENT OF HIS EMPIRE.
THE SURFACE WORLD HAS NEVER TRULY APPRECIATED THE MAGNITUDE OF THE UNDER REALM!
LOOSELY RECOGNIZED UNDER U.N. CHARTER.
AND THIS ISLE IS A PROTECTORATE OF THAT EMPIRE?
AN ISLAND FULL OF MONSTERS.
INTRIGUING, ISN'T IT?
I CAN SEE BY YOUR EXPRESSION THAT THE MYRIAD POSSIBILITIES ARE CLEAR TO YOU.
I'M LISTENING.
YOU HAVE YOUR PRECIOUS INFINITY GEMS TO PROTECT.
WOULDN'T THAT TASK GO FAR MORE SMOOTHLY IF YOU HAD A HOME BASE TO OPERATE OUT OF?
SO THAT ANY WOULD-BE GOD COULD EASILY FIND US?

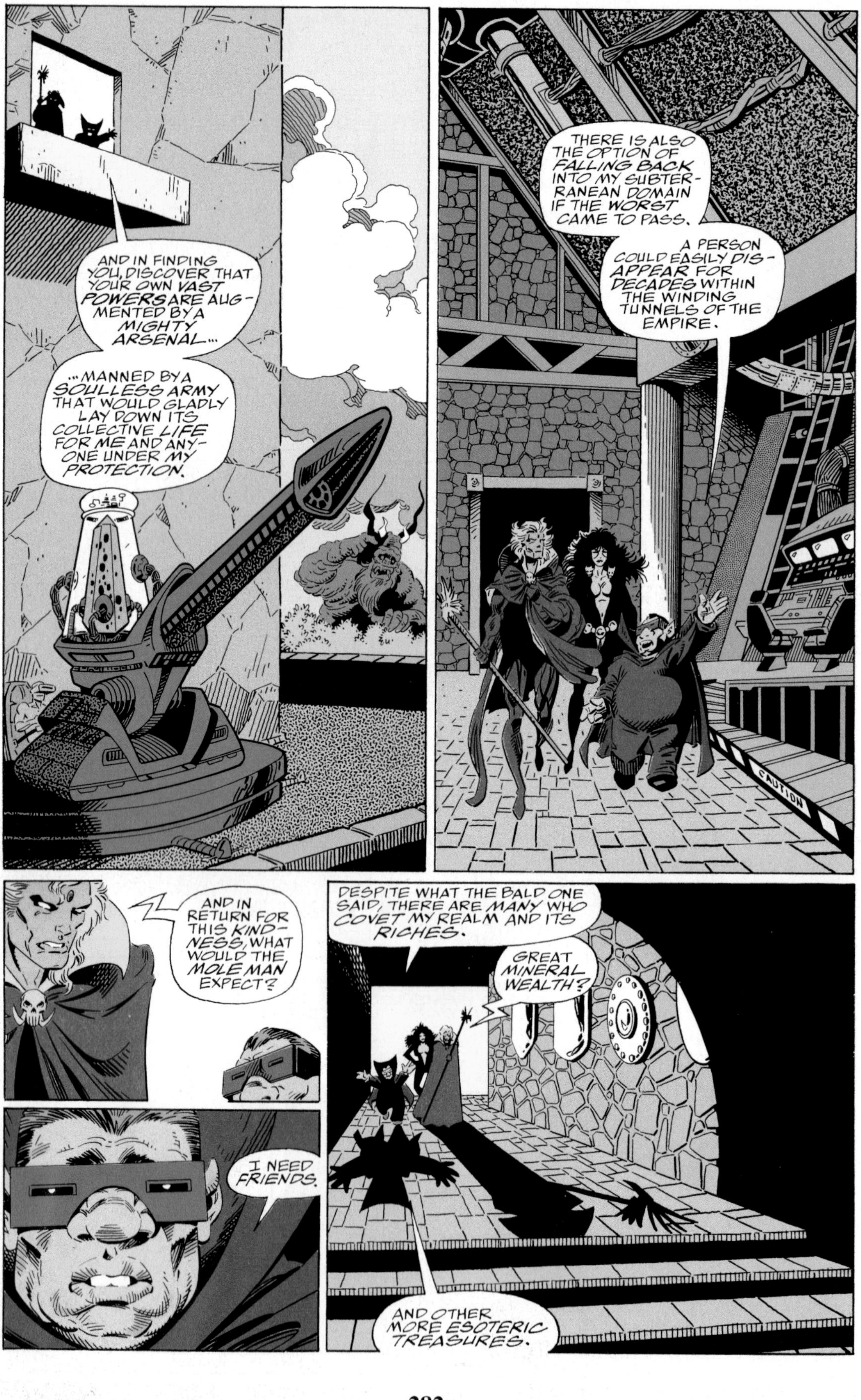
AND IN FINDING YOU, DISCOVER THAT YOUR OWN VAST POWERS ARE AUG-MENTED BY A MIGHTY ARSENAL...
...MANNED BY A SOULLESS ARMY THAT WOULD GLADLY LAY DOWN ITS COLLECTIVE LIFE FOR ME AND ANY-ONE UNDER MY PROTECTION.
THERE IS ALSO THE OPTION OF FALLING BACK INTO MY SUBTER-RANEAN DOMAIN IF THE WORST CAME TO PASS.
A PERSON COULD EASILY DIS-APPEAR FOR DECADES WITHIN THE WINDING TUNNELS OF THE EMPIRE.
CAUTION
AND IN RETURN FOR THIS KIND-NESS, WHAT WOULD THE MOLE MAN EXPECT?
I NEED FRIENDS.
DESPITE WHAT THE BALD ONE SAID, THERE ARE MANY WHO COVET MY REALM AND ITS RICHES.
GREAT MINERAL WEALTH?
AND OTHER MORE ESOTERIC TREASURES.

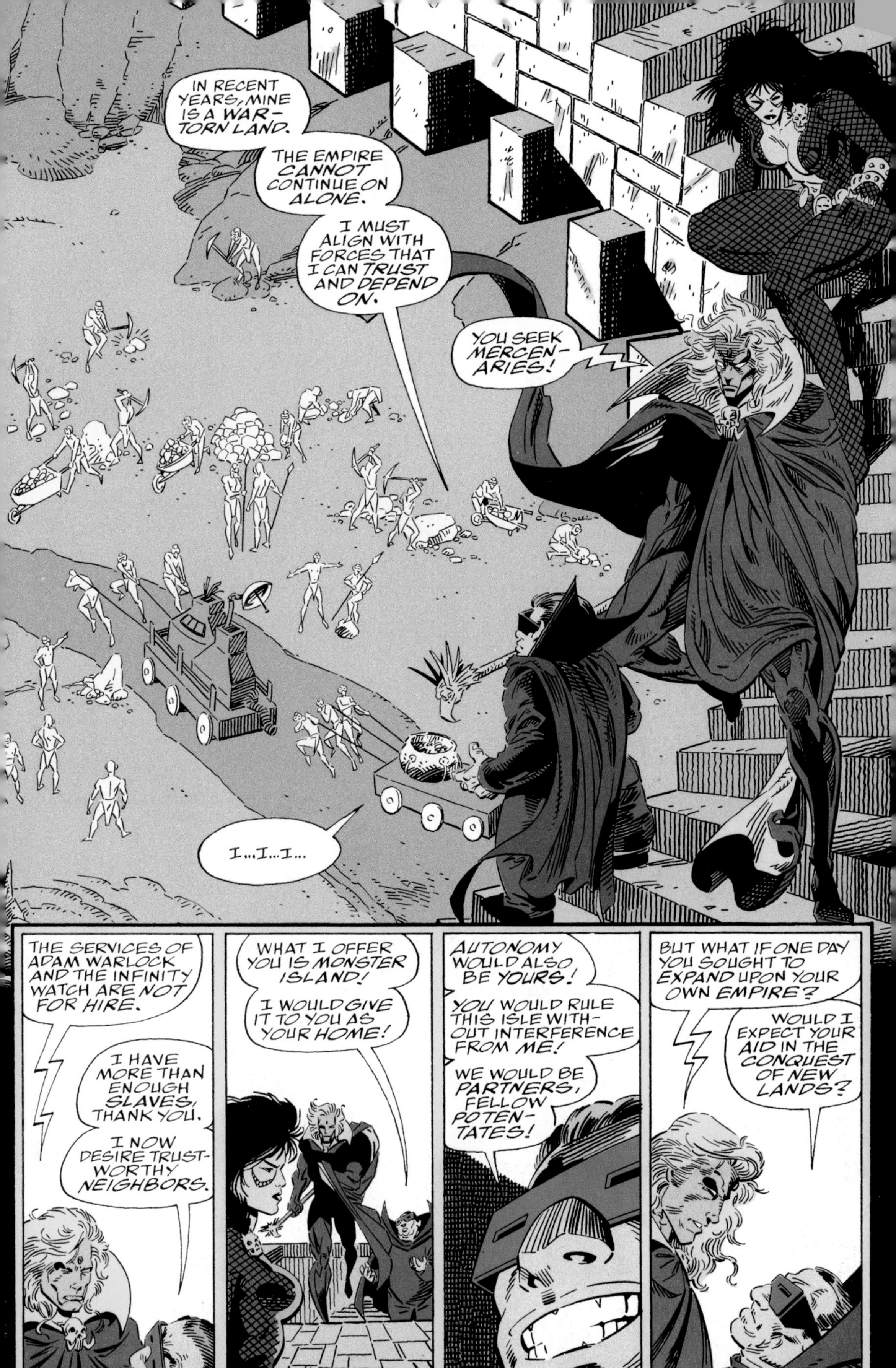
IN RECENT YEARS, MINE IS A WAR-TORN LAND.
THE EMPIRE CANNOT CONTINUE ON ALONE.
I MUST ALIGN WITH FORCES THAT I CAN TRUST AND DEPEND ON.
YOU SEEK MERCEN-ARIES!
I...I...I...
THE SERVICES OF ADAM WARLOCK AND THE INFINITY WATCH ARE NOT FOR HIRE.
I HAVE MORE THAN ENOUGH SLAVES, THANK YOU.
I NOW DESIRE TRUST-WORTHY NEIGHBORS.
WHAT I OFFER YOU IS MONSTER ISLAND!
I WOULD GIVE IT TO YOU AS YOUR HOME!
AUTONOMY WOULD ALSO BE YOURS!
YOU WOULD RULE THIS ISLE WITH-OUT INTERFERENCE FROM ME!
WE WOULD BE PARTNERS, FELLOW POTEN-TATES!
BUT WHAT IF ONE DAY YOU SOUGHT TO EXPAND UPON YOUR OWN EMPIRE?
WOULD I EXPECT YOUR AID IN THE CONQUEST OF NEW LANDS?

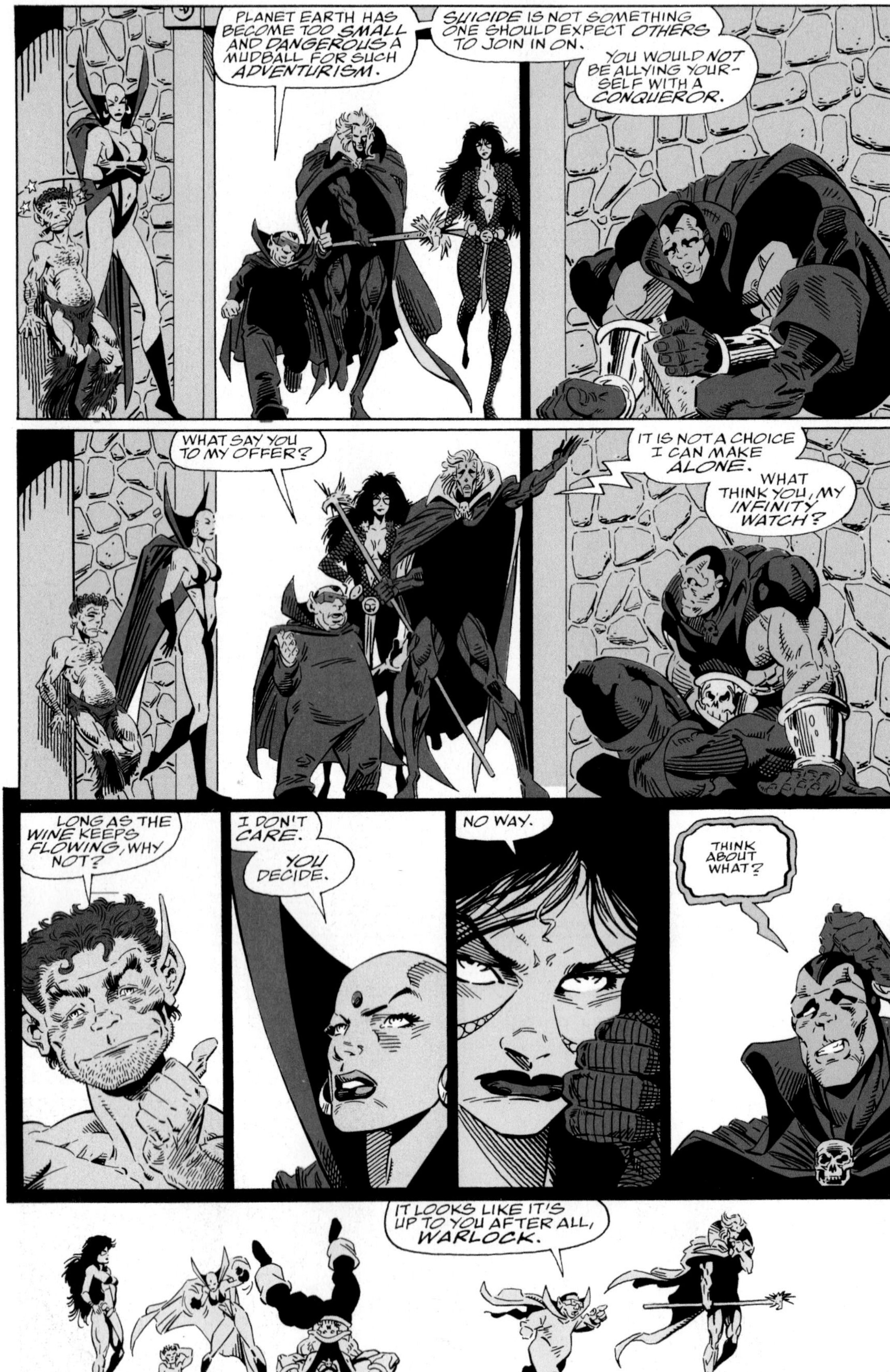
PLANET EARTH HAS BECOME TOO SMALL AND DANGEROUS A MUDBALL FOR SUCH ADVENTURISM.
SUICIDE IS NOT SOMETHING ONE SHOULD EXPECT OTHERS TO JOIN IN ON.
YOU WOULD NOT BE ALLYING YOURSELF WITH A CONQUEROR.
WHAT SAY YOU TO MY OFFER?
IT IS NOT A CHOICE I CAN MAKE ALONE.
WHAT THINK YOU, MY INFINITY WATCH?
LONG AS THE WINE KEEPS FLOWING, WHY NOT?
I DON'T CARE.
YOU DECIDE.
NO WAY.
THINK ABOUT WHAT?
IT LOOKS LIKE IT'S UP TO YOU AFTER ALL, WARLOCK.

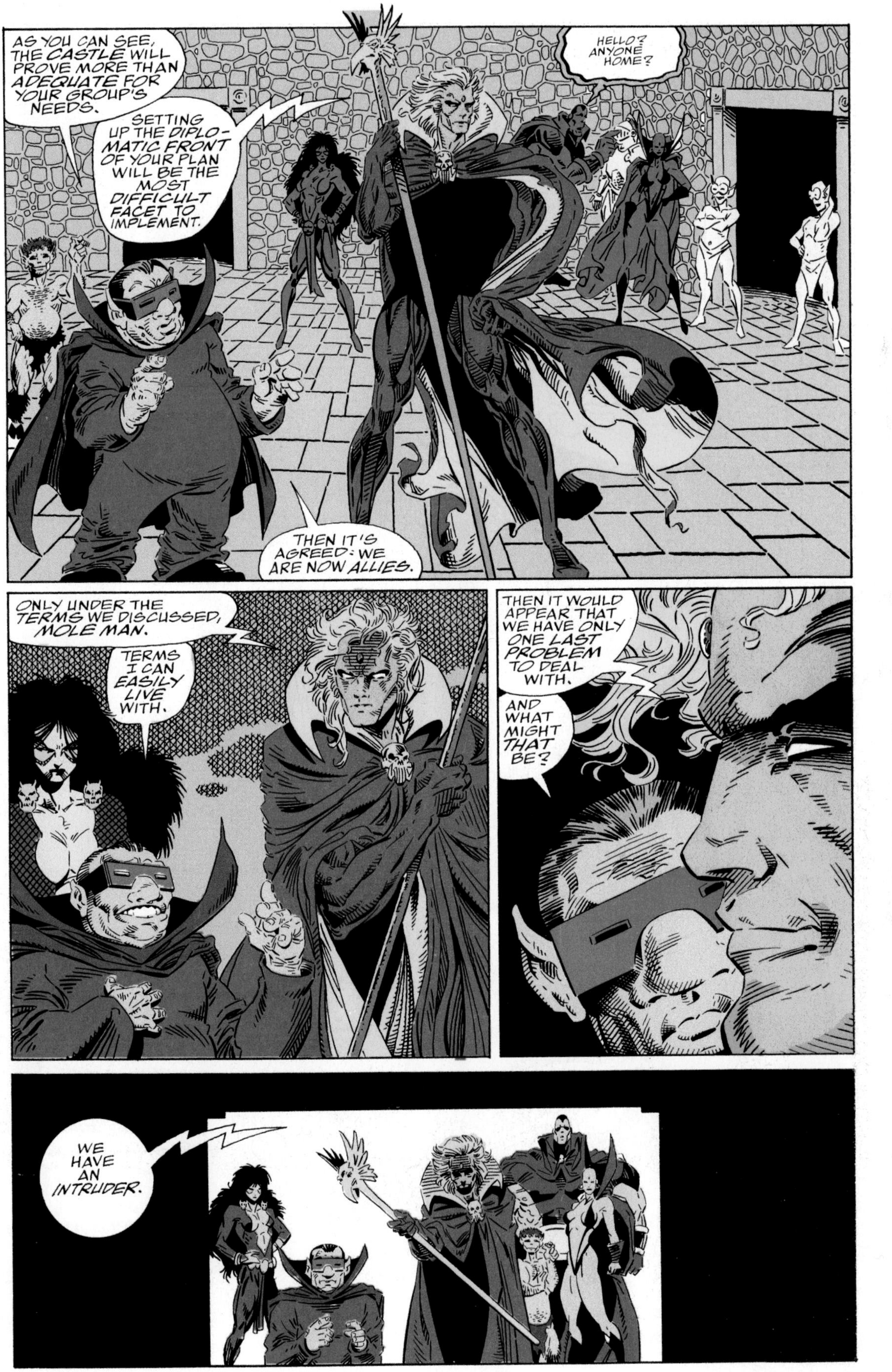
AS YOU CAN SEE, THE CASTLE WILL PROVE MORE THAN ADEQUATE FOR YOUR GROUP'S NEEDS.
SETTING UP THE DIPLOMATIC FRONT OF YOUR PLAN WILL BE THE MOST DIFFICULT FACET TO IMPLEMENT.
HELLO? ANYONE HOME?
THEN IT'S AGREED: WE ARE NOW ALLIES.
ONLY UNDER THE TERMS WE DISCUSSED, MOLE MAN.
TERMS I CAN EASILY LIVE WITH.
THEN IT WOULD APPEAR THAT WE HAVE ONLY ONE LAST PROBLEM TO DEAL WITH.
AND WHAT MIGHT THAT BE?
WE HAVE AN INTRUDER.

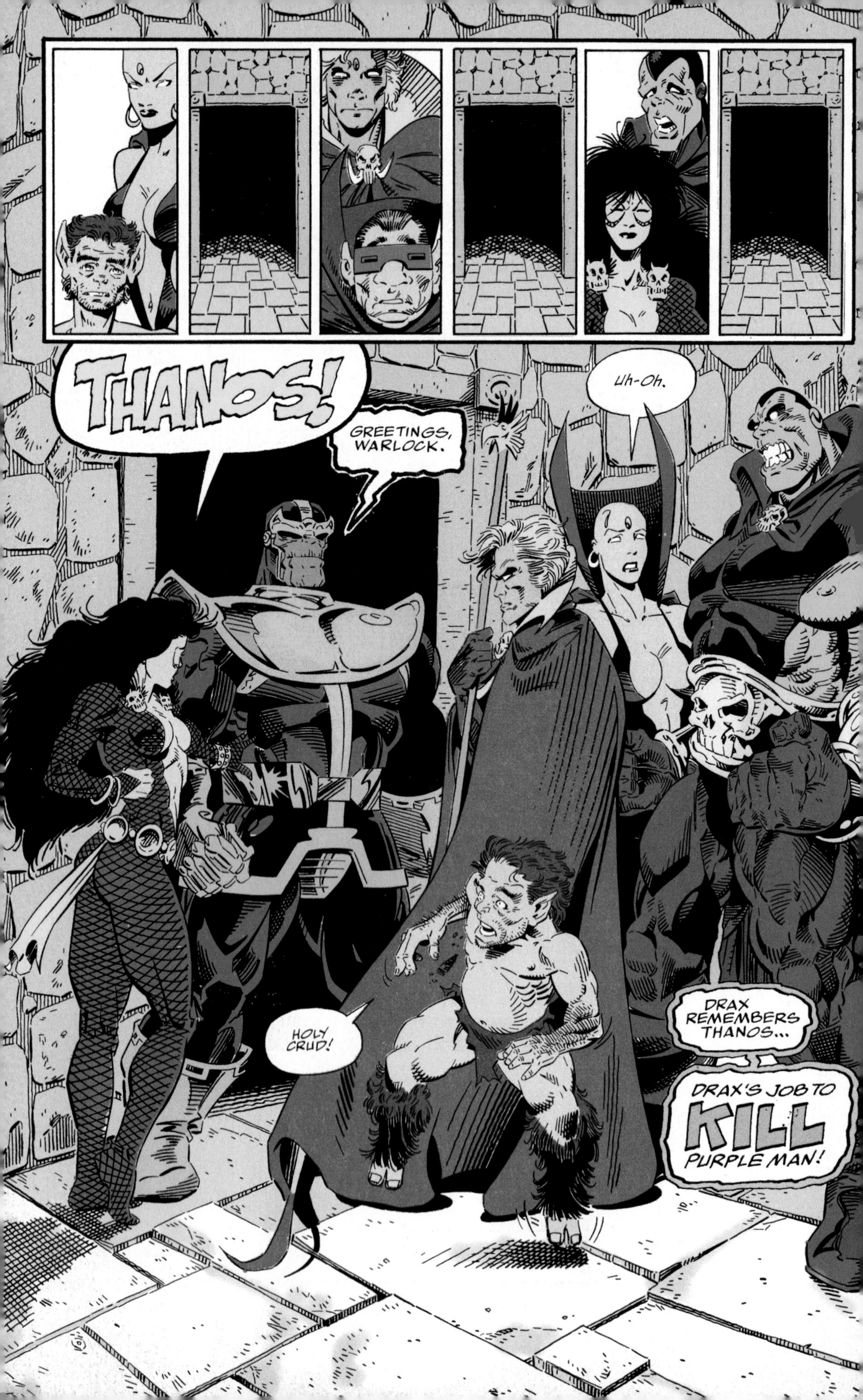
THANOS!
GREETINGS, WARLOCK.
UH-OH.
HOLY CRUD!
DRAX REMEMBERS THANOS...
DRAX'S JOB TO KILL PURPLE MAN!

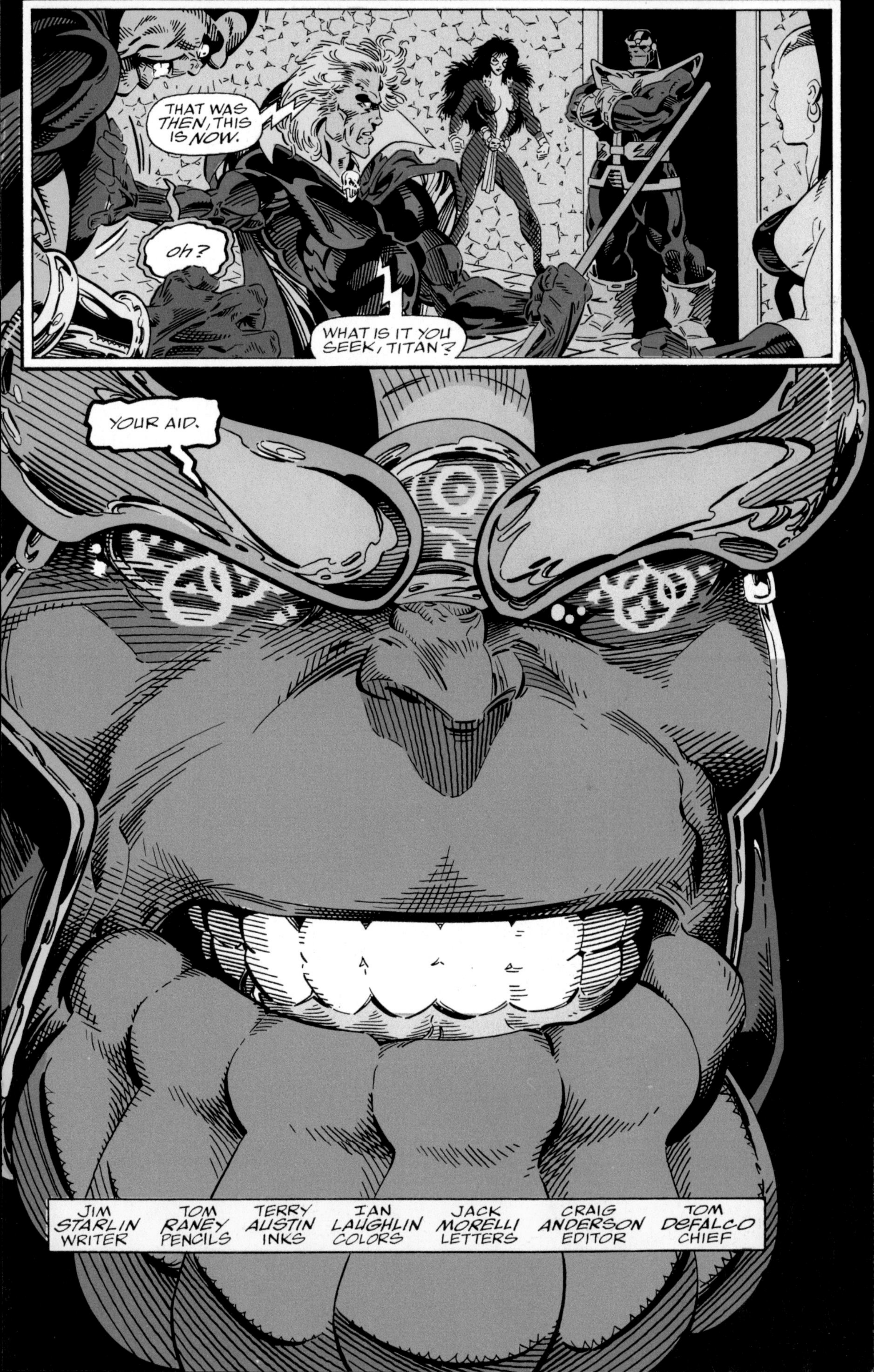
THAT WAS THEN, THIS IS NOW.
oh?
WHAT IS IT YOU SEEK, TITAN?
YOUR AID.
JIM STARLIN WRITER
TOM RANEY PENCILS
TERRY AUSTIN INKS
IAN LAUGHLIN COLORS
JACK MORELLI LETTERS
CRAIG ANDERSON EDITOR
TOM DEFALCO CHIEF

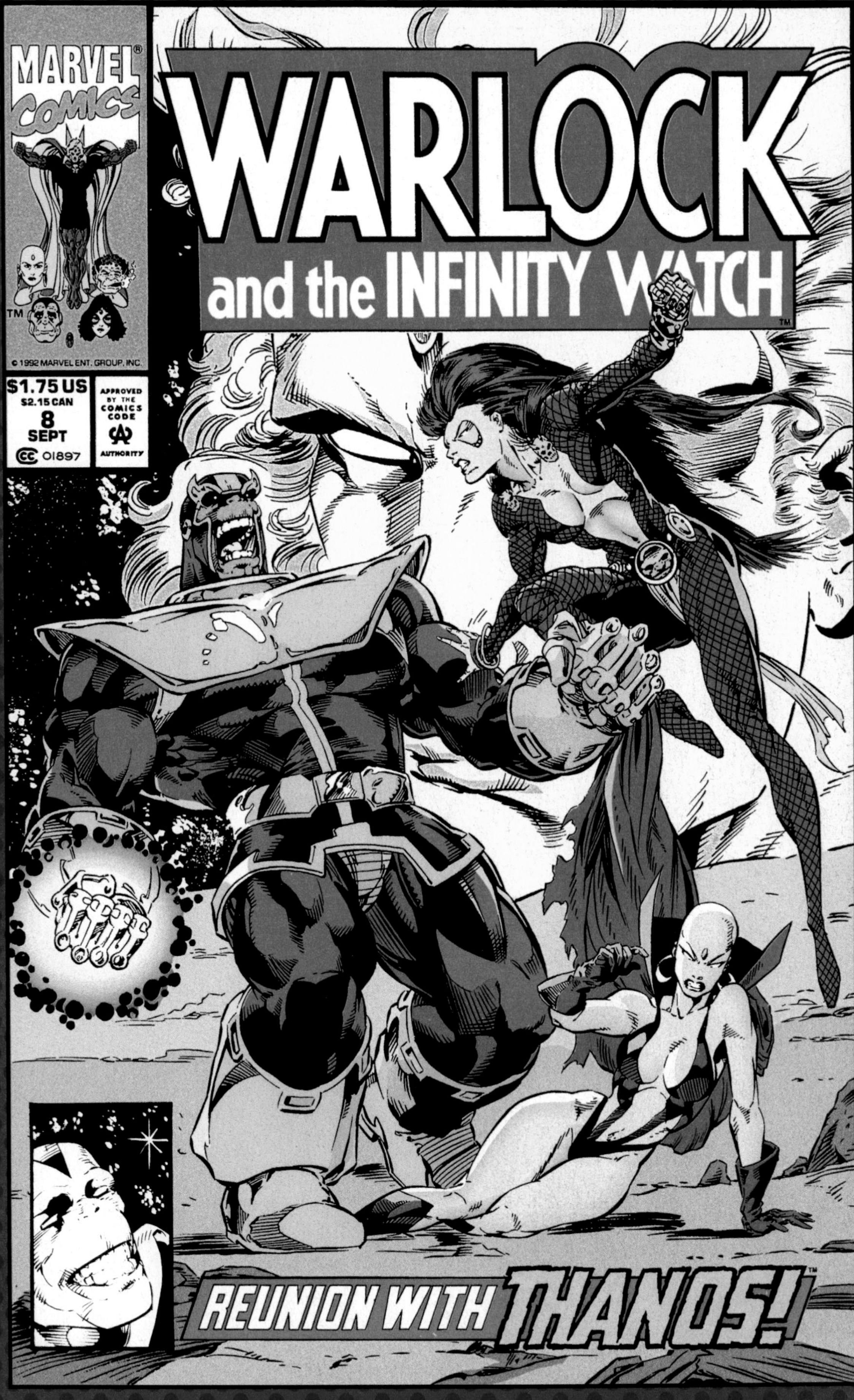

MARVEL® COMICS
WARLOCK and the INFINITY WATCH™
© 1992 MARVEL ENT. GROUP, INC.
$1.75 US
$2.15 CAN
8
SEPT
01897
APPROVED BY THE COMICS CODE AUTHORITY
REUNION WITH THANOS!™

INTERLUDE

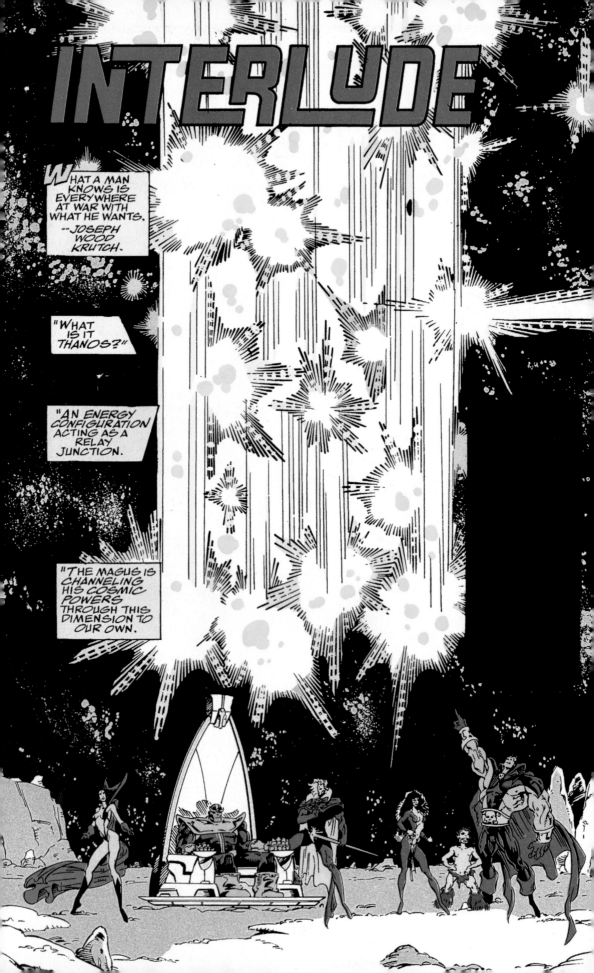

WHAT A MAN KNOWS IS EVERYWHERE AT WAR WITH WHAT HE WANTS.
--JOSEPH WOOD KRUTCH.

"WHAT IS IT THANOS?"

"AN ENERGY CONFIGURATION ACTING AS A RELAY JUNCTION.

"THE MAGUS IS CHANNELING HIS COSMIC POWERS THROUGH THIS DIMENSION TO OUR OWN.

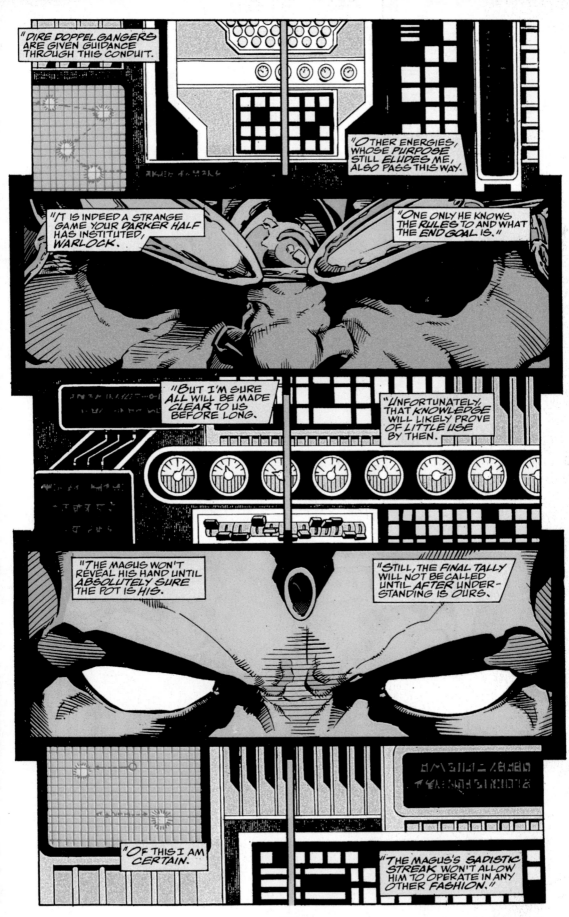

"DIRE DOPPELGANGERS ARE GIVEN GUIDANCE THROUGH THIS CONDUIT.

"OTHER ENERGIES, WHOSE PURPOSE STILL ELUDES ME, ALSO PASS THIS WAY.

"IT IS INDEED A STRANGE GAME YOUR DARKER HALF HAS INSTITUTED, WARLOCK.

"ONE ONLY HE KNOWS THE RULES TO AND WHAT THE END GOAL IS.

"BUT I'M SURE ALL WILL BE MADE CLEAR TO US BEFORE LONG.

"UNFORTUNATELY, THAT KNOWLEDGE WILL LIKELY PROVE OF LITTLE USE BY THEN.

"THE MAGUS WON'T REVEAL HIS HAND UNTIL ABSOLUTELY SURE THE POT IS HIS.

"STILL, THE FINAL TALLY WILL NOT BE CALLED UNTIL AFTER UNDER-STANDING IS OURS.

"OF THIS I AM CERTAIN.

"THE MAGUS'S SADISTIC STREAK WON'T ALLOW HIM TO OPERATE IN ANY OTHER FASHION."

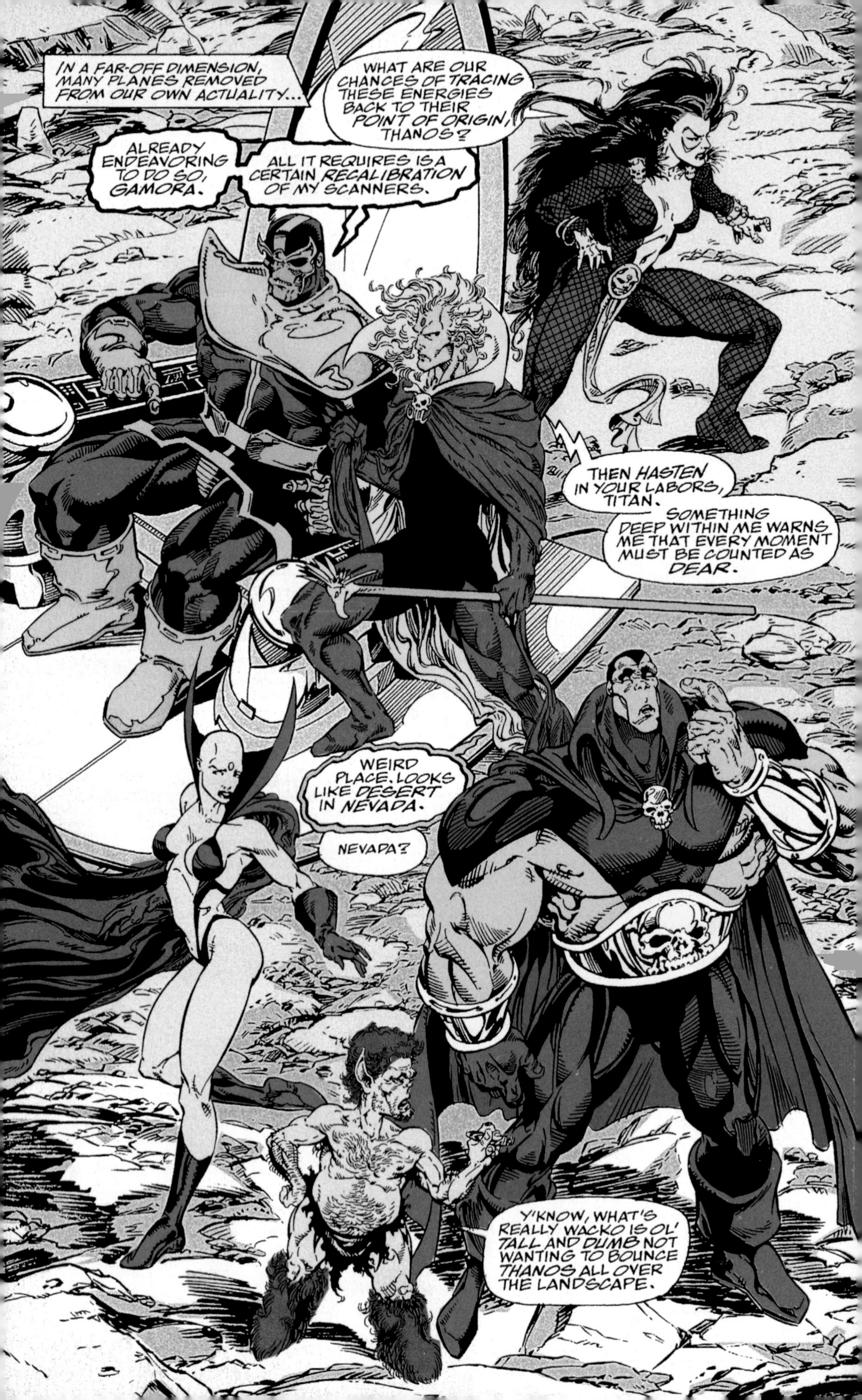
IN A FAR-OFF DIMENSION, MANY PLANES REMOVED FROM OUR OWN ACTUALITY...
WHAT ARE OUR CHANCES OF TRACING THESE ENERGIES BACK TO THEIR POINT OF ORIGIN, THANOS?
ALREADY ENDEAVORING TO DO SO, GAMORA.
ALL IT REQUIRES IS A CERTAIN RECALIBRATION OF MY SCANNERS.
THEN HASTEN IN YOUR LABORS, TITAN.
SOMETHING DEEP WITHIN ME WARNS ME THAT EVERY MOMENT MUST BE COUNTED AS DEAR.
WEIRD PLACE. LOOKS LIKE DESERT IN NEVADA.
NEVADA?
Y'KNOW, WHAT'S REALLY WACKO IS OL' TALL AND DUMB NOT WANTING TO BOUNCE THANOS ALL OVER THE LANDSCAPE.

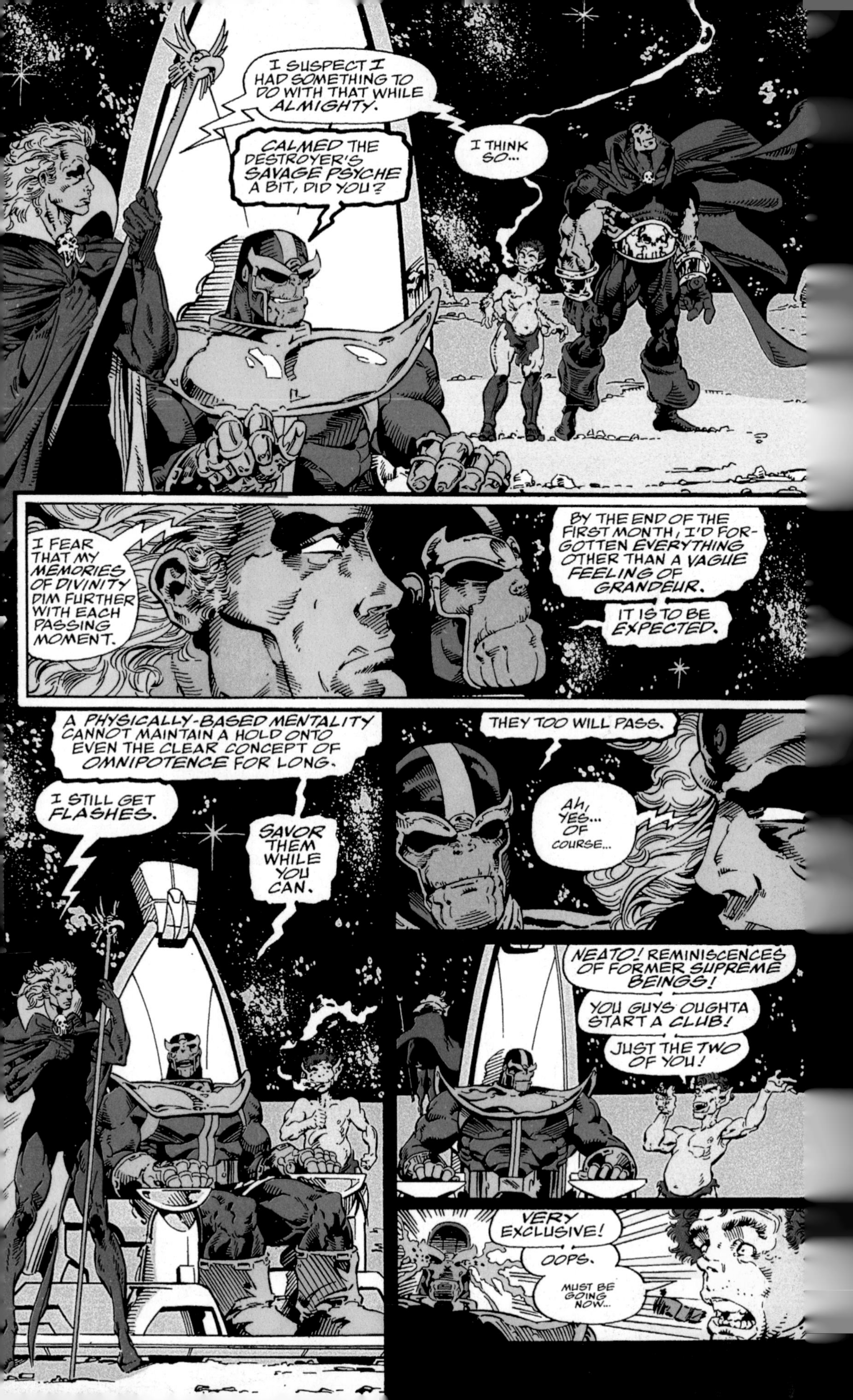

I SUSPECT I HAD SOMETHING TO DO WITH THAT WHILE ALMIGHTY.
CALMED THE DESTROYER'S SAVAGE PSYCHE A BIT, DID YOU?
I THINK SO...
I FEAR THAT MY MEMORIES OF DIVINITY DIM FURTHER WITH EACH PASSING MOMENT.
BY THE END OF THE FIRST MONTH, I'D FORGOTTEN EVERYTHING OTHER THAN A VAGUE FEELING OF GRANDEUR.
IT IS TO BE EXPECTED.
A PHYSICALLY-BASED MENTALITY CANNOT MAINTAIN A HOLD ONTO EVEN THE CLEAR CONCEPT OF OMNIPOTENCE FOR LONG.
I STILL GET FLASHES.
SAVOR THEM WHILE YOU CAN.
THEY TOO WILL PASS.
Ah, YES... OF COURSE...
NEATO! REMINISCENCES OF FORMER SUPREME BEINGS!
YOU GUYS OUGHTA START A CLUB!
JUST THE TWO OF YOU!
VERY EXCLUSIVE!
OOPS.
MUST BE GOING NOW...

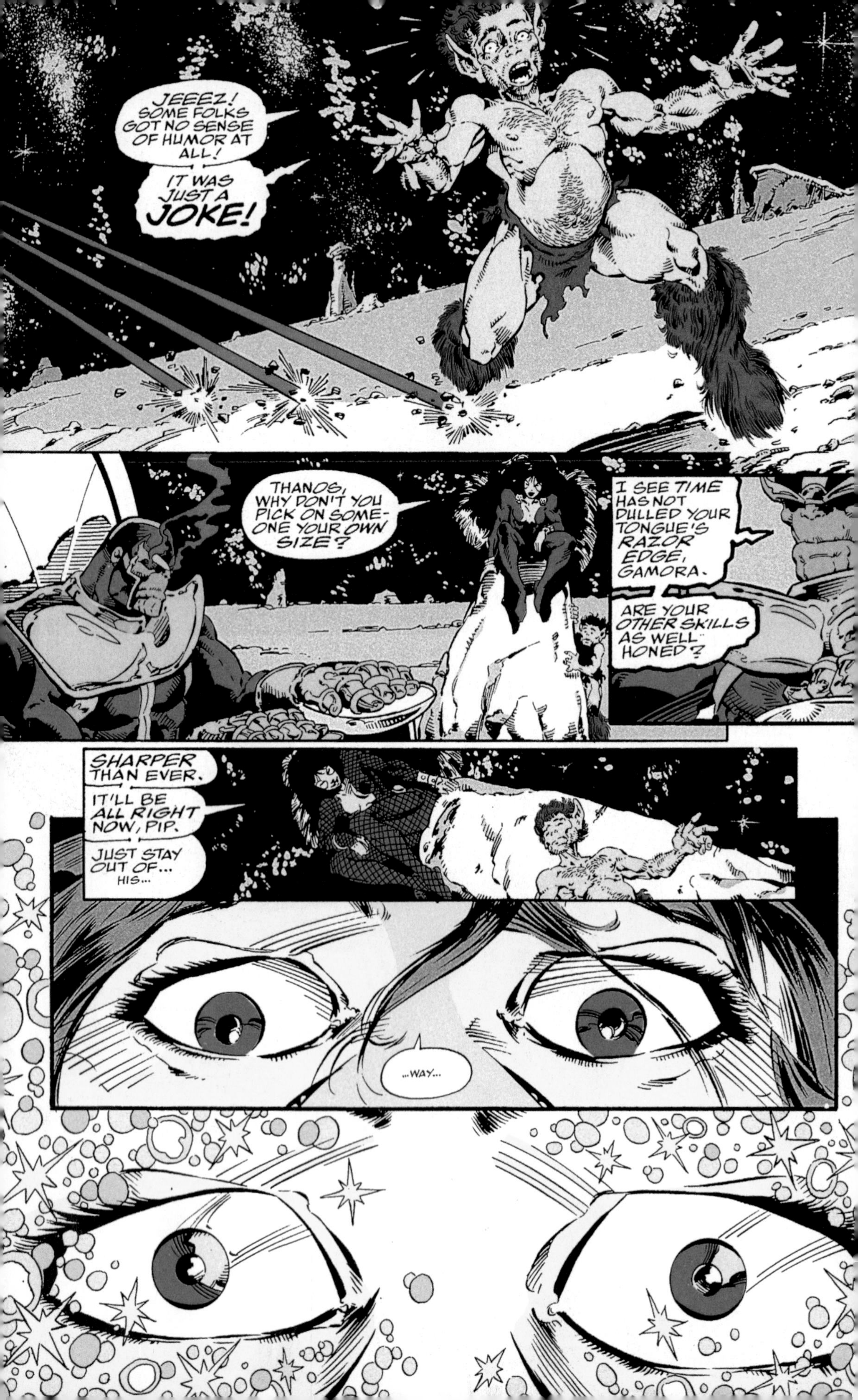
JEEEZ! SOME FOLKS GOT NO SENSE OF HUMOR AT ALL!
IT WAS JUST A JOKE!
THANOS, WHY DON'T YOU PICK ON SOME-ONE YOUR OWN SIZE?
I SEE TIME HAS NOT DULLED YOUR TONGUE'S RAZOR EDGE, GAMORA.
ARE YOUR OTHER SKILLS AS WELL HONED?
SHARPER THAN EVER.
IT'LL BE ALL RIGHT NOW, PIP.
JUST STAY OUT OF... HIS...
...WAY...

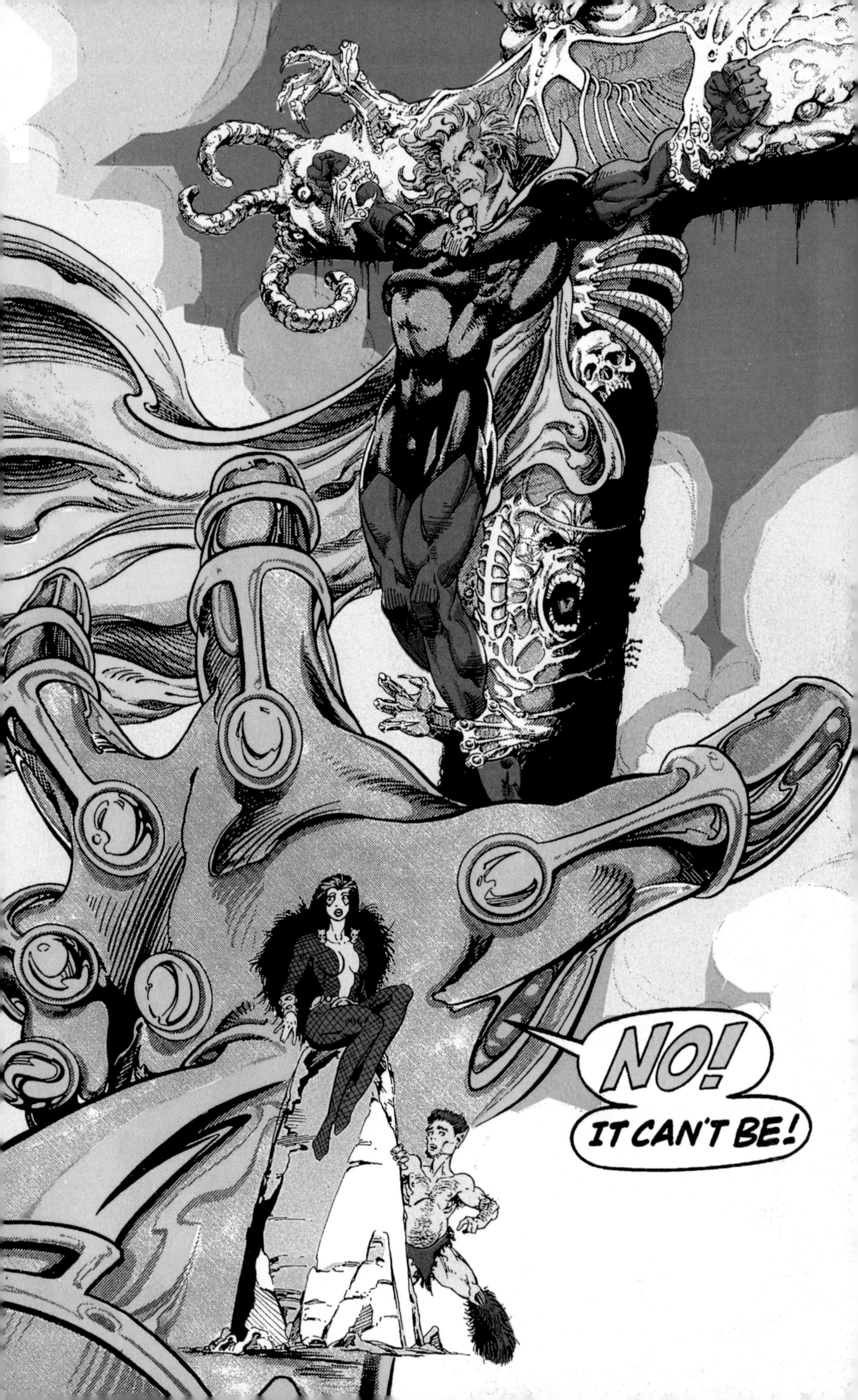
NO!
IT CAN'T BE!

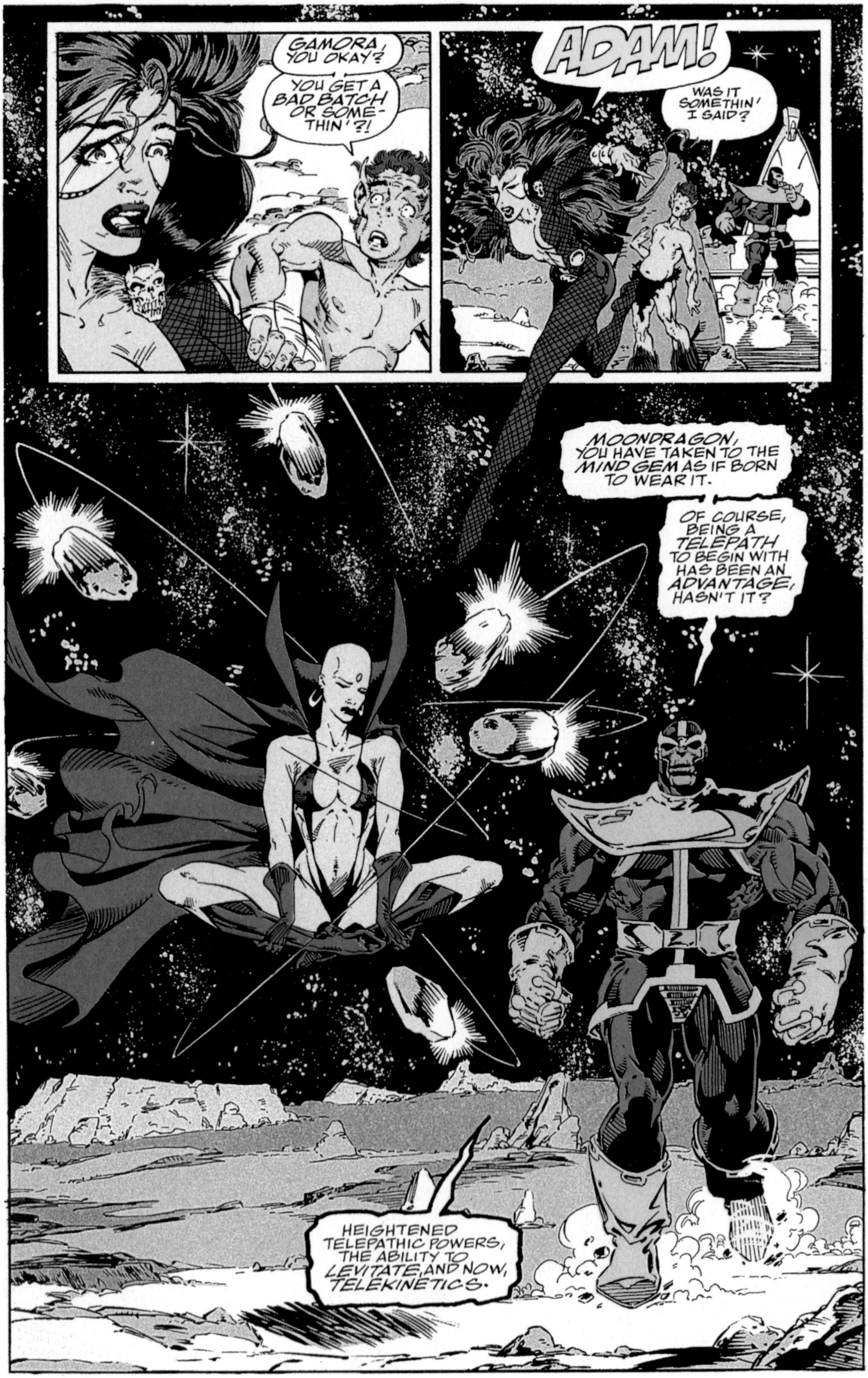
GAMORA, YOU OKAY?
YOU GET A BAD BATCH OR SOME-THIN'?!
ADAM!
WAS IT SOMETHIN' I SAID?
MOONDRAGON, YOU HAVE TAKEN TO THE MIND GEM AS IF BORN TO WEAR IT.
OF COURSE, BEING A TELEPATH TO BEGIN WITH HAS BEEN AN ADVANTAGE, HASN'T IT?
HEIGHTENED TELEPATHIC POWERS, THE ABILITY TO LEVITATE, AND NOW, TELEKINETICS.

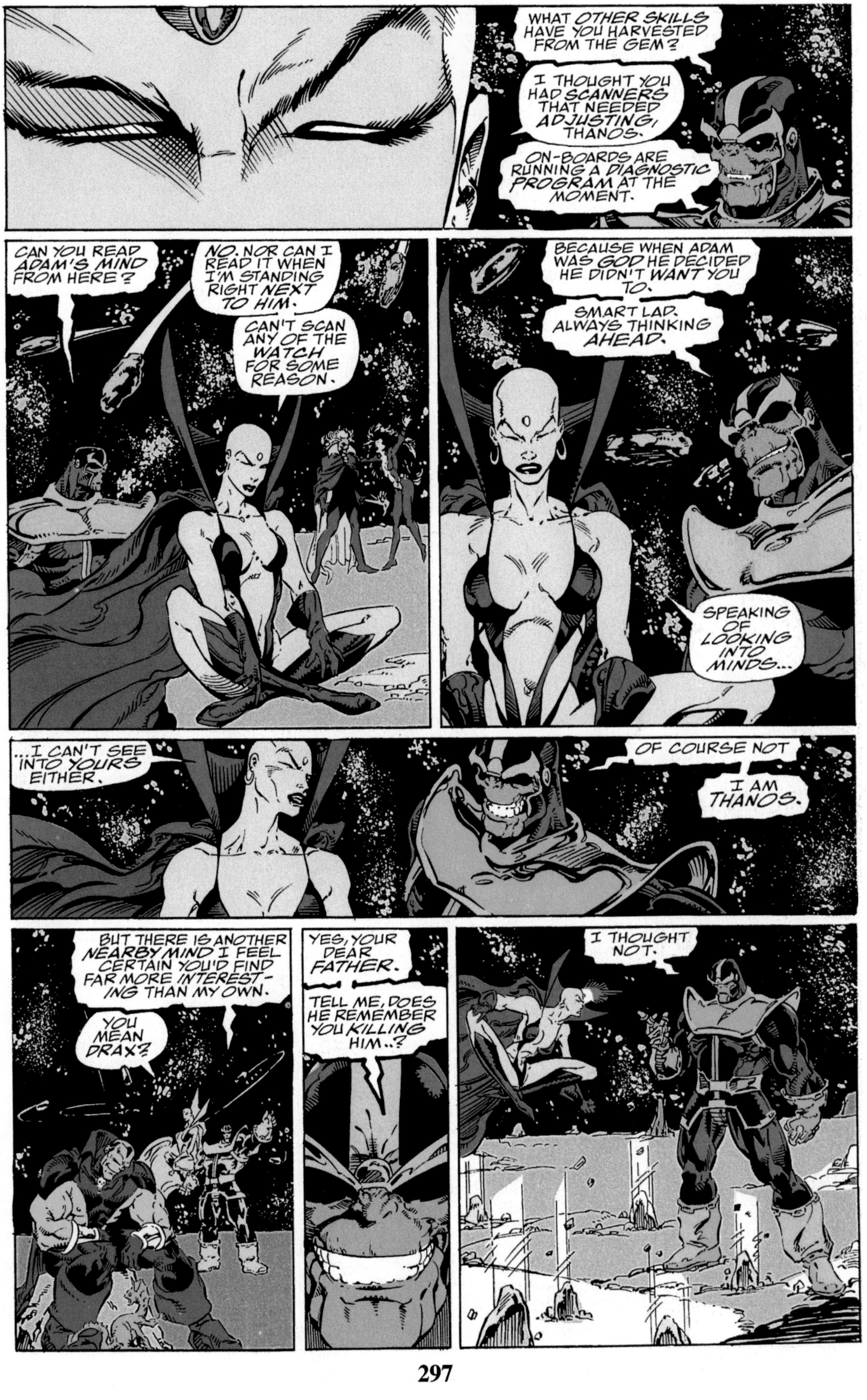
WHAT OTHER SKILLS HAVE YOU HARVESTED FROM THE GEM?
I THOUGHT YOU HAD SCANNERS THAT NEEDED ADJUSTING, THANOS.
ON-BOARDS ARE RUNNING A DIAGNOSTIC PROGRAM AT THE MOMENT.
CAN YOU READ ADAM'S MIND FROM HERE?
NO. NOR CAN I READ IT WHEN I'M STANDING RIGHT NEXT TO HIM.
CAN'T SCAN ANY OF THE WATCH FOR SOME REASON.
BECAUSE WHEN ADAM WAS GOD HE DECIDED HE DIDN'T WANT YOU TO.
SMART LAD. ALWAYS THINKING AHEAD.
SPEAKING OF LOOKING INTO MINDS...
...I CAN'T SEE INTO YOURS EITHER.
OF COURSE NOT
I AM THANOS.
BUT THERE IS ANOTHER NEARBY MIND I FEEL CERTAIN YOU'D FIND FAR MORE INTERESTING THAN MY OWN.
YOU MEAN DRAX?
YES, YOUR DEAR FATHER.
TELL ME, DOES HE REMEMBER YOU KILLING HIM..?
I THOUGHT NOT.

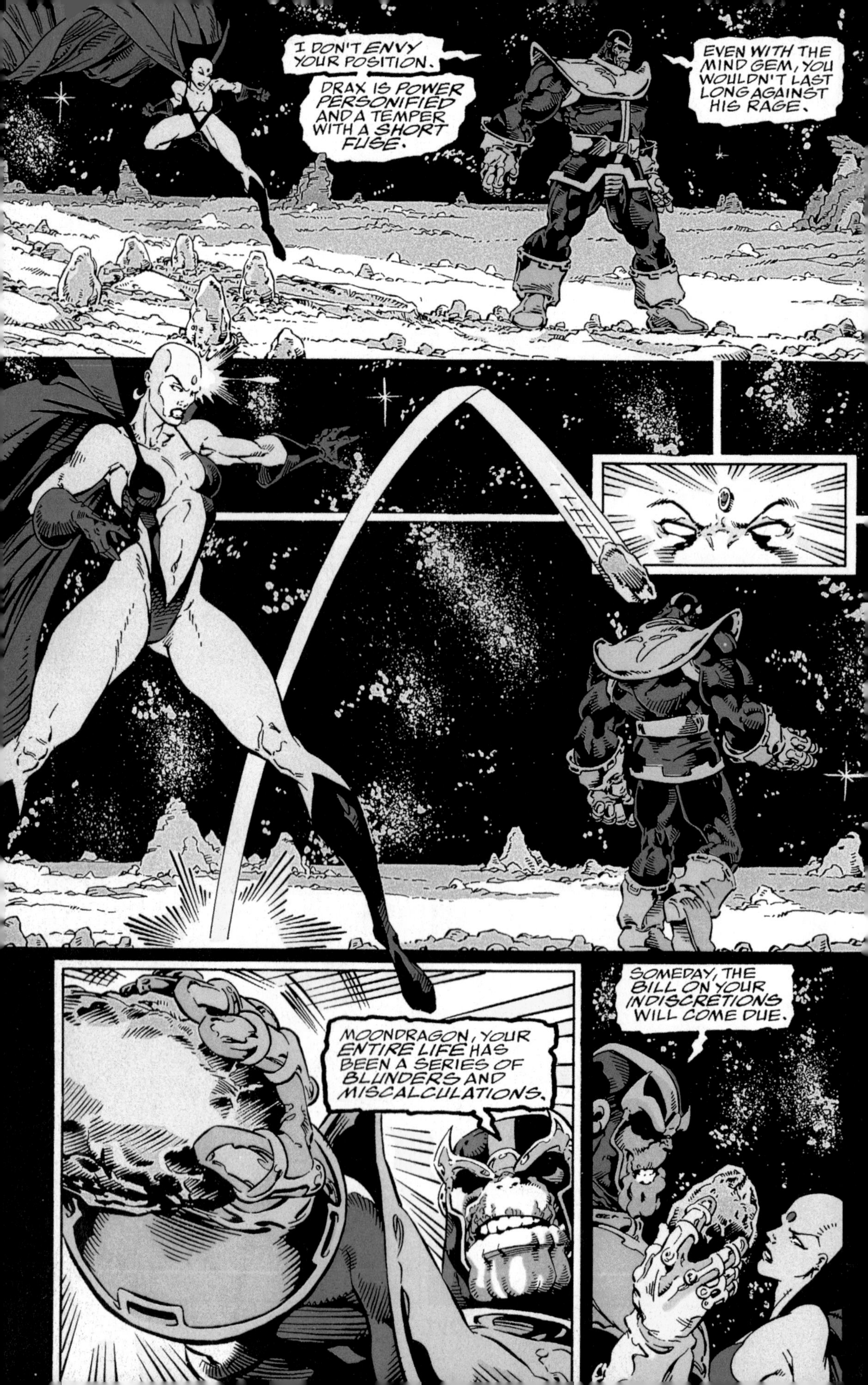
I DON'T ENVY YOUR POSITION.
DRAX IS POWER PERSONIFIED AND A TEMPER WITH A SHORT FUSE.
EVEN WITH THE MIND GEM, YOU WOULDN'T LAST LONG AGAINST HIS RAGE.
MOONDRAGON, YOUR ENTIRE LIFE HAS BEEN A SERIES OF BLUNDERS AND MISCALCULATIONS.
SOMEDAY, THE BILL ON YOUR INDISCRETIONS WILL COME DUE.

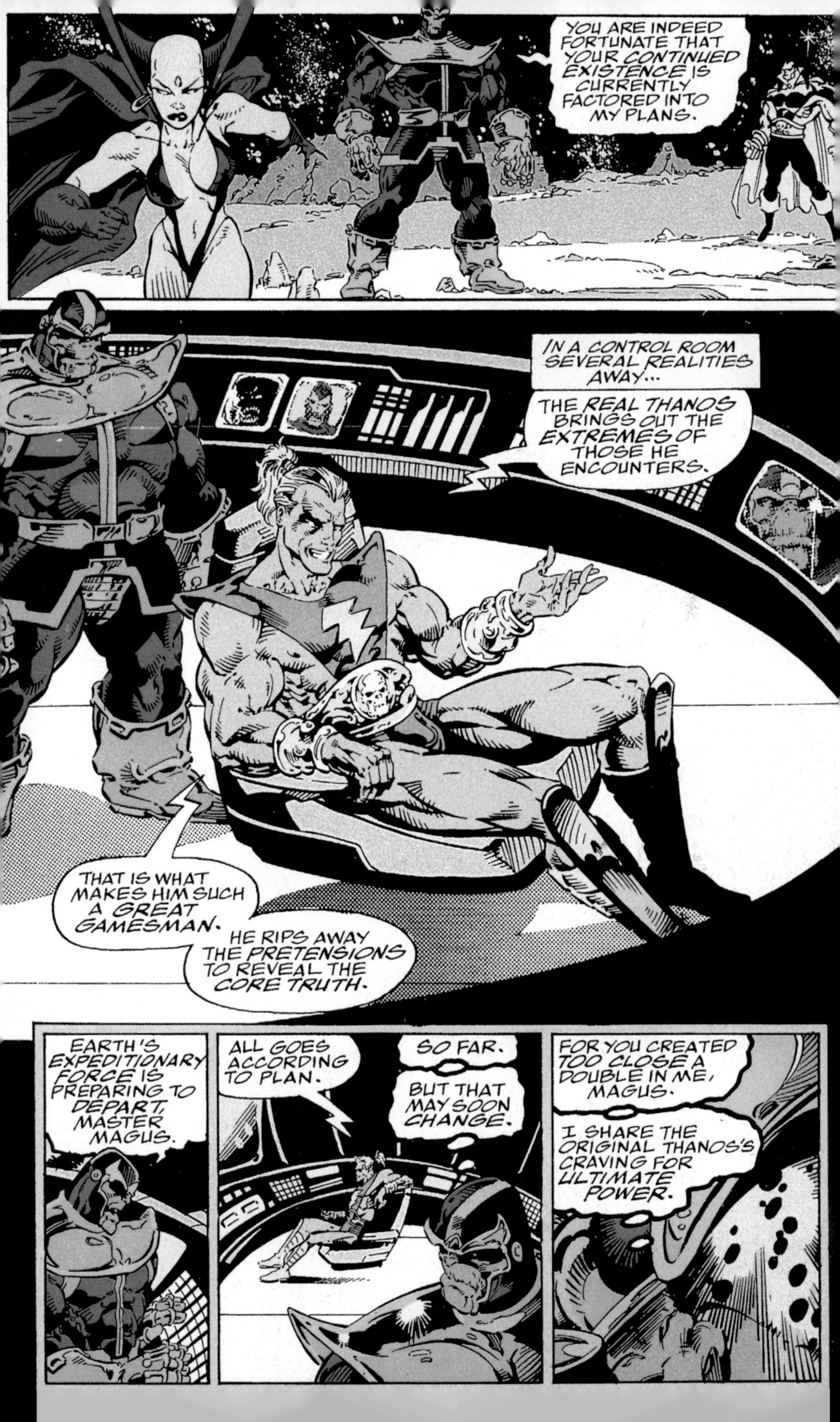
YOU ARE INDEED FORTUNATE THAT YOUR CONTINUED EXISTENCE IS CURRENTLY FACTORED INTO MY PLANS.
IN A CONTROL ROOM SEVERAL REALITIES AWAY...
THE REAL THANOS BRINGS OUT THE EXTREMES OF THOSE HE ENCOUNTERS.
THAT IS WHAT MAKES HIM SUCH A GREAT GAMESMAN.
HE RIPS AWAY THE PRETENSIONS TO REVEAL THE CORE TRUTH.
EARTH'S EXPEDITIONARY FORCE IS PREPARING TO DEPART, MASTER MAGUS.
ALL GOES ACCORDING TO PLAN.
SO FAR.
BUT THAT MAY SOON CHANGE.
FOR YOU CREATED TOO CLOSE A DOUBLE IN ME, MAGUS.
I SHARE THE ORIGINAL THANOS'S CRAVING FOR ULTIMATE POWER.

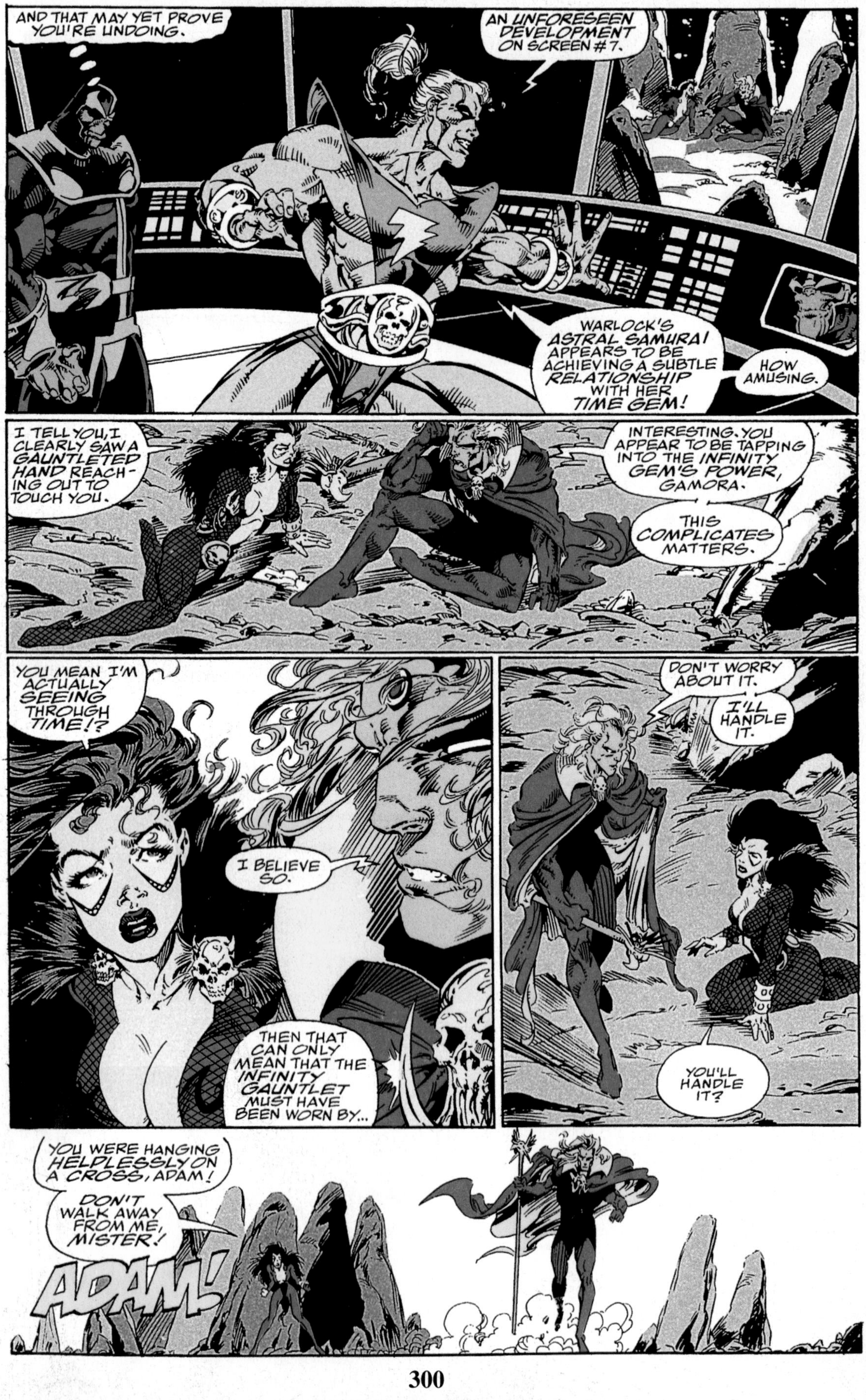
AND THAT MAY YET PROVE YOU'RE UNDOING.
AN UNFORESEEN DEVELOPMENT ON SCREEN #7.
WARLOCK'S ASTRAL SAMURAI APPEARS TO BE ACHIEVING A SUBTLE RELATIONSHIP WITH HER TIME GEM!
HOW AMUSING.
I TELL YOU, I CLEARLY SAW A GAUNTLETED HAND REACHING OUT TO TOUCH YOU.
INTERESTING. YOU APPEAR TO BE TAPPING INTO THE INFINITY GEM'S POWER, GAMORA.
THIS COMPLICATES MATTERS.
YOU MEAN I'M ACTUALLY SEEING THROUGH TIME!?
I BELIEVE SO.
THEN THAT CAN ONLY MEAN THAT THE INFINITY GAUNTLET MUST HAVE BEEN WORN BY...
DON'T WORRY ABOUT IT.
I'LL HANDLE IT.
YOU'LL HANDLE IT?
YOU WERE HANGING HELPLESSLY ON A CROSS, ADAM!
DON'T WALK AWAY FROM ME, MISTER!
ADAM!

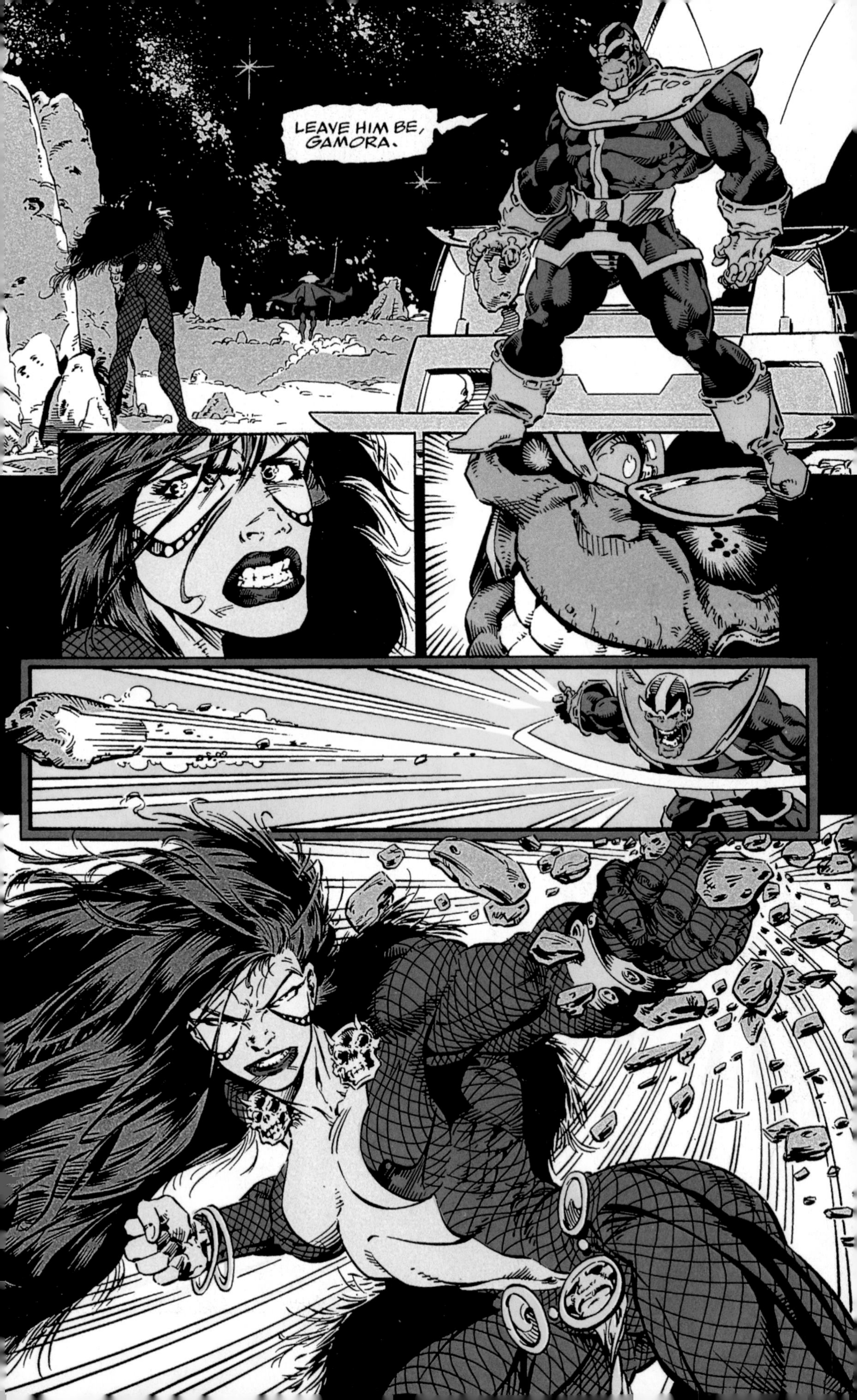
LEAVE HIM BE, GAMORA.

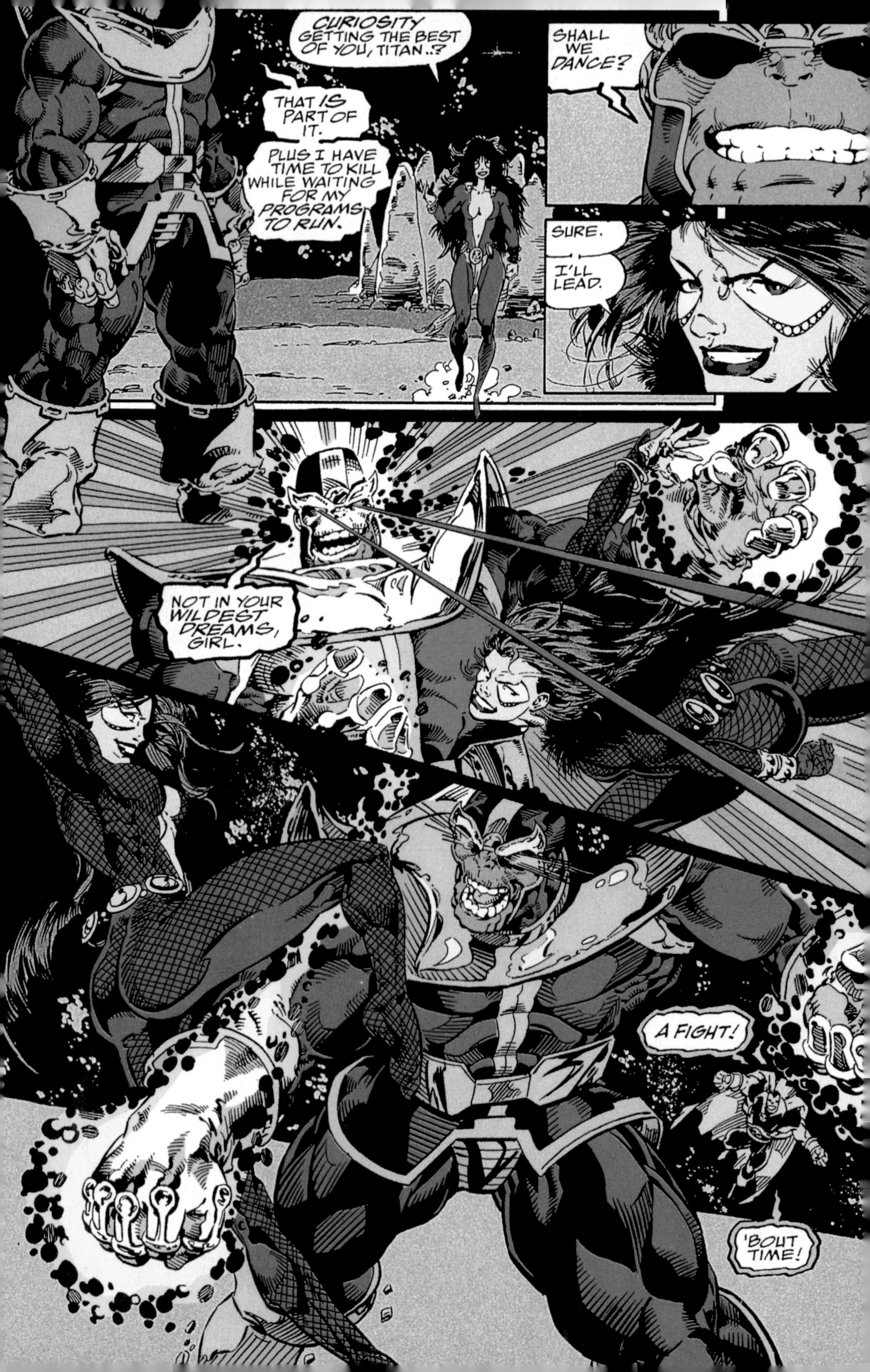
CURIOSITY GETTING THE BEST OF YOU, TITAN..?
THAT IS PART OF IT.
PLUS I HAVE TIME TO KILL WHILE WAITING FOR MY PROGRAMS TO RUN.
SHALL WE DANCE?
SURE.
I'LL LEAD.
NOT IN YOUR WILDEST DREAMS, GIRL.
A FIGHT!
'BOUT TIME!

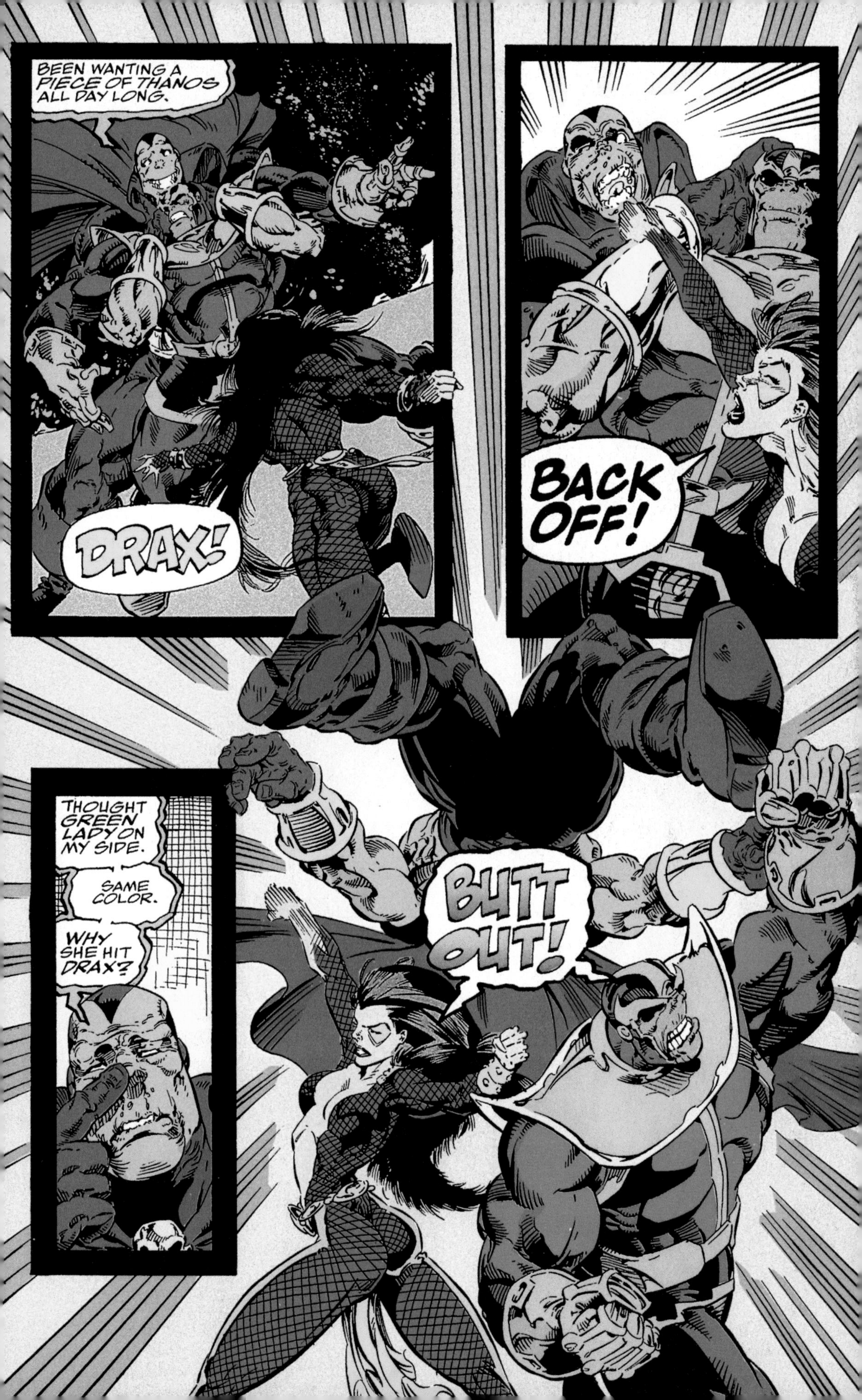
BEEN WANTING A PIECE OF THANOS ALL DAY LONG.
DRAX!
BACK OFF!
THOUGHT GREEN LADY ON MY SIDE.
SAME COLOR.
WHY SHE HIT DRAX?
BUTT OUT!

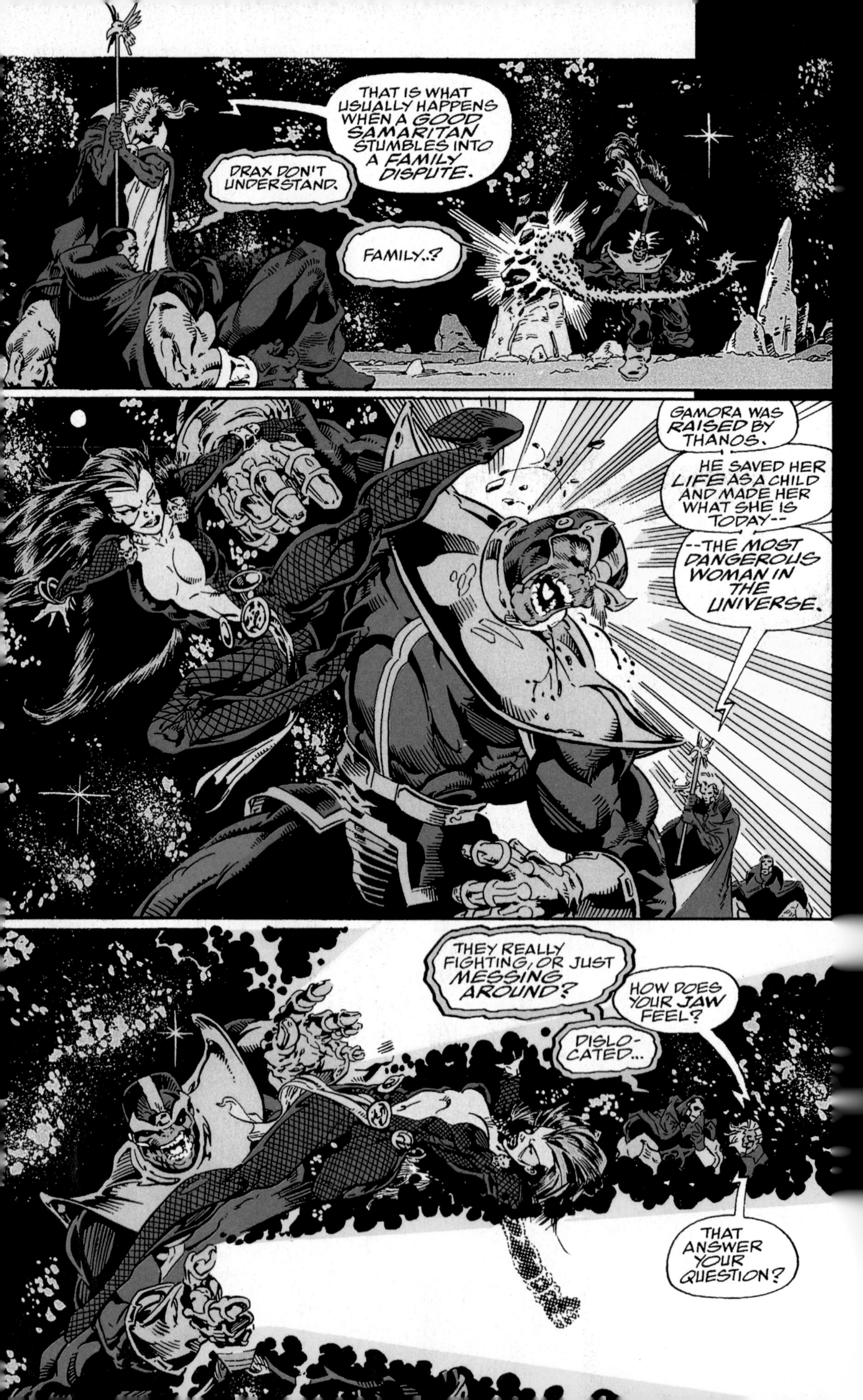
THAT IS WHAT USUALLY HAPPENS WHEN A GOOD SAMARITAN STUMBLES INTO A FAMILY DISPUTE.
DRAX DON'T UNDERSTAND.
FAMILY..?
GAMORA WAS RAISED BY THANOS.
HE SAVED HER LIFE AS A CHILD AND MADE HER WHAT SHE IS TODAY--
--THE MOST DANGEROUS WOMAN IN THE UNIVERSE.
THEY REALLY FIGHTING, OR JUST MESSING AROUND?
HOW DOES YOUR JAW FEEL?
DISLOCATED...
THAT ANSWER YOUR QUESTION?

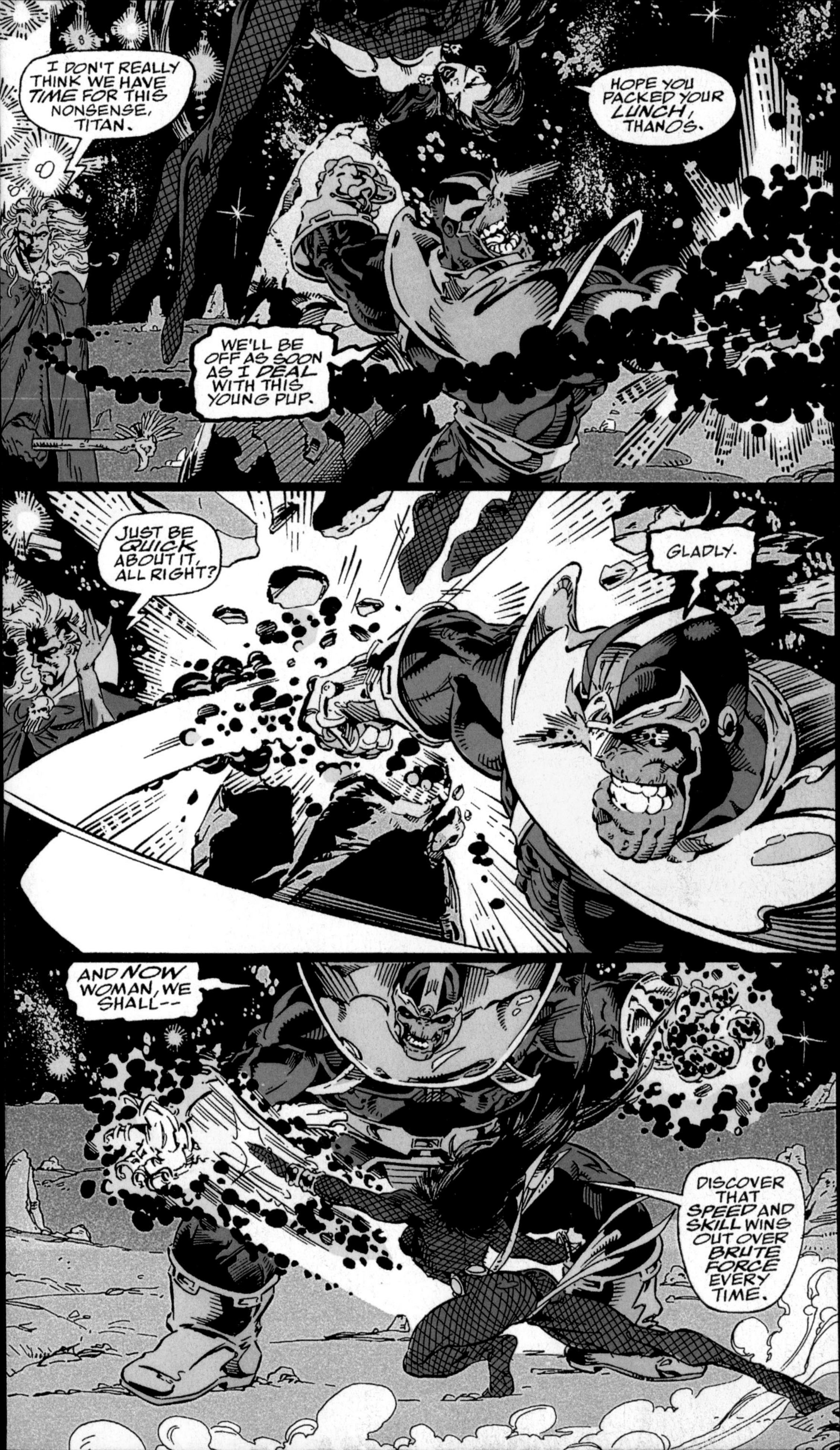
I DON'T REALLY THINK WE HAVE TIME FOR THIS NONSENSE, TITAN.
HOPE YOU PACKED YOUR LUNCH, THANOS.
WE'LL BE OFF AS SOON AS I DEAL WITH THIS YOUNG PUP.
JUST BE QUICK ABOUT IT, ALL RIGHT?
GLADLY.
AND NOW WOMAN, WE SHALL--
DISCOVER THAT SPEED AND SKILL WINS OUT OVER BRUTE FORCE EVERY TIME.

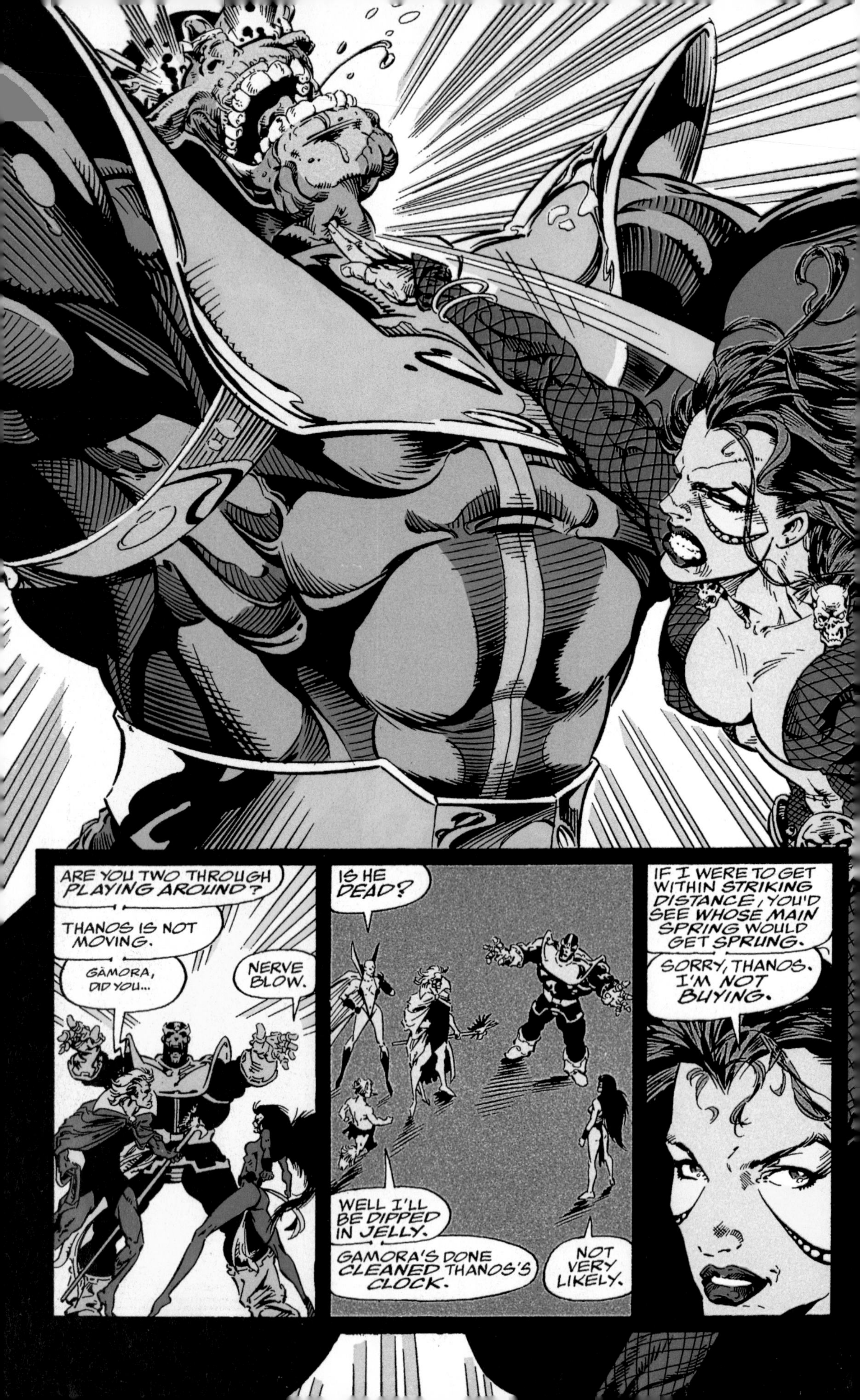
ARE YOU TWO THROUGH PLAYING AROUND?
THANOS IS NOT MOVING.
GAMORA, DID YOU...
NERVE BLOW.
IS HE DEAD?
WELL I'LL BE DIPPED IN JELLY.
GAMORA'S DONE CLEANED THANOS'S CLOCK.
NOT VERY LIKELY.
IF I WERE TO GET WITHIN STRIKING DISTANCE, YOU'D SEE WHOSE MAIN SPRING WOULD GET SPRUNG.
SORRY, THANOS. I'M NOT BUYING.

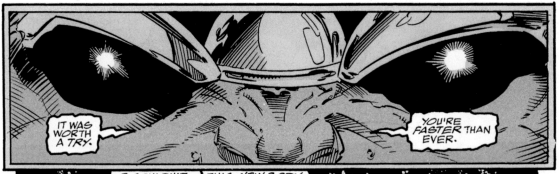

IT WAS WORTH A TRY.

YOU'RE FASTER THAN EVER.

I COULDN'T LAY A *GLOVE* ON YOU.

THIS *NEW BODY* ADAM FITTED ME WITH HELPS A *LOT.*

I SEE AND HEAR THESE TWO, BUT I STILL *DON'T BELIEVE* THEM.

THINK THIS IS BAD, YOU OUGHT TO SEE THEM PLAY *MONOPOLY.*

THAT *BLOW* WOULD'VE *KILLED* ANYONE OTHER THAN ME.

YOU SURE MADE IT *TOUGH* TO FIND AN OPENING.

WEIRD.

HANGING OUT WITH YOU, ADAM, I GET TO MEET THE *MOST INTERESTING* FOLKS.

BUT WHY ARE THEY ALWAYS TRYING TO *KILL* EACH OTHER?

POOR DIET? I DON'T KNOW.

DOUBT YOUR BUDDY THANOS MISSES MANY MEALS.

HE IS NO *"BUDDY"* OF MINE.

HOW ABOUT THE *MAGUS* THEN?

NOT IN THE *FRIEND* CATEGORY EITHER.

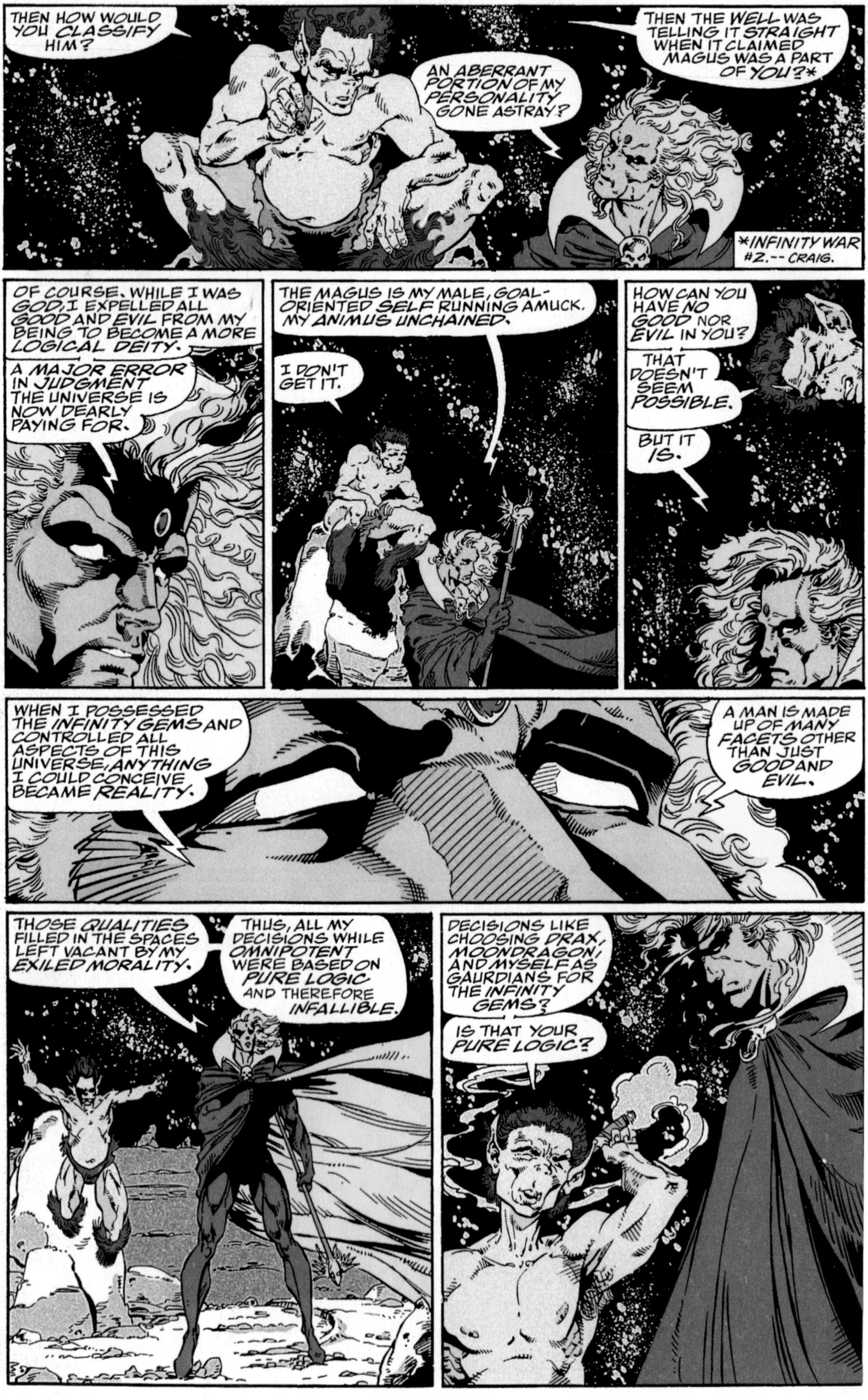

THEN HOW WOULD YOU CLASSIFY HIM?
AN ABERRANT PORTION OF MY PERSONALITY GONE ASTRAY?
THEN THE WELL WAS TELLING IT STRAIGHT WHEN IT CLAIMED MAGUS WAS A PART OF YOU?*
*INFINITY WAR #2.-- CRAIG.
OF COURSE. WHILE I WAS GOD, I EXPELLED ALL GOOD AND EVIL FROM MY BEING TO BECOME A MORE LOGICAL DEITY.
A MAJOR ERROR IN JUDGMENT THE UNIVERSE IS NOW DEARLY PAYING FOR.
THE MAGUS IS MY MALE, GOAL-ORIENTED SELF RUNNING AMUCK. MY ANIMUS UNCHAINED.
I DON'T GET IT.
HOW CAN YOU HAVE NO GOOD NOR EVIL IN YOU?
THAT DOESN'T SEEM POSSIBLE.
BUT IT IS.
WHEN I POSSESSED THE INFINITY GEMS AND CONTROLLED ALL ASPECTS OF THIS UNIVERSE, ANYTHING I COULD CONCEIVE BECAME REALITY.
A MAN IS MADE UP OF MANY FACETS OTHER THAN JUST GOOD AND EVIL.
THOSE QUALITIES FILLED IN THE SPACES LEFT VACANT BY MY EXILED MORALITY.
THUS, ALL MY DECISIONS WHILE OMNIPOTENT WERE BASED ON PURE LOGIC AND THEREFORE INFALLIBLE.
DECISIONS LIKE CHOOSING DRAX, MOONDRAGON, AND MYSELF AS GAURDIANS FOR THE INFINITY GEMS?
IS THAT YOUR PURE LOGIC?

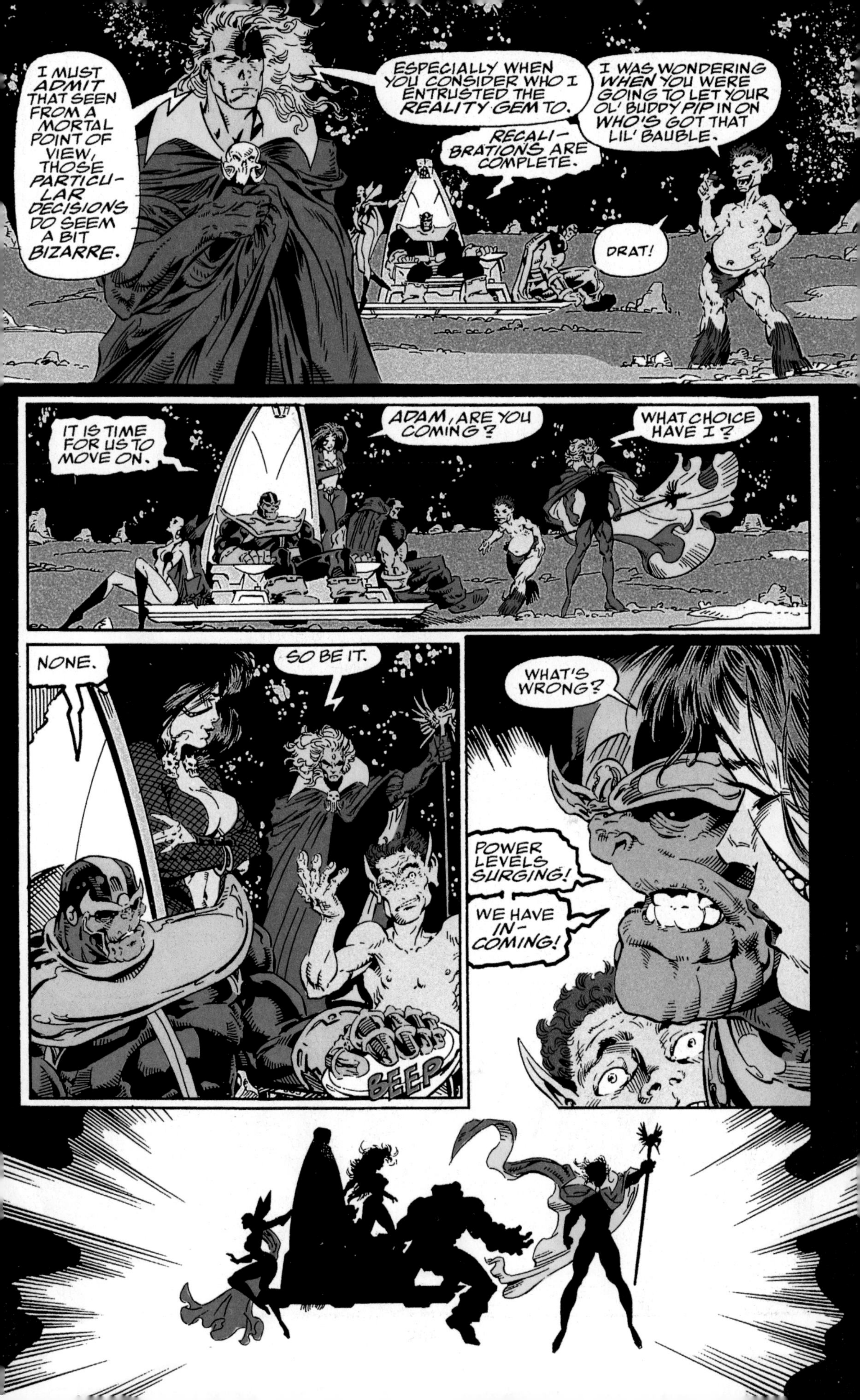
I MUST ADMIT THAT SEEN FROM A MORTAL POINT OF VIEW, THOSE PARTICULAR DECISIONS DO SEEM A BIT BIZARRE.
ESPECIALLY WHEN YOU CONSIDER WHO I ENTRUSTED THE REALITY GEM TO.
I WAS WONDERING WHEN YOU WERE GOING TO LET YOUR OL' BUDDY PIP IN ON WHO'S GOT THAT LIL' BAUBLE.
RECALIBRATIONS ARE COMPLETE.
DRAT!
IT IS TIME FOR US TO MOVE ON.
ADAM, ARE YOU COMING?
WHAT CHOICE HAVE I?
NONE.
SO BE IT.
BEEP
WHAT'S WRONG?
POWER LEVELS SURGING!
WE HAVE IN-COMING!

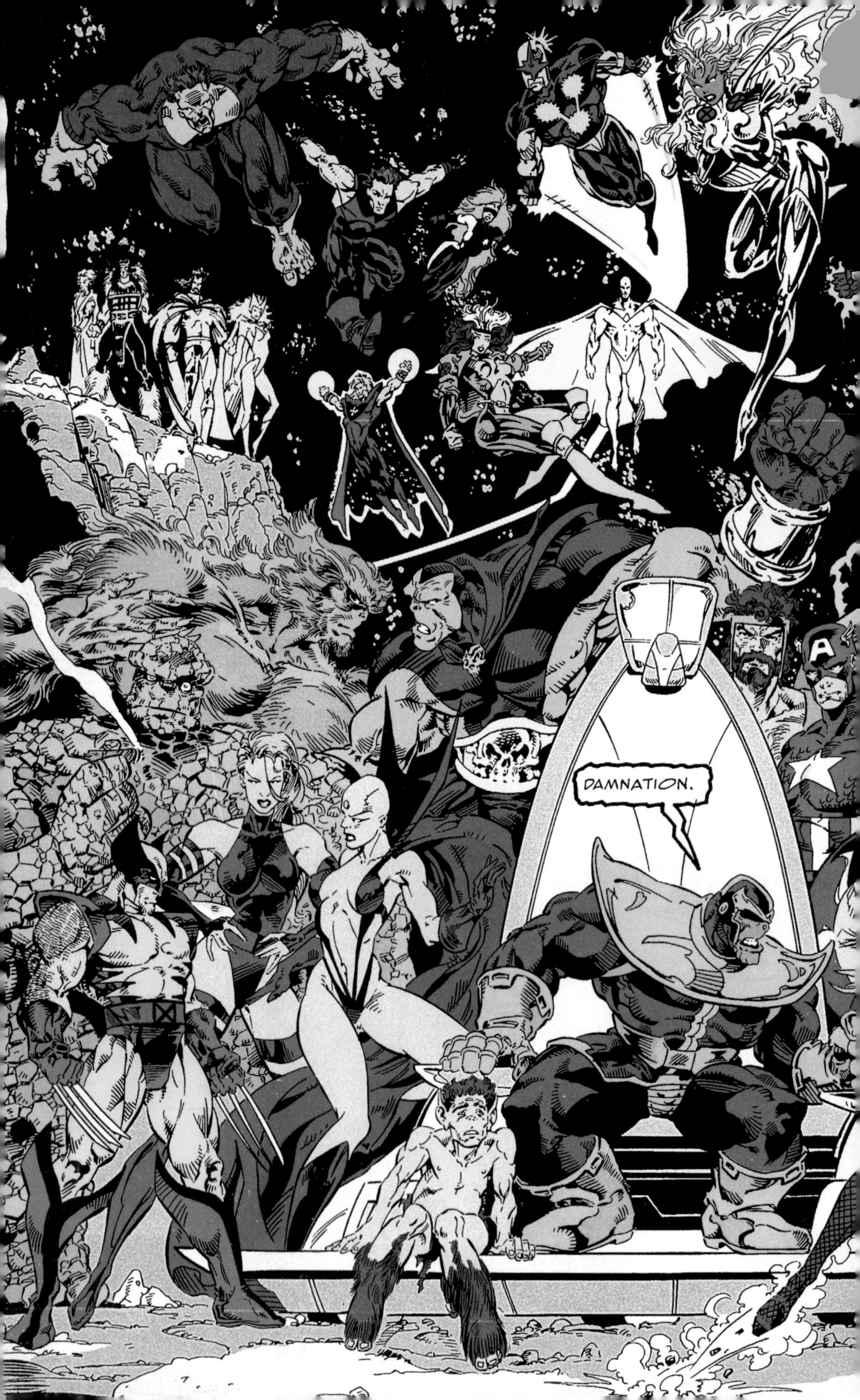
DAMNATION.

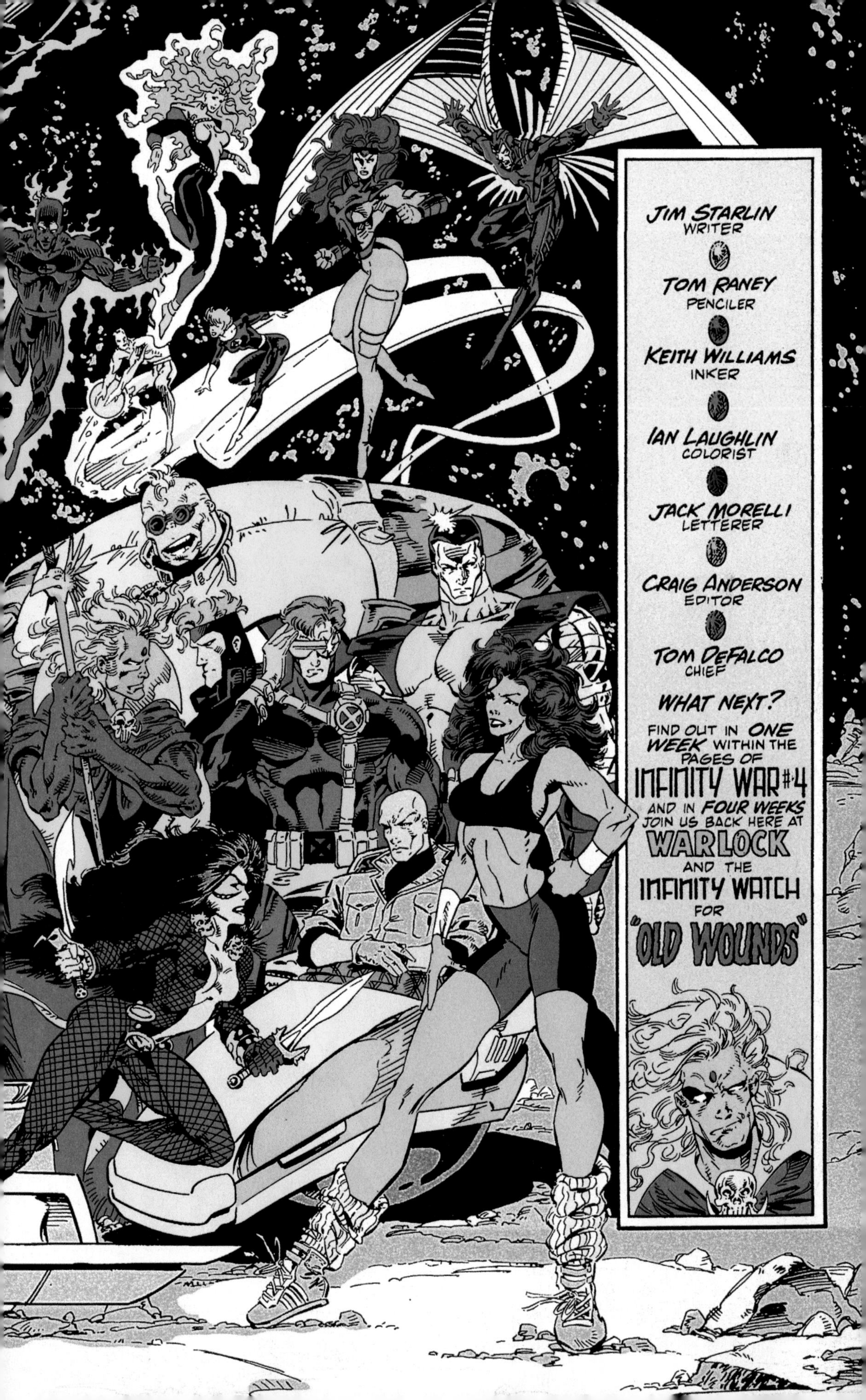
JIM STARLIN
WRITER
TOM RANEY
PENCILER
KEITH WILLIAMS
INKER
IAN LAUGHLIN
COLORIST
JACK MORELLI
LETTERER
CRAIG ANDERSON
EDITOR
TOM DEFALCO
CHIEF
WHAT NEXT?
FIND OUT IN ONE WEEK WITHIN THE PAGES OF
INFINITY WAR #4
AND IN FOUR WEEKS JOIN US BACK HERE AT
WARLOCK
AND THE
INFINITY WATCH
FOR
"OLD WOUNDS"

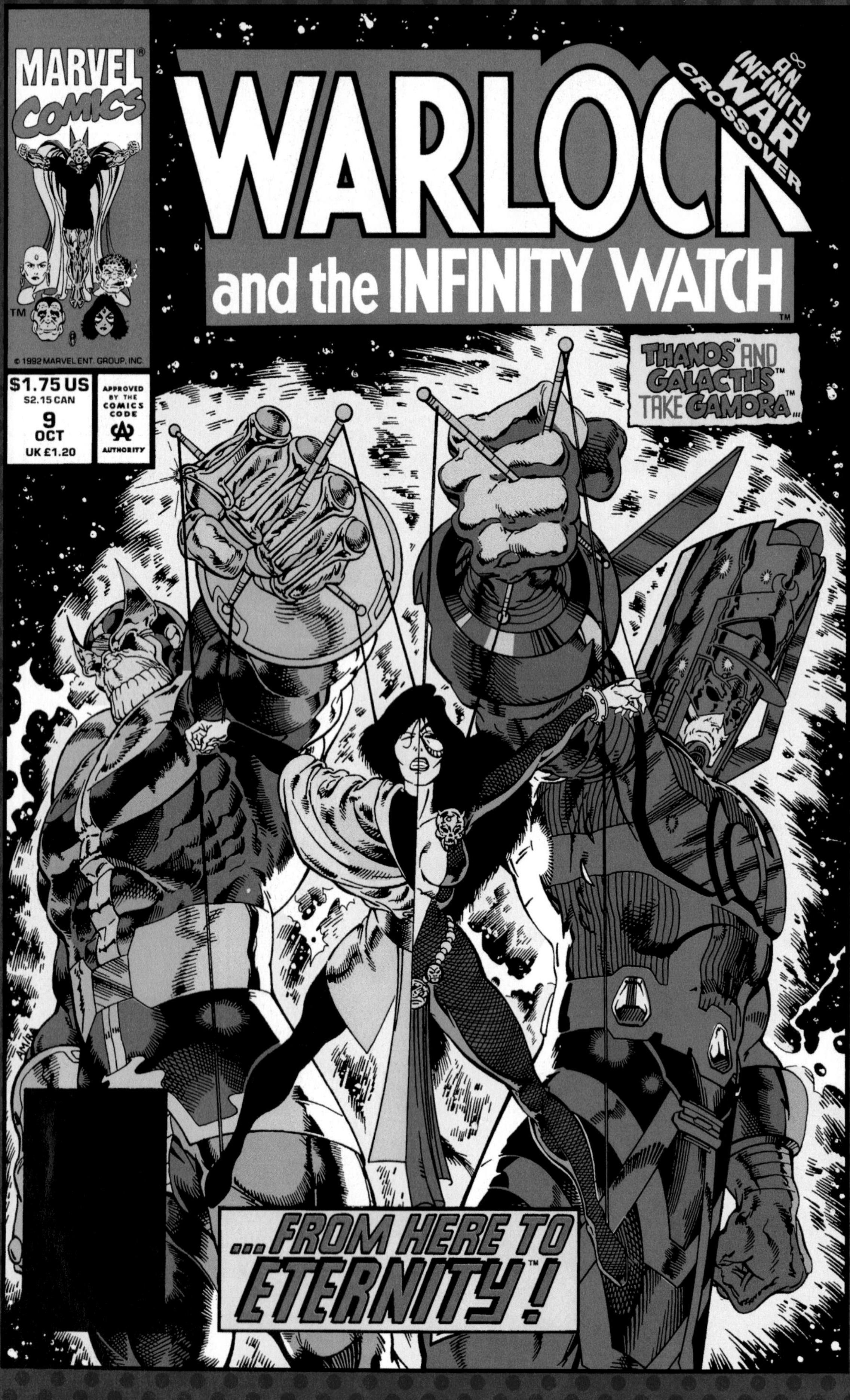
MARVEL® COMICS
WARLOCK and the INFINITY WATCH™
AN ∞ INFINITY WAR CROSSOVER
© 1992 MARVEL ENT. GROUP, INC.
$1.75 US
$2.15 CAN
9
OCT
UK £1.20
APPROVED BY THE COMICS CODE AUTHORITY
THANOS™ AND GALACTUS™ TAKE GAMORA™
...FROM HERE TO ETERNITY™!

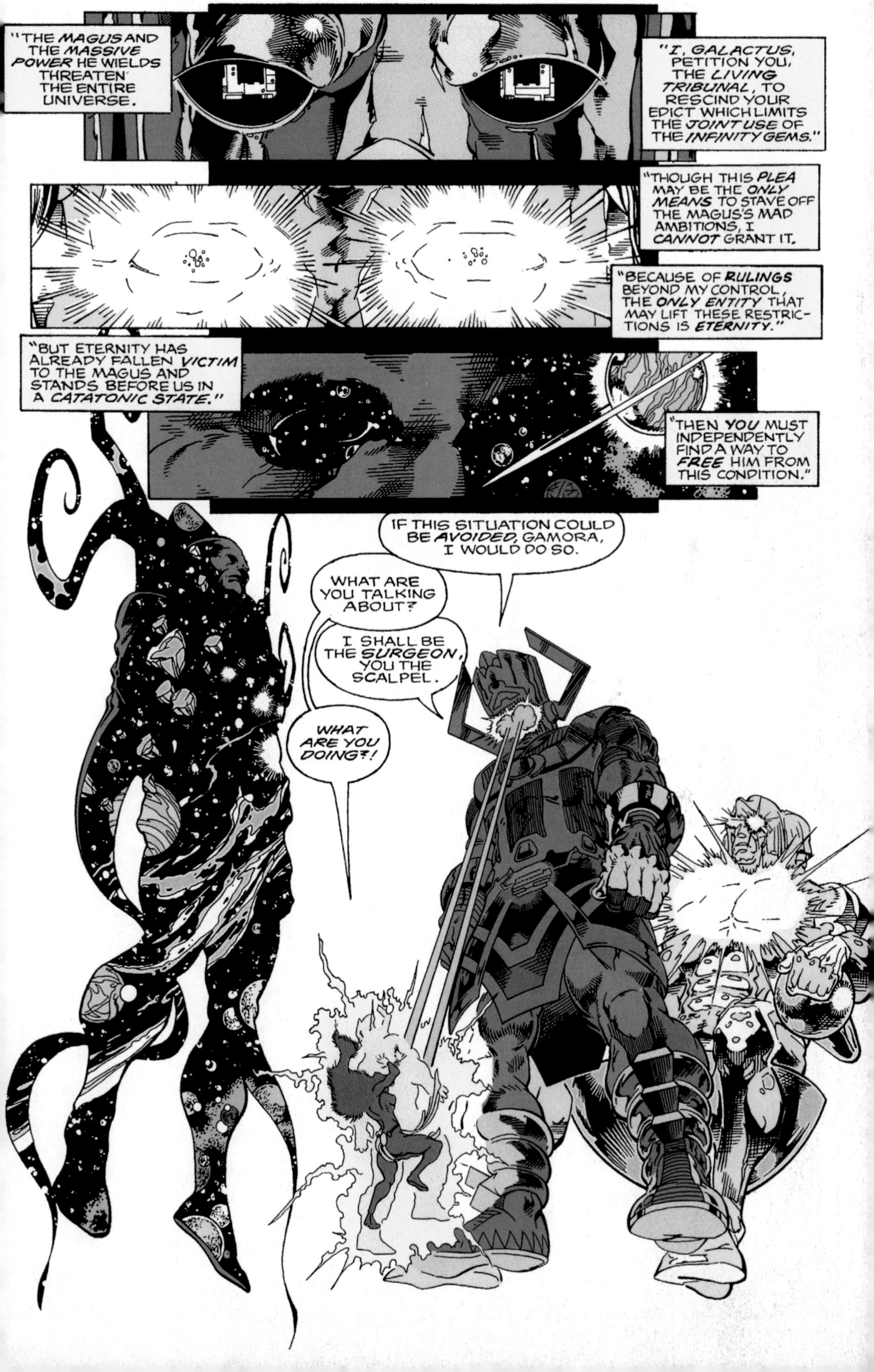
"THE MAGUS AND THE MASSIVE POWER HE WIELDS THREATEN THE ENTIRE UNIVERSE.
"I, GALACTUS, PETITION YOU, THE LIVING TRIBUNAL, TO RESCIND YOUR EDICT WHICH LIMITS THE JOINT USE OF THE INFINITY GEMS."
"THOUGH THIS PLEA MAY BE THE ONLY MEANS TO STAVE OFF THE MAGUS'S MAD AMBITIONS, I CANNOT GRANT IT.
"BECAUSE OF RULINGS BEYOND MY CONTROL, THE ONLY ENTITY THAT MAY LIFT THESE RESTRICTIONS IS ETERNITY."
"BUT ETERNITY HAS ALREADY FALLEN VICTIM TO THE MAGUS AND STANDS BEFORE US IN A CATATONIC STATE."
"THEN YOU MUST INDEPENDENTLY FIND A WAY TO FREE HIM FROM THIS CONDITION."
IF THIS SITUATION COULD BE AVOIDED, GAMORA, I WOULD DO SO.
WHAT ARE YOU TALKING ABOUT?
I SHALL BE THE SURGEON, YOU THE SCALPEL.
WHAT ARE YOU DOING?!

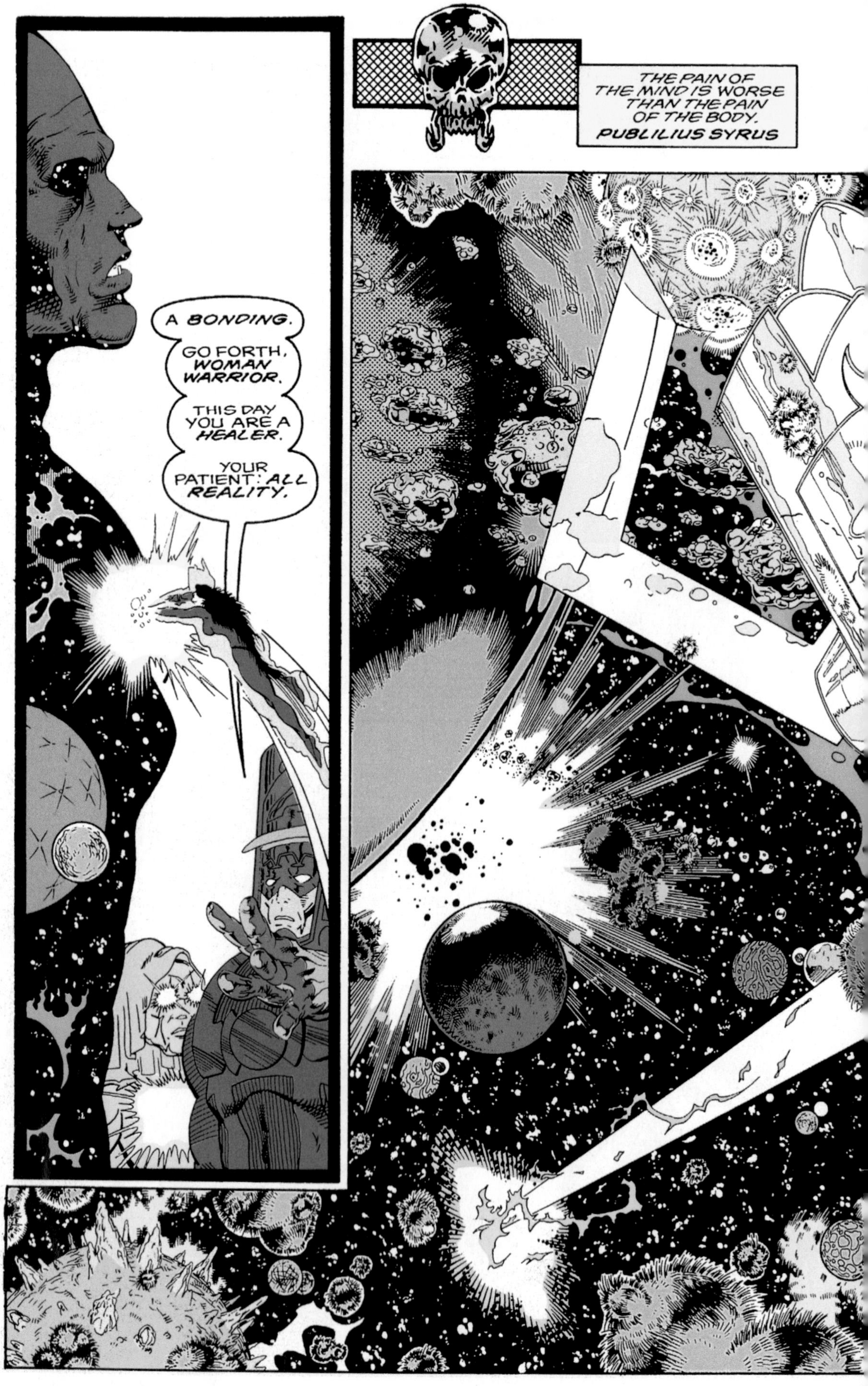
THE PAIN OF THE MIND IS WORSE THAN THE PAIN OF THE BODY.
PUBLILIUS SYRUS
A BONDING.
GO FORTH, WOMAN WARRIOR.
THIS DAY YOU ARE A HEALER.
YOUR PATIENT: ALL REALITY.

OLD WOUNDS

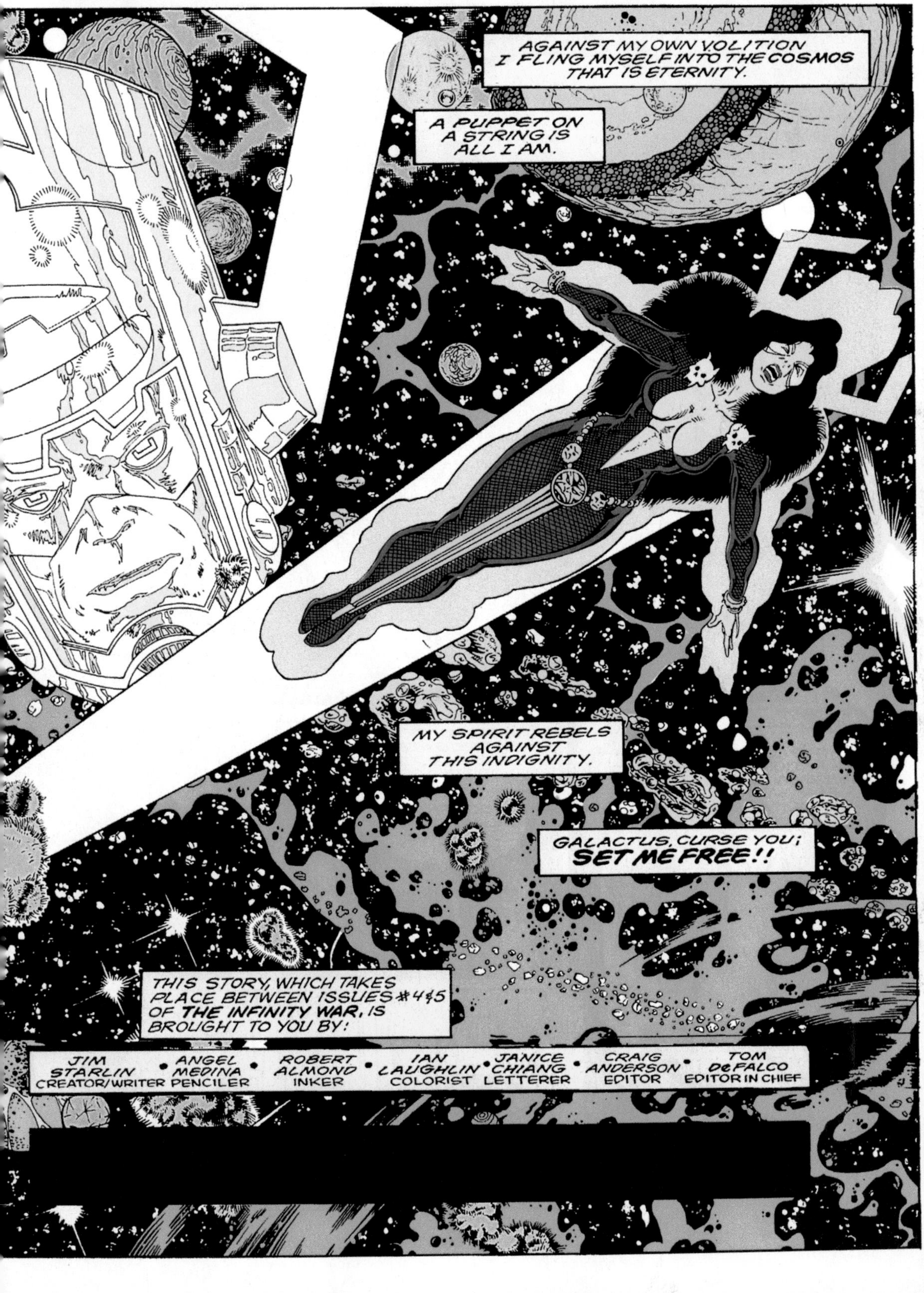

AGAINST MY OWN VOLITION I FLING MYSELF INTO THE COSMOS THAT IS ETERNITY.
A PUPPET ON A STRING IS ALL I AM.
MY SPIRIT REBELS AGAINST THIS INDIGNITY.
GALACTUS, CURSE YOU; **SET ME FREE!!**
THIS STORY, WHICH TAKES PLACE BETWEEN ISSUES #4&5 OF **THE INFINITY WAR**, IS BROUGHT TO YOU BY:
JIM STARLIN CREATOR/WRITER • ANGEL MEDINA PENCILER • ROBERT ALMOND INKER • IAN LAUGHLIN COLORIST • JANICE CHIANG LETTERER • CRAIG ANDERSON EDITOR • TOM DeFALCO EDITOR IN CHIEF
[redacted]

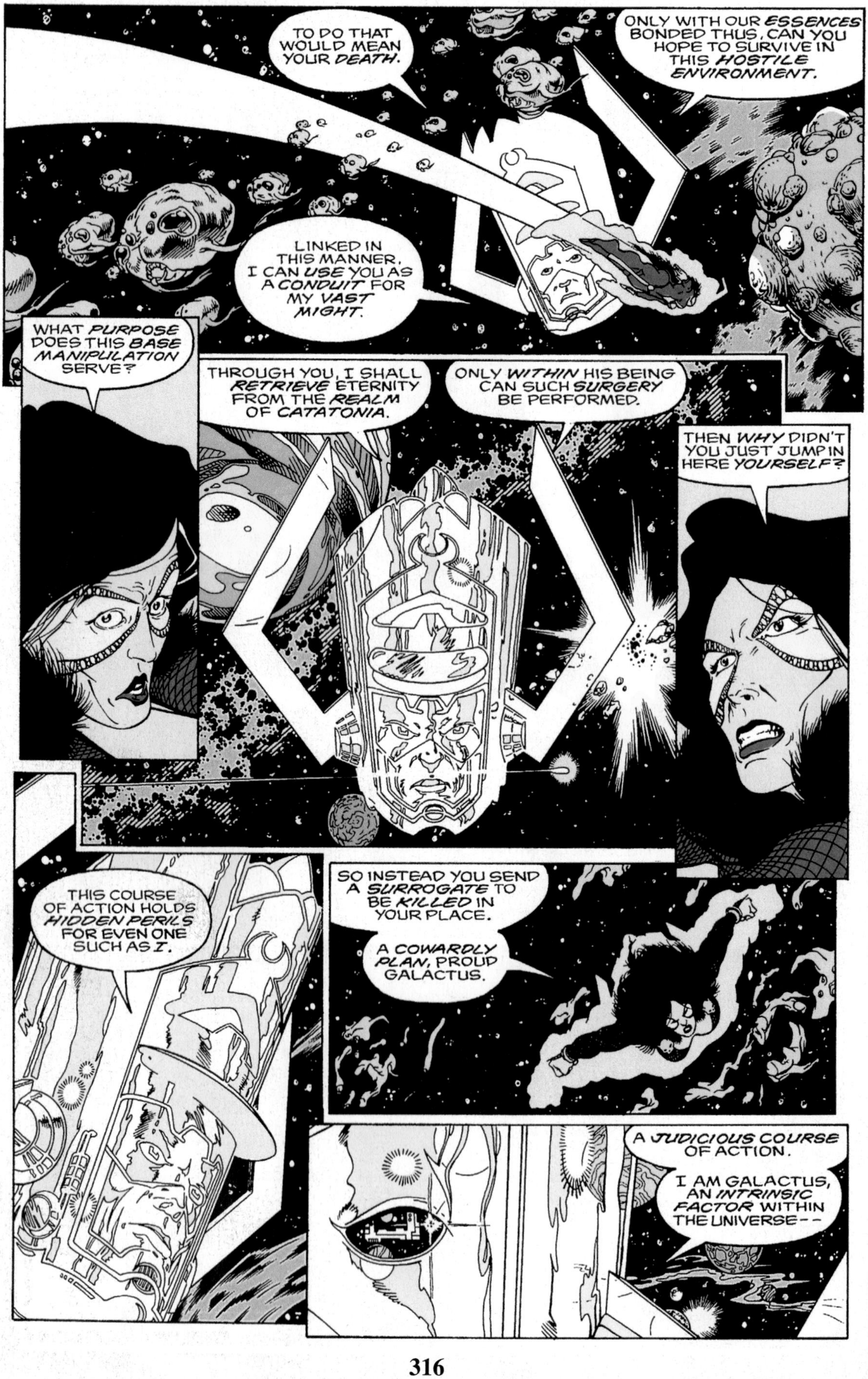
TO DO THAT WOULD MEAN YOUR DEATH.
ONLY WITH OUR ESSENCES BONDED THUS, CAN YOU HOPE TO SURVIVE IN THIS HOSTILE ENVIRONMENT.
LINKED IN THIS MANNER, I CAN USE YOU AS A CONDUIT FOR MY VAST MIGHT.
WHAT PURPOSE DOES THIS BASE MANIPULATION SERVE?
THROUGH YOU, I SHALL RETRIEVE ETERNITY FROM THE REALM OF CATATONIA.
ONLY WITHIN HIS BEING CAN SUCH SURGERY BE PERFORMED.
THEN WHY DIDN'T YOU JUST JUMP IN HERE YOURSELF?
THIS COURSE OF ACTION HOLDS HIDDEN PERILS FOR EVEN ONE SUCH AS I.
SO INSTEAD YOU SEND A SURROGATE TO BE KILLED IN YOUR PLACE.
A COWARDLY PLAN, PROUD GALACTUS.
A JUDICIOUS COURSE OF ACTION.
I AM GALACTUS, AN INTRINSIC FACTOR WITHIN THE UNIVERSE--

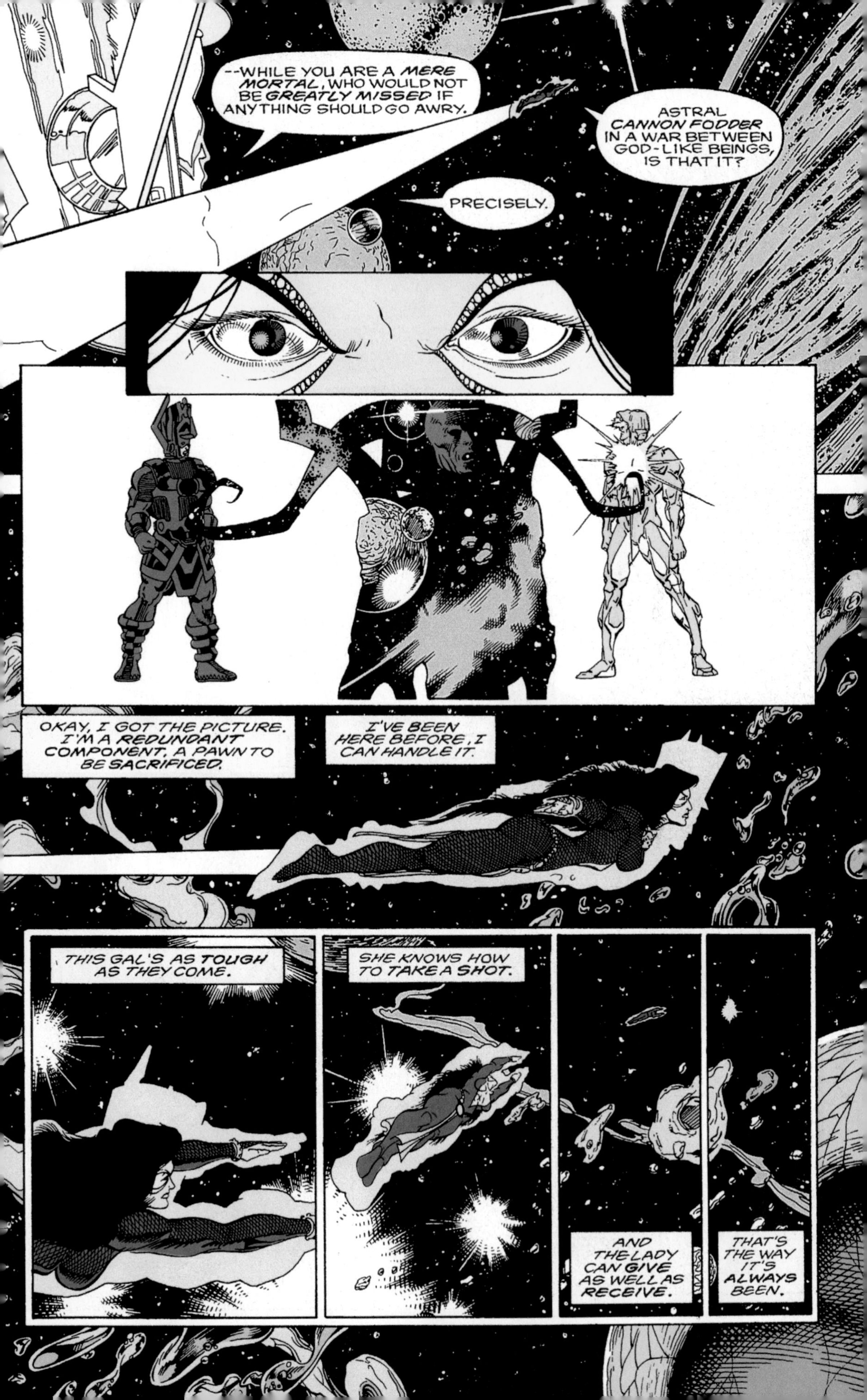
--WHILE YOU ARE A MERE MORTAL, WHO WOULD NOT BE GREATLY MISSED IF ANYTHING SHOULD GO AWRY.
ASTRAL CANNON FODDER IN A WAR BETWEEN GOD-LIKE BEINGS, IS THAT IT?
PRECISELY.
OKAY, I GOT THE PICTURE. I'M A REDUNDANT COMPONENT, A PAWN TO BE SACRIFICED.
I'VE BEEN HERE BEFORE, I CAN HANDLE IT.
THIS GAL'S AS TOUGH AS THEY COME.
SHE KNOWS HOW TO TAKE A SHOT.
AND THE LADY CAN GIVE AS WELL AS RECEIVE.
THAT'S THE WAY IT'S ALWAYS BEEN.

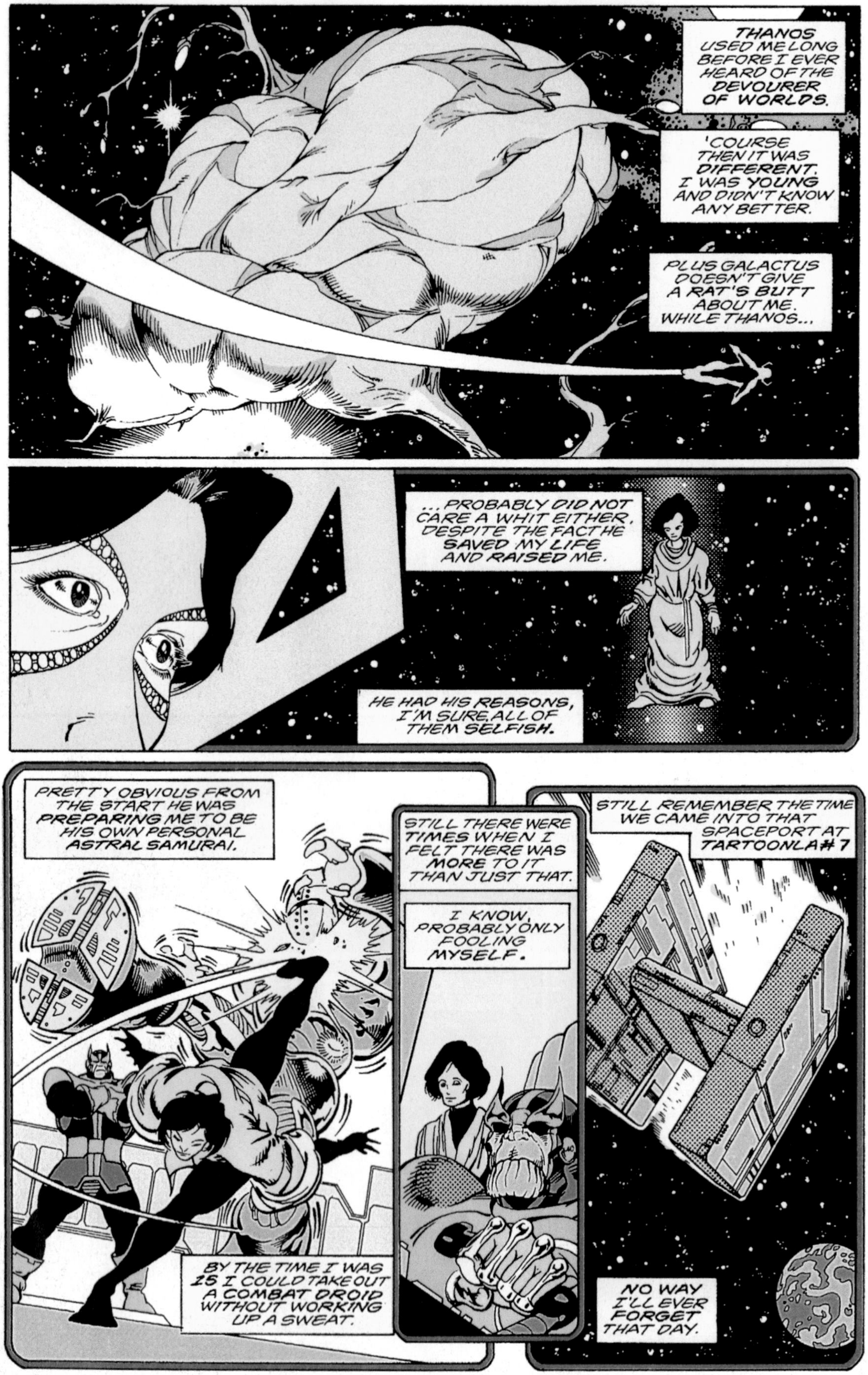
THANOS USED ME LONG BEFORE I EVER HEARD OF THE DEVOURER OF WORLDS.
'COURSE THEN IT WAS DIFFERENT. I WAS YOUNG AND DIDN'T KNOW ANY BETTER.
PLUS GALACTUS DOESN'T GIVE A RAT'S BUTT ABOUT ME. WHILE THANOS...
...PROBABLY DID NOT CARE A WHIT EITHER, DESPITE THE FACT HE SAVED MY LIFE AND RAISED ME.
HE HAD HIS REASONS, I'M SURE. ALL OF THEM SELFISH.
PRETTY OBVIOUS FROM THE START HE WAS PREPARING ME TO BE HIS OWN PERSONAL ASTRAL SAMURAI.
BY THE TIME I WAS 15 I COULD TAKE OUT A COMBAT DROID WITHOUT WORKING UP A SWEAT.
STILL THERE WERE TIMES WHEN I FELT THERE WAS MORE TO IT THAN JUST THAT.
I KNOW, PROBABLY ONLY FOOLING MYSELF.
STILL REMEMBER THE TIME WE CAME INTO THAT SPACEPORT AT TARTOONLA #7
NO WAY I'LL EVER FORGET THAT DAY.

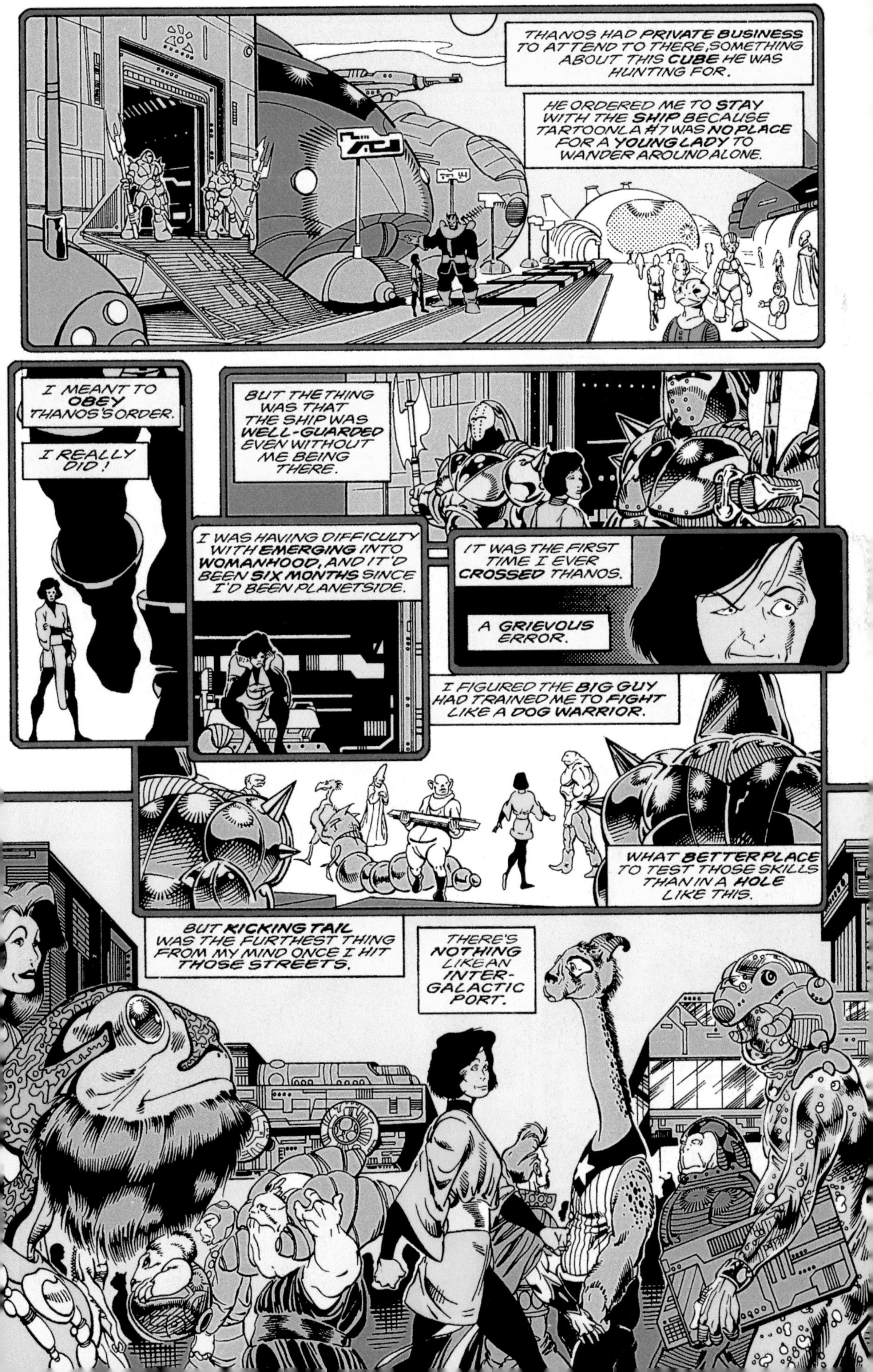
THANOS HAD PRIVATE BUSINESS TO ATTEND TO THERE, SOMETHING ABOUT THIS CUBE HE WAS HUNTING FOR.
HE ORDERED ME TO STAY WITH THE SHIP BECAUSE TARTOONLA #7 WAS NO PLACE FOR A YOUNG LADY TO WANDER AROUND ALONE.
I MEANT TO OBEY THANOS'S ORDER.
I REALLY DID!
BUT THE THING WAS THAT THE SHIP WAS WELL-GUARDED EVEN WITHOUT ME BEING THERE.
I WAS HAVING DIFFICULTY WITH EMERGING INTO WOMANHOOD, AND IT'D BEEN SIX MONTHS SINCE I'D BEEN PLANETSIDE.
IT WAS THE FIRST TIME I EVER CROSSED THANOS.
A GRIEVOUS ERROR.
I FIGURED THE BIG GUY HAD TRAINED ME TO FIGHT LIKE A DOG WARRIOR.
WHAT BETTER PLACE TO TEST THOSE SKILLS THAN IN A HOLE LIKE THIS.
BUT KICKING TAIL WAS THE FURTHEST THING FROM MY MIND ONCE I HIT THOSE STREETS.
THERE'S NOTHING LIKE AN INTER-GALACTIC PORT.

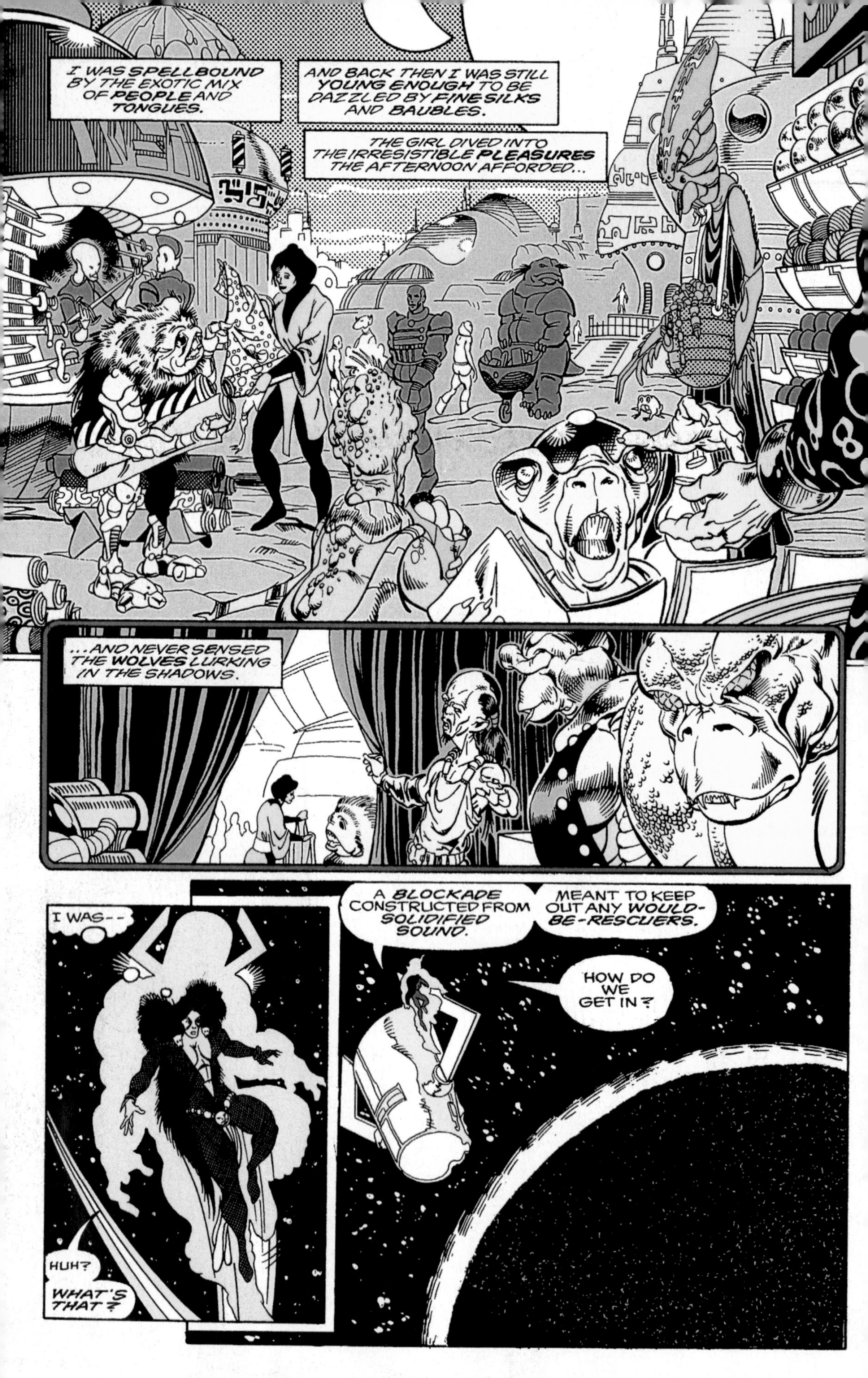
I WAS SPELLBOUND BY THE EXOTIC MIX OF PEOPLE AND TONGUES.
AND BACK THEN I WAS STILL YOUNG ENOUGH TO BE DAZZLED BY FINE SILKS AND BAUBLES.
THE GIRL DIVED INTO THE IRRESISTIBLE PLEASURES THE AFTERNOON AFFORDED...
...AND NEVER SENSED THE WOLVES LURKING IN THE SHADOWS.
I WAS--
HUH?
WHAT'S THAT?
A BLOCKADE CONSTRUCTED FROM SOLIDIFIED SOUND.
MEANT TO KEEP OUT ANY WOULD-BE-RESCUERS.
HOW DO WE GET IN?

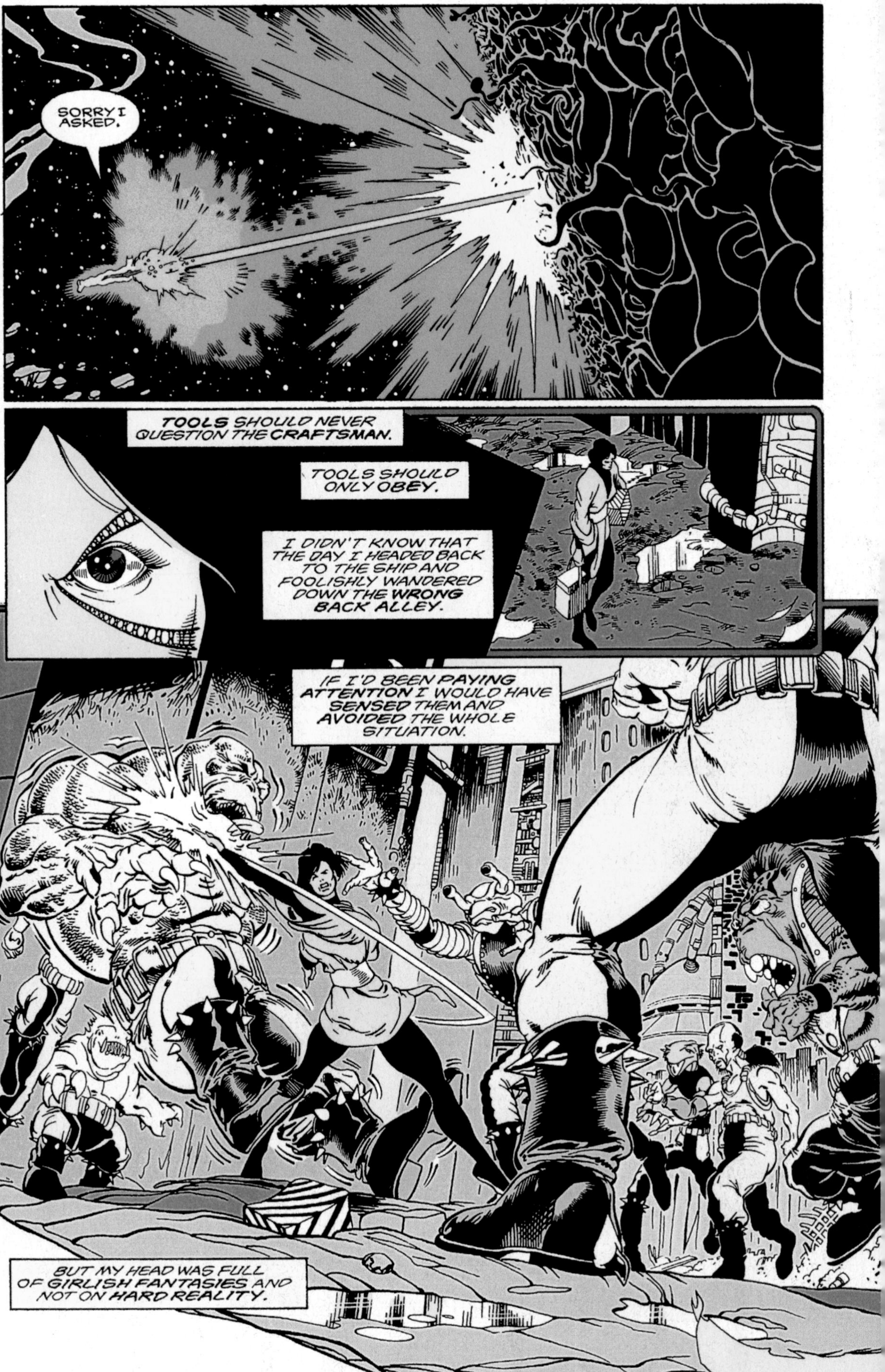
SORRY I ASKED.
TOOLS SHOULD NEVER QUESTION THE CRAFTSMAN.
TOOLS SHOULD ONLY OBEY.
I DIDN'T KNOW THAT THE DAY I HEADED BACK TO THE SHIP AND FOOLISHLY WANDERED DOWN THE WRONG BACK ALLEY.
IF I'D BEEN PAYING ATTENTION I WOULD HAVE SENSED THEM AND AVOIDED THE WHOLE SITUATION.
BUT MY HEAD WAS FULL OF GIRLISH FANTASIES AND NOT ON HARD REALITY.

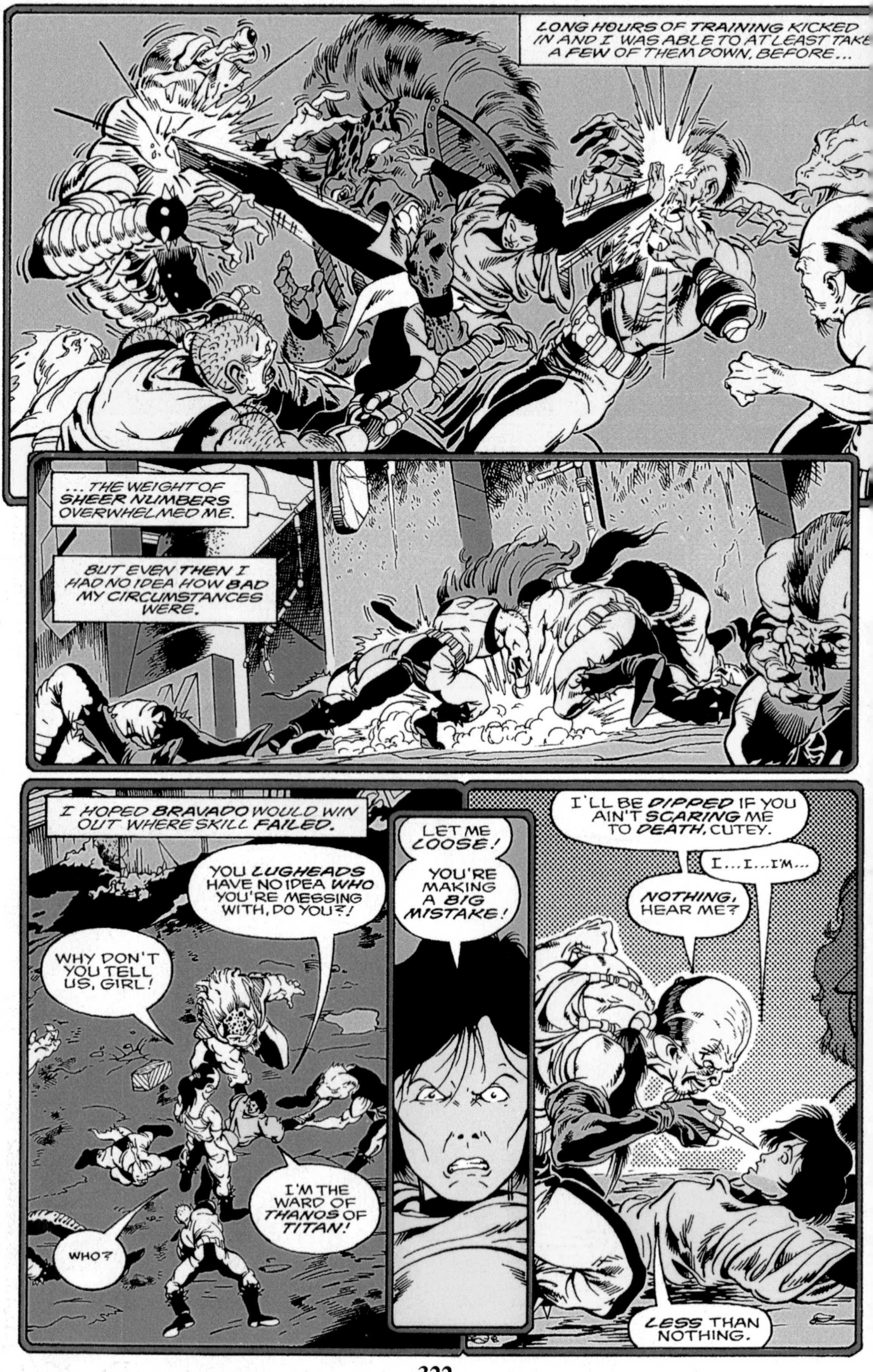

LONG HOURS OF TRAINING KICKED IN AND I WAS ABLE TO AT LEAST TAKE A FEW OF THEM DOWN, BEFORE...
...THE WEIGHT OF SHEER NUMBERS OVERWHELMED ME.
BUT EVEN THEN I HAD NO IDEA HOW BAD MY CIRCUMSTANCES WERE.
I HOPED BRAVADO WOULD WIN OUT WHERE SKILL FAILED.
YOU LUGHEADS HAVE NO IDEA WHO YOU'RE MESSING WITH, DO YOU?!
WHY DON'T YOU TELL US, GIRL!
I'M THE WARD OF THANOS OF TITAN!
WHO?
LET ME LOOSE!
YOU'RE MAKING A BIG MISTAKE!
I'LL BE DIPPED IF YOU AIN'T SCARING ME TO DEATH, CUTEY.
I...I...I'M...
NOTHING, HEAR ME?
LESS THAN NOTHING.

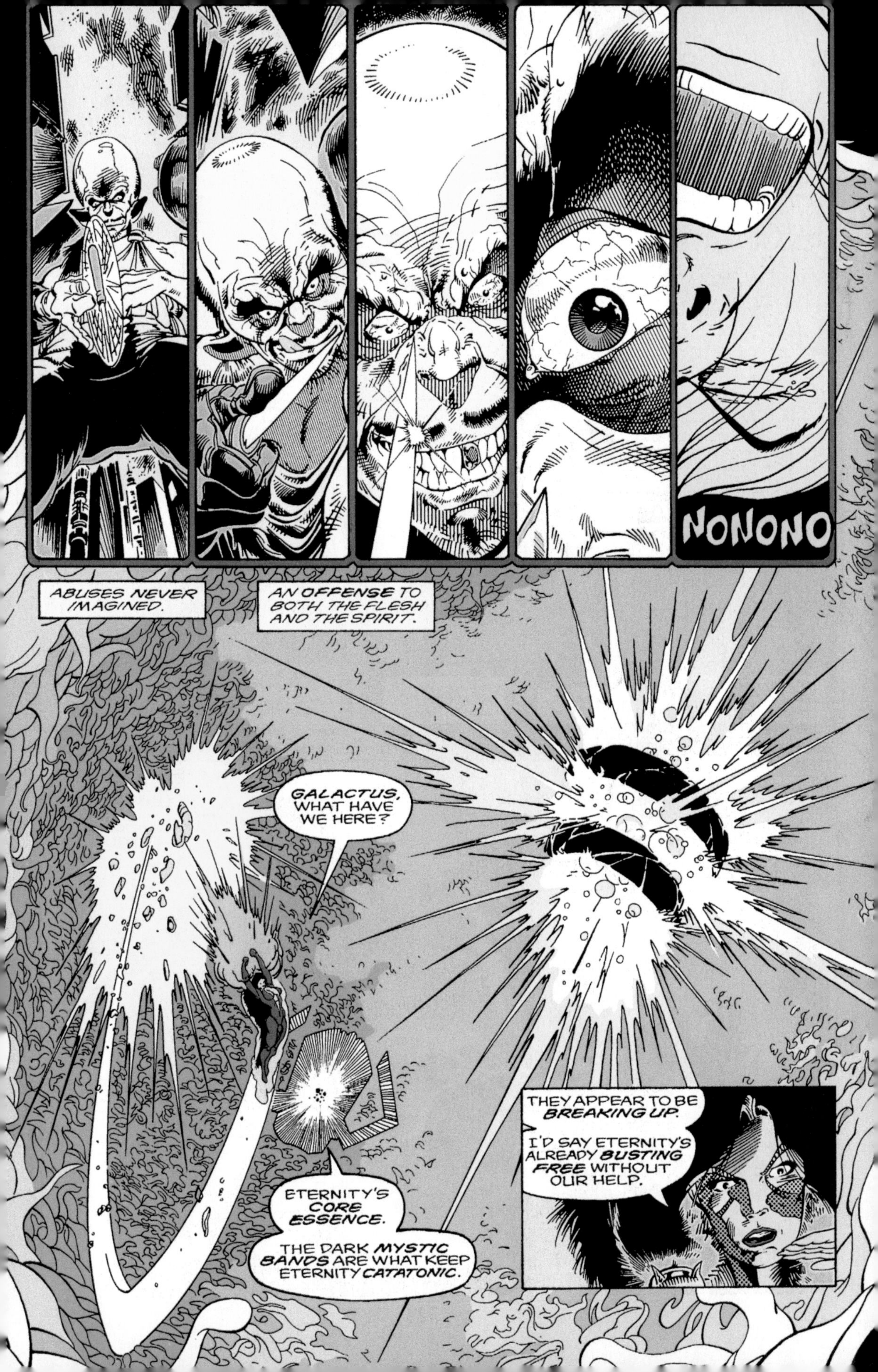
NONONO
ABUSES NEVER IMAGINED.
AN OFFENSE TO BOTH THE FLESH AND THE SPIRIT.
GALACTUS, WHAT HAVE WE HERE?
ETERNITY'S CORE ESSENCE.
THE DARK MYSTIC BANDS ARE WHAT KEEP ETERNITY CATATONIC.
THEY APPEAR TO BE BREAKING UP.
I'D SAY ETERNITY'S ALREADY BUSTING FREE WITHOUT OUR HELP.

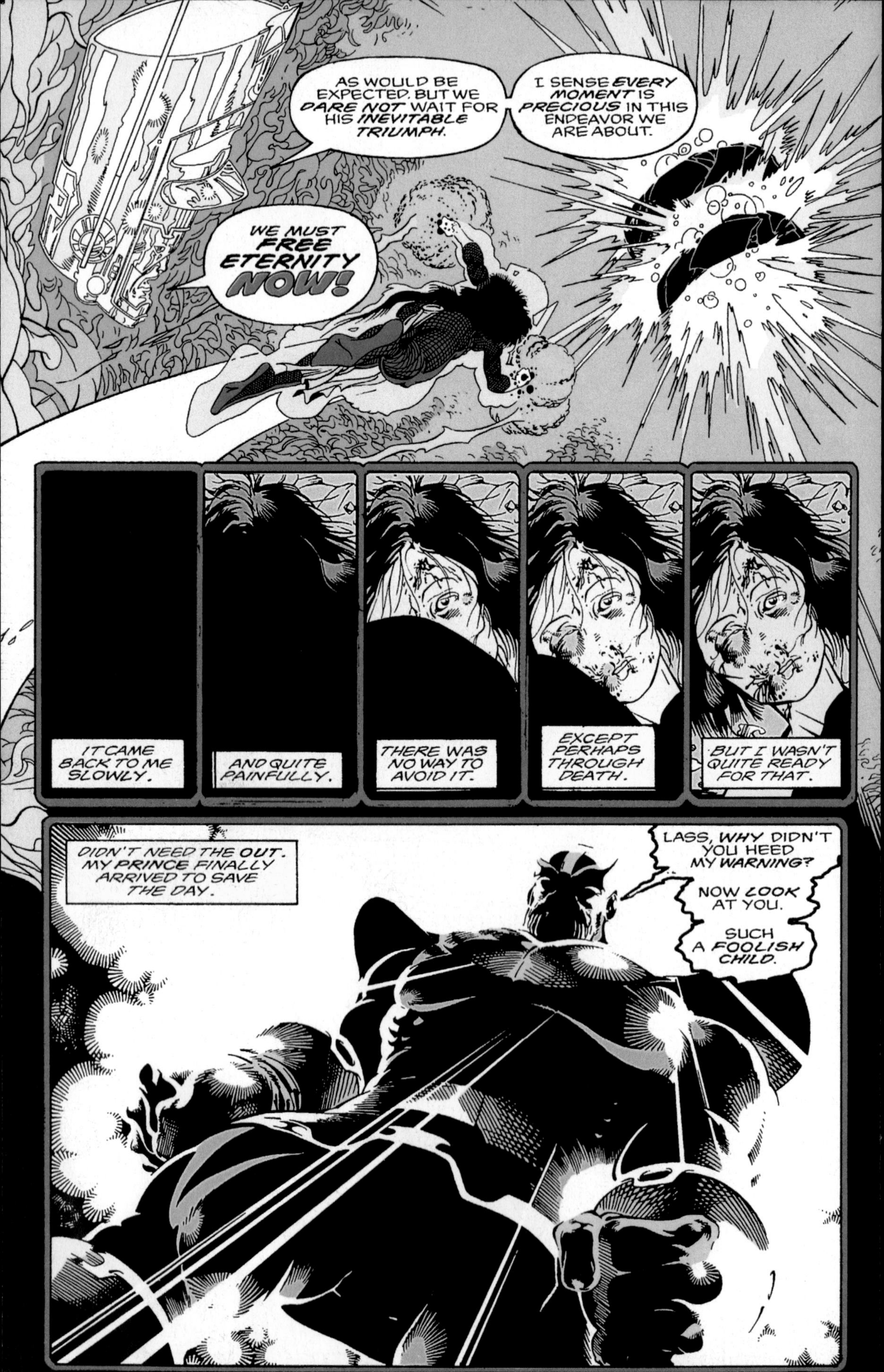
AS WOULD BE EXPECTED. BUT WE DARE NOT WAIT FOR HIS INEVITABLE TRIUMPH.
I SENSE EVERY MOMENT IS PRECIOUS IN THIS ENDEAVOR WE ARE ABOUT.
WE MUST FREE ETERNITY NOW!
IT CAME BACK TO ME SLOWLY.
AND QUITE PAINFULLY.
THERE WAS NO WAY TO AVOID IT.
EXCEPT PERHAPS THROUGH DEATH.
BUT I WASN'T QUITE READY FOR THAT.
DIDN'T NEED THE OUT. MY PRINCE FINALLY ARRIVED TO SAVE THE DAY.
LASS, WHY DIDN'T YOU HEED MY WARNING?
NOW LOOK AT YOU.
SUCH A FOOLISH CHILD.

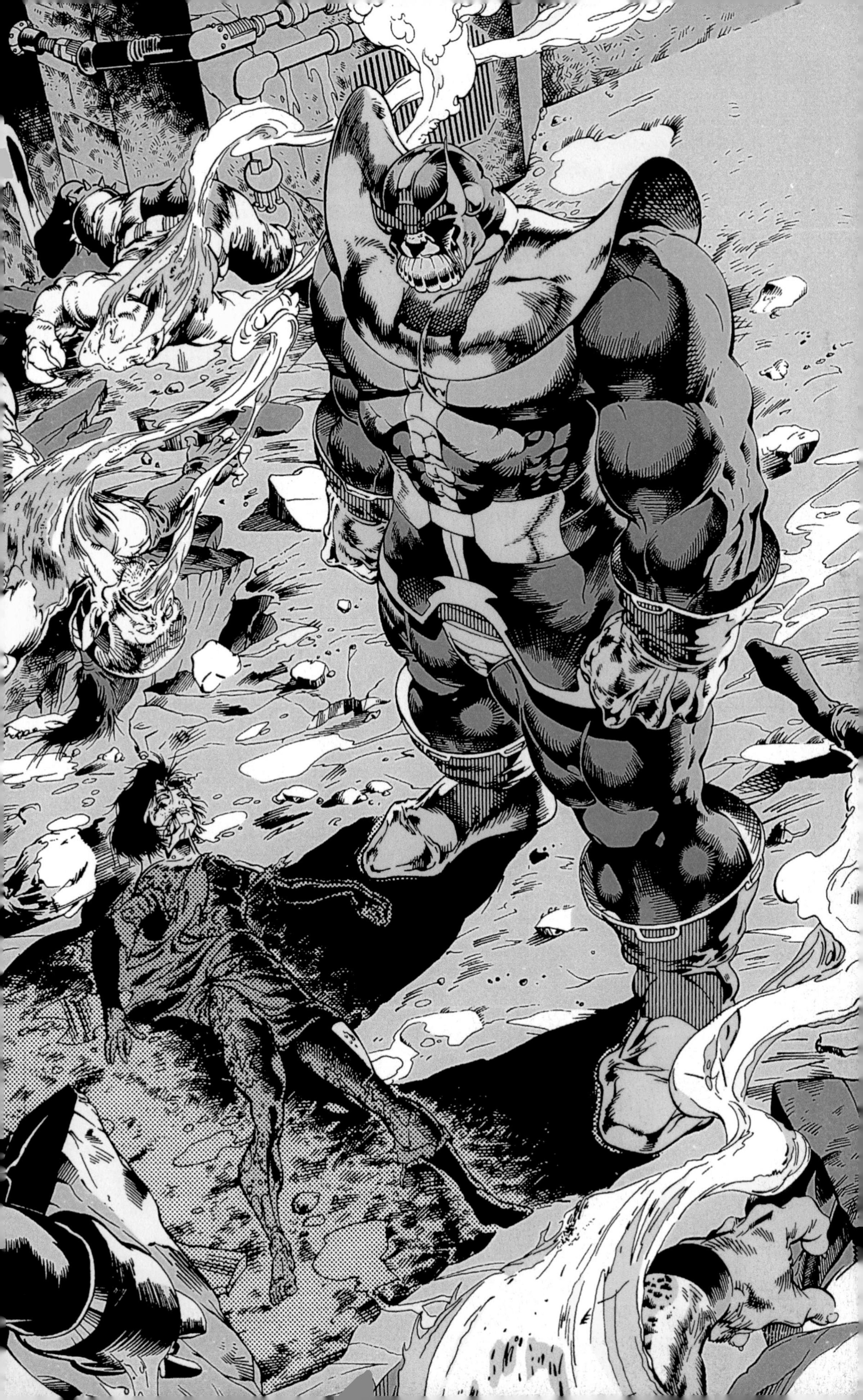

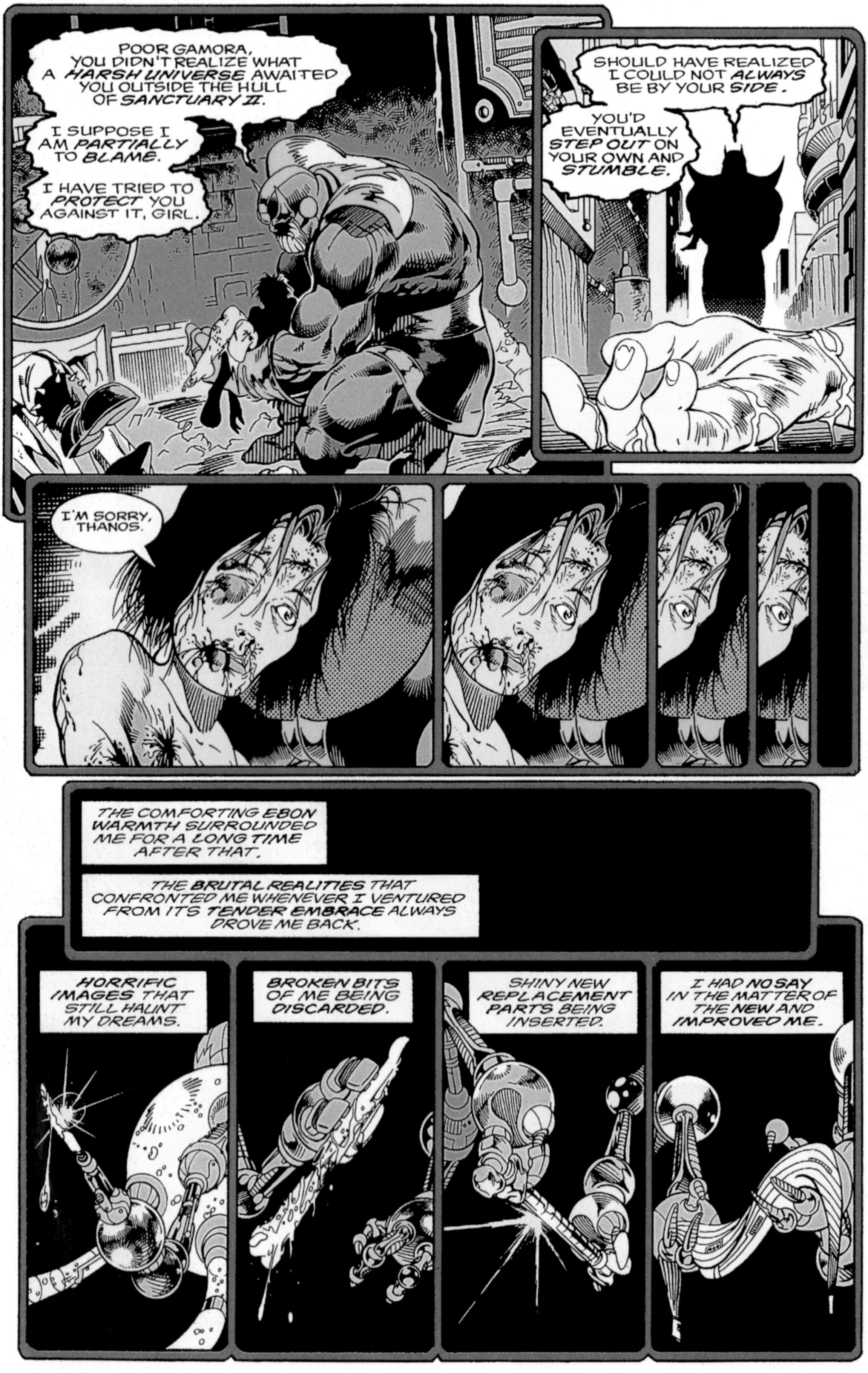
POOR GAMORA, YOU DIDN'T REALIZE WHAT A HARSH UNIVERSE AWAITED YOU OUTSIDE THE HULL OF SANCTUARY II.
I SUPPOSE I AM PARTIALLY TO BLAME.
I HAVE TRIED TO PROTECT YOU AGAINST IT, GIRL.
SHOULD HAVE REALIZED I COULD NOT ALWAYS BE BY YOUR SIDE.
YOU'D EVENTUALLY STEP OUT ON YOUR OWN AND STUMBLE.
I'M SORRY, THANOS.
THE COMFORTING EBON WARMTH SURROUNDED ME FOR A LONG TIME AFTER THAT.
THE BRUTAL REALITIES THAT CONFRONTED ME WHENEVER I VENTURED FROM ITS TENDER EMBRACE ALWAYS DROVE ME BACK.
HORRIFIC IMAGES THAT STILL HAUNT MY DREAMS.
BROKEN BITS OF ME BEING DISCARDED.
SHINY NEW REPLACEMENT PARTS BEING INSERTED.
I HAD NO SAY IN THE MATTER OF THE NEW AND IMPROVED ME.

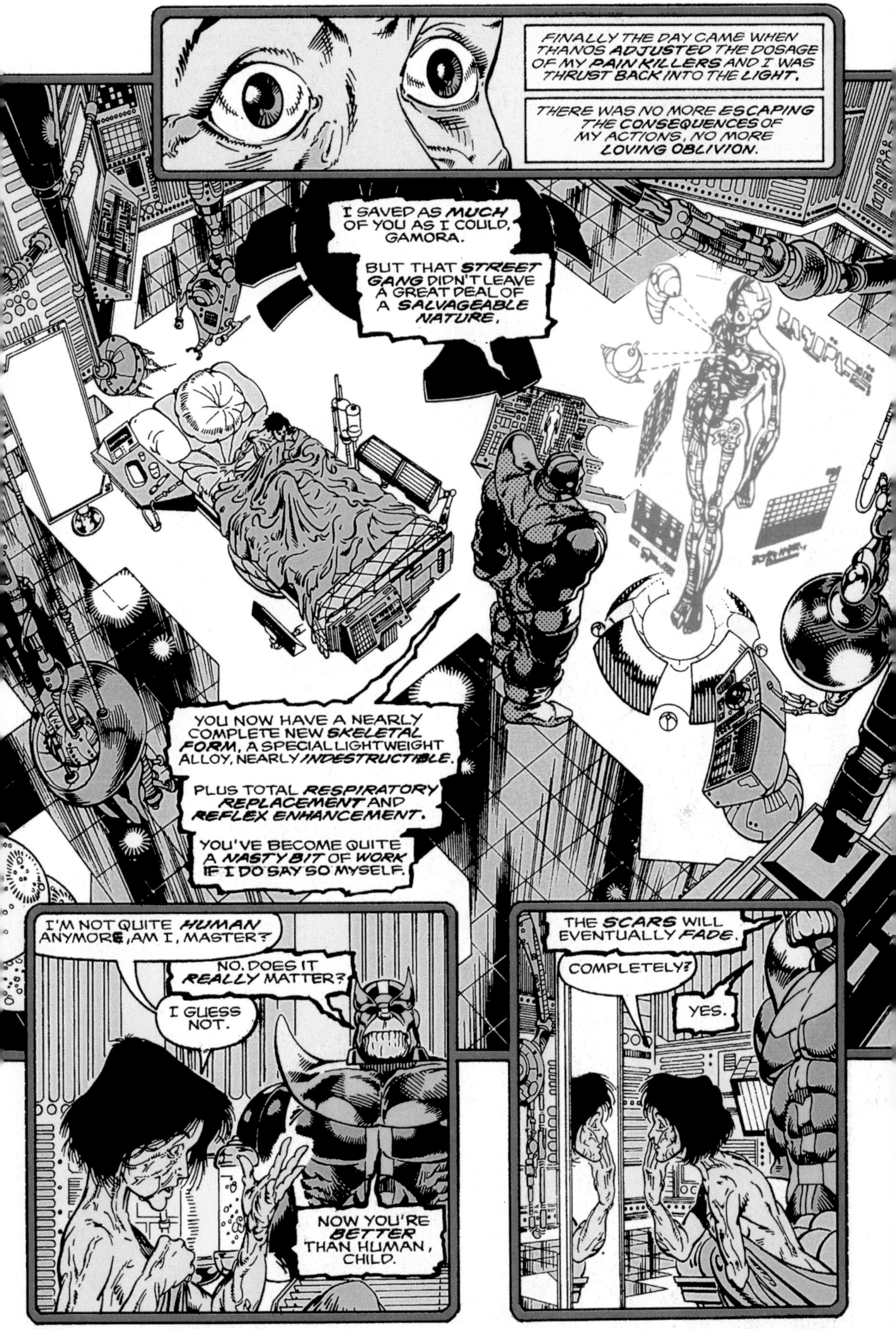

FINALLY THE DAY CAME WHEN THANOS ADJUSTED THE DOSAGE OF MY PAIN KILLERS AND I WAS THRUST BACK INTO THE LIGHT.
THERE WAS NO MORE ESCAPING THE CONSEQUENCES OF MY ACTIONS, NO MORE LOVING OBLIVION.
I SAVED AS MUCH OF YOU AS I COULD, GAMORA.
BUT THAT STREET GANG DIDN'T LEAVE A GREAT DEAL OF A SALVAGEABLE NATURE.
YOU NOW HAVE A NEARLY COMPLETE NEW SKELETAL FORM, A SPECIAL LIGHTWEIGHT ALLOY, NEARLY INDESTRUCTIBLE.
PLUS TOTAL RESPIRATORY REPLACEMENT AND REFLEX ENHANCEMENT.
YOU'VE BECOME QUITE A NASTY BIT OF WORK IF I DO SAY SO MYSELF.
I'M NOT QUITE HUMAN ANYMORE, AM I, MASTER?
NO. DOES IT REALLY MATTER?
I GUESS NOT.
NOW YOU'RE BETTER THAN HUMAN, CHILD.
THE SCARS WILL EVENTUALLY FADE.
COMPLETELY?
YES.

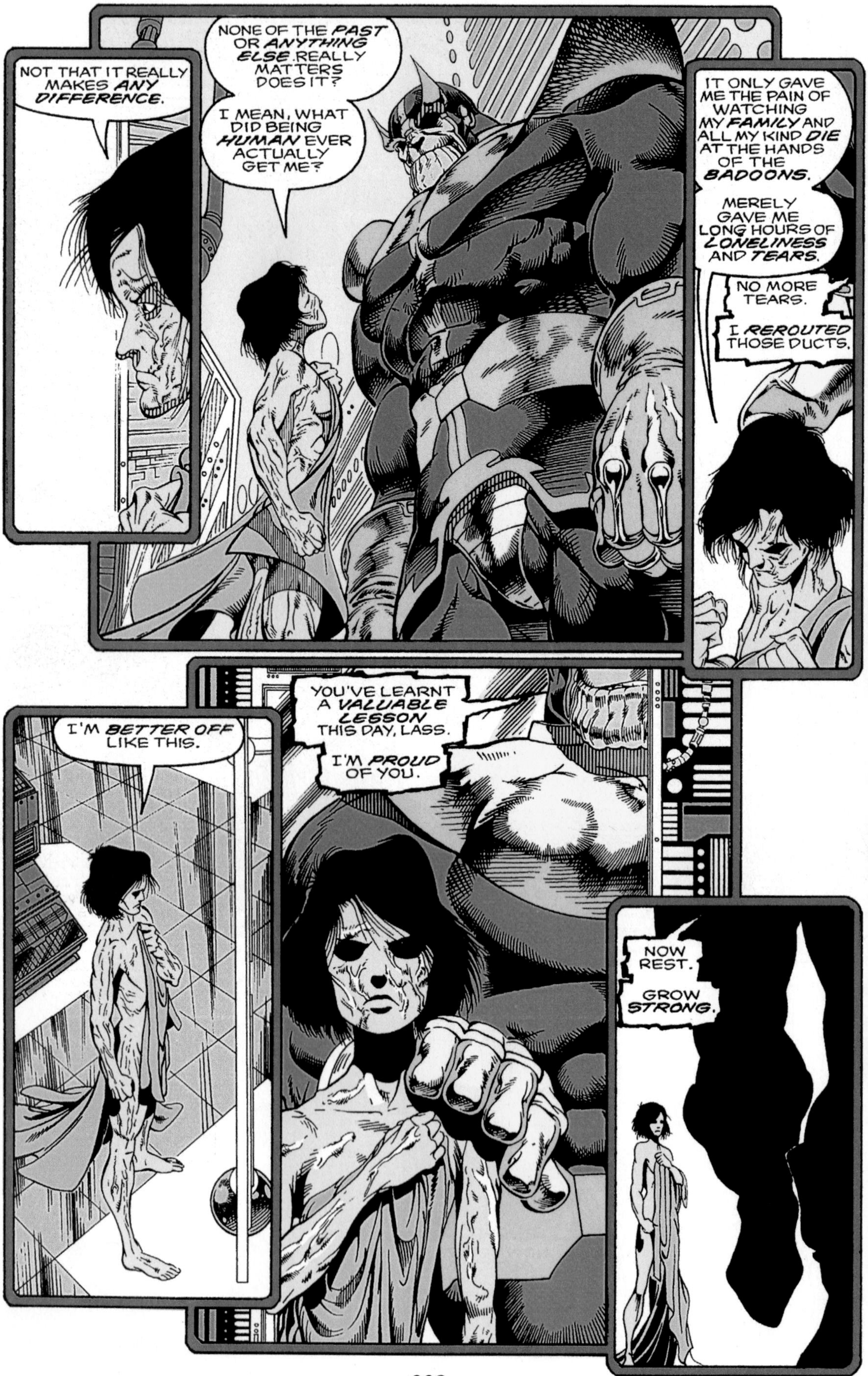
NOT THAT IT REALLY MAKES ANY DIFFERENCE.
NONE OF THE PAST OR ANYTHING ELSE REALLY MATTERS DOES IT?
I MEAN, WHAT DID BEING HUMAN EVER ACTUALLY GET ME?
IT ONLY GAVE ME THE PAIN OF WATCHING MY FAMILY AND ALL MY KIND DIE AT THE HANDS OF THE BADOONS.
MERELY GAVE ME LONG HOURS OF LONELINESS AND TEARS.
NO MORE TEARS.
I REROUTED THOSE DUCTS.
I'M BETTER OFF LIKE THIS.
YOU'VE LEARNT A VALUABLE LESSON THIS DAY, LASS.
I'M PROUD OF YOU.
NOW REST.
GROW STRONG.

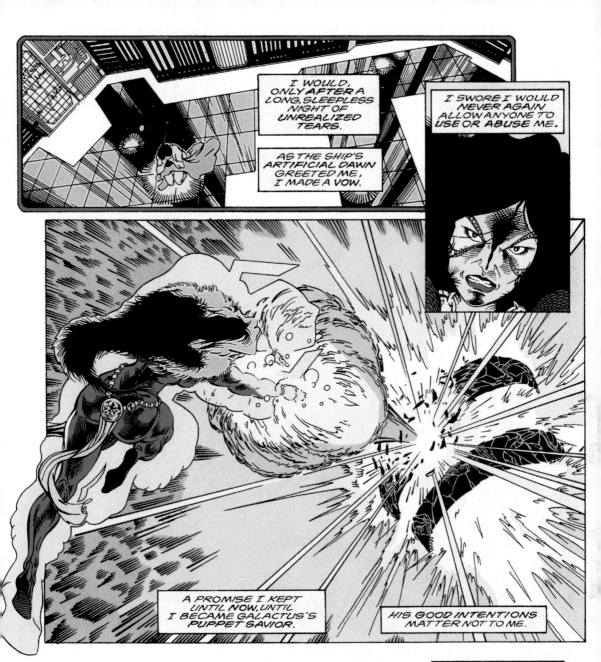

I WOULD, ONLY AFTER A LONG, SLEEPLESS NIGHT OF *UNREALIZED* TEARS.

AS THE SHIP'S *ARTIFICIAL DAWN* GREETED ME, I MADE A VOW.

I SWORE I WOULD *NEVER AGAIN* ALLOW ANYONE TO *USE* OR *ABUSE* ME.

A PROMISE I KEPT UNTIL NOW, UNTIL I BECAME GALACTUS'S *PUPPET SAVIOR.*

HIS GOOD INTENTIONS MATTER NOT TO ME.

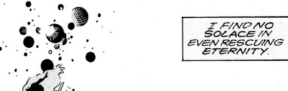

THE CURRENT STATE OF AFFAIRS IS STILL A *BITTER PILL* TO SWALLOW.

I FIND NO *SOLACE* IN EVEN RESCUING *ETERNITY.*

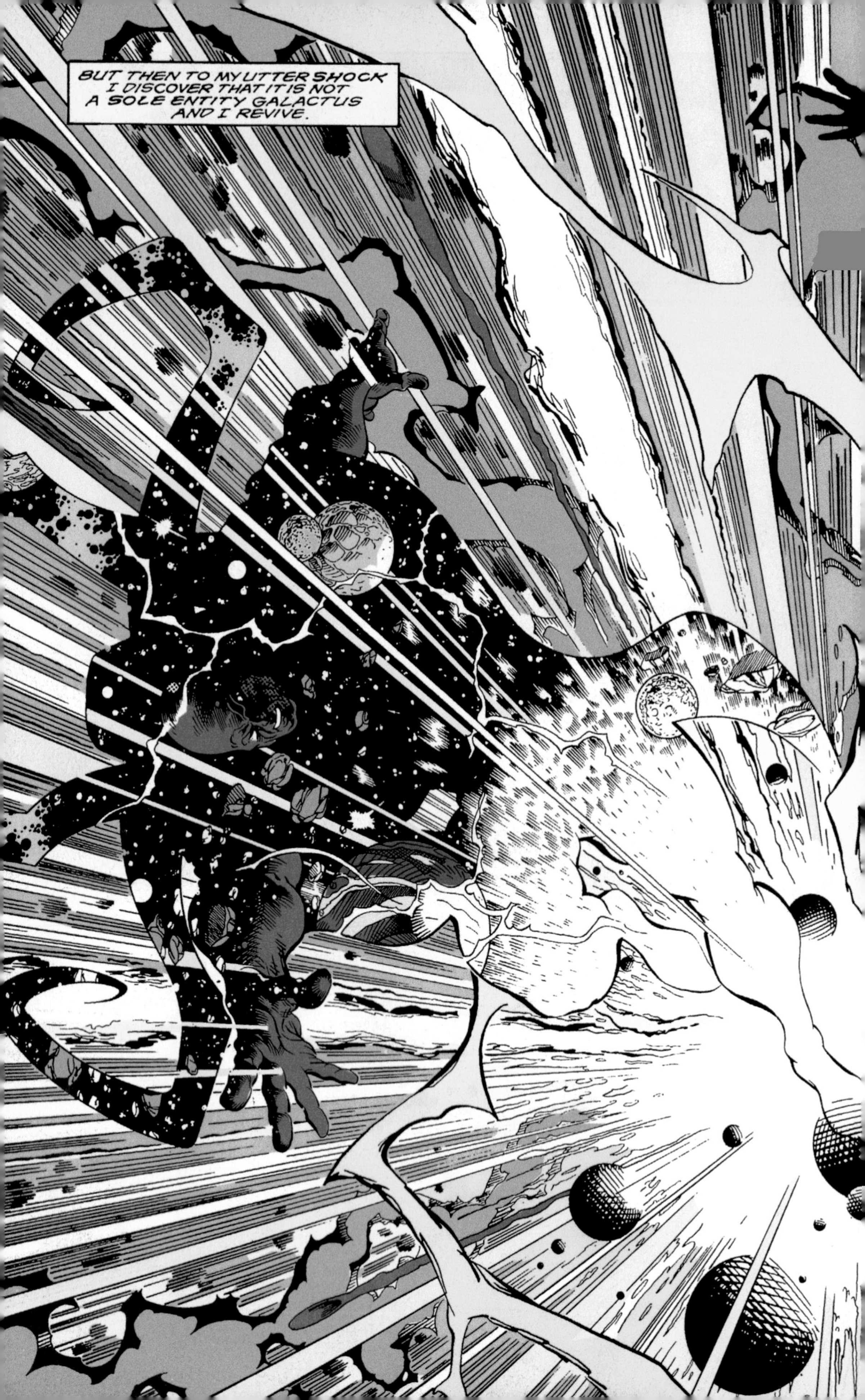
BUT THEN TO MY UTTER SHOCK I DISCOVER THAT IT IS NOT A SOLE ENTITY GALACTUS AND I REVIVE.

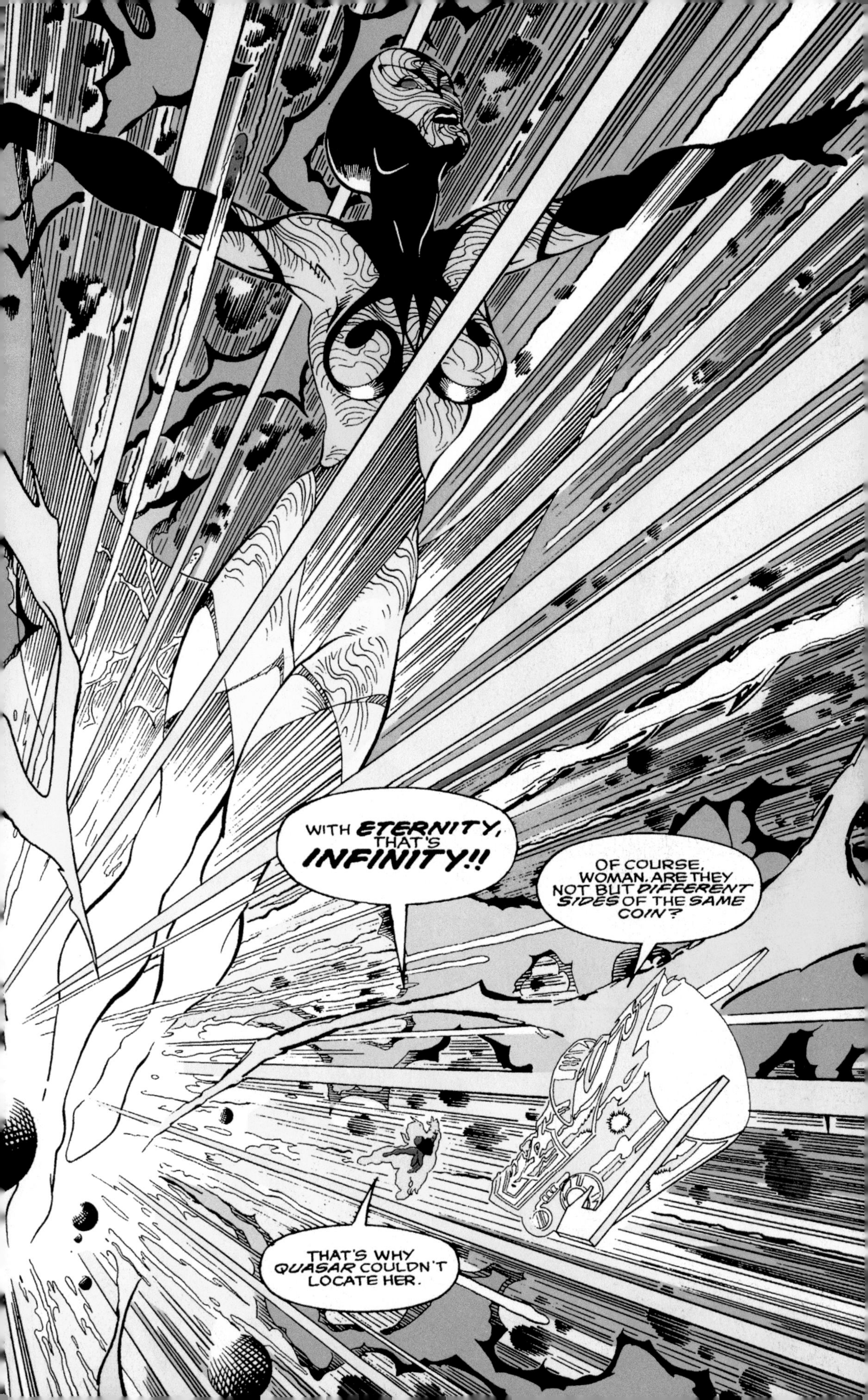
WITH *ETERNITY*, THAT'S *INFINITY*!!
OF COURSE, WOMAN. ARE THEY NOT BUT *DIFFERENT SIDES* OF THE *SAME* COIN?
THAT'S WHY *QUASAR* COULDN'T LOCATE HER.

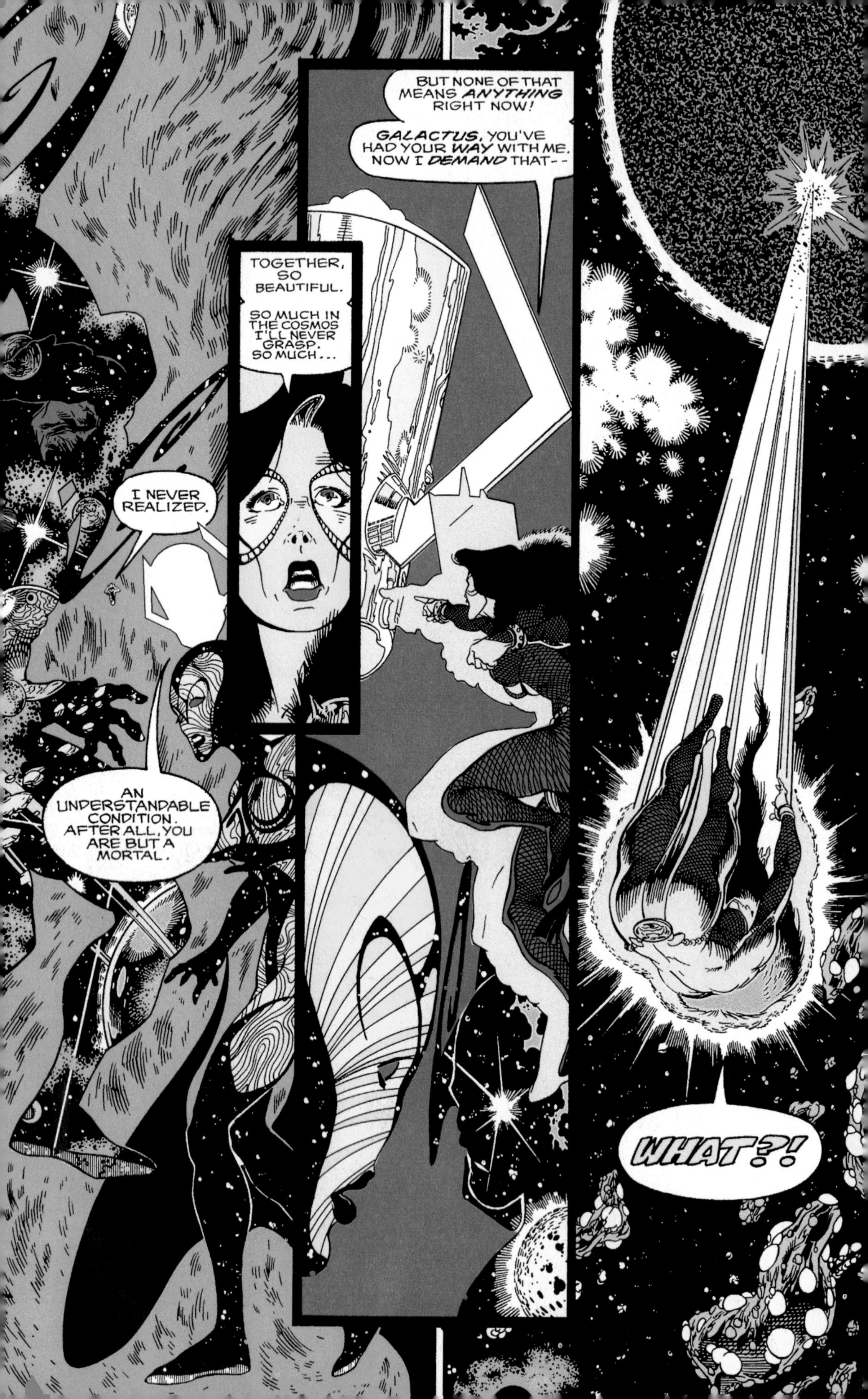
BUT NONE OF THAT MEANS ANYTHING RIGHT NOW!
GALACTUS, YOU'VE HAD YOUR WAY WITH ME. NOW I DEMAND THAT--
TOGETHER, SO BEAUTIFUL.
SO MUCH IN THE COSMOS I'LL NEVER GRASP. SO MUCH...
I NEVER REALIZED.
AN UNDERSTANDABLE CONDITION. AFTER ALL, YOU ARE BUT A MORTAL.
WHAT?!

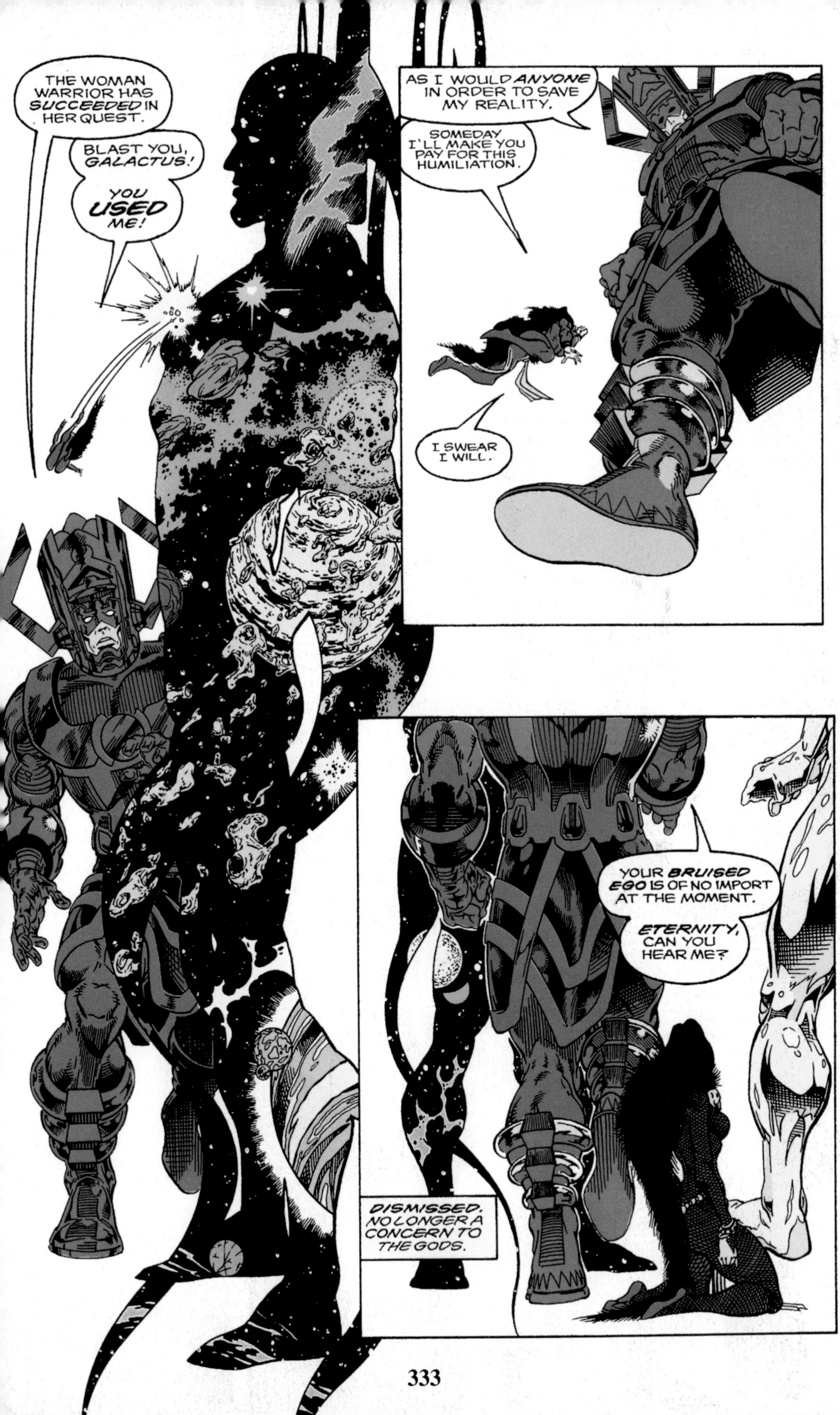
THE WOMAN WARRIOR HAS SUCCEEDED IN HER QUEST.
BLAST YOU, GALACTUS!
YOU USED ME!
AS I WOULD ANYONE IN ORDER TO SAVE MY REALITY.
SOMEDAY I'LL MAKE YOU PAY FOR THIS HUMILIATION.
I SWEAR I WILL.
YOUR BRUISED EGO IS OF NO IMPORT AT THE MOMENT.
ETERNITY, CAN YOU HEAR ME?
DISMISSED. NO LONGER A CONCERN TO THE GODS.

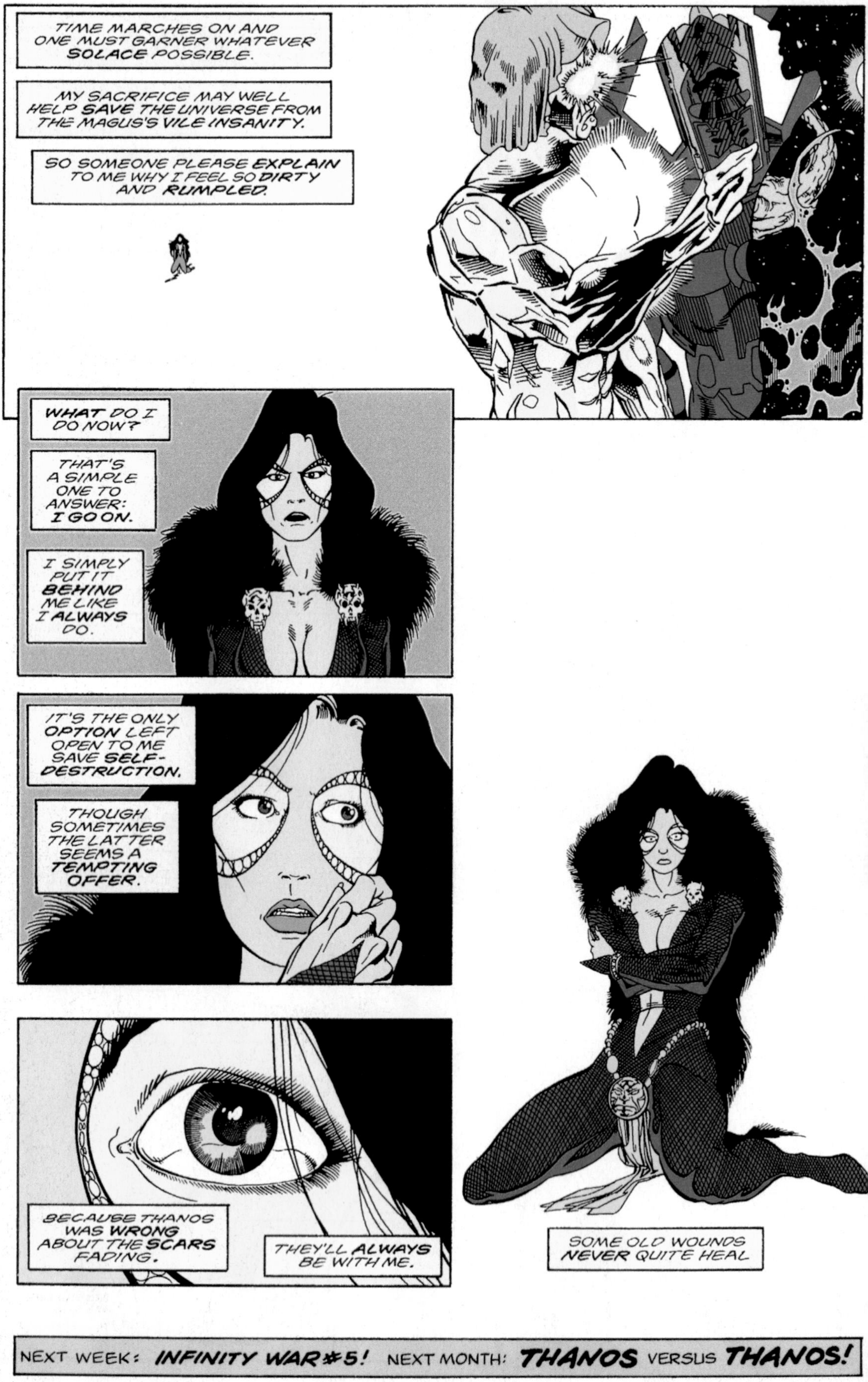
TIME MARCHES ON AND ONE MUST GARNER WHATEVER SOLACE POSSIBLE.
MY SACRIFICE MAY WELL HELP SAVE THE UNIVERSE FROM THE MAGUS'S VILE INSANITY.
SO SOMEONE PLEASE EXPLAIN TO ME WHY I FEEL SO DIRTY AND RUMPLED.
WHAT DO I DO NOW?
THAT'S A SIMPLE ONE TO ANSWER: I GO ON.
I SIMPLY PUT IT BEHIND ME LIKE I ALWAYS DO.
IT'S THE ONLY OPTION LEFT OPEN TO ME SAVE SELF-DESTRUCTION.
THOUGH SOMETIMES THE LATTER SEEMS A TEMPTING OFFER.
BECAUSE THANOS WAS WRONG ABOUT THE SCARS FADING.
THEY'LL ALWAYS BE WITH ME.
SOME OLD WOUNDS NEVER QUITE HEAL
NEXT WEEK: INFINITY WAR #5! NEXT MONTH: THANOS VERSUS THANOS!

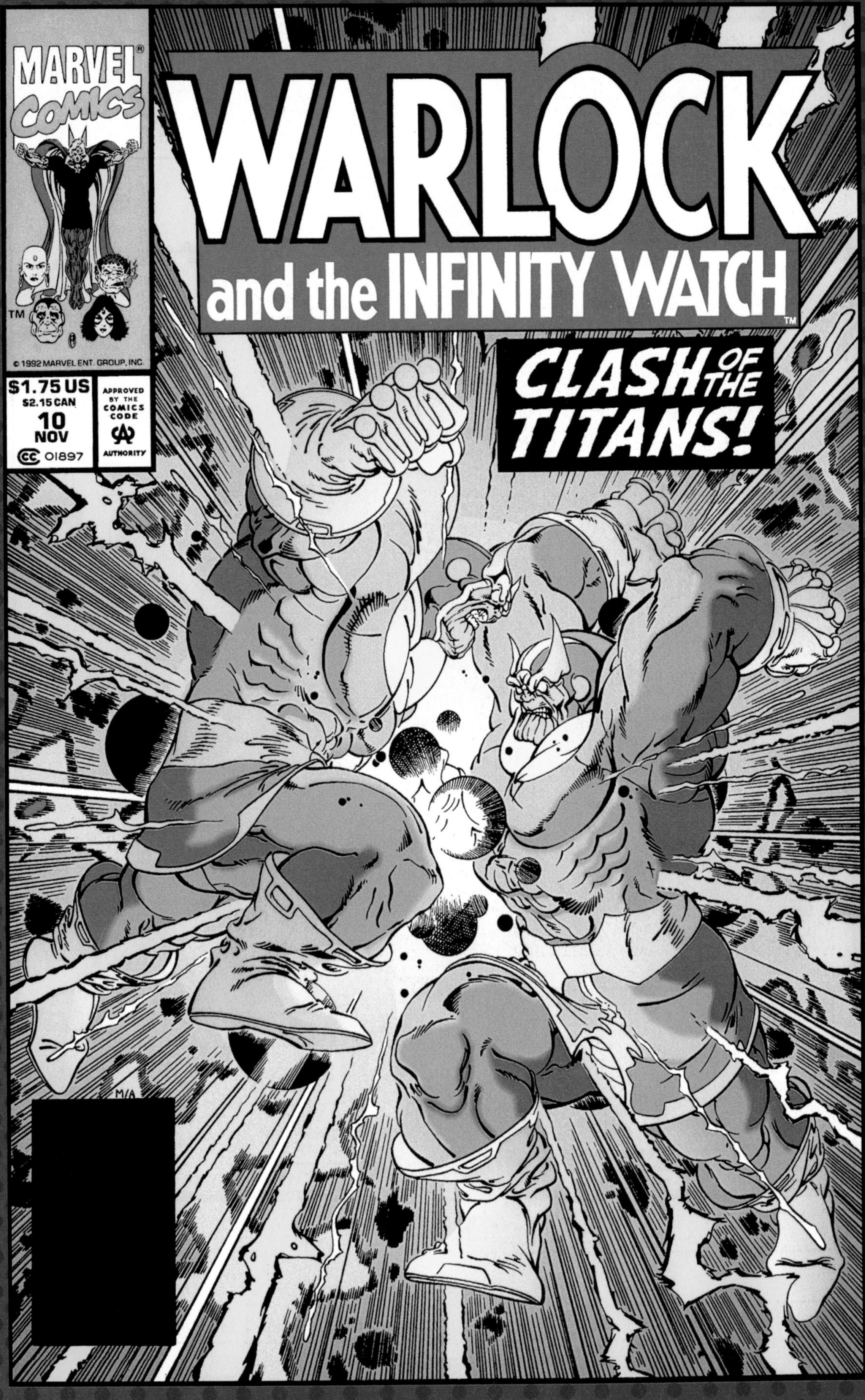
MARVEL COMICS
WARLOCK
and the INFINITY WATCH
© 1992 MARVEL ENT. GROUP, INC.
$1.75 US
$2.15 CAN
10
NOV
01897
APPROVED BY THE COMICS CODE AUTHORITY
CLASH OF THE TITANS!

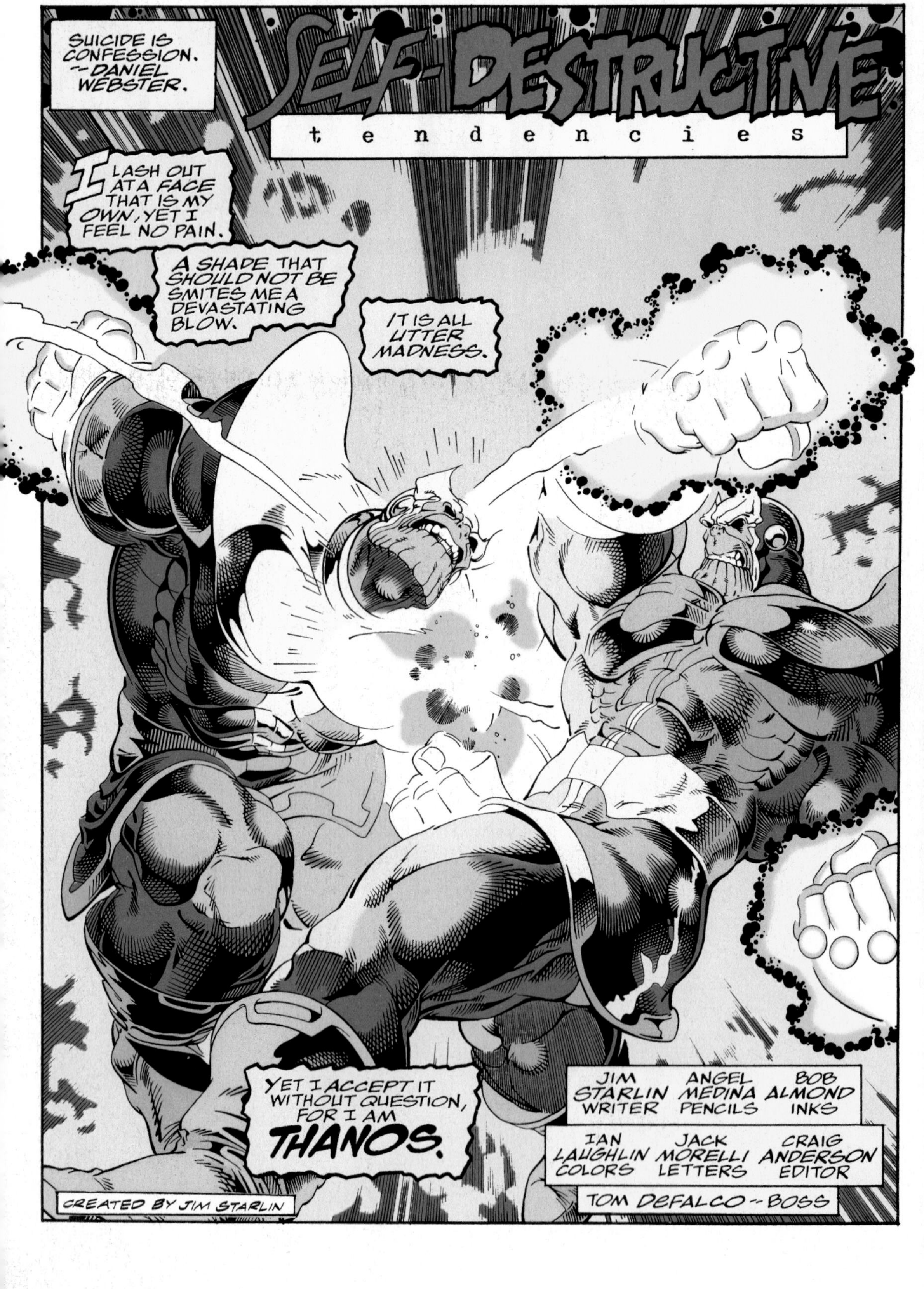

SUICIDE IS CONFESSION. --DANIEL WEBSTER.
SELF-DESTRUCTIVE
tendencies
I LASH OUT AT A FACE THAT IS MY OWN, YET I FEEL NO PAIN.
A SHADE THAT SHOULD NOT BE SMITES ME A DEVASTATING BLOW.
IT IS ALL UTTER MADNESS.
YET I ACCEPT IT WITHOUT QUESTION, FOR I AM THANOS.
JIM STARLIN WRITER
ANGEL MEDINA PENCILS
BOB ALMOND INKS
IAN LAUGHLIN COLORS
JACK MORELLI LETTERS
CRAIG ANDERSON EDITOR
TOM DEFALCO--BOSS
CREATED BY JIM STARLIN

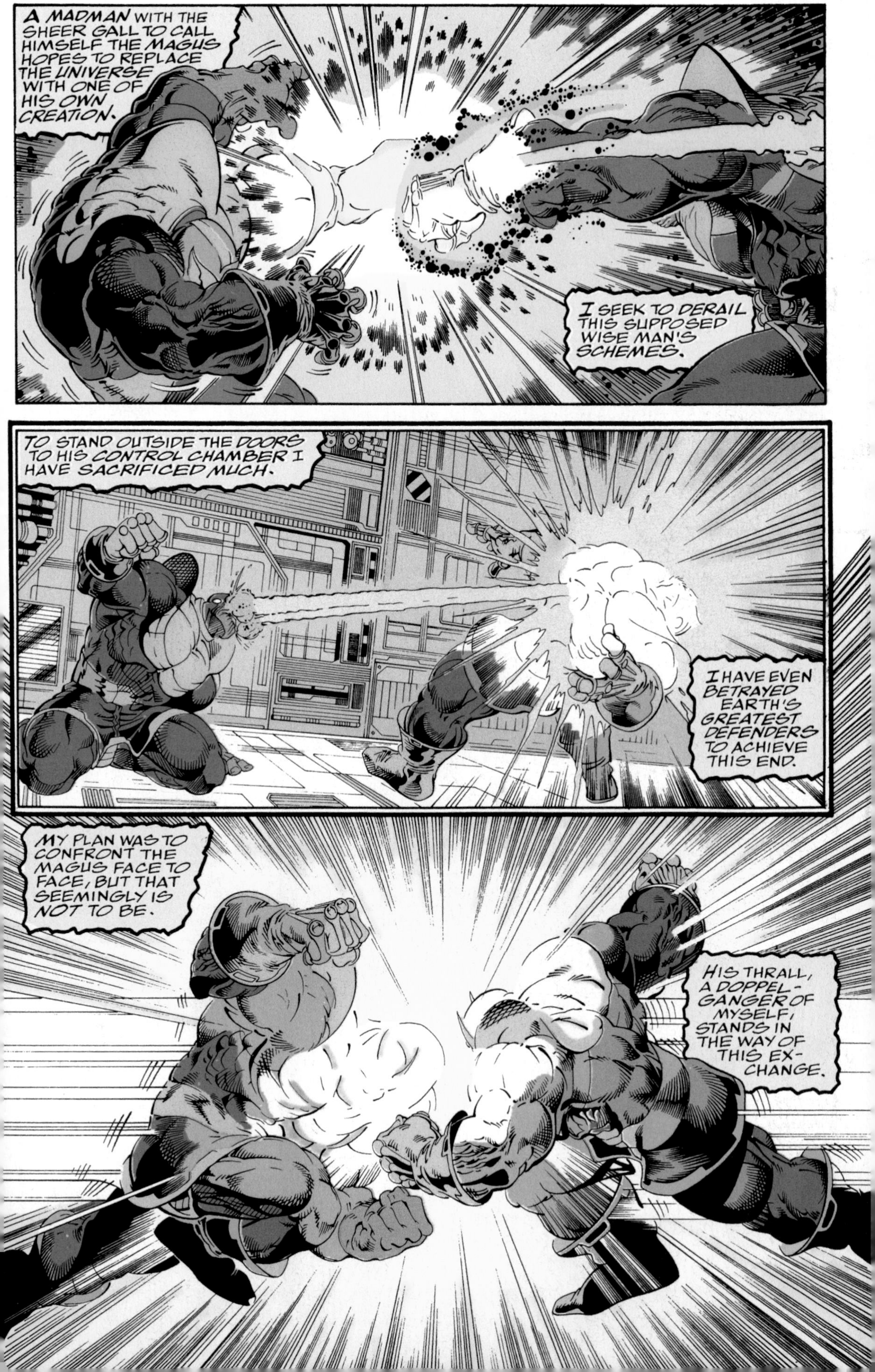
A MADMAN WITH THE SHEER GALL TO CALL HIMSELF THE MAGUS HOPES TO REPLACE THE UNIVERSE WITH ONE OF HIS OWN CREATION.
I SEEK TO DERAIL THIS SUPPOSED WISE MAN'S SCHEMES.
TO STAND OUTSIDE THE DOORS TO HIS CONTROL CHAMBER I HAVE SACRIFICED MUCH.
I HAVE EVEN BETRAYED EARTH'S GREATEST DEFENDERS TO ACHIEVE THIS END.
MY PLAN WAS TO CONFRONT THE MAGUS FACE TO FACE, BUT THAT SEEMINGLY IS NOT TO BE.
HIS THRALL, A DOPPEL-GANGER OF MYSELF, STANDS IN THE WAY OF THIS EX-CHANGE.

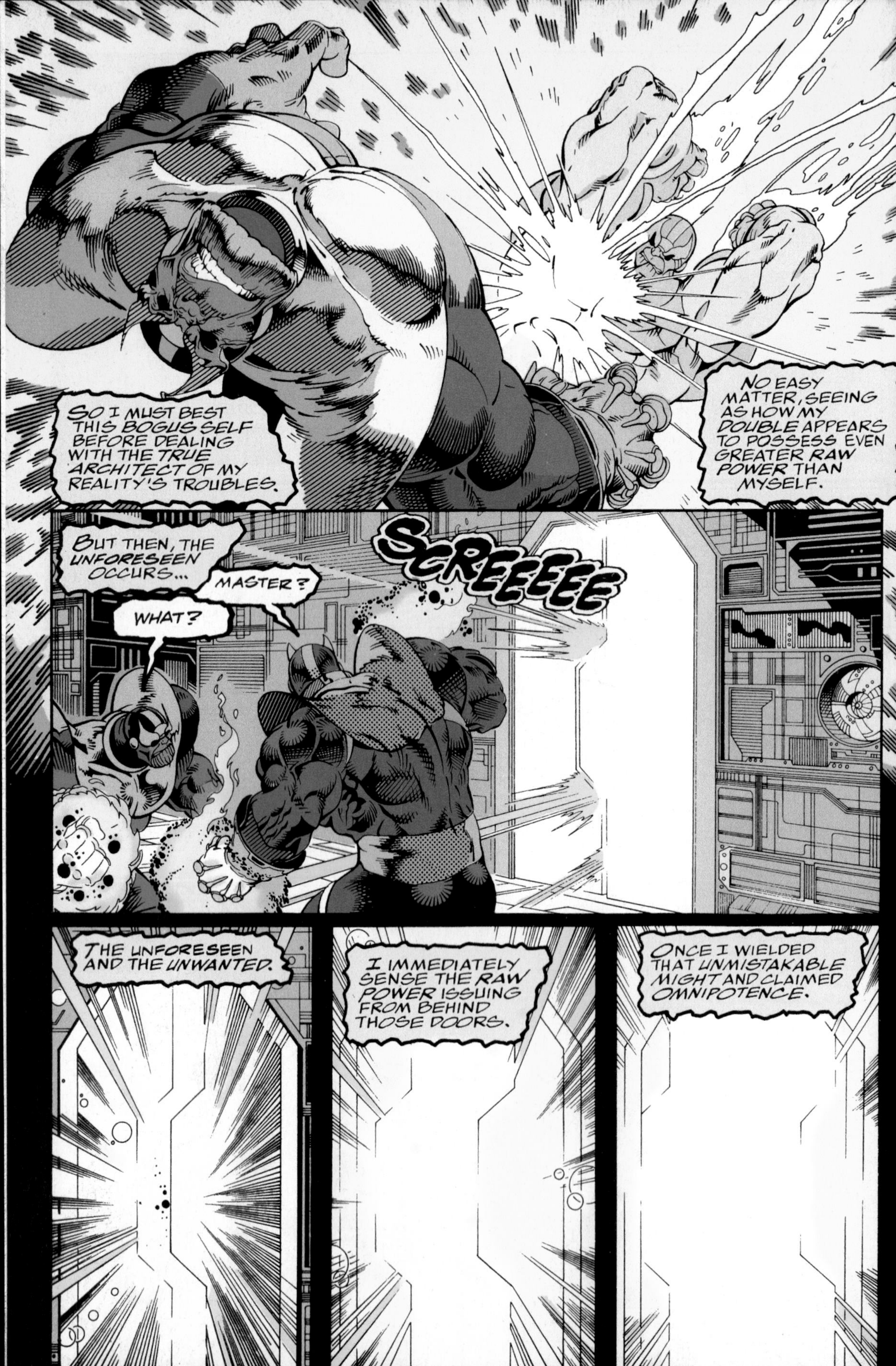

So I must best this bogus self before dealing with the true architect of my reality's troubles.
No easy matter, seeing as how my double appears to possess even greater raw power than myself.
But then, the unforeseen occurs...
SCREEEEEE
Master?
What?
The unforeseen and the unwanted.
I immediately sense the raw power issuing from behind those doors.
Once I wielded that unmistakable might and claimed omnipotence.

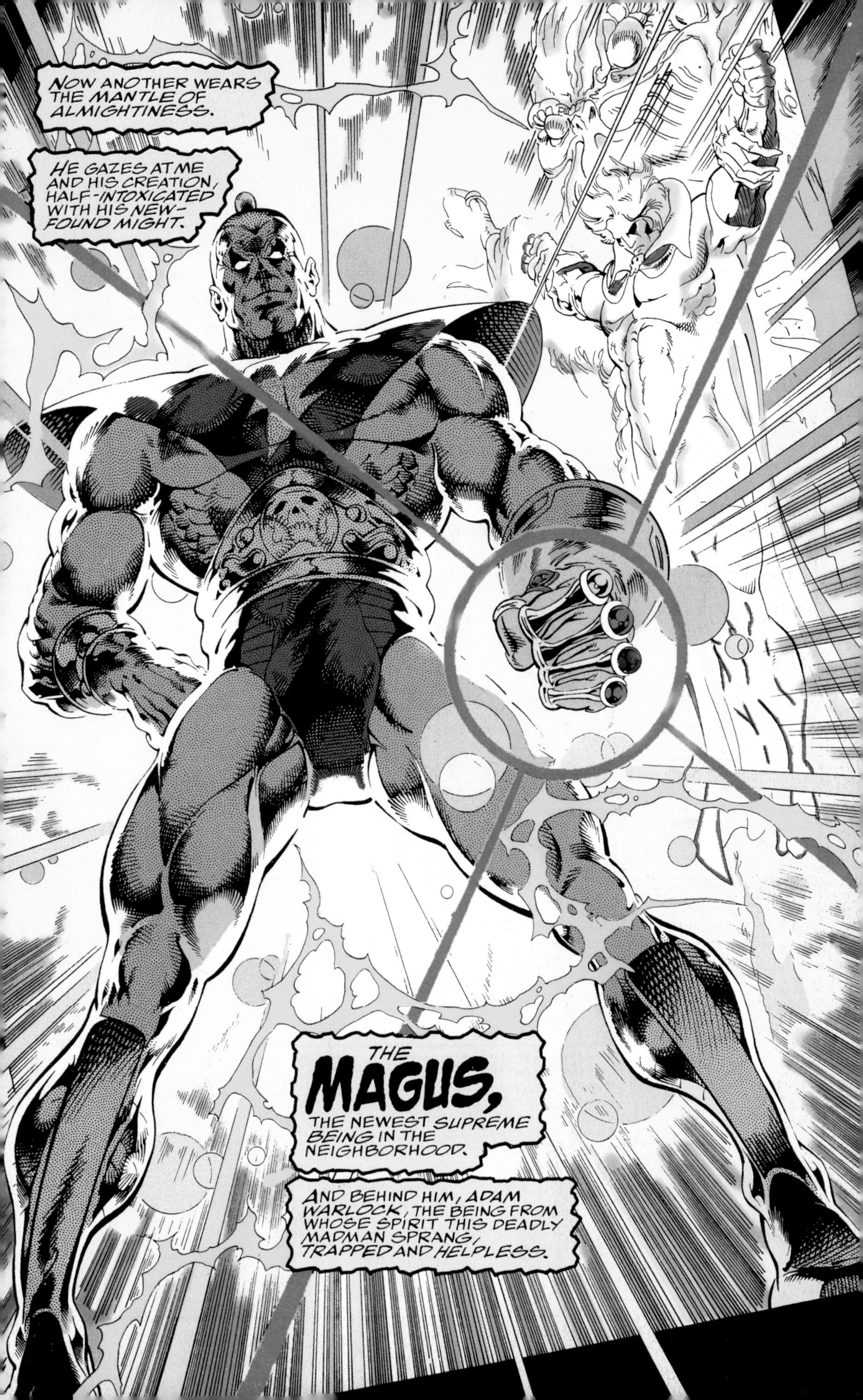
NOW ANOTHER WEARS THE MANTLE OF ALMIGHTINESS.
HE GAZES AT ME AND HIS CREATION, HALF-INTOXICATED WITH HIS NEW-FOUND MIGHT.
THE MAGUS, THE NEWEST SUPREME BEING IN THE NEIGHBORHOOD.
AND BEHIND HIM, ADAM WARLOCK, THE BEING FROM WHOSE SPIRIT THIS DEADLY MADMAN SPRANG, TRAPPED AND HELPLESS.

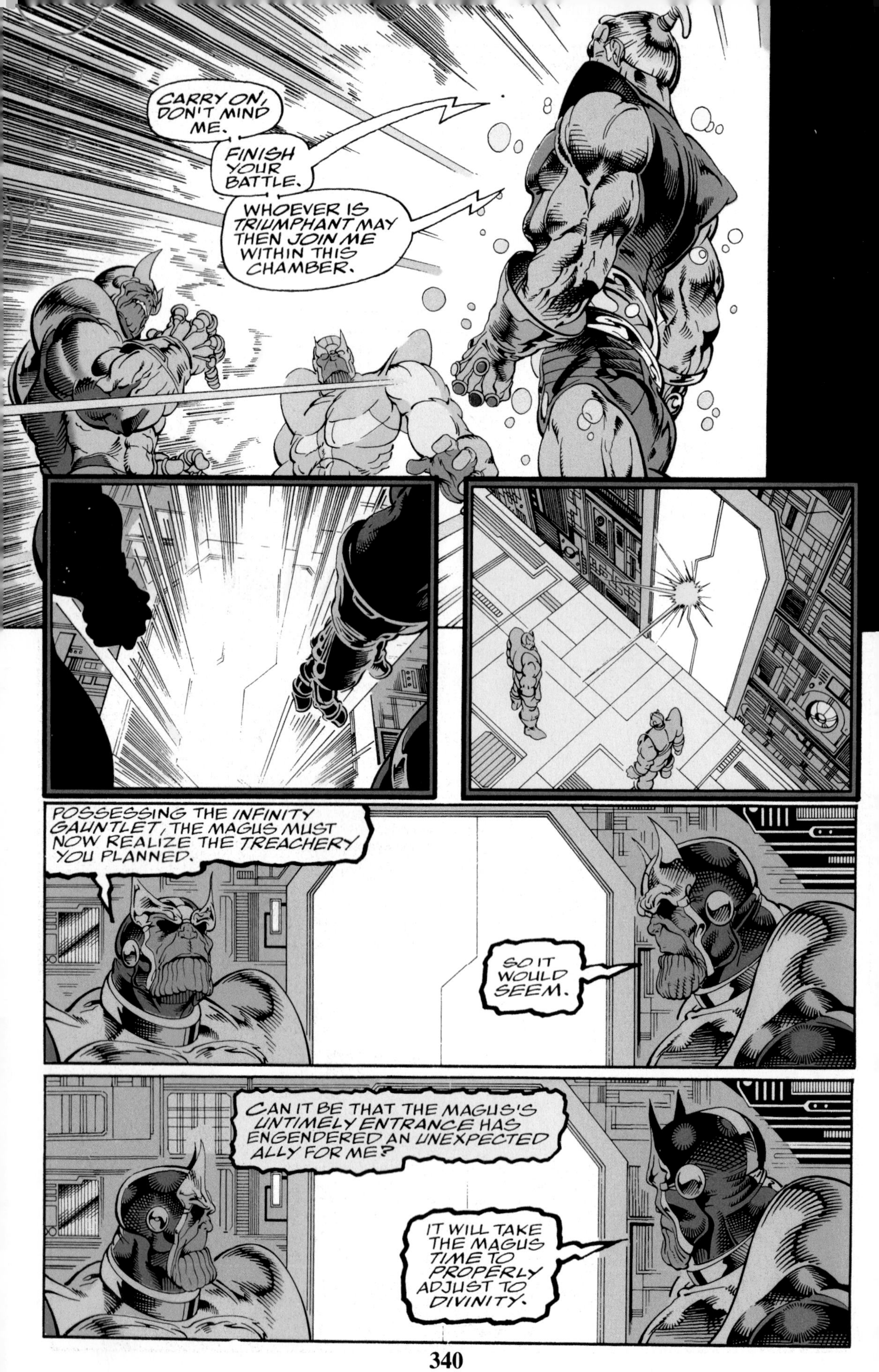

CARRY ON, DON'T MIND ME.
FINISH YOUR BATTLE.
WHOEVER IS TRIUMPHANT MAY THEN JOIN ME WITHIN THIS CHAMBER.
POSSESSING THE INFINITY GAUNTLET, THE MAGUS MUST NOW REALIZE THE TREACHERY YOU PLANNED.
SO IT WOULD SEEM.
CAN IT BE THAT THE MAGUS'S UNTIMELY ENTRANCE HAS ENGENDERED AN UNEXPECTED ALLY FOR ME?
IT WILL TAKE THE MAGUS TIME TO PROPERLY ADJUST TO DIVINITY.

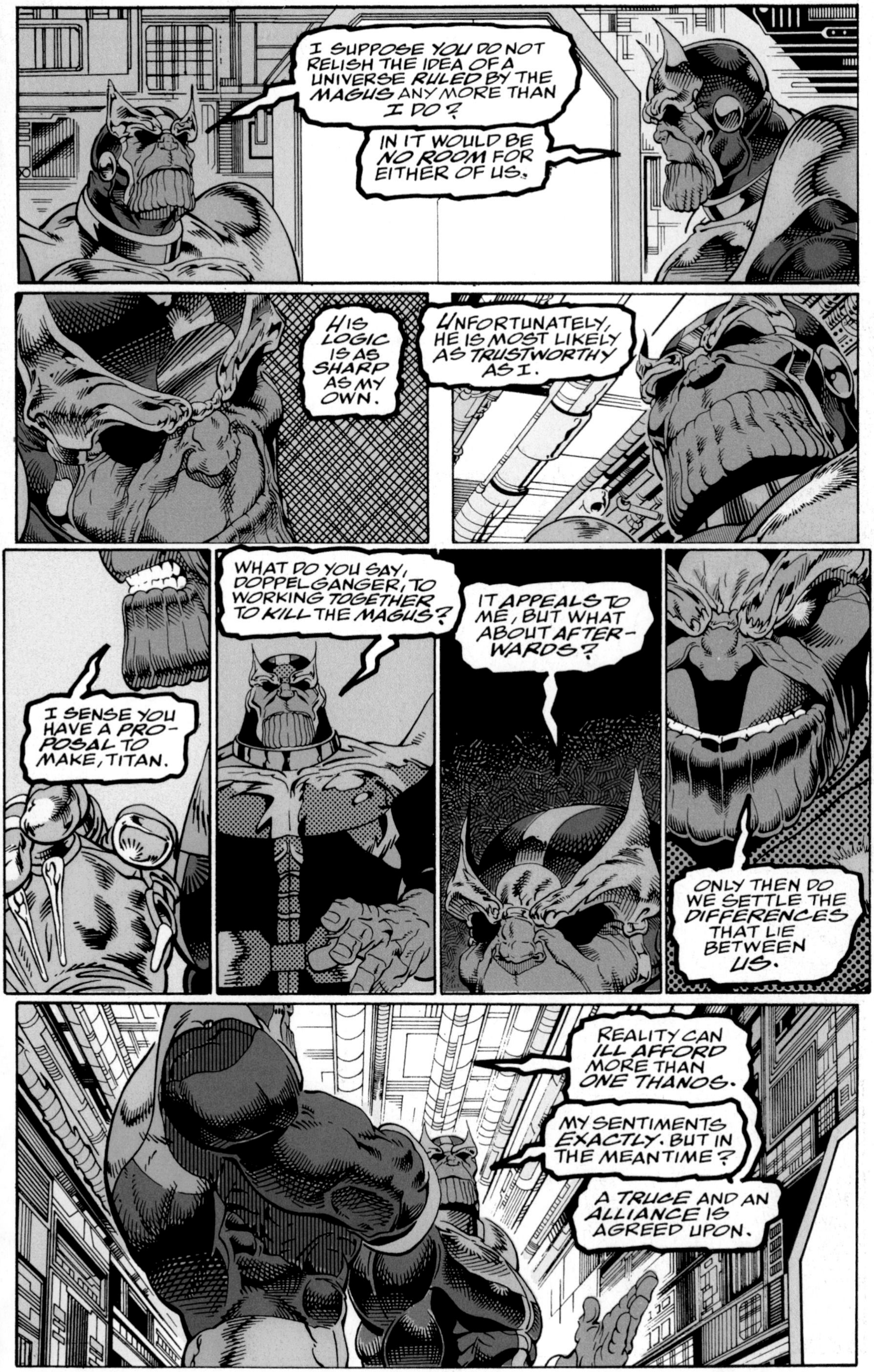
I SUPPOSE YOU DO NOT RELISH THE IDEA OF A UNIVERSE RULED BY THE MAGUS ANY MORE THAN I DO?
IN IT WOULD BE NO ROOM FOR EITHER OF US.
HIS LOGIC IS AS SHARP AS MY OWN.
UNFORTUNATELY, HE IS MOST LIKELY AS TRUSTWORTHY AS I.
I SENSE YOU HAVE A PRO-POSAL TO MAKE, TITAN.
WHAT DO YOU SAY, DOPPELGANGER, TO WORKING TOGETHER TO KILL THE MAGUS?
IT APPEALS TO ME, BUT WHAT ABOUT AFTER-WARDS?
ONLY THEN DO WE SETTLE THE DIFFERENCES THAT LIE BETWEEN US.
REALITY CAN ILL AFFORD MORE THAN ONE THANOS.
MY SENTIMENTS EXACTLY. BUT IN THE MEANTIME?
A TRUCE AND AN ALLIANCE IS AGREED UPON.

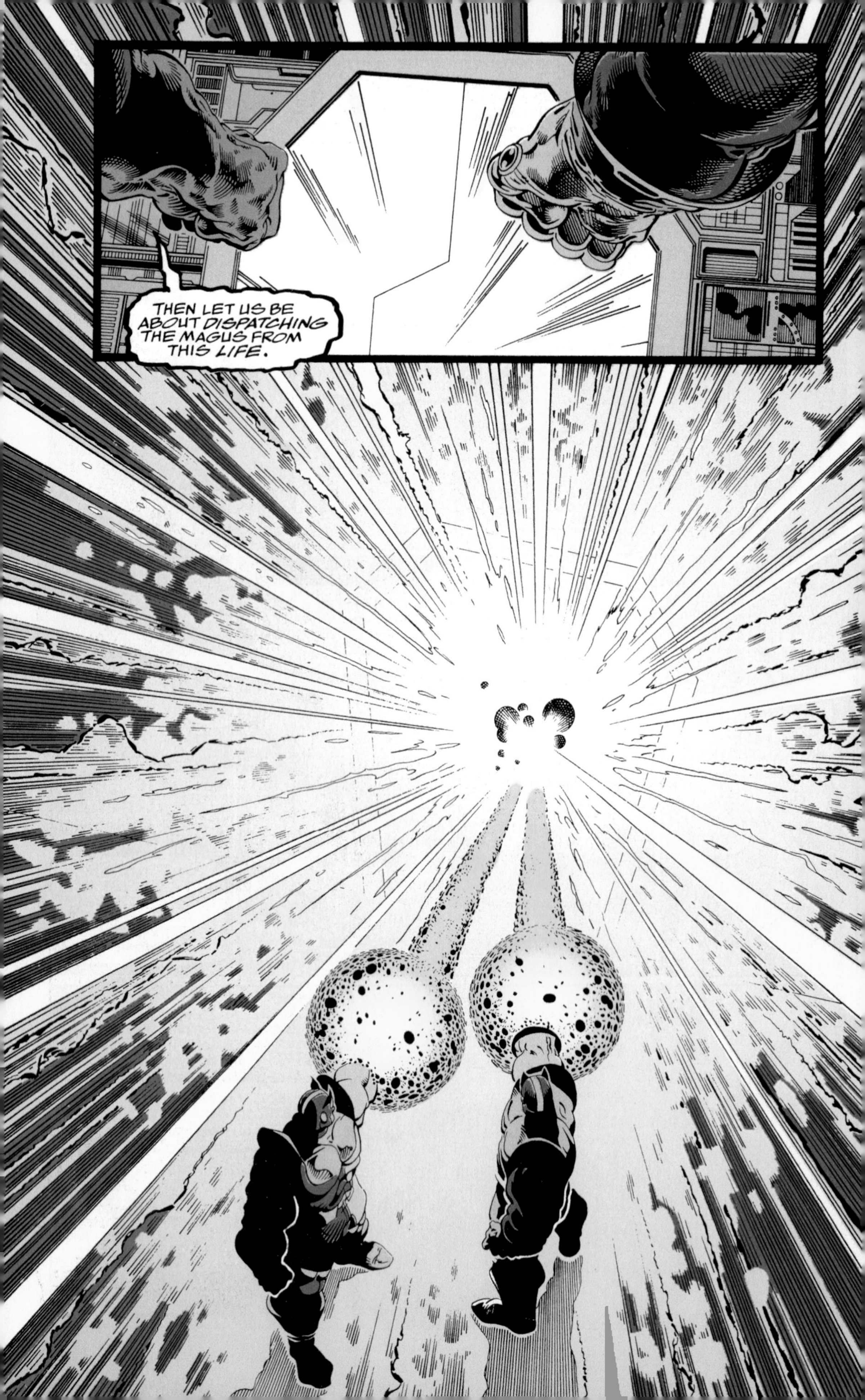
THEN LET US BE ABOUT DISPATCHING THE MAGUS FROM THIS LIFE.

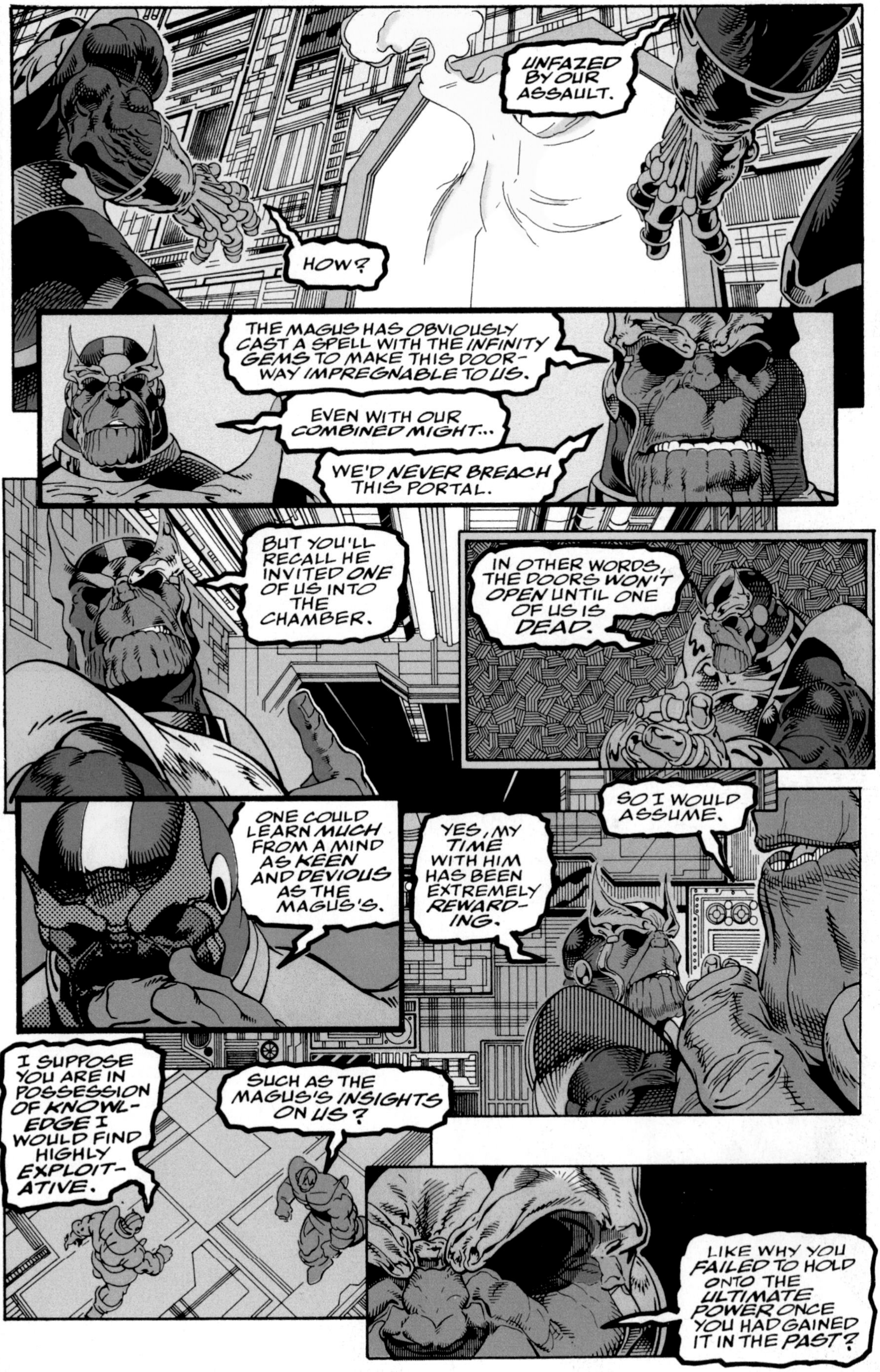
UNFAZED BY OUR ASSAULT.
HOW?
THE MAGUS HAS OBVIOUSLY CAST A SPELL WITH THE INFINITY GEMS TO MAKE THIS DOORWAY IMPREGNABLE TO US.
EVEN WITH OUR COMBINED MIGHT...
WE'D NEVER BREACH THIS PORTAL.
BUT YOU'LL RECALL HE INVITED ONE OF US INTO THE CHAMBER.
IN OTHER WORDS, THE DOORS WON'T OPEN UNTIL ONE OF US IS DEAD.
ONE COULD LEARN MUCH FROM A MIND AS KEEN AND DEVIOUS AS THE MAGUS'S.
YES, MY TIME WITH HIM HAS BEEN EXTREMELY REWARDING.
SO I WOULD ASSUME.
I SUPPOSE YOU ARE IN POSSESSION OF KNOWLEDGE I WOULD FIND HIGHLY EXPLOITATIVE.
SUCH AS THE MAGUS'S INSIGHTS ON US?
LIKE WHY YOU FAILED TO HOLD ONTO THE ULTIMATE POWER ONCE YOU HAD GAINED IT IN THE PAST?

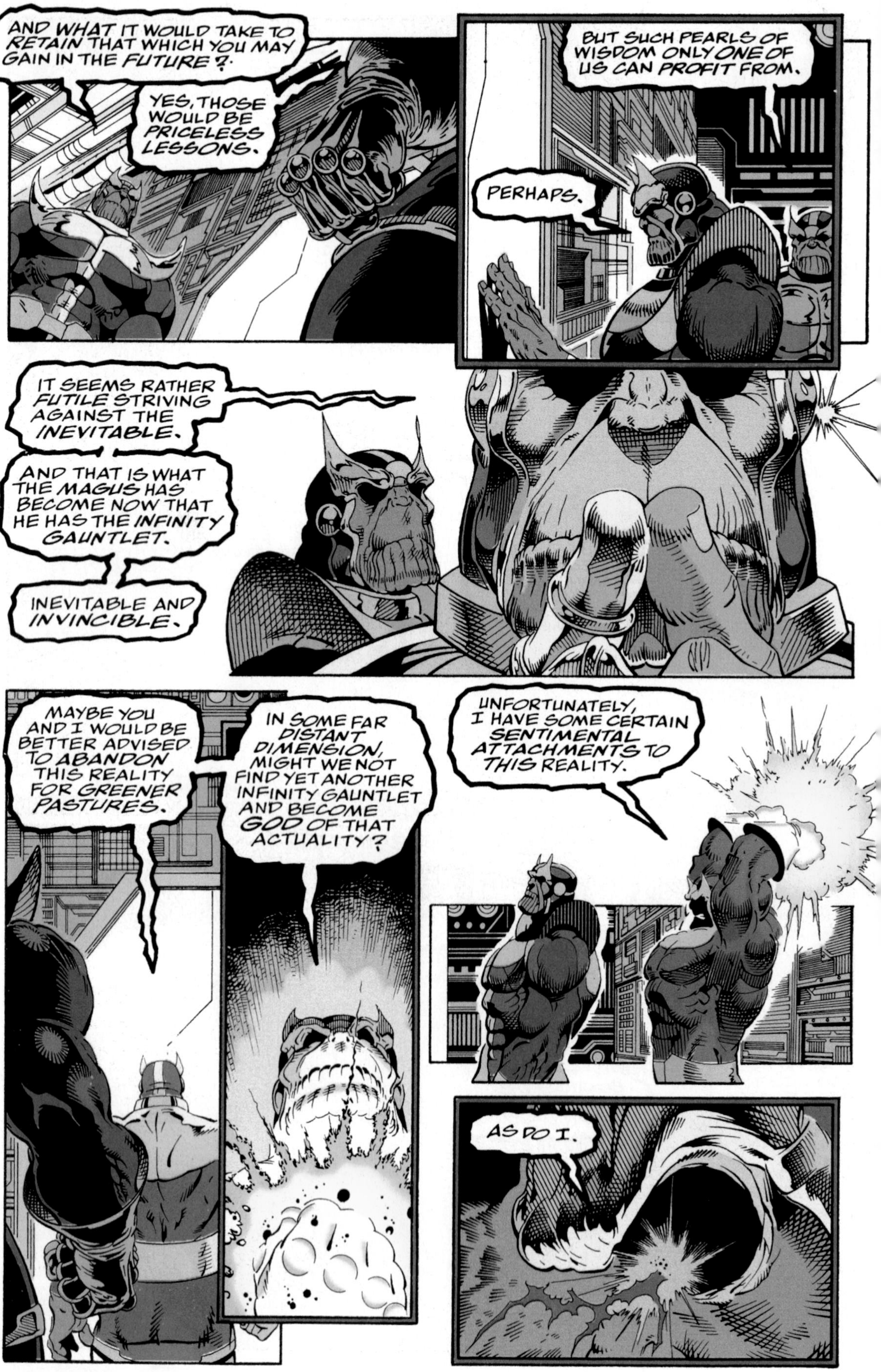
AND WHAT IT WOULD TAKE TO RETAIN THAT WHICH YOU MAY GAIN IN THE FUTURE?
YES, THOSE WOULD BE PRICELESS LESSONS.
BUT SUCH PEARLS OF WISDOM ONLY ONE OF US CAN PROFIT FROM.
PERHAPS.
IT SEEMS RATHER FUTILE STRIVING AGAINST THE INEVITABLE.
AND THAT IS WHAT THE MAGUS HAS BECOME NOW THAT HE HAS THE INFINITY GAUNTLET.
INEVITABLE AND INVINCIBLE.
MAYBE YOU AND I WOULD BE BETTER ADVISED TO ABANDON THIS REALITY FOR GREENER PASTURES.
IN SOME FAR DISTANT DIMENSION, MIGHT WE NOT FIND YET ANOTHER INFINITY GAUNTLET AND BECOME GOD OF THAT ACTUALITY?
UNFORTUNATELY, I HAVE SOME CERTAIN SENTIMENTAL ATTACHMENTS TO THIS REALITY.
AS DO I.

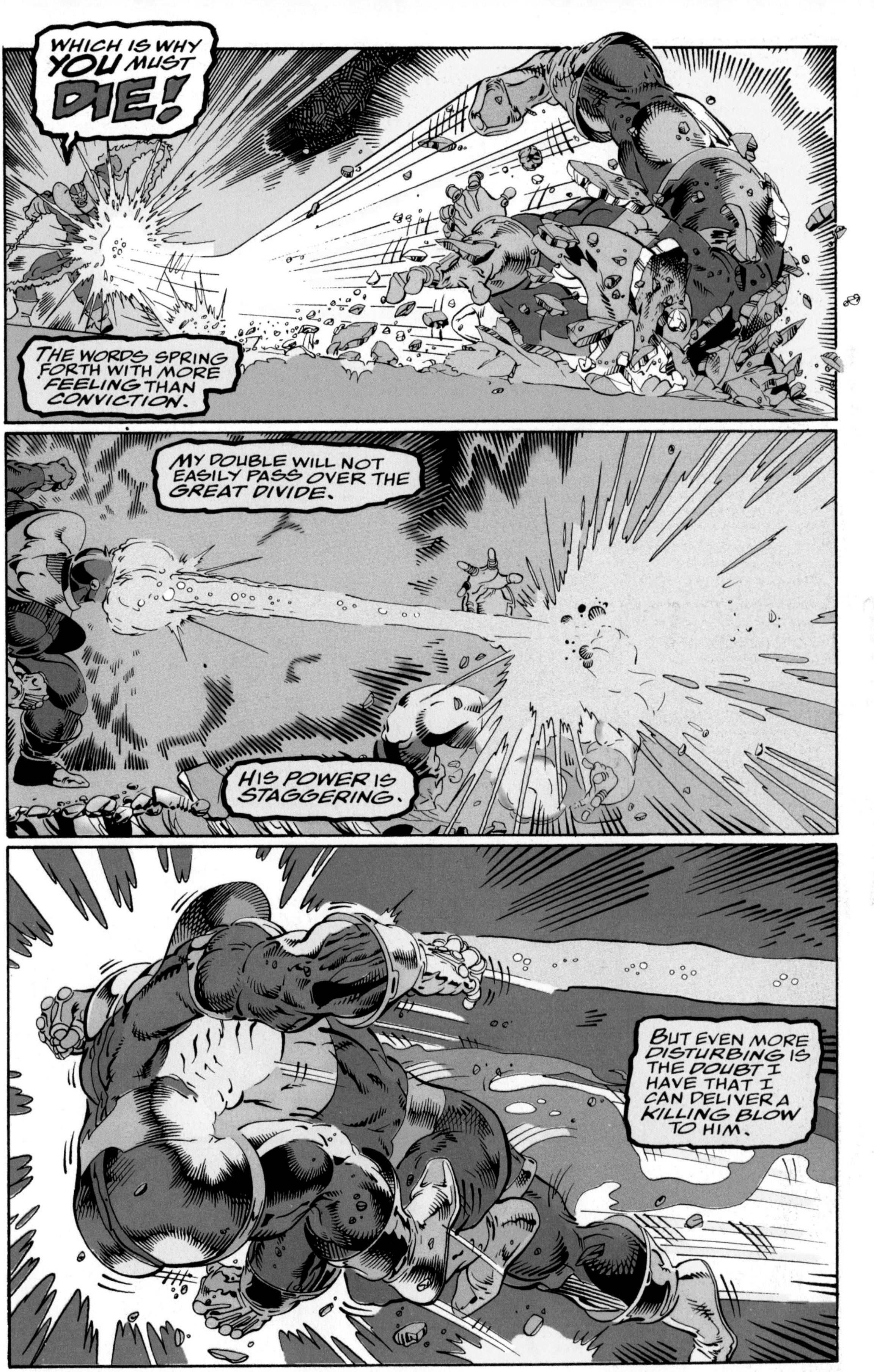
WHICH IS WHY YOU MUST DIE!
THE WORDS SPRING FORTH WITH MORE FEELING THAN CONVICTION.
MY DOUBLE WILL NOT EASILY PASS OVER THE GREAT DIVIDE.
HIS POWER IS STAGGERING.
BUT EVEN MORE DISTURBING IS THE DOUBT I HAVE THAT I CAN DELIVER A KILLING BLOW TO HIM.

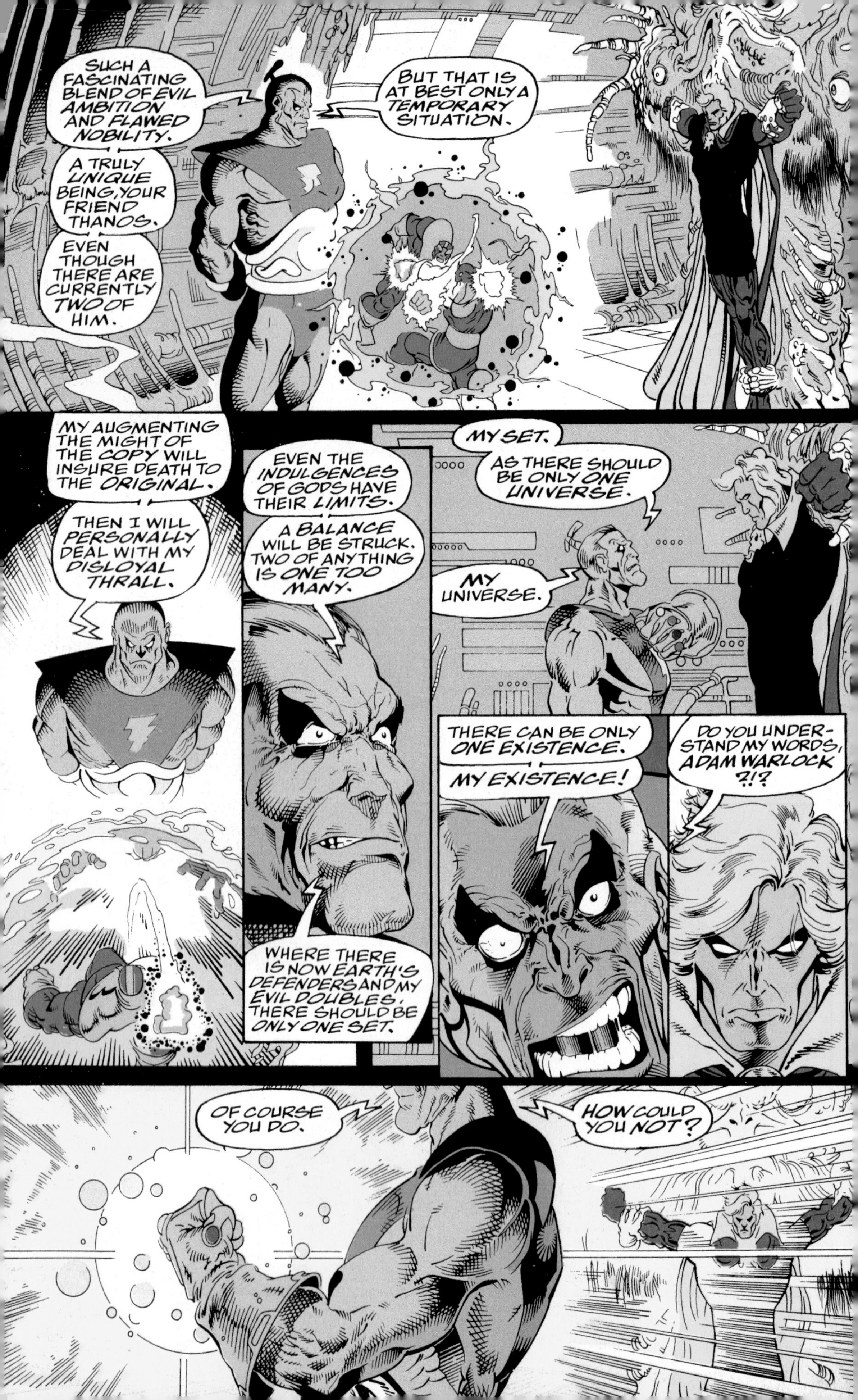
SUCH A FASCINATING BLEND OF EVIL AMBITION AND FLAWED NOBILITY.
A TRULY UNIQUE BEING, YOUR FRIEND THANOS.
EVEN THOUGH THERE ARE CURRENTLY TWO OF HIM.
BUT THAT IS AT BEST ONLY A TEMPORARY SITUATION.
MY AUGMENTING THE MIGHT OF THE COPY WILL INSURE DEATH TO THE ORIGINAL.
THEN I WILL PERSONALLY DEAL WITH MY DISLOYAL THRALL.
EVEN THE INDULGENCES OF GODS HAVE THEIR LIMITS.
A BALANCE WILL BE STRUCK. TWO OF ANYTHING IS ONE TOO MANY.
WHERE THERE IS NOW EARTH'S DEFENDERS AND MY EVIL DOUBLES, THERE SHOULD BE ONLY ONE SET.
MY SET.
AS THERE SHOULD BE ONLY ONE UNIVERSE.
MY UNIVERSE.
THERE CAN BE ONLY ONE EXISTENCE.
MY EXISTENCE!
DO YOU UNDERSTAND MY WORDS, ADAM WARLOCK ?!?
OF COURSE YOU DO.
HOW COULD YOU NOT?

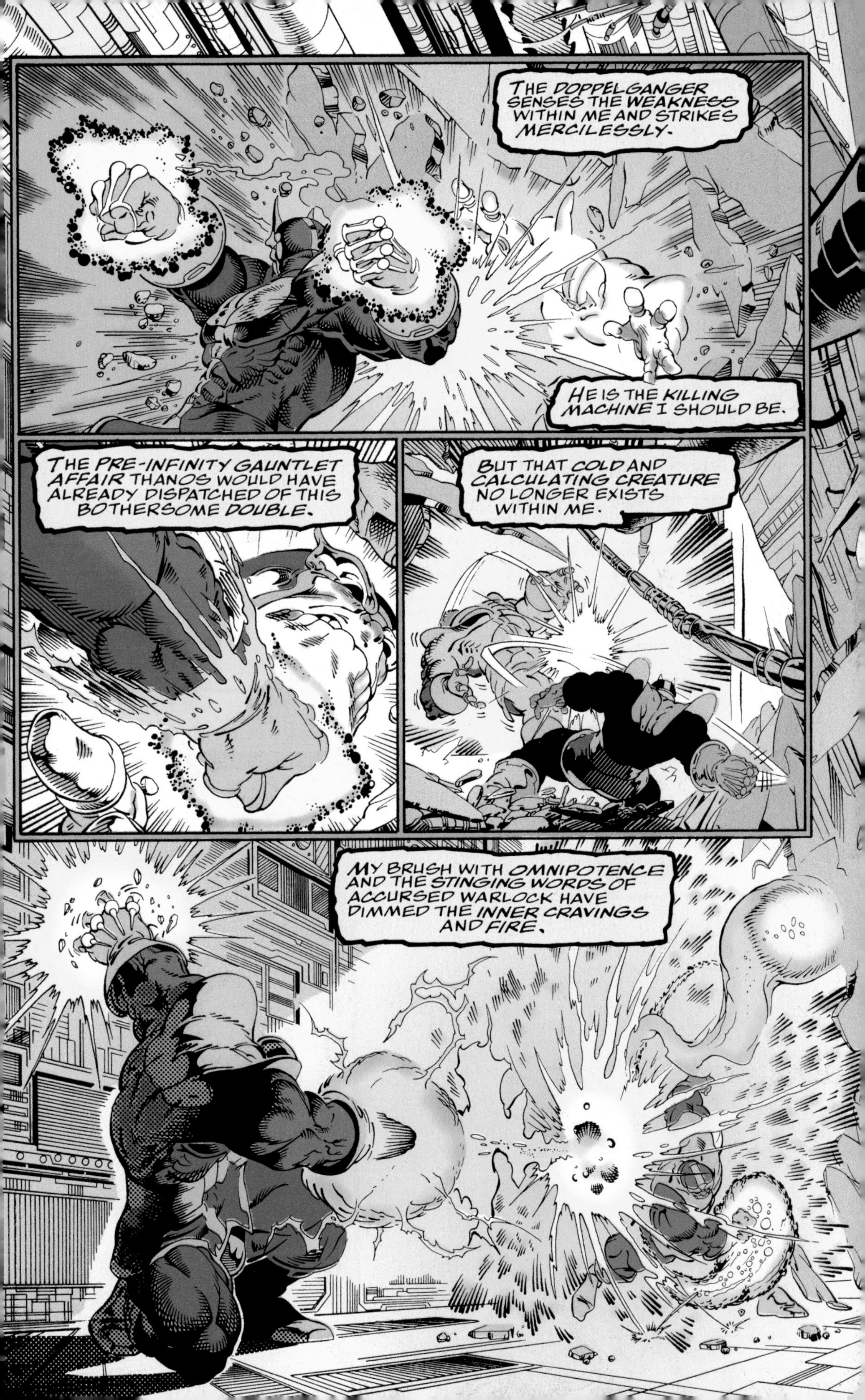
THE DOPPELGANGER SENSES THE WEAKNESS WITHIN ME AND STRIKES MERCILESSLY.
HE IS THE KILLING MACHINE I SHOULD BE.
THE PRE-INFINITY GAUNTLET AFFAIR THANOS WOULD HAVE ALREADY DISPATCHED OF THIS BOTHERSOME DOUBLE.
BUT THAT COLD AND CALCULATING CREATURE NO LONGER EXISTS WITHIN ME.
MY BRUSH WITH OMNIPOTENCE AND THE STINGING WORDS OF ACCURSED WARLOCK HAVE DIMMED THE INNER CRAVINGS AND FIRE.

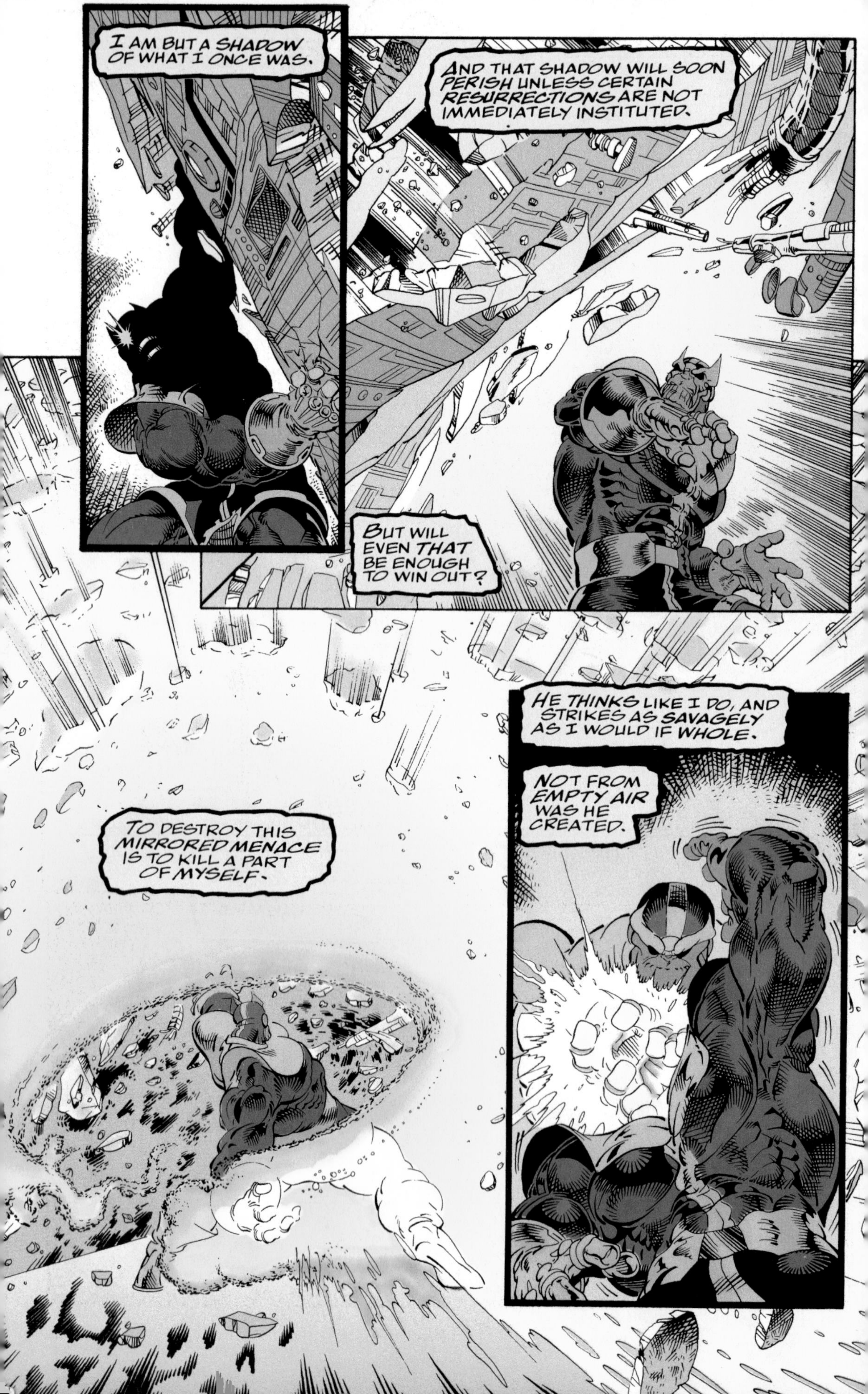
I AM BUT A SHADOW OF WHAT I ONCE WAS.
AND THAT SHADOW WILL SOON PERISH UNLESS CERTAIN RESURRECTIONS ARE NOT IMMEDIATELY INSTITUTED.
BUT WILL EVEN THAT BE ENOUGH TO WIN OUT?
HE THINKS LIKE I DO, AND STRIKES AS SAVAGELY AS I WOULD IF WHOLE.
NOT FROM EMPTY AIR WAS HE CREATED.
TO DESTROY THIS MIRRORED MENACE IS TO KILL A PART OF MYSELF.

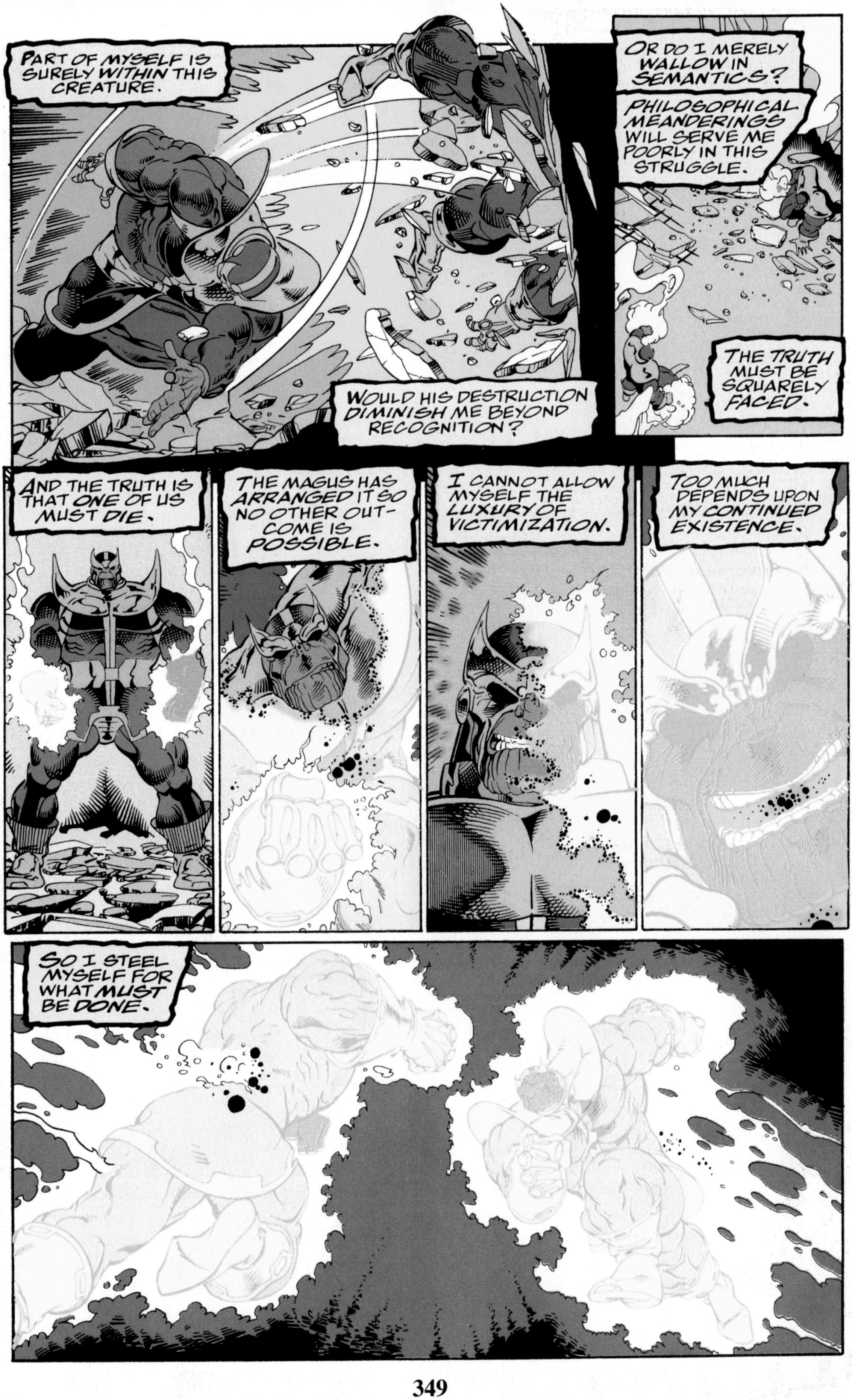
PART OF MYSELF IS SURELY WITHIN THIS CREATURE.
WOULD HIS DESTRUCTION DIMINISH ME BEYOND RECOGNITION?
OR DO I MERELY WALLOW IN SEMANTICS?
PHILOSOPHICAL MEANDERINGS WILL SERVE ME POORLY IN THIS STRUGGLE.
THE TRUTH MUST BE SQUARELY FACED.
AND THE TRUTH IS THAT ONE OF US MUST DIE.
THE MAGUS HAS ARRANGED IT SO NO OTHER OUT-COME IS POSSIBLE.
I CANNOT ALLOW MYSELF THE LUXURY OF VICTIMIZATION.
TOO MUCH DEPENDS UPON MY CONTINUED EXISTENCE.
SO I STEEL MYSELF FOR WHAT MUST BE DONE.

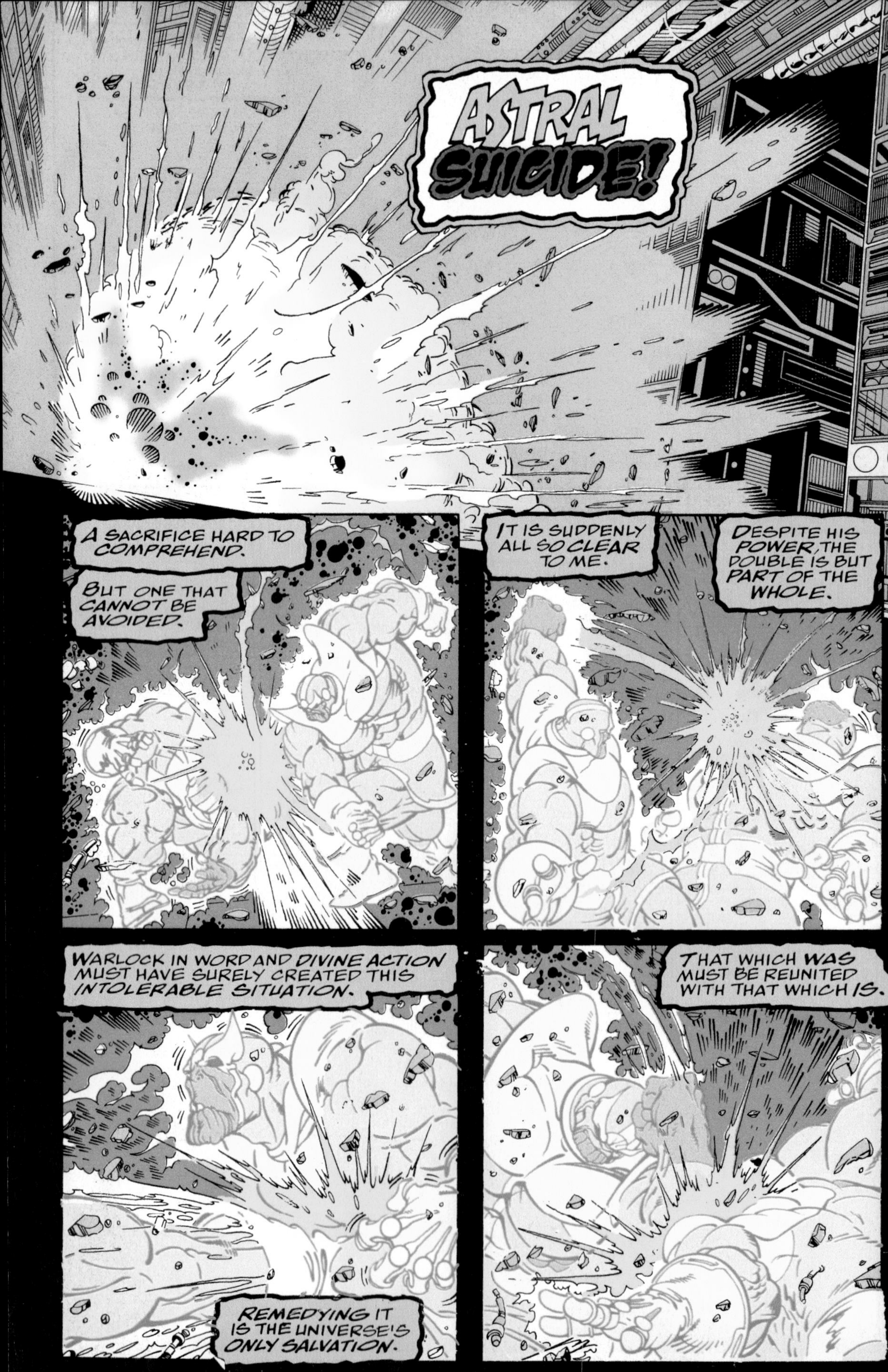
ASTRAL SUICIDE!
A SACRIFICE HARD TO COMPREHEND.
BUT ONE THAT CANNOT BE AVOIDED.
IT IS SUDDENLY ALL SO CLEAR TO ME.
DESPITE HIS POWER, THE DOUBLE IS BUT PART OF THE WHOLE.
WARLOCK IN WORD AND DIVINE ACTION MUST HAVE SURELY CREATED THIS INTOLERABLE SITUATION.
REMEDYING IT IS THE UNIVERSE'S ONLY SALVATION.
THAT WHICH WAS MUST BE REUNITED WITH THAT WHICH IS.

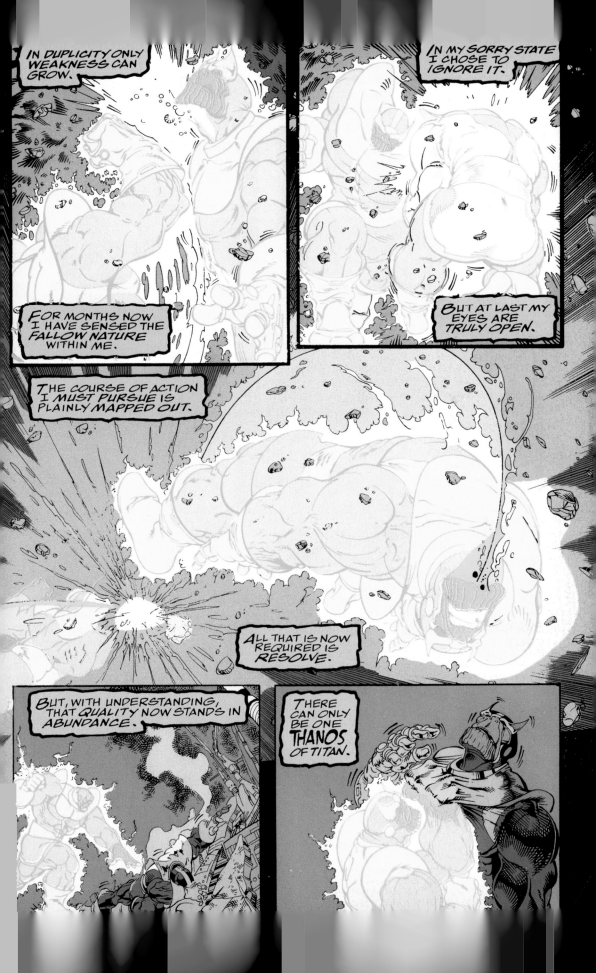

IN DUPLICITY ONLY WEAKNESS CAN GROW.

IN MY SORRY STATE I CHOSE TO IGNORE IT.

FOR MONTHS NOW I HAVE SENSED THE FALLOW NATURE WITHIN ME.

BUT AT LAST MY EYES ARE TRULY OPEN.

THE COURSE OF ACTION I MUST PURSUE IS PLAINLY MAPPED OUT.

ALL THAT IS NOW REQUIRED IS RESOLVE.

BUT, WITH UNDERSTANDING, THAT QUALITY NOW STANDS IN ABUNDANCE.

THERE CAN ONLY BE ONE THANOS OF TITAN.

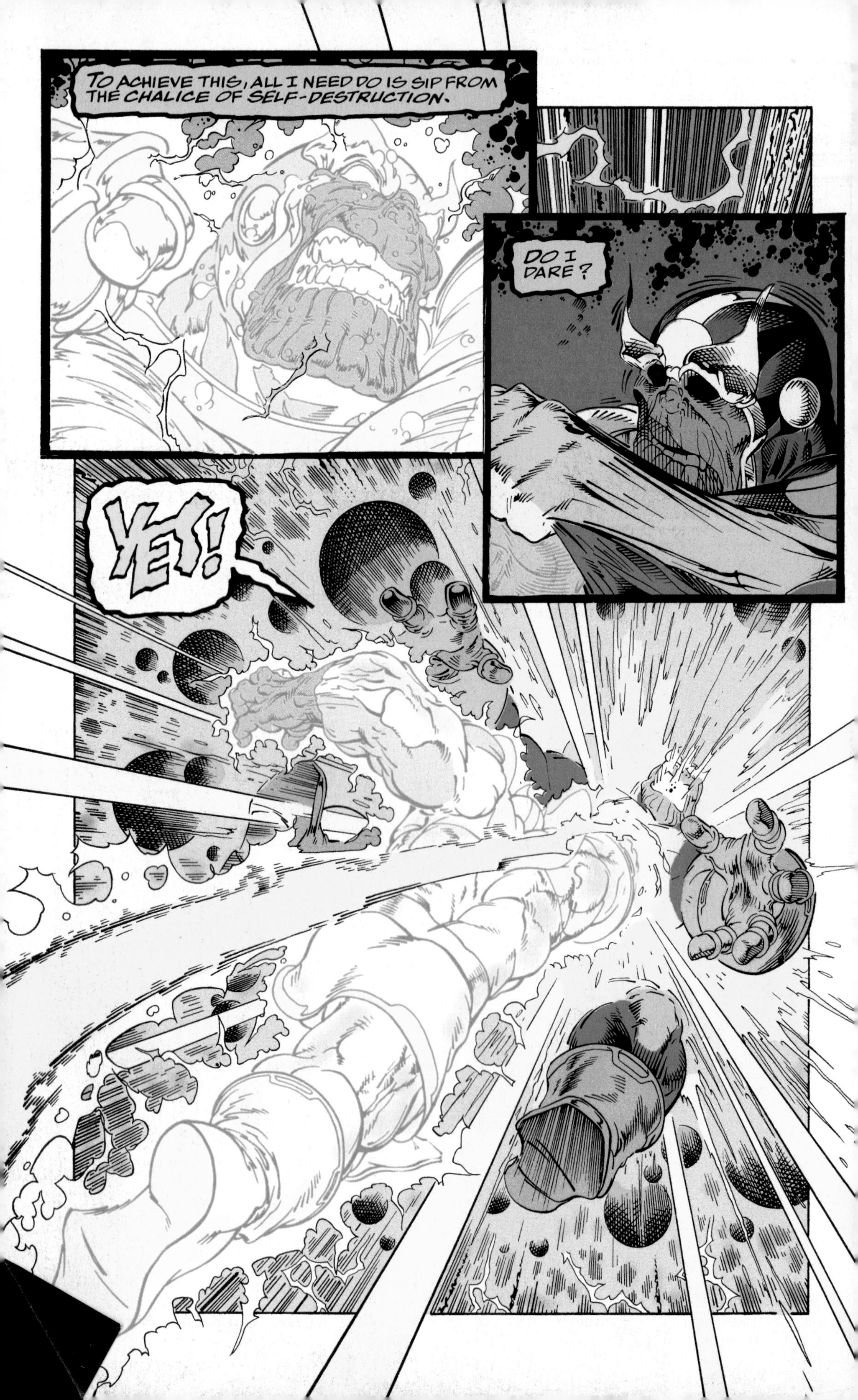
TO ACHIEVE THIS, ALL I NEED DO IS SIP FROM THE CHALICE OF SELF-DESTRUCTION.
DO I DARE?
YES!

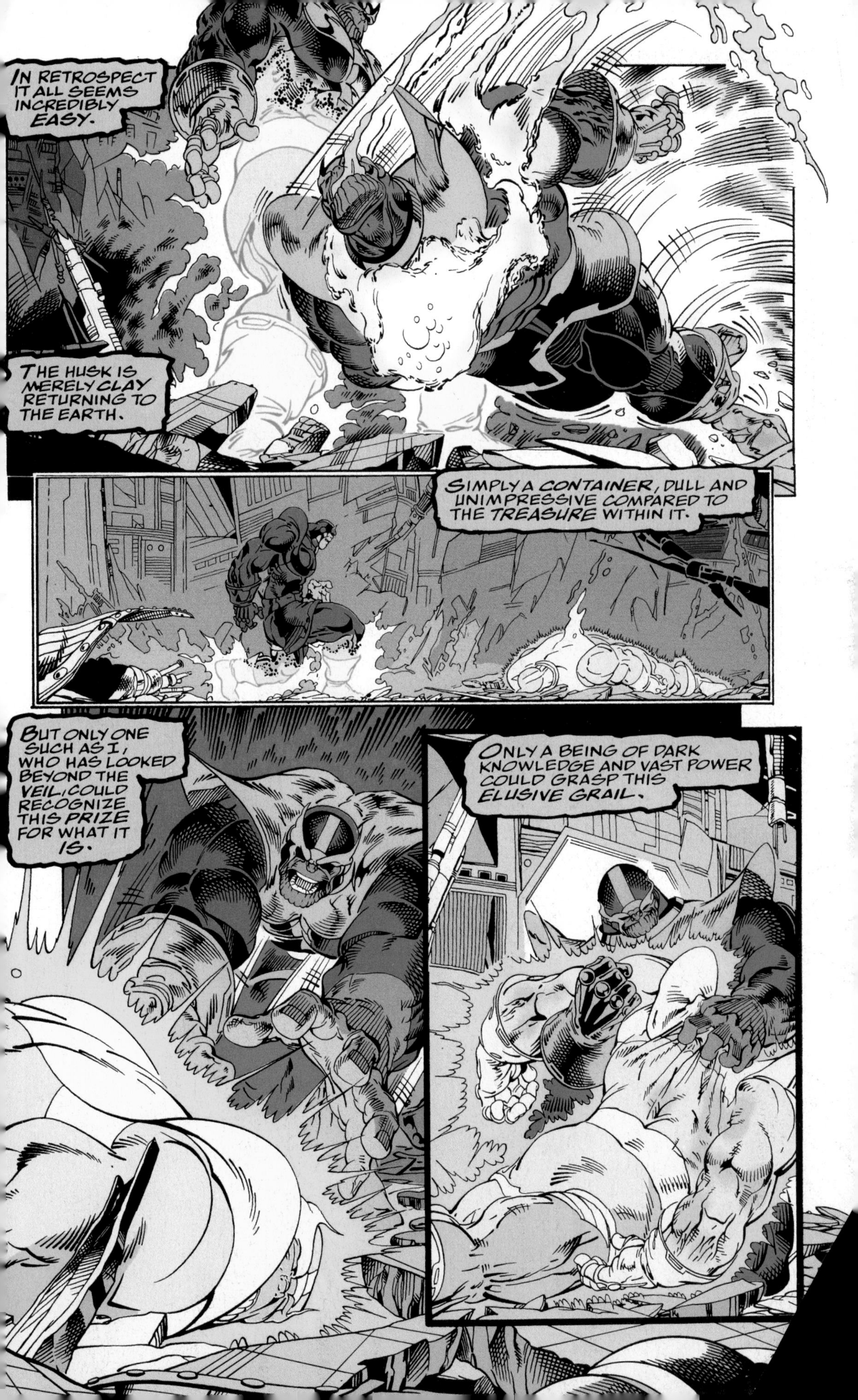
IN RETROSPECT IT ALL SEEMS INCREDIBLY EASY.
THE HUSK IS MERELY CLAY RETURNING TO THE EARTH.
SIMPLY A CONTAINER, DULL AND UNIMPRESSIVE COMPARED TO THE TREASURE WITHIN IT.
BUT ONLY ONE SUCH AS I, WHO HAS LOOKED BEYOND THE VEIL, COULD RECOGNIZE THIS PRIZE FOR WHAT IT IS.
ONLY A BEING OF DARK KNOWLEDGE AND VAST POWER COULD GRASP THIS ELUSIVE GRAIL.

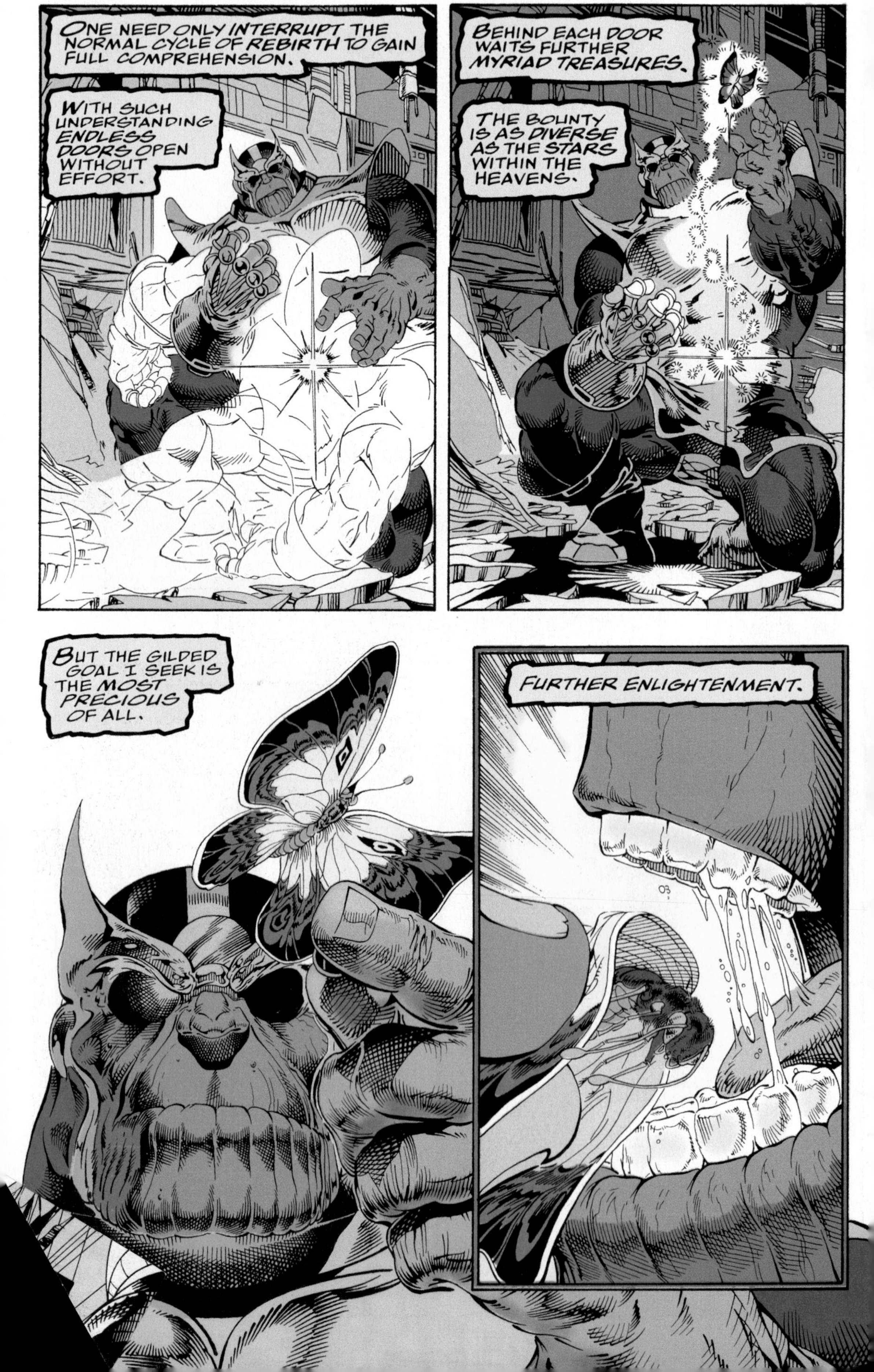

ONE NEED ONLY INTERRUPT THE NORMAL CYCLE OF REBIRTH TO GAIN FULL COMPREHENSION.
WITH SUCH UNDERSTANDING ENDLESS DOORS OPEN WITHOUT EFFORT.
BEHIND EACH DOOR WAITS FURTHER MYRIAD TREASURES.
THE BOUNTY IS AS DIVERSE AS THE STARS WITHIN THE HEAVENS.
BUT THE GILDED GOAL I SEEK IS THE MOST PRECIOUS OF ALL.
FURTHER ENLIGHTENMENT.

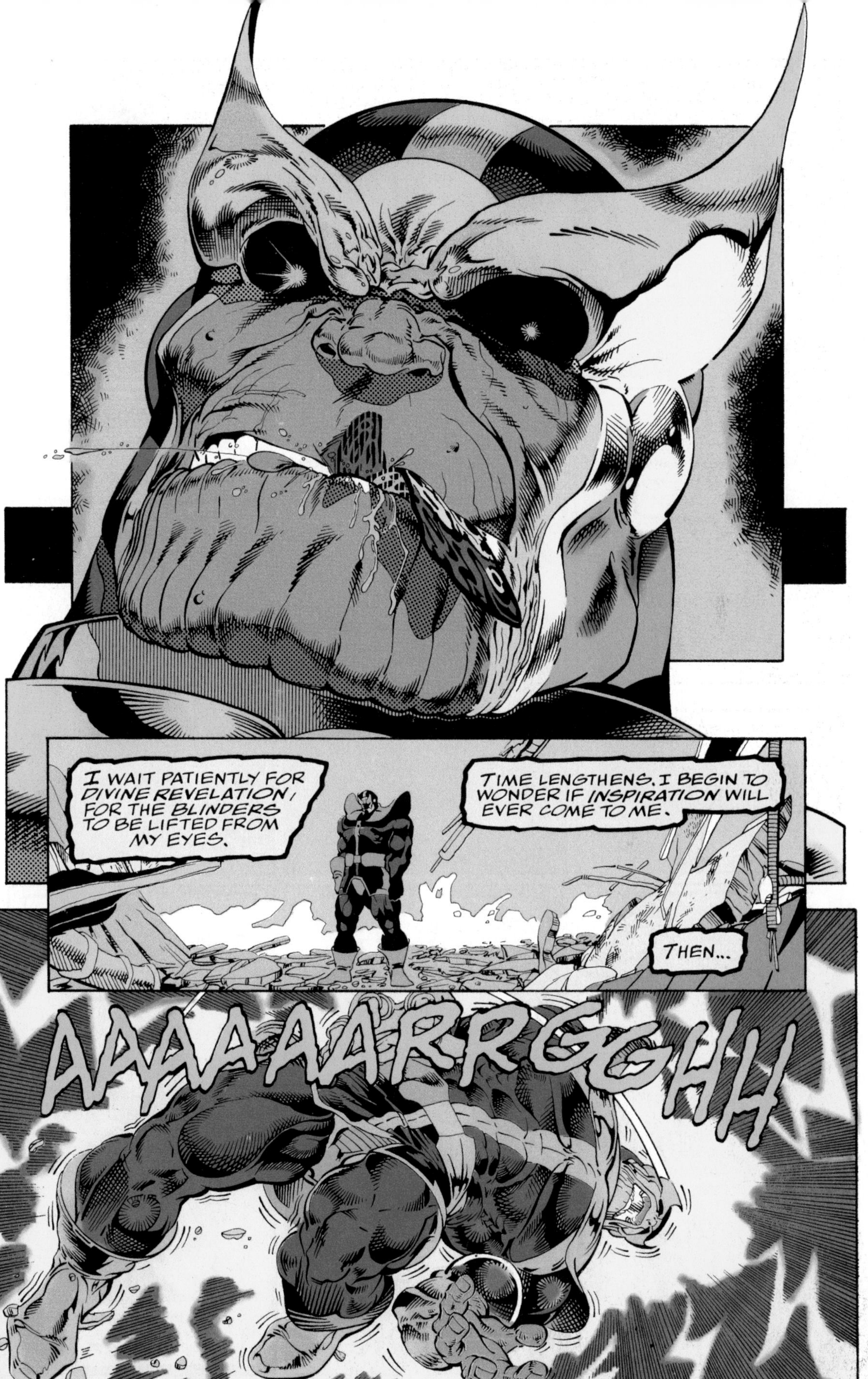
I WAIT PATIENTLY FOR DIVINE REVELATION, FOR THE BLINDERS TO BE LIFTED FROM MY EYES.
TIME LENGTHENS. I BEGIN TO WONDER IF INSPIRATION WILL EVER COME TO ME.
THEN...
AAAAAARRGGHH

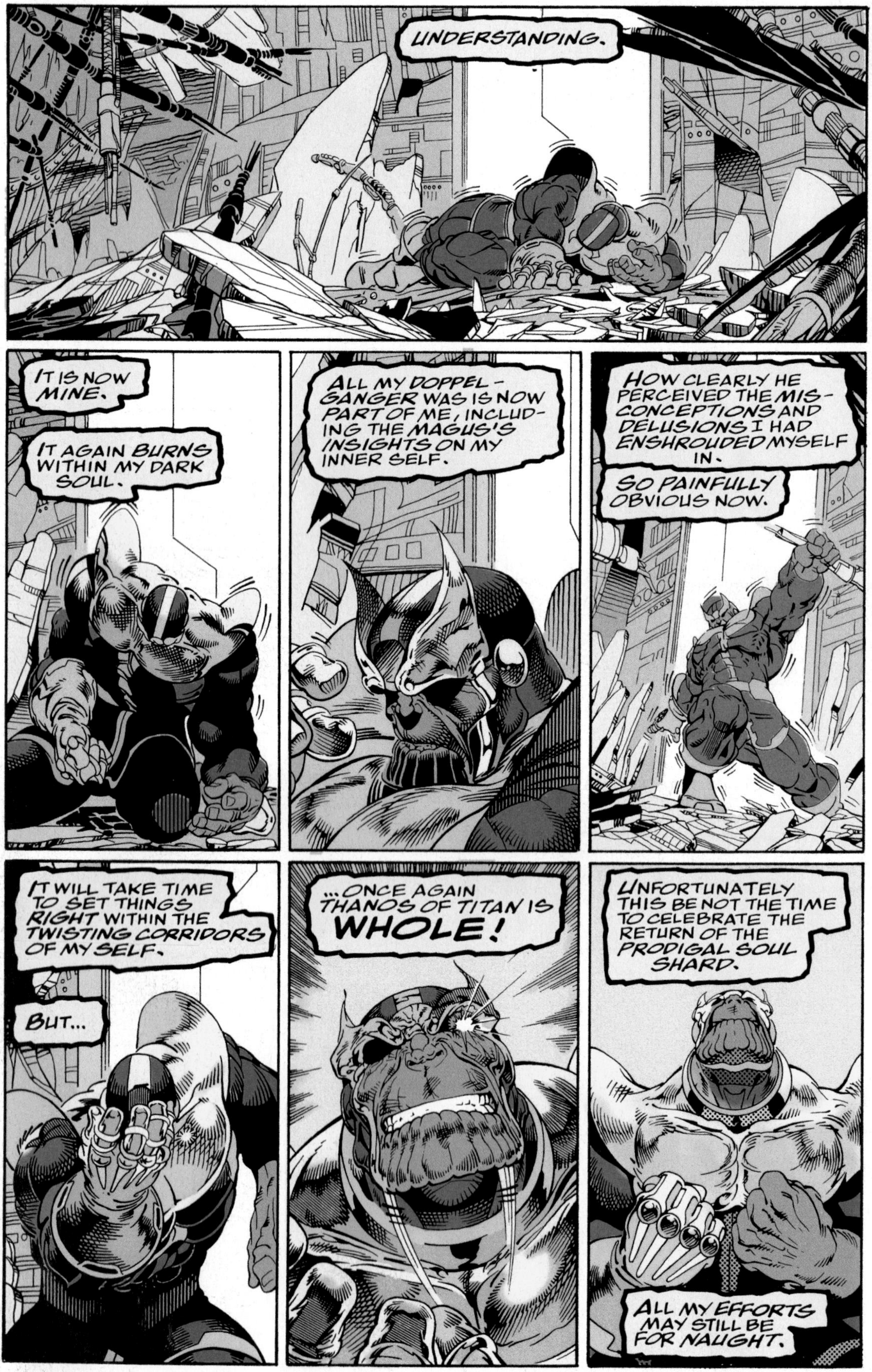
UNDERSTANDING.
IT IS NOW MINE.
IT AGAIN BURNS WITHIN MY DARK SOUL.
ALL MY DOPPELGANGER WAS IS NOW PART OF ME, INCLUDING THE MAGUS'S INSIGHTS ON MY INNER SELF.
HOW CLEARLY HE PERCEIVED THE MISCONCEPTIONS AND DELUSIONS I HAD ENSHROUDED MYSELF IN.
SO PAINFULLY OBVIOUS NOW.
IT WILL TAKE TIME TO SET THINGS RIGHT WITHIN THE TWISTING CORRIDORS OF MY SELF.
BUT...
...ONCE AGAIN THANOS OF TITAN IS WHOLE!
UNFORTUNATELY THIS BE NOT THE TIME TO CELEBRATE THE RETURN OF THE PRODIGAL SOUL SHARD.
ALL MY EFFORTS MAY STILL BE FOR NAUGHT.

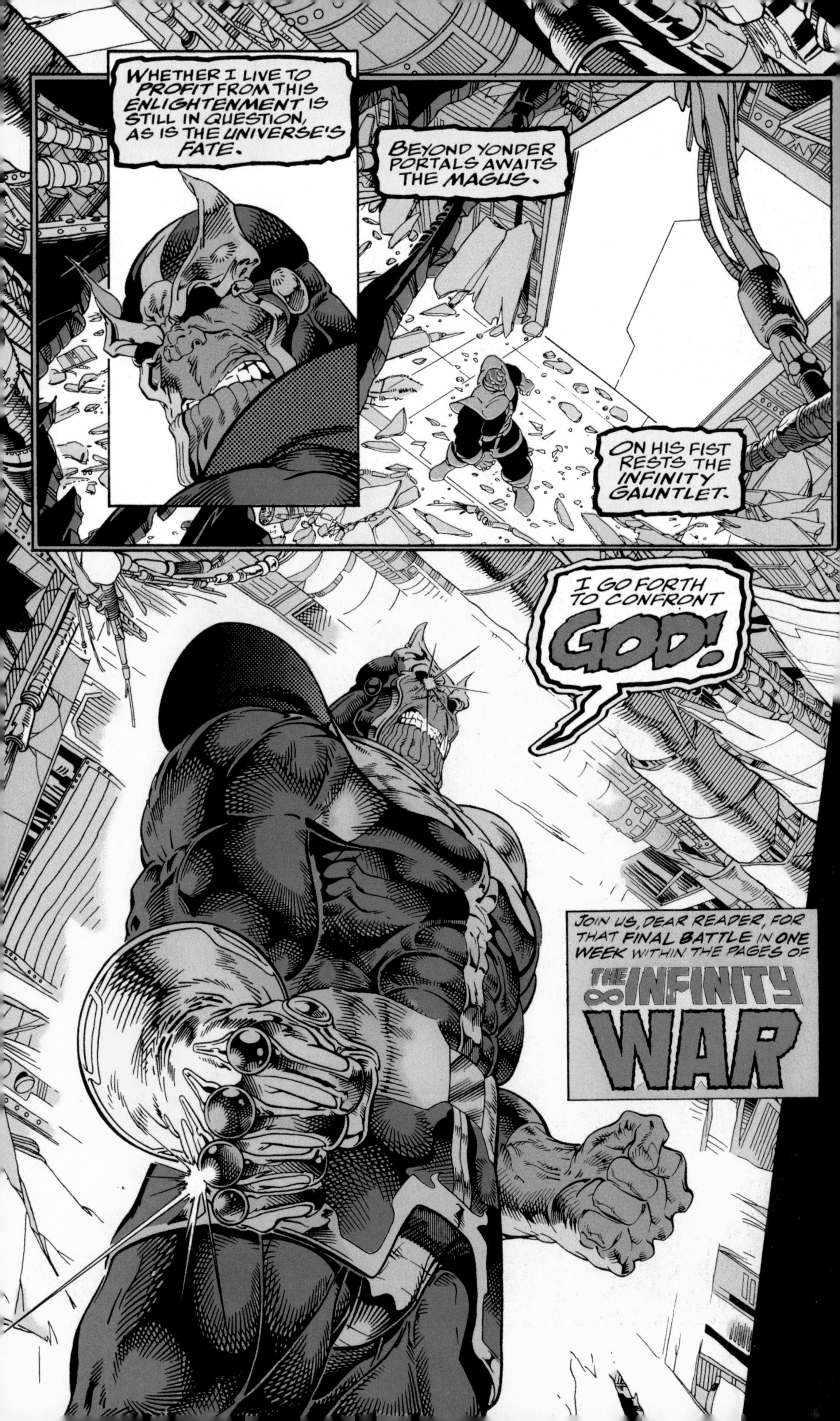
WHETHER I LIVE TO PROFIT FROM THIS ENLIGHTENMENT IS STILL IN QUESTION, AS IS THE UNIVERSE'S FATE.
BEYOND YONDER PORTALS AWAITS THE MAGUS.
ON HIS FIST RESTS THE INFINITY GAUNTLET.
I GO FORTH TO CONFRONT GOD!
JOIN US, DEAR READER, FOR THAT FINAL BATTLE IN ONE WEEK WITHIN THE PAGES OF
THE INFINITY WAR

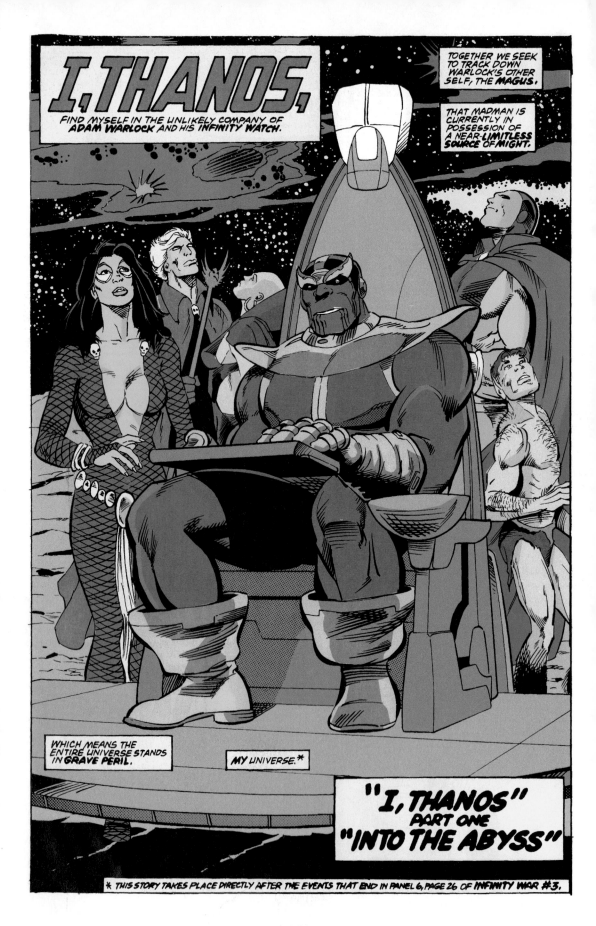

I, THANOS, FIND MYSELF IN THE UNLIKELY COMPANY OF *ADAM WARLOCK* AND HIS *INFINITY WATCH.*

TOGETHER WE SEEK TO TRACK DOWN WARLOCK'S OTHER SELF, THE *MAGUS.*

THAT MADMAN IS CURRENTLY IN POSSESSION OF A NEAR-*LIMITLESS SOURCE OF MIGHT.*

WHICH MEANS THE ENTIRE UNIVERSE STANDS IN *GRAVE PERIL.*

MY UNIVERSE. *

"I, THANOS" PART ONE **"INTO THE ABYSS"**

* THIS STORY TAKES PLACE DIRECTLY AFTER THE EVENTS THAT END IN PANEL 6, PAGE 26 OF *INFINITY WAR #3.*

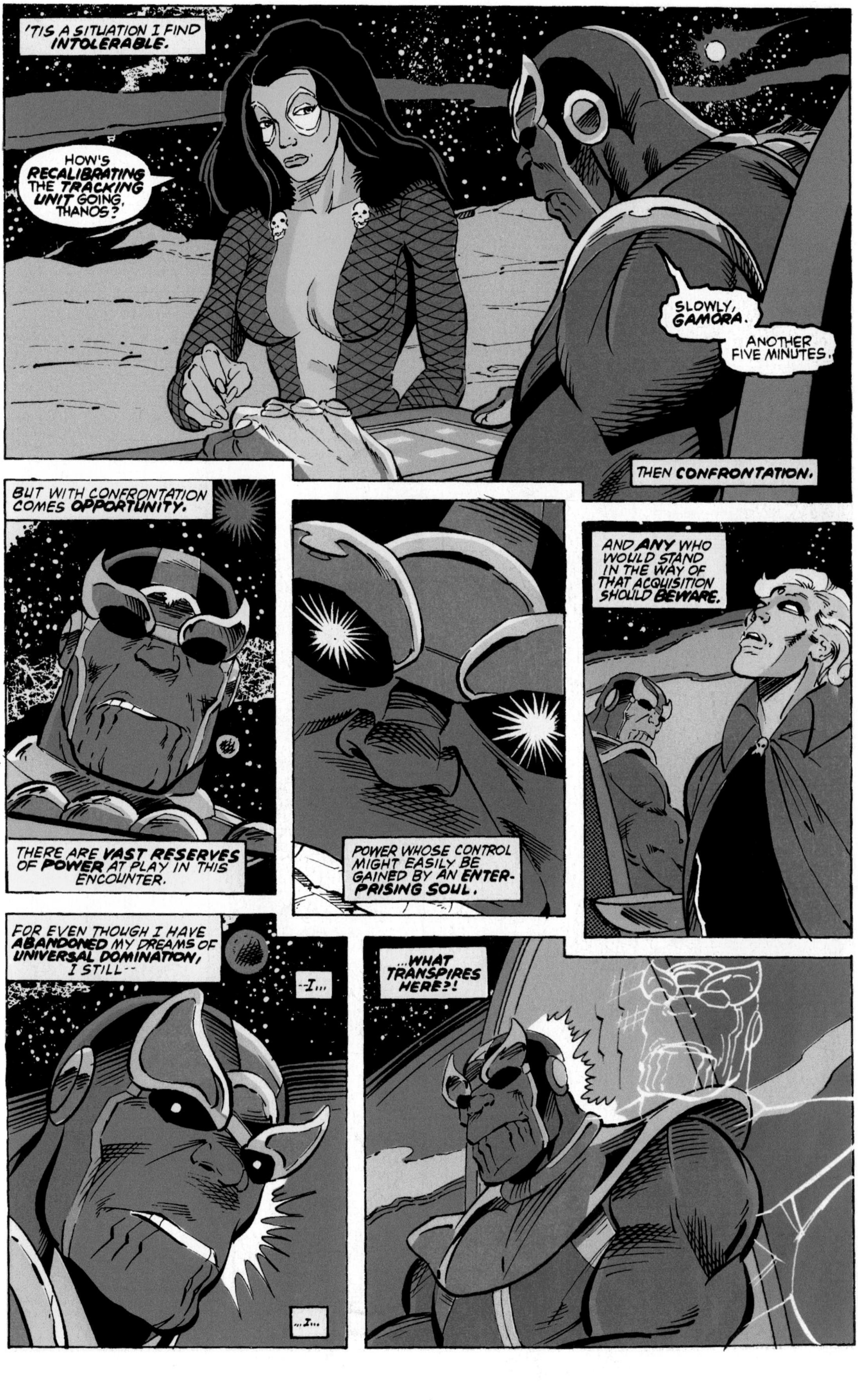
'TIS A SITUATION I FIND INTOLERABLE.
HOW'S RECALIBRATING THE TRACKING UNIT GOING, THANOS?
SLOWLY, GAMORA.
ANOTHER FIVE MINUTES.
THEN CONFRONTATION.
BUT WITH CONFRONTATION COMES OPPORTUNITY.
THERE ARE VAST RESERVES OF POWER AT PLAY IN THIS ENCOUNTER.
POWER WHOSE CONTROL MIGHT EASILY BE GAINED BY AN ENTER-PRISING SOUL.
AND ANY WHO WOULD STAND IN THE WAY OF THAT ACQUISITION SHOULD BEWARE.
FOR EVEN THOUGH I HAVE ABANDONED MY DREAMS OF UNIVERSAL DOMINATION, I STILL--
--I...
...I...
...WHAT TRANSPIRES HERE?!

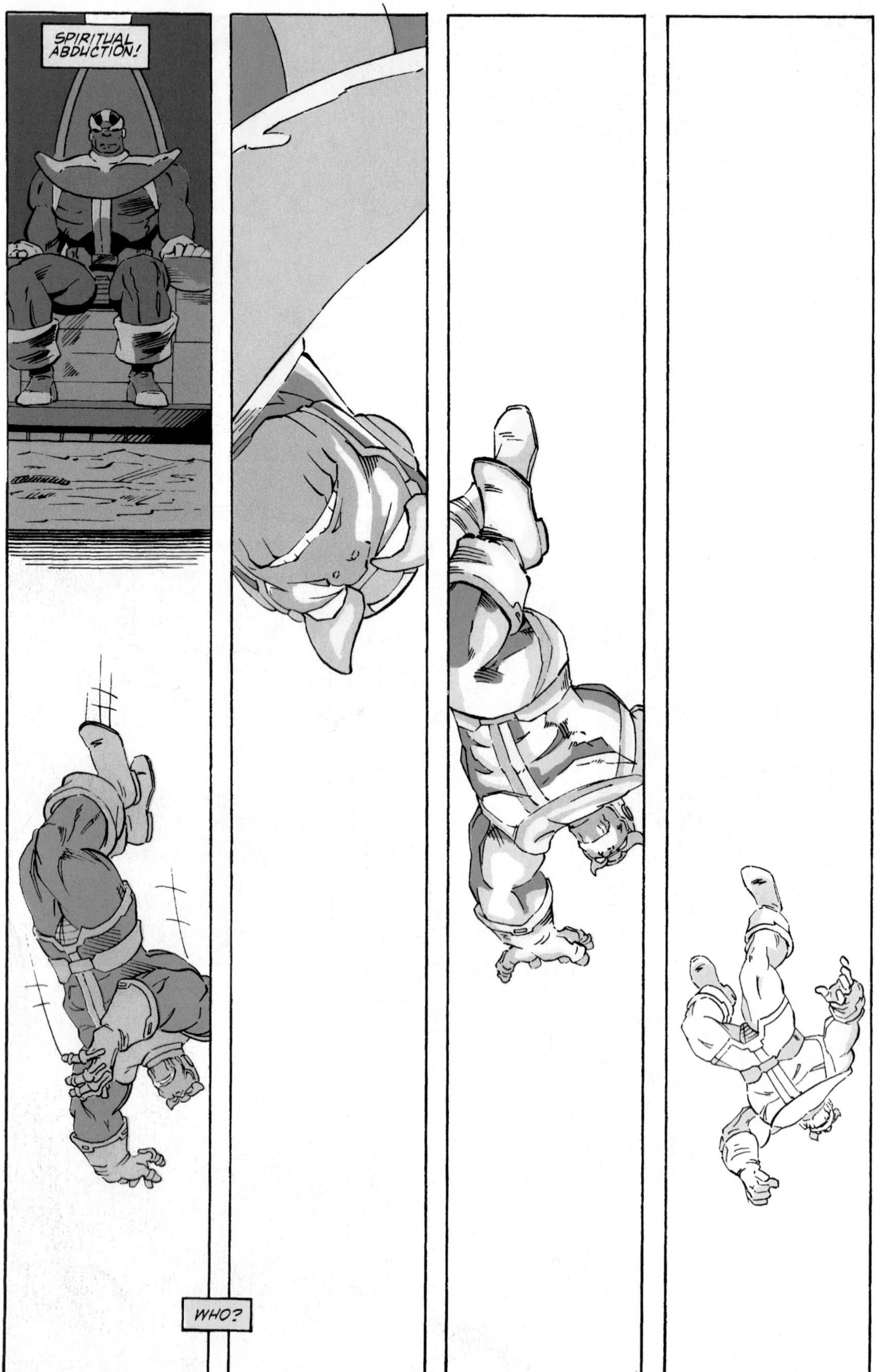
SPIRITUAL ABDUCTION!
WHO?

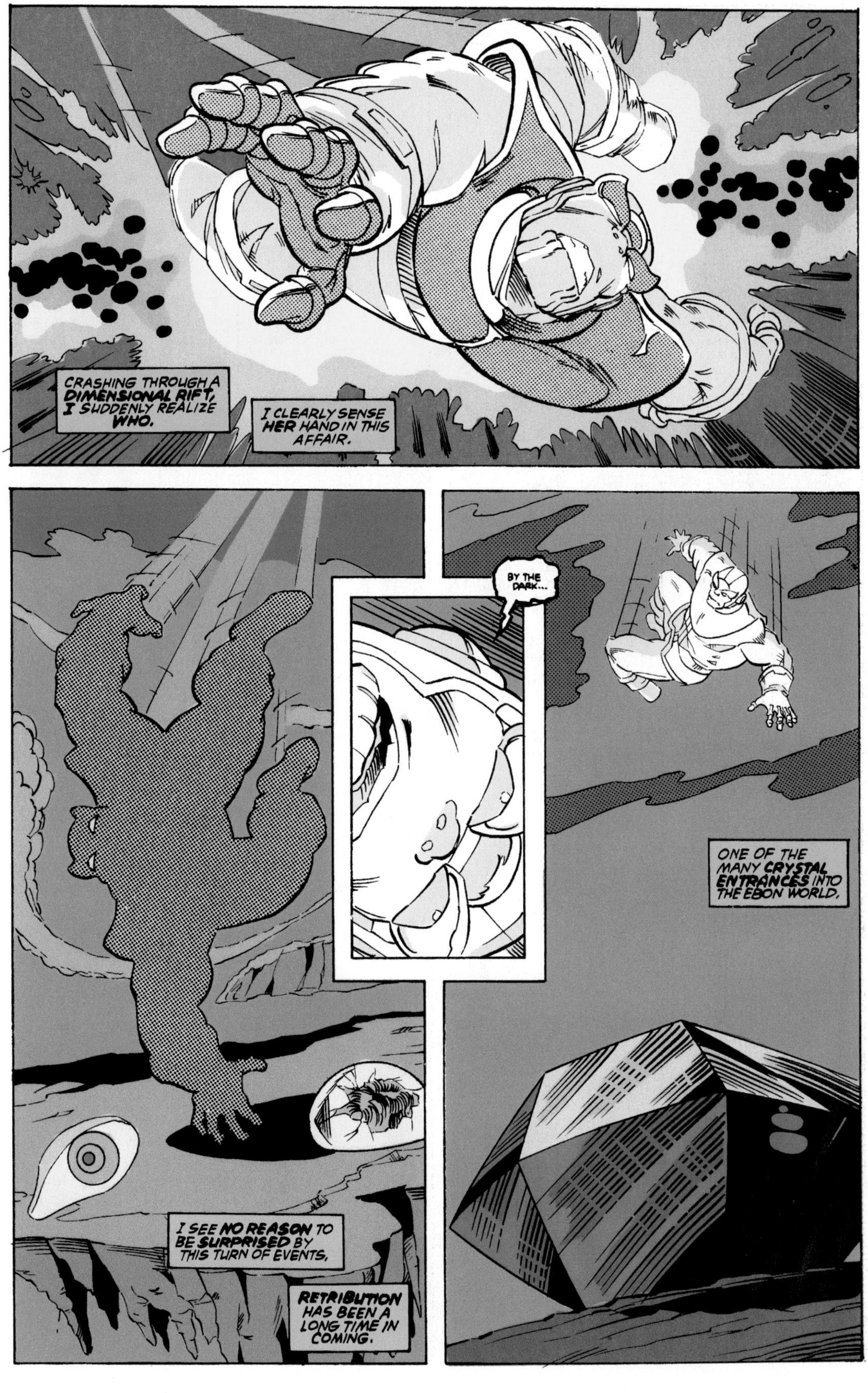
CRASHING THROUGH A DIMENSIONAL RIFT, I SUDDENLY REALIZE WHO.
I CLEARLY SENSE HER HAND IN THIS AFFAIR.
BY THE DARK...
ONE OF THE MANY CRYSTAL ENTRANCES INTO THE EBON WORLD,
I SEE NO REASON TO BE SURPRISED BY THIS TURN OF EVENTS,
RETRIBUTION HAS BEEN A LONG TIME IN COMING.

BUT IN THIS **STATE** I WILL **NOT** SURVIVE THE TRANSITION!

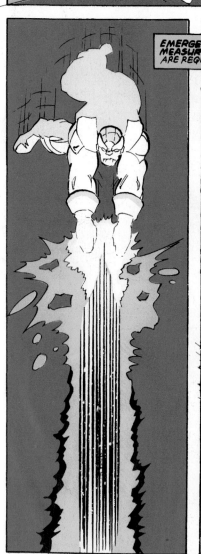

EMERGENCY MEASURES ARE REQUIRED.

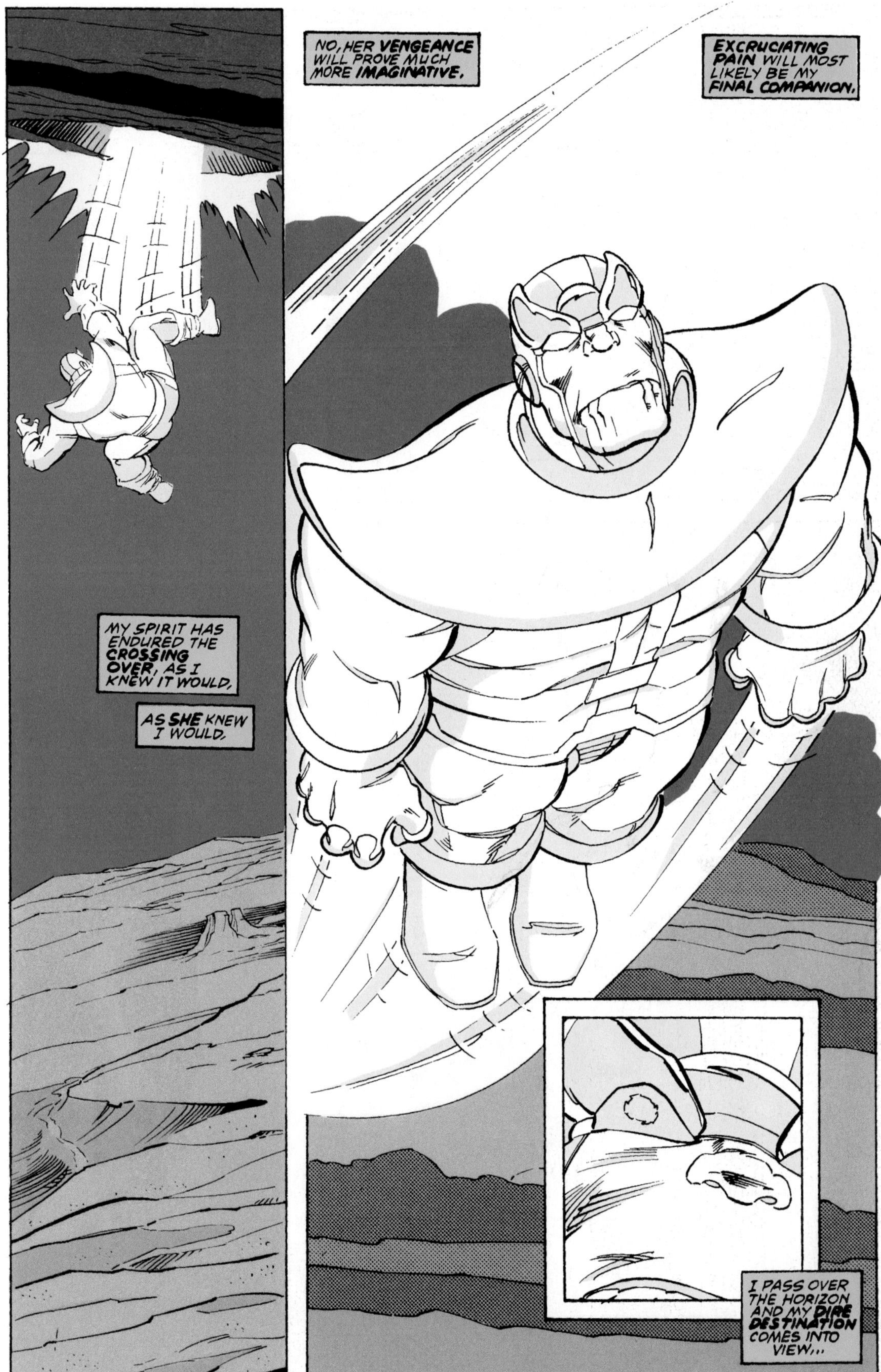
NO, HER VENGEANCE WILL PROVE MUCH MORE IMAGINATIVE.
EXCRUCIATING PAIN WILL MOST LIKELY BE MY FINAL COMPANION.
MY SPIRIT HAS ENDURED THE CROSSING OVER, AS I KNEW IT WOULD,
AS SHE KNEW I WOULD.
I PASS OVER THE HORIZON AND MY DIRE DESTINATION COMES INTO VIEW...

...THE ROYAL PALACE OF MISTRESS DEATH!

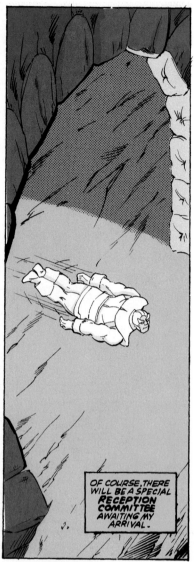

OF COURSE, THERE WILL BE A SPECIAL RECEPTION COMMITTEE AWAITING MY ARRIVAL.

EXACTLY WHO I EXPECTED.

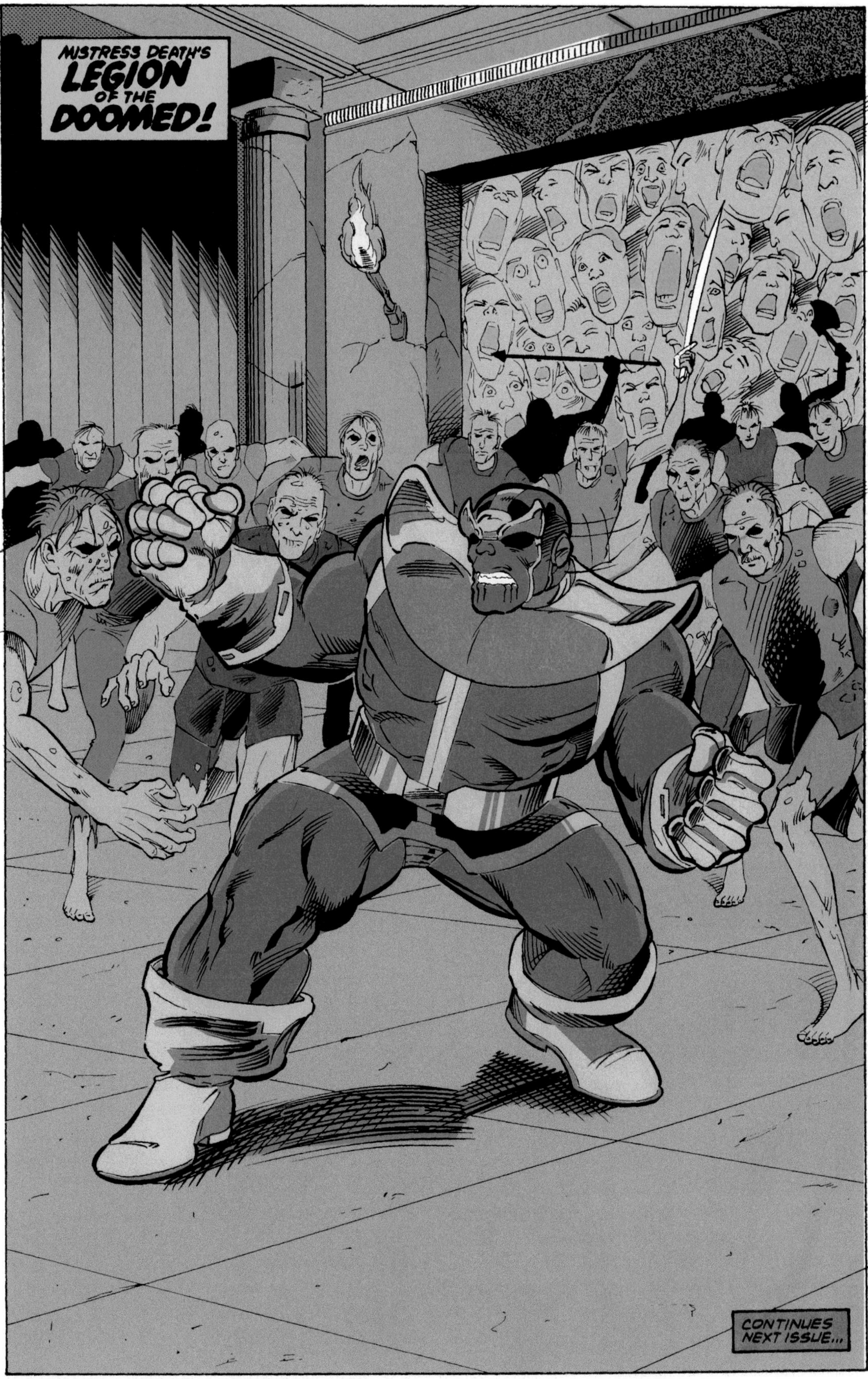
MISTRESS DEATH'S LEGION OF THE DOOMED!
CONTINUES NEXT ISSUE...

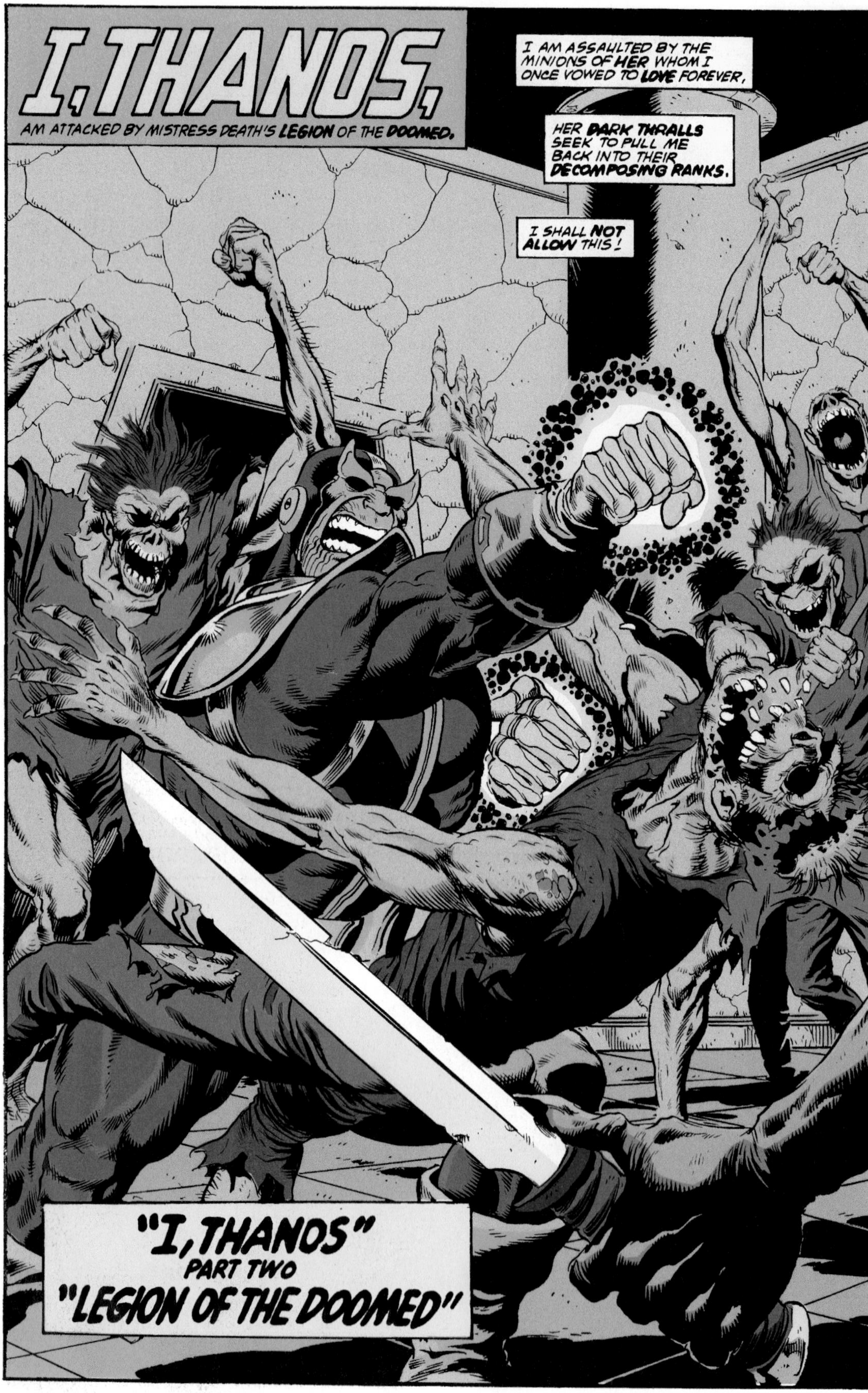
I, THANOS,
AM ATTACKED BY MISTRESS DEATH'S LEGION OF THE DOOMED.
I AM ASSAULTED BY THE MINIONS OF HER WHOM I ONCE VOWED TO LOVE FOREVER,
HER DARK THRALLS SEEK TO PULL ME BACK INTO THEIR DECOMPOSING RANKS.
I SHALL NOT ALLOW THIS!
"I, THANOS" PART TWO "LEGION OF THE DOOMED"

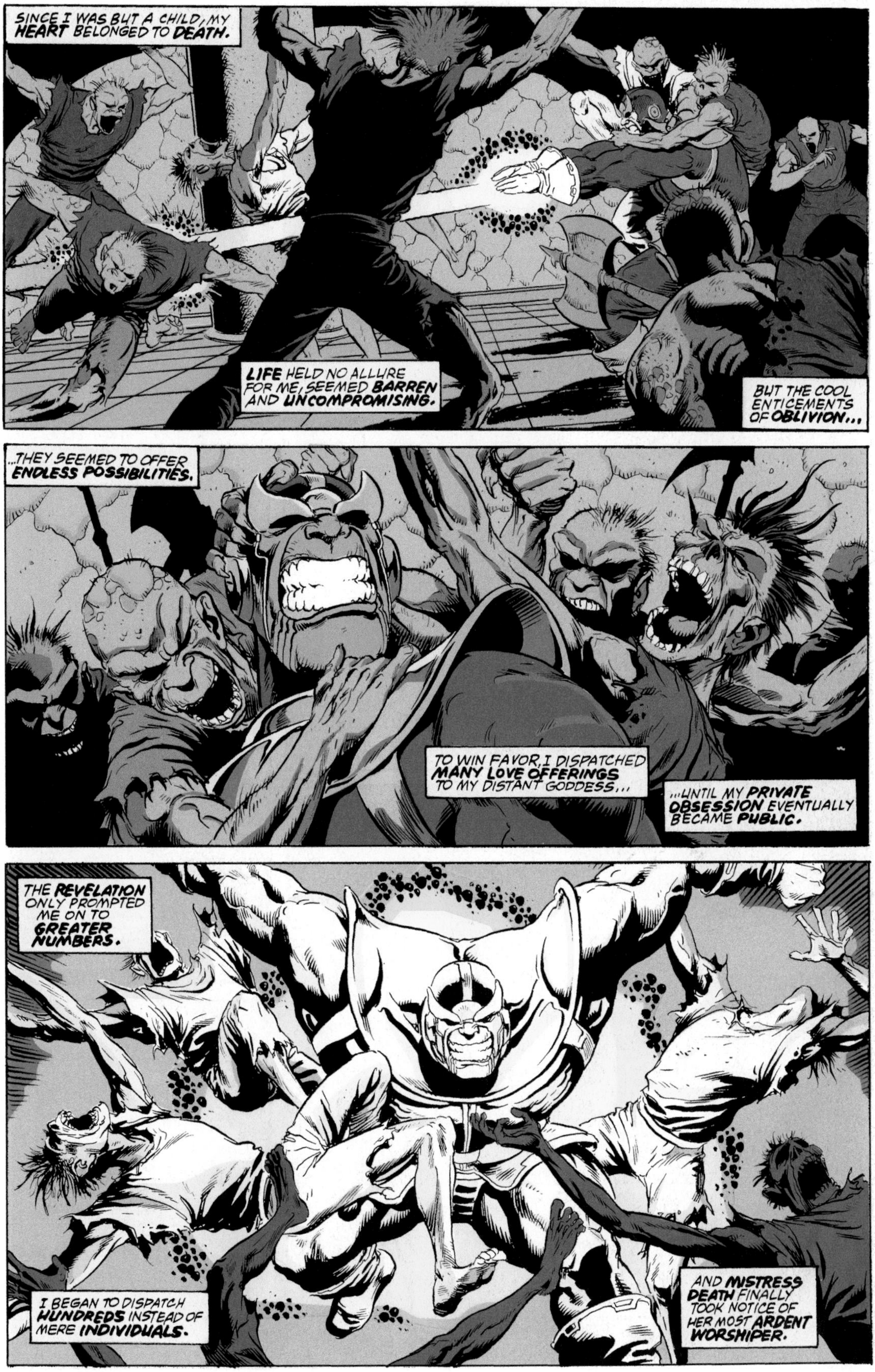
SINCE I WAS BUT A CHILD, MY HEART BELONGED TO DEATH.
LIFE HELD NO ALLURE FOR ME, SEEMED BARREN AND UNCOMPROMISING.
BUT THE COOL ENTICEMENTS OF OBLIVION...
...THEY SEEMED TO OFFER ENDLESS POSSIBILITIES.
TO WIN FAVOR, I DISPATCHED MANY LOVE OFFERINGS TO MY DISTANT GODDESS...
...UNTIL MY PRIVATE OBSESSION EVENTUALLY BECAME PUBLIC.
THE REVELATION ONLY PROMPTED ME ON TO GREATER NUMBERS.
I BEGAN TO DISPATCH HUNDREDS INSTEAD OF MERE INDIVIDUALS.
AND MISTRESS DEATH FINALLY TOOK NOTICE OF HER MOST ARDENT WORSHIPER.

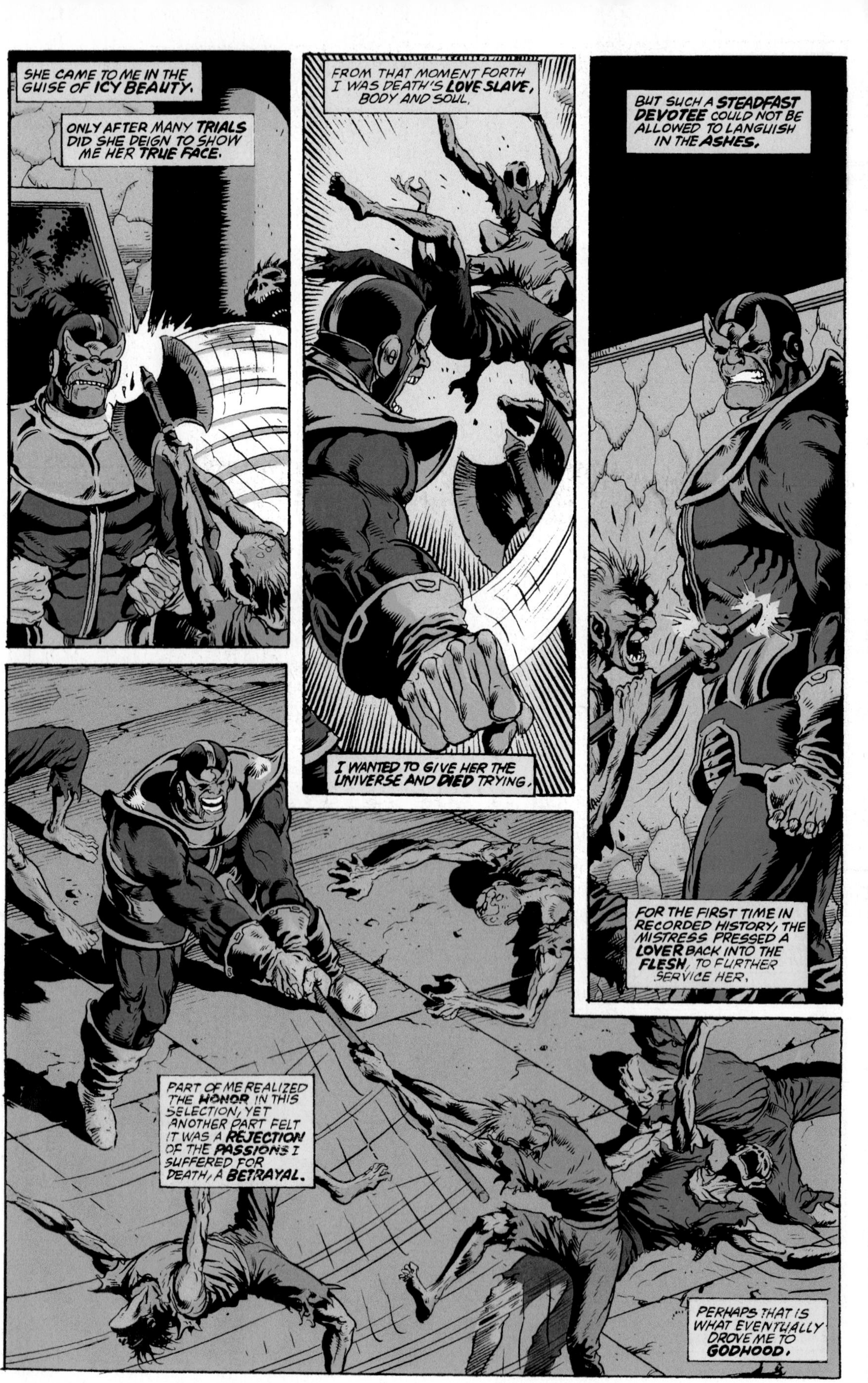

SHE CAME TO ME IN THE GUISE OF ICY BEAUTY.
ONLY AFTER MANY TRIALS DID SHE DEIGN TO SHOW ME HER TRUE FACE.
FROM THAT MOMENT FORTH I WAS DEATH'S LOVE SLAVE, BODY AND SOUL.
I WANTED TO GIVE HER THE UNIVERSE AND DIED TRYING.
BUT SUCH A STEADFAST DEVOTEE COULD NOT BE ALLOWED TO LANGUISH IN THE ASHES.
FOR THE FIRST TIME IN RECORDED HISTORY, THE MISTRESS PRESSED A LOVER BACK INTO THE FLESH, TO FURTHER SERVICE HER.
PART OF ME REALIZED THE HONOR IN THIS SELECTION, YET ANOTHER PART FELT IT WAS A REJECTION OF THE PASSIONS I SUFFERED FOR DEATH, A BETRAYAL.
PERHAPS THAT IS WHAT EVENTUALLY DROVE ME TO GODHOOD.

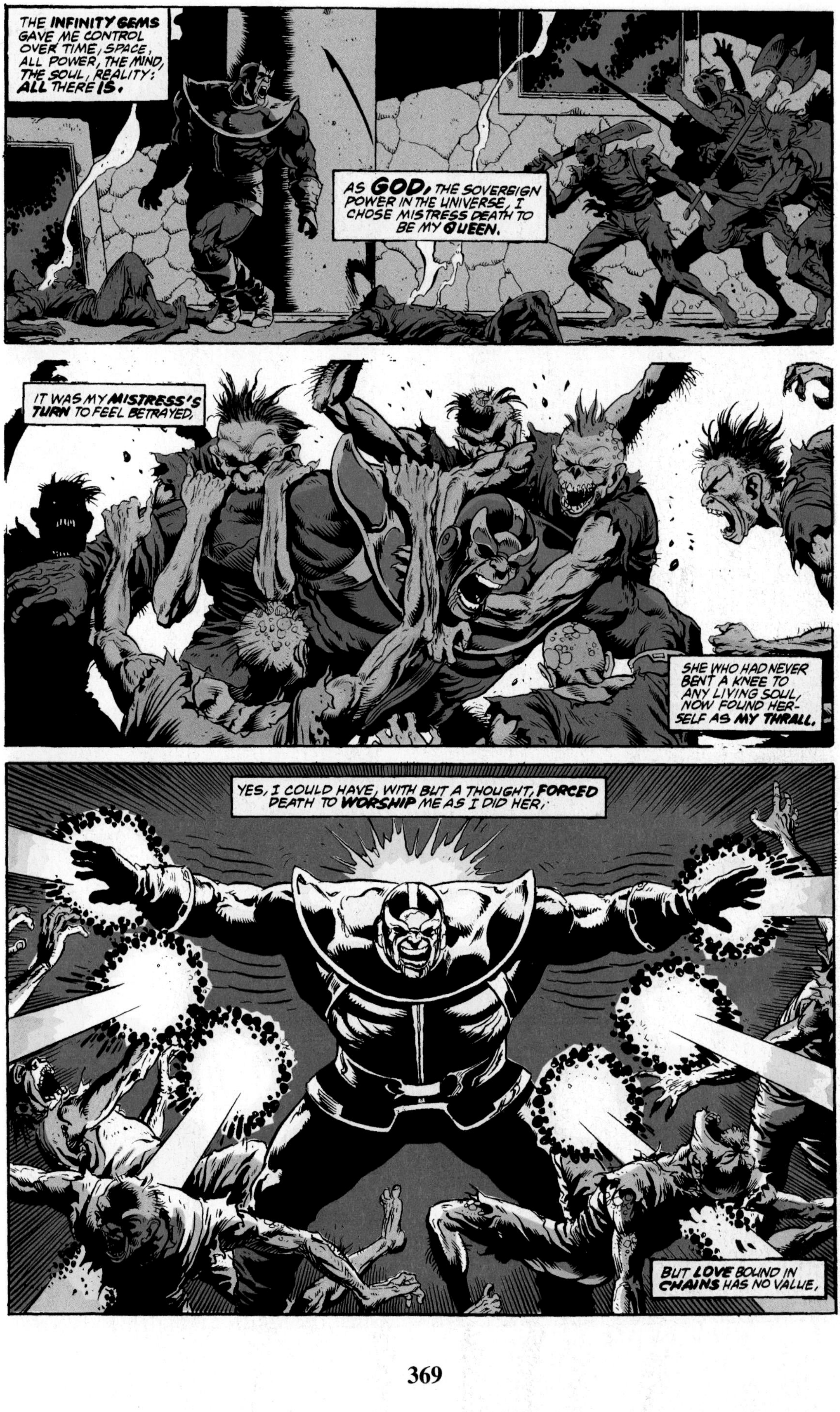
THE INFINITY GEMS GAVE ME CONTROL OVER TIME, SPACE, ALL POWER, THE MIND, THE SOUL, REALITY: ALL THERE IS.
AS GOD, THE SOVEREIGN POWER IN THE UNIVERSE, I CHOSE MISTRESS DEATH TO BE MY QUEEN.
IT WAS MY MISTRESS'S TURN TO FEEL BETRAYED,
SHE WHO HAD NEVER BENT A KNEE TO ANY LIVING SOUL, NOW FOUND HERSELF AS MY THRALL.
YES, I COULD HAVE, WITH BUT A THOUGHT, FORCED DEATH TO WORSHIP ME AS I DID HER,
BUT LOVE BOUND IN CHAINS HAS NO VALUE,

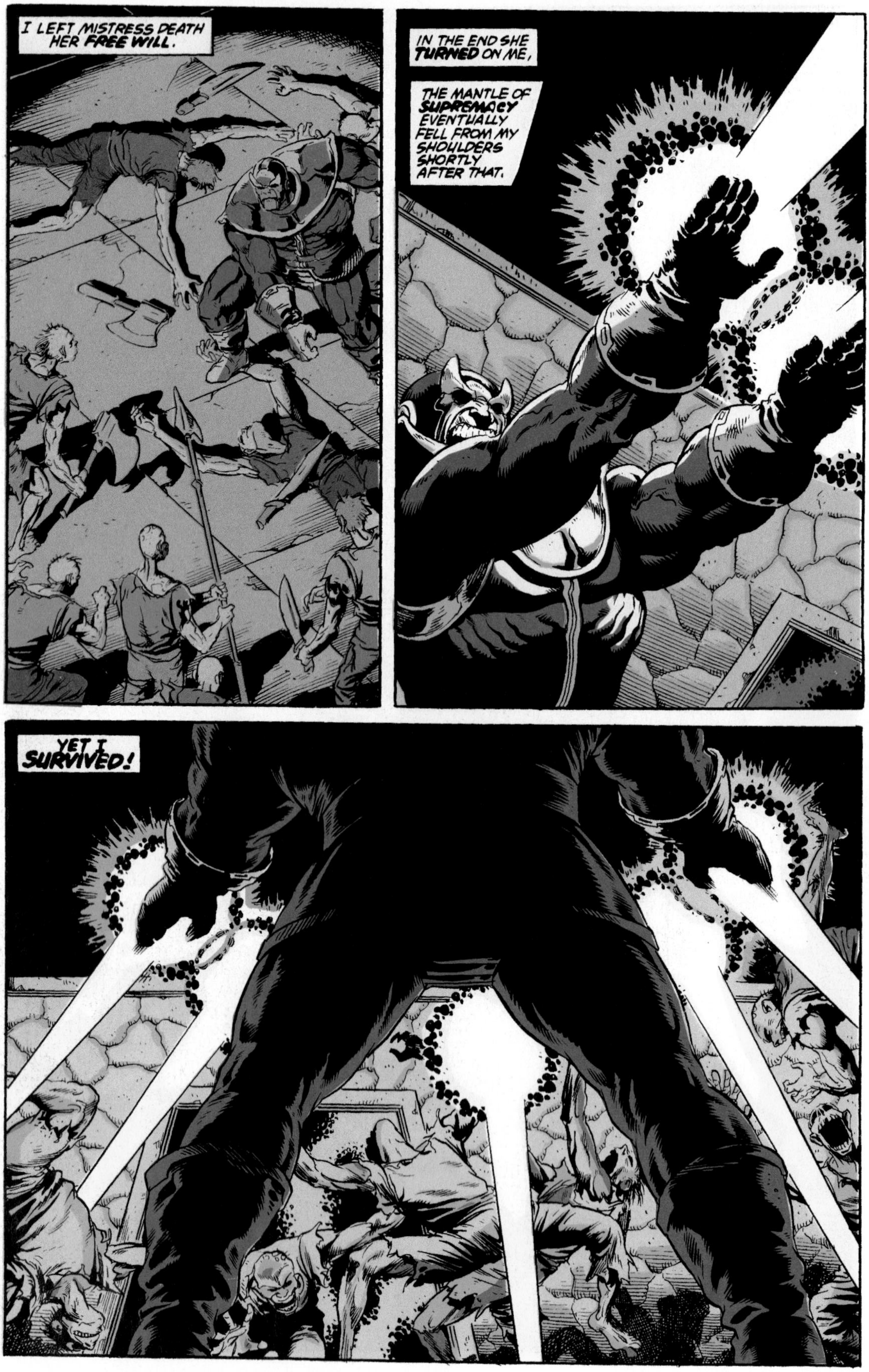
I LEFT MISTRESS DEATH HER FREE WILL.
IN THE END SHE TURNED ON ME,
THE MANTLE OF SUPREMACY EVENTUALLY FELL FROM MY SHOULDERS SHORTLY AFTER THAT.
YET I SURVIVED!

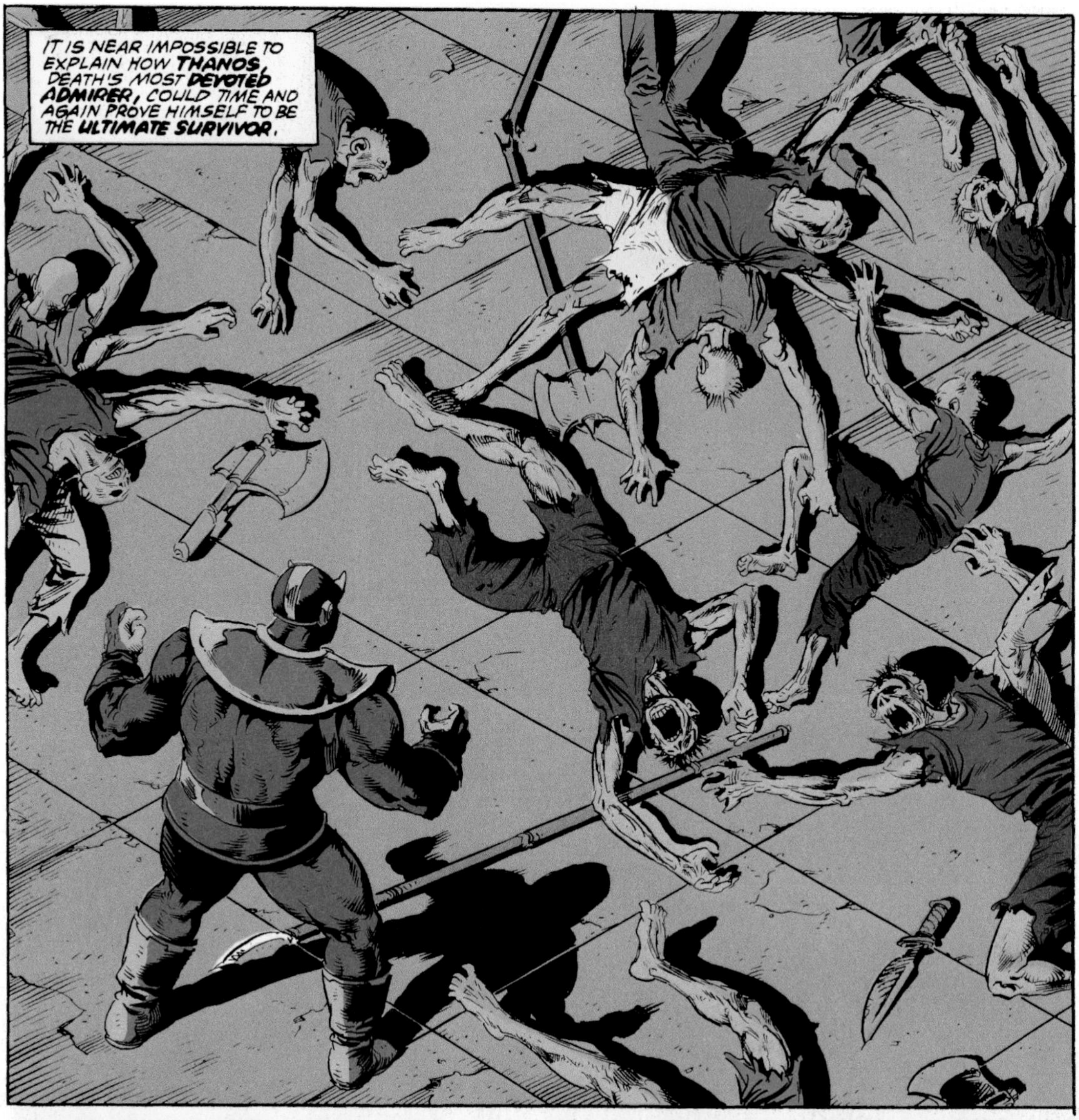
IT IS NEAR IMPOSSIBLE TO EXPLAIN HOW THANOS, DEATH'S MOST DEVOTED ADMIRER, COULD TIME AND AGAIN PROVE HIMSELF TO BE THE ULTIMATE SURVIVOR.

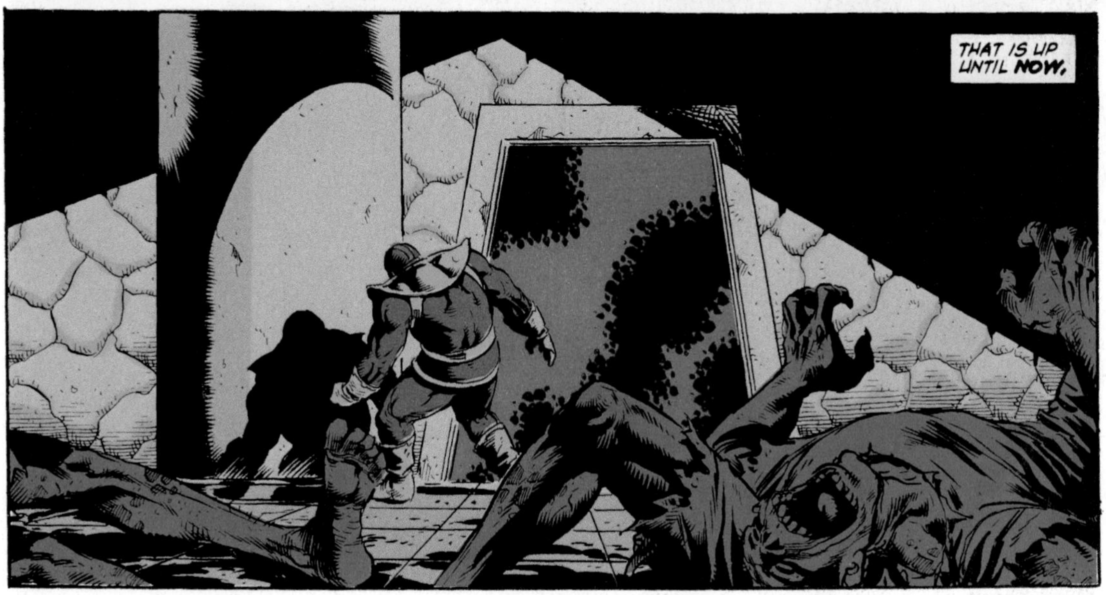
THAT IS UP UNTIL NOW.

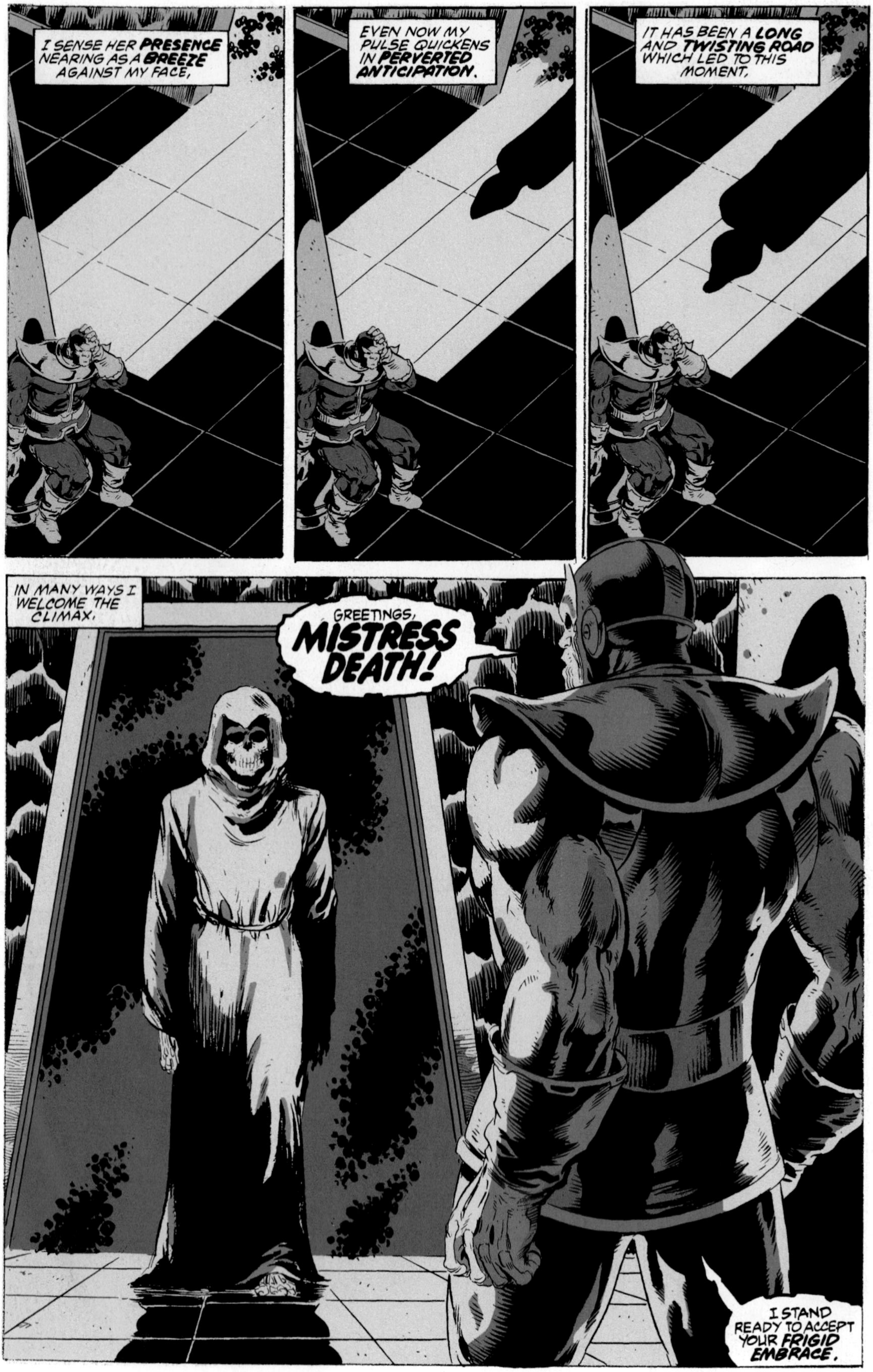
I SENSE HER PRESENCE NEARING AS A BREEZE AGAINST MY FACE,
EVEN NOW MY PULSE QUICKENS IN PERVERTED ANTICIPATION.
IT HAS BEEN A LONG AND TWISTING ROAD WHICH LED TO THIS MOMENT,
IN MANY WAYS I WELCOME THE CLIMAX,
GREETINGS, MISTRESS DEATH!
I STAND READY TO ACCEPT YOUR FRIGID EMBRACE.

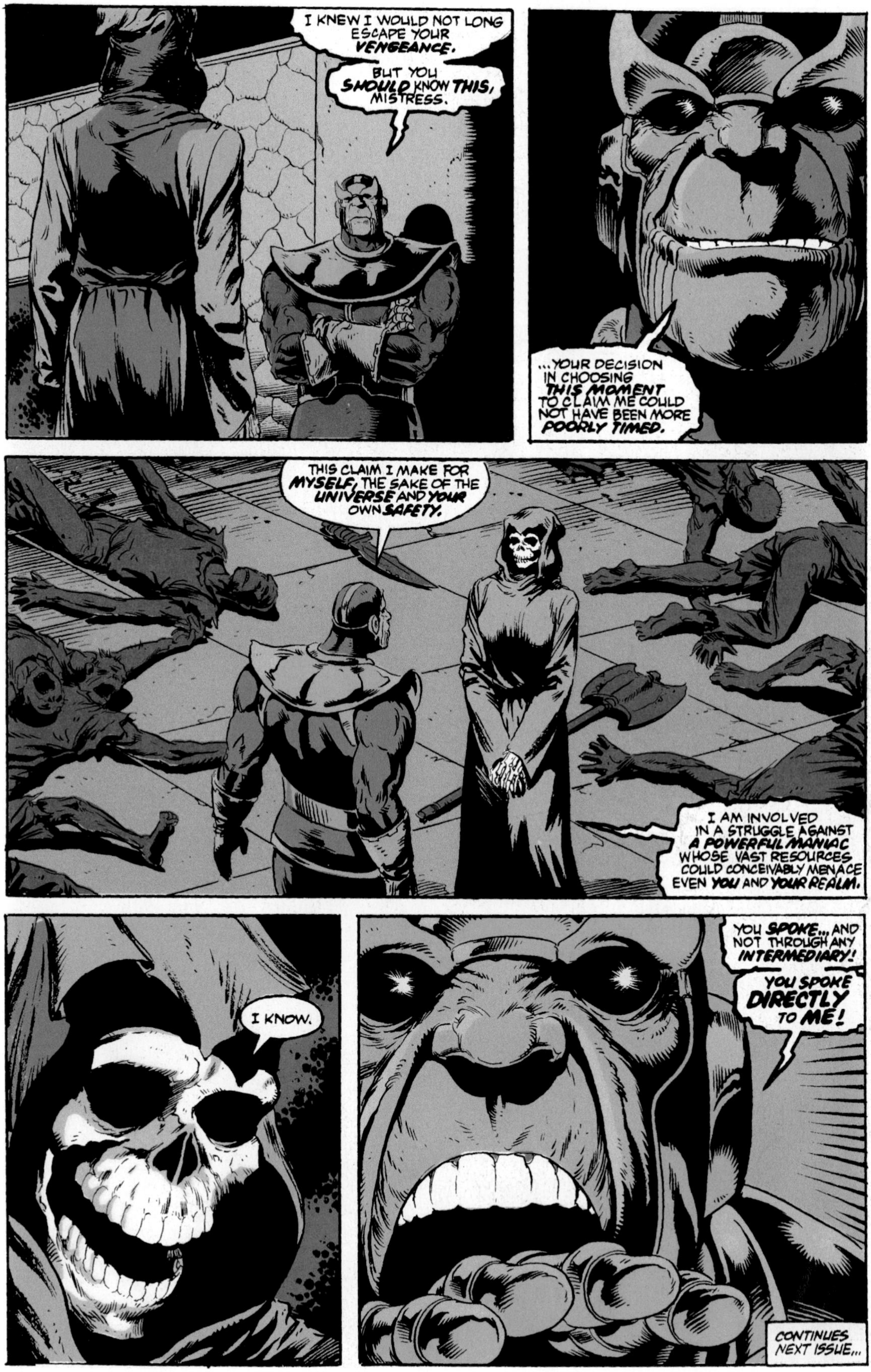
I KNEW I WOULD NOT LONG ESCAPE YOUR VENGEANCE.
BUT YOU SHOULD KNOW THIS, MISTRESS.
...YOUR DECISION IN CHOOSING THIS MOMENT TO CLAIM ME COULD NOT HAVE BEEN MORE POORLY TIMED.
THIS CLAIM I MAKE FOR MYSELF, THE SAKE OF THE UNIVERSE AND YOUR OWN SAFETY.
I AM INVOLVED IN A STRUGGLE AGAINST A POWERFUL MANIAC WHOSE VAST RESOURCES COULD CONCEIVABLY MENACE EVEN YOU AND YOUR REALM.
I KNOW.
YOU SPOKE... AND NOT THROUGH ANY INTERMEDIARY!
YOU SPOKE DIRECTLY TO ME!
CONTINUES NEXT ISSUE...

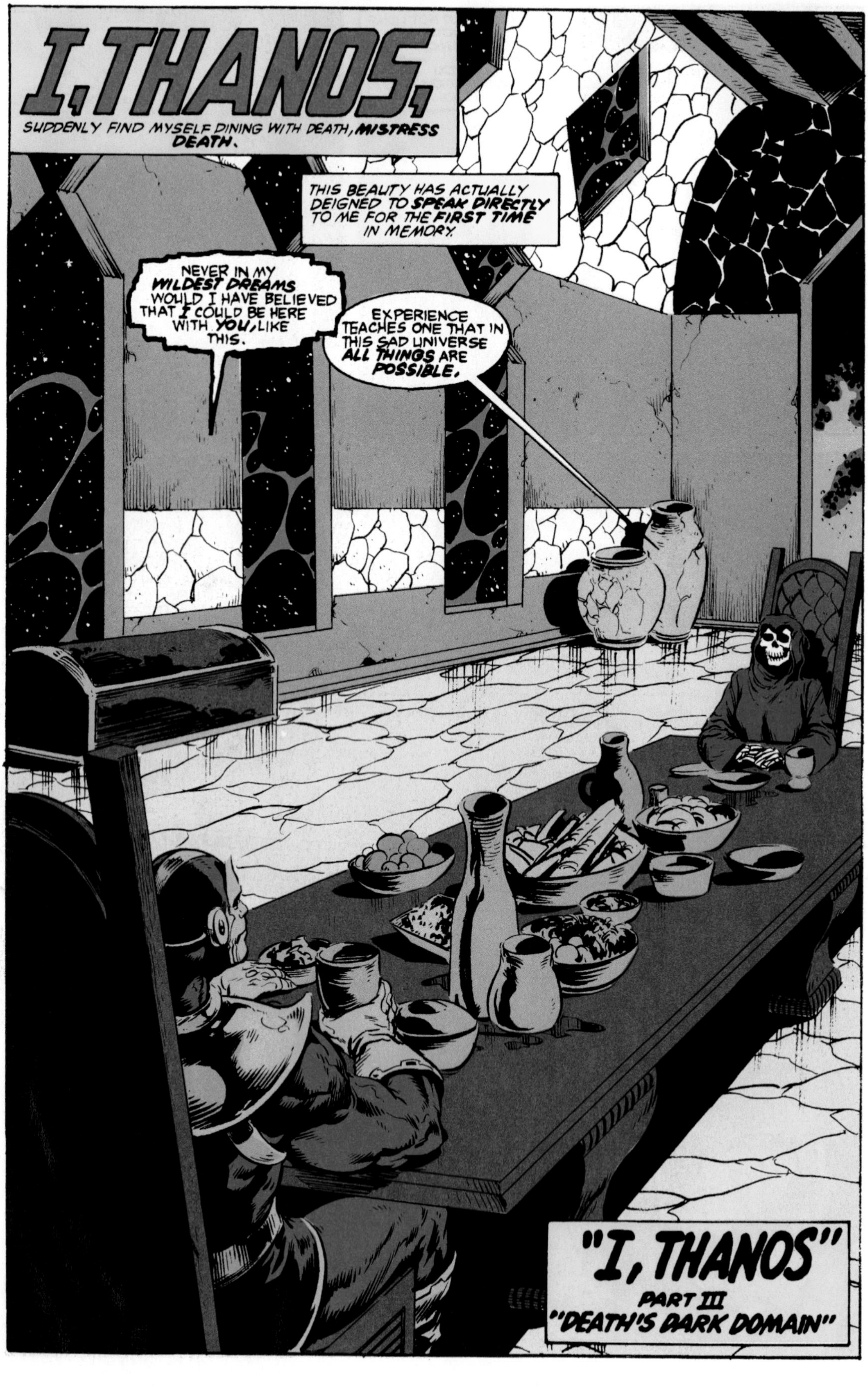
I, THANOS,
SUDDENLY FIND MYSELF DINING WITH DEATH, MISTRESS DEATH.
THIS BEAUTY HAS ACTUALLY DEIGNED TO SPEAK DIRECTLY TO ME FOR THE FIRST TIME IN MEMORY.
NEVER IN MY WILDEST DREAMS WOULD I HAVE BELIEVED THAT I COULD BE HERE WITH YOU, LIKE THIS.
EXPERIENCE TEACHES ONE THAT IN THIS SAD UNIVERSE ALL THINGS ARE POSSIBLE.
"I, THANOS"
PART III
"DEATH'S DARK DOMAIN"

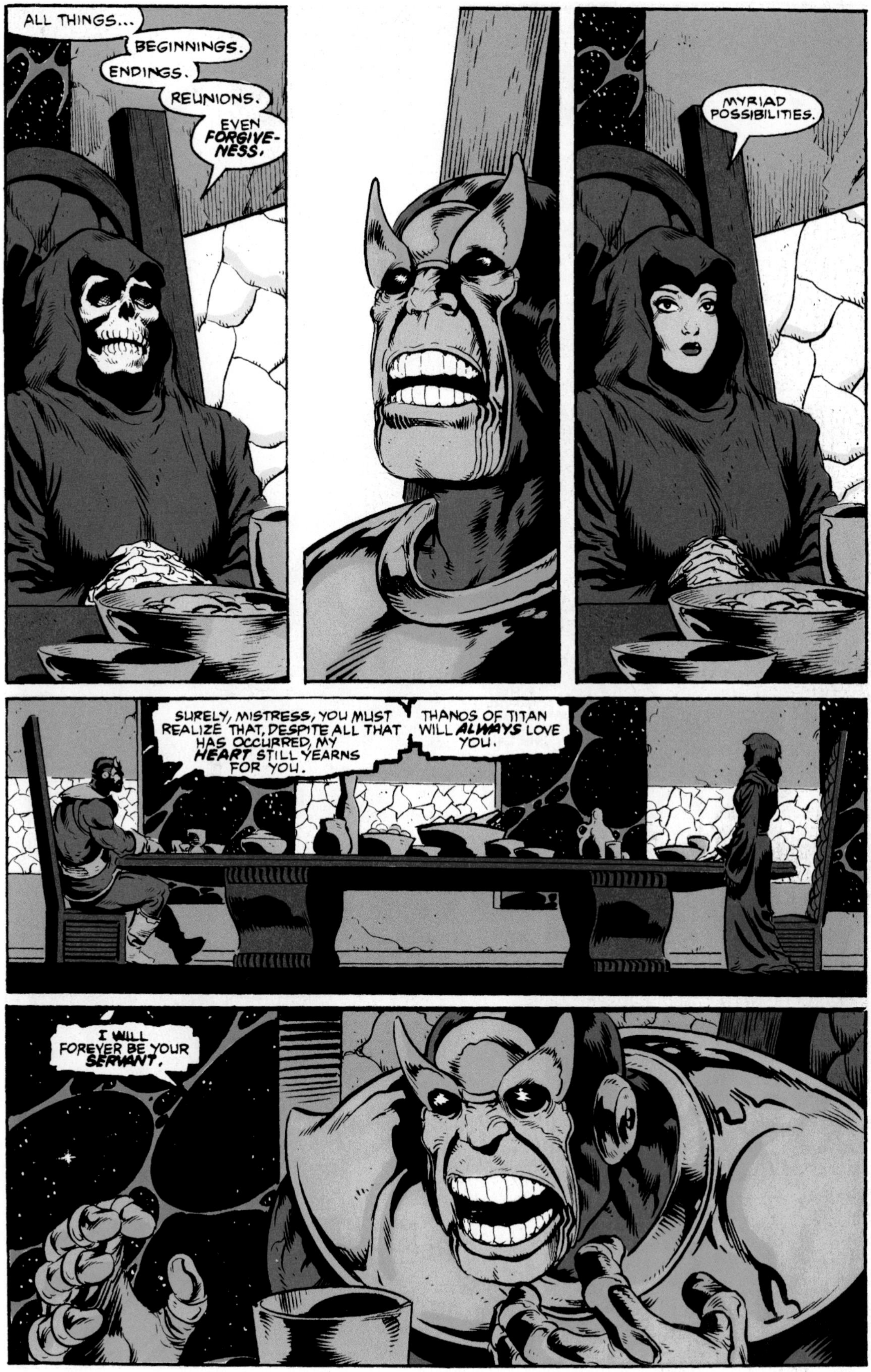

ALL THINGS...
BEGINNINGS.
ENDINGS.
REUNIONS.
EVEN FORGIVE-NESS.
MYRIAD POSSIBILITIES.
SURELY, MISTRESS, YOU MUST REALIZE THAT, DESPITE ALL THAT HAS OCCURRED, MY HEART STILL YEARNS FOR YOU.
THANOS OF TITAN WILL ALWAYS LOVE YOU.
I WILL FOREVER BE YOUR SERVANT.

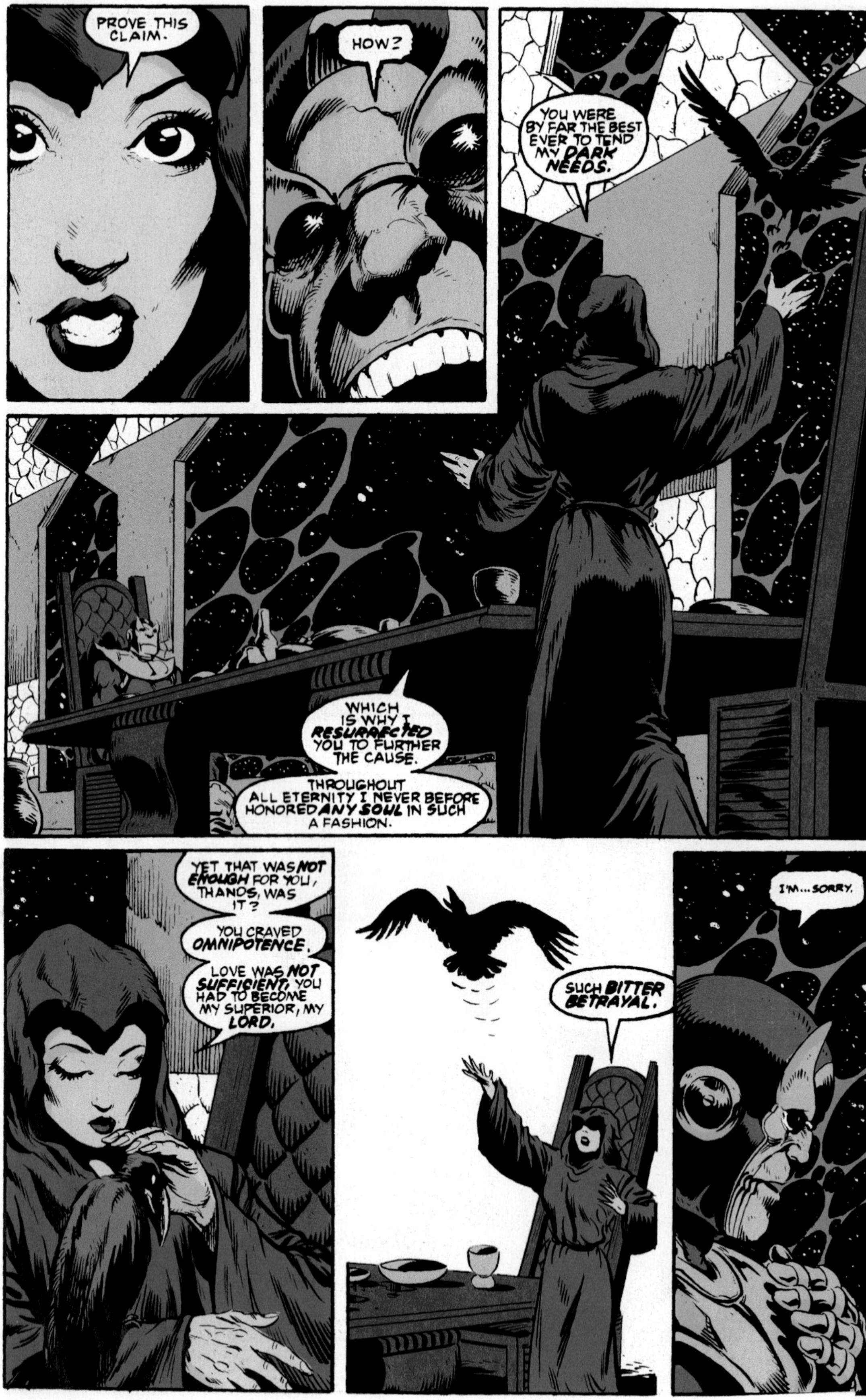
PROVE THIS CLAIM.
HOW?
YOU WERE BY FAR THE BEST EVER TO TEND MY DARK NEEDS.
WHICH IS WHY I RESURRECTED YOU TO FURTHER THE CAUSE.
THROUGHOUT ALL ETERNITY I NEVER BEFORE HONORED ANY SOUL IN SUCH A FASHION.
YET THAT WAS NOT ENOUGH FOR YOU, THANOS, WAS IT?
YOU CRAVED OMNIPOTENCE.
LOVE WAS NOT SUFFICIENT, YOU HAD TO BECOME MY SUPERIOR, MY LORD.
SUCH BITTER BETRAYAL.
I'M... SORRY.

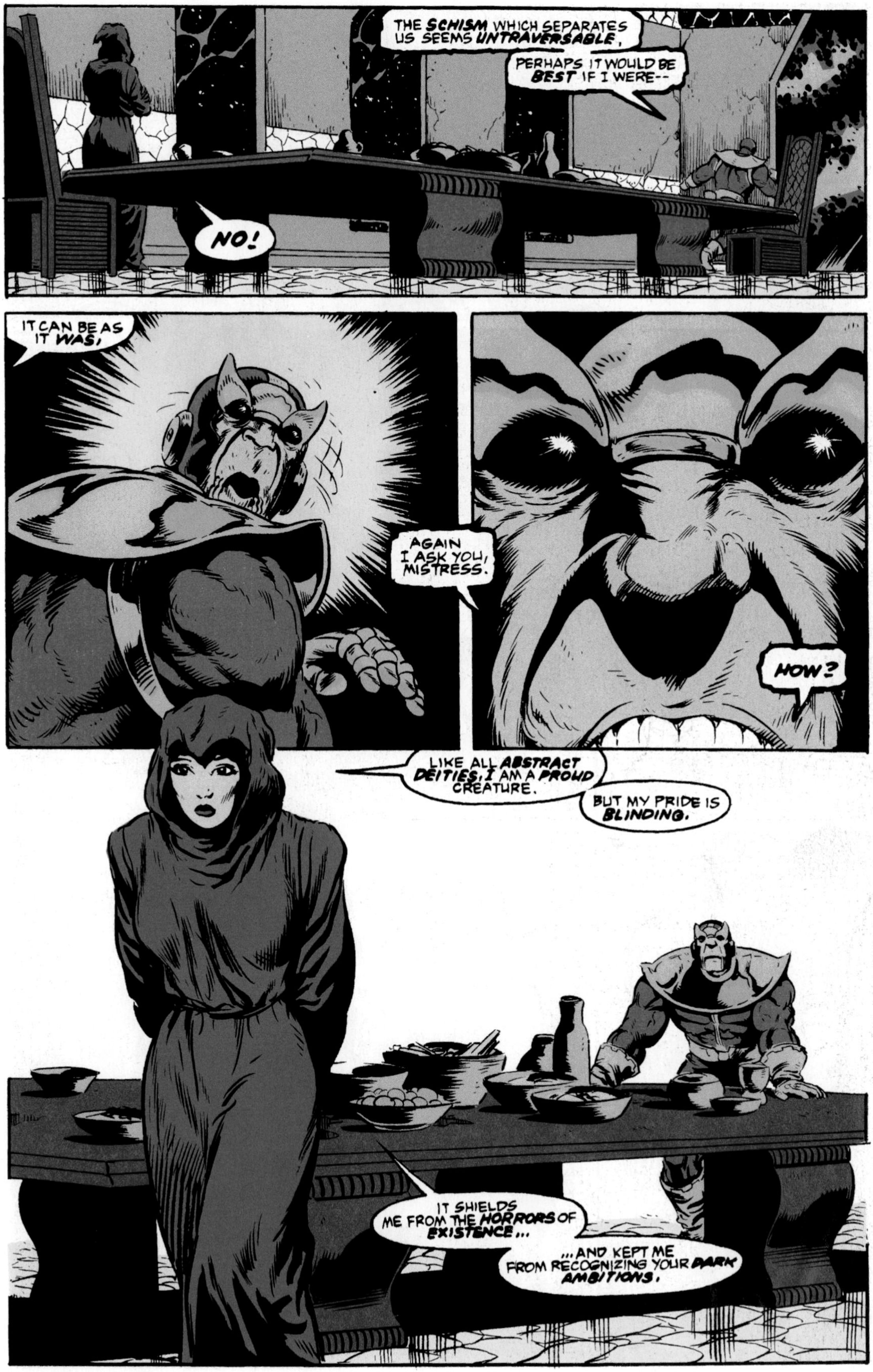

THE SCHISM WHICH SEPARATES US SEEMS UNTRAVERSABLE.
PERHAPS IT WOULD BE BEST IF I WERE--
NO!
IT CAN BE AS IT WAS.
AGAIN I ASK YOU, MISTRESS.
HOW?
LIKE ALL ABSTRACT DEITIES, I AM A PROUD CREATURE.
BUT MY PRIDE IS BLINDING.
IT SHIELDS ME FROM THE HORRORS OF EXISTENCE...
...AND KEPT ME FROM RECOGNIZING YOUR DARK AMBITIONS.

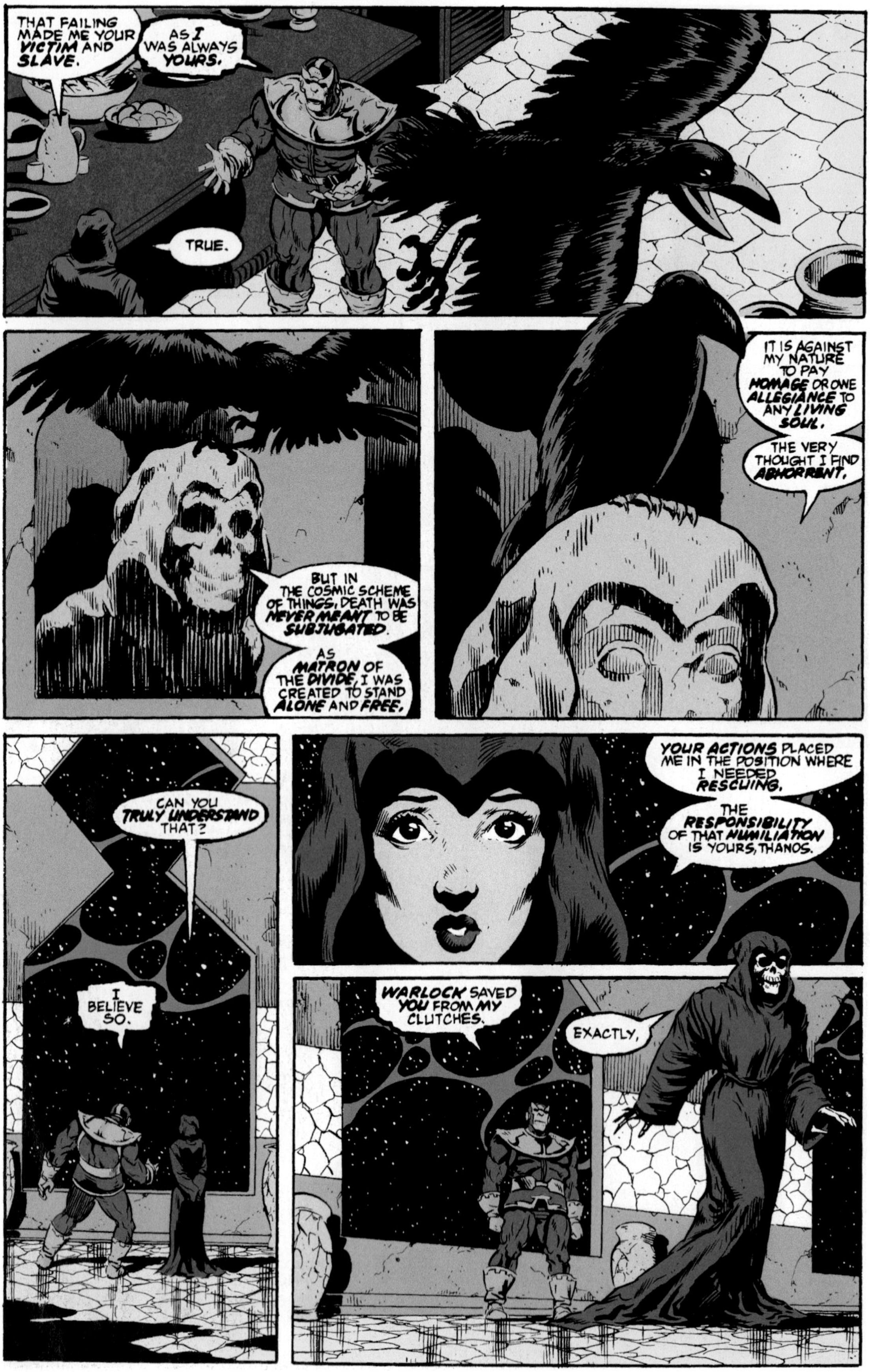

THAT FAILING MADE ME YOUR VICTIM AND SLAVE.
AS I WAS ALWAYS YOURS.
TRUE.
BUT IN THE COSMIC SCHEME OF THINGS, DEATH WAS NEVER MEANT TO BE SUBJUGATED.
AS MATRON OF THE DIVIDE, I WAS CREATED TO STAND ALONE AND FREE.
IT IS AGAINST MY NATURE TO PAY HOMAGE OR OWE ALLEGIANCE TO ANY LIVING SOUL.
THE VERY THOUGHT I FIND ABHORRENT.
CAN YOU TRULY UNDERSTAND THAT?
I BELIEVE SO.
YOUR ACTIONS PLACED ME IN THE POSITION WHERE I NEEDED RESCUING.
THE RESPONSIBILITY OF THAT HUMILIATION IS YOURS, THANOS.
WARLOCK SAVED YOU FROM MY CLUTCHES.
EXACTLY.

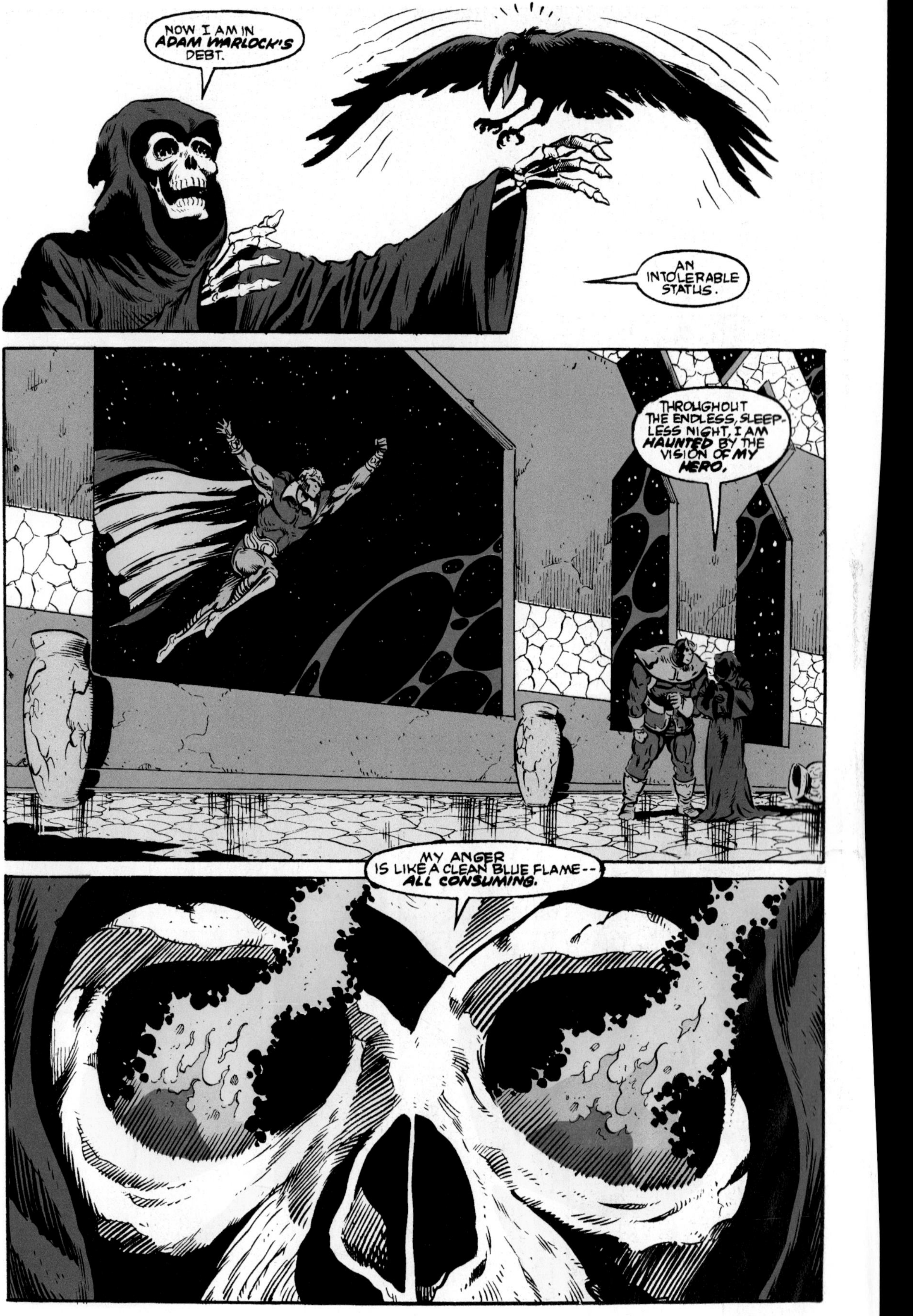
NOW I AM IN ADAM WARLOCK'S DEBT.
AN INTOLERABLE STATUS.
THROUGHOUT THE ENDLESS, SLEEPLESS NIGHT, I AM HAUNTED BY THE VISION OF MY HERO.
MY ANGER IS LIKE A CLEAN BLUE FLAME-- ALL CONSUMING.

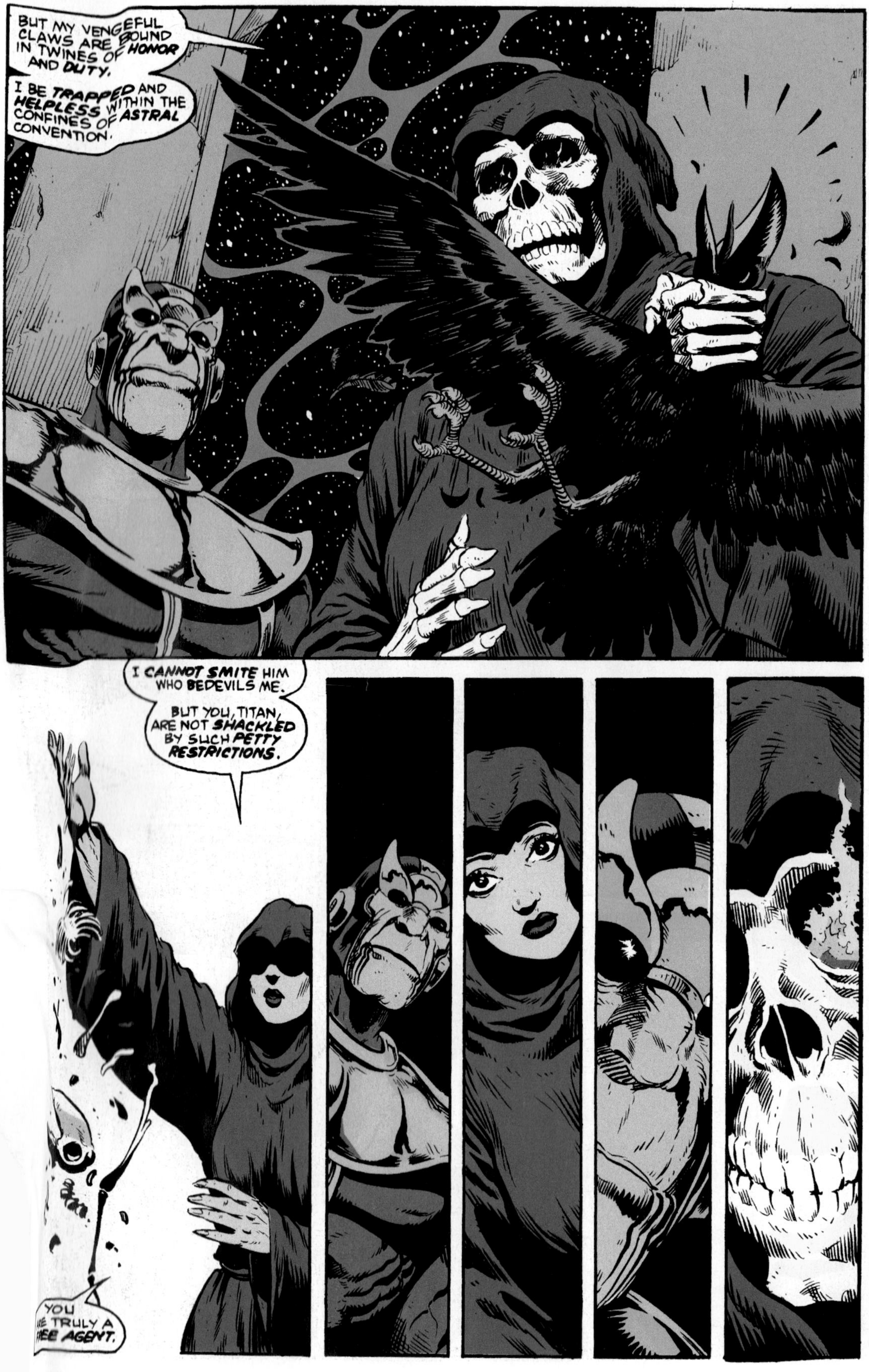
BUT MY VENGEFUL CLAWS ARE BOUND IN TWINES OF HONOR AND DUTY.
I BE TRAPPED AND HELPLESS WITHIN THE CONFINES OF ASTRAL CONVENTION.
I CANNOT SMITE HIM WHO BEDEVILS ME.
BUT YOU, TITAN, ARE NOT SHACKLED BY SUCH PETTY RESTRICTIONS.
YOU ARE TRULY A FREE AGENT.

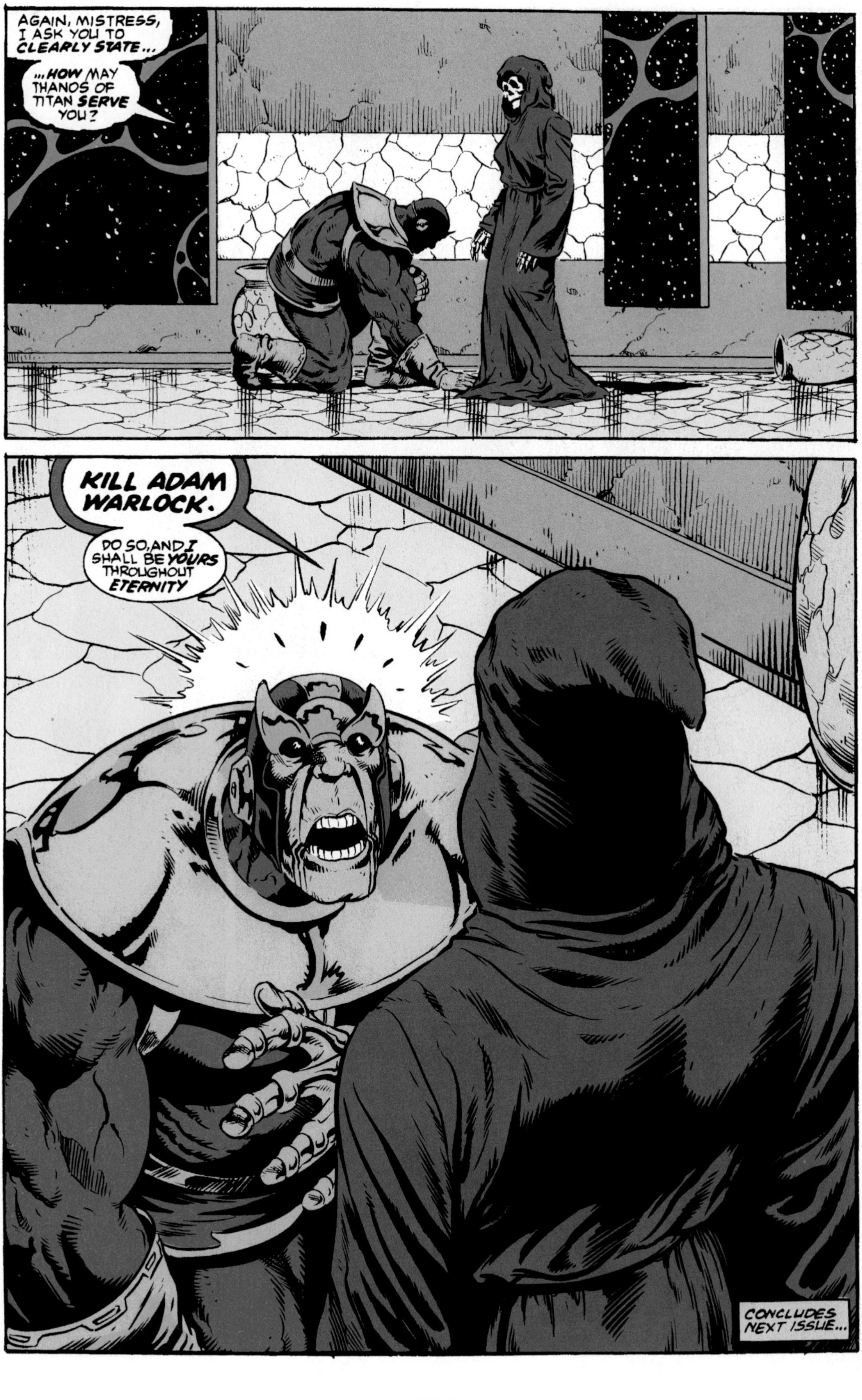
AGAIN, MISTRESS, I ASK YOU TO CLEARLY STATE...
...HOW MAY THANOS OF TITAN SERVE YOU?
KILL ADAM WARLOCK.
DO SO, AND I SHALL BE YOURS THROUGHOUT ETERNITY
CONCLUDES NEXT ISSUE...

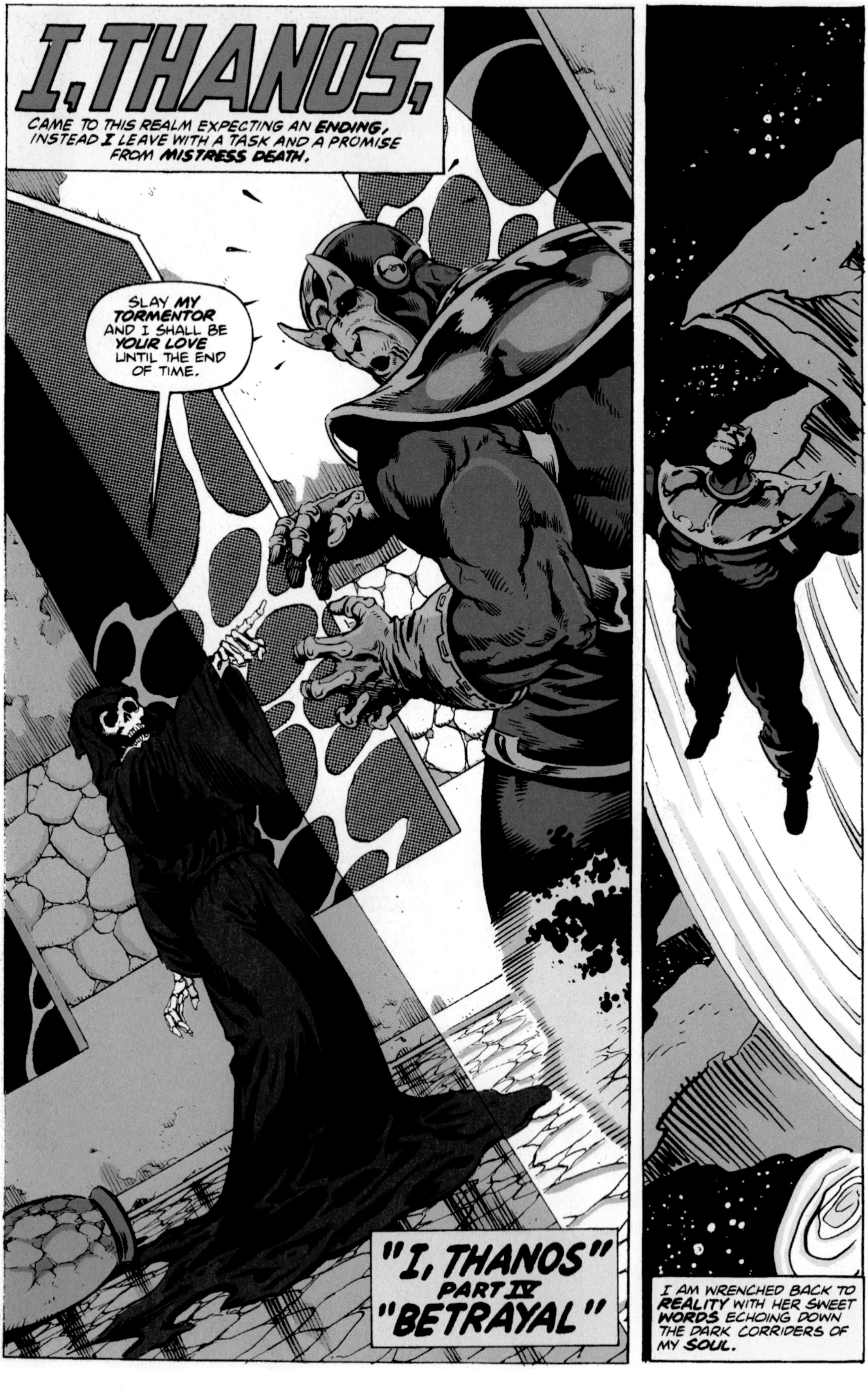
I, THANOS,
CAME TO THIS REALM EXPECTING AN ENDING, INSTEAD I LEAVE WITH A TASK AND A PROMISE FROM MISTRESS DEATH.
SLAY MY TORMENTOR AND I SHALL BE YOUR LOVE UNTIL THE END OF TIME.
"I, THANOS" PART IV "BETRAYAL"
I AM WRENCHED BACK TO REALITY WITH HER SWEET WORDS ECHOING DOWN THE DARK CORRIDERS OF MY SOUL.

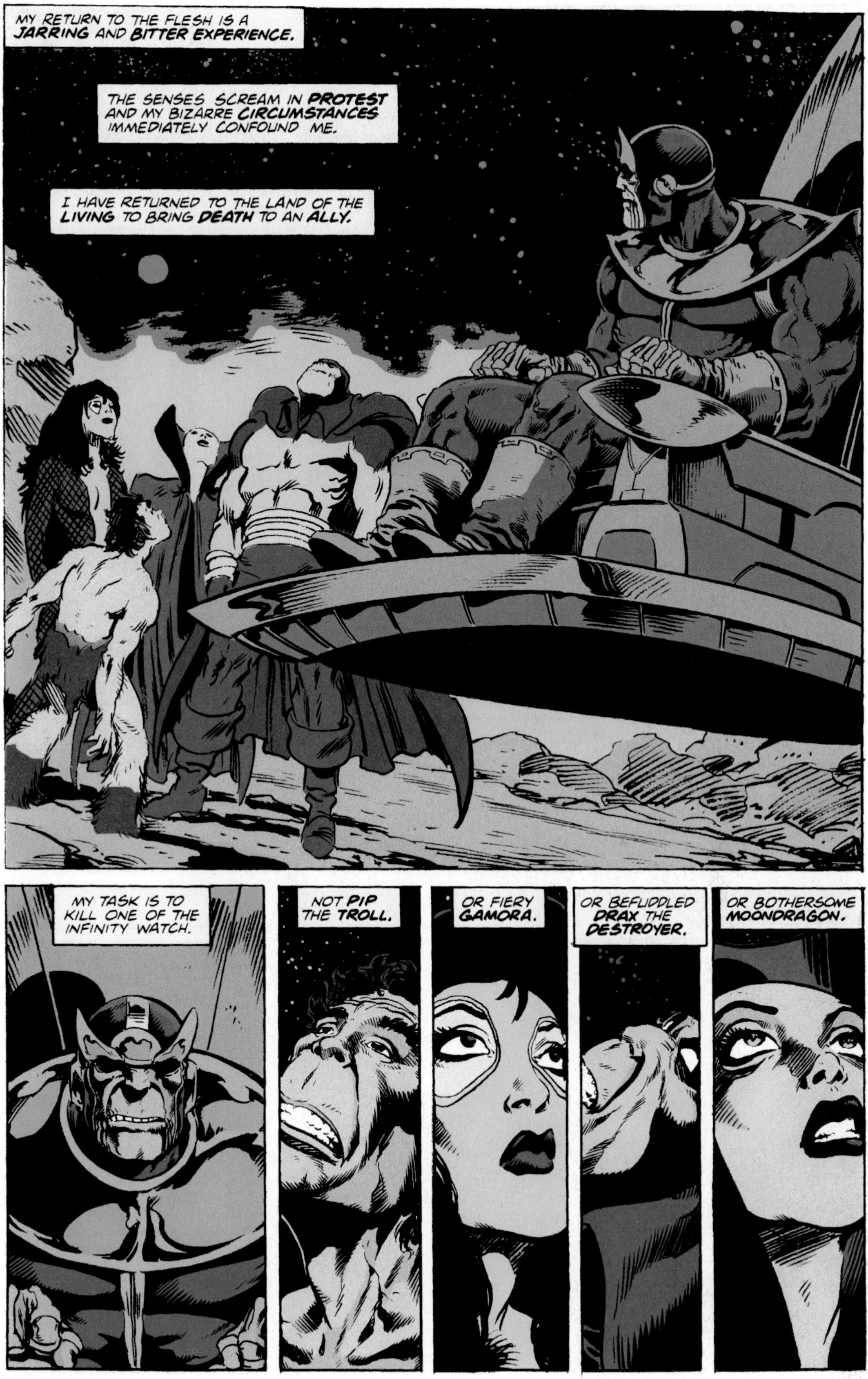
MY RETURN TO THE FLESH IS A JARRING AND BITTER EXPERIENCE.
THE SENSES SCREAM IN PROTEST AND MY BIZARRE CIRCUMSTANCES IMMEDIATELY CONFOUND ME.
I HAVE RETURNED TO THE LAND OF THE LIVING TO BRING DEATH TO AN ALLY.
MY TASK IS TO KILL ONE OF THE INFINITY WATCH.
NOT PIP THE TROLL.
OR FIERY GAMORA.
OR BEFUDDLED DRAX THE DESTROYER.
OR BOTHERSOME MOONDRAGON.

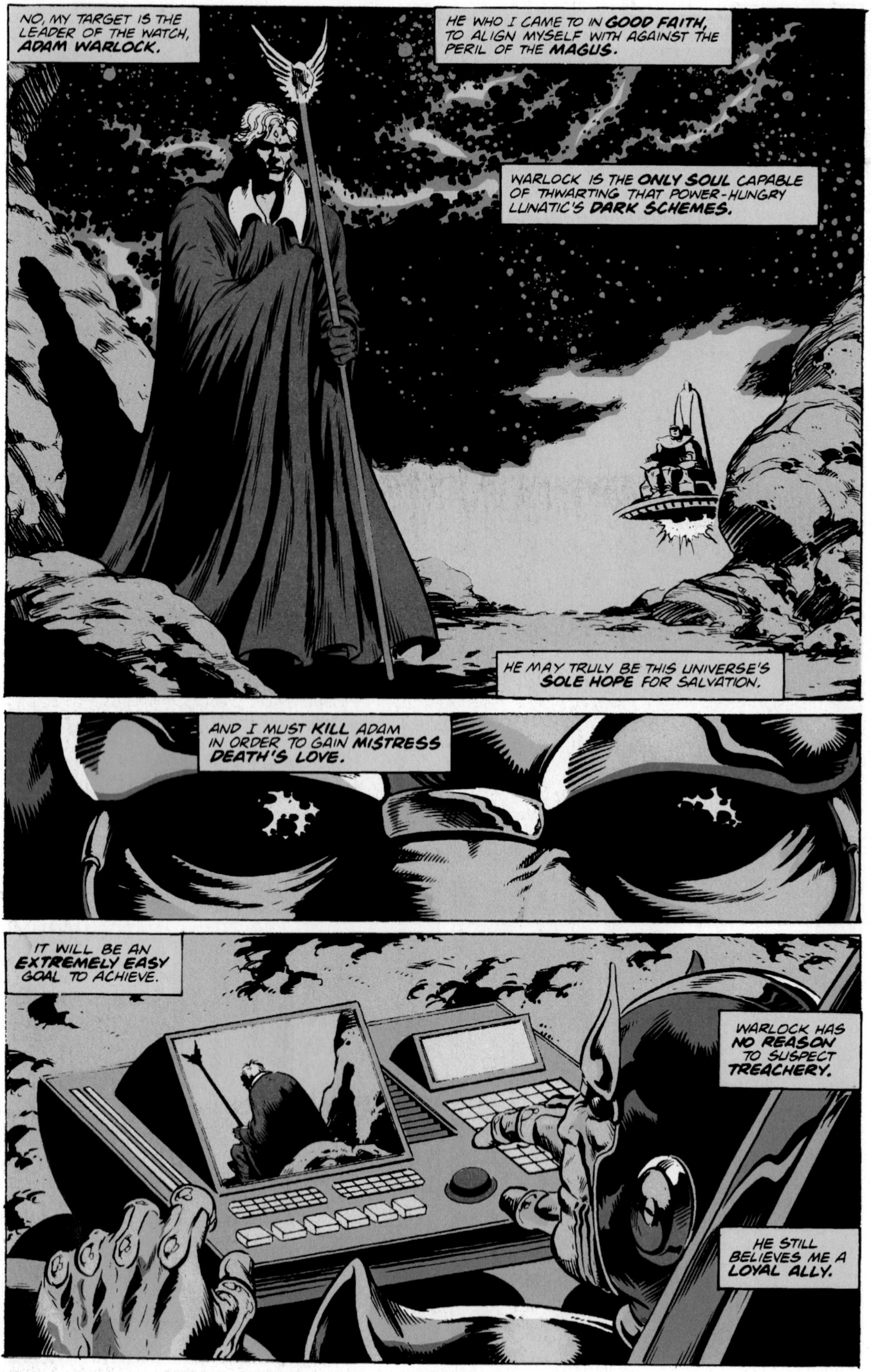
NO, MY TARGET IS THE LEADER OF THE WATCH, ADAM WARLOCK.
HE WHO I CAME TO IN GOOD FAITH, TO ALIGN MYSELF WITH AGAINST THE PERIL OF THE MAGUS.
WARLOCK IS THE ONLY SOUL CAPABLE OF THWARTING THAT POWER-HUNGRY LUNATIC'S DARK SCHEMES.
HE MAY TRULY BE THIS UNIVERSE'S SOLE HOPE FOR SALVATION.
AND I MUST KILL ADAM IN ORDER TO GAIN MISTRESS DEATH'S LOVE.
IT WILL BE AN EXTREMELY EASY GOAL TO ACHIEVE.
WARLOCK HAS NO REASON TO SUSPECT TREACHERY.
HE STILL BELIEVES ME A LOYAL ALLY.

WEAPONS SYSTEM
ACTIVATED

AN INCORRECT ASSUMPTION.

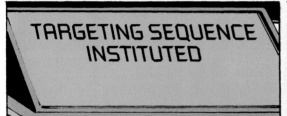

TARGETING SEQUENCE
INSTITUTED

A FATAL MISCALCULATION.

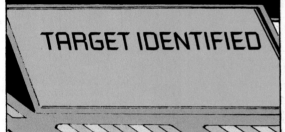

TARGET IDENTIFIED

THE FRAGILITY OF LIFE.

LOCKED ONTO TARGET

A TOUCH OF A BUTTON AND MY DREAMS CAN ALL COME TRUE.

SO EASY.

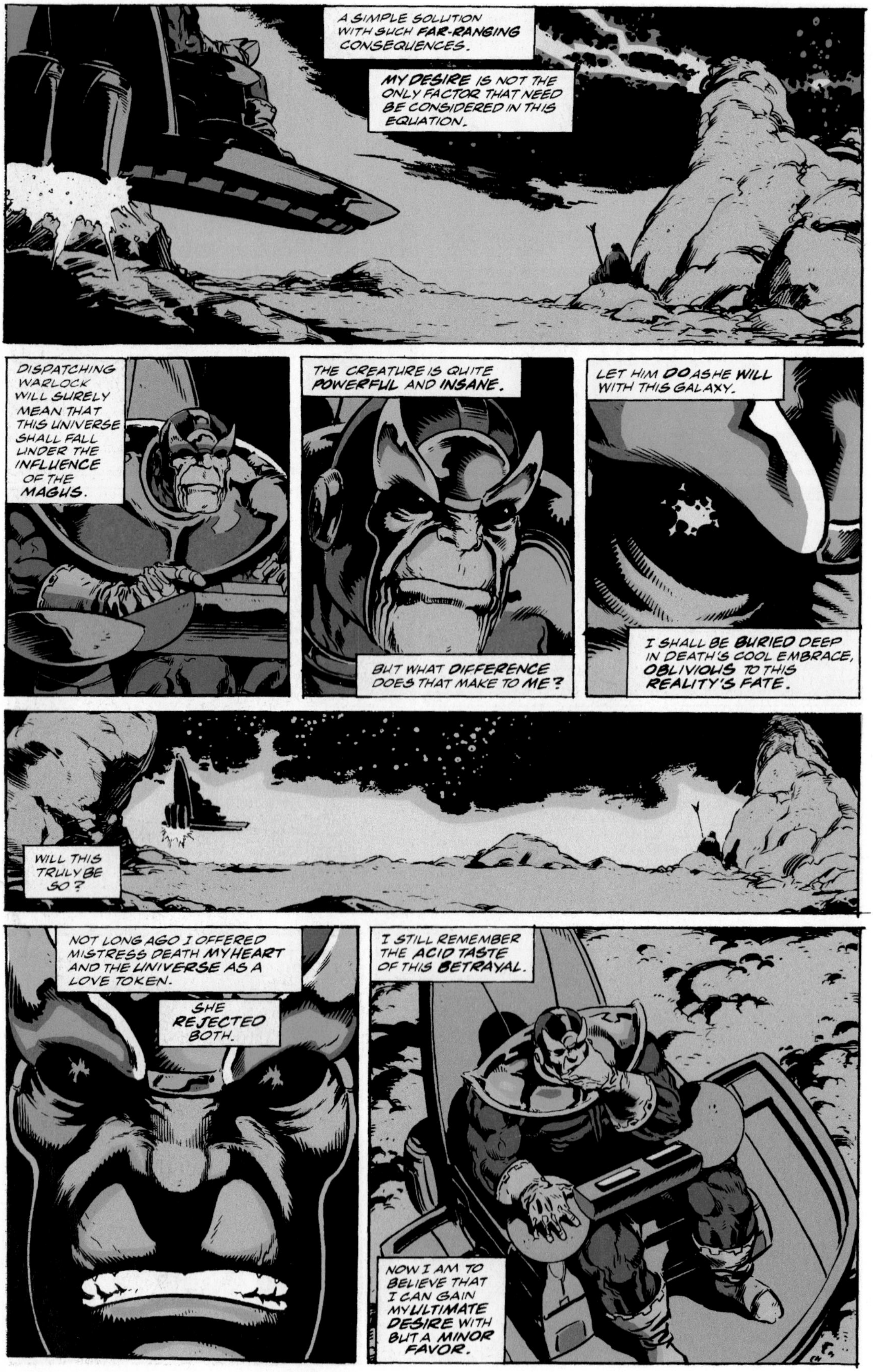
A SIMPLE SOLUTION WITH SUCH FAR-RANGING CONSEQUENCES.
MY DESIRE IS NOT THE ONLY FACTOR THAT NEED BE CONSIDERED IN THIS EQUATION.
DISPATCHING WARLOCK WILL SURELY MEAN THAT THIS UNIVERSE SHALL FALL UNDER THE INFLUENCE OF THE MAGUS.
THE CREATURE IS QUITE POWERFUL AND INSANE.
BUT WHAT DIFFERENCE DOES THAT MAKE TO ME?
LET HIM DO AS HE WILL WITH THIS GALAXY.
I SHALL BE BURIED DEEP IN DEATH'S COOL EMBRACE, OBLIVIOUS TO THIS REALITY'S FATE.
WILL THIS TRULY BE SO?
NOT LONG AGO I OFFERED MISTRESS DEATH MY HEART AND THE UNIVERSE AS A LOVE TOKEN.
SHE REJECTED BOTH.
I STILL REMEMBER THE ACID TASTE OF THIS BETRAYAL.
NOW I AM TO BELIEVE THAT I CAN GAIN MY ULTIMATE DESIRE WITH BUT A MINOR FAVOR.

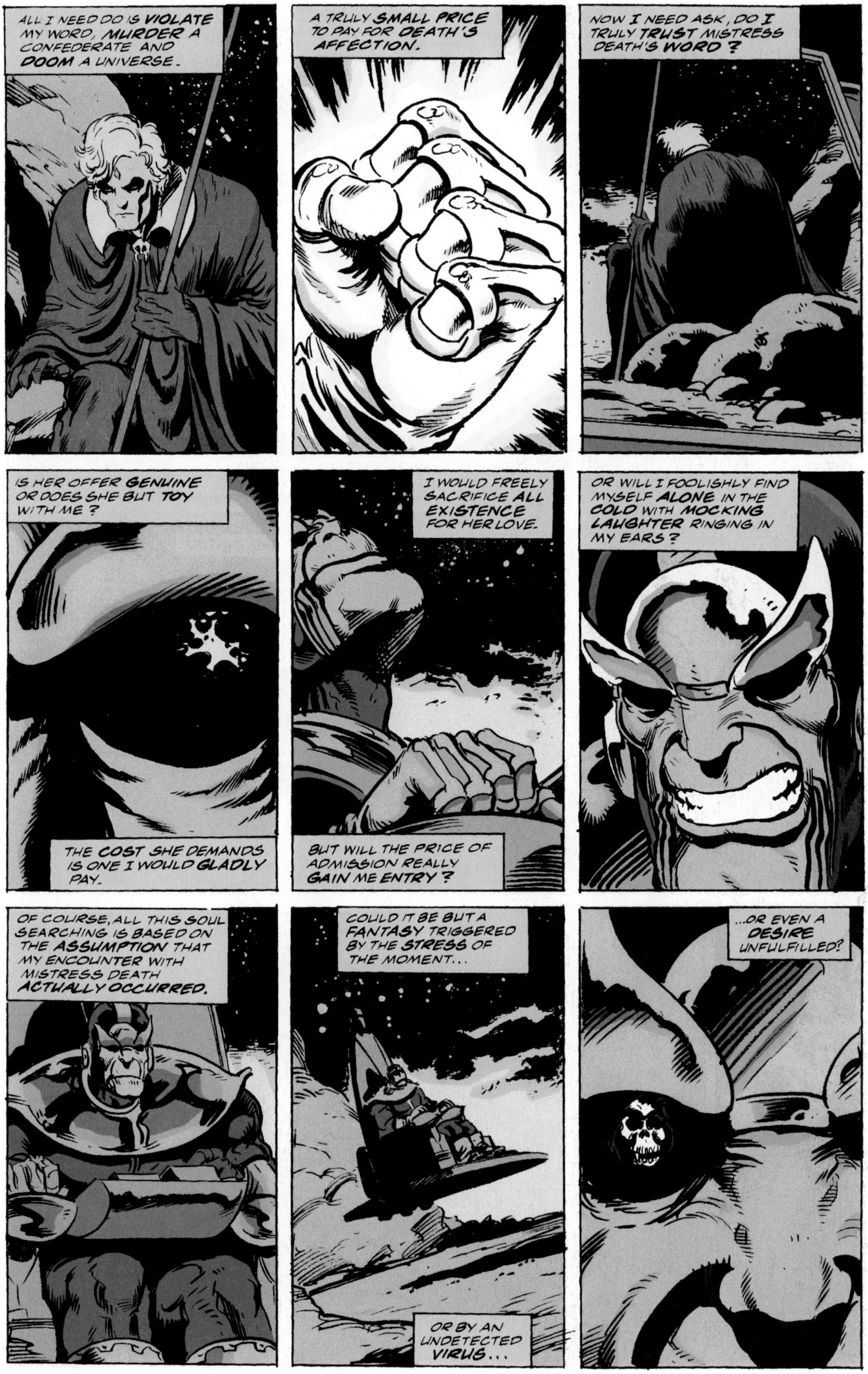
ALL I NEED DO IS VIOLATE MY WORD, MURDER A CONFEDERATE AND DOOM A UNIVERSE.
A TRULY SMALL PRICE TO PAY FOR DEATH'S AFFECTION.
NOW I NEED ASK, DO I TRULY TRUST MISTRESS DEATH'S WORD?
IS HER OFFER GENUINE OR DOES SHE BUT TOY WITH ME?
THE COST SHE DEMANDS IS ONE I WOULD GLADLY PAY.
I WOULD FREELY SACRIFICE ALL EXISTENCE FOR HER LOVE.
BUT WILL THE PRICE OF ADMISSION REALLY GAIN ME ENTRY?
OR WILL I FOOLISHLY FIND MYSELF ALONE IN THE COLD WITH MOCKING LAUGHTER RINGING IN MY EARS?
OF COURSE, ALL THIS SOUL SEARCHING IS BASED ON THE ASSUMPTION THAT MY ENCOUNTER WITH MISTRESS DEATH ACTUALLY OCCURRED.
COULD IT BE BUT A FANTASY TRIGGERED BY THE STRESS OF THE MOMENT...
OR BY AN UNDETECTED VIRUS...
...OR EVEN A DESIRE UNFULFILLED?

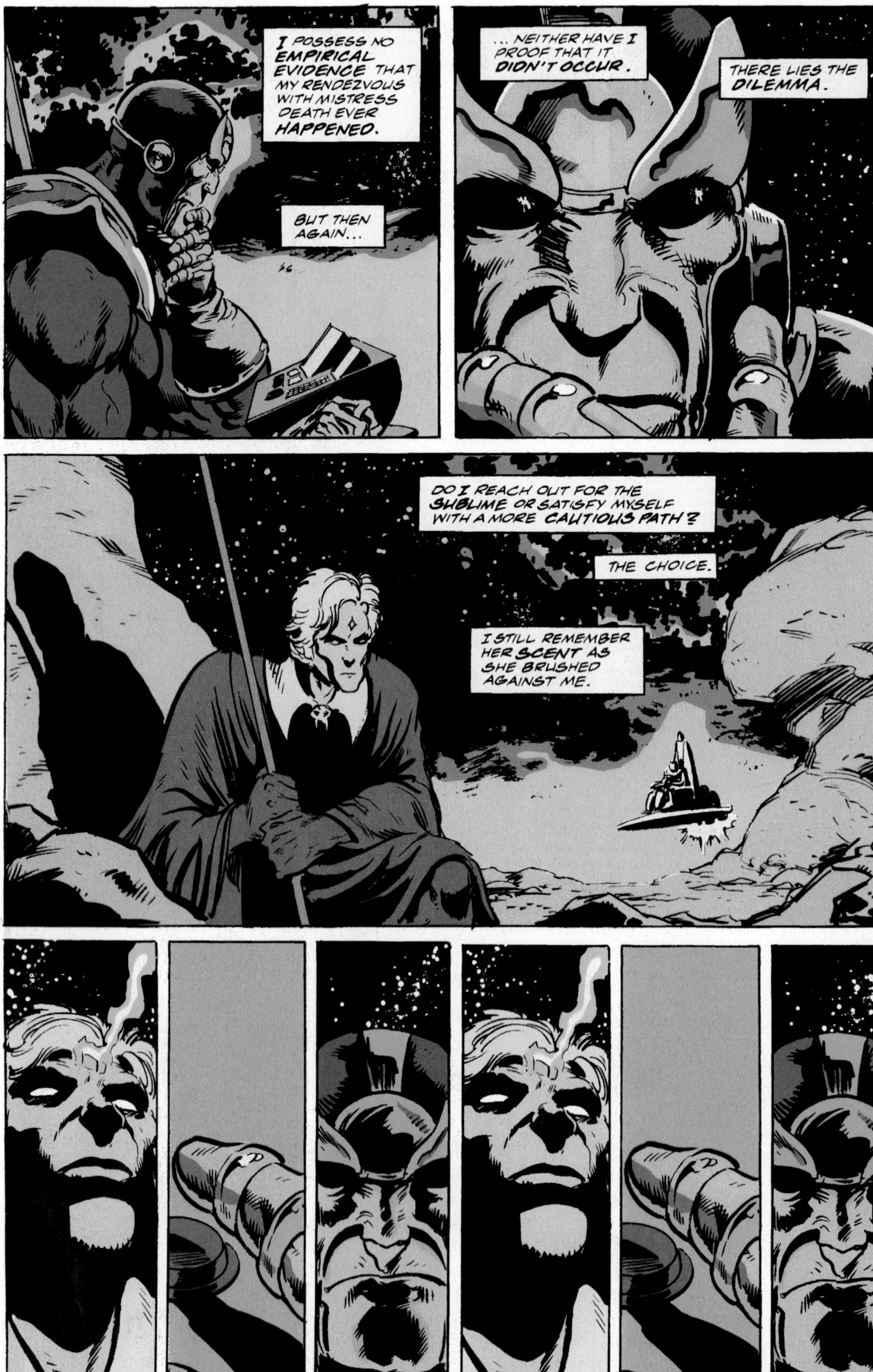
I POSSESS NO EMPIRICAL EVIDENCE THAT MY RENDEZVOUS WITH MISTRESS DEATH EVER HAPPENED.
BUT THEN AGAIN...
... NEITHER HAVE I PROOF THAT IT DIDN'T OCCUR.
THERE LIES THE DILEMMA.
DO I REACH OUT FOR THE SUBLIME OR SATISFY MYSELF WITH A MORE CAUTIOUS PATH?
THE CHOICE.
I STILL REMEMBER HER SCENT AS SHE BRUSHED AGAINST ME.

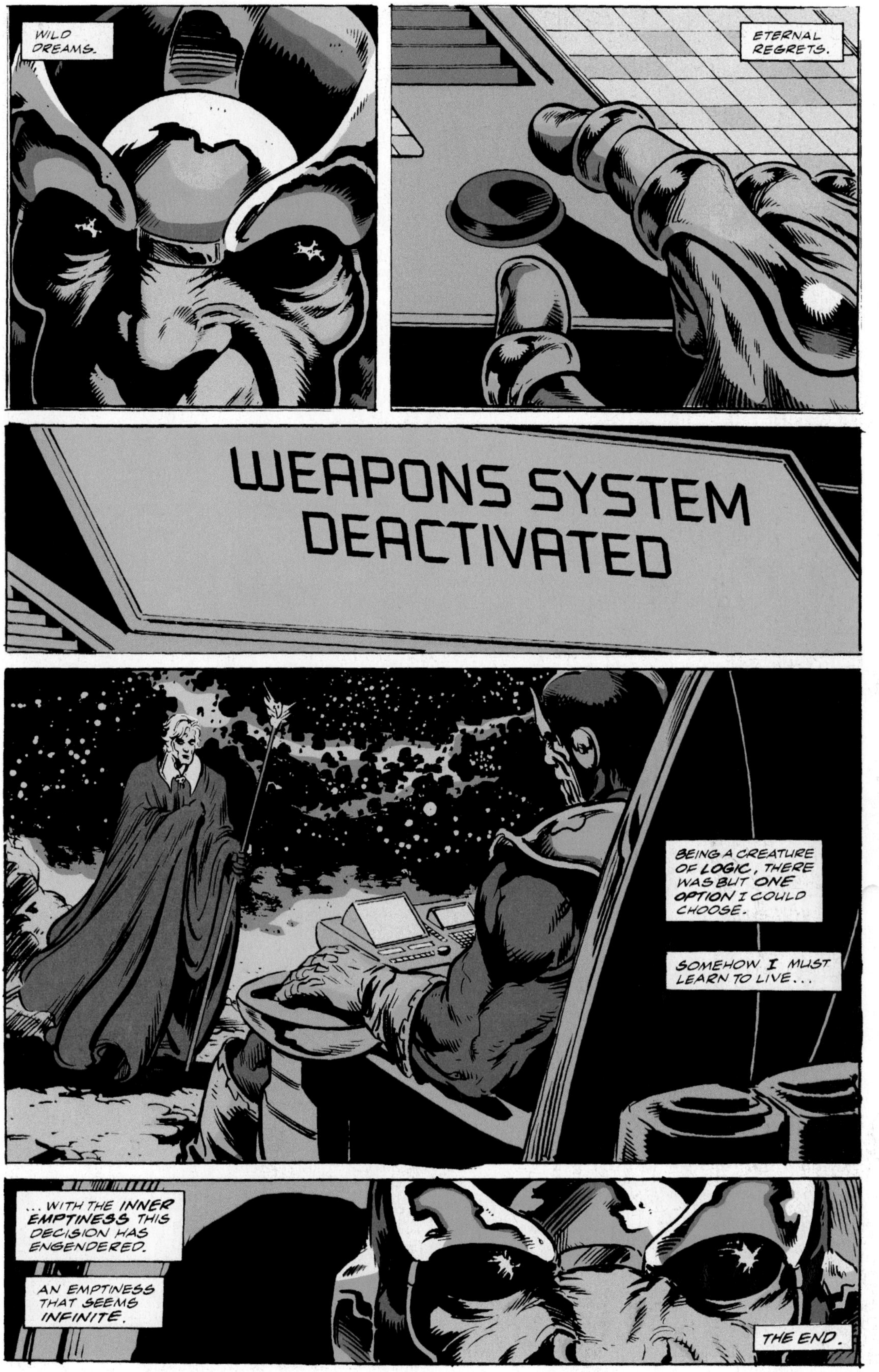

WILD DREAMS.
ETERNAL REGRETS.
WEAPONS SYSTEM DEACTIVATED
BEING A CREATURE OF LOGIC, THERE WAS BUT ONE OPTION I COULD CHOOSE.
SOMEHOW I MUST LEARN TO LIVE...
...WITH THE INNER EMPTINESS THIS DECISION HAS ENGENDERED.
AN EMPTINESS THAT SEEMS INFINITE.
THE END.

INFINITY WAR CROSSOVERS

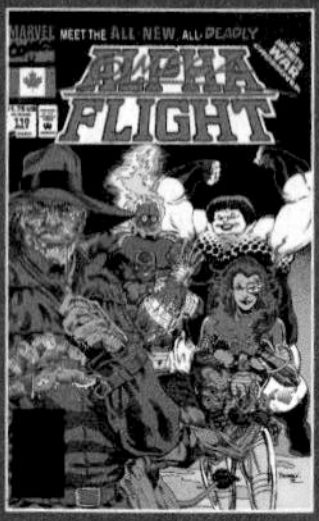
MEET THE ALL-NEW, ALL-DEADLY
ALPHA FLIGHT

ALPHA FLIGHT #110-112 (July-September, 1992)

With Alpha Flight caught up in the Infinity War, Windshear and Gamma Flight must face the Master and his all-new Omega Flight. To save the Earth from the Magus, the Master unleashes a horde of extraterrestrial Ska'r to consume Canada, while he intends to claim the rest of the world. After defeating the Ska'r, Gamma Flight is promoted to Beta Flight for their efforts.

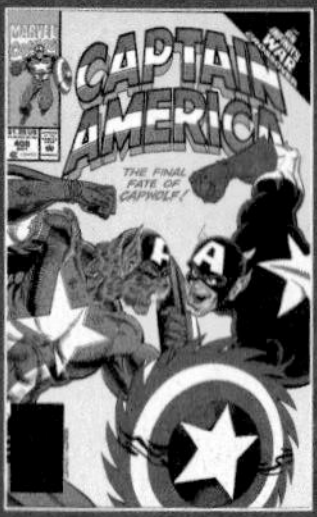
CAPTAIN AMERICA

CAPTAIN AMERICA #408 (October, 1992)

Just as he's recovering from a case of lycanthropy, Captain America is attacked by his doppelganger. When he realizes that his double isn't really alive, he beheads it. Later, Captain America's friend D-Man is attacked by his doppelganger, and winds up drifting into the community of the Night People after the fight.

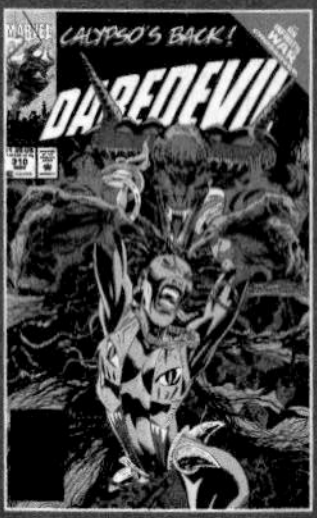
CALYPSO'S BACK!

DAREDEVIL #310 (November, 1992)

Calypso attempts to stalk and kill Daredevil, but mistakes his doppelganger ("Hellspawn") for him, and kills the doppelganger instead. Calypso would later employ a resurrected Hellspawn as her minion; it was finally slain and used by Daredevil to trick the public into thinking he was dead.

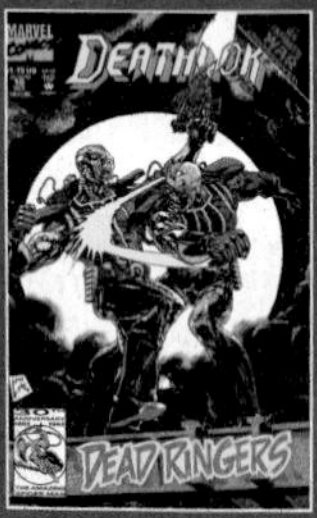
DEAD RINGERS

DEATHLOK #16 (October, 1992)

Deathlok faces his doppelganger, who is his equal in every way except for its penchant for killing. Unable to understand the creature, Deathlok finally manages to incapacitate it and hopes to find out what it really is, but it self-destructs to prevent being studied.

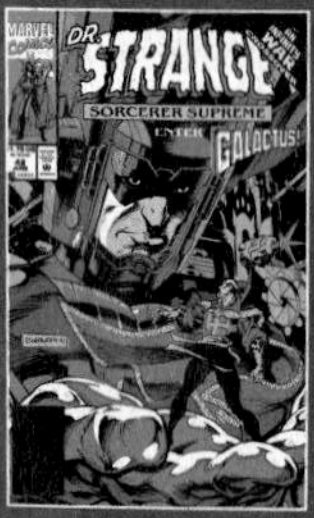
DR. STRANGE
SORCERER SUPREME
GALACTUS!

DOCTOR STRANGE, SORCERER SUPREME #42-47 (June-November, 1992)

Dr. Strange joins Nova, the Silver Surfer and Galactus on their quest to study Eternity's catatonia. Along the way Dr. Strange's patron Agamotto demands that Strange return his amulets and orb to him, but Galactus faces Agamotto in battle and the Vishanti finally make Agamotto step down. Dr. Strange is also menaced by Cyttorak, but helps defeat him with the help of the Juggernaut. Joining with fellow mystics Agatha Harkness, Dr. Druid, Shaman and the Scarlet Witch, Dr. Strange returns to Earth just as the Magus was creating his duplicate world, and found that his double from the long-destroyed Counter-Earth had taken his place as the Necromancer, and sworn allegiance to the Magus. Dr. Strange destroys the Necromancer.

FANTASTIC FOUR #366-370 **(July-November, 1992)**

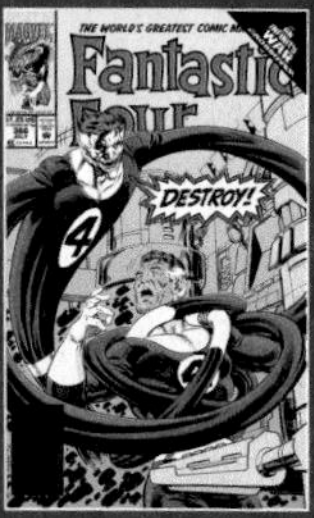
Fantastic Four
DESTROY!

Events are shown from the Fantastic Four's perspective as Reed is replaced by his doppelganger; Ben battles a Thing doppelganger, and is saved by his old enemy—the Puppet Master; Johnny slaughters a number of doppelgangers, and is told by his own double that he's already on the dark side; Susan faces a doppelganger who manifests as Malice, the identity she used while under the Psycho-Man's thrall years earlier, and absorbs Malice into herself. Over the following months, Susan exhibited increasingly troubling behavior due to Malice's influence, until she was finally completely exorcised by her son Franklin, who destroyed Malice on the psychic plane.

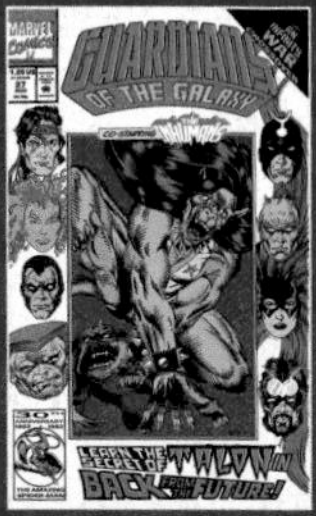
Guardians of the Galaxy

GUARDIANS OF THE GALAXY #27-29 **(August-October, 1992)**

The Guardians of the Galaxy arrive in the 20th century and stop at the city of Attilan to receive medical aid for their teammate Talon from the Inhumans. The Guardians and Inhumans are attacked by their doppelgangers, but manage to defeat them. The Guardians visit the Avengers' headquarters to learn more about the crisis, and help defend the base from an attack by Dr. Octopus' Masters of Evil, as well as more doppelgangers of the Guardians and the Masters.

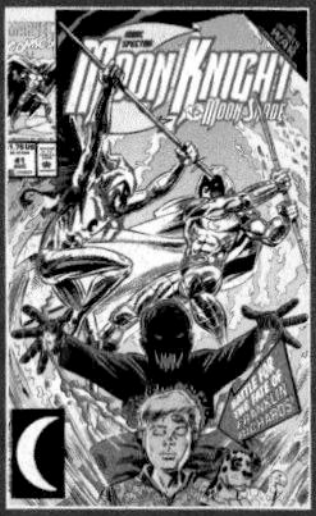
Moon Knight

MARC SPECTOR: MOON KNIGHT #41-44 **(August-November, 1992)**

As his body decays due to an infection from the Demogoblin, Moon Knight aids in the defense of Four Freedoms Plaza, saving Franklin Richards from his doppelganger. Moon Knight's double, Moonshade, attempts to become the only Moon Knight in the multiverse by killing Moon Knight's counterparts in every reality, but Moon Knight finally destroys Moonshade, then returns to Four Freedoms Plaza to aid his fellow heroes.

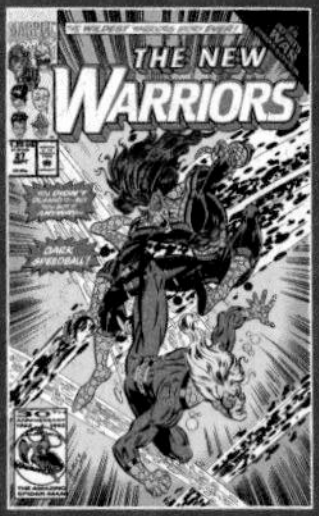
THE NEW
WARRIORS

NEW WARRIORS #27 **(September, 1992)**

Rage and Speedball face their doppelgangers, "Blackball" and "Enraged." Rage absorbs his doppelganger into his body. Blackball attacks Speedball's mother, but Speedball comes to her rescue and destroys Blackball.

NOMAD #7 **(November, 1992)**

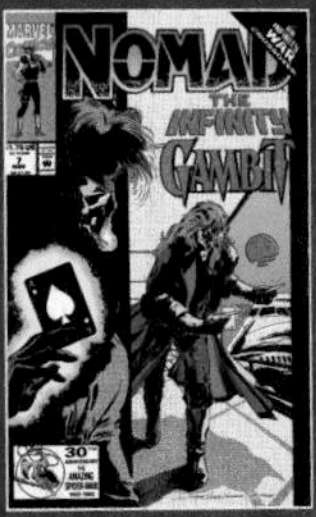
NOMAD
Gambit

Gambit's doppelganger searches for the real Gambit and hijacks a plane bound for Los Angeles, mistaking it for a flight to Louisiana. In L.A., he battles Nomad and FBI agent Vernon Hatchway at the airport. Nomad and Hatchway get the doppelganger on a plane to deliver it to Louisiana, but it bails out by parachute. Fortunately, Hatchway had loaded the chute with plastique, and the doppelganger (blows) himself up.

QUASAR #38-40 **(September-November, 1992)**

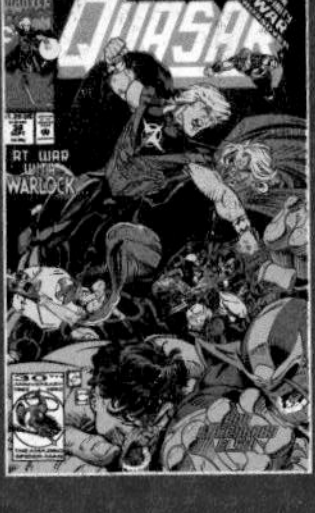
QUASAR
WARLOCK

The doppelgangers are revealed to have been created within the Dimension of Manifestations, the realm cosmic entities use to manifest physical bodies. Quasar researches the Ultimate Nullifier at the extraterrestrial University of Rus, and his enemy Deathurge encourages him to wield the device, hoping he will destroy all life with it. After being destroyed by the Ultimate Nullifier, Quasar awakens in the White Room, a dimension created by his mentor Eon to preserve a portion of the consciousnesses of his former protectors of the universe.

DOOMED!!
SILVER SABLE
& THE WILD PACK

SILVER SABLE AND THE WILD PACK #4-5 (September-October, 1992)

Dr. Doom's doppelganger misses its chance to kill him when he leaves with Kang, and so it takes Doom's place in Latveria. When Silver Sable comes to Castle Doom to meet with Doom, it pretends to be him, but she realizes the deception and fights back. Meanwhile, Sandman is replaced by his doppelganger and fights other members of the Wild Pack. Sandman and Dr. Doom's doppelgangers are both rendered inert when Galactus disrupts all of the doppelgangers on Earth.

SILVER SURFER

SILVER SURFER #67-69 (July-August, 1992)

The Silver Surfer joins Galactus, Nova and Dr. Strange as they set out to solve the mystery of Eternity's catatonia. Along the way, Galactus' vessel is attacked by a lost space traveler named Khoon who is desperate to get out of the void he has been trapped in for ages. Having no idea of who he is facing, Khoon is absorbed into Galactus' vessel, and Galactus uses Khoon's knowledge to help aid their navigation.

SLEEPWALKER

SLEEPWALKER #18 (November, 1992)

Sleepwalker is contacted by Professor X, Moondragon, Jean Grey and Psylocke, who want him to serve as the conduit by which to save the Earth from the Magus' duplication effort. He is reluctant to trust them, but after witnessing the evil of Daredevil, Firestar and the Beast's doppelgangers, he concedes and helps them, although the people of Earth remain comatose.

SPIDER-MAN

SPIDER-MAN #24 (July, 1992)

Spider-Man and the Hobgoblin are attacked by Spider-Man's doppelganger and the Demogoblin, the Hobgoblin's formerly demon half. Although the Spider-Doppelganger is seemingly slain, Demogoblin spirits away its body. It later aided Carnage in the events of Maximum Carnage before finally being destroyed. See more in the Spider-Man: Maximum Carnage trade paperback!

WONDER MAN
DOUBLE TROUBLE

WONDER MAN #13-15 (September-November, 1992)

Wonder Man's powers have altered so that now he needs to become angry to retain his abilities. Questioning his own humanity, he draws upon his hatred to battle the doppelgangers, until during the final battle, he can no longer discern friend from foe. He fights until he exhausts himself, and is then replaced by his doppelganger.

WHAT THE...?! #20 (August, 1992)

When Forbush Man gains the Infinity Wart, granting him omnipotent powers, his evil self Negative Forbush Man claims the power for himself! To save Forbush Man, Milk, Cookies, Spider-Ham and Wolverina join forces, battling Milk & Cookies' evil selves Bread & Water, and Spider-Ham's evil self Pork Grind. Wolverina saves the day by lancing the Infinity Wart from Negative Forbush Man's finger with her adamantium nails, restoring order to the universe.

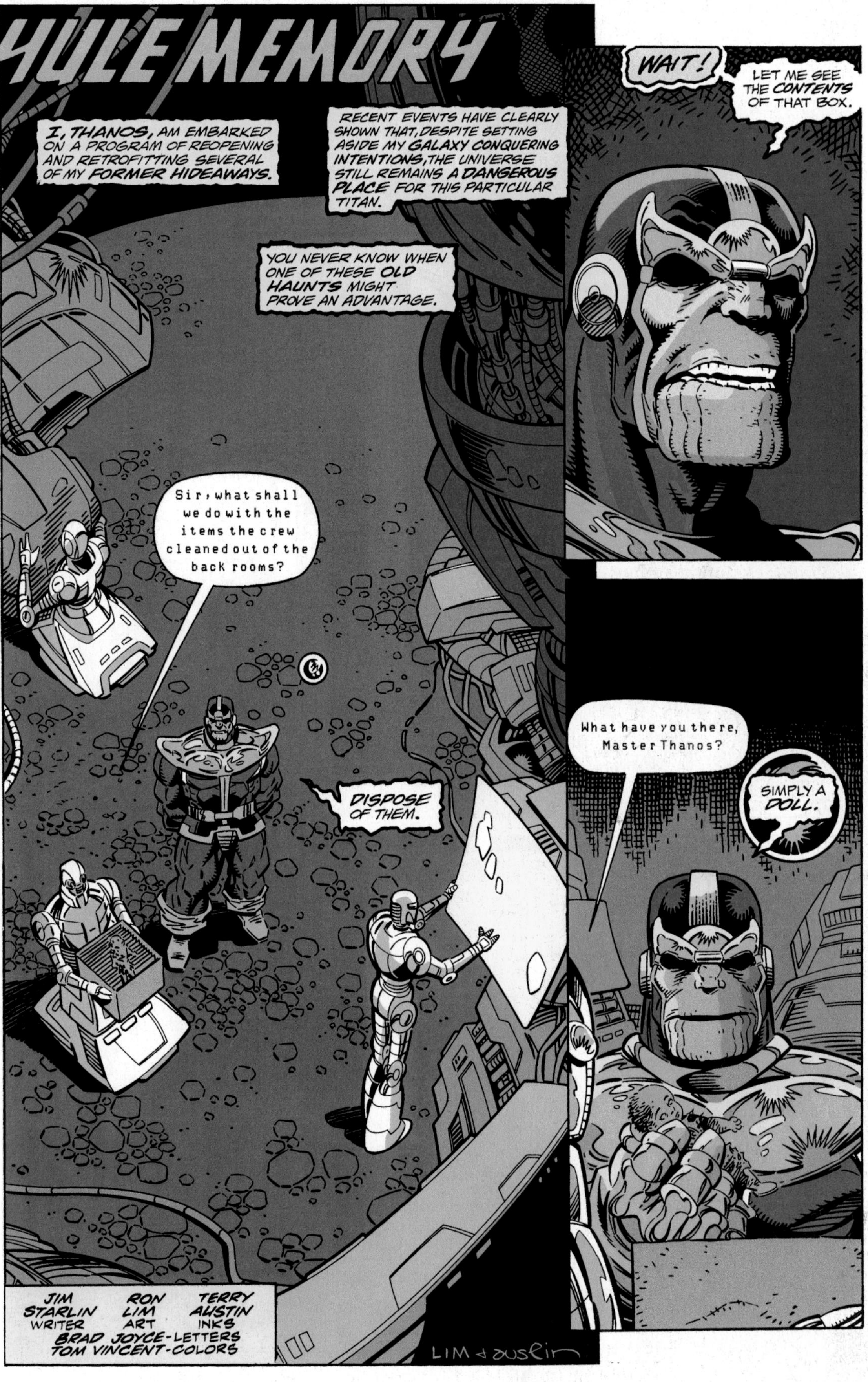
YULE MEMORY
I, THANOS, AM EMBARKED ON A PROGRAM OF REOPENING AND RETROFITTING SEVERAL OF MY FORMER HIDEAWAYS.
RECENT EVENTS HAVE CLEARLY SHOWN THAT, DESPITE SETTING ASIDE MY GALAXY CONQUERING INTENTIONS, THE UNIVERSE STILL REMAINS A DANGEROUS PLACE FOR THIS PARTICULAR TITAN.
YOU NEVER KNOW WHEN ONE OF THESE OLD HAUNTS MIGHT PROVE AN ADVANTAGE.
Sir, what shall we do with the items the crew cleaned out of the back rooms?
DISPOSE OF THEM.
JIM STARLIN WRITER
RON LIM ART
TERRY AUSTIN INKS
BRAD JOYCE-LETTERS
TOM VINCENT-COLORS
LIM & AUSTIN
WAIT!
LET ME SEE THE CONTENTS OF THAT BOX.
What have you there, Master Thanos?
SIMPLY A DOLL.

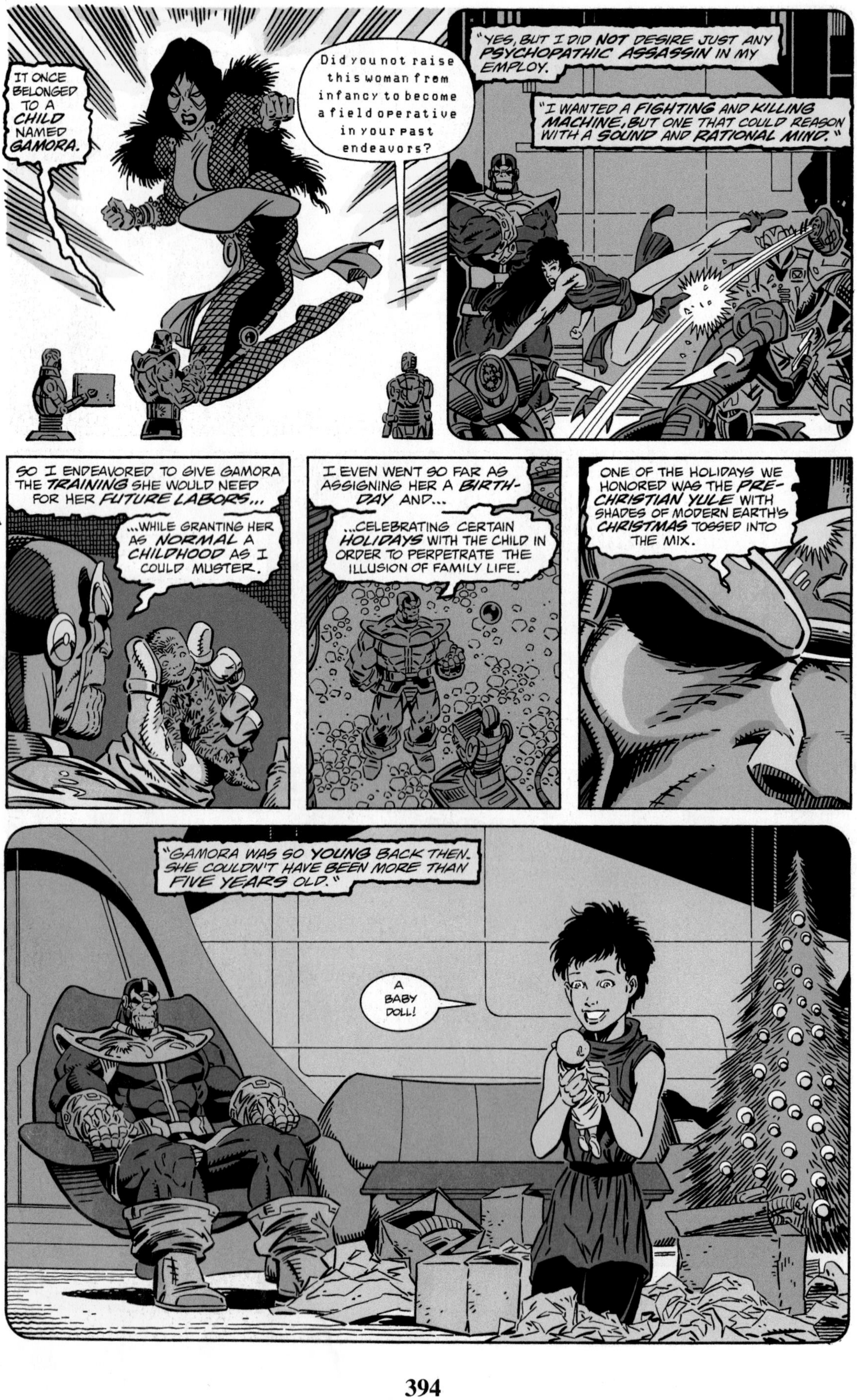

IT ONCE BELONGED TO A CHILD NAMED GAMORA.
Did you not raise this woman from infancy to become a field operative in your past endeavors?
"YES, BUT I DID NOT DESIRE JUST ANY PSYCHOPATHIC ASSASSIN IN MY EMPLOY.
"I WANTED A FIGHTING AND KILLING MACHINE, BUT ONE THAT COULD REASON WITH A SOUND AND RATIONAL MIND."
SO I ENDEAVORED TO GIVE GAMORA THE TRAINING SHE WOULD NEED FOR HER FUTURE LABORS...
...WHILE GRANTING HER AS NORMAL A CHILDHOOD AS I COULD MUSTER.
I EVEN WENT SO FAR AS ASSIGNING HER A BIRTH-DAY AND...
...CELEBRATING CERTAIN HOLIDAYS WITH THE CHILD IN ORDER TO PERPETRATE THE ILLUSION OF FAMILY LIFE.
ONE OF THE HOLIDAYS WE HONORED WAS THE PRE-CHRISTIAN YULE WITH SHADES OF MODERN EARTH'S CHRISTMAS TOSSED INTO THE MIX.
"GAMORA WAS SO YOUNG BACK THEN. SHE COULDN'T HAVE BEEN MORE THAN FIVE YEARS OLD."
A BABY DOLL!

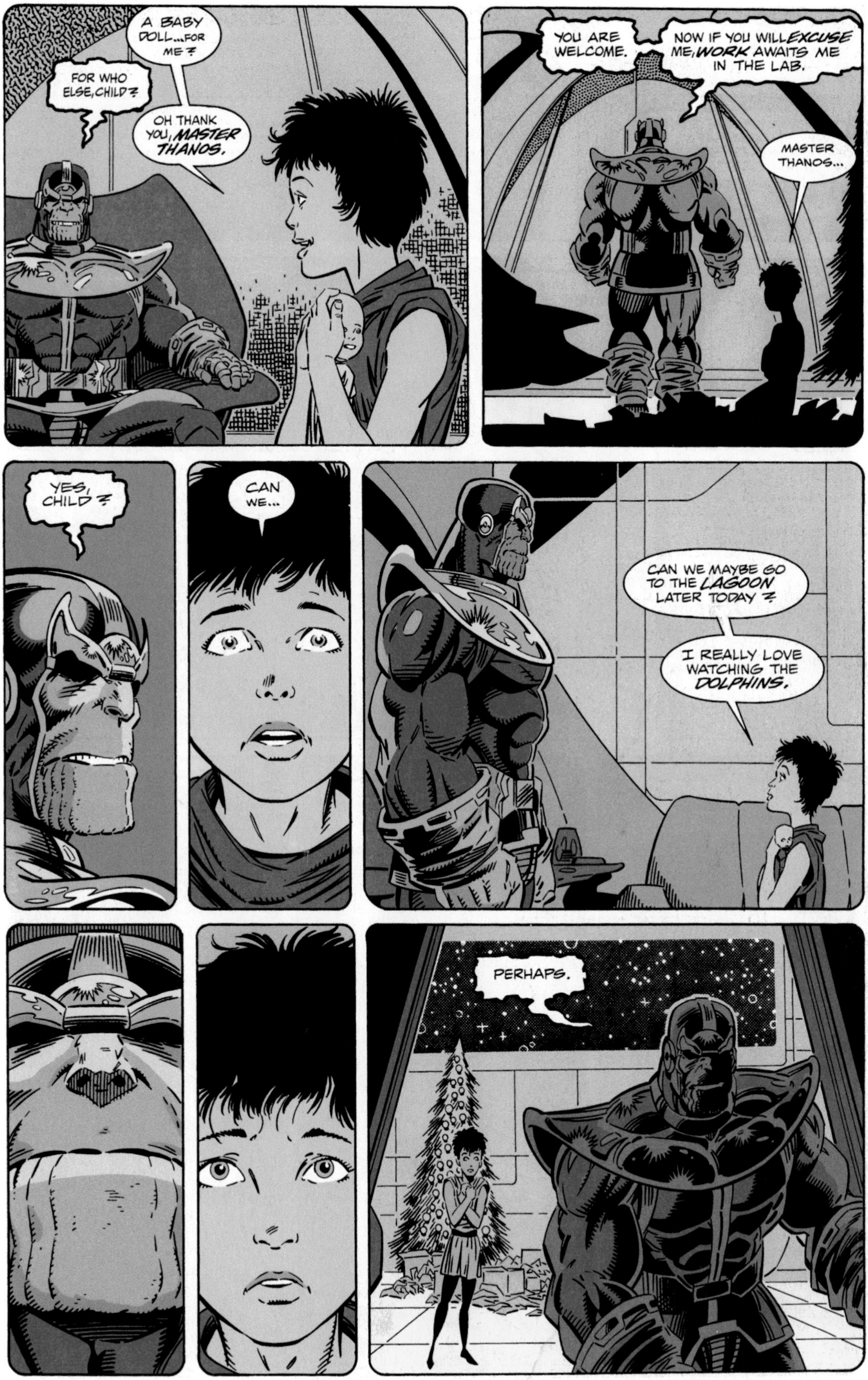
A BABY DOLL...FOR ME?
FOR WHO ELSE, CHILD?
OH THANK YOU, MASTER THANOS.
YOU ARE WELCOME.
NOW IF YOU WILL EXCUSE ME, WORK AWAITS ME IN THE LAB.
MASTER THANOS...
YES, CHILD?
CAN WE...
CAN WE MAYBE GO TO THE LAGOON LATER TODAY?
I REALLY LOVE WATCHING THE DOLPHINS.
PERHAPS.

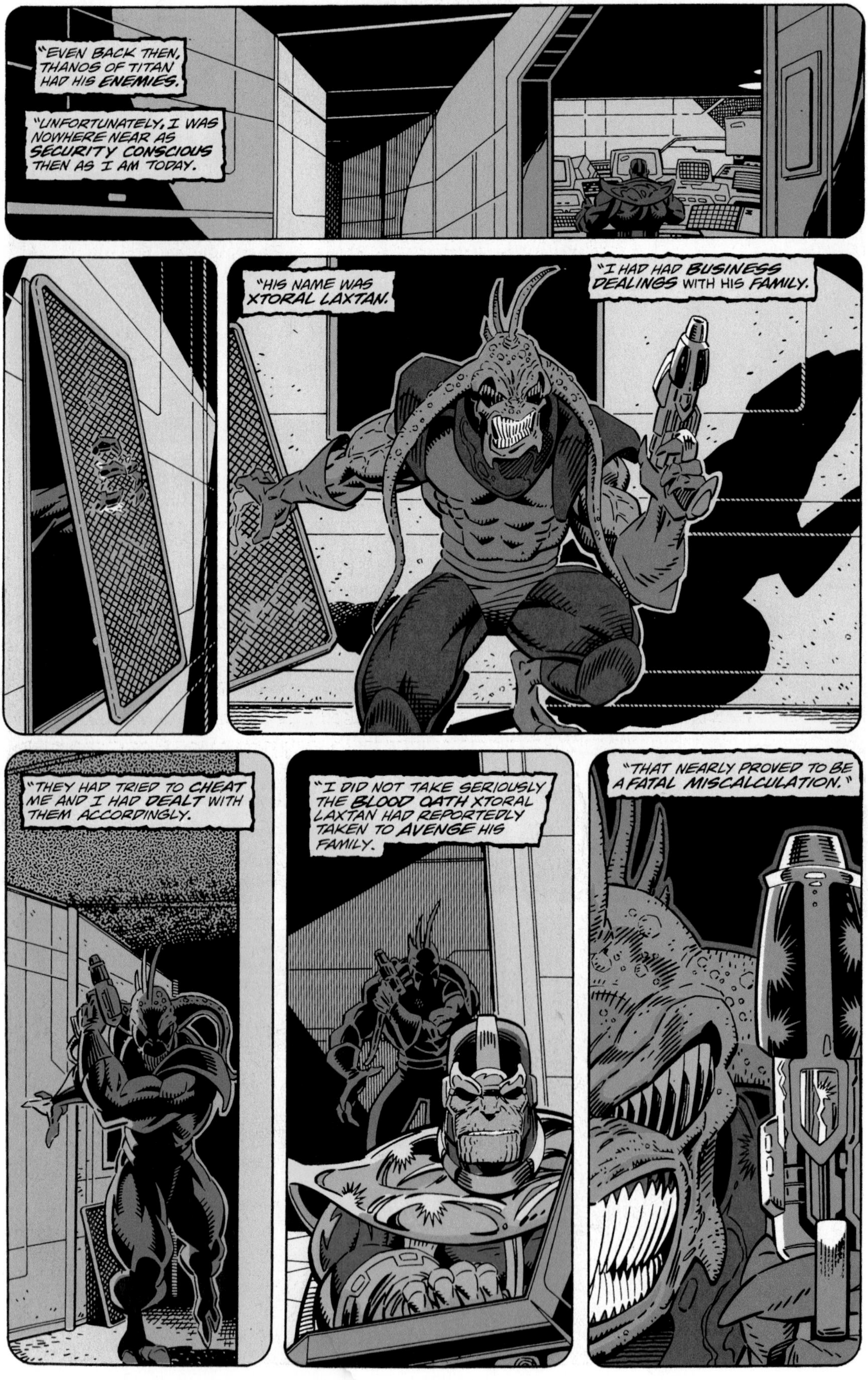
"EVEN BACK THEN, THANOS OF TITAN HAD HIS ENEMIES.
"UNFORTUNATELY, I WAS NOWHERE NEAR AS SECURITY CONSCIOUS THEN AS I AM TODAY.
"HIS NAME WAS XTORAL LAXTAN.
"I HAD HAD BUSINESS DEALINGS WITH HIS FAMILY.
"THEY HAD TRIED TO CHEAT ME AND I HAD DEALT WITH THEM ACCORDINGLY.
"I DID NOT TAKE SERIOUSLY THE BLOOD OATH XTORAL LAXTAN HAD REPORTEDLY TAKEN TO AVENGE HIS FAMILY.
"THAT NEARLY PROVED TO BE A FATAL MISCALCULATION."

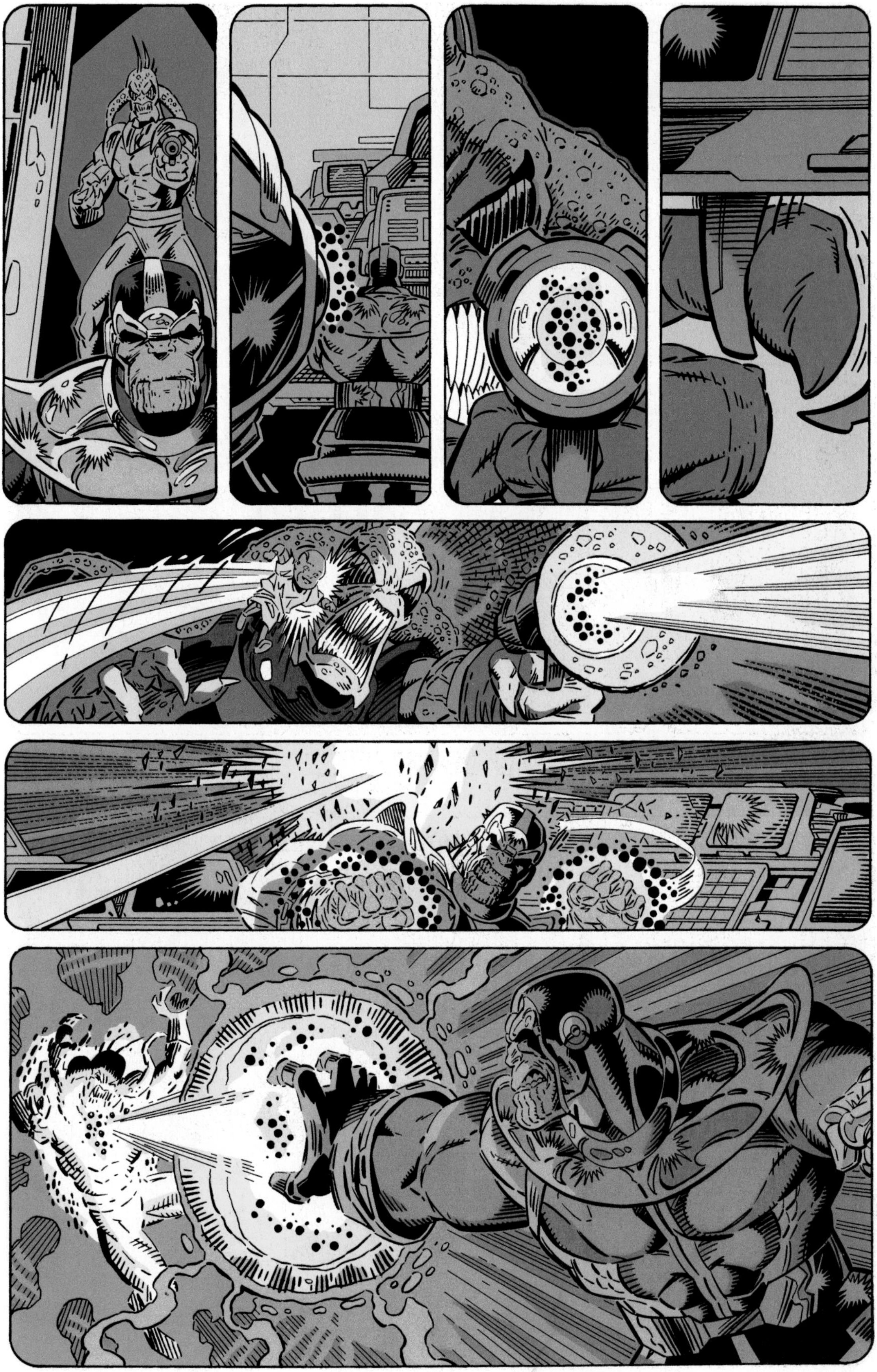

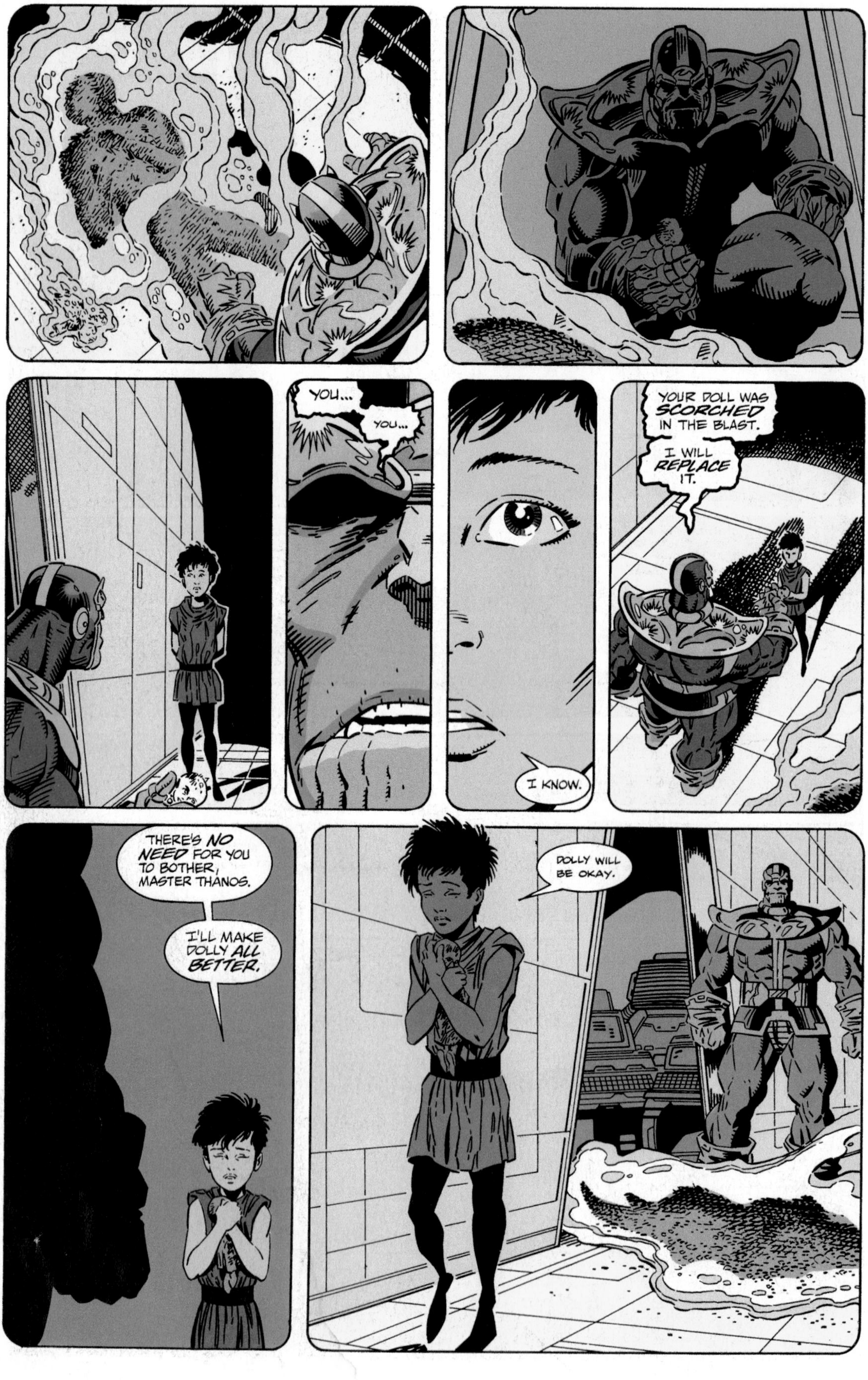
YOU...
YOU...
I KNOW.
YOUR DOLL WAS SCORCHED IN THE BLAST.
I WILL REPLACE IT.
THERE'S NO NEED FOR YOU TO BOTHER, MASTER THANOS.
I'LL MAKE DOLLY ALL BETTER.
DOLLY WILL BE OKAY.

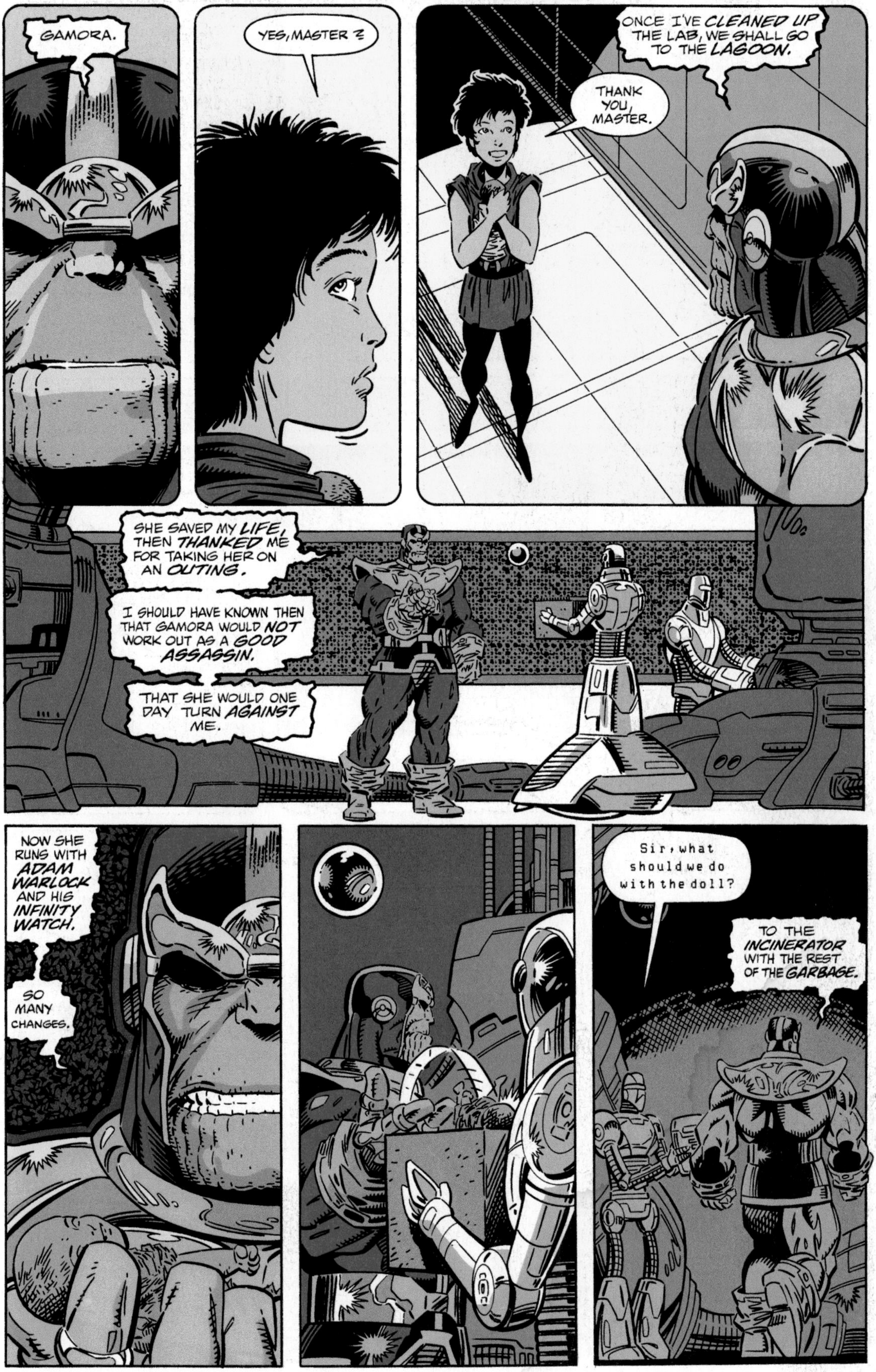
GAMORA.
YES, MASTER ?
ONCE I'VE CLEANED UP THE LAB, WE SHALL GO TO THE LAGOON.
THANK YOU, MASTER.
SHE SAVED MY LIFE, THEN THANKED ME FOR TAKING HER ON AN OUTING.
I SHOULD HAVE KNOWN THEN THAT GAMORA WOULD NOT WORK OUT AS A GOOD ASSASSIN.
THAT SHE WOULD ONE DAY TURN AGAINST ME.
NOW SHE RUNS WITH ADAM WARLOCK AND HIS INFINITY WATCH.
SO MANY CHANGES.
Sir, what should we do with the doll?
TO THE INCINERATOR WITH THE REST OF THE GARBAGE.

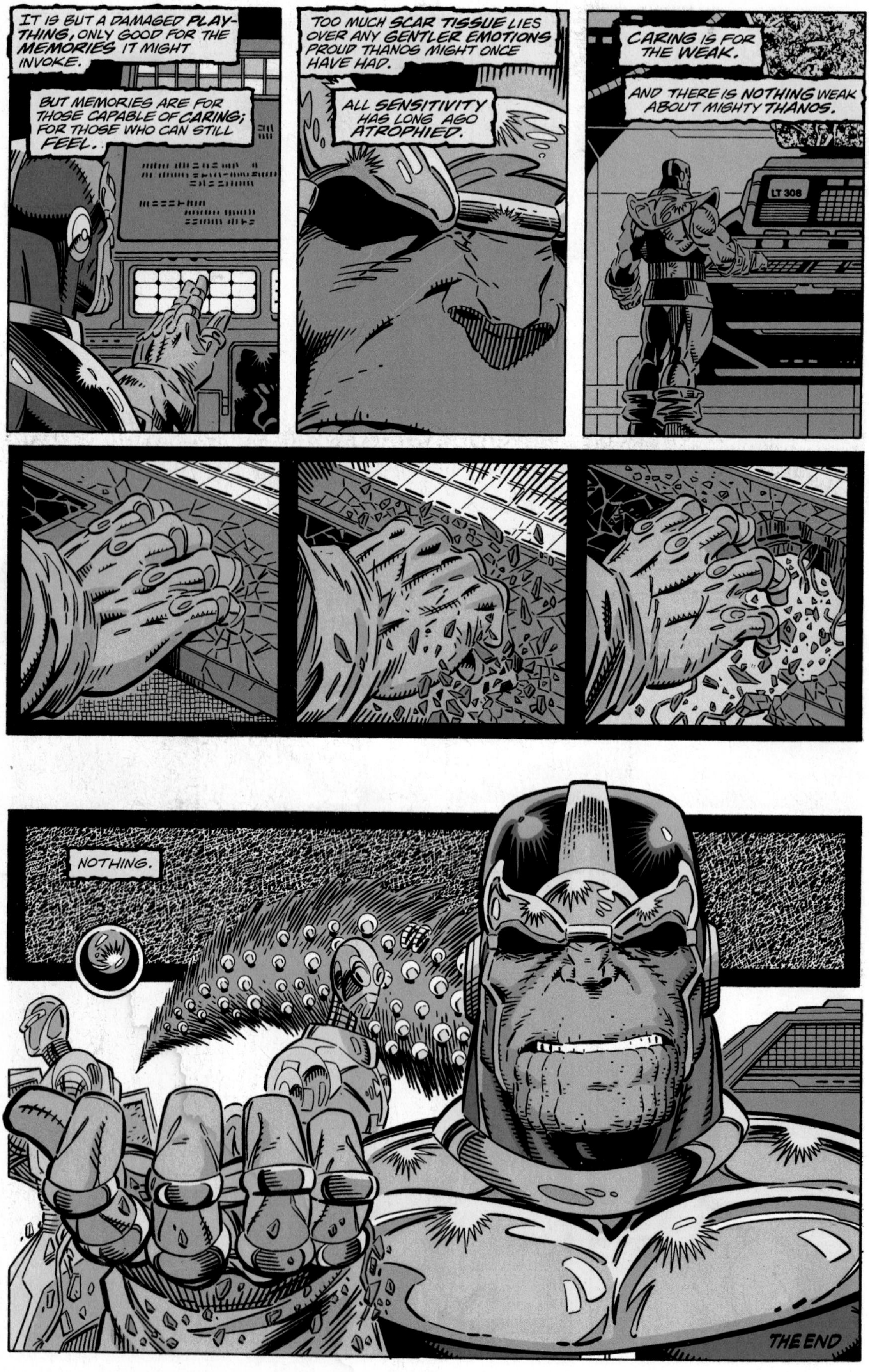

IT IS BUT A DAMAGED PLAYTHING, ONLY GOOD FOR THE MEMORIES IT MIGHT INVOKE.
BUT MEMORIES ARE FOR THOSE CAPABLE OF CARING; FOR THOSE WHO CAN STILL FEEL.
TOO MUCH SCAR TISSUE LIES OVER ANY GENTLER EMOTIONS PROUD THANOS MIGHT ONCE HAVE HAD.
ALL SENSITIVITY HAS LONG AGO ATROPHIED.
CARING IS FOR THE WEAK.
AND THERE IS NOTHING WEAK ABOUT MIGHTY THANOS.
LT 308
NOTHING.
THE END